THE *PAST & PRESENT* BOOK SERIES

*General Editor*
MATTHEW HILTON

# Islam and the European Empires

# Islam and the European Empires

Edited by
DAVID MOTADEL

OXFORD
UNIVERSITY PRESS

# OXFORD

UNIVERSITY PRESS

Great Clarendon Street, Oxford, OX2 6DP,
United Kingdom

Oxford University Press is a department of the University of Oxford.
It furthers the University's objective of excellence in research, scholarship,
and education by publishing worldwide. Oxford is a registered trade mark of
Oxford University Press in the UK and in certain other countries

First Edition published in 2014

Impression: 1

Published in the United States of America by Oxford University Press
198 Madison Avenue, New York, NY 10016, United States of America

British Library Cataloguing in Publication Data

Data available

Library of Congress Control Number: 2014939131

ISBN 978–0–19–966831–1

Printed and bound by
CPI Group (UK) Ltd, Croydon, CR0 4YY

# Acknowledgments

The idea for this book emerged during my time as a Research Fellow at Gonville and Caius College, Cambridge, and I am grateful to the Fellows of the College for providing me with an extraordinary intellectual environment in which to complete it. I am much indebted to Sir C. A. Bayly, Houchang E. Chehabi, Sir Richard J. Evans, and Rachel G. Hoffman for their invaluable comments on the introduction, and their helpful advice on the overall concept of the volume. Many thanks in particular go to James L. W. Roslington for his assistance during the final phase of the editorial process. I am also grateful to the anonymous readers, both at Oxford University Press and at Past & Present, for their insightful suggestions, which helped greatly to improve the book. It is, moreover, a pleasure to acknowledge the encouragement, advice, and guidance from the editorial board of Past & Present, especially Matthew Hilton and Alexandra Walsham, who from the outset gave the book their full support; from Cathryn Steele, Christopher Wheeler, and Fiona Barry of Oxford University Press, who ensured its smooth production; and from the team of the Wylie Agency, who oversaw the process. Finally, and most importantly, I wish to thank all the contributors for providing the fascinating essays that brought this book to life.

# Contents

# List of Figures

# List of Contributors

**Cemil Aydin** is Associate Professor of History at the University of North Carolina at Chapel Hill. He is author of *The Politics of Anti-Westernism in Asia: Visions of World Order in Pan-Islamic and Pan-Asian Thought* (Columbia University Press, 2007).

**Felicitas Becker** is a Lecturer in African History at the University of Cambridge. She is author of *Becoming Muslim in Mainland Tanzania, 1890–2000* (Oxford University Press, 2008).

**Julia Clancy-Smith** is Professor of History at the University of Arizona. She is author of *Rebel and Saint: Muslim Notables, Populist Protest, Colonial Encounters (Algeria and Tunisia, 1800–1904)* (University of California Press, 1994), *Mediterraneans: North Africa and Europe in an Age of Migration* (University of California Press, 2011), and co-author of *The Modern Middle East and North Africa* (Oxford University Press, 2013).

**Robert D. Crews** is Associate Professor of History at Stanford University. He is author of *For Prophet and Tsar: Islam and Empire in Russia and Central Asia* (Harvard University Press, 2006).

**Faisal Devji** is a Reader in Modern South Asian History at the University of Oxford. He is author of *Landscapes of the Jihad: Militancy, Morality, Modernity* (Cornell University Press, 2005), *The Terrorist in Search of Humanity: Militant Islam and Global Politics* (Columbia University Press, 2009), *The Impossible Indian: Gandhi and the Temptation of Violence* (Harvard University Press, 2012), and *Muslim Zion: Pakistan as a Political Idea* (Harvard University Press, 2013).

**Rebekka Habermas** is Professor of History at the University of Göttingen. She is author of *Frauen und Männer des Bürgertums: Eine Familiengeschichte (1750–1850)* (Vandenhoeck and Ruprecht, 2000), and co-editor of *Mission Global: Eine Verflechtungsgeschichte seit dem 19. Jahrhundert* (Böhlau, 2014).

**Benjamin D. Hopkins** is Associate Professor of History at George Washington University. He is author of *The Making of Modern Afghanistan* (Palgrave Macmillan, 2008), and co-author of *Fragments of the Afghan Frontier* (Oxford University Press, 2011).

**Gerrit Knaap** is Senior Researcher at the Huygens Institute for the History of the Netherlands, The Hague, and Professor of History at Utrecht University. He is author of *Shallow Waters, Rising Tide: Shipping and Trade in Java Around 1775* (Kitlv Press, 1996), and *Cephas, Yogyakarta: Photography in the Service of the Sultan* (Kitlv Press, 1999).

**David Motadel** is a Research Fellow in History at Gonville and Caius College, University of Cambridge. He is author of *Islam and Nazi Germany's War* (Harvard University Press, 2014).

**Michael A. Reynolds** is Associate Professor of Near Eastern Studies at Princeton University. He is author of *Shattering Empires: The Clash and Collapse of the Ottoman and Russian Empires, 1908–1918* (Cambridge University Press, 2011).

**Umar Ryad** is Associate Professor of Islamic Studies at Utrecht University. He is author of *Islamic Reformism and Christianity: A Critical Reading of the Works of Muhammad Rashid Rida and his Associates (1898–1935)* (Brill, 2009).

**John Slight** is a Research Fellow in History at St John's College, University of Cambridge. He is currently working on a book entitled *The British Empire and the Hajj, 1865–1956* (Harvard University Press).

**Eric Tagliacozzo** is Professor of History at Cornell University. He is author of *Secret Trades, Porous Borders: Smuggling and States along a Southeast Asian Frontier, 1865–1915* (Yale University Press, 2005), and editor of *Southeast Asia and the Middle East: Islam, Movement, and the Longue Durée* (Stanford University Press, 2009).

**George R. Trumbull IV** is Associate Professor of History at Dartmouth College. He is author of *An Empire of Facts: Colonial Power, Cultural Knowledge, and Islam in Algeria, 1871–1914* (Cambridge University Press, 2009).

**Knut S. Vikør** is Professor of History at the University of Bergen. He is author of *Sufi and Scholar on the Desert Edge: Muhammad b. ʿAli al-Sanusi and his Brotherhood* (Northwestern University Press, 1995), *Between God and the Sultan: A History of Islamic Law* (Oxford University Press, 2005), and *The Maghreb since 1800: A Short History* (Hurst, 2012).

# Note on Transliteration

This book generally follows a simplified version of the transliteration system used by the *International Journal of Middle East Studies*. Arabic, Persian, and Ottoman Turkish terms are transliterated without diacritical markings (macrons and dots). The use of the *ayn* and *hamza* is indicated by a ' and a, ' respectively. Arabic, Persian, and Ottoman Turkish words in common usage in English are printed according to the form given by Merriam-Webster's Collegiate Dictionary. Although Arabic, as the medium of the Qur'an, has a privileged position in the Muslim world, the languages of Islam have always been diverse, ranging from Urdu to Russian to Indonesian. In view of this linguistic diversity, regional spellings and transliterations, including for common religious terms, have been retained where appropriate in each contributor's chapter.

# Introduction

*David Motadel*

This book is about the engagement of the European empires with Islam.[1] The expansion of Europe engulfed vast parts of the Islamic world, gradually subjugating Muslims around the globe, from the West African savannah to the shores of Southeast Asia, under non-Muslim imperial rule. In the heyday of empire, Britain, France, Russia, and the Netherlands each governed more Muslim subjects than any independent Muslim state. European politicians and colonial officials believed Islam to be of considerable political significance, and were quite cautious when it came to matters of the religious life of their Muslim subjects. Governing the religious affairs of Muslims became, in fact, central to imperial rule. In the colonies, European authorities regularly employed religious leaders and Islamic institutions to enhance social and political control. At the same time, their empires were increasingly challenged by religious resistance movements and Islamic insurgencies. Towards the end of the nineteenth century, government corridors in London, Paris, and St Petersburg were haunted by the specter of pan-Islamism.

Historians have long been interested in religion and empire. Yet, the literature in the field remains overwhelmingly dominated by studies on Christian missions, which are usually seen as an integral part of the European colonial expansion— 'first the missionary, then the Consul, and at last the invading army', as it was once famously put.[2] This view can be traced back to the colonial period itself, finding one of its most profound visual expressions in Horace Vernet's *Première messe en Kabylie*, painted in 1855 (Fig. 1). A growing number of historical studies, however, suggest that the role of Christian missionary movements in the European empires was generally less significant than commonly assumed, and that mission and formal empire were, in fact, two very different endeavors. While missionaries often acted outside colonized territories, imperial rulers regularly pursued a policy of religious neutrality and noninterference and refused to give missions special status in the colonies in order to avoid religious unrest. Historians of empire have increasingly emphasized that there was often little connection between

---

[1] This introduction is based on the historiographical essay by David Motadel, 'Islam and the European Empires', *Historical Journal*, 55/3 (2012), 831–56.
[2] J. A. Hobson, *Imperialism: A Study* (London, 1902), 215, quoting Wen Ching, *The Chinese Crisis from Within* (London, 1901), 12.

Bible and flag.[3] Besides, scholars have demonstrated that the accomplishments of missionaries in terms of conversion have generally been exaggerated, and that European Christians contributed less significantly than commonly assumed to the centuries-long expansion of Christianity, which mostly depended on local agents and indigenous church movements. In short, the extensive corpus of documents produced by missionaries bears little relation to either their accomplishments in the global spread of Christianity, or their relevance within the European empires. Religious life in the European empires was shaped not by Christian missionaries but by native religious groups.

European emperors and empresses ruled over Muslims, Jews, Sikhs, Buddhists, Hindus, indigenous Christians, and followers of numerous animist beliefs.[4] Religious affiliation became an important lens through which colonial officials viewed their subjects. Across the world, the governing of religion was a pivotal concern of imperial authorities. In the European empires nowhere was this perceived to be of greater importance than in Islamic regions, as Muslims were usually regarded as especially sensitive subjects and prone to revolt.

The history of Islam within the European empires has attracted considerable attention among scholars. Studies have examined the ways in which the imperial powers engaged with Muslims and their faith, addressing the accommodation of Islam in the colonies as well as anti-colonial Islamic resistance movements. Yet, although these works have significantly increased our knowledge of the engagement of the imperial states with their Muslim subjects, they have been written primarily within the historiographical frameworks of specific empires and geographical regions. Despite addressing similar questions and problems, most scholars working on Islam and empire have taken little notice of works on different empires. Comparative studies are missing.[5] This book brings together historians who work on Islam in different imperial contexts and geographic regions, offering

---

[3] A. N. Porter, *Religion versus Empire? British Protestant Missionaries and Overseas Expansion, 1700–1914* (Manchester, 2004); A. N. Porter, 'Religion and Empire: British Expansion in the Long Nineteenth Century, 1780–1914', *Journal of Imperial and Commonwealth History*, 20/3 (1992), 370–90; Brian Stanley, *The Bible and the Flag: Protestant Missions and British Imperialism in the Nineteenth and Twentieth Centuries* (Leicester, 1990); Norman Etherington, 'Missions and Empire', in Robin W. Winks and Alaine Low (eds), *The Oxford History of the British Empire*, v: *Historiography* (Oxford, 1999), 303–14; Norman Etherington, 'Introduction', in Norman Etherington (ed.), *Missions and Empire* (Oxford, 2005), 1–18; Owen White and J. P. Daughton, 'Introduction: Placing French Missionaries in the Modern World', in Owen White and J. P. Daughton (eds), *In God's Empire: French Missionaries and the Modern World* (Oxford, 2012), 3–25; Robert P. Geraci and Michael Khodarkovsky, 'Introduction', in Robert P. Geraci and Michael Khodarkovsky (eds), *Of Religion and Empire: Missions, Conversion, and Tolerance in Tsarist Russia* (Ithaca, NY, and London, 2001), 1–15; and Paul Werth, *At the Margins of Orthodoxy: Mission, Governance, and Confessional Politics in Russia's Volga-Kama Region, 1827–1905* (Ithaca, NY, and London, 2002).

[4] Susan Bayly, *Saints, Godesses and Kings: Muslims and Christians in South Indian Society 1700–1900* (Cambridge, 1989), gives a fascinating account of the religious heterogeneity encountered by colonial officials overseas.

[5] Francis Robinson (ed.), *The New Cambridge History of Islam*, v: *The Islamic World in the Age of Western Dominance* (Cambridge, 2010), is primarily a general history of the Muslim world in the nineteenth and twentieth centuries, although a number of contributors do discuss the relationship between religion and European imperialism.

**Fig. 1** *La première messe en Kabylie* by Horace Verne (1854), depicting missionaries and Muslims in French Algeria (AKG Images).

the first comparative account of the history of Islam in the European empires. Besides providing general overviews and condensing research results, the chapters give new insights into their subjects. They are arranged according to specific themes, so that the very structure of the book provides a comparative analytical framework. The volume is by no means intended to be a comprehensive or definite account of the history of Islam and the European empires. Instead, it constitutes a first attempt to provide a bigger picture, which may be taken further by future comparative research.

The question about the ways in which the European imperial powers engaged with Muslims and their faith is addressed in three parts. Chapters in the first section of the volume examine the accommodation of Islam in the imperial order (Part I). Contributions in the following part explore the role of Islam in anti-colonial resistance movements across the Muslim world (Part II). The third and final section of the book examines the relationship between Islam, information, and colonial knowledge (Part III). There are obviously significant overlaps between the themes of these three parts, and a number of chapters explicitly allude to them. Taken together, the contributions reveal the complexities and variations of the European imperial encounter with Islam. Differences and ambiguities in the accounts are, of course, hardly surprising given not only the very different forms that imperial rule took across the globe, but also the heterogeneity of the Muslim world itself.[6] Taking these differences into account, the contributions present a story full of contradictions and discontinuities, but also, and perhaps more importantly, of remarkable similarities and parallels.

## ISLAM AND IMPERIAL RULE

Historical writing about imperialism has long been influenced by the notion of an antagonism between the Christian European empires and Islam. European colonialism has been described as just another episode in a long history of conflict between Islam and Christendom that began in the early Middle Ages. The reality was, of course, rather more complex. Muslims formed an integral part of the European empires, just as Muslim powers such as Persia or the Ottoman empire

---

[6] Clifford Geertz, *Islam Observed: Religious Development in Morocco and Indonesia* (New Haven, 1968), has famously illustrated the cultural diversity within the Islamic world. Discussions about the heterogeneity of Islam, both globally and within Muslim majority societies, can also be found in Ernest Gellner, *Muslim Society* (Cambridge, 1981); Aziz Al-Azmeh, *Islams and Modernities* (London and New York, 1993); and Dale Eikelman and James Piscatori, *Muslim Politics* (Oxford, 1996). On the emergence of modern conceptions of the 'Islamic world' among Muslims and non-Muslims, see Cemil Aydin, 'Globalizing the Intellectual History of the Idea of the "Muslim World"', in Samuel Moyn and Andrew Sartori (eds), *Global Intellectual History* (New York, 2013), 159–86; and Nile Green, 'Spacetime and the Muslim Journey West: Industrial Communications in the Making of the "Muslim World"', *American Historical Review*, 118/2 (2013), 401–29. On the construction of communities—though national, not religious—more generally, see Benedict Anderson, *Imagined Communities: Reflections on the Origin and Spread of Nationalism* (London, 1983).

had accommodated Christians and Jews as *dhimmis* for centuries.[7] From the beginning of the European expansion into Muslim lands, imperial authorities not only
made significant efforts to integrate Islam into the colonial state, but often actively
employed Islamic structures.

The chapters in the first part of the book explore various aspects of the imperial
politics of religion in the colonized Muslim world, addressing the employment
of religious dignitaries and leaders by the imperial authorities, the integration of
Islamic institutions such as mosques, law courts, waqf endowments, and madrasas
into the colonial state, and the control and regulation of religious rituals such as
the pilgrimage to Mecca. Colonial officials in Muslim lands, as elsewhere, were
usually eager to embed their rule in existing structures and hierarchies, and religion
was considered central in this respect. Religious practices, laws, and elites were
considered crucial sources of moral and political authority that could be employed
to enhance social discipline and imperial control. The first part of the book shows
the remarkable extent to which the imperial states became involved in the religious
lives of their subjects. To administer Islamic affairs, European authorities tended
to institutionalize Islam and to introduce centralized religious bureaucracies and
ecclesiastical hierarchies which had previously been unknown in most parts of the
Muslim world.

The imperial politics of Islam was first studied by historians of Napoleonic
Egypt.[8] Shortly after the invasion of 1798, French colonial authorities decided to
administer Egypt using the Islamic judicial system and employing religious leaders.
The Qur'an was repeatedly interpreted in favor of the *Grande Armée*, and procla-
mations were translated into Qur'anic Arabic to give religious legitimacy to the
occupying regime. Napoleon himself attended a public celebration of the Prophet's
birthday (*mawlid*) in Cairo. In other parts of the empire, the French continued
these policies, deploying Islam in support of their rule. In Algeria, which was
invaded in 1830, French authorities used local shari'a courts and the Islamic judiciary to sustain order.[9] Gradually, formal rules and modern bureaucratic structures
were introduced into the traditional Islamic legal system. Qadis, now paid by the

---

[7] Youssef Courbage and Philippe Fargues, *Christians and Jews under Islam* (London and New York,
1997); and articles in the classic by Benjamin Braude and Bernard Lewis (eds), *Christians and Jews
in the Ottoman Empire: The Functioning of a Plural Society*, 2 vols (New York, 1982). On the Islamic
gunpowder empires more generally, see Stephen F. Dale, *The Muslim Empires of the Ottomans, Safavids,
and Mughals* (Cambridge, 2010).

[8] Christian Cherfils, *Bonaparte et l'Islam d'après les documents français et arabes* (Paris, 1914); and,
for more recent scholarship, Christopher J. Herold, *Bonaparte in Egypt* (New York, 1962); Jean
Thiry, *Bonaparte en Égypte: Décembre 1797–24 août 1799* (Paris, 1973); and Juan Cole, *Napoleon's
Egypt: Invading the Middle East* (New York, 2007), especially 123–42; see also Jacques Frémeaux, *La
France et l'Islam depuis 1789* (Paris, 1991), 35–54; and the articles in Pierre-Jean Luizard (ed.), *Le choc
colonial et l'Islam: Les politiques religieuses des puissances coloniales en terres d'Islam* (Paris, 2006), which
mainly focus on French colonial policies towards Islam.

[9] Allan Christelow, *Muslim Law Courts and the French Colonial State in Algeria* (Princeton, 1985);
and James McDougall, 'The Secular State's Islamic Empire: Muslim Spaces and Subjects of Jurisdiction
in Paris and Algiers, 1905–1957', *Comparative Studies in Society and History*, 52/3 (2010), 553–80.
Charles-Robert Ageron, *Les Algériens musulmans et la France (1871–1919)*, 2 vols (Paris, 1968), provides a more general account.

state, were placed under strict surveillance. Merging French legal principles and shariʿa, a hybrid Islamic–French law, the *droit musulman algérien*, was created. As scripturalist interpretations of Islam seemed easier to control, the shariʿa was strengthened at the expense of customary law. Although it thereby lost much of its flexibility and autonomy, in the end the Islamic judicial system survived. Later the French adopted similar, though not identical, policies to integrate religious structures within the French protectorates of Tunisia and Morocco.[10] In her chapter, 'Islam and the French Empire in North Africa', Julia Clancy-Smith compares the accommodation of Islam in all three French possessions in the Maghrib, pointing out that, although colonial officials generally sought to respect religious structures and practices, their engagement with Islam could differ considerably across the region. While more interventionist policies were pursued in Algeria—reflected in attempts to integrate religious courts, schools, and pious endowments into the colonial state—in Tunisia and Morocco colonial authorities meddled less in religious matters. Looking more closely at the intersection of Islam and empire in the protectorate of Tunisia, Clancy-Smith shows that French policies varied over time, oscillating between interventionism and non-interference. In any case, colonial officials in Tunisia tried to keep (pre-colonial) religious institutions in place to bolster their rule. The Husaynids were allowed to maintain their hold over Islamic affairs, with the bey continuing to act as the highest judicial authority, and the ʿulama maintained, on the whole, control over courts, schools, and funds. Although their responses to the imperial conquest were mixed, Islamic dignitaries did not issue any major call for resistance, while the French were at pains to cultivate good relations with them. Anxious to avoid religious tensions, colonial authorities in Tunisia would even ensure (in contrast to their counterparts in Algeria) that the 1905 Law of Separation of church and state did not affect Islamic institutions. Major religious conflicts only emerged in the interwar period, when Catholic revivalism, culminating in the Tunisian Eucharistic Congress of 1930, provoked massive anti-colonial protests.

The policies in the Maghrib eventually served as a model for French officials in colonial West Africa, which was conquered at the end of the nineteenth century. The French engagement with Islam in West Africa has attracted interest from historians for decades.[11] Although cautiously monitored by the colonial administration,

---

[10] Arnold H. Green, *The Tunisian Ulama 1873–1915: Social Structure and Response to Ideological Currents* (Leiden, 1978), 129–230; and Moshe Gershovich, *French Military Rule in Morocco: Colonialism and its Consequences* (London and Portland, OR, 2000), 63–121; and, on the coordination of French policies in North Africa, see William A. Hoisington, 'France and Islam: The Haut Comité Méditerranéen and French North Africa', in George Joffé (ed.), *North Africa: Nation, State, and Region* (London and New York, 1993), 78–90.

[11] Christopher Harrison, *France and Islam in West Africa, 1860–1960* (Cambridge, 1988). On the question of the coherence of French policies towards Islam in nineteenth-century West Africa, see Donal Cruise O'Brien, 'Towards an "Islamic Policy" in French West Africa', *Journal of African History*, 8/2 (1967), 303–16; and, in response, David Robinson, 'French "Islamic" Policy and Practice in Late Nineteenth-Century Senegal', *Journal of African History*, 29/3 (1988), 415–35; see also Jean-Louis Triaud, 'Islam in Africa under French Colonial Rule', in Nehemia Levtzion and Randall L. Pouwels (eds), *The History of Islam in Africa* (Athens, OH, 2000), 169–88; Gregory Mann, 'Fetishizing Religion: Allah Koura and French "Islamic Policy" in Late Colonial French Soudan (Mali)', *Journal*

Muslims were granted full religious autonomy and could run their own law courts, pious endowments, and schools. In their search for local allies, the French soon became convinced that it was more useful to cooperate with the shaykhs of the Sufi brotherhoods than with the seemingly less influential traditional chiefs.[12] The shaykhs and their lodges were granted full autonomy and in return they endorsed the colonial regime. Some of them even legitimized French rule in religious terms and helped to promote the secular Third Republic as a 'Muslim power', a *puissance musulmane*. This cooperation with the colonial regime helped the Sufi shaykhs to consolidate their position in French West Africa. Under foreign rule, their Islamic institutions grew.[13] The French even sponsored the hajj of loyal religious leaders and soon expanded this policy to wider parts of the population. By the mid-twentieth century, French authorities supported the hajj of hundreds of ordinary West African Muslims.[14] Of course, these policies had their limits. Despite the notable efforts made by the colonial administration to employ Islam, historians have pointed out that, particularly in the early phase of conquest, French interference frequently undermined and even destroyed Islamic structures.[15]

French policies toward Islam in West Africa, which at any time relied on the close surveillance of Islamic structures, have often been compared with British rule in the region, which has usually been described as less interventionist.[16] Indeed, the classic example of the accommodation of Islam in the British empire is West Africa. In the protectorate of Northern Nigeria, established at the turn of the twentieth century in the territories of the former Sokoto caliphate, Islamic leaders and institutions enjoyed remarkable autonomy. The system of colonial government established by Frederick Lugard, high commissioner of the protectorate from 1899

*of African History*, 44/2 (2003), 263–82; and Hélène Grandhomme, 'La politique musulmane de la France au Sénégal (1936–1964)', *Canadian Journal of African Studies*, 38/2 (2004), 237–78.

[12] David Robinson, *Paths of Accommodation: Muslim Societies and French Colonial Authorities in Senegal and Mauritania, 1880–1920* (Oxford and Athens, OH, 2000); and also David Robinson, 'France as a Muslim Power in West Africa', *Africa Today*, 46, 3/4 (1999), 105–27; David Robinson, 'The Murids: Surveillance and Accommodation', *Journal of African History*, 40/2 (1999), 193–213; the articles in David Robinson and Jean-Louis Triaud (eds), *Le temps des marabouts: Itinéraires et stratégies Islamiques en Afrique occidentale française v. 1880–1960* (Paris, 1997); the articles of David Robinson in David Robinson and Jean-Louis Triaud (eds), *La Tijâniyya: Une confrérie musulmane à la conquête de l'Afrique* (Paris, 2000); and Lucy Behrman, 'French Muslim Policy and the Senegalese Brotherhoods', in Daniel F. McCall (ed), *Aspects of West African Islam* (Boston, 1971), 185–208.

[13] Robert Launay and Benjamin F. Soares, 'The Formation of an "Islamic Sphere" in French Colonial West Africa', *Economy and Society*, 28/4 (1999), 497–519.

[14] Gregory Mann and Baz Lecocq, 'Between Empire, *Umma*, and the Muslim Third World: The French Union and African Pilgrims to Mecca, 1946–58', *Comparative Studies of South Asia, Africa and the Middle East*, 27/2 (2007), 167–81.

[15] Martin A. Klein, *Islam and Imperialism in Senegal: Sine-Saloum, 1847–1914* (Stanford, 1968); and Cheikh Anta Babou, *Fighting the Greater Jihad: Amadu Bamba and the Founding of the Muridiyya of Senegal, 1853–1913* (Athens, OH, 2007), have shown the less accommodating side of French policies toward Islam.

[16] Michael Crowder, *West Africa under Colonial Rule* (London, 1968); William F. S. Miles, *Hausaland Divided: Colonialism and Independence in Nigeria and Niger* (Ithaca, NY and London, 1994); and William F. S. Miles, 'Partitioned Royalty: The Evolution of Hausa Chiefs in Nigeria and Niger', *Journal of Modern African Studies*, 25/2 (1987), 233–58. A concise comparison is given by Mervyn Hiskett, *The Development of Islam in West Africa* (London and New York, 1984), 202–301.

to 1906, has often been described as the major example not only of indirect rule, but also of the accommodation of Islam in the colonial state.[17] Under the control of only a few British officials, Muslim authorities of the caliphate, most notably the local judges and the powerful amirs, were employed to govern on a local level. Their autonomy was, of course, not absolute. Recent studies have noted the limits of British indirect rule in Islamic Northern Nigeria and pointed out that religious leaders and the 'ulama were far less loyal to the British than usually assumed.[18] And even though colonial officials accepted Islamic law within their jurisdiction, their presence affected various Islamic legal practices, and many of their edicts and rulings even destroyed Islamic institutions.

While research has focused on the intersection of Islam and empire in West Africa, the eastern part of the continent has remained surprisingly neglected.[19] In the chapter, 'Islam and Imperialism in East Africa', Felicitas Becker shows that most Islamic leaders in East Africa did not call for resistance against European intrusion, but instead sought cooperation. This response, she points out, was not surprising, given the history of exchange, pluralism, and interaction with foreigners in the Indian Ocean setting. After all, many Muslim leaders believed that they could benefit from cooperation. In German East Africa, colonial officials took the Muslim population and their religious structures quite seriously. Indeed, among the richest files from the German period in the archives are the folders on 'religious movements'. Yet Becker points out that even though anxious about the political impact of Sufi orders, Mahdist movements, and the 'ulama, the Germans ultimately showed considerable pragmatism, pursuing a policy of religious neutrality,

---

[17] Frederick D. Lugard, *The Dual Mandate in British Tropical Africa* (Edinburgh and London, 1922), is the foundational text; see also Margery Perham, Lugard, 2 vols (London, 1956–60), ii: *The Years of Authority 1898–1945*, 1–280 and 375–638. Scholars have long questioned Lugard's alleged policy of indirect rule, see Hubert Deschamps, 'Et Maintenant, Lord Lugard?', *Africa: Journal of the International African Institute*, 33/4 (1963), 293–306; and, in response, Michael Crowder, 'Indirect Rule: French and British Style', *Africa: Journal of the International African Institute*, 34/3 (1964), 197–205; and I. F. Nicolson, *The Administration of Nigeria 1900–1960: Men, Methods, and Myths* (Oxford, 1969), 124–79; on the spread of Islam under British rule, see C. N. Ubah, 'Colonial Administration and the Spread of Islam in Northern Nigeria', *The Muslim World*, 81/2 (1991), 133–48; on the conflict between missionaries and colonial authorities over Islam, see Andrew E. Barnes, '"Religious Insults": Christian Critiques of Islam and the Government in Colonial Northern Nigeria', *Journal of Religion in Africa*, 34/1–2 (2004), 62–81.

[18] Muhammad S. Umar, *Islam and Colonialism: Intellectual Responses of Muslims of Northern Nigeria to British Colonial Rule* (Leiden, 2006). On British interference in Muslim matters, see also Muhammad S. Umar, 'The Tijâniyya and British Colonial Authorities in Northern Nigeria', in Triaud and Robinson (eds), *La Tijâniyya*, 327–55; Peter Kazenga Tibenderana, 'The Role of the British Administration in the Appointment of the Emirs of Northern Nigeria, 1903–1931: The Case of Sokoto Province', *Journal of African History*, 28/2 (1987), 231–57; Peter Kazenga Tibenderana, 'The Irony of Indirect Rule in Sokoto Emirate, Nigeria, 1903–1944', *African Studies Review*, 31/1 (1988), 67–92; Auwalu Hamsxu Yadudu, 'Colonialism and the Transformation of the Substance and Form of Islamic Law in the Northern States of Nigeria', *Journal of Law and Religion*, 9/1 (1991), 17–47; and Jonathan Reynolds, 'Good and Bad Muslims: Islam and Indirect Rule in Northern Nigeria', *International Journal of African Historical Studies*, 34/3 (2001), 601–18.

[19] Said S. Samatar (ed.), *In the Shadow of Conquest: Islam in Colonial Northeast Africa* (Trenton, NJ, 1992), contains studies on some aspects of the intersection of Islam and imperialism in the northern parts of East Africa.

cooperating with Islamic leaders, and employing Muslims in their colonial administration. In the British parts of East Africa, colonial bureaucrats adopted a similar policy, although they were more experienced and less excitable when dealing with Islamic affairs than their German counterparts. British officials in the region made considerable efforts to integrate Islamic judicial structures into the colonial state. To control the religious courts, they subordinated them to European colonial courts, creating a hybrid legal system. In the process, the emphasis of Islamic law shifted from 'law as process' to 'law as structure'. Becker's chapter also demonstrates that the role of missionaries in colonial East Africa was quite complex. Whereas the Germans were anxious not to give missions too much room, the British did not impede missionaries (as they did in other parts of their Muslim empire), though their general policy of noninterference still provided the framework for the expansion of Islam.

The largest Muslim population of the British empire lived, of course, in the Indian subcontinent. Influenced by the events of 1947, historians have long focused on Muslim political representation and separatist activism in British India.[20] From the middle of the nineteenth century the British increasingly treated the Muslim population of India as a distinct group, thereby contributing to the rise of modern Muslim community consciousness. British endorsement of the foundation of the All-India Muslim League in 1906, and the introduction of separate electorates in 1909 provided, albeit unintentionally, an environment in which Muslim separatism could develop. Colonial officials made significant efforts to cooperate with loyal Muslim leaders such as Sayyid Ahmad Khan, and were at pains to accommodate Muslims in the colonial state. Studies on Muslim political representation and activism in British India have been primarily concerned with social and political aspects, rather than with religion as such. Only recently have scholars begun to enquire more deeply into British policies towards the religion of their Muslim subjects in India, addressing themes such as the role of the Islamic judiciary system and the creation of the colonial 'Anglo-Mohammedan law',[21] the

---

[20] P. Hardy, *The Muslims of British India* (Cambridge, 1972); Francis Robinson, *Separatism among Indian Muslims: The Politics of the United Provinces' Muslims, 1860–1923* (Cambridge, 1975); and, more recently, Francis Robinson, 'The British Empire and Muslim Identity in South Asia', *Transactions of the Royal Historical Society*, 6/8 (1998), 271–89; see also the studies by David Page, *Prelude to Partition: The Indian Muslims and the Imperial System of Control 1920–1932* (Delhi, 1982); David Gilmartin, *Empire and Islam: Punjab and the Making of Pakistan* (Berkeley, 1988); and Farzana Shaikh, *Community and Consensus in Islam: Muslim Representation in Colonial India, 1860–1947* (Cambridge, 1989). Shaikh gives a good overview of the complex historiographical debate about Islam, British rule, and communalism in the subcontinent (pp. 1–9). On the special role of Shi'i politics in British India, see Justin Jones, *Shi'a Islam in Colonial India: Religion, Community and Sectarianism* (Cambridge, 2012), especially 147–85.

[21] Michael R. Anderson, 'Islamic Law and Colonial Encounter in British India', in Chibli Mallat and Jane Connors (eds), *Islamic Family Law* (London, 1990), 205–23; Scott Alan Kugle, 'Framed, Blamed and Renamed: The Recasting of Islamic Jurisprudence in Colonial South Asia', *Modern Asian Studies*, 35/2 (2001), 257–313; Muhammad Qasim Zaman, *The Ulama in Contemporary Islam: Custodians of Change* (Princeton, 2002), 17–37; and Nandini Chatterjee, 'Muslim or Christian? Family Quarrels and Religious Diagnosis in a Colonial Court', *American Historical Review*, 117/4 (2012), 1101–22; for a comparison with the *droit musulman algérien* in French Algeria, see David S. Powers, 'Orientalism, Colonialism, and Legal History: The Attack on Muslim Family Endowments in Algeria and India', *Comparative Studies in Society and History*, 31/3 (1989), 535–71; and for a

role of Islam in the colonial army,[22] and the engagement of the colonial authorities with specific religious rituals, most importantly the hajj.[23] British officials were concerned about the pilgrimage for medical reasons, fearing the spread of diseases, as experienced with the massive cholera epidemic during the 1865 hajj. Moreover, they suspected that the annual gathering facilitated pan-Islamic ideas and anti-colonial radicalism. In the chapter 'British Imperial Rule and the Hajj', John Slight addresses London's policies towards the yearly ritual. Slight demonstrates that British involvement with the pilgrimage was not only prompted by anxieties about the spread of dangerous germs and ideas, but also by a wide range of other considerations, generally overlooked by historians. Of major concern to the authorities were the so-called 'pauper pilgrims', who could only afford a one-way ticket to the Hijaz. Stranded on the Arabian peninsula, the presence of these destitute Muslims from British-controlled lands troubled colonial officials, who were anxious about their empire's prestige in the Islamic world. After all attempts to regulate the group's travels proved unsuccessful, the British routinely repatriated them at considerable expense. Indeed, Slight shows that Britain developed a global administrative apparatus to deal with the flow of pilgrims to Mecca. Its involvement in the hajj echoed, to some extent, the practices of the older Islamic empires, although it took place in the modern world of steamships, railways, and telegraphed pilgrimage reports. Employed in the hajj administration were also a significant number of Muslim intermediaries, who, as Slight points out, extensively shaped imperial policies. Finally, the chapter shows how Britain's relationship with the hajj was complicated by the political situation in the Arabian peninsula. During the Arab Revolt of 1916–18, for instance, British authorities grew ever more concerned about the hajj, as they believed that their policies towards the pilgrimage had political and propagandistic consequences. And following the Saudi-Wahhabi conquest of 1924, Whitehall even ignored the protests of its own Muslim subjects—especially those from India—about Wahhabi doctrine in order to establish an alliance with the new guardians of the Ka'ba.

comparison with colonial West Africa, see Lauren Benton, *Law and Colonial Cultures: Legal Regimes in World History, 1400–1900* (Cambridge, 2002), 127–66.

[22] Nile Green, *Islam and the Army in Colonial India: Sepoy Religion in the Service of Empire* (Cambridge, 2009); see also Nile Green, 'The Faqir and the Subalterns: Mapping the Holy Man in Colonial South Asia', *Journal of Asian History*, 41/1 (2007), 57–84; and Nile Green, 'Jack Sepoy and the Dervishes: Islam and the Indian Soldier in Princely Hyderabad', *Journal of the Royal Asiatic Society*, 18/1 (2008), 31–46.

[23] John P. Slight, 'The British Empire and the Hajj, 1865–1956' (PhD, University of Cambridge, 2011); see also William R. Roff, 'Sanitation and Security: The Imperial Powers and the Nineteenth-Century Hajj', *Arabian Studies*, 6 (1982), 143–60; Takashi Oishi, 'Friction and Rivalry over Pious Mobility: British Colonial Management of the Hajj and the Reaction to it by Indian Muslims, 1870–1920', in Kuroki Hidemitsu (ed.), *The Influence of Human Mobility in Muslim Societies* (London, 2003), 151–79; Michael B. Miller, 'Pilgrims' Progress: The Business of the Hajj', *Past and Present*, 191/1 (2006), 189–228; Michael Christopher Low, 'Empire and the Hajj: Pilgrims, Plagues, and Pan-Islam under British Surveillance, 1865–1908', *International Journal of Middle Eastern Studies*, 40/2 (2008), 269–90; and Saurabh Mishra, *Pilgrimage, Politics and Pestilence: The Haj from the Indian Subcontinent, 1860–1920* (Delhi, 2011).

In Southeast Asia, British officials ultimately pursued similar policies to those in India. In British Malaya, the involvement of the imperial administration with religious courts, schools, waqf endowments, and the hajj resulted in an increasing institutionalization and bureaucratization of Islam.[24] Yet the most important power in the region was the Dutch empire. Although in the Dutch East Indies confrontations between Christian conquerors and Muslim subjects were frequent, Islamic institutions continued to function within the imperial framework.[25] The colonial government maintained Islamic schools and courts and tried to administer Islam in a modern bureaucracy. And just like their British counterparts, Dutch officials became heavily involved in the organization of the annual pilgrimage to Mecca. In the chapter 'The Dutch Empire and the Hajj', Eric Tagliacozzo examines the Dutch engagement with pilgrims from the East Indies. Although the first Dutch who arrived on the shores of the Indies archipelago in the sixteenth century were still bewildered by their encounters with people called 'hajjis', the pilgrimage increasingly became a subject of colonial policy as Dutch control over the region tightened. In the nineteenth century, a complex bureaucracy was established to regulate the hajj and to cope with issues such as pauper pilgrims, sanitary problems, and the threat of anti-colonial and pan-Islamic extremism. Colonial officials became main facilitators of the hajj, supplying steamships and even battling banditry in the Arabian peninsula. Under imperial rule, greater numbers of Indies pilgrims could embark on the hajj than ever before. At the same time, as Tagliacozzo points out, the bureaucracy provided colonial officials, afraid of Muslim militancy, with an instrument of surveillance and control. As in the French and British empires, the hajj was seen as a political matter by Dutch authorities.

Yet, it was not only the overseas empires, but also some of the European continental empires that expanded into Muslim regions. Following the involvement of Franz Josef I in the Balkans in 1878, Habsburg authorities encountered a significant Muslim population.[26] Eager to establish religious institutions independent from those of the Ottomans and keen to monitor and control Islam in the Balkans, imperial officials under the ambitious and able bureaucrat Benjamin Kállay, governor of Bosnia and Herzegovina, introduced an elaborate religious administration. The faithful were organized under the authority of a single religious leader, the

[24] Moshe Yegar, *Islam and Islamic Institutions in British Malaya: Policies and Implementation* (Jerusalem, 1979).
[25] Karel Steenbrink, *Dutch Colonialism and Indonesian Islam: Contacts and Conflicts 1596–1950* (Amsterdam, 1993); see also Muhammad Hisyam, *Caught Between Three Fires: The Javanese Pangulu under the Dutch Colonial Administration 1882–1942* (PhD, Leiden University, 2001); and the classic Georges Henri Bousquet, *La politique musulmane et coloniale des Pays-Bas* (Paris, 1939).
[26] Robert J. Donia, *Islam under the Double Eagle: The Muslims of Bosnia and Hercegovina, 1978–1914* (New York, 1981); Ferdinand Hauptmann, 'Die Mohammedaner in Bosnien-Hercegovina', in Adam Wandruzka and Peter Urbanitsch (eds), *Die Habsburgermonarchie 1848–1918*, iv: *Die Konfessionen* (Vienna, 1985), 670–701; Muhamed Mufaku al-Arnaut, 'Islam and Muslims in Bosnia 1878–1918: Two Hijras and Two Fatwas', *Journal of Islamic Studies*, 5/2 (1994), 242–53; Mark Pinson, 'The Muslims of Bosnia-Herzegovina under Austro-Hungarian Rule, 1878–1918', in Mark Pinson (ed.), *The Muslims of Bosnia and Herzegovina: Their Historical Development from the Middle Ages to the Dissolution of Yugoslavia* (Cambridge, MA, 1994), 84–128; and Rupert Klieber, *Jüdische—Christliche—Muslimische Lebenswelten der Donaumonarchie 1848–1918* (Vienna, 2010), 157–68.

*Reis-ul-Ulema* (head of the 'ulama), who was assisted by a council of religious dignitaries, the *Ulema-Medžlis* (council of the 'ulama), which oversaw the waqf endowments, madrasas, and shari'a courts, as well as the work of the local imams, 'ulama,
and *hodžas*. Habsburg officials would also employ religious authorities when
recruiting thousands of Muslims into their armies.[27] In 1882, the Mufti of Sarajevo
(who would soon become the first *Reis-ul-Ulema*), Mustafa Hilmi Omerović, even
issued a fatwa encouraging the faithful to serve in the Austro-Hungarian ranks.

The situation in the tsarist empire was remarkably similar, although it contained
a much larger Muslim population.[28] Muscovy had already begun expanding into
the Muslim areas of the Volga-Ural region in the sixteenth century. With Russia's
annexation of the Caucasus and the Crimea in the eighteenth and nineteenth centuries and its nineteenth-century expansion into the heart of Central Asia, many
more Muslims came under the tzar's rule. In the chapter 'The Russian Worlds of
Islam', Robert D. Crews examines the relationship between state and mosque in
the Muslim lands of the tsarist empire, arguing that the Russian rule of Muslims
was more tolerant and successful than has often been assumed. After a period of
suppression under Peter the Great, marked by the destruction of mosques and
forced conversions, in the late eighteenth century Catherine II introduced a policy of religious tolerance. Although Russian rulers saw themselves as the leaders
of Orthodox Christendom, they also promoted themselves as patrons of Islam.
In fact, tsarist rule was heavily based on confessional foundations, and Islam
was an important pillar of the imperial order. Officials and bureaucrats, such
as the famous Konstantin von Kaufmann, the first governor-general of Russian

---

[27] Richard B. Spence, 'Die Bosniaken kommen! The Bosnian-Hercegovinian Formations of the
Austro-Hungarian Army, 1914–1918', in Richard B. Spence and Linda L. Nelson (eds), *Scholar,
Patriot, Mentor: Historical Essays in Honor of Dimitrije Djordjević* (Boulder, CO, 1992), 299–314;
and, on the fatwa of the Mufti of Sarajevo, see Fikret Karčić, *The Bosniaks and the Challenge of
Modernity: Late Ottoman and Hapsburg Times* (Sarajevo, 1999), 119–20.

[28] Robert D. Crews, *For Prophet and Tsar: Islam and Empire in Russia and Central Asia* (Cambridge,
MA and London, 2006); see also Robert D. Crews, 'Empire and the Confessional State: Islam and
Religious Politics in Nineteenth-Century Russia', *American Historical Review*, 108/1 (2003), 50–83;
Robert D. Crews, 'Islamic Law, Imperial Order: Muslims, Jews, and the Russian State', *Ab Imperio*,
3 (2004), 467–90; Allen J. Frank, *Muslim Religious Institutions in Imperial Russia: The Islamic World
of Novouzensk District and the Kazakh Inner Horde, 1780–1910* (Leiden, 2001); Elena I. Campbell,
'The Autocracy and the Muslim Clergy in the Russian Empire (1850s–1917)', *Russian Studies in
History*, 44/2 (2005), 8–29; Vladimir Bobrovnikov, 'Islam in the Russian Empire', in Dominic Lieven
(ed.), *The Cambridge History of Russia*, ii: *Imperial Russia, 1689–1917* (Cambridge, 2006), 202–23;
and Paolo Sartori, 'An Overview of Tsarist Policy on Islamic Courts in Turkestan: Its Genealogy and
its Effects', in Svetlana Gorshenina and Sergey Abashin (eds) *Le Turkestan russe: Une colonie comme
les autres?* (Paris, 2009), 477–507. These works have emphasized the accommodation of Islam in
the tsarist empire. Studies that have stressed the less accommodating side of Russian rule in its
Islamic periphery are Firouzeh Mostashari, *On the Religious Frontier: Tsarist Russia and Islam in the
Caucasus* (London, 2006); Kelly O'Neill, 'Between Subversion and Submission: the Integration of
the Crimean Khanate into the Russian Empire, 1783–1853' (PhD, Harvard University, 2006); Kelly
O'Neill, 'Constructing Russian Identity in the Imperial Borderland: Architecture, Islam, and the
Transformation of the Crimean Landscape', *Ab Imperio*, 2 (2006), 163–92; A. S. Morrison, *Russian
Rule in Samarkand 1868–1910: A Comparison with British India* (Oxford, 2008), especially 51–87;
and also articles in part I in Stéphane A. Dudoignon and Komatsu Hisao (eds), *Islam in Politics in
Russia and Central Asia (Early Eighteenth to Late Twentieth Centuries)* (London, 2001).

Turkestan, made significant attempts to accommodate Islamic structures in the empire. They employed trusted Muslim dignitaries and members of the 'ulama, who were to act as intermediaries and to exert power in their local communities. Paid by St Petersburg, they became government officials and part of the imperial state. Crews shows that tsarist Russia can also serve as a good example of the imperial bureaucratization of Islam. In 1788, Catherine II created the Orenburg Muslim Ecclesiastical Assembly in Ufa. Headed by a mufti who was on St Petersburg's payroll, the body was to administer and control Muslims across the empire. The assembly had authority over the local 'ulama, but was subordinated to the tsarist Ministry of Internal Affairs. In the following decades, similar bodies were founded in different regions of the empire—in 1831 in the Crimea, and in 1872 in the Caucasus, where assemblies for the Sunni community and for the Shi'a were established. The institutionalization of Islam in hierarchical and ecclesiastical structures had a considerable impact on the religious practice of Muslims under Russian rule. Through this system, the imperial state tried to control almost every part of Muslim life, including marriage and funerary rites, the number of mosques and imams, and the hajj. Yet, Muslim leaders, too, could exploit the new bureaucracy to their own advantage, using it to petition the state and to employ tsarist authorities to settle disputes, enforce the shari'a, and exert authority in their communities. Crews also discusses the place of Islam in the Romanovs' multi-confessional armed forces. Curbing the army chaplains' drive to convert non-Christian soldiers, from the late eighteenth century onwards military officials established posts for field imams who were not only responsible for overseeing religious observance in the units, but were also used to monitor the political mood in the ranks.

Overall, the contributions in the first part of the book show that European authorities adopted a wide range of means to accommodate Islamic structures within their empires. Islamic institutions were not only tolerated, but regularly used to enhance and bolster colonial rule. Yet, the history of Islam and imperialism also had a more violent side—the expansion of European powers into the Muslim world also provoked conflict and religious unrest.

## ISLAM AND ANTI-COLONIAL RESISTANCE

Throughout the high age of empire, European authorities were confronted with religious insurgency and Islamic anti-colonialism. Across Africa and Asia, religious leaders called for holy war against non-Muslim rule over the *dar al-Islam*. At times, this call was preceded by the appeal for emigration from the colonized territories, drawing on the concept of hijra. Though we must be cautious not to adopt an essentialist view of these resistance movements, there seem to be some striking similarities between them.[29] They were led by religious authorities. Their

[29] William R. Roff (ed.), *Islam and the Political Economy of Meaning: Comparative Studies of Muslim Discourse* (London, 1987), and other works have stressed the importance of specific social and political

slogans were religiously charged. Religious forms of organization and Islamic polities were promoted as viable alternatives to non-Muslim rule. The movements were usually rooted in the pre-colonial era and regularly went along with internal struggles and attempts to transform local communities and to establish theocratic states. Emphasizing the significance of religion should by no means imply that socioeconomic forces and material conditions were unimportant.[30] Nevertheless, the role of religion needs to be taken seriously in order to fully understand these movements. Islam often played a crucial part in shaping social and political life in Muslim communities and proved to be a highly effective legitimizing, organizing, and mobilizing force in a considerable number of popular anti-colonial movements. Islam could be used to overcome ethnic, social, and linguistic disunity. And after all, religion provided one of the most obvious demarcations between invaders and invaded, thus offering an attractive vehicle of protest against foreign rule rooted in indigenous culture.

There were different types of Islamic resistance movements, most notably Sufi brotherhoods and networks, Mahdist movements, and reformist groups, all on occasion backed by the traditional 'ulama.[31] To be sure, there were many varieties and streams within each of these movements, and the lines that can be drawn between them are not clear-cut. Some scholars have, in fact, described them as part of the same wave of Islamic renewal and reformism that spread across the world from the eighteenth century onwards.[32] The chapters in the second part of this book examine various anti-colonial uprisings in the Muslim parts of the European empires, enquiring into the role that religion and religious violence played in them, and examining the forms of Islam by which they were dominated.

Messianic movements arguably posed one of the most potent threats to imperial rule.[33] Centered on a charismatic leader and driven by millennial expectations, entire societies could rise in revolt against foreign intrusion. The most prominent example is the late nineteenth-century Mahdi uprising in Sudan, when self-proclaimed Mahdi Muhammad Ahmad waged holy war against Ottoman-Egyptian rule and

---

contexts in shaping Islamic movements and discourses across the world, although the emphasis on diversity bears the risk of overlooking crucial similarities. On more general discussions about diversity in the Muslim world, see the literature in footnote 6.

[30] Edmund Burke III, 'Islam and Social Movements: Methodological Reflections', in Edmund Burke III and Ira M. Lapidus (eds), *Islam, Politics, and Social Movements* (Berkeley, 1988), 17–35.

[31] For a comparison between various Islamic anti-colonial movements, see Rudolph Peters, *Islam and Colonialism: The Doctrine of Jihad in Modern History* (The Hague, 1979), 39–104; and Nikki R. Keddie, 'The Revolt of Islam, 1700 to 1993: Comparative Considerations and Relations to Imperialism', *Comparative Studies in Society and History*, 36/3 (1994), 463–87, especially 481–5. Peters (pp. 41–4) and Keddie (pp. 466–7 and 481), mainly distinguish between 'messianic' and 'Wahhabi type' revolts. Part IV of Sohail H. Hashmi (ed.), *Just Wars, Holy Wars, and Jihads: Christian, Jewish, and Muslim Encounters and Exchanges* (Oxford, 2012), also provides some comparative insights into anti-colonial jihad movements.

[32] John Obert Voll, 'Foundations of Renewal and Reform: Islamic Movements in the Eighteenth and Nineteenth Centuries', in John L. Esposito (ed.), *The Oxford History of Islam* (Oxford, 1999), 509–47.

[33] For the general context, see Michael Adas, *Prophets of Rebellion: Millenarian Protest Movements against the European Colonial Order* (Chapel Hill, NC, 1979); and the classic by Bryan R. Wilson, *Magic and the Millennium: A Sociological Study of Religious Movements of Protest among Tribal and Third-World Peoples* (London, 1973).

its British protectors, conquered Khartoum, and established a theocratic state, banning smoking, alcohol, and dancing. In 1896, London sent an army under the ruthless Herbert Kitchener against the Islamic state, now led by Ahmad's successor, 'Abd Allah al-Ta'ayishi. The campaign took more than three years and ended with the total defeat of al-Ta'ayishi. A topic of continued fascination, the revolt has been the subject of numerous popular books.[34] Historians, too, for decades have been drawn to the subject, examining the wider social and political circumstances of the Sudanese Mahdiyya and its legacy, the role of reformist puritanical ideas that shaped the movement, and British official assessments of millennial Islam.[35] Studies have also explored the structure of the theocratic regime itself, including its organization, its eschatological propaganda, its ceremonies and rituals of power, and its ambivalent relationship with the local Sufi brotherhoods.[36] But although the Sudanese Mahdiyya continues to be a subject of particular fascination, it was by no means the only anti-colonial rebellion in Africa that was fueled by messianism. After the turn of the century, various Mahdist revolts challenged British rule in Northern Nigeria, specifically the uprisings in Burmi (1903), Satiru (1906), and Dumbulwa (1923).[37] In 1907, German troops waged a colonial war against

---

[34] Dominic Green, *Armies of God: Islam and Empire on the Nile, 1869–1899* (London, 2007); Fergus Nicoll, *Mahdi of Sudan and the Death of General Gordon* (London, 2005); Michael Asher, *Khartoum: The Ultimate Imperial Adventure* (London, 2005); and Robin Neillands, *The Dervish Wars: Gordon and Kitchener in the Sudan, 1880–1898* (London, 1996). Popular fascination with the Mahdiyya goes back to the times of the revolt itself. Famous contemporary accounts are F. R. Wingate, *Mahdism and the Egyptian Sudan* (London, 1891); and Winston S. Churchill, *The River War: An Historical Account of the Reconquest of the Soudan* (London, 1899); on Churchill's views of the Mahdi revolt, see Richard Toye, *Churchill's Empire: The World That Made Him and the World He Made* (London, 2010), 50–60.

[35] Alice Moore-Harell, *Gordon and the Sudan: Prologue to the Mahdiyya 1877–1880* (London and Portland, OR, 2001), on preconditions of the Mahdiyya; Gabriel Warburg, *Islam, Sectarianism, and Politics in Sudan since the Mahdiyya* (London, 2003), on the legacy of the movement; John Obert Voll, 'The Sudanese Mahdi: Frontier Fundamentalist', *International Journal of Middle East Studies*, 10/2 (1979), 145–66, on the influence of reformist ideas; and David Steele, 'Lord Salisbury, the "False Religion" of Islam, and the Reconquest of the Sudan', in Edward M. Spiers (ed.), *Sudan: The Reconquest Reappraised* (London, 1998), 11–34, on British perceptions of the Mahdi.

[36] P. M. Holt, *Mahdist State in the Sudan, 1881–98: A Study of Its Origins, Development and Overthrow* (Oxford, 1958), provides the most comprehensive account; see also A. B. Theobald, *The Mahdīya: A History of the Anglo-Egyptian Sudan, 1881–1899* (London, 1951); and Kim Searcy, *The Formation of the Sudanese Mahdist State: Ceremony and Symbols of Authority: 1882–1898* (Leiden, 2011).

[37] Paul E. Lovejoy and J. S. Hogendorn, 'Revolutionary Mahdism and Resistance to Colonial Rule in the Sokoto Caliphate, 1905–6', *Journal of African History*, 31/2 (1990), 217–44; Thea Büttner, 'Social Aims and Earlier Anti-Colonial Struggles: The Satiru Rising of 1906', in Thea Büttner and Gerhard Brehme (eds), *African Studies* (Berlin, 1973), 1–18; R. A. Adeleye, 'Mahdist Triumph and British Revenge in Northern Nigeria: Satiru 1906', *Journal of the Historical Society of Nigeria*, 6 (1972), 193–214; C. N. Ubah, 'British Measures against Mahdism in Dumbulwa in Northern Nigeria, 1923: A Case of Colonial Overreaction', *Islamic Culture*, 50/3 (1976), 169–83; Asma'u G. Saeed, 'The British Policy Towards the Mahdiyya in Northern Nigeria: A Study of the Arrest, Detention and Deportation of Shaykh Sa'id b. Hayat, 1923–1959', *Kano Studies*, 2/3 (1982–5), 95–119; John Fisher, 'British Responses to Mahdist and Other Unrest in North and West Africa, 1919–1930', *Australian Journal of Politics and History*, 52/3 (2006), 347–61; Muhammad S. Umar, 'Muslims' Eschatological Discourses on Colonialism in Northern Nigeria', *Journal of the American Academy of Religion*, 67/1 (1999), 59–84; and Peter B. Clarke, *Mahdism in West Africa: The Ijebu Mahdiyya Movement* (London, 1995), 35–44.

Mahdist movements in northern Cameroon.[38] In other parts of the world, too, Mahdism served as a vehicle for anti-imperial agitation. The Dutch empire in the East Indies had already been confronted with anti-colonial messianism in the early nineteenth century. During the Dipanagara revolt of the 1820s, Javanese rebels drew not only on mystical Islam but also on various messianic ideas to mobilize resistance.[39]

The most prevalent forces of armed anti-colonial struggle in the Islamic world, however, were Sufi orders.[40] Among the best known of these movements was ʿAbd al-Qadir and his Qadiri brotherhood, which led the jihad against French colonial troops in Algeria in the 1830s and 1840s.[41] But al-Qadir and his followers were not the only anti-colonial force in the country.[42] The Rahmaniyya brotherhood, for instance, also confronted the French invaders and later continued its resistance within the framework of the colonial state.[43] Across the Maghrib, Sufi orders played a crucial role in anti-colonial resistance. After the turn of the twentieth century, French troops became embroiled in a war with the followers of the Sanusi brotherhood in the Sahara.[44] Led by Sanusi shaykh Ahmad al-Sharif

[38] Thea Büttner, 'Die Mahdi-Erhebungen 1907 in Nordkamerun im Vergleich mit antikolonialen islamischen Bewegungen in anderen Regionen West- und Zentralafrikas', in Peter Heine and Ulrich van der Heyden (eds), *Studien zur Geschichte des deutschen Kolonialismus in Afrika* (Pfaffenweiler, 1995), 147–59; and, more generally, Martin Z. Njeuma, 'The Foundation of Radical Islam in Ngaoundere, 1835–1907', in Jean Boutrais (ed.), *Peuples et cultures de l'Adamaoua (Cameroun)* (Paris, 1993), 87–101.

[39] Peter Carey, *The Power of Prophecy: Prince Dipanagara and the End of an Old Order in Java, 1785–1855* (Leiden, 2007). Dipanagara's millenarism was based on a syncretism of various strains of centuries-old Javanese folkloric eschatology, most importantly the idea of the prophet *ratu adil*, and newer ideas of the Islamic Mahdi, see Adas, *Prophets of Rebellion*, 93–9; and Justus M. van der Kroef, 'Javanese Messianic Expectations: Their Origin and Cultural Context', *Comparative Studies in Society and History*, 1/4 (1959), 299–323, especially 308–9.

[40] On the general context, see Jamil M. Abun-Nasr, *Muslim Communities of Grace: The Sufi Brotherhoods in Religious Life* (London, 2007), 200–35, especially 202–14; and Nile Green, *Sufism: A Global History* (Oxford, 2012), 187–238, especially 191–214.

[41] Raphael Danziger, *Abd al-Qadir and the Algerians: Resistance to the French and Internal Consolidation* (New York, 1977), remains the most authoritative account; see also the classic by Colonel Paul Azan, *L'Émir Abd El Kader, 1808–1883: Du fanatisme musulman au patriotisme français* (Paris, 1925); and articles published in Marcel Émérit (ed.), *L'Algérie à l'époque d'Abd-El-Kader* (Paris, 1951); on the role of religion in his struggle, see Pessah Shinar, "Abd al-Qadir and ʿAbd al-Krim: Religious Influences on their Thought and Action', *Asian and African Studies*, 1 (1965), 139–74; and on the pre-colonial roots of al-Qadir's jihad, see Amira K. Bennison, *Jihad and its Interpretations in Pre-Colonial Morocco: State-Society Relations during the French Conquest of Algeria* (London and New York, 2002).

[42] Benjamin Brower, *A Desert Named Peace: The Violence of France's Empire in the Algerian Sahara, 1844–1902* (New York, 2009), gives a broad overview; see also Peter von Sivers, 'The Realm of Justice: Apocalyptic Revolts in Algeria (1849–1879)', *Humaniora Islamica*, 1 (1973), 47–60; the articles in part II of Burke and Lapidus (eds), *Islam, Politics, and Social Movements*; and, more generally, Fanny Colonna, 'Cultural Resistance and Religious Legitimacy in Colonial Algeria', *Economy and Society*, 3/3 (1974), 233–52.

[43] Julia Clancy-Smith, *Rebel and Saint: Muslim Notables, Populist Protest, Colonial Encounters* (Berkeley, 1994).

[44] Jean-Louis Triaud, *La légende noire de la Sanûsiyya: Une confrérie musulmane saharienne sous le regard français (1840–1930)*, 2 vols (Paris, 1995), especially vol. ii; Jean-Louis Triaud, *Tchad 1900–1902: Une guerre franco-libyenne oubliée? Une confrérie musulmane, la Sanusiyya, face à la France* (Paris, 1987); and Russell McGuirk *The Sanusi's Little War: The Amazing Story of a Forgotten Conflict in the Western Desert, 1915–1917* (London, 2007); see also the classic of E. E. Evans-Pritchard, *The Sanusi of Cyrenaica* (Oxford, 1949); and, on the origins of the order, Knut S. Vikør, *Sufi and Scholar on the*

al-Sanusi, they would later also oppose the Italian occupation of Cyrenaica. While Italian authorities officially sought to accommodate Islam in Libya, they waged a merciless colonial war against the Muslim rebels and everyone they suspected to be supporting them.[45] When, in 1931, they hanged the elderly Sanusi commander 'Umar al-Mukhtar, waves of outrage spread across the Islamic world.[46]

In his chapter 'Religious Revolts in Colonial North Africa', Knut S. Vikør provides a comparative study of 'Abd al-Qadir's war against the French in Algeria and the conflicts between the Sanusiyya and the French and Italians, enquiring more generally into the role of Sufi networks in anti-colonial resistance in North Africa. Both 'Abd al-Qadir and Ahmad al-Sharif al-Sanusi drew their authority and won their initial tribal support through their leadership of a regional Sufi order. Both were pious Sufis who only took temporary leadership of the local forces, and returned to a life of scholarship and piety after the war. Yet Vikør also points to some crucial differences between Sanusi and Qadiri resistance. Whereas Ahmad al-Sharif al-Sanusi turned the Sufi lodges into centers of resistance and drew on their shaykhs to lead the jihad, the Algerian Qadiriyya provided less stringent structures to draw on and 'Abd al-Qadir, as a consequence, founded a theocratic polity based on Islamic and modernist Ottoman models during his struggle. On the whole, the Sufi orders were more instrumental in mobilizing and unifying support among the tribes in Libya than they were in Algeria. Examining the reasons for the prominent role of the brotherhoods in various anti-colonial struggles more generally, Vikør points out that the relationship between religion and resistance was often more complex than is usually assumed. He stresses that only some aspects of the organizational framework of particular Sufi orders, under specific political and social circumstances, could generate militant resistance. The involvement of the brotherhoods in anti-colonial struggles in times of crisis required a considerable, though temporary, transformation from usually purely religious organizations into political ones.

The intersection of Sufi brotherhoods and anti-imperialism has also been studied by historians of Islam in sub-Saharan Africa. In the mid-nineteenth century, the legendary al-Hajj 'Umar Tal and the Tijaniyya confronted the French expansion in the West African savannah.[47] In French Senegal, another famous Sufi shaykh,

*Desert Edge: Muhammad b. 'Ali al-Sanusi and his Brotherhood* (London, 1995). A fascinating contemporary account of Ahmad al-Sharif al-Sanusi's resistance is G. F. Abbott, *The Holy War in Tripoli* (London, 1912).

[45] Salvatore Bono, 'Islam et politique coloniale en Libye', *The Maghreb Review*, 13 (1988), 70–6; and Anna Baldinetti, 'Italian Colonial Rule and Muslim Elites in Libya: A Relationship of Antagonism and Collaboration', in Meir Hatina (ed.), *Guardians of Faith in Modern Times: 'Ulama' in the Middle East* (Leiden, 2009), 91–108, give insights into attempts to accommodate Islam in colonial Libya. Anna Baldinetti, 'Italian Colonial Studies on the Sufi Brotherhoods in Libya', in Anna Baldinetti (ed.), *Modern and Contemporary Libya: Sources and Histogriographies* (Rome, 2003), 125–39, explores the underlying conceptions of this policy.

[46] Romain Rainero, 'La Capture: L'exécution d'Omar El-Muktar et la fin de la guérilla libyenne', *Cahirs de Tunisie*, 28/111–2 (1980), 59–74.

[47] David Robinson, *Holy War of Umar Tal: The Western Sudan in the Mid-Nineteenth Century* (Oxford, 1985), is the definitive study on the subject; see also David Robinson, *Chiefs and Clerics: Abdul Bokar Kan and Futa Toro 1853–1891* (Oxford, 1975), especially 28–53; Fernand Dumont, *L'Anti-Sultan, ou Al-Hajj Omar Tal du Fouta, combattant de la foi (1794–1864)* (Paris,

Amadu Bamba, and his order, the Muridiyya, engaged (at least initially) in anti-colonial resistance.[48] Equally important was militant Sufi opposition to European rule in East Africa. In Somaliland, the 'Dervish movement' of Salihi shaykh Muhammad 'Abd Allah Hasan, the 'mad mullah' as the British called him, confronted Italian, British, and Ethiopian troops after the turn of the twentieth century.[49] Hasan's Salihiyya also stood in conflict with the rival Qadiri brotherhood, which itself opposed the German presence in East Africa.[50]

Sufi resistance has long also attracted the attention of scholars of the tsarist empire. In the second half of the nineteenth century, the three legendary imams Ghazi Muhammad, Hamza Bek, and Shamil called for holy war, or *ghazawat*, against Russian troops in the Northern Caucasus. Imam Shamil, a reckless military genius immortalized in Tolstoy's *Hadji Murad*, fought the tsarist army for almost thirty years. Enforcing shari'a legislation, the imams merged the local communities of the northern Caucasus into an imamate. The Russians confronted the rebels with extreme brutality.[51] Studying these conflicts, historians have long tended to emphasize the role of the Naqshbandi brotherhood in organizing the anti-tsarist struggle and unifying Muslims in the imamate.[52] Only recently have scholars begun questioning the importance of the Sufi brotherhood in the anti-Russian resistance, arguing that the Naqshbandiyya had no crucial influence on the jihad movement or, indeed, the organization of the imamate.[53] Moreover, they have pointed out that Sufi ideas played only a marginal

1971); Murray Last, 'Reform in West Africa: The Jihād Movement of the Nineteenth Century', in J. F. A. Ajayi and Michael Crowder (eds), *History of West Africa*, ii (London, 1974), 1–29, especially 17–23; and Christian Coulon, 'Prophets of God or of History? Muslim Messianic Movements and Anti-Colonialism in Senegal', in Wim van Binsbergen and Matthew Schoffeleers (eds.), *Theoretical Explorations in African Religion* (London, 1985), 346–66.

[48] Babou, *Fighting the Greater Jihad*; and Cheikh Anta Babou, 'Contesting Space, Shaping Places: Making Room for the Muridiyya in Colonial Senegal, 1912–45', *Journal of African History*, 46/3 (2005), 405–26.

[49] Abdi Sheik-Abdi, *Divine Madness: Mohammed Abdulle Hassan (1856–1920)* (London, 1993), is the most comprehensive study; see also Robert L. Hess, 'The "Mad Mullah" and Northern Somalia', *Journal of African History*, 5/3 (1964), 415–33; and John P. Slight, 'British and Somali views of Muhammad Abdullah Hassan's Jihad, 1899–1920', *Bildhaan: An International Journal of Somali Studies*, 10/7 (2010), 16–35; for contemporary interpretations, see H. G. C. Swayne, *Seventeen Trips through Somaliland and a Visit to Abyssinia: With Supplementary Preface on the 'Mad Mullah' Risings* (London, 1903); and Douglas J. Jardine, *The Mad Mullah of Somaliland* (London, 1923).

[50] B. G. Martin, 'Muslim Politics and Resistance to Colonial Rule: Shaykh Uways B. Muhammed Al-Barawi and the Qadiriya Brotherhood in East Africa', *Journal of African History*, 10/3 (1969), 471–86; and Michael Pesek, 'Islam und Politik in Deutsch-Ostafrika', in Albert Wirz, Andreas Eckert, and Katrin Bromber (eds), *Alles unter Kontrolle: Disziplinierungsverfahren im Kolonialen Tanzania (1850–1960)* (Cologne, 2003), 99–140.

[51] Moshe Gammer, *Muslim Resistance to the Tsar: Shamil and the Conquest of Chechnia and Daghestan* (London, 1994); Moshe Gammer, 'Shamil's Most Successful Offensive: Daghestan 1843', *Journal of Muslim Minority Affairs*, 12/1 (1991), 41–54; and, on the early history of Russian imperialism in the Caucasus, Michael Khodarkovsky, 'Of Christianity, Enlightenment, and Colonialism: Russia in the North Caucasus, 1550–1800', *Journal of Modern History*, 71/2 (1999), 394–430.

[52] Gammer, *Muslim Resistance to the Tsar*; and, most strongly, Anna Zelkina, *In Quest of God and Freedom: Sufi Responses to the Russian Advance in the North Caucasus* (London, 2000).

[53] Alexander Knysh, 'Sufism as an Explanatory Paradigm: The Issue of the Motivations of Sufi Resistance Movements in Western and Russian Scholarship', *Die Welt des Islams*, 42/2 (2002), 139–73; Michael Kemper, *Herrschaft, Recht und Islam in Daghestan: Von den Khanaten und Gemeindebünden zum ğihād-Staat* (Wiesbaden, 2005); and Clemens P. Sidorko, *Dschihad im Kaukasus: Antikolonialer*

role and that the three imams were in fact mainly concerned about the enforcement of shariʻa, the abolishment of the *adat*, and the foundation of an Islamic polity, and thus acted in the tradition of the reformist 'shariʻa movement' of the seventeenth and eighteenth centuries. Indeed, confronting the North Caucasian Islamic resistance, the Russian imperial state consciously tried to strengthen *adat* law.[54] In his chapter 'Muslim Mobilizaton in Imperial Russia's Caucasus', Michael Reynolds reassesses the nineteenth-century *ghazawat* against Imperial Russia. Reynolds underlines the importance of reformist ideas and the lack of Sufi influence on the imams' resistance movements, although he warns against dismissing the influence of Sufism entirely. In contrast to earlier scholarship, Reynolds argues that the 'shariʻa movement' was not a distinctly Caucasian phenomenon devoid of external influence, but since the late seventeenth century had been strongly influenced by puritanical ideas from the Middle East. After all, Islam in the Caucasus was far from homogeneous and even within one group interpretations of faith and doctrine were rather diverse. Moving beyond the discussion of the particular religious influences that shaped the *ghazawat*, Reynolds presents a broad account of the imams' two distinct, though linked, struggles—the war against empire and the internal battle against un-Islamic practices. The chapter gives detailed insights into the rigidly regulated life of the imamate with its segregation of the sexes, bans on alcohol and tobacco, restrictions on music and dancing, and interference in sartorial norms, and shows that these policies were anything but popular among the mountain communities. Overall, it demonstrates that religion defined the conflict between the imams and Russia. The legitimacy and legislation of the imamate were based on religion, and Islamic slogans enabled the warlords to mobilize Muslims across tribal lines. At the same time, Reynolds points out that the *ghazawat* also needs to be seen as part of the broader historical phenomenon of clashes generally generated by imperial expansion.

The question of the importance of Sufi influences on anti-colonial revolts has been discussed by historians in more general terms. Some have even suggested rethinking the role of Sufism in anti-colonial resistance altogether, arguing that the influence of Sufi brotherhoods in Islamic anti-colonial movements has been widely overestimated, and instead emphasizing reformist influences.[55]

There is no doubt that Islamic reformism was highly influential in various anti-colonial struggles. Many of the Islamic reformist movements emerged in the eighteenth century, most famously perhaps Wahhabism in the Arabian peninsula, and became powerful forces against European colonialism in the nineteenth and early twentieth centuries. Muslim revivalists preached a renewal and purification of Islam, putting new emphasis on the Qur'an and the hadith. Only the return to

---

*Widerstand der Dagestaner und Tschetschenen gegen das Zarenreich (18. Jahrhundert bis 1859)* (Wiesbaden, 2007). Sidorko gives an excellent historiographical overview on pp. x–vii.

[54] Michael Kemper, 'Adat Against Shariʻa: Russian Approaches Toward Daghestani "Customary Law" in the 19th Century', *Ab Imperio*, 3 (2005), 147–74.

[55] Kemper, *Herrschaft, Recht und Islam in Daghestan*; Michael Kemper, 'The Changing Images of Jihad Leaders: Shamil and Abd al-Qadir in Daghestani and Algerian Historical Writing', *Nova Religio: Journal of Alternative and Emergent Religions*, 11/2 (2007), 28–58; and Knysh, 'Sufism as an Explanatory Paradigm'.

an 'authentic' and 'uncorrupted' Islam would prevent the perceived global decline of their faith. Others, Islamic modernists, urged the adoption of Western sciences, technologies, and forms of learning to strengthen Islam from within. The ideas of Islamic reformers—revivalist or modernist—implied a significant degree of secular reflection about faith and a conceptionalization of religion in abstract terms. In fact, this formalization of religion could be observed globally, and has been described as part of the 'birth of the modern world'.[56]

To be sure, Islamic reform movements were not inevitably connected to anti-colonial militancy. The major movements of religious reformism and renewal in British India, such as the puritan and revivalist Deoband school (founded in 1866) and their modernist and rationalist rival, the Aligarh school (founded in 1875), were firmly accommodated within the colonial state.[57] Scholars have shown that British rule in South Asia in fact had a considerable impact on reformist schools, reflected in the systematization of teaching and the introduction of new bureaucratic structures such as an examination system, the establishment of institutions such as a central library, and the use of modern technologies such as the printing press, the telegraph, and the postal system, which revolutionized the spread of religious knowledge.[58] Similarly, Jadidism, a reform movement of Muslim intellectuals and scholars in late nineteenth-century Central Asia, never sought violent confrontation with Russian imperialism—even though tsarist officials remained suspicious.[59] In French Algeria, too, colonial officials were equally uneasy when dealing with the reformist 'ulama, who, since 1931, had organized themselves into the influential Association of Reformist 'Ulama.[60] Imperial authorities were aware that reformist ideas could, under certain circumstances, fuel armed revolt.

---

[56] C. A. Bayly, *The Birth of the Modern World, 1780–1914: Global Connections and Comparisons* (Oxford, 2004), 325–65, especially 333–43.

[57] David Lelyveld, *Aligarh's First Generation* (Princeton, 1978); C. W. Troll, *Sayyid Ahmad Khan* (New Delhi, 1978); Ziya-ul-Hasan Faruqi, *The Deoband School and the Demand for Pakistan* (Bombay, 1963); and Barbara Metcalf, *Islamic Revival in British India: Deoband, 1860–1900* (Princeton, 1982); see also Barbara Metcalf, 'Islam and Power in Colonial India: The Making and Unmaking of a Muslim Princess', *American Historical Review*, 116/1 (2011), 1–30, on the intersection of Islamic reformism (Siddiq Hasan Khan's Ahl-i Hadith movement) and British imperialism in Shah Jahan Begum's Bhopal. An antipode to these reformist groups was the Barelvi movement, rooted in traditional folk Islam, see Usha Sanyal, *Devotional Islam and Politics in British India: Ahmed Riza Khan Barelwi and his Movement, 1870–1920* (Delhi, 1996).

[58] Metcalf, *Islamic Revival*; and Francis Robinson, 'Technology and Religious Change: Islam and the Impact of Print', *Modern Asian Studies*, 27/1 (1993), 229–51.

[59] Adeeb Khalid, *The Politics of Muslim Cultural Reform: Jadidism in Central Asia* (Berkeley, 1998); for an earlier perspective, see Hélène Carrère d'Encausse, *Réforme et révolution chez les musulmans de l'empire russe* (Paris, 1966); and for a broader examination of Islamic reformism under tsarist rule, see Michael Kemper, *Sufis und Gelehrte in Tatarien und Baschkirien, 1789–1889: Der islamische Diskurs unter russischer Herrschaft* (Berlin, 1998).

[60] Ali Merad, *Le réformisme musulman en Algérie de 1925 à 1940: Essai d'histoire religieuse et sociale* (Paris and The Hague, 1967); and Allan Christelow, 'Ritual, Culture and Politics of Islamic Reformism in Algeria', *Middle East Studies*, 23/3 (1987), 255–73. James McDougall, 'The Shabiba Islamiyya of Algiers: Education, Authority, and Colonial Control, 1921–57', *Comparative Studies of South Asia, Africa and the Middle East*, 24/1 (2004), 147–54, discusses the role of Islamic reformist education in Algeria.

Revivalist Islam was a particularly strong force in the anti-colonial resistance in British India.[61] Among the first was the reformist movement of Sayyid Ahmad Barelwi and his successors, who battled the Sikhs and, later, the British in Northern India. Throughout the nineteenth century, a main concern of colonial officers on the subcontinent was revolt on the notorious Northwest Frontier, waged by (allegedly) Wahhabi-inspired insurgents—the 'Hindustani fanatics' or 'Hindostan Wahabees' as the British called them. While clashes in the region could simply be a product of the raiding that was fundamental to the frontier economy, a result of geostrategic conflict, most notably the Anglo-Afghan Wars, or a response to the brutal collective punishment inflicted by the British, a number of rebellions were unmistakably religiously inspired—often, of course, these different factors were interwoven. The frontier region remained a hotbed of rebels, among them the legendary mullahs Saidulla, Najmuddin and Sayyid Akbar, the Syrian imam Shami Pir, and Mirza Ali Khan, known as the 'Faqir of Ipi', until the end of the colonial period. Benjamin D. Hopkins' chapter, 'Islam and Resistance in the British Empire', gives a thorough account of the frontier wars, demonstrating that in times of revolt the rebels frequently employed the language of Islam to unify the region's fractious tribal communities and to legitimize the war against colonial rulers and non-Muslims, although the meanings of religious concepts used in this resistance were fluid and changed over time. Hopkins ultimately looks beyond British India, comparing the frontier frictions with the Mahdist uprising in Sudan, the rebellions in Northern Nigeria, and the revolt of 'mad mullah' Muhammad 'Abd Allah Hasan in Somaliland. Providing the first comparative account of these revolts in the Muslim fringes of the British empire, Hopkins argues that religion played a strikingly similar role in all of these conflicts. Islam was a source of unity in fragmented and destabilized societies, as well as an idiom of anti-colonial resistance. On a more general level, he is critical that scholars have all too often tended

[61] Qeyamuddin Ahmad, *The Wahabi Movement in India* (Calcutta, 1966); J. G. Elliott, *The Frontier 1839–1947: The Story of the North-West Frontier of India* (London, 1968); Milan Hauner, 'One Man Against the Empire: The Faqir of Ipi and the British in Central Asia on the Eve of and during the Second World War', *Journal of Contemporary History*, 16/1 (1981), 183–212; Alan Warren, *Waziristan, the Faqir of Ipi, and the Indian Army: The North West Frontier Revolt of 1936–37* (Oxford, 2000); Hugh Beattie, *Imperial Frontier: Tribe and State in Wazirisan* (London, 2001); Christian Tripodi, *Edge of Empire: the British Political Officer and Tribal Administration on the North-West Frontier 1877–1947* (Farnham and Burlington, VT, 2011); and, more generally, Ghulam Mohammad Jaffar, 'The Repudiation of Jihad by the Indian Scholars in the Nineteenth Century', *Hamdard Islamicus*, 15/3 (1992), 93–100; Ayesha Jalal, *Partisans of Allah: Jihad in South Asia* (Cambridge, MA, 2008); and, for a study of the global connection of Indian Muslim 'outlaws', Seema Alavi, '"Fugitive Mullahs and Outlawed Fanatics": Indian Muslims in Nineteenth-Century Trans-Asiatic Imperial Rivalries', *Modern Asian Studies*, 45/6 (2011), 1337–82. Popular accounts are Michael Barthorp, *The North-West Frontier: British India and Afghanistan: A Pictorial History 1839–1947* (Poole, 1982); Michael Barthorp, *Afghan Wars and the North-West Frontier 1839–1947* (London, 2002); Jules Stewart, *The Savage Border: The Story of the North-West Frontier* (Gloucestershire, 2007); and popular contemporary accounts include E. A. P. Hobday, *Sketches on Service During the Indian Frontier Campaigns of 1897* (London, 1898); and Winston Spencer Churchill, *The Story of the Malakand Field Force: An Episode of Frontier War* (London, 1898); on Churchill's views of the Northwest Frontier, see David B. Edwards, 'Mad Mullahs and Englishmen: Discourse in the Colonial Encounter', *Comparative Studies in Society and History*, 31/4 (1989), 649–70; and Toye, *Churchill's Empire*, 34–50.

to prioritize economic and material motives in inspiring resistance, while not taking seriously the religious sensibilities and intellectual investment of the rebels and
the sincerity of their religious discourse.

In the Dutch East Indies, too, Islamic revivalism played a significant role in
anti-colonial mobilization. Fighting colonial troops, Muslim guerrilla groups in
the Padri War (after the Dutch intervention of 1821–37), the Banten Uprising
(1888), and the Aceh War (1873–1913) called for jihad and used Islamic revivalist
rhetoric as a unifying motive against both internal rivals and colonial domination.
The Dutch were particularly nervous of the connections of Indonesian Muslims
with Islamic movements and centers of religious learning in the Middle East, fearing reformist and anti-colonial ideas brought to the East Indies by Mecca pilgrims and students who had studied in Egypt, Syria, or the Hijaz.[62] The imperial
authorities considered the Islamic anti-colonial agitation of reformist activists a
profound threat and introduced various instruments of surveillance. In his chapter,
'Islamic Resistance in the Dutch Colonial Empire', Gerrit Knaap examines the
intersection of religion and anti-colonialism in the Dutch empire in Southeast
Asia, assessing three forms of resistance. First, in the era of the Dutch East India
Company, local Muslim rulers fought conventional wars against the invaders, frequently employing religious slogans to rally their subjects. Second, in the period
of formal Dutch rule, insurgency, rebellions, and guerrilla wars were organized
by Islamic movements within the colonial territory. Knaap discusses a number of
conflicts, including the Padri War, the Banten Uprising, and the Aceh War, assessing the involvement of religious authorities and the role played by Islamic slogans in mobilizing support. Third, after the turn of the twentieth century (largely
non-violent) anti-colonialism was promoted by Islamic organizations within the
Indonesian nationalist movement, most importantly the Sarekat Islam ('Islamic
Union'). The chapter examines the development of Islamic resistance, considering changes within Indonesian Islam, from popular to more orthodox forms, and
transformations in the nature of colonial rule. More generally, Knaap argues that,
although Islam played a crucial role, the actual outbreak of anti-colonial violence
was usually triggered by a combination of religious, economic, and political causes.

In other parts of Southeast Asia as well, Islam played a crucial role in anti-colonial
resistance. In the Philippines, the confrontations between the 'Moros' and Imperial
Spain, which lasted for three centuries, were considered by both sides to be not
only colonial, but also religious wars.[63] In the quest for martyrdom, some Muslim
warriors even launched suicide attacks on their Christian enemies, who came to

---

[62] Michael Francis Laffan, *Islamic Nationhood and Colonial Indonesia: The Umma Below the Winds*
(London and New York, 2003); and, for an earlier account, Deliar Noer, *The Modernist Muslim
Movement in Indonesia, 1900–1942* (Singapore, 1973).

[63] T. J. S. George, *Revolt in Mindanao: The Rise of Islam in Philippine Politics* (Kuala Lumpur, 1980),
28–48; Luis Camara Dery, *The Kris in Philippine History: A Study of the Impact of Moro Anti-Colonial
Resistance, 1571–1896* (Manila, 1997); and Thomas M. McKenna, *Muslim Rulers and Rebels: Everyday
Politics and Armed Separatism in the Southern Philippines* (Berkeley, 1998), 80–5; on the *juramentados*,
see J. Franklin Ewing 'Juramentado: Institutionalized Suicide among the Moros of the Philippines',
*Anthropological Quarterly*, 28/4 (1955), 148–55.

fear them as *juramentados*. Spain was also opposed by Muslim resistance fighters in Morocco, men such as Muhammad bin 'Abd al-Karim al-Khattabi, who in the early 1920s called for jihad against the Spanish occupation of the Rif, provoking declarations of solidarity around the world.[64]

Colonial officials widely perceived Islamic renewal movements as a global threat. At the end of the nineteenth century, they became terrified by the perceived dangers of pan-Islamism.[65] Across the world, pan-Islamist agitators spread their ideas of religious solidarity and a united Islamic front against European domination. Although pan-Islamism was mainly an urban intellectual project, it could indeed inspire violent revolt. In Egypt, the 'Urabi rebels used pan-Islamist rhetoric to mobilize the faithful against British involvement in 1882. In the following years, Lord Cromer fought vigorously against pan-Islamist propaganda, banning, for instance, the popular Paris-published pan-Islamic journal *al-'Urwa al-Wuthqa* (*The Firmest Bond*). In Persia, the Tobacco Protest of 1891 was to some extent also inspired by pan-Islamist preachers. Pan-Islamic propaganda and networks also influenced Moroccan urban resistance to French colonial penetration in the early twentieth century. After the First World War, the British struggled with the pan-Islamic Khilafat movement in India. Unsurprisingly, pan-Islamist activists and thinkers, most importantly the triad of Jamal al-Din al-Afghani, Muhammad 'Abduh, and Rashid Rida, continue to capture the attention of scholars.[66] In the chapter, 'Anti-Imperialism and the Pan-Islamic

---

[64] David S. Woolman, *Rebels in the Rif: Abd el Krim and the Rif Rebellion* (Stanford, 1968); C. R. Pennell, *A Country with a Government and a Flag: The Rif War in Morocco, 1921–1926* (Wisbech, 1986); and, on the global responses, James L. W. Roslington, 'The Rif War (Morocco, 1921–26) and the coming World Crisis' (PhD, University of Cambridge, 2013).

[65] Jacob M. Landau, *The Politics of Pan-Islam: Ideology and Organization* (Oxford, 1990); and Adeeb Khalid, 'Pan-Islamism in Practice: The Rhetoric of Muslim Unity and its Uses', in Elisabeth Özdalga (ed.), *Late Ottoman Society: The Intellectual Legacy* (Abingdon, 2005), 201–24, provide general accounts; see also Anthony Reid, 'Nineteenth Century Pan-Islam in Indonesia and Malaysia', *Journal of Asian Studies*, 26/2 (1967), 267–83; Nikki R. Keddie, 'Pan-Islam as Proto-Nationalism', *Journal of Modern History*, 41/1 (1969), 17–28; Naimur Rahman Farooqi, 'Pan-Islamism in the Nineteenth Century', *Islamic Culture*, 57/4 (1983), 283–96; Martin Kramer, *Islam Assembled: The Advent of the Muslim Congresses* (New York, 1986); and the classic by Dwight E. Lee, 'The Origins of Pan-Islamism', *American Historical Review*, 47/2 (1942), 278–87. On pan-Islam and anti-French resistance in Morocco, see Edmund Burke, 'Pan-Islam and Moroccan Resistance to French Colonial Penetration, 1900–1912', *Journal of African History*, 13/1 (1972), 97–118. On the Khilafat movement, see Albert Christiaan Niemeijer, *The Khilafat Movement in India, 1919–1924* (The Hague, 1972); Gail Minault, *The Khilafat Movement: Religious Symbolism and Political Mobilisation in India* (New York, 1982); Azmi Özcan, *Pan-Islamism: Indian Muslims, the Ottomans and Britain (1877–1924)* (Leiden, 1997), 184–204; M. Naeem Qureshi, *Pan-Islam in British Indian Politics: A Study of the Khilafat Movement, 1918–1924* (Leiden, 1999); and Hasan Mushirul and Margrit Pernau (eds), *Regionalizing Pan-Islamism: Documents on the Khilafat Movement* (New Delhi, 2005); and, on British policies toward the caliphate more generally, Saad Omar Khan, 'The "Caliphate Question": British Views and Policy Toward Pan-Islamic Politics and the End of the Ottoman Caliphate', *American Journal of Islamic Social Sciences*, 24/4 (2007), 1–25. On the imperial fears of pan-Islam, see in particular John Darwin, *The Empire Project: The Rise and Fall of the British World System 1830–1970* (Cambridge, 2009), 295–7; and, for the interwar period, Martin Thomas, *Empires of Intelligence: Security Services and Colonial Disorder After 1914* (Berkeley, 2008).

[66] Nikki R. Keddie, *Sayyid Jamāl ad-Dīn 'al-Afghānī': A Political Biography* (Berkeley, 1972); Nikki R. Keddie, 'The Pan-Islamic Appeal: Afghani and Abdülhamid', *Middle Eastern Studies*, 3/1 (1966), 46–67; Nikki R. Keddie, *An Islamic Response to Imperialism: Political and Religious Writings of Sayyid Jamāl ad-Dīn 'al-Afghānī'* (Berkeley, 1968), 1–97; Homa Pakdaman, *Djemal-ed-Din Assad Abadi dit Afghani* (Paris, 1966); Malcolm Kerr, *Islamic Reform: The Political and Legal*

Movement', Umar Ryad examines the anti-colonial discourses and activities of these men and shows that the movement was anything but homogeneous. Although all three are usually considered to represent the same school of thought, Ryad emphasizes that their programs differed considerably. While al-Afghani believed in revolution from above and in cooperation with the powerful, 'Abduh promoted reform from below. Rida, finally, advocated a puritanical revolution, inspired by his nostalgia for the early years of Islam. Ryad shows that the ideas and strategies of pan-Islamic figures were, though directed against European imperialism, heavily influenced by the colonial experience. Pan-Islam's proponents, moreover, often lived remarkably global lives. Al-Afghani propagated pan-Islamic unity in British India, Egypt, and Russia, consulted with the rulers in Constantinople, Tehran, and Kabul, and mingled with Muslim exiles in Paris, London, and Munich. 'Abduh worked from Cairo, Beirut, and Paris. Rida moved from Ottoman Syria to Cairo, and traveled across Europe. Their ideas, too, were global in reach. Rida's paper *al-Manar* (*The Lighthouse*) had subscribers around the world, including, as Felicitas Becker shows in her chapter, in the protectorate of Zanzibar.

The pan-Islamic movement can be situated in the wider context of anti-colonial rhetoric and propaganda in the non-European world.[67] Just like many other non-European intellectuals, pan-Islamic thinkers began developing alternative visions of world order once they realized, in the middle of the nineteenth century, that European ideas of world order proved anything but universal in practice. Pan-Islamic ideas also found reception among Muslim rulers. Since the reign of Abdülhamid II, pan-Islamic rhetoric was famously employed by the Sublime Porte as both a domestic and a geopolitical strategy, and was eventually used to foment Muslim revolt in their enemies' empires during the First World War.

Throughout the imperial age, European empires regularly employed religious propaganda to stir up the Muslim subjects of rival colonial powers. Islam, it seemed, provided a powerful mobilizing force that could be exploited to provoke Islamic revolt for political and military aims. Already Napoleon had hoped for a united Islamic front against Orthodox Russia.[68] In the Crimean War, the British, French, and Ottomans made various attempts to incite the Muslims in the Crimean peninsula and in the

*Theories of Muḥammad 'Abduh and Rashīd Riḍā* (Berkeley, 1966); Mark Sedgwick, *Muhammad Abduh* (Oxford, 2009); and Umar Ryad, *Islamic Reformism and Christianity: A Critical Reading of the Works of Muḥammad Rashīd Riḍā and His Associates (1898–1935)* (Leiden, 2009); and also the survey chapters in Ali Rahnema (ed.), *Pioneers of Islamic Revival* (London, 1994).

[67] Cemil Aydin, *The Politics of Anti-Westernism in Asia: Visions of World Order in Pan-Islamic and Pan-Asian Thought* (New York, 2007); and Pankaj Mishra, *From the Ruins of Empire: The Revolt Against the West and the Remaking of Asia* (London, 2012). On the Ottoman sponsorship of pan-Islamism, see Hasan Kayalı, *Arabs and Young Turks: Ottomanism, Arabism, and Islamism in the Ottoman Empire, 1908–1918* (Berkeley, 1997); Selim Deringil, *The Well-Protected Domains: Ideology and Legitimation of Power in the Ottoman Empire, 1876–1909* (London and New York, 1998); Kemal H. Karpat, *The Politicization of Islam: Reconstructing Identity, State, Faith, and Community in the Late Ottoman State* (Oxford, 2001); and, more generally, Frederick F. Anscombe, 'Islam and the Age of Ottoman Reform', *Past and Present*, 208/1 (2010), 159–89.

[68] Note pour le Moniteur, 30 December 1806, Pultusk, in *Correspondance de Napoléon Ier, publiée par ordre de l'Empereur Napoléon III*, xiv (Paris, 1863), 123–4, 124.

Caucasus mountains.[69] One of the most significant efforts to use the Muslim faith for geopolitical purposes was made by the Central Powers in the First World War.[70] In November 1914, the German and Ottoman governments published five fatwas by the Shaykh al-Islam, the highest religious authority of the caliphate in Constantinople, calling for holy war against the Entente. The text was translated into numerous languages and distributed across the world. In a massive propaganda campaign, Islamic rhetoric and imperatives were employed to give religious legitimacy to the involvement of Muslims on the side of the Central Powers. The British, French, and Russians responded with their own religious propaganda campaigns, which, however, remain less studied.[71] Similar attempts to mobilize Muslims were made by the Axis states during the Second World War.[72]

[69] Orlando Figes, *Crimea* (London, 2010). On the anxieties of tsarist officials and their reactions, see Mara Kozelsky, 'Casualties of Conflict: Crimean Tatars during the Crimean War', *Slavic Review*, 67/4 (2008), 862–91; and on Islam and the cross-imperial exodus of Crimean Tatars after the Crimean War, see Alan W. Fisher, 'Emigration of Muslims from the Russian Empire in the Years after the Crimean War', *Jahrbücher für Geschichte Osteuropas*, 35/3 (1987), 356–71; Brian Glyn Williams, 'Hijra and Forced Migration from Nineteenth-Century Russia to the Ottoman Empire: A Critical Analysis of the Great Crimean Tatar Emigration of 1860–1861', *Cahiers du Monde Russe*, 41/1 (2000), 79–108; and, for the wider context, Kemal H. Karpat, 'The Hijra from Russia and the Balkans: The Process of Self-Definition in the Late Ottoman State', in Dale F. Eickelman and James Piscatori (eds), *Muslim Travelers: Pilgrimage, Migration and Religious Imagination* (London, 1990), 131–52.

[70] Fritz Fischer, *Germany's Aims in the First World War* (New York, 1967), 120–31, first explored this campaign; Edmund Burke, 'Moroccan Resistance, Pan-Islam and German War Strategy, 1914–1918', *Francia*, 3 (1975) 434–64; Jide Osuntokun, 'Nigeria's Colonial Government and the Islamic Insurgency in French West Africa, 1914–1918', *Cahiers d'Études Africaines*, 15/57 (1975), 85–93; Werner Ende, 'Iraq in World War I: The Turks, the Germans and the Shi'ite Mujtahids' Call for Jihâd', in Rudolf Peters (ed.), *Proceedings of the Ninth Congress of the Union Européenne des Arabisants et Islamisants* (Leiden, 1981), 57–71; William Deakin, 'Imperial Germany and the "Holy War" in Africa, 1914–1918', *University of Leeds Review*, 28 (1985/6), 75–95; Mahmoud Abdelmoula, *Jihad et colonialism: La Tunisie et la Tripolitaine (1914–1918)* (Tunis, 1987); Herbert Landolin Müller, *Islam, Gihâd ('Heiliger Krieg') und Deutsches Reich: Ein Nachspiel zur Wilhelminischen Weltpolitik im Maghreb 1914–1918* (Frankfurt M., 1992); Peter Hopkirk, *On Secret Service East of Constantinople: The Plot to Bring Down the British Empire* (London, 1994); Gerhard Höpp, *Muslime in der Mark: Als Kriegsgefangene und Internierte in Wünsdorf und Zossen, 1914–1924* (Berlin, 1997); Donald McKale, *War by Revolution: Germany and Great Britain in the Middle East in the Era of World War I* (Kent, OH, 1998); Wolfgang G. Schwanitz, 'Djihad "made in Germany": Der Streit um den Heiligen Krieg (1914–1915)', *Sozial.Geschichte*, 18/2 (2003), 7–34; Gottfried Hagen, 'German Heralds of Holy War: Orientalists and Applied Oriental Studies', *Comparative Studies of South Asia, Africa and the Middle East*, 24/2 (2004), 145–62; Michael Pesek, 'Für Kaiser und Allah: Ostafrikas Muslime im Großen Krieg für die Zivilisation, 1914–1919', *Bulletin der Schweizerischen Gesellschaften Mittlerer Osten und Islamische Kulturen*, 19 (2005), 9–18; Tilman Lüdke, *Jihad Made in Germany: Ottoman and German Propaganda and Intelligence Operations in the First World War* (Münster, 2005); Salvador Oberhaus, *'Zum wilden Aufstande entflammen': Die Deutsche Propagandastrategie für den Orient im Ersten Weltkrieg am Beispiel Ägypten* (Saarbrücken, 2007); Sean McMeekin, *The Berlin–Baghdad Express: The Ottoman Empire and Germany's Bid for World Power, 1898–1918* (London, 2010); and Michael A. Reynolds, *Shattering Empires: The Clash and Collapse of the Ottoman and Russian Empires, 1908–1918* (Cambridge, 2011), 82–139. A critical reassessment of the German and Ottoman roles in the campaign is given by Mustafa Aksakal, '"Holy War Made in Germany"? Ottoman Origins of the 1914 Jihad', *War in History*, 18/2 (2011), 184–99.

[71] William L. Cleveland, 'The Role of Islam as Political Ideology in the First World War', in Edward Ingram (ed.), *National and International Politics in the Middle East: Essays in Honour of Elie Kedourie* (London, 1986), 84–101, provides an account of the use of Islam by both Ottomans and British-backed Sharifian rebels, describing the Arab Revolt as a religious uprising.

[72] David Motadel, 'Germany's Policy Towards Islam, 1941–1945' (PhD, University of Cambridge, 2010); and, on Southeast Asia, Harry J. Benda, *The Crescent and the Rising Sun: Indonesian Islam under*

## ISLAM AND COLONIAL KNOWLEDGE

Colonial officials produced an extensive body of texts about Islam. These writings provide an insight into the wide range and evolution of ideas about Islam that informed European imperial administrators, military officials, and politicians.[73] Islam was usually understood to be an organized religion that could be studied and understood. Muslim communities seemed to be governed by a coherent system of values, norms, and conventions, and characterized by a specific mentality and set of manners. Above all, Islamic imperatives appeared to provide an ideal framework to legitimize claims to power and authority that could be employed not only by Islamic rebels but also by the European rulers. The chapters in the final part of this volume explore different colonial conceptions of Islam, revealing the diversity and complexity of ideas about the religion that shaped policymaking processes in the colonies and in the European centers of power.

Over the past decades, questions about the relationship between empire, power, and knowledge have attracted much interest among scholars.[74] Seminal works by Bernard Cohn, C. A. Bayly, and Saul Dubow have examined information-gathering, and the production, ordering, and distillation of colonial knowledge, the language and terminology used to convey this information and, ultimately, the relationships between this knowledge, political decisions, and the exertion of colonial control. Historians have enquired into cartographic, linguistic, ethnographic, and ecological knowledge. Among the most important categories used by colonial authorities to map and understand local populations, though, was religion.[75] Religion became a central analytic and bureaucratic category applied to colonial subjects throughout empires, no matter how pious they were or how different their notion of religion.

Much, though not all, historical scholarship on the connections between knowledge and colonial power has been influenced by Foucauldian and Saidian ideas. In one of the most intriguing parts of *Orientalism*, Said discussed the employment of Islam by French authorities during the Napoleonic occupation of Egypt, stressing the crucial role played by Orientalist scholars in this endeavor, most notably the students of Sylvestre de Sacy.[76] Studies of Islam and French colonialism have examined in great detail the ways in which experts shaped political practice.[77] They,

---

the Japanese Occupation, 1942–1945 (The Hague, 1958); and Abu Talib Ahmad, *Malay-Muslims, Islam and the Rising Sun 1941–1945* (Selangor, 2003).

[73] General studies about European perceptions of the Muslim faith in the imperial age are Norman Daniel, *Islam, Europe and Empire* (Edinburgh, 1966); more broadly, Norman Daniel, *Islam and the West: The Making of an Image* (Edinburgh, 1960); and Albert Hourani, *Islam in European Thought* (Cambridge, 1991).

[74] Bernard Cohn, *Colonialism and its Forms of Knowledge* (Princeton, 1996); C. A. Bayly, *Empire and Information: Intelligence Gathering and Social Communication in India, 1780–1870* (Cambridge, 1997); and Saul Dubow, *A Commonwealth of Knowledge: Science, Sensibility, and White South Africa, 1820–2000* (Oxford, 2006). A good overview is provided by Tony Ballantyne, 'Colonial Knowledge', in Sarah Stockwell (ed.), *The British Empire: Themes and Perspectives* (Oxford, 2008), 177–98.

[75] Ballantyne, 'Colonial Knowledge', 190–2.

[76] Edward Said, *Orientalism* (London, 2003 (1978)), 80–7.

[77] Christelow, *Muslim Law Courts*; Harrison, *France and Islam*; and Robinson, *Paths of Accommodation*.

too, have emphasized the importance of scholars, men such as Alfred Le Chatelier, Robert Arnaud, Xavier Coppolani, and Paul Marty, who not only studied the Muslim societies under French rule, but also took part in drafting colonial policies towards them. The French considered Muslims in sub-Saharan Africa to be quite distinct from those in North Africa and the Arab world. Although perceived as superior to African animist beliefs, Islam in sub-Saharan Africa was deemed to be different from the 'original' and 'pure' Arab Islam. Merging notions of race and religion, French experts, most importantly Paul Marty, invented the notion of 'black Islam', or *Islam noir. Islam noir* was imagined as a mixture of 'pure' Arab Islam and pre-Islamic African beliefs and customs, which were increasingly studied by scholars such as Émile Durkheim and Lucien Lévy-Bruhl. On the other side, the concepts of 'white Islam', *Islam bidan*, and 'Moorish Islam', *Islam maure*, were created to categorize Muslims of Mauritania, the Maghrib, and the wider Arab world. While 'white Islam' was considered to be more 'fanatical' and dangerous, French scholars and colonial officials believed that 'black Islam' was easier to rule. Still, also in sub-Saharan Africa fears of Islam, *le péril de l'Islam*, never really vanished from the colonial records.

More recently, historians have, moreover, shown increasing interest in French perceptions of popular religion and mysticism in their Muslim colonies, particularly the Maghrib.[78] In the chapter 'French Colonial Knowledge of Maraboutism', George R. Trumbull demonstrates that colonial officials and experts became obsessed with popular and mystical forms of religion. Marabouts, Islamic holy people, were of particular concern to imperial bureaucrats and scholars, Trumbull argues. Afraid that these wandering religious figures could escape their control, the French observed them with utmost caution. In fact, marabouts became even more popular objects of surveillance than the urban 'ulama and the Sufi orders, which seemed somewhat easier to govern. Although they studied various aspects of the lives of marabouts, colonial observers were naturally most interested in their political and legal authority among the Muslim population. Indeed, marabouts often played a central role in the settling of disputes or the sheltering of the poor and outcast. Although the French assessed the marabouts to be both enemies and potential allies, administrative documents and scholarly writings were predominantly concerned with the potential threat they posed. In an age of rationality, their practices were perceived as illogical, absurd, and, hence, potentially subversive. At times, marabouts were even defined through concepts of madness, deviance, and insanity. Ultimately, the French were anxious that the holy figures would cause religious unrest or even incite revolt. Trumbull shows that attempts by experts and officials to conceptualize this very particular form of popular religion were usually motivated by the desire to control it.

Just like French texts, British colonial documents about Islam reflect a wide range of assumptions and ideas. Imperial historians have studied, for instance,

---

[78] George R. Trumbull IV, *An Empire of Facts: Colonial Power, Cultural Knowledge, and Islam in Algeria, 1870–1914* (Cambridge, 2009).

the variety of British colonial conceptions of Islam in Africa.[79] They have also explored the fascinating debate among British officials about Islam and the abolition of slavery across their formal and informal empire.[80] Scholars of colonialism in India have long debated the role of British conceptions of religious differences in fostering religious communalism on the subcontinent. While some historians have argued that the British understood Indian society in terms of religious divisions and therefore pursued a policy that created religious communalism, others have stressed the fact that religious categories such as 'Sikh', 'Hindu', and 'Muslim' already had a political meaning in pre-colonial India, and that religiou Find all people named "Sumitha Kumar" s communalism was not an invention of the British colonial mind.[81] Islam, in any case, played a significant role in British perceptions of colonial India and in Victorian thought more generally.[82] In his chapter, 'Islam and British Imperial Thought', Faisal Devji addresses British ideas about the role of Islam in the empire. He argues that it was India, home of the largest Muslim population in the empire, and not the Middle East, that shaped British conceptions of Islam. Overall, these conceptions were rather ambivalent. On the one side, they reflected fears of Islamic militancy and pan-Islamism, fueled by sensationalist books such as W. W. Hunter's classic *The Indian Musalmans: Are They Bound in Conscience to Rebel Against the Queen?* (1871), which dealt with religious 'fanaticism' on the Northwest Frontier. A civil servant in the Raj, Hunter's views reflected, at least to some extent, general concerns about Islam prevalent not only among colonial administrators and officials, but also among political and military leaders such as Lord Kitchener and Lord Salisbury. And yet, there was another current of thought about Islam that shaped the official mind of empire. A number of British thinkers advanced the idea of Britain as a patron

[79] Holger Weiss, 'Variations in the Colonial Representation of Islam and Muslims in Northern Ghana, *ca.*1900–1930', *Journal of Muslim Minority Affairs*, 25/1 (2005), 73–95. For a comparison between British, French, and German colonial conceptions of Islam in West Africa, see Holger Weiss, 'European Images of Islam in the Northern Hinterlands of the Gold Coast through the Early Colonial Period', *Sudanic Africa*, 12 (2001), 83–110; and Rüdiger Seesemann, '"Ein Dialog der Taubstummen": Französische vs. Britische Wahrnehmungen des Islam im spätkolonialen Westafrika', *Africa Spectrum*, 37/2 (2002), 109–39.

[80] William Clarence-Smith, 'The British "Official Mind" and Nineteenth-Century Islamic Debates Over the Abolition of Slavery', in Keith Hamilton and Patrick Salmon (eds), *Slavery, Diplomacy and Empire: Britain and the Suppression of the Slave Trade, 1807–1975* (Brighton, 2009), 125–42; and, more generally, William Clarence-Smith, *Islam and the Abolition of Slavery* (New York, 2006).

[81] For the first group, see Gyanendra Pandey, *The Construction of Communalism in Colonial North India* (Delhi, 1990); for the second group see C. A. Bayly, 'The Pre-History of "Communalism?" Religious Conflict in India 1700–1860', *Modern Asian Studies*, 19/2 (1985), 177–203; Katherine Prior, 'Making History: The State's Intervention in Urban Religious Disputes in the North-Western Provinces in the Early Nineteenth Century', *Modern Asian Studies*, 27/1 (1993), 179–203; and Cynthia Talbot, 'Inscribing the Other, Inscribing the Self: Hindu-Muslim Identities in Pre-Colonial India', *Comparative Studies in Society and History*, 37/4 (1995), 692–722.

[82] Alex Padamsee, *Representations of Indian Muslims in British Colonial Discourse* (New York, 2005); and Katherine Watt, 'Thomas Walker Arnold and the Re-Evaluation of Islam, 1864–1930', *Modern Asian Studies*, 36/1 (2002), 1–98. On popular Victorian images of Islam, see Philip C. Almond, *Heretic and Hero: Muhammad and the Victorians* (Wiesbaden, 1989); Clinton Bennett, *Victorian Images of Islam* (London, 1992); and Shahin Kuli Khan Khattak, *Islam and the Victorians: Nineteenth Century Perceptions of Muslim Practices and Beliefs* (London, 2008).

of Islam. Among them were Wilfred Scawen Blunt who, in *The Future of Islam* (1882), promoted Britain as the 'protector' of Islam, and R. G. Corbett who, in *Mohammedanism and the British Empire* (1902), described the empire as a 'Moslem power'. During the First World War, Lloyd George advocated exploiting this very idea of the British empire as the greatest Muslim power as an instrument in geopolitics against the Ottoman Porte, while, in practice, officers such as T. E. Lawrence propagated among Arab bedouins the slogan that Arab Islam had to be liberated from Turkish domination. Devji's contribution finally also points to the significant role Muslims played in shaping British ideas about the relationship between Islam and the empire.

German official conceptions of Islam and colonial policies were influenced by British, Dutch, and French texts, but also by the works of German experts such as Carl Heinrich Becker, Martin Hartmann, and Diedrich Westermann.[83] In her chapter, 'Debates on Islam in Imperial Germany', Rebekka Habermas shows that following the German involvement in the Muslim areas of its colonies Togo, Cameroon, and German East Africa, experts, colonial pressure groups, and officials in Berlin began engaging in a broad debate about Islam. At colonial congresses, Islam and colonial policies towards Muslims were at the top of the agenda. The question about the place of Islam in the German empire caused fierce conflict between missionaries, who spread fears about an Islamic threat to German imperial rule, and scholars, who advocated the use of Islam to bolster the colonial state. Yet Habermas argues that, despite different perspectives on Muslims, both sides shared the same assumptions about the ontological nature of Islam. The discussion was generally informed by the idea of an essentialist difference between the Islamic and the Christian world. Moreover, most writers articulated the same notions of Islam, most importantly the equation of Islam with slavery, the assumption that Islam was vigorously expanding across Africa, and the idea that African Islam was more superficial than Middle Eastern Islam, though still superior to animist religions. After the turn of the century, German scholars became involved in a number of large-scale research projects in their Muslim colonies to collect empirical data. Although they drew on modern methods of investigation and surveying, Habermas emphasizes that due to their structure and questions, the surveys often simply reproduced pre-existing stereotypes. Most of the German experts in Islamic studies advocated the active use of Islam to strengthen colonial rule, a policy that was generally reflected on the ground. Despite frictions and conflicts with Islamic groups in Africa, German colonial officials generally made every effort to accommodate Islam. Finally, as Wilhelm II embraced his new strategy of *weltpolitik*, Islam was also seen as an opportunity to advance German geopolitical interests. This was reflected most prominently when the emperor spectacularly declared himself a 'friend' of the world's '300 million Mohammedans' after visiting Saladin's tomb in Damascus in 1898, and in Imperial Germany's campaign for Islamic mobilization during the First World War.

---

[83] Holger Weiss, 'German Images of Islam in West Africa', *Sudanic Africa*, 11 (2000), 53–93; and, on the role of missionaries in German colonial debates about Islam, Per Hassing, 'Islam at the German Colonial Congresses', *The Muslim World*, 67/3 (1977), 165–74.

The role German experts played in shaping these schemes to stir up the faithful against its enemies did not remain unnoticed in the international world of scholarship. The eminent Dutch Islam expert Christiaan Snouck Hurgronje furiously accused his German colleagues of spreading religious hatred.[84] Becker was unimpressed, rebutting the attempt to 'denounce' German policies toward Islam. Just as in Imperial Germany, Dutch experts such as Karel Frederik Holle, L. W. C. van der Berg, and Christiaan Snouck Hurgronje played a crucial role in formulating their country's colonial policies. Snouck was certainly the most colorful of these figures, and has been studied in depth by historians.[85] An eminent scholar, he was posted to Mecca and Jidda, where he monitored the hajj and anti-colonial and pan-Islamic activism, and was later transferred to the Dutch East Indies.

Ultimately, however, it was not just the European imperial officials who developed a political interest in Islam. In the final chapter of this volume, 'Islam and the European Empires in Japanese Imperial Thought', Cemil Aydin examines the ways in which early twentieth-century Japanese scholars of Islamic studies as well as diplomatic and military officials developed an increasing political interest in Islam, which they identified as the Achilles heel of the European empires. Aydin shows that scholarship of Islam and imperial politics were often tightly interwoven. Islam was regularly studied and discussed in terms of its practical implications for Japan's quest for supremacy in Asia and its policies towards the wider Muslim world. Japanese political discussions about Islam drew heavily, as Aydin points out, on European scholarship and the schemes of European imperial policies, most importantly those of Germany and Italy. Although Japanese authors claimed to have a better, unprejudiced, and more nuanced understanding of Islam than their European counterparts, their writings reflected the classic Orientalist East–West dichotomy and the notion of a unified 'Islamic world'. In the end, these views also influenced Japan's imperial policies toward the Muslims in China and Southeast Asia and its imperial propaganda for solidarity between the Muslim world and Japan against the Europeans.

Overall, the following chapters point to the centrality of religion in the encounters between the European empires and their Muslim subjects across the world, and at the same time illustrate that this encounter was not dominated by

---

[84] Peter Heine, 'C. Snouck Hurgronje versus C. H. Becker: Ein Beitrag zur Geschichte der Angewandten Orientalistik', *Die Welt des Islams*, 23–24 (1984), 378–87, quotation on 381.

[85] Harry J. Benda, 'Christian Snouck Hurgronje and the Foundation of Dutch Islamic Policy in Indonesia', *Journal of Modern History*, 30/4 (1958), 338–47; P. S. van Koningsveld, *Snouck Hurgronje alias Abdoel Ghaffar: Enige historisch-kritische Kanttekeningen* (Leiden, 1982); P. S. van Koningsveld, *Snouck Hurgronje's 'Izhaar oel-Islam': Een veronachtzaamd Aspect van de Koloniale Geschiedenis* (Leiden, 1982); P. S. van Koningsveld (ed.), *Snouck Hurgronje dan Islam* (Jakarta, 1989); Ulrike Freitag, 'Der Orientalist und der Mufti: Kulturkontakt im Mekka des 19. Jahrhunderts', *Die Welt des Islams*, 43/1 (2003), 37–60; Eric Tagliacozzo, 'The Skeptic's Eye: Snouck Hurgronje and the Politics of Pilgrimage from the Indies', in Eric Tagliacozzo (ed.), *Southeast Asia and the Middle East: Islam, Movement, and the Longue Durée* (Stanford, 2009), 135–55; Michael Laffan, *The Makings of Indonesian Islam: Orientalism and the Narration of a Sufi Past* (Princeton, 2011); and, for an excellent case study on Dutch colonial perceptions of Islam, Michael Laffan, 'A Watchful Eye: The Meccan Plot of 1881 and Changing Dutch Perceptions of Islam in Indonesia', *Archipel*, 63 (2002), 79–108.

missionaries and the promotion of Christianity. Drawing on the expertise of historians from various fields, this volume provides the first comparative account of the engagement of the European empires with Islam. It presents a wide range of perspectives on various aspects of these encounters. It shows that, despite the differences between geographic regions and empires, the questions and themes raised by scholars of all these imperial histories are in many ways remarkably similar. The book thereby offers a picture only possible through a global and comparative history of empire.

# PART I

# ISLAM AND IMPERIAL RULE

# 1

# The Russian Worlds of Islam

*Robert D. Crews*

## INTRODUCTION

In December 1908, telegraph reports of the opening of the Ottoman parliament in Istanbul reached Irkutsk, a town in eastern Siberia not far from the Mongolian and Chinese frontiers of the Russian empire. Commenting on the arrival of this news, the famous pan-Islamic thinker and activist Abdurreshid Ibrahim (1857–1944), who was traveling in the region, marveled at the outpouring of enthusiasm among the local Muslim inhabitants. They rejoiced, he recalled, at the restoration of the Ottoman constitution and gathered for prayers and speeches. Although these revelers were, like Ibrahim, subjects of the Russian tsar, they felt a close affinity with 'all of their Ottoman Muslim brothers'. They tried to reply with their own telegrams expressing solidarity with the Ottoman constitutionalists, only to be thwarted by the meddling of Russian officials. Still, Ibrahim lauded the emotional ties that linked these Siberian Muslims with their co-religionists in the Ottoman capital: 'It was as if the wireless telegraph bound their hearts together.'[1]

In Ibrahim's account of his travels across Russia and Asia in the early twentieth century, we encounter many such affirmations of Muslim unity in the face of tsarist oppression. In multiple respects, these representations took on a life of their own. Ibrahim's portrayal of trans-imperial Muslim solidarity stoked myth-making among pan-Islamist activists like himself and heightened paranoia in imperial capitals such as London, St Petersburg, and even Istanbul.[2] Active in émigré circles in Turkey, Japan, Germany, and elsewhere before and after the First World War, figures such as Ibrahim played a critical role in naturalizing the story of Muslim

---

[1] Abdürreşid İbrahim, *Yirminci Asrın Başlarında Âlem-i İslam ve Japonya'da İslamiyet'in Yayılması* (*The World of Islam and the Spread of Islam in Japan in the Early Twentieth Century*), ed. Mehmed Paksu (Istanbul, 2012), 197. On Ibrahim, see Mikhail Meyer, 'An Islamic Perspective in Russian Public Opinion: The Russian Tatar Thinker Abdurrashid Ibrahim (1857–1944)', *Archiv Orientální*, 80/2 (2012), 259–72.

[2] Volker Adam, *Russlandmuslime in Istanbul am Vorabend des Ersten Weltkrieges: Die Berichterstattung osmanischer Periodika über Russland und Zentralasien* (Frankfurt M., 2002); Selçuk Esenbel, 'Japan's Global Claim to Asia and the World of Islam: Transnational Nationalism and World Power, 1900–45', *American Historical Review*, 109/4 (2004), 1140–70. On Ottoman mistrust of the activities of Muslims under Christian rule, see Selim Deringil, *The Well-Protected Domains: Ideology and the Legitimation of Power in the Ottoman Empire, 1876–1909* (London and New York, 1998), 44–67.

disaffection from Russia and its politics, a perspective that continues to frame historical interpretations of Russian–Muslim relations.[3] From the perspective of the diaspora, Muslims had always been victims and outsiders. Their destiny was the world of Islam beyond the borders of the tsarist and Soviet empires. Yet they were not alone. Émigré Muslims shared this perspective with Jewish émigré communities from Russia: both remembered the tsarist empire as a harrowing backdrop for emigration and exile.

Although the tsarist polity was a land empire that spread across contiguous territory in Eurasia over the course of the sixteenth to twentieth centuries, it emerged, like other contemporary imperial states, out of war and conquest. Throughout many centuries of imperial expansion, the monarchy steadfastly guarded the privileged status of Orthodox Christianity. In the case of the Muslim populations that tsarist rulers encountered along their southern and eastern frontiers, state violence periodically took the form of forced conversions and mass deportations. Decades before hundreds of thousands of Jews abandoned the Pale of Settlement in the late nineteenth and early twentieth centuries, Muslim communities suffered collective expulsions from the Crimean Peninsula and the Caucasus at the hands of tsarist military forces. In its lengthy struggle to control the North Caucasus and stamp out local resistance movements, especially among Avars, Chechens, and other communities inhabiting the highlands, the regime practiced forcible removals and relocations.[4] The authorities unleashed what Russian generals called 'terror' against communities they suspected of challenging tsarist power or of clandestinely siding with their co-religionists abroad.[5] On other occasions, however, the regime attempted to prevent Muslim emigration, and many who emigrated to the Ottoman empire ultimately tried to return to Russia.[6]

As in the case of Jewish emigration, moreover, violence was only one kind of catalyst. Diverse networks had long connected Russia's southern borderlands to Europe, the Middle East, North Africa, and South Asia. Trade, slavery, pilgrimage, and study were among the principal modes of sustained contact across imperial boundaries.[7] And like the inhabitants of borderlands elsewhere, these populations faced the challenges—and opportunities—that came with close proximity to multiple imperial patrons. Tsarist military expansion brought destruction for some

---

[3] See, for example, Michael Khodorkovsky, *Russia's Steppe Frontier: The Making of a Colonial Empire, 1500–1800* (Bloomington, 2004); and Adeeb Khalid, *The Politics of Muslim Cultural Reform: Jadidism in Central Asia* (Berkeley, 1999).

[4] Charles King has astutely observed that 'Russia's expansion into the Caucasus was always a matter of altitude rather than latitude', see Charles King, *The Ghost of Freedom: A History of the Caucasus* (Oxford, 2008), 38. On Islamic resistance in the Caucasus, see the chapter by Michael A. Reynolds in this volume.

[5] Peter Holquist, 'To Count, to Extract, and to Exterminate: Population Statistics and Population Politics in Late Imperial and Soviet Russia', in Ronald Grigor Suny and Terry Martin (eds), *A State of Nations: Empire and Nation-Building in the Age of Lenin and Stalin* (Oxford, 2001), 111–44, 118.

[6] James H. Meyer, 'Immigration, Return, and the Politics of Citizenship: Russian Muslims in the Ottoman Empire, 1860–1914', *International Journal of Middle East Studies*, 39 (2007), 15–32.

[7] Megan Dean Farah, 'Mobility, Commerce and Conversion in the Caucasus' (PhD, Stanford University, 2013).

**Fig. 2** *Tatar School for Children* by Carlo Bossoli (1856) (Public Domain).

elites, but new possibilities for others, particularly when the regime began to establish administrative capacity in newly seized territories.

Russian empire-building hinged on Muslims' engagement with the institutions of the regime, and on the state's management of Islam. In the fifteenth century, Muslims were among the first non-Christian subjects of Muscovy. By the reign of Nicholas II (1894–1917), they numbered some twenty million, making Muslims the second largest confessional group in the empire after the Orthodox Christians. Taking into account geopolitics, demography, and evolving understandings of religion and clerical authority, tsarist officials adopted a variety of approaches to their Muslim subjects. These policies shifted over time and in response to specific challenges posed by diverse populations that the regime grouped, beginning in the late eighteenth and early nineteenth centuries, under the rubric of Islam. During this period, Russian officials periodically utilized violence where they deemed it necessary, especially in highland borderland regions. However, in the day-to-day governance of the empire, they simultaneously pursued various kinds of accommodation with their Muslim subjects, first in the Volga River and Ural Mountains regions and, later, along the frontiers of the Kazakh steppe, the Crimean Peninsula, the Caucasus Mountain range, and Central Asia (Fig. 2).

This chapter focuses on the practice of institutional accommodation. I concentrate on venues where Muslims made claims on the state, and where the regime in turn conferred particular rights on its Muslims. As a number of scholars have recently observed, there was nothing precisely like the Western European conception of 'citizenship' in the tsarist empire.[8] But a closer examination of tsarist juridical institutions, on the one hand, and those of the estate system, civilian bureaucracy, and army, on the other, reveals the emergence of spaces where Muslims could call on the regime to defend property, honor, and religion, and where they could perform service for the tsar and the empire as Muslims. The last generation of tsarist Muslim subjects increasingly imagined themselves as citizens in an empire with a highly contested rights regime.

## ENLIGHTENMENT, TOLERATION, AND EMPIRE

Under Catherine the Great (1762–96), tsarist law began to treat Islam as something more than a faith either to be persecuted, as some Orthodox churchmen would have preferred, or to be endured in pragmatic fashion. Cross-border ties that might strengthen the Ottoman challenge appeared threatening, and St Petersburg's expansion to the East necessitated some alternative to exclusively repressive policies. Much contemporary European thought, especially that of German thinkers in Central Europe, suggested that utility to the state should be the chief factor in guiding enlightened rulers' approach to other faiths. Orthodox Christianity would continue as the dominant faith of the dynasty and empire. Yet, Islam could prove useful, especially if its potential as a source of social discipline could be enhanced, and if its informal notions of religious authority could be made more hierarchical, like the Ottoman religious establishment or, even better, the Orthodox Church.

Among peoples who were far from Christianity but closer to Islam, it could even serve the empire as a civilizing influence. Toward this end, in the eastern provinces, governors built mosques and schools to attract Kazakh nomads from the steppe to trading centers. Catherine hoped to transform this frontier people just beyond her control into loyal merchants and peasants—like the Muslims whom she ruled along the Volga River in Kazan and neighboring provinces. Islam appeared to be a way to end their raids on Russian frontier towns and tie them to the land and settled agriculture. In 1788, she established an official Islamic hierarchy, the Orenburg Muhammadan Ecclesiastical Assembly in the town of Ufa. Its head, with the title of mufti, issued fatwas enjoining Muslims to take up agricultural livelihoods. Muslim clerics and merchants acted as intermediaries for the state. State-sponsored imams issued oaths sworn on the Qur'an to Kazakh elders, binding them as 'loyal subjects' to the empire.[9] In the nineteenth century, the tsars saw Islam as a foundation of dynastic loyalty and state patriotism. The Orenburg mufti would command the Muslim faithful to 'be obedient to the

---

[8] Valerie Kivelson, 'Muscovite "Citizenship": Rights Without Freedom', *Journal of Modern History*, 74/3 (2002), 465–89; and Meyer, 'Immigration, Return, and the Politics of Citizenship'.

[9] Michael Kemper, *Sufis und Gelehrte in Tatarien und Baschkirien, 1789–1889: Der islamische Diskurs unter russischer Herrschaft* (Berlin, 1998); Allen J. Frank, *Muslim Religious Institutions in Imperial Russia: The Islamic World of Novouzensk District and the Kazakh Inner Horde, 1780–1910* (Leiden, 2001); and Robert D. Crews, *For Prophet and Tsar: Islam and Empire in Russia and Central Asia* (Cambridge, MA and London, 2006).

Sovereign Emperor' and to 'obey all commands emanating from him; to serve the Tsar and Fatherland by faith and justice, in accordance with sworn oath and loyal duty, without sparing one's life'.[10]

Russian officials held the Orenburg Assembly to be a church-like structure that would mobilize Islamic religious authority on behalf of the empire. Aided by three Muslim judges, the state-appointed mufti issued directives insisting that obedience to the laws of Islam compelled fealty to the Russian empire and its law. Muslims were to remember the dynasty in their prayers and carefully fulfill all of their obligations to the state. And like other 'churches', the assembly oversaw what Russian officialdom took to be a 'clergy' in mosque communities. The assembly summoned prayer-leaders, teachers, and preachers to its seat in Ufa to have their qualifications examined. Clerics who passed these exams received licenses and official appointments in villages and towns under its jurisdiction. Over the course of the nineteenth century, a growing body of tsarist legislation defined with greater detail the duties and responsibilities of a group of Muslim clerics that came to resemble more closely a social estate separated from lay men and women. Though never placed on a par with Orthodox clergymen, state-licensed Muslim clerics enjoyed the backing of the state in receiving maintenance from their community and, most importantly, in policing the morality and piety of their communities. Muslims enjoyed toleration for their faith—but they remained dependent on the legal interpretations of Muslim authorities. The Orenburg mufti stood at the pinnacle of this hierarchy of interpretation, but at the level of the mosque community it was the local imam who had the power to draw in the district or provincial police authorities to enforce his writ. Disputed cases ended up on the desk of the governor, who in turn, sent them on to the Orenburg mufti and his superiors in the Ministry of Internal Affairs. The regime was invested in establishing the *true* rules of Islam, even if this was an arduous process involving multiple layers of bureaucracy, dialogue with the scholars in the assembly, and, from the second half of the nineteenth century, the state's own Orientalist experts.

Tsarist officials privileged clerical authority in all of the confessions that they sought to involve in the policing of the empire, but in the case of Islam, they left the door open to anti-clerical challenges. Local police and governors welcomed complaints against prayer-leaders who shirked their duties or cavorted with the young women of the village.[11] Charges of false belief were particularly alarming to Orthodox officials who may not have understood the nuances of Islamic thought and practice—but who understood well from the history of Russian sectarian movements the challenges such heterodoxy might pose to the regime. For their part, lay people actively pursued denunciations against clerics—and against one another. Men and women, fathers and sons, neighbors and kinfolk all approached local courts and police, presenting arguments about honor, Islamic orthodoxy, and their loyalty to imperial law. Much the same pattern emerged beyond the Volga River and Ural Mountains region, the primary jurisdiction of the Orenburg

---

[10] Crews, *For Prophet and Tsar*, 77.    [11] Crews, *For Prophet and Tsar*, especially 92–142.

Assembly, when the state established a regionally based hierarchy in the Crimea in 1831 and two more in the Caucasus in 1872. There, too, Muslim communities appealed to the state to mediate disputes over clerical authority and submitted denunciations to their regional Islamic authorities. Even Persian merchants, who were theoretically subordinate to their own Shi'i spiritual guides in Persia or Ottoman Iraq, turned to clerics licensed by the Russian state or directly to the tsarist Shi'i hierarchy.[12] Thus tsarist institutions became a key venue for the litigation of various disputes involving marriage and the family as well as the arbitration of religious controversies. This dense network of Islamic institutions did not capture every aspect of Muslim life, of course, but it drew Muslim subjects into the project of tsarist governance, creating relations of interdependence between mosque communities and imperial authorities and transforming Muslim communities in the process.

In addition to relying on Islamic institutions, the state turned to Muslim communities to supply men of authority who could amplify the power of the regime in its vulnerable periphery. As in other empires, imperial officials sought out intermediaries who could embed tsarist rule in existing hierarchies.[13] Here, too, geopolitics and demography were factors, alongside Islam, that complicated the tsarist imperial project. Despite treaty agreements that formally marked the Russo-Ottoman and Russo-Persian borders in Transcaucasia, for instance, tsarist officials continued to view the challenge of administration in its new territories as a trans-border proposition. Bureaucratic discussions of the integration of the khanate of Erivan in 1827 centered on this difficulty. In principle, officials aspired to break up all existing social, political, and economic relations of dependence that subordinated Christians to Muslims. At the same time, they feared the wider consequences of breaking with the old order. 'From the Black Sea to the Caspian, in territories belonging to Russia', General Lieutenant A. A. Vel'iaminov noted:

> at least two-thirds of the inhabitants profess the Muhammadan faith and...it would be extremely unfavorable to introduce a decree that may shake the loyalty to us of such a powerful population. The Ottoman Porte and the Persian government, which have never favored us, will through their secret agents present such a decree to all the Muslims under our rule as a violation of their rights and as an institution intended for their oppression. For these Muhammadan states that are hostile to us such a decree will serve as a spark to kindle, at the first convenient opportunity, a general mutiny in our Muslim provinces.

To ease the disruption caused by the wartime annexation and to disarm propaganda from Russia's neighbors, moreover, officials proclaimed religious toleration for Muslims and Christians, alongside temporary exemptions from taxation. The new regime also invited Christians and Muslims who had fled Erivan (presumably

---

[12] See the correspondence between the viceroy of the Caucasus and Shi'i religious figures in Central State Historical Archive of Azerbaijan (CSHAA), f. 44, op. 1, d. 180 and f. 290, op. 1, dd. 1828 and 1701; and Abdollah Mostofi, *The Adminstrative and Social History of the Qajar Period*, trans. Nayer Mostofi Glenn, 3 vols (Costa Mesa, CA, 1997), ii, 519–20.

[13] Andreas Kappeler, *Russland als Vielvölkerreich: Entstehung—Geschichte—Zerfall* (Munich, 1993).

with the Persian retreat) to return. While Christians were offered a period of five years within which they could return, reclaim property, and become tsarist subjects, Muslims were given two years, with the added proviso that they 'take an oath of subjecthood and loyalty'.[14] Loyal notables were incorporated into the lower ranks of the administration responsible for policing and the collection of taxes, but these new institutions were an amalgam of personnel and legal principles drawn from new and old repertoires. As General I. F. Pashkevich complained in 1830, 'Everywhere the administrative organs are provisional, a unique mixture of Russian, Georgian, and Muslim forms of government; there is unity neither in the forms of administration nor in law or finances.'[15] The regime needed Muslim police officers, tax collectors, scribes, and translators to link the administration to local communities. But its officials never resolved tensions over the pace of changes designed to make uniform imperial institutions and laws. And, as seen in the uprisings in the North and South Caucasus in the 1830s and 1840s, local elites frequently pushed back against attempts to marginalize them from positions of prominence in local life.[16]

Another central goal of tsarist patronage of Islamic religious institutions along the eastern and southern borderlands was to cultivate a class of Muslim traders who would be integrated into the imperial estate system, an elaborate set of juridical categories defining rights and obligations for various social groups. Tiflis, Astrakhan, Orenburg, and Tobol'sk served as cosmopolitan hubs of this trade, drawing Muslim merchants from the Ottoman empire, Qajar Persia, Bukhara, Tashkent, Khiva, Kashgar, and elsewhere. Russian officials relied, in turn, on Muslim subjects to carry on trade with their southern and eastern neighbors, gather (and circulate) intelligence, and, on occasion, conduct diplomacy on behalf of the empire.[17] A number of these merchants settled in the frontier village of Kargala (Seitovskii posad) in Orenburg province and intermarried with Tatar

---

[14] Warning that Armenians, 'a cunning, pushy, and crafty people' filled with hatred toward Muslims, would abuse broader autonomy from Muslim masters, Vel'iaminov proposed that the status quo be maintained, though with the provision that Armenians be allowed to complain to Russian authorities or, alternatively, that the state compensate Muslims for the loss of their Christian dependants, see Ts. P. Agaian (ed.), *Prisoedinenie Vostochnoi Armenii k Rossii: sbornik dokumentov* (*Russia's Annexation of Eastern Armenia: A Collection of Documents*), 2 vols (Erevan, 1978), ii, 421–6.

[15] Eva-Maria Auch, *Muslim—Untertan—Bürger: Identitätswandel in gesellschaftlichen Transformationsprozessen der muslimischen Ostprovinzen Südkaukasiens (Ende 18.—Anfang 20. Jh.)* (Wiesbaden, 2004), 109; see also V. O. Bobrovnikov and I. L. Babich (eds), *Severnyi Kavkaz v sostave Rossiiskoi imperii* (*The Northern Caucasus within the Russian Empire*) (Moscow, 2007), 189–210; and S. N. Abashin, D. Iu. Arapov, and N. E. Bekmakhanova (eds), *Tsentral'naia Aziia v sostave Rossiiskoi imperii* (*Central Asia within the Russian Empire*) (Moscow, 2008), 86–131.

[16] Auch, *Muslim—Untertan—Bürger*, 106–47.

[17] Khamamato Mami, 'Sviazuiushchaia rol' tatarskikh kuptsov Volgo-Ural'skogo regiona v Tsentral'noi Evrazii: zveno "Shelkogo puti novogo vremeni" (vtoraia polovina XVIII–XIX v.)' ('The Mediating Role of Tatar Merchants between the Volga-Ural Region and Central Asia: A Link in the "Silk Road of Modern Times" (Second Half of the Eighteenth to Nineteenth Centuries)'), in Naganava Norikhiro, D. M. Usmanova, and Khamamato Mami (eds), *Volgo-Uralskii region v imperskom prostranstve: XVIII–XX vv.* (*The Volga Ural Region in Imperial Space: From the Eighteenth to Twentieth Centuries*) (Moscow, 2011), 39–58; and R. A. Silant'ev, *Musul'manskaia diplomatiia v Rossii: istoriia i sovremennost'* (*Muslim Diplomacy in Russia: Past and Present*) (Moscow, 2010).

women whose families had migrated, with the encouragement of tsarist authorities, from towns along the Volga River in the mid-1740s. By the mid-nineteenth century, Muslims made up more than half of the merchant guilds of Orenburg province. Their commercial activities added to the imperial treasury while supplying the capital that would fund the construction of numerous mosques and schools in the early nineteenth century.[18]

The tsarist nobility was another avenue of integration. In 1784, Catherine opened up the noble estate by reversing early eighteenth-century legislation that had stripped Muslims of noble rank. On the eastern frontier, more than a dozen Muslim families in Ufa province demonstrated that their ancestors had enjoyed this status in the past and were registered in the Noble Assembly.[19] Where the imperial government did not find social groups that appeared to fit in the empire's cosmopolitan noble estate, it sought out tribal and clan notables. At the end of the eighteenth century, the tsarist government introduced a cantonal administrative system that led to the formation of a service elite among the Bashkirs and smaller neighboring Muslim groups. Subordinate to the governor-general of Orenburg, state-appointed Bashkir leaders headed up territorial administrative units and organized military service. Like other privileged groups in imperial society, these Bashkir elders secured exemption from military service and corporal punishment; some among them earned ennoblement for their service.[20]

For other Muslims, nobles in particular, military service was an attractive means to enter into the imperial elite. As Charles Steinwedel has shown, the Tevkelev family was among the most prominent ethnic Tatar families to serve the Russian state from the seventeenth century. Employed as translators and diplomats, they mediated between the tsarist government and the Muslim peoples along the eastern frontier. In the mid-eighteenth century, Kutlu-Mukhammad Tevkelev became a major landowner in the Ural Mountain region. In 1755, Empress Elizabeth (1741–62) promoted him to the rank of general and assigned him an important administrative position in Orenburg province.[21] Catherine the Great confirmed the family's noble status. In the nineteenth century, Selim-Girei Tevkelev (1805–55) fought against the Ottomans and rebellious Poles and held the title of marshal of the nobility in Samara province before being appointed in 1865 to head the official Islamic hierarchy. Treading a similar path, many young Muslim nobles entered state service through officer training at the elite Corps of Pages in St Petersburg.[22] Over the course of the nineteenth century the officer corps integrated the sons of elite families from the Muslim borderlands, the relatives of the Imam

[18]  Khamamoto, 'Sviazuiushchaia rol' tatarskikh kuptsov'.

[19]  Charles Steinwedel, 'How Bashkiriia Became Part of European Russia, 1762–1881', in Jane Burbank, Mark von Hagen, and Anatoly Remnev (eds), *Russian Empire: Space, People, Power, 1700–1930* (Bloomington, IN, 2007), 94–124, 98–9.

[20]  Steinwedel, 'How Bashkiriia Became Part of European Russia', 103–4.

[21]  Charles Steinwedel, 'Kutlu-Mukhammad Batyr-Gireevich Tevkelev (1850–?) and Family', in Stephen M. Norris and Willard Sunderland (eds), *Russia's People of Empire: Life Stories from Eurasia, 1500 to the Present* (Bloomington, IN, 2012), 189–97.

[22]  Steinwedel, 'Kutlu-Mukhammad Batyr-Gireevich Tevkelev (1850–?) and Family'.

Shamil among them. His son, Magomet-Shefi, entered tsarist service while in exile with his father.[23] Their ranks included princes who emigrated from Qajar Persia, embarking on lengthy careers in tsarist military service.[24] On the eve of the First World War, ten Muslims held the rank of general in the Russian army, while over 200 served as officers of various ranks.[25]

At the same time, the state recruited non-elite Muslims to serve in the heterogeneous bodies that made up the armed forces. Tatars served in regular units from the early eighteenth century, including in the Russian navy founded by Peter the Great (1689–1725) and various regionally based Cossack regiments. Under Catherine the Great, policies that sought to incorporate local elites into the nobility drew Muslims from the Crimea in the south and even Poland in the west into the officer corps. However, Muslims serving in the military were not immune from periodic proselytization and pressure to convert to Orthodoxy. Priests stood at the ready to receive soldiers and sailors seeking to convert to the tsar's faith. Nevertheless, instructions issued by St Petersburg in 1742 mandated that this be a voluntary choice on the part of the convert.[26]

As an extension of its instrumentalist conception of toleration, Catherine's government reasoned that the faith that the empress and her advisers had newly found to be useful in civil and diplomatic affairs could be useful in the military world as well. From the late eighteenth century, the state appointed (and paid) mullahs to fulfill the religious needs of Muslim soldiers. Official mullahs served in garrisons from Finland and Poland in the west, to the steppe frontier in the east. Among other duties, they buried Muslims and administered oaths of loyalty to the tsar. Later tsarist legislation permitted oaths in 'Chagatay-Tatar dialect, the Persian language, the Turkish language, the Arabic language, [or] the Azerbaijani Turkish dialect'.[27]

---

[23] Austin Jersild, *Orientalism and Empire: North Caucasus Mountain Peoples and the Georgian Frontier, 1845–1917* (Montreal and Kingston, 2002), 120–5.

[24] E. E. Ismailov, *Persidskie printsy iz doma Kadzharov v Rossiiskoi imperii* (*Persian Princes from the Qajar Dynasty in the Russian Empire*) (Moscow, 2009).

[25] I. K. Zagidullin, 'Osobennosti sobliudeniia religioznykh prav musul'man v rossiiskoi sukhoputnoi reguliarnoi armii v 1874–1914 g.' ('The Particularities of the Religious Practices of Muslims in the Russian Imperial Army, 1874–1918'), *Journal of Power Institutions in Post-Soviet Societies*, 10 (2009), online.

[26] Kh. M. Abdullin, *Musul'mane i musul'manskoe dukhovenstvo v voennom vedomstve Rossiiskoi imperii: Sbornik zakonodatel'nykh aktov, normativno-pravovykh dokumentov i materialov* (*Muslims and the Muslim Clergy in the Military of the Russian Empire: A Collection of Legislative Acts, Normative-Legal Documents and Materials*) (Kazan, 2009), 15.

[27] Naganava Norikhiro, 'Musul'manskoe soobshchestvo v usloviiakh mobilizatsii: uchastie volgo-ural'skikh musul'man v voinakh poslednego desiatiletiia sushchestvovaniia Rossiiskoi imperii' ('Mobilizing the Muslim Community: The Participation of Volga-Ural Muslims in the Wars of the Last Decades of the Russian Empire'), in Naganava Norikhiro, D. M. Usmanova and Khamamato Mami (eds), *Volgo-Uralskii region v imperskom prostranstve*, 198–228. On Muslims in imperial armies more generally, see Nile Green, *Islam and the Army in Colonial India: Sepoy Religion in the Service of Empire* (Cambridge, 2009); and the articles in David Killingray and David Omissi (eds), *Guardians of Empire: The Armed Forces of the Colonial Powers, c.1700–1964* (Manchester, 1999); and on the ways that European notions of race and ethnicity shaped the conscription of Muslims, see Joe Lunn, '"Les Races Guerrières": Racial Preconceptions in the French Military about West African Soldiers During

Like Muslims in other European colonial armies, Muslim soldiers and officers fought in wars of imperial conquest. Originally from Dagestan, Maksud Alikhanov (1846–1907) served in the campaign against Khiva in 1871, received a medal for his role in the Russo-Ottoman War of 1877–78, and then fought in the Akhal-Teppe expedition against the Turkmen in 1879, the seizure of Merv in 1884, and the border skirmish with the Afghans in 1885.[28] In 1901, Alikhanov was promoted to the rank of major-general, serving as military governor charged with imposing order on the volatile Caucasus region of Kutaisi during the revolutionary upheaval of 1905. In 1907, he was killed by a terrorist's bomb in Aleksandropol'. Muslim generals also commanded tsarist troops in the Russo-Japanese War, earning medals for valor.[29] Although most of these men hailed from the Caucasus and Central Asia, the descendants of aristocratic Lithuanian and Polish Tatars were also to be found serving in the Kiev military district and elsewhere.[30]

In 1874, the introduction of universal military service, a cornerstone of the 'Great Reforms' of Alexander II (1855–81), further expanded the number of Muslims serving in the tsar's armed forces, although Russian authorities did not judge Muslims from recently conquered regions suitable for military service. More Muslims in the army brought an expansion in the number of officially sponsored Muslim clerics. In 1896, however, St Petersburg reversed course and abolished the post of military mullah. Nevertheless, the regime reinstituted the post in response to the Russo-Japanese War of 1904–05. Muslim clerics were then directed to monitor and direct the 'political mood' of Muslim soldiers. According to the report of one such cleric cited by the Japanese scholar Norihiro Naganawa, the mullah's exhortations convinced Muslim soldiers to sit out the soldiers' protests that shook Vladivostok in the autumn of 1905.[31] During the revolutionary events of 1905–07, Muslim communities pushed the regime to accommodate Islam further in military institutions. Petitioners complained of exposure to prohibited food and drink and argued that Muslim clerics should enjoy the same privileges as their Orthodox Christian counterparts, including exemption from conscription.[32] They gained this privilege finally in 1912, a development that left fewer clerics to lead Muslims in prayer and bury the dead during the First World War, when the regime was forced to expand the clerical establishment within military ranks once again.[33]

the First World War', *Journal of Contemporary History*, 34/4 (1999), 517–36; Myron Echenberg, *Colonial Conscripts: The Tirailleurs Sénégalais in French West Africa, 1857–1960* (Portsmouth, NH, and London, 1991); and the contributions in Karl Hack and Tobias Rettig (eds), *Colonial Armies in Southeast Asia* (London, 2006). I thank Sean Hanretta for recommending many of these sources.

[28] K. V. Zhil'tsov, 'Generaly musul'manskogo veroispovedaniia v Rossiiskoi armii v 1905–1914 godakh' ('Generals of Muslim Religious Confession in the Russian Imperial Army, 1905–14'), *Voprosy istorii*, 12 (2007), 130–5.

[29] Zhil'tsov, 'Generaly musul'manskogo veroispovedaniia v Rossiiskoi armii v 1905–1914 godakh'.

[30] Zhil'tsov, 'Generaly musul'manskogo veroispovedaniia v Rossiiskoi armii v 1905–1914 godakh', 133.

[31] Norikhiro, 'Musul'manskoe soobshchestvo v usloviiakh mobilizatsii', 205.

[32] Norikhiro, 'Musul'manskoe soobshchestvo v usloviiakh mobilizatsii', 207.

[33] In selecting these military mullahs, authorities in Kazan province favored clerics who appeared to side with traditionalists against reformist advocates of 'new method' schools, but officials in Ufa were not guided by the same concerns; Norikhiro, 'Musul'manskoe soobshchestvo v usloviiakh mobilizatsii', 209.

During the second half of the nineteenth century, Russian nationalist thinkers agitated against Muslims, Poles, Jews, and other non-Russians, but the 'Great Reforms' broadened opportunities for Muslim civic and social integration into the institutions of the empire. In civilian life, Muslim elites such as the Tevkelevs served in bodies formed by Russian nobles as well as in the organs of provincial self-government (*zemstvos*) that emerged in the countryside as part of Alexander II's reforms. In the 1880s, Muslims made up more than half of the deputies to the *zemstvo* of the Muslim-majority Belebei County of Ufa Province.[34] Muslim merchants and entrepreneurs founded charities for Muslim orphans and schoolchildren. Simultaneously, they joined civic organizations that were multi-confessional.[35] In 1905, some Muslim elites were drawn to a Muslim political party, while others joined liberal or leftist parties with a mixed membership of Russians, Jews, Poles, and others. Muslim turnout for elections to the State Duma was high, and twenty-five Muslims became deputies (five percent of the total). In the second Duma, the number of Muslim deuties increased to thirty-seven. In 1907, however, the imperial government sharply reduced the number of peasant deputies and increased the representation of nobles. The Third Duma included ten deputies, some forty percent of whom were nobles from Ufa. In 1912, the Fourth Duma had just six. Similar restrictions appeared in local government, where governors acted on charges directed by Orthodox Christian clerics and Russian nationalists against Muslim participation.[36]

From the reign of Alexander II the regime had explored, in a somewhat haphazard fashion, policies intended to make the empire look more like an emergent nation-state, but these largely incoherent moves coincided with an expansion in state sponsorship and management of Islamic religious institutions. Following on the conquest of Central Asia between the 1860s and 1880s, authorities in the Ministry of War resisted the establishment of a state-backed hierarchy resembling the Orenburg assembly. Arguing that the absence of official support would weaken Muslim institutions, administrators still found themselves drawn in, often at the initiative of local communities, in transforming and directing Islamic law courts and waqf endowments. On the ground, astute officials such as Konstantin von Kaufmann, the first governor-general of Russian Turkestan, sought to accommodate Central Asian Islamic structures in the imperial state. Meanwhile in 1872, in the Caucasus, the Ministry of Internal Affairs created two new administrative bodies, one for the oversight of Shi'i matters, another for the Sunnis. The regime now oversaw a total of four regional Islamic hierarchies designed to domesticate Muslim religious authority, sealing off harmful foreign influences, and to deploy it in the wider project of policing the family and disciplining imperial subjects.

---

[34] Steinwedel, 'Kutlu-Mukhammad Batyr-Gireevich Tevkelev', 192. The counter-reform of 1892 reduced these numbers significantly.

[35] Steinwedel, 'Kutlu-Mukhammad Batyr-Gireevich Tevkelev', 192; see also Christian Noack, *Muslimischer Nationalismus im Russischen Reich: Nationsbildung und Nationalbewegung bei Tataren und Baschkiren, 1861–1917* (Stuttgart, 2000).

[36] Steinwedel, 'Kutlu-Mukhammad Batyr-Gireevich Tevkelev', 194.

However, the challenge of the inter-imperial dimensions of Islam remained. Russia relied on Muslim merchants to trade with Asia, and tsarist policymakers were always concerned with presenting a benevolent face to the Muslim subjects of neighboring empires. Nonetheless, tsarist authorities viewed the regulation of the movement of people and texts as a crucial means of mitigating Russian Muslims' exposure to potentially threatening ideas. Yet the goal was more to manage than to sever entirely transborder connections. Seeking to protect Russian Muslims from the 'fanaticism' of their foreign co-religionists, the regime issued decrees in the 1830s banning 'dervishes' and pilgrims on the way to Mecca from entering Russian territory.[37] Marriage was another matter the regime was keen on regulating. As of 1847, men who were subjects of Bukhara, the Ottoman empire, or Persia could return to their homelands with Russian Muslim wives with the consent of the women's parents. Tsarist law permitted them to leave their wives in Russia, but only after specifying the length of their absence and after providing maintenance.[38] In the Caucasus, the tsarist administration regulated marriage between Russians and foreigners; there, officials tended to offer formal approval for marriage with Qajar subjects.[39] More generally, the regime permitted an array of religious and cultural associations and institutions, including schools, founded by Persians in the Caucasus.[40] From the last two decades of the nineteenth century, the state-directed development of the oil industry and railway in the wider Caspian region brought tens of thousands of Muslim migrants from neighboring states.[41] Simultaneously encouraging the separation and mixing of domestic and foreign Muslim populations, Russian policies produced contradictory outcomes. But inciting mobility did not mean surrendering control.

The hajj highlighted the dilemmas facing the state. Anxious about pan-Islamic contacts but sensitive to charges of repressing Islam, the empire responded like a number of rival European empires and opted to give institutional form to the pilgrimage.[42] As with other policies, the authorities devised conservative policies aimed at establishing control, but ended up unleashing sweeping changes in the lives of the empire's Muslim subjects. In the first decade of the twentieth century, more and more Russian Muslims joined pilgrims from neighboring Afghanistan, China, and Persia in availing themselves of an expanding tsarist railway and steamship

[37] D. Iu. Arapov, *Islam v Rossiiskoi imperii: zakonodatel'nye akty, opisaniia, statistika (Islam in the Russian Empire: Legislative Acts, Descriptions, and Statistics)* (Moscow, 2001), 119–21.
[38] Arapov, *Islam v Rossiiskoi imperii*, 140–1.
[39] See, for example, the journals of the Shi'i administration relating to the regulation of marriage in CSHAA, f. 290, op.1, d. 18.
[40] Nizam 'Ali Dihnavi, *Iraniyan-i muhajir dar Qafqaz: fa'aliyatha-yi farhangi-i anan dar salha-yi 1900 M–1931 M (Iranian Migrants in the Caucasus: Their Cultural Activities Between 1900 and 1931)* (Tehran, 2004).
[41] N. K. Belova, 'Ob otkhodnichestve iz Severo-Zapadnogo Irana v kontse XIX—nachale XX veka' ('On Seasonal Migration from Northwestern Iran at the End of the Nineteenth and Beginning of the Twentieth Centuries'), *Voprosy istorii*, 10 (1956), 112–21; and Touraj Atabkai, 'Disgruntled Guests: Iranian Subalterns on the Margins of the Tsarist Empire', in Touraj Atabaki (ed.), *The State and the Subaltern: Modernization, Society and the State in Turkey and Iran* (London, 2007), 31–52.
[42] See the chapters by John Slight and Eric Tagliacozzo in this volume.

network to travel to Mecca. In 1908, the Ministry of Transport organized 'hajj cars' running from Tashkent to Odessa. In the following year, state-funded ships designated for pilgrims steamed directly from Odessa to Jeddah. For a period, a merchant from Tashkent, Said Gani Saidazimbaev, enjoyed the backing of Prime Minister Peter Stolypin, who appointed him 'head of the Muslim pilgrimage in Russia' and allowed him to run a vast complex of ticket sales, halal concessions, dormitories, prayer rooms, and guides for Russian pilgrims. 'By investing in railroads and steamship navigation', Eileen Kane has shown, 'the tsarist regime helped facilitate Muslim mobility within the empire, bringing its Muslim subjects into closer contact with the wider Muslim world.'[43]

## RIGHTS WITHOUT BORDERS

From the late eighteenth century, the expansion of tsarist power at the expense of the Ottomans and Qajars established new forms of interdependence between Russian authorities and Muslim merchants. For these tsarist subjects, traversing the Black Sea or crossing the border from the Caucasus did not mean leaving the empire behind. Following Russian military victories, St Petersburg imposed capitulations on the Ottomans in 1783 and the Qajars in 1828, establishing extra-territorial rights for Russian subjects. These included immunity in most criminal matters. Local authorities were obliged to turn over suspected criminals to Russian officials. In commercial disputes, they gained access to a consular network and separate court system in which representatives of the tsarist Ministry of Foreign Affairs were to safeguard the interests of Russian subjects, including Muslims.[44]

The Ministry of Foreign Affairs devised administrative structures, like those within the empire, to forge hierarchical links with the Russian trading diasporas abroad. This network had two principal functions. Consular staff exercised oversight over tsarist subjects, while representing their interests before local authorities. Consuls appointed elders nominated by merchant communities in trading centers such as Tabriz and Mashhad to police their members and to represent their concerns to the imperial bureaucracy. Moreover, given the weakness of the central government in Tehran and near-anarchic conditions in many regional capitals, the offices of the Russian (or British) consulates often functioned as shadow government institutions. Such institutions did not capture all Russian subjects abroad, of course. Many different kinds of tsarist subjects were on the move, pilgrims, escaped conscripts, runaway serfs, fugitives from the law, itinerant preachers, and debtors, among them.

[43] Eileen Kane, 'Odessa as a Hajj Hub, 1880s–1910s', in John Randolph and Eugene M. Avrutin (eds), *Russia in Motion: Cultures of Human Mobility Since 1850* (Urbana, IL, and Chicago, 2010), 107–25, 120.

[44] Robert D. Crews, 'Muslim Networks, Imperial Power, and the Local Politics of Qajar Iran', in Uyama Tomohiko (ed.), *Asiatic Russia: Imperial Power in Regional and International Contexts* (London, 2012), 174–88.

Tsarist subjects on Ottoman and Persian territory frequently evaded tsarist consular control but readily turned to these same agents seeking advantage against local business partners and officials. They turned to consular personnel to gain assistance in recovering debts and enforcing contracts and appealed for intervention in disputes with Qajar authorities and notables. Equipped with their own police and military forces and a small treasury, they became actors in highly factionalized political struggles waged among local government and commercial elites, the religious classes, and the tribes. While pressing claims before Tehran against Shahsavan nomads who waged cross-border raids into Russian territory and attacked trade caravans, Russian diplomats also intervened in Persian domestic politics.[45] As in the Russian empire, tsarist officials received petitions and delegations from local populations seeking justice and protection. Consular institutions became parastatal institutions that pledged to defend vulnerable groups, whether Russian (Christians and Muslims with tsarist passports) or Persian, during recurring periods of crisis. Throughout its borderlands, Russia played the 'dissident' card on behalf of Christians. In Persian Azerbaijan, they frequently pressed Tehran over the insecurity of Nestorians and Armenian Christians. At the same time, Russians interceded with the central government on behalf of Sunni Muslims from the Russian empire as well.[46] Asserting a universal commitment to humanitarianism and toleration, St Petersburg offered its protection to Sunnis and Shi'a, alongside Christians and Jews, when such activism expanded the reach of tsarist influence.

From at least the 1830s, Persians also sought affiliation with Russian power as a safeguard against the endemic insecurity of life under the Qajars. At mid-century, when the area around Tabriz was plagued by political instability and social unrest, villagers appealed to the Russian consul general seeking aid against soldiers and officials whom they accused of oppressing them. In 1849, the consul general, Nikolai Anichkov, reported that Shi'i clerical factions and their followers began to confront one another in armed street confrontations, and that each party appealed to him for backing against its rivals. Anichkov professed neutrality in their disputes. In the following months, however, the security in Tabriz deteriorated further. When rumors spread of the miraculous healing of a blind man, Anichkov began to fear for the safety of the Russian Armenians and other Christians in the town. The new governor of Tabriz initially replied to Anichkov's requests for attention to the safety of Christians by refusing to guarantee their safety should they leave their homes. Anichkov protested this as an offense to the honor of Russian subjects and apparently won them immunity from an official curfew. Still fearing violence against his Christian charges at the hands of politically active Shi'i mullahs, he set up meetings

[45] Firuz Kazemzadeh, *Russia and Britain in Persia, 1864–1914: A Study in Imperialism* (New Haven, 1968); and articles in Stephanie Cronin (ed.), *Iranian-Russian Encounters: Empires and Revolutions Since 1800* (London, 2013).

[46] P. P. Bushev, *Posol'stvo Artemiia Volynskogo v Iran v 1715–1718 gg. (The Embassy of Artemii Volynskii in Iran, 1715–1718)* (Moscow, 1978), 250–1 and 270.

with the senior 'ulama of Tabriz and extracted promises that they would offer sermons aimed at diffusing the communal tensions in the town.[47]

The various protections afforded by a Russian passport were significant enough to generate a flood of demands on Qajar territory for documents proving tsarist subjecthood. However, the government of Nasir al-Din Shah (1848–96) protested the expansion of Russian authority over individuals it regarded as Qajar subjects, pointing to the Russo-Persian convention of 1844, which allowed the shah's government to weigh in on the applications of Persians seeking tsarist nationality.[48] Authorities on both sides of the border struggled to identify the legal identities of persons who claimed subjecthood in different contexts as applicants turned to the Russian imperial mission in Tehran and to consular officials elsewhere with stories of lost or stolen passports. Similarly, in the Ottoman empire, Muslim travelers and émigrés from the tsarist empire also appealed to the Russian consular network for assistance against Ottoman authorities, giving rise to similar disputes about who was an Ottoman and who was a tsarist subject.[49] Here, too, political loyalty, not confessional identity, was the chief tsarist concern.

In practice, archival records reveal that contrary to the formal wording of the diplomatic texts, Russian merchants in Qajar Persia did not always enjoy a privileged status in civil or criminal law. For example, the Persian Interior Minister Mirza Said Khan was intransigent when it came to prosecuting the murder of Russian subjects. Russian authorities conducted their own crime investigations and frequently turned over the names of the victims and suspects to the Persian police. In 1860, the Russian ambassador protested the robbery and murder of Meshedi Magomed (Mashhadi Muhammad in Persian) and named a suspect, but the interior minister refused to act on what he dismissed as unfounded allegations. Over a dozen such murders remained uninvestigated, despite Russian pressure to arrest figures they named in official communiqués.[50]

Still, these difficulties did not stem the tide of merchants and other actors seeking Russian papers. Aspiring Russian subjects, such as a certain Mirza Yahya Khan Ilyasov of the central Persian town of Soltanabad who applied for a Russian passport, even traveled to the Caucasus to secure an exit visa before presenting a claim in Tehran and, ultimately, to the Senate in St Petersburg. In 1908 the investigation into his application stretched from Tehran to the district of Kuba in Baku province. Citing a 'multitude' of cases in which Shi'i Persians had acquired Russian passports illegally, the Russian authorities increasingly treated them with suspicion. In Kuba, local authorities interviewed all residents of the village that the applicant from Soltanabad had claimed as his home. The elderly inhabitants

---

[47] Nikolai Anichkov to Mikhail Vorontsov, 16 April 1850, Tabriz, Central State Historical Archive of the Republic of Georgia (Sakartvelos sakhelmtsipo saistorio arkivi, hereafter SSSA), f. 11, op. 1, d. 2004.

[48] Qajar subjects, particularly in southern Persia, also frequently sought recognition as British subjects.

[49] Meyer, 'Immigration, Return, and the Politics of Citizenship'.

[50] Russian Imperial Mission, Report, 2 April 1860, Tehran, SSSA, f. 11, op. 1, d. 3254; and see also Crews, 'Muslim Networks, Imperial Power, and the Local Politics of Qajar Iran'.

of the village remembered his father, who had emigrated to Persia some fifty years ago, where the applicant was born. His name did not appear in the records of the village, but it did appear on the lists of state employees maintained by Tehran. Citing his state service, the fact that the Persian government insisted he was a Qajar subject, and evidence that he had severed ties to his ancestral village, the Russian authorities rejected his claim.[51] Such cases suggest that Russian authorities were hesitant to extend the protections of a tsarist passport freely. Consular officials may have acted independently, on behalf of particular Armenians or even Jews, but the archives record many more cases, at least by the early twentieth century, when Russian authorities tended to take seriously the terms of the 1844 convention— and the fragile legitimacy of the Qajar dynasty.[52]

For Qajar subjects, another pathway to the limited rights regime of the tsarist empire was emigration, a practice that St Petersburg cultivated in specific cases that seemed to advance tsarist policy. Indeed, Russian officials cultivated Islamic dignitaries as émigrés who might serve as trans-imperial power-brokers. Following the Russo-Persian War of 1826–28, for instance, tsarist authorities identified a senior cleric in Tabriz whom they credited with keeping the population of Persian Azerbaijan 'in complete obedience and submission' during their brief occupation of the territory. When this Mir Fatah Aga asked to accompany Russian forces on their retreat, the Russian authorities resolved to capitalize on his ostensible influence. General I. F. Pashkevich sought to use him, as the head of all Shi'a in Russian-controled territory, to exercise 'supervision over the teaching and conduct in relation to our government' of Shi'i clerics, who, in the past had often incited 'hatred of our government'. To demonstrate the value of loyalty to the Russian cause, Pashkevich proposed to award Mir Fatah Aga with an annual pension and property to compensate him for the wealth he left behind in Persia. In August 1831, Nicholas I (1825–55) awarded him possession of fifteen villages in Shirvan province. The mullah managed the area as his personal fiefdom. He issued rules on marriage, trade, and order among his dependents, threatening them with fines and corporal punishment.[53] Russian officials valued him as a counterweight to the region's Sunnis, especially against rebellious Dagestani tribes in 1832–33, and as a lever in Qajar politics across the Aras River. However, such relations proved unstable. The mullah fled back to Persia in 1843, and Russian spies traced his movements there, pressuring Tehran to keep him far away from the Russian border.[54]

---

[51]  Mirza Yahya Khan Ilyasov to Governor of Baku, 15 July1911, CSHAA f. 44, op. 1, d. 555.

[52]  See, for example, the unsuccessful petition of a Persian subject who lacked documentation from the shah's government approving of his petition in CSHAA f. 44, op. 1, d. 537.

[53]  Institut Istorii (Akademiia nauk SSSR) (ed.), *Kolonial'naia politika Rossiiskogo tsarizma v Azerbaidzhane v 20-60-kh gg. XIX v.* (*The Colonial Policies of Russian Tsarism in Azerbaijan, 1820s–1860s*), 2 vols (Moscow and Leningrad, 1937), ii, 311–14.

[54]  Institut Istorii (Akademiia nauk SSSR) (ed.), *Kolonial'naia politika Rossiiskogo tsarizma v Azerbaidzhane*, 327–8 and 332–6. For their part, the British frequently voiced anxieties about Russian influence among Persian 'ulama. See, for example, a report from Captain Picot in Tehran of 1894, which claimed that 'Russian agents are increasing their influence amongst the Mollahs in the northern provinces, and that this influence is extending southwards towards Seistan', in R. M. Burrell (ed.), *Iran Political Diaries 1881–1965*, 14 vols (London, 1997), i, 237; and also Marina Alexidze, 'Fazel-Khan Garrusi and Tbilisi', *Iran and the Caucasus*, 7/1–2 (2003), 125–31.

Other Muslim Qajar subjects attempted to gain access to tsarist subjecthood by encouraging the expansion of Russian territorial sovereignty. Across the Caspian Sea, the frontier between eastern Persia and another newly incorporated territory of the Russian empire emerged in the 1850s and 1860s as an object of particular concern for both the Qajar and tsarist states. This was a borderland distinguished by mobile populations whom Persian Qajar officials had struggled to control. Whether on horseback or boat, Turkmen eluded taxation and conscription and frequently faced repression from Qajar authorities. They frequently raided villages throughout Khorasan, taking people and livestock to markets in Khiva and elsewhere. Here the fault-line was not only between nomadic and settled world, but between Sunni and Shi'a. The Russians arrived brutally on the scene in the 1870s and 1880s with a complex agenda. They ruthlessly slaughtered some Turkmen populations (officials even used the term 'pogrom' to characterize this violence) in areas they sought to control.[55] But they assumed a different posture towards Turkmen on or bordering Qajar territory. Their presence had an immediate effect on the political horizons of many Turkmen lineages inhabiting the border zone. A letter written by a group of Salor Turkmen to the governor of Khorasan in June 1884 offers a window on this shifting terrain. The letter, which appeared above the stamps of seventeen khans, 'ulama, and elders, complained of forced relocation and of material deprivation. In the previous year they had sought the intercession of Nasir al-Din Shah who had visited the province, but they were denied access to him. Moreover, they complained, the government had placed over them a state official, Nusrat al-Mulk Ali Mardan Khan, a 'short' man who had turned 'brother against brother' and who had caused dissatisfaction within their community. Despite their protests, nothing was done about this official. They resolved, at the first sight of Russian troops, to gather their people and go over to them. The letter concluded by announcing that the Russian government had been sympathetic to their 'pathetic condition' and that Russians 'take under their protection Sunni people'—and that 'we, who are also among the Sunnis' had decided to become tsarist subjects.[56] The tsarist discourse of religious toleration and protection for persecuted communities could prove useful to tsarist authorities and aspiring imperial subjects alike.

## CONCLUSION

The story of Islam in the Russian empire is more than one of repression and emigration. Tsarist policy toward its heterogeneous Muslim populations was dynamic and complex. Geopolitics and regional specificities were as important as shifting conceptions of Islam and 'the Orient'.[57] However, one persistent thread of tsarist

---

[55] A. Il'iasov (ed.), *Prisoedinenie Turkmenii k Rossii (sbornik arkhivnykh dokumentov)* (*The Russian Annexation of Turkmeniia (A Collection of Archival Documents)*) (Ashkhabad, 1960), 114–15 and 118.

[56] Il'iasov (ed.), *Prisoedinenie Turkmenii k Rossii*, 114–15 and 118.

[57] David Schimmelpenninck van der Oye, *Russian Orientalism: Asia in the Russian Mind from Peter the Great to the Emigration* (New Haven and London, 2010).

political thought understood Islamic rites, law, and personnel as potential instruments of social discipline and spiritual as well as moral authority that the regime might appropriate for the imperial project of mapping and ruling ethnically, linguistically, and socially diverse peoples. At the same time, tsarist elites constructed multiple paths of integration for Muslim subjects both within and beyond the borders of the empire. The Romanov dynasty presided over an illiberal polity, but its subjects nonetheless enjoyed limited rights. Membership in social estates and appointment to state offices entailed particular privileges, as did integration in the hierarchical order of religious institutions established by tsarist law. At critical nodes in the institutions of civil and military administration and throughout the tsarist estate system, Muslims occupied positions of authority over local populations because of the active support or, at a minimum, the tacit approval of the tsarist regime. Whether Muslim Cossacks on the Caucasian and steppe frontiers, Turkmen sailors on the Caspian, merchants in Persia, Bashkir peasants in the Urals, or townspeople in Samarkand, the various Muslim communities of the empire were subordinated to Muslim religious as well as secular elites with ties to the state. In the late nineteenth century, these connections grew more dense, and the power of state institutions expanded. However, toleration in the tsarist context did not mean freedom of conscience per se. Instead it meant being bound to the norms of a state-sanctioned confession and its 'clergy'. Such policies did not forestall locally based uprisings or occasional resistance. Yet, the appeal of this limited rights regime emerges most starkly when we follow the movement of Russian Muslim subjects beyond the frontiers of the empire into neighboring Muslim countries where they made claims to the extraterritorial rights acquired by Russian imperial supremacy against Muslim co-religionists. Though discriminatory and incomplete, the tsarist accommodation of Islam—and Muslim subjects' active engagement with the institutions and practices of tsarist subjecthood—reinforced the stability of the empire and shaped the possibilities of being a Russian Muslim, both within and beyond its borders.

# 2

# British Imperial Rule and the Hajj

*John Slight*

## INTRODUCTION

This chapter addresses the policies of the British empire towards the hajj, from the 1865 cholera epidemic, which was the catalyst for imperial involvement with the ritual, to the outbreak of the Second World War in 1939, which ushered in a new and final phase of Britain's association with the pilgrimage. In the territories of Britain's empire where Islam was an important faith—the Gambia, Sierra Leone, the Gold Coast, Northern Nigeria, Sudan, Zanzibar, Egypt, Somaliland, Palestine, Transjordan, Iraq, Kuwait, the Trucial States, Aden, India, Malaya, Brunei, and Sarawak—the hajj was an area of Muslim religious practice that came to command the attention of British officials.[1] Thousands of pilgrims who lived under British imperial rule traveled to the Hijaz to perform the hajj every year. During the 1937 pilgrimage, for example, out of a total of approximately 76,000 pilgrims, over 10,500 were from India, 4,500 from Nigeria, 1,600 from Sudan, 1,200 from Somalia, and 105 were Indians from South Africa.[2] Britain's 'Muslim empire' has only been noted by a few historians.[3] As chapters in this volume and other works demonstrate, the governance of religious practices, central to the exercise and legitimation of imperial power, is a vital framework of enquiry in assessing the history of empire.[4] The most significant unintended

---

[1] To give a sense of the growth of Britain's Muslim empire, what follows are the dates of acquisition of these territories: India (1765), Sierra Leone (1787), Gambia (1821), Gold Coast (1821), Aden (1839), Sarawak (1841), Malaya (1874), Egypt (1882), Somaliland (1884), Trucial States (1887), Brunei (1888), Zanzibar (1890), Sudan (1899), Kuwait (1899), Northern Nigeria (1900), Iraq (1914), Palestine (1918), and Transjordan (1921). However, these dates are inevitably imprecise, given the complex and sometimes lengthy processes of British conquest and expansion.

[2] Report on the Hajj of 1937, enclosed in British Legation, Jidda to Foreign Office, London, FO 371/20840, in Alan Rush (ed.), *Records of the Hajj: A Documentary History of the Pilgrimage to Mecca*, 10 vols (Slough, 1993), vii, 209–15.

[3] John Darwin, *The Empire Project: The Rise and Fall of the British World-System, 1830–1970* (Cambridge, 2009), 295–7; Ronald Hyam, *Britain's Declining Empire: The Road to Decolonisation, 1918–1968* (Cambridge, 2006), 154–62; and Francis Robinson, 'The Muslim World and the British Empire' in Wm Roger Louis and Judith M. Brown (eds), *The Oxford History of the British Empire*, 5 vols (Oxford, 1999), iv: *The Twentieth Century*, 398–420: see also Faisal Devji's chapter in this volume.

[4] The centrality of religion and religious practice to empires throughout world history has been emphasized in Jane Burbank and Frederick Cooper, *Empires in World History: Power and the Politics of Difference* (Princeton, 2010), 2, 4, 15, 332.

consequence of the British empire's involvement with the hajj was its *facilitation* of the pilgrimage, in an ultimately futile attempt to gain legitimacy as a ruler of Muslims. In doing so, it echoed the practices of older Islamic empires, but within the context of subsidized passages on steamships and railways and telegraphed pilgrimage reports.[5]

The British empire's interactions with the hajj were more complex than existing accounts suggest.[6] One area these works focus on is the attempts by British authorities to regulate the pilgrimage on a medical basis, given the threat of epidemic disease posed by the annual movement of large numbers of pilgrims. This was an important sphere of activity.[7] However, couched in a Foucauldian model of surveillance and sanitary control, these studies tend to overestimate the *overall* effectiveness and impact of British imperial policies towards the hajj. Another focus of these works is on the hajj as a catalyst for numerous anti-colonial resistance movements and an incubator for pan-Islamic activities. As Nile Green cogently argues, the actions of Muslims in such movements became 'so thoroughly registered in the imagination and archive of empire as to offer historians the double attraction of being automatically "important" and abundantly documented in colonial records'.[8] To be sure, these aspects were important, but the existing emphasis on their activities has obscured other no less significant facets of the pilgrimage. Consequently, this chapter moves beyond these interpretative

---

[5] Stephen F. Dale, *The Muslim Empires of the Ottomans, Safavids and Mughals* (Cambridge, 2010); Suraiya Faroqhi, *Pilgrims and Sultans: The Hajj under the Ottomans, 1517–1683* (London, 1996); M. N. Pearson, *Pilgrimage to Mecca: The Indian Experience 1500–1800* (Princeton, 1996); Naimur Farooqi, *Mughal–Ottoman Relations: A Study of Political and Diplomatic Relations between Mughal India and the Ottoman Empire, 1556–1748* (Delhi, 1989); William Ochsenwald, *Religion, Society and the State in Arabia: The Hijaz under Ottoman Control, 1840–1908* (Athens, OH, 1984); and Karl K. Barbir, *Ottoman Rule in Damascus, 1708–1758* (Princeton, 1980).

[6] Saurabh Mishra, *Pilgrimage, Politics and Pestilence: The Haj from the Indian Subcontinent, 1860–1920* (Delhi, 2011); Saurabh Mishra, 'Beyond the Bounds of Time? The Hajj Pilgrimage from the Indian Subcontinent, 1865–1920', in Mark Harrison and Biswamoy Pati (eds), *The Social History of Health and Medicine in Colonial India* (London, 2009), 31–44; Saurabh Mishra, 'Pilgrims, Politics and Pestilence: The Hajj from the Indian Sub-Continent, 1860–1920', (DPhil, University of Oxford, 2008); M. C. Low, 'Empire and the Hajj: Pilgrims, Plagues and Pan-Islam, 1865–1908', *International Journal of Middle Eastern Studies*, 40, 2 (2008), 269–90; M. C. Low, 'Empire of the Hajj: Pilgrims, Plagues and Pan-Islam under British Surveillance 1865–1926', (MA, University of Georgia, 2007); Michael Miller, 'Pilgrim's Progress: The Business of the Hajj', *Past and Present*, 191/1 (2006), 189–228; Sugata Bose, *A Hundred Horizons: The Indian Ocean in the Age of Global Empire* (Cambridge, MA, 2006), 193–233; Takashi Oishi, 'Friction and Rivalry over Pious Mobility: British Colonial Management of the Hajj and the Reaction to it by Indian Muslims, 1870–1920', in Kuroki Hidemitsu (ed.), *The Influence of Human Mobility in Muslim Societies* (London, 2003), 151–79; F. E. Peters, *The Hajj: The Muslim Pilgrimage to Mecca and the Holy Places* (Princeton, 1994); Mark Harrison, *Public Health in British India: Anglo-Indian Preventative Medicine, 1859–1914* (Cambridge, 1994), 117–38; and William Roff, 'Sanitation and Security: The Imperial Powers and the Nineteenth Century Hajj', *Arabian Studies*, 6 (1982), 143–61.

[7] See Eric Tagliacozzo's chapter in this book.

[8] Nile Green, *Bombay Islam: The Religious Economy of the West Indian Ocean, 1840–1915* (Cambridge, 2011), 7.

frameworks by analyzing under-studied areas of enquiry, such as Britain's policies towards 'pauper pilgrims', the vital role played by Muslim employees in Britain's hajj administration, Anglo-Hashemite relations and the hajj during the period of the First World War, and the impact of Wahhabism on pilgrims from 1924 to the outbreak of the Second World War. This survey begins with a brief appraisal of Britain's involvement in the Hijaz up to the 1865 cholera epidemic and its after-math, which prompted a more active British engagement with the hajj.

## BRITAIN AND THE HIJAZ, 1837–69

In October 1837, the East India Company appointed British agents—elevated to vice-consuls by the Foreign Office in October 1838—to Suez, Qusayr, and Jidda, in order to 'facilitate steam communication' between Egypt and India.[9] The age of steam reached the Red Sea in 1830 with the seminal voyage of the vessel *Hugh Lindsay* from Bombay to Suez. This venture, backed by the Bombay Presidency, cut the journey time to only twenty-one days.[10] By the 1860s, European ship-ping companies had a dominant position in the pilgrim traffic from South and Southeast Asia to Jidda (Fig. 3).[11]

Steamships made the cost of a passage to the Hijaz affordable to a larger number of pilgrims than ever before.[12] This led to a 'plebianization' of the hajj, as many were only able to afford a one-way passage—travelers branded 'pauper pilgrims' by the British.[13]

The exasperated correspondence of Charles Cole, Britain's consul in Jidda, to the Bombay authorities in 1853 illustrates how little concerned officials in India were with destitute pilgrims. Cole was concerned that unless action was taken to pre-vent 'absolute paupers' leaving India to go on hajj, the Indian government would be liable for the financial cost of repatriation.[14] That same year, Victorian explorer Richard Burton (1821–90) was in Mecca and Medina. Within his account of the pilgrimage, Burton put forward the view that pilgrims should be required to prove they could afford the journey before receiving a travel permit for hajj. Through this permit, Burton felt that Cole could then assist 'our' Indian pilgrims: 'though men die of starvation in the streets, he [Cole] was unable to relieve them. The highways of Meccah abound in pathetic Indian beggars, who affect . . . all the circumstance

---

[9] Roff, 'Sanitation and Security', 145; and Saleh Muhammad al-Amr, *The Hijaz under Ottoman Rule 1869–1914: Ottoman Vali, the Sharif of Mecca, and the Growth of British Influence* (Riyadh, 1978), 169 and 175–6.

[10] Low, 'Empire and the Hajj', 273.

[11] William Ochsenwald, *Religion, Society and the State in Arabia: The Hijaz under Ottoman Control, 1840–1908* (Athens, OH, 1984), 201; and Miller, 'Pilgrim's Progress', 98.

[12] C. A. Bayly, *The Birth of the Modern World, 1780–1914: Global Connections and Comparisons* (London, 2004), 354–5.

[13] Saurabh Mishra, 'Pilgrims, Politics and Pestilence', 77.

[14] Charles Cole to Arthur Malet, Chief Secretary to the Foreign Department, Government of Bombay, 7 December 1853, Foreign Department, Political—External Affairs—A, 5 May, 1854, National Archives of India, Delhi, India (hereafter NAI).

**Fig. 3** Mecca pilgrims from British India, arriving in Jidda, *c*.1930 (Royal Geographical Society).

of misery, because it supports them in idleness.'[15] Burton and Cole's beliefs in the necessity of British involvement with the hajj, primarily to staunch the flow of 'pauper' pilgrims, were in stark contrast to officials' views in India. The Earl of Dalhousie, India's governor-general, firmly believed that the hajj had nothing to do with the British authorities, and thought the government had no right to prevent anyone from going on pilgrimage.[16] Dalhousie's response reflected the prevailing administrative doctrine in India. Liberal 'reforms' and 'improvements' undertaken by the colonial state were confined to what officials considered 'secular' affairs.[17]

While the 1857 Uprising did not have a direct impact on Britain's interactions with the hajj, it did exacerbate British suspicions towards Muslims.[18] Initially,

[15] Richard Burton, *Personal Narrative of a Pilgrimage to Al-Madinah and Meccah*, 2 vols (London, 1855–56), ii, 185–6.

[16] Secretary, Foreign Department, Government of India, to H. L. Anderson, Secretary, Government of Bombay, 5 May 1854, NAI, Foreign Department, Political—External Affairs—A, 5 May, 1854.

[17] Thomas R. Metcalf, *Ideologies of the Raj* (Cambridge, 1994), 36.

[18] Peter Hardy, *The Muslims of British India* (Cambridge, 1972), 60, 62, and 81. A partial selection of the principal works on the Uprising are the articles in Biswamoy Pati (ed.), *The Great Rebellion of 1857* (London, 2010); Biswamoy Pati (ed.), *The 1857 Rebellion* (Oxford, 2007); and Rosie Llewellyn-Jones, *The Great Uprising in India, 1857–58: Untold Stories, Indian and British* (Woodbridge, 2007); Rajat Kanta Ray, 'Race, Religion and Realm: The Political Theory of "The Reigning Indian Crusade", 1857', in Mushirul Hasan and Narayani Gupta (eds), *India's Colonial Encounter: Essays in Memory of Eric Stokes* (Delhi, 1993), 133–82; Eric Stokes and C.A. Bayly (eds), *The Peasant Armed* (Oxford, 1986); and Gautam Bhadra, 'Four Rebels of 1857', in Ranajit Guha (ed.), *Subaltern Studies IV* (Delhi, 1985), 229–75; and Rudrangshu Mukherjee, *Awadh in Revolt* (Oxford, 1984).

Britons in India thought the revolt was the result of Muslim resentment at their loss of political power. The speed and scale of events led some to think it was an Islamic conspiracy, a view expounded by various officials, although scant evidence for this interpretation emerged afterwards.[19] After Queen Victoria's 1858 proclamation, religion was one of the foremost arenas where Indians could contest British power, which was apparent in relation to the hajj, as will be shown later.[20] British ambivalence towards Islam in this period was exemplified by official monitoring for seditious activities, combined with a strategy of cooperation with Indian Muslims elites from the 1870s.[21]

The reason for Britain's initial interest in the pilgrimage was the threat of epidemic disease. A devastating cholera epidemic in 1865, which killed 15,000 out of 90,000 pilgrims in the Hijaz and then spread to Europe, prompted Britain—and other European powers—to note that the hajj was a significant conduit for disease.[22] Britain's Cholera Commissioners reported that these epidemics always originated in India.[23] The 1866 international sanitary conference directed that preventative measures to protect Europe from cholera should be linked to arresting its development in India. These would be similar to hygiene measures undertaken by colonial authorities for Hindu pilgrimages. Quarantine stations would be established in the Red Sea, and pilgrim steamship traffic would receive 'especial attention' given the hajj's role in spreading cholera in 1865. Although Britain was opposed to sanitary intervention in the pilgrimage, the Cholera Commissioners noted the 'pitiable condition' of Indian pilgrims in the Hijaz, and proposed that there should be measures to prevent 'such disastrous scenes' in the future.[24] The Cholera Commissioners' report reflected Britain's cautionary attitude towards intrusions in Indian public health in the later nineteenth century, informed by the perceived risk of civil unrest. Any sanitary regulation of the pilgrimage threatened to damage the Indian government's strategy of cooperation with Muslim leaders. Regulations were seen as vulnerable to misinterpretation by 'lower-class' Muslims, who would supposedly view them as interfering with religious practices, a viewpoint held by some of the local Muslim notables consulted by the British, such as liberal lawyer and university lecturer Sayyid Amir Ali and Maulvi Abdul Latif,

---

[19] Thomas R. Metcalf, *Aftermath of Revolt: India 1857–1870* (Princeton, 1964), 55–6; Metcalf, *Ideologies,* 139–40; see also Salahuddin Ahmad, *Mutiny, Revolution or Muslim Rebellion? British Public Reaction to the Indian Crisis of 1857* (Delhi, 2008); Gautam Chaktravarty, *The Indian Revolt and the British Imagination* (Cambridge, 2005); and William Dalrymple, *The Last Mughal: The Fall of a Dynasty: Delhi, 1857* (London, 2007).

[20] Kama MacLean, *Pilgrimage and Power: The Kumbh Mela in Allahabad, 1765–1954* (Oxford, 2008), 111.

[21] Harrison, *Public Health in British India,* 117; and Hardy, *Muslims of British India,* 79, 118, and 125. This policy was mirrored in the Sudan in the 1900s, see M. W. Daly, *Empire on the Nile: The Anglo-Egyptian Sudan 1898–1934* (Cambridge, 1986), 122.

[22] Peters, *Hajj,* 301.

[23] British Cholera Commissioners, Constantinople, to Lord Stanley, Secretary of State for Foreign Affairs, 3 October 1866, London, p. 2, The National Archives, London (hereafter TNA), PC 1/2672.

[24] British Cholera Commissioners, Constantinople, to Lord Stanley, Secretary of State for Foreign Affairs, 3 October 1866, London, pp. 4–7, TNA, PC 1/2672; on the British administration of Hindu pilgrimages, see Maclean, *Pilgrimage and Power.*

deputy magistrate in the 24 Pargannahs in Bengal.[25] Although sanitation and quarantine remained important concerns and were an impetus for the growth of an imperial 'hajj bureaucracy', the British empire's engagement with the pilgrimage after 1865 rapidly encompassed many other aspects, such as destitute pilgrims.[26]

### 'PAUPER' PILGRIMS AND MUSLIM EMPLOYEES

There were many tensions and paradoxes that informed Britain's policies towards the hajj, such as a perceived need to appease Muslim 'religious sentiment' through a policy of 'non-interference' with religious practices, to forestall any potential unrest. This jostled with an inconsistent desire to exercise varying degrees of control over pilgrims' movements, and the increasing need to uphold British 'prestige' in the Hijaz. A good example of this was Britain's engagement with destitute pilgrims. The cheaper cost of long-distance travel gave rise to large numbers of Indian 'pauper' pilgrims in the Hijaz, rued by administrators as a stain on British 'prestige'.[27] Britain's engagement with destitute pilgrims developed in complexity from the 1870s, as British authorities in Jidda and India attempted to grapple with the seemingly intractable question of how to deal with the presence of these pilgrims, stranded in Jidda after each hajj's conclusion. No clear official policy developed on this issue. Attempts to regulate 'pauper' pilgrims met with repeated failure. There was never really any effective attempt to prevent such people going on hajj, if such action was ever possible, precisely because of British sensitivity to Muslim opinion.

Officials first seriously grappled with the issue of destitute pilgrims during the 1875–76 pilgrimage seasons. In 1876, Beyts, the British consul at Jidda, drew his superiors' attention to the plight of destitute pilgrims.[28] While he recognized that the Indian authorities were unwilling to impose travel restrictions on its subjects, Beyts suggested these pilgrims' predicament could be alleviated through using a 'respectable, intelligent and unbigoted' Muslim, who would warn pilgrims of the dangers in going on hajj without enough money.[29] As other officials came to realize, any governmental action regarding destitute pilgrims, and the hajj more widely, could only be effective through employing Muslim intermediaries.

---

[25] Harrison, *Public Health in British India,* 118 and 130; and John P. Slight, 'The British Empire and the Hajj, 1865–1956' (PhD, University of Cambridge, 2012), 69–72.

[26] Early pilgrimage reports by the consul in Jidda merely recorded pilgrim numbers and the incidence of epidemic disease, see Reports on the conclusion of the Hajj, Jidda to Foreign Office, 29 March 1869 and 18 March 1870, London, TNA, FO 195/956.

[27] The only detailed treatment of this topic is Radhika Singha, 'Passport, Ticket and India-rubber Stamp: "The Problem of the Pauper Pilgrim" in Colonial India, *c.*1882–1925', in Ashwini Tambe and Harald Fischer-Tiné (eds), *The Limits of British Colonial Control in South Asia: Spaces of Disorder in the Indian Ocean Region* (London, 2009), 49–84.

[28] Capt. G. Beyts, Consul, Jidda, to Earl of Derby, Secretary of State for Foreign Affairs, London, 1 December 1876, Foreign Department, General—A, 1877, No. 125–192, NAI.

[29] Capt. G. Beyts, Consul, Jidda, to Brig. Gen. J. W. Schneider, Political Resident, Aden, 27 May 1875, Foreign Department, General—A, 1877, No. 125–192, NAI.

Beyts' theory that poor pilgrims went on hajj because wealthy Muslims gave *zakat* in the form of an outward passage to Jidda and food for the voyage—leaving them penniless in the Hijaz—sparked a lengthy investigation ordered by the India Office to find solutions to the problem.[30] The enquiry's results unsurprisingly debunked Beyts' theory.[31] Overall, these documents confirmed British officials' reluctance to introduce any restrictive travel measures on pilgrims for fear of upsetting Muslim opinion, a perception skillfully played upon by the Muslim elites consulted by the British.[32] Moreover, it was believed that government repatriation of poor pilgrims would encourage more of their kin to go on hajj. Any restrictions on the pilgrimage were 'specially inopportune' because of the heightened state of Indian Muslim feeling in support of the Ottoman empire, then at war with Russia.[33]

Although only a small number of Muslims were consulted, their views were influential in shaping Britain's policy of inaction towards destitute pilgrims. Some officials and Muslim notables used Queen Victoria's 1858 proclamation that Britain would not interfere in Indian religious practices to successfully oppose any proposed curtailment of poor pilgrims' travels.[34] Some of the Muslims consulted suggested that an English-speaking Indian Muslim official working at the Jidda consulate should assist Indian pilgrims in the Hijaz.[35] While British authorities in Calcutta initially rejected this, the eventual appointment of a Muslim official in Britain's Jidda consulate demonstrates how Muslims played an influential role in defining the contours of Britain's administrative involvement with the pilgrimage.

The expansion of Muslim employment in Britain's growing hajj administration began in 1878, when the Indian government sent Assistant Surgeon Dr Abdur

---

[30] Capt. G. Beyts, Consul, Jidda, to Brig. Gen. J. W. Schneider, Political Resident, Aden, 27 May 1875, Foreign Department, General—A, 1877, No. 125–192, NAI; Secretary of State for India, London, to Government of India, Calcutta, 8 July 1875, Foreign Department, General—A, 1877, No. 125–192, NAI.

[31] B. W. Colvin, Secretary to Government, North Western Provinces, Agra, to Secretary to the Government of India, Home Department, Calcutta, 26 July 1876; Lindsay Neill, Assistant Secretary to Chief Commissioner, Central Provinces, Nagpur, to Secretary to the Government of India, Home Department, Calcutta, 5 April 1876; and E. J. Sinkinson, Junior Secretary to Chief Commissioner, British Burmah, Rangoon, to Secretary to the Government of India, Home Department, Calcutta, 17 December 1875, Foreign Department, General—A, 1877, No. 125–192, NAI.

[32] Moulvie Abdool Luteef, Khan Bahadoor, Deputy Magistrate of 24 Pergunnahs, Alipore, to R. H. Wilson, Magistrate, 24 Pergunnahs, Alipore, 14 February 1876, Foreign Department, General—A, 1877, No. 125–192, NAI.

[33] Government of India, Calcutta, to Secretary of State for India, London, 2 July 1877, Foreign Department, General—A, 1877, No. 125–192, NAI. On Indian Muslim relations with the Ottomans in this period, see Azmi Özcan, *Pan-Islamism: Indian Muslims, the Ottomans and Britain, 1877–1924* (Leiden, 1997).

[34] One large cache of letters from Muslim notables and leaders to I.C.S. officials can be found in Foreign Department, General—A, 1877, No. 125–192, NAI.

[35] Moulvie Abdool Luteef, Khan Bahadoor, Deputy Magistrate of 24 Pergunnahs, Alipore, to R. H. Wilson, Magistrate, 24 Pergunnahs, Alipore, 14 February 1876, Foreign Department, General—A, 1877, No. 125–192, NAI; Secretary, Government of India, Delhi, to Secretary, Government of Bombay, Bombay, 28 March 1878, Government of Bombay, Bombay to Government of India, Home Department, Calcutta, 23 April 1878, General Department, 1878 Vol. 51, File 360, Maharashtra State Archives, Mumbai (hereafter MSA).

Razzack on hajj with Indian pilgrims to monitor their sanitary situation and to assess the impact of quarantine *lazarets* at al-Tur on the Sinai Peninsula, established in 1877.[36] Abdur Razzack's value to the British, because of his ability to travel to Mecca and Medina—closed to non-Muslims—led to the doctor's appointment as vice-consul in Jidda in 1882 after accompanying Indian pilgrims every year since 1878.[37] Although Abdur Razzack began his hajj-related employment dealing with sanitary and quarantine matters, his work rapidly encompassed many other areas, not least his attempts to ameliorate the issue of destitute pilgrims.

Abdur Razzack now became a key voice calling for further British intervention in the pilgrimage, while his British imperial employers adhered to a stance of non-interference. In 1885, Abdur Razzack argued that a fund should be established at Jidda by prominent Indian Muslims to assist indigent pilgrims.[38] To side-step official policy, Abdur Razzack wrote that the fund could be operated 'without giving any publicity to our intentions'.[39] The issue of destitute pilgrims was a major preoccupation of Abdur Razzack's throughout the duration of his employment in the Hijaz.[40] Improving this group's pilgrimage experience was one of his most important tasks. For example, nearly fifty percent of pilgrims from India on the 1887 hajj were destitute.[41] The shibboleth of governmental non-interference in religious affairs was being subtly critiqued and eroded by a Muslim employee within the British bureaucracy. When Abdur Razzack was tragically murdered by Bedouin tribesmen outside Jidda on 30 May 1895, his superior felt that his death was a 'very great, irreparable loss for the Consulate...H.M.G. have lost a good faithful public servant'.[42] The multifaceted functions of Muslim employees as intercessors between British officials in India, Jidda, and pilgrims crucially enhanced Britain's administration of the pilgrimage. Muslim employees possessed a considerable degree of agency in their interactions with the British, a trend especially apparent in the years running up to the outbreak of the First World War.

Despite their relatively junior position, Muslim vice-consuls at Jidda drove the government of India to re-examine British policy towards destitute pilgrims from

---

[36] Government of India, Calcutta, to Secretary of State for India, London, 15 June 1880, Foreign Department, Secret, June 1881, No. 425-6, NAI.

[37] On indigenous collaboration with European imperialism, see Ronald E. Robinson, 'Non-European Foundations of European Imperialism: Sketch for a Theory of Collaboration', in Roger Owen and Bob Sutcliffe (eds), *Studies in the Theory of Imperialism* (London, 1972), 117–42. Other relevant works include, for example, James Onley, *The Arabian Frontier of the British Raj: Merchants, Rulers and British in the Nineteenth-Century Gulf* (Oxford, 2007); and Sarah Ansari, *Sufi Saints and State Power: The Pirs of Sind, 1843–1947* (Cambridge, 1992).

[38] Consul Jago, Jidda, to Secretary to the Government of India, Foreign Department, 21 January 1885, Calcutta, p. 1, TNA, FO 881/5113 in *Records of the Hajj*, iii, 585.

[39] Dr Abdur Razzack, Report on the 1884 Hajj, Inclosure 2, 10 January 1885, p. 6, within Consul Jago, Jidda, to Secretary to the Government of India, Foreign Department, 21 January, 1885, Calcutta, TNA, FO 881/5113, in *Records of the Hajj*, iii, 588.

[40] Dr Abdur Razzack, Report on the 1886 Hajj, undated, TNA, FO 195/1583, in *Records of the Hajj*, iii, 747–8.

[41] 4,955 out of 10,324 in total. Dr Abdur Razzack, Report on the 1887 Hajj, 15 February 1888, TNA, FO 195/1610, in *Records of the Hajj*, iii, 761, 783–5.

[42] W. S. Richards, Consul, Jidda, to Secretary of the Foreign Department, Government of India, Calcutta, 17 June 1895, Foreign Department, Secret—E, September 1895, No. 44–64, NAI.

1909–14. These debates took place amidst rising tensions in Anglo-Ottoman and Anglo-Muslim relations, exemplified by trends such as Indian Muslim support for the Ottomans during the Italo-Turkish War (1911–12) and the wars in the Balkans (1912–13) through measures such as aid to the Red Crescent, and the pan-Islamic policies of the Young Turks from 1908.[43] Vice-Consul Dr Hussein's proposal for compulsory return tickets in 1905 to eliminate destitute pilgrims led to a consultation exercise among Muslim notables across India, but their recourse to highlighting the potential backlash from 'ignorant masses' of Muslims to such a scheme meant the authorities abandoned the proposal.[44] Undeterred by this setback, from 1909–11 Vice-Consul Dr Abdur Rahman successfully revived the issue of destitute pilgrims as a matter that warranted urgent attention, which he presented as an affront to imperial—and Islamic—prestige: 'a disgrace to Islam as well as to the British community'. Abdur Rahman was particularly appalled that British inaction led to censure from the Ottoman authorities.[45]

For officials tasked with the 1912 review of the destitute pilgrim issue, concerns about imperial prestige and British relations with the Ottoman authorities in the Hijaz were paramount.[46] The 'scandal' of poor pilgrims was especially humiliating to Britain, because other European powers did not face the same problem.[47] The viceroy felt the status quo was unsustainable, but felt the government, at this point, should avoid compulsory return tickets because this would create the impression the authorities were preventing people from going on hajj.[48] The appearance of 4,000 destitute pilgrims in Jidda after that year's pilgrimage changed everything. In a state of panic, the consul in Jidda asked Bombay's Hajj Committee to allocate 25,000 rupees for repatriation, and officials in Delhi were forced to apply, begrudgingly, to the Finance Department to foot the bill. Related to this, Dr Abdur Rahman's policies were adopted: hajj committees would be established across India, and rulers such as the Begum of Bhopal would be asked to establish a relief fund.[49] Governmental policy regarding destitute pilgrims had been swiftly overturned.

Rising tensions between Britain, Indian Muslims, and the Ottoman empire, created a climate in which the views and proposals of Muslim employees gained

---

[43] Özcan, *Pan-Islamism*, 127–83.

[44] See the large cache of letters from Muslim notables and local leaders to I.C.S. officials in Foreign Department, External—B, September 1907, No. 111–140, NAI; and Secretary, Government of Bombay, Bombay, to Secretary, Government of India, Calcutta, 9 July 1906, General Department, 1912, Vol.132, File 768, MSA.

[45] Government of Bombay, Bombay, to Government of India, Delhi, 15 March 1912, Foreign Department, Internal—B, August 1913, No. 349–352, NAI; and Dr S. Abdurrahman, Vice-Consul Jidda, Hajj Report 1910–11, General Department, 1911, Vol. 160, File 768, MSA.

[46] Maharaj Singh, Note, Delhi, 11 July 1912, Foreign Department, Internal—B, August 1913, No. 349–352, NAI.

[47] L. Porter, Note, Delhi, 27 June 1912, Foreign Department, Internal—B, August 1913, No. 349–352, NAI.

[48] L. Porter, Note, Delhi, 6 August 1912, Foreign Department, Internal—B, August 1913, No. 349–352, NAI.

[49] L.M.R. and P.A.C., Delhi, Note, 7 January 1913, Foreign Department, Internal—B, August 1913, No. 349–352, NAI.

traction, contributing to the swift and significant change in policy towards destitute pilgrims in 1912–13: Britain's *facilitation* of the hajj for its poorer subjects.
Muslim officials frequently complicated Britain's overall stance of non-interference
with the hajj; the views expressed by these men, especially regarding destitute pilgrims, were generally more interventionist than their employers. This was a complicated set of interactions and negotiations, which demonstrates the capacity of
Muslims within the imperial bureaucracies to shape the experience of the hajj for
pilgrims. While the outbreak of the First World War temporarily halted the process
of repatriation for destitute pilgrims, a Rubicon had been crossed.

## THE HASHEMITE INTERREGNUM

The importance of the hajj to Britain's Muslim empire sharply increased when it
went to war with the Ottoman empire in 1914. A (mostly unsuccessful) jihad was
declared in the Ottoman sultan-caliph's name against Britain and its allies on 14
November 1914.[50] Britain's riposte, in a December 1914 proclamation to the Arab
people, paid close attention to its relationship with Islam, and stressed how the
British supply of much-needed grain to Mecca and Medina showed an acute concern for the well-being of these Holy Places.[51] In London and Delhi, the future of
the Holy Places was seen as vitally important to imperial security. Earl Kitchener's
address to the War Committee in London in February 1915 emphasized that it
was in Britain's interest to 'secure all the approaches to the Mahomedan Holy
Places. This, in [Britain's] position as the greatest of Moslem states, would greatly
enhance our prestige amongst the many millions of our Mahomedan subjects.'[52] In
May 1915, India's viceroy proclaimed that Mecca and Medina would be 'immune
from attack' provided there was 'no interference' with Indian pilgrims. When the
war ended, moreover, Britain would guarantee Hijaz 'independence'.[53] British
officials also contemplated the prospect of an Arab caliphate centered on Mecca.
Sharif Hussein (1854–1931) of Mecca's aspirations for an empire of his own in
Arabia, coupled with British encouragement, caused the Arab Revolt against the
Ottomans in June 1916. The British empire now played an active engagement in
remaking the political landscape. Hussein received a huge financial subsidy from

---

[50] Peter Hopkirk, *On Secret Service East of Constantinople: The Plot to Bring Down the British
Empire* (London, 1994), 60–2; Donald McKale, *War by Revolution: Germany and Great Britain
in the Middle East in the Era of World War I* (Kent, OH, 1998), 85–7; Tilman Lüdke, *Jihad Made
in Germany: Ottoman and German Propaganda and Intelligence Operations in the First World War*
(Münster, 2005), 55–114 and throughout; Jacob M. Landau, *The Politics of Pan-Islam: Ideology and
Organization* (Oxford, 1990), especially 100–3 and also 103–42; and Geoffrey Lewis, 'The Ottoman
Proclamation of Jihad in 1914', *Islamic Quarterly*, 19/3–4 (1975), 157–63.

[51] Official Proclamation to the Arab People, 3 December 1914, TNA, FO 141/710.

[52] Chairman Maurice de Bunsen, Report of the Committee on Asiatic Turkey, 30 June 1915,
Appendix X (folios 100–5), TNA, CAB 27/1, quoted in Polly Mohs, *Military Intelligence and the Arab
Revolt: The First Modern Intelligence War* (London, 2008), 15.

[53] Proclamation by the Viceroy of India, 27 May 1915, Delhi, TNA, FO 141/710, quoted in
Singha, 'Passport, Ticket and India-rubber Stamp', 65.

Britain; although mainly spent on arms, it also financed the Hijaz's pilgrimage administration. While Britain proclaimed its 'non-interference' in the Holy Places of Islam, Hussein's kingdom was, in effect, a British client state, although the degree to which Britain exercised authority over the mercurial Hussein was highly circumscribed.[54]

The reaction of Britain's Muslim subjects to the Arab Revolt was intricately bound up with the pilgrimage. In Sudan's Sennar Province, the provincial governor Angus Hamilton reported that 'interest in any outside news is very slight... the fact that the Arab Revolt will enable pilgrim routes to be re-opened is favorably commented upon'.[55] By contrast, the news 'exploded like a bombshell' in India; many suspected British involvement and condemned Hussein's revolt.[56] Worryingly for Britain, many 'loyal' Indian Muslims were ambivalent about the revolt.[57] Officials across Britain's Muslim empire concluded that facilitating the pilgrimage was vital to increase Muslim support for the fledgling British-sponsored Hashemite regime in the Hijaz.[58]

This policy was vital given the threat wartime conditions posed to the hajj. Anglo-Ottoman hostilities, the Arab Revolt, and insecure shipping conditions effectively caused the temporary suspension of the hajj.[59] The Arab Bureau, a British intelligence organization established in Cairo in January 1916, thought that the Hashemite capture of Jidda in June 1916 was a vital first step in facilitating the hajj for Britain's Muslim subjects.[60] Sir Reginald Wingate, governor-general of Sudan, who was deeply involved in the planning and organization of the Arab Revolt, remarked: 'I see no reason why we should not mark the new era by somewhat encouraging the pilgrimage.'[61] The resumption of the pilgrimage under Hashemite control meant Britain, as Hussein's paymaster, would hold greater influence over the hajj's management. Consequently,

[54] Timothy J. Paris, *Britain, the Hashemites, and Arab Rule, 1920–1925: The Sherifian Solution* (London, 2003); Joshua Teitelbaum, *The Rise and Fall of the Hashemite Kingdom of Arabia* (New York, 2001); Efraim Karsh and Inari Karsh, *Empires of the Sand: The Struggle for Mastery in the Middle East, 1789–1923* (Cambridge, MA, 1999); Bruce Westrate, *The Arab Bureau: British Policy in the Middle East, 1916–1920* (University Park, PA, 1992); and Randall Baker, *King Husain and the Kingdom of Hejaz* (Cambridge, 1979).

[55] Angus Cameron, Governor of Sennar Province, Sinja, to Wingate, Khartoum, 24 July 1916, Sudan Archive, University of Durham Library (hereafter SAD) Wingate 138/16/52.

[56] Angus Cameron, Governor of Sennar Province, Sinja, to Wingate, Khartoum, 24 July 1916, Sudan Archive, University of Durham Library (hereafter SAD) Wingate 138/16/52.

[57] *Arab Bulletin*, 6 (July 9, 1916).

[58] See, for example, R. S., Note on the present position at Jidda, 30 June, 1916, TNA, FO 141/803. A copy of this memo can also be found in Reel 5 Box Number II/4, Private Letters and Diaries of Sir Ronald Storrs, Pembroke College, Cambridge.

[59] The hajj was a potent topic used in German propaganda efforts towards the Muslim world. One example was German secret agent Wilhelm Wassmuss's work in Persia during 1915; he explained to tribesmen around Bushire that Kaiser Wilhelm had converted to Islam and had ordered all his subjects to do so, and had made a secret pilgrimage to Mecca, which allowed him to adopt the title of 'Hajji' Wilhelm Muhammad, see Hopkirk, *On Secret Service East of Constantinople*, 105–6.

[60] *Arab Bulletin*, 5 (18 June 1916).

[61] Wingate, Khartoum, to Wilson, Jidda, 19 June 1916, SAD Wingate 137/4/29–30.

there was a temporary extension of British control over the hajj in Jidda. Ronald Storrs, Oriental Secretary in Cairo, assessed Jidda's administrative arrangements in June 1916, and argued that there should be 'an Englishman in charge'.[62] This official's primary duties were to act as an unofficial adviser to Hussein and assist the Hashemite authorities in maintaining Jidda's pilgrimage-related administration. In August 1916, Colonel Cyril Wilson, the governor of Sudan's Red Sea Province, became Britain's 'Pilgrimage Officer' in Jidda. Wilson was joined by Indian Army officers with experience of the Northwest Frontier and Iraq who monitored Indian pilgrim traffic and also acted to counter the Arab Bureau's influence over British policy regarding the Hijaz.[63] One of Wilson's colleagues wrote that the position was of 'utmost difficulty and delicacy—he had to look after British and Allied subjects...and make arrangements for furthering the pilgrimage, including the safe reception and escort of the Egyptian *mahmal* to Mecca'.[64]

The Arab Revolt created a decidedly unusual administrative situation with the Hijaz hajj administration. British officials across the empire showed a heightened concern with the pilgrimage, and attempted to use the ritual as a propaganda tool to popularize Hussein's standing and legitimacy throughout Britain's Muslim empire.[65] For example, a 1917 Government of India communiqué emphasized the difficulties of undertaking the pilgrimage due to a shortage of ships during wartime, yet stated that the government's 'extreme anxiety' to help Indian Muslims perform the hajj meant several ships were made available.[66] Britain also presented itself as a facilitator of the hajj by using the Royal Navy for traditional ceremonies related to the pilgrimage, which rested on older Ottoman practices.[67] The first hajj under Hashemite rule began on 19 September 1916, with the arrival of HMS *Hardinge* at Jidda, which was carrying the Egyptian *mahmal*, a ceremonial palanquin carried on a camel that was the centerpiece of the pilgrim caravan from Cairo.[68] British reports from 1916–18 emphasized the successful nature of the pilgrimage; one such report from November 1916 stated there were 'no untoward incidents' unlike those that plagued the hajj under Ottoman rule.[69]

[62] R. S., Note on the present position at Jidda, 30 June 1916, Jidda, TNA, FO 141/803, and Reel 5, Box Number II/4, Storrs Papers, Pembroke College, Cambridge.

[63] Foreign Office, London, to Government of India, 10 July 1916, Delhi, TNA, FO 141/803; and Martin Thomas, *Empires of Intelligence: Security Services and Colonial Disorder After 1914* (Berkeley, 2007), 129.

[64] Young, 'A Little to the East: Memoirs of an Anglo-Egyptian Official', 137–8, Middle East Centre Archive, St Antony's College, Oxford (hereafter MECA) Young GB-0165-0310.

[65] Minute paper, Political Department, Government of India, Delhi, 9 and 10 April 1917, British Library, India Office Records (hereafter BL IOR) IOR/PS/11/122/P1670.

[66] Viceroy of India, Delhi, to India Office, London, 27 April 1917, BL IOR/PS/11/122/P1670.

[67] Jacques Jomier, *Le Mahmal et la caravane égyptienne des pèlerins de la Mecque (XIIIe–XXe siècles)* (Cairo, 1953); Ibrahim Rif'at Basha, *Mir'at al-Haramayn* (*Mirror of the Two Sanctuaries*) (Cairo, 1925); Muhammad Labib Batanuni, *Rihla al-Hijaziya* (*Travels in the Hijaz*) (Cairo, 1909).

[68] *Arab Bulletin*, 24 (5 October 1916).

[69] *Arab Bulletin*, 28 (1 November 1916), for example.

In the postwar period, the hajj was one of the main reasons for Britain's deteriorating relations with King Hussein.[70] The pilgrimage was not only a vital source of income for King Hussein's impoverished kingdom, but a key part of his campaign for legitimacy as ruler of the Hijaz, and his wider pretensions to be king of the lands of the Arabs, *malik bilad al-'arab*, and, in 1924, caliph. Britain's withdrawal of subsidies to King Hussein in February 1920, in exasperation at his refusal to recognize the postwar Anglo-French-dominated political landscape in the Middle East, meant Hussein was forced to over-tax pilgrims, his only source of revenue. The chaotic nature of the hajj in this period contributed to Britain's rejection of the 'Hashemite solution' in Arabia.

Alongside these developments, the Indian Khilafat movement, especially in 1919–22, was probably the most important over-arching event that Britain had to factor in to its relationship with the pilgrimage, which militated against greater imperial involvement with the hajj. The Khilafat movement was forged out of Indian Muslim opposition to the 1919 Rowlatt Act, Britain's treatment of the Ottoman empire in the Paris peace talks, and the issue of the caliphate's future.[71] The alliance of Abdul Bari and the Ali brothers with Gandhi in September 1920 led to India's first non-cooperation movement, but its grievances related to the Holy Places were swiftly rendered irrelevant by postwar peace treaties and Mustafa Kemal's (1881–1938) abolition of the caliphate in 1924. The movement's roots partly derived from general Indian Muslim hostility to King Hussein.[72] The Khilafat movement was extremely influential in shaping British—especially British Indian—policy towards the hajj.[73] From 1919–22, almost every proposal or action undertaken by the various British officials involved with the hajj was colored by the Khilafat movement, and it was often mentioned—implicitly or explicitly—as the reason for supporting or opposing various schemes or policies. For example, India subsidized return passages for pilgrims from 1919–20 at a cost of over 1,150,000 rupees and maintained a pilgrimage officer at Jidda for Indian pilgrims.[74] This piecemeal repatriation and the continued presence of destitute pilgrims in 1922, meant that the compulsory return ticket proposal resurfaced.[75] India remained opposed to this, citing opposition from Muslim members on India's legislative council. After the Khilafat movement subsided from 1923, Indian officials were 'no longer in favor of subsidizing... [Muslims]... who visited the Holy Places',

---

[70] *Arab Bulletin*, 28 (1 November 1916), 311.

[71] For the principal works on the Khilafat movement, see M. Naeem Qureshi, *Pan-Islam in British Indian Politics: A Study of the Khilafat Movement, 1918–1924* (Leiden, 1999); Özcan, *Pan-Islamism*; Gail Minault, *The Khilafat Movement: Religious Symbolism and Political Mobilization in India* (Oxford, 1982); and Francis Robinson, *Separatism among Indian Muslims: The Politics of the United Provinces' Muslims, 1860–1923* (Cambridge, 1974).

[72] Briton Cooper Busch, *Britain, India, and the Arabs, 1914–1921* (Berkeley, 1971), 166–8; Low, 'Empire of the Hajj', 156; and Timothy J. Paris, *Britain, the Hashemites, and Arab Rule, 1920–1925: The Sherifian Solution* (London, 2003), 326.

[73] Paris, *Sherifian Solution*, 302; Qureshi, *Pan-Islam*, 423–4; and Robinson, *Separatism*, 208–11.

[74] Paris, *Sherifian Solution*, 306–7.

[75] Report for October 1922, in Robert L. Jarman (ed.), *The Jedda Diaries*, 4 vols (London, 1990), ii, 82–3.

although this continued in practice, with a 35,000 rupees subsidy for repatriation that same year.[76]

Britain's financial outlay towards facilitating the hajj for its poorer subjects formed part of a wider context whereby conditions in the Hijaz were viewed as 'intolerable' for pilgrims who were British subjects. Major Marshall, the Hijaz's inspector-general of quarantine and public health in 1919, believed that the crisis could only be resolved by King Hussein's abdication or a suspension of the pilgrimage, because conditions in the Hijaz 'expose pilgrims to risks to which it would be inhuman to allow them to take'.[77] Vickery, Marshall's colleague, thought that 'it is through the pilgrimage that we can strike at the King'. However, it was realized that London and Delhi would not agree to such dramatic moves because of the potential backlash across Britain's Muslim empire.[78] In response, Hussein was adamant that the phenomenon of destitute Indian pilgrims was Britain's fault, castigating them as a 'burden' on his kingdom.[79] The descendant of Muhammad and Guardian of the Holy Cities wanted to limit pilgrim numbers; conversely, the British empire facilitated the hajj for its Muslim subjects for pragmatic and self-interested reasons arising from the difficult political situation it faced during this period.

Exasperation with Hussein's perceived mismanagement of the hajj, seen as a combination of incompetent administration and extortion of pilgrims, was widely shared among British officials. Palestine's High Commissioner Sir Herbert Samuel wrote in June 1922 that Britain now 'felt tired of Hussein' and believed that any change of regime in the Hijaz would be 'an improvement on the existing state of affairs'.[80] Sir Arthur Hirtzel at the India Office commented that 'the feeling is growing that it would be a good thing if Ibn Saud did establish himself at Mecca'.[81] Imperial authorities in India preferred the ruler of Nejd in Eastern Arabia, Ibn Saud (1856–1933), with whom they had relations with since the first decade of the twentieth century, over Hussein, who had been supported by officials in Cairo.[82] In Jidda, British Vice-Consul Lawrence Grafftey-Smith described Hussein as 'a monster of our own creation', after a particularly chaotic pilgrimage in October 1923.[83] Hussein's proclamation of himself as caliph in March 1924 was a fatal move, an excuse for Britain to abrogate its responsibilities towards their erstwhile ally. The British consul at Jidda, Reader Bullard, described this declaration as

[76] Paris, *Sherifian Solution*, 306–7.

[77] Report on Hajj 1337AH/1919, pp. 1–4, TNA, FO 371/4195 in *Records of the Hajj*, v, 159–62; and *Notes on the Middle East*, 7 December 1919, No. 1. Secret appendix to Report for 20 September 1920, *Jedda Diaries*, i, 383–4.

[78] Secret appendix to Report for 20 September 1920, *Jedda Diaries*, i, 383–4.

[79] Report for 1–10 January 1921, *Jedda Diaries*, i, 474–5.

[80] High Commissioner Palestine, Jerusalem, to Colonial Office, London, 5 June, 1922, BL IOR/L/PS/10/936.

[81] Minutes by Arthur Hirtzel, India Office, London, 10 June 1922, BL IOR/L/PS/10/936.

[82] Askar Al-Enazy, 'Ibn Saud's Early Foreign Policy Towards the Rashidi Emirate and the Kingdom of Hijaz, in Light of British Imperial Policy, 1914–1927' (PhD, University of Cambridge, 2006), 195.

[83] Bullard, Jidda, to Foreign Office, London, 19 October 1923, with enclosed Note by Grafftey-Smith, 17 October 1923, TNA, FO 800/253, quoted in Paris, *Sherifian Solution*, 309.

'exceedingly unpopular, and was one of the reasons why, when he was attacked by the Wahhabis, he found no friends'.[84] British officials felt that any ruler in Mecca was better than King Hussein.

## WAHHABI RULE AND THE HAJJ

Ibn Saud's frustration with Hussein's administration of the hajj, the king's repeated prohibition on Ibn Saud's Wahhabi soldiers performing the pilgrimage, and finally, Hussein's audacious proclamation of himself as caliph, led to the outbreak of war between these two British allies. The British Treasury had also informed the Saudi ruler that his subsidy would end in March 1924. Astutely, Saud recognized that the hajj was the most lucrative source of income in Arabia, although revenue from the pilgrimage fluctuated according to the political situation in the Hijaz and economic conditions across the Muslim world. Oil was only discovered in eastern Saudi Arabia in 1938 and limited exports began in 1939. The Saudis successfully occupied the Hijaz in 1924–25. The Saudi-Wahhabi takeover of Mecca and Medina caused the hajj's character and meaning to change profoundly. Britain cultivated the Saudis as allies as anti-colonial nationalism in its Muslim territories increased from the later 1920s. Muslims—especially from India—reacted strongly against Wahhabi doctrines, which they thought contrary to customary Islamic practices. These included acts of devotion that occurred around the pilgrimage, such as the *ziyara*, visiting the shrines of saints. The enforcement of Wahhabi religious orthodoxy was noted in a neutral fashion by the British, who gradually withdrew from active involvement in the Hijaz's internal religious affairs. Britain's accommodation of Wahhabism after the First World War highlighted official flexibility in dealing with militant fundamentalist forms of Islam when faced with the paramount importance of ensuring—as far as possible—a safe pilgrimage for its Muslim subjects. Britain's historical aversion to Indian Wahhabis, highlighted by paranoia among officials in India about their activities, belonged in the nineteenth century. The threat of Indian Wahhabi 'fanaticism', however real or chimerical, had lessened by the 1920s.[85] British reports repeatedly drew a distinction between Ibn Saud, who was often lauded as an astute, pragmatic ruler, and his more 'fanatical' Wahhabi 'ulama and soldiers, the *ikhwan*.[86]

---

[84] Bullard, 'Notes for memoirs—1924', File 4, Box 3, MECA Bullard GB-0165-0034.

[85] Ayesha Jalal, *Partisans of Allah: Jihad in South Asia* (Cambridge, MA, 2008); Seema Alavi, '"Fugitive Mullahs and Outlawed Fanatics": Indian Muslims in Nineteenth-Century Trans-Asiatic Imperial Rivalries', *Modern Asian Studies*, 45/6 (2011), 1337–82; see also the chapter by Benjamin D. Hopkins in this volume.

[86] D. G. Hogarth, 'Wahabism and British Interests', *Journal of the British Institute of International Affairs*, 4/2 (1925), 70–81. Hogarth foresaw that while the Wahhabis would 'discourage relics of pre-Islamic cult and non-Koranic local associations honoured by the vulgar among the faithful' and may force 'Nejdean austerities' on Mecca, 'they can hardly be more unpopular than...the recent control of King Hussein'. In his final analysis, pilgrims' experiences were 'little likely to be seriously altered by the present access of Wahhabism' (Hogarth, 'Wahabism and British Interests', 77–9).

During the conflict between Hussein and Ibn Saud, officials across Britain's Muslim empire adhered to a policy of non-intervention. The viceroy of India reported to London that although some Indian Muslims were vehemently opposed to any British support to Hussein, many also 'did not regard the Wahhabis very highly'.[87] In September 1924, Reader Bullard presciently foretold that if Ibn Saud conquered Mecca, there would be 'longer-lived complications arising from the difference between the tenets of the Wahhabis and those of the bulk of the pilgrims'.[88] Ibn Saud entered Mecca in October 1924, clad in the pilgrim's garb of the *ihram*.[89] Britain's success in gleaning information about the new regime's religious policies and their impact on pilgrims, would have been impossible without using Muslims in their consular bureaucracy, who could travel freely to the Holy Cities of Mecca and Medina. The main author of the voluminous imperial archive on Britain's interactions with the hajj in this period was an Indian Punjabi Muslim, Munshi Ihsanullah, who worked for the British in Jidda. Ihsanullah migrated to Medina, where he became a merchant and banker. Ruined by the war, he went to Damascus, where he subsequently served in British intelligence. He was well acquainted with officials, merchants, pilgrim guides, and 'ulama in the Holy Places, as well as Bedouin tribes around Medina, and spoke English, Arabic, Turkish, and Bengali.[90] Many of the views espoused by officials at Jidda regarding Britain's policy towards the hajj and administration originally came from Ihsanullah. Many, such as Bullard, were perfectly willing to admit to this fact: 'He became invaluable and many suggestions he made were adopted and became law in India to the great advantage of pilgrims.'[91]

Ihsanullah went to Mecca in April 1925 and reported that Ibn Saud had come under 'the influence of religious fanatics'. Only Wahhabi imams were allowed to conduct prayers in the Holy Mosque at Mecca. These actions caused consternation amongst many pilgrims who were British subjects. For example, one group of Indian Muslims at Mecca returned home before the hajj, as they believed that pilgrimage 'under such circumstances could not be regarded as lawful'.[92] Eldon Rutter, a British convert to Islam on hajj in 1925, explained how it was dangerous to look at Islamic shrines in Mecca and Medina because 'a passing Wahhabi, seeing one so occupied, would be quite capable of laying about him with his camel stick, calling down curses the while upon those who make supplication to the Prophet'.[93]

---

[87] Viceroy of India, Delhi, to Secretary of State for India, London, 25 September 1924, Telegram No. 3890, BL IOR/L/PS/10/3665/1924 Part I, quoted in Gary Troeller, *The Birth of Saudi Arabia: Britain and the Rise of the House of Sa'ud* (London, 1976), 219.

[88] Reader Bullard, Consul, Jidda, to Foreign Office, London, 21 September 1924, Foreign and Political Department, External, 1924, No. 4 (2), NAI.

[89] Mai Yamani, *Cradle of Islam: The Hijaz and the Quest for an Arabian Identity* (London, 2004), 8.

[90] Note by Bullard on Indian Clerk, 17 June 1925, BL IOR/L/E/7/1146.

[91] Reader Bullard, Jidda, to Foreign Office, London, 28 July 1937, in Reader Bullard and E. C. Hodgkin (eds), *Two Kings in Arabia: Letters from Jeddah 1923–5 and 1936–9* (Reading, 1993), 165.

[92] Extracts from précis of Munshi Ihsanullah's Report, April 1925, TNA, FO 371/11436.

[93] Eldon Rutter, *Holy Cities of Arabia* (London, 1930), 270–1.

Despite such events, British officials generally regarded the hajj under Wahhabi rule as a success in the interwar period.[94]

The complex dynamics of the politico-religious economy of Ibn Saud's realm were complicated by the fact that many Muslims who came to the Hijaz for hajj held a variety of interpretations of Islam at odds with Wahhabism. Indian Muslim pilgrims particularly deplored the Saudi policy of tomb demolition. They sent telegrams addressed to Ibn Saud denouncing Saudi policies to the British consulate at Jidda. One telegram recounted how, during a mass meeting in a Bombay mosque, those present considered Wahhabi actions 'deserving of the whole of Muslim hatred and curses for irreligious acts'.[95] Indian intelligence officials felt the gathering force of complaints against Ibn Saud meant he could lose Indian Muslim sympathy among those who were generally favorable towards him.[96] Ihsanullah continued to receive many complaints from pilgrims who were admonished, arrested, and fined by Wahhabis in Mecca, whose duty was to enforce the prohibition on tomb worship.[97] Ibn Saud's reputation in India appeared to have been damaged.

The British consular authorities were sanguine about these developments.[98] Reports from across Britain's Muslim empire, such as Delhi, London, Khartoum, and Kano, showed that Britain was unwilling to intervene with the intricacies of religious practice in Ibn Saud's domains. British officials were more preoccupied with the need to delineate the boundaries between Ibn Saud's territories and Iraq, Transjordan, Kuwait, and the Persian Gulf emirates—a task made all the more difficult by *ikhwan* raiders who refused to recognize the tentatively demarcated borders. The Government of India's 1930 *Confidential Report of the Hajj Enquiry Committee* confirmed Britain's continued policy of non-interference towards religious practices in the Hijaz. The report highlighted complaints from pilgrims that stemmed from 'the fact that Nejdis are reactionary and intolerant in matters of religion and are at pains to interfere with certain observances and practices, which have been customary as part of the pilgrimage among Indian and other pilgrims'. It was considered 'undesirable' to address these concerns. Sensitivity to Muslim opinion went hand-in-hand with British self-interest: 'If even diplomatic representations on any of these points are made which are in the least likely to prejudice the harmonious relations that exist at present between both governments, we would certainly prefer that no action be taken.'[99] Britain's priority was to maintain good relations with Ibn Saud—who was perceived as a better ally to Britain in the Hijaz than his predecessor—rather than placate their Indian Muslim subjects, who were angered by Saudi-Wahhabi religious policies during the hajj.

---

[94] Report for 21 July–10 August, 1925, *Jedda Diaries,* ii, 325.
[95] Report for 21 July 10 August, 1925, *Jedda Diaries,* ii, 346.
[96] Extract from Weekly Report of Director of Intelligence, Home Department, 13 August 1925, BL L/PJ/12/111.
[97] Report on the Hajj 1344AH/1926, p. 11, TNA, FO 371/11436, in *Records of the Hajj,* vi, 49.
[98] Extract from Report for March 1926, Jidda Consulate, TNA, FO371/11442.
[99] Confidential Report of the Hajj Enquiry Committee on arrangements in the Hejaz, p. 1, TNA, FO371/15290 in *Records of the Hajj,* vi, 313.

The Great Depression of the 1930s had a marked effect on the hajj as many Muslims could no longer afford the journey. The Jidda consulate reported that: 'the heart of Islam is now beginning to feel the reflex action of world conditions'.[100] The Depression affected the hajj in two ways.[101] First, the issue of destitute Indian pilgrims was complicated by the appearance of pilgrims who attempted to reach Mecca by traveling overland, avoiding the Bombay–Jidda steamship route. Britain remained powerless to prevent poor Indian pilgrims from reaching their goal, and continued to facilitate these pilgrims' journeys by repatriating them to India. Secondly, because the Depression led to a slump in pilgrim numbers, Saudi-Wahhabi policies moved toward a cautious form of religious compromise with non-Wahhabi pilgrims.

The Jidda consulate conceded that, even with strict controls in India, destitute pilgrims would continue to arrive in Mecca from the overland route. This involved pilgrims landing on the Persian Gulf coast or traveling from India across Persia and Iraq before striking out across the desert to Mecca.[102] Despite British attempts to staunch this flow of pilgrims by mounting patrols, Reader Bullard realized that: 'nothing could prevent a penniless Indian Moslem from begging his way across northern India and Baluchistan, getting a lift in a dhow across the Persian Gulf, and setting out to walk to Mecca'.[103] In 1938, Lal Shah, a Muslim official at the consulate, was able to gain a unique insight into this world. Delayed at a coffee shop on the road to Mecca when his car broke down, Shah's conversations with several poor pilgrims revealed tales of the routes they took into the Hijaz, which evaded all administrative formalities and payments. Unaware of Shah's occupation, these pilgrims cheerfully told him the Government of India would repatriate them.[104] Officials in Jidda opined that the issue should be taken up by 'some influential Indian' so the Indian vice-consul would 'no longer have to work with destitute lady pilgrims lying on the floor of his office or pulling his hair'.[105] The zeal of poor pilgrims to perform the hajj triumphed over British attempts to regulate this group's travels towards Mecca. Indeed, British repatriation efforts encouraged such people to attempt the journey.

Britain's accommodation of Wahhabi Islam was underlined by the consular authorities' adherence to the Saudi government's instructions to pilgrims when they arrived in Jidda. But the acute economic pressure on Ibn Saud's kingdom— the Depression had caused an estimated seventy-five percent drop in Saudi pilgrimage revenue—meant the application of Wahhabi practice was lessened.[106] For

---

[100] Report for September–December 1929, *Jedda Diaries*, iii, 153.

[101] Briefly covered in Sugata Bose, *A Hundred Horizons: The Indian Ocean in the Age of Global Empire* (Cambridge, MA, 2006), 214–16.

[102] Report for August–September 1930, *Jedda Diaries*, iii, 148–9; Report for May–June 1931, *Jedda Diaries*, iii, 267. Many pilgrims from Britain's West African territories walked to Mecca, which typically took several years.

[103] Report for September 1936, *Jedda Diaries*, iv, 124; Sir Reader Bullard, *The Camels Must Go: An Autobiography* (London, 1961), 202–3.

[104] Report for April 1938, *Jedda Diaries*, iv, 289–90.

[105] Report for February 1939, *Jedda Diaries*, iv, 402–3.

[106] Notes on Saudi Arabia for Dr Hugh Scott, 1944, 1/4/9/3/28, Box 18, MECA Philby GB-0165-0229.

example, pilgrims were able to take advantage of the Nejdi soldiers' lack of pay and bribed them so they could kiss the Prophet's tomb in Medina 'to their heart's content'.[107] Nevertheless, Ihsanullah advised Indian pilgrims to avoid visiting shrines that might 'lead to unpleasant incidents'.[108]

The retirement of Khan Bahadur Ihsanullah, MBE, in 1937 further underscored the importance of Muslim employees within Britain's hajj administration to the empire's overall engagement with the pilgrimage. Reader Bullard noted how Ibn Saud relied heavily on Ihsanullah's expertise regarding hajj administration after he conquered Mecca in 1924.[109] Bullard also praised Ihsanullah's efforts with Indian pilgrims: 'he has worn himself out trying to make Indian pilgrims safer from exploitation in the Hejaz than Wigan cotton operatives on holiday in Blackpool'.[110] Ihsanullah was a crucial interlocutor in Britain's association with the hajj.

The wider context of Britain's Muslim empire in this period informed Britain's policy of studied neutrality towards Saudi-Wahhabi practices in relation to the hajj. The rising nationalist tide in India, Iraq, Egypt, and especially in Palestine, where British forces engaged in violent suppression of the 1936–39 Arab Revolt, meant Saudi Arabia was increasingly seen as a trusted conservative Muslim ally.[111]

## CONCLUSION

Although the Second World War and the postwar period fall outside the scope of this survey, those years saw a continuance of Britain's interactions with the hajj, notwithstanding India's independence in 1947 Indeed, the empire's long association with the ritual only reached a terminal point during the 1956 Suez Crisis.[112] Saudi Arabia's suspension of diplomatic relations with Britain as a result of that crisis meant the closure of the British Embassy in Jidda. Consequently, with British approval, Mohammed Effendi al-Awin Saleh, head of the Nigerian Pilgrimage Mission, coordinated the empire's hajj administration from the empty British embassy, dealing with over 22,000 pilgrims from across Britain's Muslim empire in cooperation with officials from the Pakistani embassy.[113] The Suez crisis was an enormous loss of British prestige, which

---

[107] Report on the Hajj of 1348 AH/1930, pp. 16–7, TNA, FO 371/14456 in *Records of the Hajj*, vi, 270–1.

[108] Report on the Hajj of 1933/1351, p. 18, TNA, FO 371/16857, in *Records of the Hajj*, 559.

[109] Reader Bullard, Jidda, to Foreign Office, London, 28 July 1937, in Reader Bullard and E. C. Hodgkin (eds), *Two Kings in Arabia: Letters from Jeddah, 1923–5 and 1936–9* (Reading, 1993), 165.

[110] Reader Bullard, Jidda, to Foreign Office, London, 26 April 1937, in Hodgkin (ed.), *Two Kings in Arabia*, 153.

[111] Reader Bullard, Jidda, to Anthony Eden, Foreign Office, London, copied to Palestine, Cairo, and Baghdad, 7 December 1937, TNA, FO 371/20786.

[112] Simon C. Smith (ed.), *Reassessing Suez 1956: New Perspectives on the Crisis and its Aftermath* (London, 2008); Barry Turner, *Suez 1956* (London, 2006); Wm Roger Louis and Roger Owen (eds), *Suez: The Crisis and its Consequences* (Oxford, 1989); Mahmoud Fawzi, *Suez 1956: An Egyptian Perspective* (London, 1986); Saad Zaghlul Fuad, *Al-qital fi'l-qawal* (*The Story of the Fighting*) (Cairo, 1969); and Kamil Isma'il Al-Sharif, *Al-Muqawama fi Qanat al-Suwais* (*The Resistance in the Suez Canal*) (Beirut, 1957).

[113] Commonwealth Relations Office, London, to Molyneux, Karachi, 31 December 1956; Molyneux, Karachi, to CRO, London, 5 February 1957; Colonial Office, London, to Foreign Office,

in turn meant a real loss of power.[114] It also marked an effective conclusion to British involvement with the pilgrimage on any meaningful scale. Shortly after 1956, the complex bureaucratic apparatus involved with the annual flow of pilgrims to Mecca from across the breadth of Britain's Muslim empire—from the Atlantic to the Straits of Malacca—passed into the control of newly independent nations.[115]

The British empire's interactions with Islam in the shape of the hajj formed a series of extraordinary episodes in the history of British imperialism, an experience that transcended multiple colonial boundaries. Indeed, this chapter has a wider comparative utility when placed alongside similar works dealing with other European (and Muslim) empires and their involvement with the hajj and other facets of Islamic practice.[116] While the British empire was concerned to 'accommodate' the hajj, it is necessary to appreciate the multilayered complexity of this relationship. Collaboration and conflict were equally important features of this relationship, yet two features demand sustained reflection: the vital role played by Muslim employees of the British in the development of imperial policies towards the hajj, and the ultimate inability of the British empire to 'regulate' the flow of its pilgrim subjects to the Hijaz to perform one of the most important rituals of the Islamic faith.

London, 25 February 1957; Foreign Office, London to Colonial Office, 1 March 1957, London, TNA, CO 371/127173 in *Records of the Hajj*, viii, 337–41. Colonial Office, London, to Foreign Office, 25 February 1957, London, TNA, CO 371/127173 in *Records of the Hajj*, viii, 339.

[114] John Darwin, *Britain and Decolonisation: The Retreat from Empire in the Post-War World* (London, 1988), 72.

[115] The dates of independence for the remainder of Britain's Muslim empire are: Malaya (1957), Nigeria and Somaliland (1960), Kuwait (1961), Sierra Leone (1961), Zanzibar (1963), Gambia (1965), Aden (1967), the Persian Gulf States (1971), Brunei (1984).

[116] For the Mughal and Ottoman Empires, see Suraiya Faroqhi, *Pilgrims and Sultans: The Hajj under the Ottomans, 1517–1683* (London, 1996); M. N. Pearson, *Pilgrimage to Mecca: The Indian Experience 1500–1800* (Princeton, 1996); Naimur Farooqi, *Mughal–Ottoman Relations: A Study of Political and Diplomatic Relations Between Mughal India and the Ottoman Empire, 1556–1748* (Delhi, 1989); William Ochsenwald, *Religion, Society and the State in Arabia: The Hijaz under Ottoman Control, 1840–1908* (Athens, OH, 1984); and Karl K. Barbir, *Ottoman Rule in Damascus, 1708–1758* (Princeton, 1980). for the Netherlands, see E. Tagliacozzo, 'The Skeptic's Eye: Snouck Hurgronje and the Politics of the Pilgrimage from the Indies', E. Tagliacozzo (ed.), *South East Asia and the Middle East* (Stanford, 2009), 135–55; and Karel A. Steenbrink, *Dutch Colonialism and Indonesian Islam* (Amsterdam, 2006); for France, see George R. Trumbull IV, *Empire of Facts: Colonial Knowledge, Cultural Power, and Islam in Algeria, 1870–1914* (Cambridge, 2009); G. Mann and B. Lecoq, 'Between Empire, *Umma*, and the Muslim Third World: The French Union and African Pilgrims to Mecca, 1946–58', *Comparative Studies of South Asia, Africa and the Middle East*, 27/2 (2007), 167–81; G. Mann, 'Fetishizing Religion: Allah Koura and French "Islamic Policy" in Late Colonial French Soudan (Mali)', *Journal of African History*, 44/2 (2003), 263–82; David Robinson, 'France as a Muslim Power in West Africa', *Africa Today*, 46/3–4 (1999), 105–27; Laurent Escande, 'D'Alger à la Mecque: l'administration française et le contrôle du pèlerinage 1894–1962', *Revue d'histoire maghrébine*, 26/95-96 (1999), 277–92; A. S. Kanya-Forstner, *Pilgrims, Interpreters and Agents: French Reconnaissance Reports on the Sokoto Caliphate and Borno, 1891–1895* (Madison, WI, 1997); and Vincent Joly, 'Un Aspect de la politique musulmane de la France: l'administration et le pèlerinage de la Mecque 1930–1950', *Annales du Levant*, 5, (1992), 37–58. For Russia and the USSR, see Robert D. Crews, *For Prophet and Tsar: Islam and Empire in Russia and Central Asia* (Cambridge, MA, 2006); Daniel Brower, 'Russian Roads to Mecca: Religious Tolerance and Muslim Pilgrimage in the Russian Empire', *Slavic Review*, 55/3 (1996), 567–84; A. S. Morrison, *Russian Rule in Samarkand 1868–1910: A Comparison with British India* (Oxford, 2008), 63–66; and Yaacov Ro'i, *Islam in the Soviet Union* (London, 2000). For China, see Ho-Dong Kim, *Holy War in China* (Stanford, 2004); and Raphael Israeli, *Islam in China: Religion, Ethnicity, Culture and Politics* (Westport, CT, 1994).

# 3

# The Dutch Empire and the Hajj

*Eric Tagliacozzo*

## INTRODUCTION

The Dutch came to the Indonesian archipelago around the turn of the seventeenth century, and shortly thereafter began to take stretches of local territory in their quest to control the international spice trade.[1] Colonization proceeded in fits and starts, but eventually—over the course of three centuries—covered nearly the entirety of the archipelago, some 17,000 islands. Though much of the rationale behind colonization was economic, one of the main issues the Netherlands had to deal with in this conquest and subsequent consolidation of rule was the religion of Islam. Today, Indonesia is the world's largest Muslim country, and maintaining some sort of control over the conduct of Islam in their empire was a constant source of concern for Dutch imperial planners in Batavia, their Asian capital, and back in the Netherlands itself.[2] This concern was manifested in philanthropic and coercive ways, but in both cases a strong hand in the facilitation of local Islam was seen as an important item on the colonial agenda of consolidating the Indies as a Dutch colony. A large paper trail echoing these concerns is proof of how important this issue was for the tiny number of Dutch administrators and scholars who ended up ruling this very large colonial dominion.[3]

This chapter looks at one aspect of this control: the supervision by the Netherlands of the hajj pilgrimage to Mecca (Fig. 4) from the Dutch East Indies. The first part of the chapter examines the beginnings of this process in the days of the Dutch East India Company (VOC), which was the main political presence of the Dutch from roughly 1600 to 1800. The second part of the chapter looks at the ways in which the Netherlands tried to facilitate the hajj for its Indonesian

[1] Some material in this chapter has appeared in Eric Tagliacozzo, *The Longest Journey: Southeast Asians and the Pilgrimage to Mecca* (New York, 2013).

[2] A good starting point for untangling this long relationship is Michael Laffan, *The Making of Indonesian Islam: Orientalism and the Narration of a Sufi Past* (Princeton, 2011); and Karel Steenbrink, *Dutch Colonialism and Indonesian Islam: Contacts and Conflicts, 1596–1950* (Amsterdam, 1993). For the sake of brevity, I use 'Indies' to refer to the 'Dutch East Indies' throughout this piece. I also use the term 'Indonesia' occasionally to refer to the entire archipelago in my own text, even though the country now known as 'Indonesia' did not yet exist.

[3] Two of the earliest studies include S. Keijzer, *De Bedevaart der Inlanders naar Makka: Volledige Beschrijving van Alles wat op de Bedevaart-gangers uit Nederlandsch-Indie Betrekking Heeft* (Leiden, 1871); and J. D. van Herwerden, *Toenemende Bedevaart naar Mekka* (The Hague, 1875), but the list of scholars writing on Islam in the Indies over the course of the next hundred years is very large indeed.

**Fig. 4** Mecca in 1910 (Library of Congress).

subjects in the colonial period, when company rule gradually shifted to state rule over the islands after the turn of the nineteenth century. The final part of the chapter then focuses on the opposite of facilitation and examines how Dutch surveillance increasingly regarded the hajj as a potentially dangerous transmitter of Muslim militancy back to the Dutch colony along the sea routes in Southeast Asia. Throughout the chapter, I argue that these twin impulses of benevolence and surveillance were constantly at work in Dutch attempts to oversee the hajj, from the times of the VOC to the high colonial age in the middle of the twentieth century.

## THE HAJJ AND THE DUTCH EAST INDIA COMPANY

The Dutch began to notice the appearance of people called 'hajjis' soon after their arrival in the Indies archipelago at the end of the sixteenth century, though there was some confusion about what this term actually meant. From as early as 1612, however, hajjis were showing up in places such as Banda in the spice-laden Moluccas, one of the Netherlands' primary economic targets in the Indies, and by 1642 they were described in Dutch records in Bantam, West Java as well.[4] The

---

[4] Pieter Both, Fort Mauritius Nabij Ngofakiaha op het Eiland Makean, VI, 26 July 1612, W. Ph. Coolhaas (ed.), *Generale Missieven van Gouverneurs-Generaal en Raden aan Heren XVII der Verenigde*

Dutch realized that these people were well respected because of their journeys to Mecca. That same year Arabs were recorded by them in the Indies for the first time, and ominously from the Dutch point of view, this first Arab 'priest' arrived on an English ship.[5] As the seventeenth century wore on, the Dutch connected these personages with other hajjis they were seeing on other Indian Ocean trade routes, including Indian hajjis for the first time in 1656, the pilgrimages of royalty from the subcontinent in 1662, and hajjis on the way to Yemeni ports in the Red Sea in 1679.[6] They also began to note that a certain number of hajjis seemed to be implacably against the establishment and growth of a Dutch presence in the Indies, and that these men propagated 'hate' against the Dutch, before fleeing the forces that Batavia had at its disposal in the islands.[7] Perhaps the most famous among them was Shaykh Yusuf of Makassar (1626–99), whose long itinerant career between Sulawesi, Bantam, and Mecca eventually caused some wary VOC officials to exile him to South Africa.[8]

Even if Europeans in Southeast Asia knew fairly well by the end of the seventeenth century that Muslim pilgrims were moving back and forth across the Indian Ocean, they still had only a vague idea of what the hajj was about. Many Dutchmen assumed that the great pilgrimage was to 'Muhammad's grave in Mecca', and despite this inaccuracy, it eventually became the easiest way to explain a mass movement of human beings across still partially unknown global spaces.[9] Latent in much of this thinking was the implied 'threat' of the hajj, about which the Dutch, in particular, spilled much ink. In 1690, the Dutch commented on 'troublemaking hajjis' from Ternate who had sprouted up in Rembang, East Java, while in 1725 they noted again the secret movement of hajjis to Semarang in Central Java, a matter of some concern as the latter was by now a major Dutch commercial port.[10] This 'threat' stretched all the way west to Sumatra. In 1726, the Dutch wrote about hajjis leading armed resistance fighters against VOC forces in the mountains outside Padang. One of these men had been the subject of an intensive manhunt by Batavia for

*Oostindische Compagnie* ('s –Gravenhage, 1960; 7 folios) (hereafter VOC, Gen. Miss.) (Kolonial Archief (hereafter K.A.) 961), 10; and Van Diemen, Caen, Van der Lijn, Maetsuycker, Schouten, Sweers en Witsen, XVIII, 12 December 1642, VOC, Gen. Miss. (K.A. 1047, folio 1–116), 180.

[5] Van Diemen, Van der Lijn, Maetsuyker, Schouten en Sweers, XX, 13 January 1643, VOC, Gen. Miss. (K.A. 1050, folio 1–13), 193.

[6] Maetsuyker, Hartzinck, Cunaeus, Van Oudtshoorn, Verburch en Steur, XII, 4 December 1656, VOC, Gen. Miss. (K.A. 1104, folio 1–80), 96; Maetsuyker, Hartsinck, Verburch, Steur en Joan Thijsz., 26 December 1662, VOC, Gen. Miss. (K.A. 1128, 1–467), 447; and Van Goens, Speelman, Bort, Hurdt, Blom, Van Outhoorn, XI, 11 December 1679, VOC, Gen. Miss. (K.A. 1230, folio 155–671), 356.

[7] Van Goens, Speelman, Bort, Van Outhoorn en Camphuys, VI, 21 December 1678, VOC, Gen Miss. (K.A. 1220, folio 1–94), 248.

[8] Speelman, Bort, Hurdt, Van Outhoorn, Camphuys, VII, 1 and 9 March 1683, VOC, Gen Miss. (K.A. 1260, folio 722–35), 496. His body was eventually moved back to Sulawesi, though there is still a grave in Cape Town.

[9] Van Outhoorn, Van Hoorn, Pijl, De Haas, Van Riebeeck, XV, 30 November 1697, VOC, Gen. Miss. (K.A. 1475, folio 13–398), 855.

[10] Camphuys, Van Outhoorn, Pit, Van Hoorn, De Saint-Martin, XXI, 14 March 1690, VOC, Gen. Miss. (K.A. 1347, folio 8–228), 351; and De Haan, Huysman, Hasselaar, Blom, Durven, Vuyst, IV, 30 November 1725, VOC, Gen. Miss. (K.A. 1911, folio 541–965).

over seven years.[11] These connections between Dutch outposts in the Indies and the religious connection of the hajj all the way to the Arabian peninsula conditioned much thinking about the nature of the early modern hajj and set the stage for a web of interactions for many years to come.

The VOC records known as the *Generale Missieven* first mentioned the hajj as such (*bedevaart* or 'pilgrimage', as opposed to the title 'hajji') in 1699, when the Dutch noted that Emperor Aurangzeb (1618–1707) in India had prepared a huge ship to help the pilgrimage from his own Mughal lands to the Hijaz.[12] After this, references became more numerous and regular. In 1705, the Dutch were concerned that Muscati Arabs had imprisoned Persian hajjis on their way back to their own country in the Persian Gulf, and made notes on this situation for several years running in the *Missieven*.[13] The following year, the 90-year-old Emperor Aurangzeb appeared again in the Dutch ledgers when he informed them that he was going to commence his own hajj with fifty-seven ships in attendance upon him and was in need of a Dutch sea pass to make the journey.[14] The emperor, as it turned out, also wished to bring many of his wives with him. Ten years later, fugitive hajjis from the East Indies were being commented upon, and notes were being taken on the fact that Bantam hajjis were proselytizing Islam in Cirebon, an observation which was echoed again in 1729.[15] The links with trade and profit were never far from VOC minds, however. In 1737, the Dutch expressed the hope that the ruler of Ceram would release more sappanwood for sale after he returned from his own hajj to the Hijaz.[16] These notices underscore a world of Muslims in motion along the sea routes, often with economic or political undertones in the reporting, but with the hajj as an important spoke of observation in Dutch record-keeping in Asia.

Many people were in motion along the trade routes of the early modern Indian Ocean: Sufi mystics, spice merchants, and Hadrami wanderers in diaspora among numerous other groups. Pilgrims made up only a subset of these earliest voyagers, but they were an important subset in terms of numbers and the impact they had on these trans-regional connections. Noting the apparent waffling of the VOC on a policy involving hajjis from their own Indies territories, the nineteenth-century British writer and colonial administrator Sir Thomas Stamford Raffles famously

---

[11] De Haan, Huysman, Hasselaar, Blom, Durven, Vuyst, IV, 27 March 1726, VOC, Gen. Miss. (K.A. 1915, folio 2669–2858), 49 and 50.

[12] Van Outhoorn, Van Hoorn, Pijl, De Haas, Van Riebeeck, XXIII, 23 November 1699, VOC, Gen. Miss. (K.A. 1503, folio 12–237), 88.

[13] Van Hoorn, Van Riebeeck, Van Swoll, De Wilde, Douglas, IX, 30 November 1705, VOC, Gen. Miss. (K.A. 1588, folio 16–381A), 380; Van Hoorn en Raden van Indie, XIII, 31 March 1706, VOC, Gen. Miss. (K.A. 1608, folio 516–70), 409; Van Hoorn, Van Riebeeck, Van Swoll, De Wilde, Douglas, XVI, 30 November 1706 VOC, Gen. Miss. (K.A. 1608, folio 23–488), 458.

[14] Van Hoorn, Van Riebeeck, Van Swoll, Douglas, De Vos, XXI, 30 November 1707, VOC, Gen. Miss. (K.A. 1627, folio 406–729), 504. Such sea passes were common by this time.

[15] Van Swoll, Castelijn, De Haan, Zwaardecroon, Timmerman, XV, 30 November 1717, VOC, Gen. Miss. (K.A. 1779, folio 14–600), 312; Zwaardcroon, Castelijn, De Haan, Timmerman, Faes, VIII, November 30, 1720, VOC, Gen. Miss. (K.A. 1824, folio 472–954), 509; and Diderik Durven V, November 30, 1729, VOC, Gen. Miss. (K.A. 2005, VOC 2113., folio 2521–3260), 60.

[16] Abraham Patras, IX, 2 April 1737, VOC, Gen. Miss. (K.A. 2257, VOC 2365, folio 2030–303), 815.

said of the company that 'their sole objects appear to have been the safety of their own power, and the tranquility of the country'.[17] In fact, VOC policy towards hajjis was closely connected to the company's business interests. In the first half of the seventeenth century the VOC, often under the influence of missionary circles, actively tried to make converts to Christianity east of the Cape, and also placed bans on Muslim proselytizing within its Asian dominions in 1642 and 1651.[18] By 1680, however, the company seemed to have realized that these religious proscriptions were bad for business, and thereafter it was less energetic in pursuing attempted bans on local pilgrims. Instead, the hajj was frowned upon if pilgrims did not have the money to pay their passage on Dutch ships. This was a pecuniary rationale much more in line with the *geist* of the company, even if it overrode certain instructions from the emerging state-based religious establishment back in the Netherlands.[19] Pilgrims were occasionally dissuaded from embarking for Mecca on political grounds, but more often than not the VOC stated that hajjis were welcome, partially because the sums of money they spent on such voyages helped the company's exchequer in increasingly lean times.[20] The lure of cash made the hajj a deeply paradoxical phenomenon for the Dutch, since it was thought potentially to spread Islamic militancy, but also was a magnet for trade and profit.

Because the VOC was increasingly involved in the commercial orbits of the Red Sea and Southeast Asia over the course of the seventeenth century, it seems natural that Dutch records provide examples of how the Indian Ocean economy started to have a more unitary character during this period. A Dutch VOC servant, Pieter van den Broeke, noted these connections in the 1620s when he was charged with an expedition to the Red Sea.[21] Van den Broeke, who already had experience in Yemeni waters by the time of this expedition, established a small trading post on the Tihama coasts of Yemen and had at least one of his crew, Abraham Crabee, learn enough Arabic so that they could deal profitably with local people. Among the products that he brought to sell were cloves, benzoin resin, and camphor, all from the VOC's new trading posts in the Indies.[22] He noted in passing the presence of Malays on these same Yemeni coasts, some of whom were trading in similar commodities to his own. A number of these men, he surmised, were trading while on pilgrimage voyages to the Red Sea.

Yet the most detailed records on the hajj from the 'lands beneath the winds' in this early period come primarily from Java. Javanese went on the hajj for religious purposes, but they also knew that the pilgrimage was invested with political and

---

[17] Thomas Stamford Raffles, *The History of Java*, 2 vols (London, 1817), ii, 3.

[18] Johan Eisenberger, 'Indie en de Bedevaart naar Mekka' (PhD, Leiden University, 1928), 11.

[19] Johan Eisenberger, 'Indie en de Bedevaart naar Mekka', 12 and 13.

[20] Johan Eisenberger, 'Indie en de Bedevaart naar Mekka', 14 and 15.

[21] C. G. Brouwer, 'Le Voyage au Yemen de Pieter van den Broecke (serviteur de la VOC) en 1620, d'après son livre de resolutions' in F. E. Peters et al. (eds), *The Challenge of the Middle East* (Amsterdam, 1982), 175–82.

[22] C. G. Brouwer, 'Pieter van den Broecke's Original Resulutieboeck Concerning Dutch Trade in Northwest India, Persia, and Southern Arabia, 1620–1625', in C. G. Brouwer (ed.), *Dutch-Yemeni Encounters: Activities of the United East India Company (VOC) in South Arabian Waters Since 1614* (Amsterdam, 1999), 77–102.

economic opportunities. The sultanate of Banten in West Java is one of the earliest places we see this at work. One of Banten's rulers in the late seventeenth century called himself simply 'Sultan Haji' (r.1682–87) as a mark of his voyage to Mecca. He performed the pilgrimage twice before ascending the throne in Banten, and made sure this experience was memorialized in his title.[23] Undertaking the hajj cost money, of course, but he recouped those funds by increasing the number of followers available to him as a result of his raised status as a successful pilgrim. Other Javanese also knew the many different values of the hajj. One of the Central Javanese sultans made vessels ready on the northern coast of the island in order to go on hajj, but then decided not to go himself, sending others on his behalf in 1700 and 1701. It is unclear what was at work in this decision, but it seems plausible that it may have been dangerous to be away from Java during this period of early VOC aggression. In contrast with the more direct role that the Dutch played in the Indies hajj as explored later in this chapter, in this period their influence could often be an indirect one, though nevertheless one of consequence. As a ruler, sending one's subjects conferred merit and made economic and even political opportunities for others who could be recruited subsequently, but it also left one's own *kraton* (palace) defended in case of Dutch adventurism. When this adventurism did come a few decades later, the Surakarta Major Babad wrote that hajjis were at the forefront of Javanese forces in fighting the Europeans, alongside the 'ulama, who were also praised for their bravery.[24] By the middle of the eighteenth century, Sultan Mangkubumi was sending missions to repair his own houses in Mecca— an economic perquisite that he could provide to followers—so that these could be used by his subjects in their travels across the width of the Indian Ocean.[25] And on the eve of the comprehensive Dutch takeover of Java, the legendary rebel leader Prince Dipanagara (1785–1855) was having hajjis appear in his dreams as he planned and shortly afterward executed his five-year rebellion against colonial authority of the Netherlands in Java.[26]

## FACILITATING THE HAJJ

After 1799 and the collapse of the company, when the Dutch began direct rule in the East Indies, the Batavia administration tried to regulate the hajj as much as possible, keeping detailed records on this subject throughout the course of the nineteenth century. Local *controleurs*—mid-level civil servants, usually European but often assisted by indigenous helpers—were told by their superiors to record the details of the pilgrimage to Mecca from their residencies. Though the impetus

---

[23] Merle Ricklefs, *A History of Modern Indonesia* (Stanford, 1993), 78–9.
[24] Merle Ricklefs, *Mystic Synthesis in Java: A History of Islamization From the Fourteenth to the Early Nineteenth Centuries* (Norwalk, CT, 2004), 75–6 and 94.
[25] P. B. R. Carey, 'Pangeran Dipanagara and the Making of the Java War' (DPhil, University of Oxford, 1975), i, 76.
[26] Carey, 'Pangeran Dipanagara and the Making of the Java War', 359–81.

for these directives was often political, much of this reporting ended up being financial in nature. The reports from a single place, the residency of Banten in West Java, for the year of 1860 alone, are illustrative in this respect. The reports were written by the local resident, who informed Batavia of the names of local people who had returned from Mecca that same year, among them villagers such as Mochamad Markoem, Inam, Hadjie Djamiel, and Hadji Daham. In addition to recording the names of many illiterate farmers and fishermen, the records show that 222 of these people came back to the residency from Mecca that year, a very high number considering the costs and difficulties of travel in 1860.[27] Since 1858, almost a quarter of a million guilders had left the residency on these trips, as pilgrims took whatever funds they could to facilitate their trips. This was a cause for some alarm to local officials, and the problem of 'silver drain' became one commented upon at every level of government reportage examining the mechanics of the hajj.[28] Finally, these reports spelled out exactly how much money each pilgrim was bringing on his or her person for the trip. Kardja brought 150 Spanish dollars in 1860, Kaman brought 100, and Abdulah and Oesman from Petier and Dragem villages respectively, brought 200 dollars each.[29] The level of detail in the reporting is quite astonishing, and given that this was happening across all the more settled districts of the Dutch Indies, a large cache of data exists to flesh out the conduct of the Indonesian hajj, even at this early date.[30]

Fees were charged for the right to go on pilgrimage, and these escalated from 110 guilders at mid-century to 200 guilders in 1873, and then to 300 guilders in 1890. Shortly after this, the price was lowered to 100 guilders again, but a return ticket on a steamer was a condition for being allowed to leave the Indies so that pilgrims would not be stranded in the Middle East.[31] An enormous system of brokers developed to take care of the ever-burgeoning Indies pilgrim traffic, most of which went through Singapore. In 1880, there were 180 shaykhs in charge of the Indies' flow alone, a number that grew to 400 by the eve of the First World War and 600–700 in 1926, according to the chronicler Haji Abdul Majid, who made the trip himself in that year.[32] Many of these Indies pilgrims were leaving

[27] Residentie Bantam Algemeen Verslag, Appendix: Opgave van de Personen die ter Bedevaart naar Mekka zijn Teruggekeerd (1860), National Archives of Indonesia, Jakarta (Arsip Nasional Republik Indonesia, hereafter ANRI).

[28] Residentie Bantam Algemeen Verslag (1860), ANRI.

[29] Residentie Bantam Algemeen Verslag, Appendix: Opgave van de Personen die ter Bedevaart naar Mekka zijn Vertrokken (1860), ANRI.

[30] For an incredible example of the depth of this reportage, see the archive bundle titled 'Rapporten Dari Perkara Hadji Hadja njang Minta Pas dan njang Baru Datang dari Mekka, 1860/61/62/63/64', in the Arsip Nasional Indonesia (Jakarta) Tegal archive (no. 196/5, 'Laporan Pergi dan Pulang Haji'). This is only one of a number of 500-page bundles of local letters and reports on the hajj in Tegal alone—just one small residency in Java. A small book could be written simply on the basis of this one archival bundle alone.

[31] Eisenberger, 'Indie en de Bedevaart', 27 and 175.

[32] Jacob Vredenbregt, 'The Hadj: Some of its Features and Functions in Indonesia', *Bijdragen tot de Taal-, Land-, en Volkenkunde*, 118 (1962), 91–154; and Haji Abdul Majid, 'A Malay's Pilgrimage', *Journal of the Malaysian Branch of the Royal Asiatic Society*, 4/2 (1926), 270. Keeping track of all of these shaykhs and the various dangers they represented to the colonial Dutch government was a small but very active group of diplomats scattered across several Indian Ocean ports.

the archipelago for the first time and had little idea of the vagaries of international commerce on the great shipping lanes stretching across the vast Indian Ocean. As a result, many of these hajjis were charged much more than their Malay counterparts, despite the fact that they were ultimately leaving from the same Southeast Asian ports.[33] A steady stream of pilgrims found their way to the Hijaz via these intricate connections, leaving the Indies from a series of Dutch harbors and stopping over in British dominions (usually Singapore or Penang), before making the big jump across the sea to the Arabian peninsula.

Yet just as with the Malay pilgrims, many Indies hajjis suffered at the hands of middlemen, who took advantage of their comparative naiveté and powerlessness as they tried to complete their hajj.[34] An 1876 Dutch consular report suggested that approximately thirty percent of all Indies pilgrims eventually found themselves destitute in the Hijaz, in number and percentage far higher than for Malay pilgrims.[35] Many of the archipelago hajjis entered into contracts in order to raise cash for their journeys, agreeing to work in Singapore, Malaya, or even in the Arabian peninsula for years so that sufficient funds could be raised.[36] The rate of return on these menial jobs—usually on plantations—was so low that some pilgrims could find themselves in a perpetual cycle of debt from which they could never hope to escape.[37] Shaykhs who perpetuated this cycle of indebtedness were often Arabs resident in Southeast Asia, but after several decades indigenous archipelago returnees also entered this very profitable business. When the Dutch gradually restricted the numbers of Indies pilgrims allowed to go on the pilgrimage for economic and security reasons, many started to go illegally by way of Singapore, putting themselves even more at the mercy of the shaykhs since they had little recourse to colonial laws meant to protect them. A report in the *Indische Gids* in 1897 cataloged some of the deceptions that were practiced on Indies pilgrims, but offered little by way of practical solutions.[38] Even if the Dutch knew their subjects were being fleeced, often on a systemic basis, doing something about it seemed beyond the organizational powers of Batavia's administrators.

The other big issue, besides the welfare of hajjis vis-à-vis the shaykhs, concerned medical oversight of the hajj. Large numbers of the pilgrims who sailed into the Red Sea came from the Dutch East Indies, so knowledge and cognizance of the health situation in the Hijaz was a matter of keen concern in distant colonial Indonesia. The *Koloniaal Verslag* (*Colonial Report*), published annually in the Indies, makes careful mention that chiefs of residencies were responsible for letting the population within their administrative orbits know the state of cholera in Mecca. This information included the charges for sanitary control in the Red Sea,

---

[33] Mary McDonnell, 'The Conduct of the Hajj from Malaysia' (PhD, Columbia University, 1986), 76.

[34] For a partial overview of some of the legislation against this, see Eisenberger, 'Indie en de Bedevaart', 31–7.

[35] Marcel Witlox, 'Met Gevaar voor Lijf en Goed: Mekkagangers uit Nederlands-Indie in de 19de Eeuw', in Willy Jansen and Huub de Jonge (eds), *Islamitische Pelgrimstochten* (Muiderberg, 1991), 30.

[36] William R. Roff, *The Origins of Malay Nationalism* (New Haven, 1967), 38–9.

[37] Vredenbregt, 'The Hadj', 113–15.        [38] *Indische Gids* (1897), 390.

as well as the possibility in certain years that Indies pilgrims would not be allowed in the Hijaz at all.[39] In 1875 in Japara (Java), for example, cholera statistics were kept on each village, and local Javanese there made decisions on whether or not to go on hajj partially based on the rumors they heard about health conditions in Arabia.[40] A few years later in Besoeki, the numbers of pilgrims dropped off, apparently because of the fear of cholera then prevalent in the Hijaz, the resident said.[41] The local colonial legal edifice in the Indies for dealing with this cycle of disease and transport eventually enacted laws requiring all hajj-aspirants to be inoculated against cholera and typhus before they left the Indies.[42] These rules were often ignored, however, and enforcement was not uniform. Yet even by the late 1930s, there was a steady transport of medical officers from the Indies to the Red Sea, including one Javanese named Manjoedin, a civil servant first class at the Batavia Central Laboratory, who was sent to Kamaran to look after Dutch interests there. By this time, the British and Dutch were consolidating their operations on the island in an effort to save costs in the event a war broke out.[43]

What happened in the Indies was one thing; regulating health on the long voyages across the Indian Ocean was quite another. These vessels became incubation chambers for the spread of the worst infections, so strict care was paid to those factors that might affect the health of travelers. Doctors on board were required to have certain qualifications and experiences by Indies colonial law.[44] The decks of the steamships were to be made of wood, iron, or steel, and the upper decks needed to be covered to protect pilgrims from sun exposure.[45] Adequate provisions had to be brought on board for the whole voyage, not just the roughly three weeks for one ocean crossing, but also the ten days to two weeks earmarked for quarantine. Canned foods such as sardines and salmon were favored, as were dry goods such as biscuits, which did not go off in the heat of the Red Sea.[46] Rice, sugar, and meat were also reckoned into these calculations by weight per person.[47] Medicines down to individual dosages and chemical minutiae of prophylaxis as well as drug treatments were also legislated so that outbreaks of infection could be dealt with quickly and efficiently by trained medical personnel on board.[48] Finally, a system

[39] *Koloniaal Verslagen*, 98 (1872) and 122 (1875).

[40] Japara no. 59: in K. 18: Japara, no. 59. Tahun 1875, Aankomende brieven (Vendu kantoor; Bedevaart; ziekte rapport; politiezaken), Jan.–Apr. 1875, 30, ANRI.

[41] Algemeen Verslag over het Jaar 1883, Residentie Besoeki, in K. 23: Besuki, no. 78 (Nomor lama 9/14) (1883). B.b. Uitbreiding van het Mohamedanisme toe–en afname van het aantal bedevaart-gangers, ANRI.

[42] *Bijblad*, 44114 (1885), 376–7; *Bijblad*, 10236 (1922), 387–8; and *Bijblad*, 11780 (1928), 605.

[43] Chief of Health, Kamaran, to Batavia Central Laboratory, 31 October 1937, 1.2.4 Medische Aangelegenheden, Fiche 164, Djeddah Archives, National Dutch Archives, The Hague (Nationaal Archief, hereafter ARA); and 'Uitreksel van het Register der Besluiten van het Hoefd van den Dienst der Volksgezondheid', Batavia, 26 July 1939 (no. 24724).

[44] *Bijblad*, 11018 (1926), 362.

[45] *Staatsblad*, 557 (1912), 3; and *Staatsblad*, 507 (1937), 3.

[46] Inspector for NEI to Captains of Pilgrimships of the Rotterdamsche Lloyd, 30 January 1922, 1.2.4 Medische Aangelegenheden, Fiche 156, Djeddah Archives, ARA.

[47] 'Regeling Betreffende Extra Voeding Pelgrims' (enclosed in letter in n. 45), 1.2.4 Medische Aangelegenheden, Fiche 156, Djeddah Archives, ARA.

[48] *Staatsblad*, 597 (1923), 4–5.

was instituted by the European colonial powers which stipulated that any ship approaching a port, or indeed other vessels, must fly a yellow flag, immediately signaling that cholera or some other contagious disease had spread on board and that everyone should maintain a strict distance.[49]

When the Dutch ships finally docked at Kamaran, most pilgrims were exhausted from weeks at sea living in very close quarters. Although Dutch sponsorship had transported them this far on their journey, there were still serious hurdles to be faced. While every care was made to protect passengers against epidemics, often there were a number of sick people on board. The Dutch consul at Jidda would spend time at Kamaran during the pilgrimage seasons, collecting information about ships coming in. One representative report from January 1938 recorded data from multiple pilgrim ships that year. The *Clytoneus*, which arrived from Singapore, carried 680 passengers sub-divided by gender and age, and included the number of sick on board as well as the nature and outcomes of the illnesses. The *El Amin*, a much smaller ship, arrived the next day from Aden, and the *Buitenzorg* arrived on 4 January from Batavia, with several deaths reported.[50] Like colonial armed forces elsewhere in the world at the time, the Dutch took a keen interest in finding out the routes of contagion across the sea ways.[51] If nothing else, this was seen as a measure for epidemiological survival.

The entire system at Kamaran and its health procedures for Southeast Asian and other pilgrims became public knowledge. Another Dutch report, also from the 1930s, gives a sense of the numbers of afflicted: 223 new patients and 322 repeat patients for the month of December alone.[52] A variety of authors—writing in Dutch, French, and English, primarily—debated this vast medical apparatus which stretched its radials of surveillance, maintenance, and care across the oceans.[53] Some of the actual travelers, such as the regent of Bandung, Raden Adipati Aria Wiranata Koesoma, wrote accounts that provide a human sense of the scope of Kamaran and its operations. He finished his narrative of travels through Kamaran with the notice of two Indies children who died en route to Mecca, and who were buried in Jidda only a few miles from the destination they had traveled so far to see.[54] The Dutch therefore facilitated the travels of the regent, these two children, and everyone else coming on the East Indies Hajj from a variety of vantages, erecting steamship networks and passport controls, and linking a number of ports across vast, oceanic distances. Batavia and The Hague did this out of genuinely philanthropic instincts, but also out of self-interest, assuaging existing

---

[49] *Staatsblad*, 208 (1911), 1–2.

[50] Maandrapport, Dutch Consul in Jidda (Kamaran, Jan./Feb. 1938), 1.2.4 Medische Aangelegenheden, Fiche 157, Djeddah Archives, ARA.

[51] P. Adriani, 'De Bedevaart naar Arabie en de Verspreiding der Epidemische Ziekten', *Nederlandse Militair Geneeskundige Archief*, 23 (1899) 7, 156, 245 and throughout.

[52] Medical Services, 31 December 1933 (no. 5), 1.2.4 Medische Aangelegenheden, Fiche 158, Djeddah Archives, ARA.

[53] Eisenberger, 'Indie en de Bedevaart', 103–11.

[54] G. A. van Bovene (ed.), *Mijn Reis Naar Mekka: Naar het Dagboek van het Regent van Bandoeg Raden Adipati Aria Wiranata Koesoma* (Bandung, 1924), 38.

colonial anxieties about the potentially dissident nature of Islam, and also in order to have the colonial state appear as a patron of the religion.

## SURVEILLING THE HAJJ

Though the Dutch East Indies were technically the Muslim-majority location furthest away from Mecca on the planet, from a relatively early date these islands were supplying large numbers of pilgrims to the holy cities. By the eve of the First World War these numbers had risen to over 20,000 (24,025 in 1911, 26,321 in 1912, and 28,427 in 1913), but the more telling statistic is that these were roughly a quarter of the global total of pilgrims to Mecca for these years.[55] In the eyes of the Dutch, this remarkable fact—in concert with the perceived rise of pan-Islamic sentiments and the emergence of certain cities in the Middle East such as Mecca and Cairo as markets for 'radical' ideas—necessitated the beginnings of a surveillance network on these subjects. From the mid-nineteenth century in Java, especially, voluminous files were produced to keep track of the hajj, with much of the information centered on a community-level basis. From Besoeki in the 1850s, for example, there exist notations on whether the pilgrimage was deemed a threat by local administrators at this time.[56] From Tegal came records of the routes taken by some of the ships, often jumping from the Java coasts to places such as Pontianak, Riau, and Singapore, human collection depots along the maritime routes within the archipelago.[57] The Tegal pilgrims were away for two years at a time in the 1850s according to these statistics, while others were gone for three and occasionally for six years or more.[58] One document bundle from this residency in the early 1860s, *Rapporten Dari Perkara Hadji Hadja njang Minta Pas dan njang Baru Datang dari Mekka, 1860–64* ('Reports on Hajjis Requesting Passes and on Those Who Just Returned from Mecca'), chronicles in Rumi (Romanized Malay) and Dutch the comings and goings to Mecca from this single regency in over 500 pages. It gives little away about the feelings or details of individuals, but as a source for data compilation it is an astonishing record of movement from a very small place.[59]

Documents of a more personal nature from this period also exist. Writing primarily in Rumi, local indigenous officials supplied information about individual pilgrims who were leaving the Java coasts for Mecca in large numbers. Other documents in Dutch, record the names of those leaving in short, patterned details.[60]

[55] Puuhena, 'Historiografi Haji', 413.

[56] Resident Besoeki to Gov. Gen. NEI, 23 February 1856 (no. 541), in K23: Daftar Arsip Besuki (1819–1913), ANRI. This and all of the following ANRI citations are from the Gewestilijke Stukken Archive.

[57] Regent Tegal to Resident, Tegal, 5 June 1857 (no. 571), in K8: Tegal (1790–1872), ANRI.

[58] Resident Tegal, Opgave der Uitgereiktepassen voor de Bedevaart naar Mekka voor 1856, 2 January 1857 in K8: Tegal (1790–1872), ANRI.

[59] 'Rapporten Dari Perkara Hadji Hadja njang Minta Pas dan njang Baru Datang dari Mekka, 1860/61/62/63/64' in K8: Tegal (1790–1872), ANRI.

[60] 'Rapport, Residentie Tegal, No. 27' in 'Laporan Pergi dan Pulang Haji' (no. 196/5), in K8: Tegal (1790–1872), ANRI.

A number of pilgrims decided to change their names after coming back from their hajj, a personal act that was sometimes committed at the conclusion of a successful trip to Mecca. Fasilan, the Dutch censors in Semarang in the 1850s noted, became Abdullah; Fasidjan wanted to be known as Abdulmajid; and Arseah turned into Abdusjamad.[61] This kind of very personal, individual attention to hajjis and hajjas even in small villages started early according to the Indonesian records, but eventually became more detailed as surveillance and record-gathering became more important to the Dutch later in the nineteenth century. By the early twentieth century, Batavia was using this hajj-reportage apparatus to look for connections between the pilgrimage and Sarekat Islam party membership on a local level, using the information for political ends, and eventually for repression.[62] At least one scholar has commented in detail on the potentially dangerous 'radical' links that were constantly being sought and evaluated by Dutch servants in Arabia, as Batavia and even The Hague carefully calibrated the connections of Mecca to the Indies as a market for potentially 'seditious' notions, both religious and non-religious in nature.[63]

If the Jakarta archives provide a glimpse into local surveillance, in nineteenth-century Java other repositories demonstrate how Dutch oversight of the hajj became more trans-oceanic in nature. The archive of the *Ministrie van Buitenlandse Zaken*, the ministry of foreign affairs, in The Hague, is one such place. Here, surveillance material was gathered from the other side of the Indian Ocean when dealing with the Dutch-administered hajj. As such, a certain amount of the information reflects Middle Eastern reporting. An active Dutch spy network was activated, as in 1881 when The Hague was informed that a man purporting to be the 'second coming of Muhummad' had stepped forward in Arabia ('his name is Imam Imhabil, 38 years of age, born in Mecca'). The Dutch minister for foreign affairs was warned that the Ottoman sultan had already sent out letters to Muslim lands to prepare for a jihad in two years as a result of Imhabil's birth, and the Dutch consul in Singapore performed a similar version of this preparation by writing to Batavia, as the rumors were 'quite enough to justify precautions' locally.[64] That same year, diplomatic correspondence warned of the arrival of three Meccan shaykhs—Syed Hussein Alkoods, shaykh Abdul Hamid Murdad, and shaykh Ahmed Salawi—in Singapore, which put the Dutch hajj-surveillance network on high alert. All three men 'occupy so important a role in the Mahomedan world that their movements seldom fail to have a political object', the governor-general of the Indies was told.[65] They needed to be watched, particularly if they were planning a

---

[61] Regent of Tegal to Resident of Tegal, 5 June 1857 (no. 571) in K8: Tegal (1790–1872), ANRI.

[62] Resident Batavia to Assistant Resident Tangerrang, 18 May 1914, in 'Stukken Betreffende Mohammedanaansche Zaken, o.a. Mekkagangers, 1913–1914' in K2: Tangerrang, ANRI.

[63] Michael Laffan, *Islamic Nationhood and Colonial Indonesia: The Umma Below the Winds* (London and New York, 2003).

[64] W. H. Read, Dutch consul, to Count de Bylandt, Dutch Minister, 19 March 1881, in Ministerie van Buitenlandse Zaken (MvBZ) archive, ARA.

[65] UK Gov. Weld, Singapore, to Gov Gen NEI, 13 May 1881, Confidential, in MvBZ archive, ARA; and Michael Laffan, 'A Watchful Eye: The Meccan Plot of 1881 and Changing Dutch Perceptions of Islam in Indonesia', *Archipel*, 63 (2002), 79–108.

move into the Indies to preach hate against Europeans. In this they were seen as part of a long line of 'rabble-rousers and demagogues'.[66]

Yet for an even more nuanced feel for how transnational Hajj surveillance had become in Dutch circles in the fin-de-siècle period, other sources can be examined, all of which comment on this enormous oceanic undertaking. Some of this material was public and was put into the realm of public discourse by officials writing in their capacity as officials, but also as experts who could translate the 'threat' of the hajj for a public eager to know about this phenomenon's huge global contours. Dutch journals such as the *Indische Gids* fall into this category.[67] The *Koloniaal Verslag*, a dense report of many hundreds of pages published in the Indies, also put out yearly composites of information on the Indies hajj, showing the public the trends and directions of the pilgrimage. All of this information was important in setting a tone, and also in preserving information and a record of such carefully gleaned data.[68] Yet the majority of the material in question was private and intended only for the use of civil servants in order to keep tabs on a phenomenon that was thought to be potentially dangerous to the stability of the Dutch overseas empire. Dutch consular reports from places such as Penang and Singapore were crucial in this respect. They provided a yearly template for policy planners in The Hague to know what the hajj looked like in ports just outside Dutch jurisdiction, but very much on the doorstep of the Indies. Religious 'demagogues' were thought to use these places as bases to agitate in the Indies, for example.[69] The massive run of Colonial Office records known as *mailrapporten* ('mail reports') were also crucial in this regard, as they provide an unbroken record of many decades connecting Dutch authority in the Indies, the Hijaz, and Europe on the question of the hajj. Dutch officials could follow the *mailrapporten* through various colonial record offices, giving them a long-term view as they contemplated changes in policy.[70]

Ultimately, the root of Dutch uncertainty, anxiety, and fear in controling the hajj centered on the Indies, however, as the Dutch maintained only a tiny coterie of officials and traders in the face of a huge subject population of Muslims. The hajj might be a peaceful, unthreatening phenomenon that the Dutch were 'required' to manage at the best of times, but if 'extremists' did succeed in poisoning the relationship between masters and subjects in the Indies, as many Dutchmen feared

---

[66] Eric Tagliacozzo, *Secret Trades, Porous Borders: Smuggling and States along a Southeast Asian Frontier* (New Haven, 2005), 149–51 and 171–5.

[67] 'De Bedevaart naar Mekka, 1919/10', *Indische Gids*, 2 (1910), 1637–8. For a larger view on Islam, danger, and the pilgrimage at this time, see Michael Low, 'Empire and the Hajj: Pilgrims, Plagues, and Pan-Islam under British Surveillance, 1965–1908', *International Journal of Middle Eastern Studies*, 40/2 (2008), 269–90.

[68] *Koloniaal Verslag*, 120–1 (1878), 104–5 (1881), and 102–3 (1884).

[69] *Consulaat-General der Nederlanden te Singapore, Verslag*, 354 (1872), 544 (1874), 490 (1875); see also *Consulaat-General der Nederlanden te Penang, Jaarlijksh Verslag*, 971 (1904).

[70] The number of *mailrapporten* in the Ministerie van Kolonien (hereafter 'MvK') archive, ARA, dealing with the Hajj and 'dissident Islam' and surveillance is too large to list in full here, but the most important files that I have made use of include: MR 1872, no. 820+; MR 1878, no. 474; MR 1879, no. 668+; MR 1881, no. 259+; no. 563+, no. 709+, no. 839+; no. 860; no. 1107; no. 1139+; MR 1883, no. 252+; no. 1075+; no. 1173; MR 1885, no. 638+.

in the early twentieth century, it would be the Dutch in the Indies who would pay the price. For this reason, colonial officials in Batavia tried to learn all they could about Islam and its permutations in every corner of the archipelago, wherever such knowledge was available. Almost every 'general report', 'administrative report', and 'political report' in every residency in the Indies had space for civil servants to comment on the nature of Islam in their particular area.[71] Specialized political reports were also commissioned for the so-called *Buitenbezittingen* (or residencies outside of Java and Madura, the latter comprising the 'heartland' of Dutch rule), so that Islam in the fringes of the colony could be examined with special rigor. Some of these districts, such as Aceh, had long histories of resistance against occupation by a foreign power.[72] Finally, in the documents known as *Memories van Overgaven*, Dutch provincial officials were asked to comment on the *geest* or spirit of Islam in their particular residency, when they finished their tours in a particular place, and were about to hand over 'their' landscape to another official. They noted at great length the details and trends in the hajj in a vast array of Indies locales across the archipelago. All these documents show changes over time as events unfolded in the East Indies.[73]

Acting on the knowledge claimed by all of this surveillance was the province of the law. The Indies legal edifice set up to deal with the pilgrimage to Mecca required large numbers of codes, laws, and statutes to manage its sheer size and volume. From the *Staatsbladen* and *Bijbladen*, vast legal and policy compendia, it is evident that acquiring knowledge about the pilgrims themselves was deemed important by Batavia. This was so before they set out from the Indies and once they reached the Hijaz, especially for hajjis who wanted to stay longer in the Middle East.[74] Other

[71] Residentie Bangka, Politiek Verslag 1872, and Algemeen Verslag, 1890; Residentie Billiton, Algemeen Verslagen 1874, 1880, 1885, and 1890, ANRI; Residentie Lampong, Politiek Verslagen 1864, 1867, 1886, 1887, 1888, and 1890, ANRI; Residentie Ternate, Diverse Stukken 1892, ANRI; Residentie Riouw, Administratief Verslagen 1867–74, ANRI, and Residentie West Borneo, Algemeen Verslagen, 1875, 1886, and 1891, ANRI, for details. Residentie Borneo Zuidoost, Algemeen Verslag 1889/90, ANRI, has a particularly good table on local hajjis en route to Mecca for the entire decade of the 1880s from southeastern Borneo.

[72] The Political Reports from the Outer Islands ('Politieke Verslagen van de Butengewesten') give us a huge arc of reporting on Dutch visions of Islam across the outer edges of the Indies archipelago in the late nineteenth and early twentieth centuries. For the northern half of Sumatra alone, for example, we have reporting on the ongoing insurgency from Aceh; armed 'Muslim gangs' in Tapanuli; the spillage of Muslim violence into the plantation districts of East Sumatra; and 'troublemaking' of Muslim chiefs such as Djandi Radja, whose attacks solicited the response that 'our prestige demands that we make an end to this matter'. See Gov. Atjeh G. Van Daalen to Buitenzorg, 4 June 1907 (telegram no. 608), MvK, ARA; 'Extract uit het dagboek van het Controleur van Toba', 10 June 1906', MvK, ARA; Resident, Sumatra OK to Buitenzorg, 3 December 1904 (telegram no. 117), MvK, ARA; and Resident Tapanoeli to Gov. Sumatra WK, 9 November 1901 (telegram no. 7502), MvK, ARA. On Islamic resistance in Aceh, see the chapter by Gerrit Knaap in this volume.

[73] Memories van Overgaven from West, Central, and East Java, MvK, ARA, for example, tell us of the context of Muslim 'fanaticism' as revealed in Banten; of the situation of Indies Arabs in urban places such as Semarang, Pekalongan, and Tegal; and the growth of Sarekat Islam alongside the nascent nationalist parties, among other things. See West-Java, MMK 1, Hardeman, J.A. (resident) Memorie van Overgave (1906), MvK, ARA; Midden-Java, MMK 40, Gulik, P. J. van (Gouverneur) Memorie van Overgave (1931), MvK, ARA; and Oost-Java, MMK 83, Hardeman, W. Ch. (Gouverneur) Memorie van Overgave (1931), MvK, ARA.

[74] *Bijblad*, 5741 (19 August 1902); and *Staatsblad*, 15 (17 January 1923).

laws stipulated that pilgrims were required to pay 100-guilder fines if they flouted the Netherlands East Indies pass laws, and dictated pilgrims' responsibilities to check in with Dutch port officials in the Indies cities of their departure, then again in Jidda with the Dutch consul, and finally back in Indies ports upon their return to Asia.[75] Because the majority of the journey was maritime, Dutch naval authorities got involved in adjudication as well. They determined rules regarding the requisition of ships for the express purpose of the hajj (safety matters, such as the provisioning of an adequate number of lifeboats and safety vests), and the amounts of cubic space allowed to each passenger, to try to stave off the dangers of epidemic disease.[76] Finally, it was also legislated that the Dutch were not legally obligated to help pilgrims financially in the Middle East, which was only partially effective at pre-empting cost-savings to protect them against shaykhs.[77] These legal protections and enforcements were eventually extended to a large number of Indies ports serving as hajj depots, including Batavia, Surabaya, Makassar, Palembang, Jambi, Belawan (Deli), Padang, Sabang, Banjarmasin, and Pontianak by 1930.[78]

One of the most important Dutch civil servants tasked with explaining the nuances of the Indies hajj and enacting policy on its functional parameters, including surveillance, was C. Snouck Hurgronje. Snouck had lived in Mecca for six months as a young man and developed a reputation (in no small part disseminated by himself, though he did indeed deserve the plaudits) as being the Netherlands' foremost interpreter of Islam and of the Indies connections with the Arabian peninsula. He wrote a vast number of articles and reports on the hajj, and he also produced hundreds of hand-written letters, all triangulating the importance of the pilgrimage as part of everyday Indies life, as well as discussing its potential danger to Dutch rule. He also had numerous arguments in print with other scholars and statesmen on this topic. Snouck assumed a role of *primus inter pares* in Dutch policy circles in dealing with the hajj. His pronouncements were eagerly sought by the Dutch government in determining ways to keep an eye on pan-Islamic anti-colonialism, a phenomenon that was seen to be facilitated by the wings of the hajj. Because Indies pilgrims came in such numbers to Mecca during Snouck's lifetime, his views carried great weight in decision-making circles in Europe and in the colonies. His familiarity with the Red Sea coasts of Arabia, the Indies, and the corridors of power in the Netherlands made him the single most important figure in the conduct of the hajj throughout the Dutch empire.[79]

By the mid-1930s, the Dutch consular office in Jidda had acquired the primary status as a body surveilling the Indies hajj. By this time, most of the reportage was

---

[75] *Bijblad*, 11689 (15 June 1928); and *Bijblad*, 7130 (27 July 1909).
[76] *Staatsblad*, 236 (29 April 1906); and *Staatsblad*, 531 (25 October 1912).
[77] *Bijblad*, 7469 (16 May 1911); and *Staatsblad*, 554 (18 November 1932).
[78] *Staatsblad*, 44 (26 January 1931).
[79] For Snouck and his world, see among other publications the following: Eric Tagliacozzo, 'The Skeptic's Eye: Snouck Hurgronje and the Politics of Pilgrimage from the Indies', in Eric Tagliacozzo (ed.), *Southeast Asia and the Middle East: Islam, Movement, and the Longue Durée* (Stanford, 2009), 135–55; and Harry J. Benda, 'Christian Snouck Hurgronje and the Foundation of Dutch Islamic Policy in Indonesia', *Journal of Modern History*, 30/4 (1958), 338–47.

concerned with politics, rather than protection of pilgrims. Some of these reports concerned great power maneuvering, such as Russian movements and oil shipments in conjunction with the Russian hajj, and the dissemination of German propaganda (in Turkish) to local Hijazi populations in an attempt to stir up hate against the Allies in the years leading up to the Second World War.[80] Much of it had to do with ideas of Muslim linkages and potential subversion that traveled alongside the hajj, especially vis-à-vis a number of brotherhoods and reformist sects that shuttled between the Holy Cities and places such as the al-Azhar in Cairo.[81] The largest single set of documents after the turn of the twentieth century focused on Dutch espionage on Indies communities in the Hijaz. These provided translations of 'subversive' Rumi-language letters found in Arabia and identified new organizations such as the *Comite Pembela Islam Indonesia-Malaya*, or 'Committee for the Defense of Islam in Indonesia and Malaya', that were set up in an attempt to speed the independence of an Indonesian nation.[82] Recruitment of the *Jawa* community was said to be high in the Hijaz during this period and the Dutch kept careful tabs on their subjects in the Hijaz as a result of these suspicions.[83] Ultimately, some of these people and parties did play a part in the decolonization of the Indies, though the onset of the Second World War disrupted many of these forces.


## CONCLUSION

The Netherlands maintained an uneasy relationship with the Muslim faith of the majority of its colonial subjects over the course of three-and-a-half centuries of imperial rule. Islam was noted very early on in this relationship—in the seventeenth century, when the Dutch began to arrive in the Indies—but in the beginning the Muslim observances of most Indonesians was not a huge problem, as Dutch concerns were predominantly economic (and then political) in nature. Yet as the Dutch began to consolidate territory, they were forced to come face to face with Islam in Indonesia in ways that were only seldom required in the first years of their residency in the archipelago. Ruling over populations and having Muslim sultanates as neighbors implied a deepening of contact with Islam that proved to

---

[80] Dutch Consul to MvBZ, 18 February 1932 (no. 10/P42), 1.2.6 Politieke Aangelegenheden, Fiche 182, Djeddah Archives, ARA; and Dutch Consul, Jidda, to MvBZ, 7 January 1941 (no. 9/P-8), 1.2.6 Politieke Aangelegenheden, Fiche 197, Djeddah Archives, ARA.

[81] Dutch Consul to MvBZ, 8 June 1937 (no. 497/P-105), 1.2.6 Politieke Aangelegenheden, Fiche 88, Djeddah Archives, ARA; and Dutch Consul, Jidda, to MvBZ, 27 April 1929 (no. 695/98), 1.2.6 Politieke Aangelegenheden, Fiche 200, Djeddah Archives, ARA.

[82] Dutch Consul, Jidda, to GGNEI, 26 April 1931 (no. 511/H), 1.2.6 Politieke Aangelegenheden, Fiche 199, Djeddah Archives, ARA; and Adviser for Internal Affairs, NEI, to GGNEI, 14 August 1939 (no. 1048/K-1), 1.2.6 Politieke Aangelegenheden, Fiche 201, Djeddah Archives, ARA.

[83] Dutch Consul, Bombay, to Dutch Consul, Jidda, 22 November 1944 (no. 2754), 1.2.6 Politieke Aangelegenheden, Fiche 202, Djeddah Archives, ARA; and 'Memorandum on Terms of Employment', 1.2.6 Politieke Aangelegenheden, Fiche 203, Djeddah Archives, ARA. For the context, see Tom van den Berge, 'Indonesiers en het door hen Gevolgde Onderwijs in Mekka, 1926-1940', *Jambatan*, 7/1 (1989), 5–22.

be problematic. Perhaps through no single window can this be seen as clearly as through that of the hajj. The Dutch facilitated this obligatory voyage of Muslims across the huge spaces of the Indian Ocean, but also did so with some reluctance, and with eyes carefully peeled for signs of 'trouble'. Indonesians, for their part, were able to make use of Dutch shipping and Dutch organization to go on hajj in greater numbers than ever before, but also clearly resented having to perform this signal rite of their religion under the auspices and examining gaze of their colonial overlords.

The Dutch ultimately tried to play both sides in administering their 'empire of pilgrims'. Dutch assistance and philanthropy in helping the hajj was real and significant. Muslims in the Indies traveled to Mecca in their hundreds of thousands in the Dutch colonial age, and the increase in numbers as time went on is directly attributable to structural conditions that the Dutch laid down. Steamship travel, inoculations, quarantine stations, and the selective suppression of banditry in the Arabian peninsula all made the pilgrimage a much more likely reality for Indies Muslims than before the Dutch arrived. Yet there was a price to be paid for these advantages and the Dutch expected their subject populations to pay it as part of the bargain. Registration, surveillance, and political oversight were all instituted so that the Dutch colonial regime could better 'see' its own populace and keep careful tabs on what their pilgrims were doing, both in the Indies and once they had left its shores. This was a balance that had to be careful calibrated over time. Ironically, even as the numbers of Indies pilgrims rose to unprecedented levels in the early twentieth century, the seeds were being sown to undo some of these controls. Pilgrims returning to the Indies from Mecca helped spread some of the ideologies that ultimately formed part of the 'stew of protest' that signaled the birth of the anti-colonial movement. In this, their voyages to Arabia fulfilled at least two functions: the completion of rites to fulfill obligations to one higher power and the accumulation of contacts, connections, and new ideas to throw off the yoke of another.

# 4

# Islam and the French Empire in North Africa

*Julia Clancy-Smith*

## INTRODUCTION

In 1930, as part of the centenary celebrations of French Algeria, an International Eucharistic Congress was convened in Carthage in Tunisia.[1] Initiated in 1881 to reinvigorate the Catholic Church in the face of increasingly strident anti-clericalism under the Third Republic, the first Congress had opened in Lille and was followed by subsequent celebrations in Catholic regions across Europe. The Tunisian Congress of 1930 was the only occasion when a colonial state with a large Muslim population hosted such an event. Protectorate authorities approved the plans of the Church for the Congress after intense negotiations between the Quai d'Orsay and the resident-general's office. Ahmad II (*r.*1929–42), the bey of Tunis, agreed, however reluctantly, to serve as honorary president of the Congress, while taxes imposed on Muslims partially bankrolled the affair. It is unlikely that Tunisian officials, including 'ulama serving the protectorate, had any inkling of how this commemoration would be staged. Included in the week-long festivities were Catholic youth garbed in crusader outfits, Arabic-language pamphlets advocating conversion, and an incendiary public sermon by the papal legate on the nefarious effects of Islam upon North African history and civilization.[2] A boon to the faltering nationalist movement, the Congress swelled anti-colonial dissent. Indeed, Habib Bourguiba (1903–2000), the Neo-Dustur leader who later became the first president of Tunisia, claimed to have experienced his own political epiphany during the furor generated in 1930.[3]

It is tempting to interpret the Congress as merely the logical outcome of colonial prejudices and domineering policies toward Muslim subjects as well as the result of a more deeply rooted European antipathy toward Islam long predating the imperial age. Yet, three decades earlier, when church–state disestablishment, legislated in 1905, was extended to French colonies and possessions, Catholic personnel

---

[1] The author wishes to thank Joshua Cox, an indefatigable research assistant whose assistance proved invaluable in the preparation of this chapter.

[2] Ali Mahjoubi, 'Le Congrès Eucharistique de Carthage et le mouvement national tunisien', *Les Cahiers de Tunisie: Revue de sciences humaines*, 26/101–2 (1978), 109–32; and Kenneth J. Perkins, *A History of Modern Tunisia* (Cambridge, 2004), 89–90.

[3] Pierre-Albin Martel, *Habib Bourguiba: Un homme, un siécle* (Paris, 1999), 23.

and institutions came under vigorous attack from the protectorate authorities in Tunisia. Missionary schools and clinics were forcibly closed, sisters banished from classrooms and hospitals, and the resident-general declined to participate in church activities. Thus, the story of religion and empire is much less linear than presumed, mainly because a range of historical actors, forces, and relationships incubated in the pre-colonial period shaped later imperial interventions aimed at Islam and Muslims.[4]

The two major questions that arise from this episode are how scholars of modern empire have approached religion, and, more specifically, how historians of the Maghrib have addressed Islam and French rule. Regarding the first question, the older literature differentiated 'interventionist' policies from 'non-interference' or benign neglect which often, at the same time, referred to alleged differences between the French and British empires: assimilation versus association, or indirect versus direct rule. More recent work has recast these binaries as a continuum representing the highly variable ways that European empires managed, ruled over, or accommodated colonial subjects. But it should be noted that even purportedly 'non-interventionist' policies often constituted a form of interference in Islam.[5] In addition, religion as practiced and preached by the colonizers has largely been identified with Christian missions whose ambiguous, if not contradictory, roles in imperial expansion, domination, and ideology is currently the subject of vigorous reinterpretation.[6] The most recent scholarship deploys biography as a point of entry into the constantly evolving 'mental maps' of officials and missionaries in the field, as well as those of politicians and intellectuals in the metropolis.[7] For the most part, the abundant and generally excellent corpus on Muslim encounters with Christian missionaries has concentrated on the periods of incipient or full-blown imperialism, with less attention to the era of imperial demise. Research on the end of empire and decolonization—processes that should not be conflated—emphasize the fraught nature of post-colonial legacies in Asia and Africa, as well as within Europe itself, where Islam came to represent a significant, if contested, presence in former imperial centers.[8]

---

[4] Julia Clancy-Smith, *Mediterraneans: North Africa and Europe in an Age of Migration, c.1800–1900* (Berkeley, 2011).

[5] On the nearly intractable difficulties of defining empire, see Jane Burbank and Frederick Cooper, *Empires in World History: Power and the Politics of Difference* (Princeton, 2010); and Felipe Fernández-Armesto, 'Imperial Measures: Grand Delusions in Defining the Dominators of the World', *Times Literary Supplement* (24 September 2010), 8–9.

[6] See the articles in Owen White and J. P. Daughton (eds), *In God's Empire: French Missionaries and the Modern World* (Oxford, 2012). Jay Riley Case, *Unpredictable Gospel: American Evangelicals and World Christianity, 1812–1920* (Oxford, 2012), demonstrates that missionaries often operated as ineffectual agents of empire; see also the introduction by David Motadel in this volume.

[7] See articles in Martin Thomas (ed.), *The French Colonial Mind*, 2 vols, i: *Mental Maps of Empire and Colonial Encounters*; and ii: *Violence, Military Encounters, and Colonialism* (Lincoln, NE, 2011).

[8] Ahmet Yukleyen, *Localizing Islam in Europe: Turkish Islamic Communities in Germany and the Netherlands* (Syracuse, NY, 2011); and Marcel Maussen and Veit Bader, 'Introduction', in Veit Bader, Annelies Moors, and Marcel Maussen (eds), *Changes in Colonial and Post-Colonial Governance of Islam: Continuities and Ruptures* (Amsterdam, 2011), 9–26; for a definition of 'governance', see 15–17, where the authors argue for 'studies of regulation of religious diversity' that connect the colonial with the post-colonial.

In regard to the second question—the treatment of Islam by historians of imperial rule in the Maghrib—studies of imperialism during the long nineteenth century must consider the role of the Ottoman empire, given its critical guardianship over Islam's holiest spaces and shrines and the fact that the sultan was the most powerful Muslim ruler of his day. As European empires expanded around the Mediterranean rim, Muslim, Christian, and Jewish populations long under Ottoman authority were subjected, often with great violence, to foreign rule. Moreover, the growing panic over 'pan-Islam' meant that the Ottoman empire was demonized—not as weak and ripe for dismemberment, but because it nurtured transnational religious–political associations and identities. That Muslims across the Maghrib decried the 1911 Italian invasion of Tripolitania only proved the imminent dangers posed by the Ottomans and pan-Islam.

Scholarship on Islam in the colonial Maghrib has not yet produced a systematic comparative treatment of France's rule over North African Muslims.[9] Nor has missionary activity in the Maghrib attracted the scholarly attention it merits until very recently.[10] With some exceptions, the older literature gave the misleading impression of a more or less unified French stance across the two former Ottoman regencies and the sultanate of Morocco.[11] Nevertheless, a recent study argues that the very idea of something called 'Algerian Islam' became thoroughly normalized during the nineteenth century, thereby in effect fashioning a new style of religion and a new target for colonial policy.[12] In contrast, colonial polemicists generally did not evoke similar constructions of 'Tunisian Islam'.[13] On the other hand, it has been demonstrated that amateur anthropologists and protectorate officials, influenced by variants of European Orientalism, created a 'Moroccan Islam', which differed in some respects from its Algerian and Tunisian counterparts, a trend that survived into the post-colonial era.[14] Yet, beyond these national frameworks, historians have recognized that regional and global trends were crucial in shaping

---

[9] Mounira M. Charrad, *States and Women's Rights: The Making of Postcolonial Tunisia, Algeria, and Morocco* (Berkeley, 2001), provides a comparative analysis of colonial laws and practices affecting Muslim women's status.

[10] For examples of recent work, see Sarah A. Curtis, 'Emilie de Vialar and the Religious Reconquest of Algeria', *French Historical Studies*, 29/2 (2006), 261–92; Sybille Chapeu, *Des chrétiens dans la guerre d'Algérie: L'action de la Mission de France* (Paris, 2004); and articles in Dominique Borne and Benoit Falaze (eds) *Religions et colonisation XVIe–XXe siècle* (Paris, 2009).

[11] William A. Hoisington, 'France and Islam: The Haut Comité Méditerranéen and French North Africa', in George Joffé (ed.), *North Africa: Nation, State, and Region* (London, 1993), 78–90, pointed out long ago the 'lack of an overall French policy'.

[12] Raberh Achi, '"L'Islam authentique appartient à Dieu, 'l'Islam algerién' à César." La mobilisation de l'association des oulémas d'Algérie pour la séparation du culte musulman et de l'État (1936–1956)', *Genèses*, 69 (2007), 49–69.

[13] Julia Clancy-Smith, 'Islam, Gender, and Identities in the Making of French Algeria, 1830–1962', in Julia Clancy-Smith and Frances Gouda (eds), *Domesticating The Empire: Languages of Gender, Race, and Family Life in French and Dutch Colonialism, 1830–1962* (Charlottesville, VA, 1998), 154–74. A truly comprehensive treatment of Islam and empire in North Africa would have to consider in-depth the question of women and gender.

[14] The staying power of the work by Clifford H. Geertz, *Islam Observed: Religious Development in Morocco and Indonesia* (New Haven, 1968) is noteworthy; see also Edmund Burke III and David Prochaska, *Genealogies of Orientalism: History, Theory, Politics* (Lincoln, NB, 2008).

the religious sphere. The recent literature has drawn attention to revolutions in communications and transnational capitalism, which were both the cause and the consequence of imperial expansion, and which also impacted Islamic worldviews and practices.[15]

Building on these trends in the literature, the first part of this chapter gives a broad overview of the relationship between Islam and empire in the three French possessions in colonial North Africa: Algeria, Tunisia, and Morocco. The themes described in this section are then developed in the second part, which comprises a more detailed study of Islam and colonial rule in the case of Tunisia. It argues that the early protectorate, superimposed upon the Tunisian state and the Husaynid dynasty (*c.*1705–1956) preserved to some extent older political and social arrangements during roughly its first two decades and that this continuity influenced the governance of Islam. It further explores key spheres of empire, including religious courts, property, schools, and processions, triangulating between those spaces and the politics of resident Europeans in relation to Muslim colonial subjects.

## ISLAM, THE MAGHRIB, AND FRANCE

France's rule over Islam displayed significant variations across its three North African possessions. As Georges Leygues, the French prime minister, admitted to the Chamber of Deputies in Paris in 1912, France 'had no Muslim policy'.[16] This variable governance in the states of the Maghrib owed to a range of intersecting factors: the nature of pre-colonial states and relations with Europe and the Ottomans prior to 1830; the timing of conquest and the degrees and forms of violence; the place of ethnic and religious minorities; different migratory flows, the composition of settler communities, and their internal rivalries; local intermediaries and conflicts; modes of appropriation of property and land, including religious resources; and transformations in ecological and environmental conditions, to name the most crucial.

Overall, it might be argued that the variable nature of French policy owed largely to the framing of Algeria as a colony whose coastal regions were, from 1848, administered as *départements* of France, in contrast with the protectorate status accorded to Tunisia and Morocco. Partly this was a question of administrative boundaries: Tunisia and Morocco were attached to the Ministry of Foreign Affairs, while Algeria was under the Ministry of the Interior, which impeded the elaboration of a unified Islamic policy or even a single *politique indigène*.

Yet, more than this, the divide between Algeria on the one hand and Tunisia and Morocco on the other signaled a significant ideological difference. By the late nineteenth century, Algeria had begun to serve as a counter-model for France's future imperial adventures; indeed, for Tunisia and Morocco it came to represent

---

[15] Philip Scranton and Janet Davidson (eds), *The Business of Tourism: Place, Faith, and History* (Cambridge, 1990), on the case of mass tourism.

[16] Hoisington, 'France and Islam', 79.

an abject lesson in what not to do.[17] Greatly aiding this realization was the role of former Algerian officials such as Louis Machuel (1848–1921), who disapproved of French policies towards Islam and relocated to Tunisia, where they influenced early protectorate structures and institutions.[18] As the first protectorate, Tunisia did to some extent operate as a model of 'indirect rule' over Muslims and their religious institutions in other countries, most importantly in Morocco and, perhaps by mediated filiation, in the French mandates of Syria and Lebanon after the First World War. Even if Morocco's first resident-general, Hubert Lyautey, was loath to cooperate with colonial peers elsewhere in the Maghrib, it seems that Islam and the protectorate 'formula' were intimately intertwined.[19]

At the initiation of each phase of formal occupation—in 1830, 1881, and 1912—French authorities on the ground, mainly military officers, pledged respect for Muslims and their practices, beliefs, and institutions: a pledge honored in the breach in many, but not all, cases. Subject to military conquest for decades, Algeria suffered the most drastic legal interventions that gradually incorporated Islamic courts, madrasas, and charitable institutions into the colonial order.

This interventionist policy was also evident in the treatment of religious practices. Officials in Algeria actively interfered in the pilgrimage as it became a source of growing colonial anxiety, employing the pretext of epidemics expressed in the discourse of public health to curtail the movements of pilgrims.[20] In contrast, although the colonial authorities in Tunisia and Morocco nervously monitored the hajj and surveyed the movements of pilgrims, they refrained from overt interference for the most part.

Similarly, the expulsion of Muslim leaders and religious dignitaries became an important tactic for the colonial government in Algeria. Individual and mass expulsions of Algerians occurred, usually after the ceaseless revolts that endured until 1871. The best known exile was Amir 'Abd al-Qadir (1808–83), who led determined resistance to the invading French army between 1832 and 1847.[21] He and his large retinue were forcibly transported to France in 1847. Thousands more were deported to distant parts of the French Empire, such as New Caledonia and Guyana, which served as penal colonies. By way of contrast, expulsion was indeed routinely employed in Tunisia and Morocco, but on a smaller scale. Among the

---

[17]  James McDougall, *History and the Culture of Nationalism in Algeria* (Cambridge, 2006).

[18]  Louis Machuel, *L'enseignement public dans la régence de Tunis* (Paris, 1889). Born in Algiers in 1848, Machuel arrived before the French army in Tunisia, where he held the post of Directeur de l'Enseignement Public after 1883. Educated in Algerian religious schools as a youth, he had served as a professor of Arabic in Constantine and Oran.

[19]  Louis Chauvot, *Le Comité Méditerranéen et les organismes de la politique musulmane* (Paris, 1938), 102–4; and William A. Hoisington, *Lyautey and the French Conquest of Morocco* (New York, 1995).

[20]  Allan Christelow, *Muslim Law Courts and the French Colonial State in Algeria* (Princeton, 1985); Allan Christelow, 'The Mosque at the Edge of the Plaza: Islam in the Algerian Colonial City', *Maghreb Review*, 25/3–4 (2000), 289–319; Allan Christelow, *Algerians without Borders: The Making of a Global Frontier Society* (Gainesville, FL, 2012), 72, 84, 177; and Gregory Mann, 'What Was the *Indigénat*? The "Empire of Law" in French West Africa', *Journal of African History*, 50/3 (2009), 331–53; see also the chapters of John Slight, Eric Tagliacozzo, and Robert D. Crews in this book for policies on the hajj in the British, Dutch, and Russian empires, respectively.

[21]  See the chapter of Knut S. Vikør in this volume.

most famous examples is the leader of the jihad in the Rif War, 'Abd al-Karim (1882–1963) who, following his surrender to France in 1926, was dispatched to Réunion in the Indian Ocean.

Significantly, missionaries arrived in Algiers with the French army. While forced conversions rarely happened, missionaries were given a free hand in some regions of Algeria. One area was the Amazigh region of Kabylia in north-eastern Algeria, which attracted competing Catholic and Anglo-American missionaries but produced relatively few converts.[22] In contrast, missionaries were largely excluded from pre-colonial Moroccan territories, aside from Tangier, until the end of the nineteenth century. In Tunisia, local political elites entertained harmonious ties with Christian missions from 1840 on, although that changed drastically in 1881. Ranging from amity to hostility, relations between missions and colonial bureaucracies in all three French possessions determined the nature and scope of missionary contacts with Muslim and Jewish communities. More often than not, secular-minded French officials and settlers disapproved of muscular proselytizing among Muslims because of the alleged dangers of religious unrest.

Nevertheless, it is too simplistic to ascribe differences in policy merely to the distinction between Algeria on the one hand and Tunisia and Morocco on the other. First, despite their common status, Tunisia and Morocco differed substantially from one other. They had distinct pre-colonial state structures, notably in terms of religious legitimacy. Drawing on recognized Sharifian descent, the sultans of the 'Alawi dynasty enjoyed the title of 'Commander of the Faithful', which the Husaynid dynasty never claimed. A striking difference in modalities of rule was that the Tunisian beys were vastly more accessible to their subjects and foreign visitors or diplomats. In contrast, the sultan's sacred person rendered him unapproachable. These distinct styles of rule influenced French policy in relation to the sacral character of the Sharifian dynasty. Following the turmoil of the years leading up to 1912, Lyautey prudently kept the new Moroccan sultan in a sort of 'Babylonian captivity', away from public scrutiny to restore the dynasty's religious legitimacy and thus fortify the protectorate.[23]

Moreover, although the Muslim population may have appeared homogeneous across French North Africa, each state was subject to different demographic trends. It was certainly true that the vast majority of North Africans were Sunni Muslims of the Maliki rite. Muslim scholars from prestigious centers of Islamic law and study, notably the Zaytuna mosque and university in Tunis and the Qarawiyyin university in Fez, circulated around learned religious circles in the Maghrib (and Egypt), conferring a degree of coherence in the administration and interpretation of the shari'a, especially in urban areas.[24] Nevertheless, by the late nineteenth

---

[22] Karima Dirèche-Slimani, *Chrétiens de Kabylie: Histoire d'une communauté sans histoire: Une action missionnaire de l'Algérie coloniale* (Paris, 2004).

[23] C. R. Pennell, *Morocco since 1830: A History* (London, 2000), 12–14 and 160–1; and Mohammed Kenbib, 'The Impact of the French Conquest of Algeria', in George Joffé (ed.), *North Africa: Nation, State, and Region* (London, 1993), 34–48.

[24] Mohamed El Mansour, 'Maghribis in the Mashriq During the Modem Period: Representations of the Other Within the World of Islam', in Julia Clancy-Smith (ed.), *North Africa, Islam, and the Mediterranean World: From the Almoravids to the Algerian War* (London, 2001), 81–104.

century, the population of the Maghrib was becoming increasingly diverse. While Algeria imported the largest population of colonial settlers, pre-colonial and colonial Tunisia and Morocco also attracted numerous Europeans. Immigration to Morocco differed in nature, coming as it did many decades after the migratory fluxes to Tunisia and Algeria. Partially in consequence, colonial urbanism, so critical to Islamic institutions and communal affairs, differed significantly in Tunis and Rabat, and even more so in Algiers.[25] In addition, by the modern era, Tunisia no longer contained a highly visible Muslim 'minority' population comparable to the Amazigh (Berber) minorities in Algeria and Morocco, which were targeted by both colonial regimes in divide-and-rule strategies. In the end, the divergent demographics of the three states thus inevitably affected local policies towards Islam.

Furthermore, French colonial engagement with Islam in North Africa was affected by changes inside France itself. A rich but unexplored vein of comparison, discussed below, arises from the diverse and sundry applications of the 1905 Law of Separation across colonial North Africa. Although in metropolitan theory the separation of church and state should have been enacted uniformly, in colonial practice the application of the law differed widely. In Algeria, the Law of Separation was manipulated to despoil Muslims and Islamic institutions further, whereas in Tunisia, officials closed Catholic institutions, at least for a while, while keeping Islamic structures mainly intact.[26] Overall, French policies towards Islam differed considerably across North Africa, and even within a single possession it could vary and change significantly over time.

The following pages will examine in more detail the relationship between Islam and empire in the protectorate of Tunisia. This close study of French policy towards Islam in a single territory reveals the uneven nature of a colonial agenda replete with internal contradictions. From the reign of Ahmad Bey on, the Husaynid dynasty's relative tolerance had transformed the practice of Christianity in Tunisia into a public presence with churches, bells, social welfare structures, and street processions. This meant that coexistence between Islam and Christianity was already established before the advent of the protectorate, thereby offering good foundations for a more accommodating religious policy on the part of the colonial authorities. Nevertheless, even if Islam in Tunisia was not subjected to the same crude policies as in Algeria, there were still episodes of marked hostility towards the religion. An example of this hostility is the period after zealous imperialist Charles-Martial Lavigerie (1825–92) was named Cardinal of the Holy See of Carthage in 1882. His officials sought to expel Italian clergy and congregations and embarked on a virulent anti-Islamic campaign.[27] Yet, such episodes alternated with others when colonial thinking favored the pragmatic accommodation of Islam.

[25] Janet Abu-Lughod, *Rabat: Urban Apartheid in Morocco* (Princeton, 1980); Zeynep Çelik, *Urban Forms and Colonial Confrontations. Algiers under French Rule* (Berkeley, 1997); and articles in Zeynep Çelik, Julia Clancy-Smith, and Frances Terpak (eds), *The Walls of Algiers: Narratives of the City in Text and Image* (Los Angeles, CA, 2009).

[26] Clancy-Smith, *Mediterraneans*, 247–87.     [27] Clancy-Smith, *Mediterraneans*, 247–87.

## THE CONQUEST OF TUNISIA AND THE
## RESPONSES OF RELIGIOUS AUTHORITIES

In many respects, France's imposition of protectorate constituted a rupture with the pre-colonial Tunisian polity. Following decades of European encroachment on Tunisian autonomy, the treaty of Bardo imposed on Muhammad al-Sadiq Bey (*r*.1859–82) in 1881 made major concessions which awarded France a privileged position in commerce, diplomacy, and policing.[28] The persistence of militant opposition from tribal communities along the southern and western frontiers was manipulated by France in order to force the new ruler, ʿAli Bey (*r*.1881–1902) to sign the La Marsa Convention in 1883, thereby establishing the protectorate. France now claimed far greater powers and jurisdiction, notably over 'public works, finance, defense, and foreign affairs'.[29]

The Husaynids nevertheless theoretically retained internal sovereignty including control over the religious sphere. The bey as the head of state continued to represent the highest Muslim judicial authority, enshrined in the traditional title of *qadi al-quda* ('judge of judges'). The Tunisian religious and political class likewise maintained control over Islamic law courts, education, and pious endowments.[30] However, the significant limitations upon Husaynid authority were still viewed by many in existential terms as an attack on Islam, even if the triad of violent lengthy conquest, massive expropriations, and missionary-military collaboration that could be observed in Algeria did not mark the early years of France's rule in Tunisia.

The architect of the French protectorate in Tunisia, Paul Cambon, resident-general between 1882 and 1886, boasted that the protectorate constituted 'an instrument at once strong and meek with which, when it is necessary, we can strike without giving rise to Muslim fanaticism'.[31] Initially, French officials in Tunisia attempted to deploy Algerian precedents: civilian rule prevailed in cities and coastal regions. The south was under permanent military occupation even after rebellion was quelled. In the northern highly urbanized provinces, however, the force of tradition soon reasserted itself. Here, the system of *contrôleurs civils* replicated earlier Husaynid provincial administration which had depended on *quwwad* (governors) drawn from locally prominent, often 'clerical' families, to administer justice, collect taxes, keep the peace, and ensure the flow of essential information to the political center. Indeed, many of the same clans served France as they had the beys.[32]

The protectorate encroached on pre-colonial religious institutions, particularly those established by Prime Minister Khayr al-Din (*c*.1822–90) between 1874 and 1878. These had included major reforms in Islamic higher learning, notably the

[28] Arnold H. Green, *The Tunisian Ulama, 1873–1915: Social Structures and Response to Ideological Currents* (Leiden, 1978), 129–61, remains the classic work on the early years of the protectorate, especially its impact upon the Tunis and provincial ʿulama.
[29] Green, *Tunisian Ulama*, 129–30.    [30] Green, *Tunisian Ulama*, 129–30.
[31] Green, *Tunisian Ulama*, 135 and 143–6.
[32] Moreover, labor recruitment, structures, and policies after 1881 followed patterns of work already in place, although this legacy was often ignored in colonial studies.

reorganization of the Zaytuna mosque and university whose only competitor was al-Azhar in Cairo, and the establishment of the Sadiqi College in 1874 to educate capable Muslim administrators. At first, colonial authorities dared not tamper with these institutions. Nevertheless, many Sadiqi faculty resigned teaching positions in protest at the French conquest.[33]

The reaction of Tunisia's religious establishment—the leading 'ulama, both Maliki and Hanafi—to the occupation of the capital was ambivalent. While a few, including the director of the Sadiqi College, urged the bey to resist militantly or to refuse to sign the 1881 Bardo Treaty, most counseled restraint, realizing the futility of militant opposition. Indeed, Shaykh al-Islam Ahmad ibn al-Khuja claimed to have 'preached assiduously, both publicly and privately, patience, forbearing, non-resistance, and implicit obedience to the bey in the mosques of Tunis'.[34] It appears that the majority of the Tunis 'ulama did not call for jihad, nor did they hold the bey responsible for France's invasion. They did, however, beseech religious leaders in Cairo and elsewhere to lend moral support through public condemnations. In contrast, across the south and border regions, including Sfax, Tunisia's second-largest city, rebels looked to provincial 'ulama for leadership, support, and legitimation in opposing the French army, which triggered bombardments and street fighting. But even there, the response of the leading 'ulama was mixed.

While no large-scale emigration of religious figures and their followers to Islamic lands occurred, some urban elites chose the path of hijra, self-exile in the Mashriq, though some returned once the situation settled down. Overall, the 'ulama appeared to have been placated by the protectorate's initially cautious approach towards religious institutions. The colonial authorities were careful at first not to tamper with pre-colonial religious institutions, such as the Zaytuna mosque and university and the Sadiqi College. Muslims and Jews were assured that religious schools and legal systems would remain untouched, especially for matters of personal status.

This policy of allowing the religious sphere to remain intact was enacted in the rhetoric and representation of the protectorate. For example, after debates within the highest colonial and metropolitan circles, the French authorities decided that imams could mention the Ottoman sultan—formerly the nominal suzerain of the beylik—in the Friday sermon (*khutba*), as they had done for centuries.[35] As a part of the same strategy, Arabic was systematically used in official correspondence as a junior partner to French, in stark contrast with Algeria. Thus beylical decrees contained *hijri* dates and coins were struck with French and Arabic inscriptions.

This initial attempt to win over elite Muslim opinion was also evident in the relationship between the first French residents-general in Tunisia (Paul Cambon, Justin Massicault, Maurice Rouvier, and René Millet) and the religious elites. These residents-general were generally favorable, or at least not openly hostile,

[33] Abdurrahman Çaycı, *La question tunisienne et la politique ottomane (1881–1913)* (Istanbul, 1963), 69–85.

[34] Green, *Tunisian Ulama*, 130–5, quotation on 131.

[35] Green, *Tunisian Ulama*, 134–7.

to Islam, as well as mildly anti-clerical. Indeed, in 1885 Cambon invited Shaykh al-Islam Ahmad ibn al-Khuja to the residency to participate in New Year's festivities. When the shaykh eventually accepted—after spurning initially contacts with officials—Cambon explained to Paris the significance of this social act by 'this prominent individual' whose influence was crucial in assuring tranquility in Tunisia. Moreover, the resident-general emphasized to the foreign minister that Shaykh al-Khuja's highly public visit was the talk of Tunis, widely commented on by the Muslim population.[36]

As well as placating religious elites in Tunisia, the protectorate authorities worked hard to maintain the appearance of the bey's religious legitimacy. The colonial regime's repertoire of imperial performances after 1881 drew on those conveying Husaynid dynastic legitimacy that once again were grounded in Islam. The most essential was the *bay'a* (investiture) or oath of loyalty, a two-part act; the first was private and involved leading 'ulama and the Husaynid family, the second was public.[37] In addition, Husaynid rulers assumed religious prominence during Islamic festivals, particularly the *'Id al-Fitr* and *'Id al-Adha*. After 1883, the residents-general shared in these performances alongside the reigning beys as French consuls had done before colonialism.

In staging these displays, protectorate officials circumspectly seated the ruler on the same level as the resident-general to symbolize co-sovereignty, intending thereby to avoid what they saw as the potential for outbreaks of 'Muslim fanaticism'. During the enthronement of 'Ali Bey in October 1882, the contentious issue of the Ottoman sultan's firman of investiture arose. Diplomatic interventions by the French ambassador to the Sublime Porte quashed the firman, avoiding negative repercussions in a Tunisia still in the throes of rebellion. Cambon accompanied the new prince to the traditional palace, where the resident-general invested 'Ali Bey in the name of France, sweetening the bitter pill with the much-coveted *Légion d'Honneur*.[38] However, the fundamental question of how Tunisians read these ceremonies remains largely unknown. It seems that the beys, despite their political compromises, were viewed as legitimate Muslim rulers by most.[39]

Performances of power were directly related to socio-spatial continuities as well as colonial urban interventions. Much of the protectorate machinery was situated within Husaynid structures in the heart of the medina, whose fabric resonated with Islamic institutions and culture—and not in the emerging modern city. Dating to the early seventeenth century, the Dar al-Bey communicated religious

[36] Green, *Tunisian Ulama*, 136–7.

[37] Julia Clancy-Smith, 'Ruptures? Expatriates, Law, and Institutions in Colonial-Husaynid Tunisia, 1870–1914', in Veit Bader, Annelies Moors, and Marcel Maussen (eds), *Changes in Colonial and Post-Colonial Governance of Islam: Continuities and Ruptures* (Amsterdam, 2011), 65–87.

[38] Perkins, *History*, 39; and Charles Haddad De Paz, *Juifs et arabes au pays de Bourguiba* (Aix-en-Provence, 1977), 85, noted that after the Second World War, the bey demanded, during a well-established public ritual, that his seat be more elevated than that of the resident-general, which sparked a controversy.

[39] Kimberly Katz, 'The City of Qayrawan in the Works of Salih Suwaysi: A Place of Memory', *Journal of North African Studies*, 17/2 (2012), 257–73.

and political meanings tied to Islamic legitimacy, justice, and social order.[40] The protectorate eliminated some governing aspects of the Dar al-Bey, while retaining its executive importance. Judicial functions, the *Imprimerie Officielle* (founded by Muhammad al-Sadiq Bey in 1876), police, and the secretariat were installed there, but some older Tunisian offices remained in a 'doubling' principle.

Overall, this policy of non-interference and cooptation by the protectorate served to reinforce the notion among the Tunisian elite that the Husaynids had indeed retained a measure of internal sovereignty, thereby convincing most religious leaders to remain in their posts. Hostility continued to be palpable but resistance assumed other guises, including withdrawal and avoidance, refusal to cooperate, and obstruction.

## RELIGION AND LAW

If relations with the religious elite and the bey had improved gradually after the initial shock of conquest, there remained potential areas of tension, particularly with regard to the issues of jurisdiction. The multiplicity of legal systems within Tunisia made the assignation of jurisdiction and enforcement a complicated process, rife with political danger for the colonial power. In the following, it will be shown how the relationship between religion and law posed particular problems for the colonial authorities, partly due to this legal labyrinth, but above all as a result of the 1905 Law of Separation, which legislated for a secularization of the state.

Because of trans-Maghrib and trans-Mediterranean movements of peoples, the legal landscape in pre-colonial Tunisia included Islamic law, beylical law, capitulatory concessions, consular codes and practices, military law, and international treaty law. French courts appeared in Tunis from 1883 onwards and French law theoretically applied to all foreign residents, but only after acrimonious negotiations with other states. Granted special legal status by the much-debated 1896 Italo-French convention, Italians lived and worked according to the terms of the older 1868 Italo-Tunisian treaty. In short, the protectorate inherited a number of legal legacies, above all the 'poisoned chalice' of pre-colonial settlement and an exceedingly tangled regime (or regimes) of legal pluralism, both of which greatly impacted policies toward Islamic institutions, the 'ulama overseeing those institutions, and ordinary Muslims and Jews.[41]

---

[40] Faiza Matri, *Tunis sous le protectorat: Histoire de la conservation du patrimoine architectural et urbain de la médina* (Tunis, 2008), 142–64.

[41] Alain Messaoudi, 'Être Algérien en Tunisie (1830–1962): La construction d'une catégorie nationale', *Correspondances*, 54 (1999), 10–14. When viewed from below, the protectorate's legal system remained multicentric in the extreme, particularly when it came to 'love with the wrong person'. Colonial officials constantly quarreled over what status Algerian Muslims resident in Tunisia merited or if marriage between a Tunisian Jew, who was also a beylical subject, and an Italian or Algerian Jew could be legally recognized. Lauren Benton, *Law and Colonial Cultures: Legal Regimes in World History, 1400–1900* (Cambridge, 2002) traces the historical movement from truly plural legal regimes to state-dominated legal orders characteristic of colonial states. While provocative, this model needs to

Despite initial claims to be preserving the integrity of the Islamic legal system, it is clear that over time, more and more Tunisians were brought within the jurisdiction of the French courts. This was particularly fraught in relation to land ownership, as the protectorate began circumscribing systematically the Islamic legal establishment's jurisdiction in litigation over land and other coveted resources.[42]

This hollowing out of religious prerogatives by the colonial state was accompanied by changes in both Tunisia and France. Judged by colonial lobbies as 'too well disposed toward Islam', the resident-general Réné Millet lost his post in 1900 because of his desire to protect Tunisian religious and property rights in order to avoid creating another Algeria.[43] In 1901, a new resident-general, Stephen Pichon (1857–1933) began to wage battle against three declared enemies: Islam and Muslims, the Catholic Church, and the Italians.[44] The protectorate even began meddling in the critical matter of succession to the Husaynid throne. By then, two interdependent processes became manifest. The uneasy cooperation between colonial officials and Tunisian political and religious elites, notably the Tunis 'ulama who had served as intermediaries for Muslim constituencies, frayed, giving way to antagonism and political protests; and it became apparent that the protectorate could no longer maintain the fiction of simultaneously advancing the cause of settler colonialism while protecting the interests of Tunisians. The breakdown in relations worsened existing tensions between French colonial rule and the Islamic legal system. In the end, this tense situation formed the backdrop to a series of laws enacted in Paris dissolving the pact between church and state dating to 1801. The 1901 Law of Associations declared Catholic congregations illegal and the 1905 Law of Separation ended state recognition of and funding for religious entities. Catholic schools in France were closed and their properties expropriated.[45] When the laws were applied in the colonies, local outcomes varied due to the persistence of older contracts and bargains. In Tunisia, protectorate officials had to sort out Church property deeds dating from the pre-colonial era. This situation was complicated by the well-established Catholic missionary presence for which the beys had acted as a benevolent patrons and landlords from the 1840s onwards. The

---

be juxtaposed with closely historicized ethnographic case studies because in certain, or perhaps many, instances colonial states failed or perhaps chose not to dismantle cultures of legal pluralism, see Sarah Stein, 'Protected Persons? The Baghdadi Jewish Diaspora, the British State, and the Persistence of Empire', *American Historical Review*, 116/1 (2011), 80–108.

[42] Nouraddine Sraïeb, *Le Collège Sadiki de Tunis, 1875–1956: Enseignement et nationalisme* (Tunis, 1990).

[43] Quoted in Perkins, *Tunisia*, 56–7; and Julia Clancy-Smith, 'L'école rue du pacha, Tunis: L'enseignement de la femme arabe et la plus grande France, *c.*1900–1914', *Clio: Histoire, femmes et sociétés*, 12 (2000), 33–55.

[44] Pichon espoused radical Left politics and was a member of the Republican Socialist Alliance, which explains his anti-clerical position. Prior to his 1901 nomination as resident-general of Tunisia, he had served as a French diplomat in China during the Boxer rebellion (1898–1901).

[45] Françoise Rochefort, *Le pouvoir du genre: Laïcités et religions 1905–2005* (Toulouse, 2007); Sarah S. Curtis, *Educating the Faithful: Religion, Schooling, and Society in Nineteenth-Century France* (DeKalb, IL, 2000); Sarah S. Curtis, *Civilizing Habits: Women Missionaries and the Revival of the French Empire* (Oxford, 2011); and J. P. Daughton, *An Empire Divided: Religion, Republicanism, and the Making of French Colonialism, 1880–1914* (Oxford, 2006).

Husaynid dynasty owned or held in various ways most of the prime real estate, especially in the Tunis region.[46] Many of the buildings occupied by Catholic or Protestant missionaries had been loans or leases from the beys. For example, the French Catholic Sisters of Saint-Joseph arrived in Tunisia in 1840 (after the bishop of Algiers had expelled them from Algeria), where they benefited greatly from Husaynid patronage for buildings needed to house medical, social welfare, and educational works.[47] In a sense, Catholic congregations had become protégés of a Muslim dynasty, a situation which would vastly complicate disestablishment after 1905.[48]

France's Law of Separation raised not only a legal mare's nest but also the delicate issue of public manifestations of faith—whether Islam or Christianity. The most important annual Catholic events were Corpus Christi devotions and the Sicilian processions in honor of the Virgin of Trapani, both celebrated with elaborate street pageants; even some Muslims participated in the Trapani parade, which took place in every city or town with a Sicilian community. In the words of an eyewitness:

> The annual procession to honor of Our Lady of Trapani in La Goulette is not the sort where the faithful walk in rows, chanting prayers or reciting the rosary. Instead a large statue of the Virgin posed on a wooden stretcher is carried through the streets by a dozen men who take turns. And all around the Virgin, a diverse crowd presses, seeking to touch the statue either with hands or with pieces of cloth. Mixed in this crowd are veiled Muslim women who have also come to pray to the Madonna.[49]

In 1905, Pichon implemented the Law of Separation by refusing to attend Sunday mass at the cathedral, a tradition that had long symbolized the alliance between religion and empire. Corpus Christi processions, authorized by the Husaynid beys before 1881, were banned. Paradoxically the boisterous Sicilian festivities held on August 15 were permitted, something that French clergy found difficult to take. In effect, Pichon had applied the laws of disestablishment selectively for fear of stirring up local Sicilian resentment.[50]

Moreover, despite disestablishment, the Sufi orders (*turuq* or *confréries*) were allowed to process through the streets of Tunis as they had done for centuries. This was all the more remarkable in an era when French imperial (and European) intelligence forces were consumed by visions of subversive political associations in the guise of the Islamic brotherhoods. Protectorate authorities explained away the contradiction with the old saw of not wanting to excite Muslim fanaticism, the same excuse deployed for the Sicilians. In the end, the Tunisian Sufis had never been attacked to the same degree as the brotherhoods in Algeria.

---

[46] Rochefort, *Le Pouvoir du genre*; Curtis, *Educating the Faithful*; and Curtis, *Civilizing Habits*; Daughton, *An Empire Divided*.

[47] Currently, the Sidi Saber building, leased by Ahmad Bey to the Catholic sisters in 1842, houses the library and records of the Catholic diocese of Tunis.

[48] Clancy-Smith, *Mediterraneans*, 247–87.

[49] Francois Dornier, *La vie des catholiques en Tunisie au fil des jours* (Tunis, 2000), 217.

[50] Dornier, *La vie des catholiques en Tunisie au fil des jours*, 52.

But one wonders about processions in honor of the Virgin of Trapani. When the cortege passed in the streets, Muslims showed respect by standing at attention—did officials not want to hurt local Muslim sensibilities regarding veneration for Mariam?[51] Protectorate officials continued to take part in Husaynid ceremonies tied to the practice of Islam, for example, visiting high-ranking 'ulama and receiving the heads of the guilds (*umana'*) during holy days; and they now participated in new educational events, such as visiting the School for Muslim Girls during commencement celebrations.[52]

Therefore it is clear that despite the promulgation in Tunisia of the 1905 Law of Separation, the colonial state applied disestablishment selectively in order to avoid a potentially explosive confrontation with its Muslim subjects. Yet, such a conflict could not be postponed indefinitely, as was to become evident in the linked issue of the appropriation of religious resources, whether by the colonial state or by private companies.

## ISLAM, WAQF PROPERTY, AND COLONIAL EXPROPRIATION

Empire represents an inherently exploitative enterprise with an arsenal of means for expropriating resources, both human and natural. Particularly with respect to the fate of religious waqf endowments, this could prove to be an area of religious tension within the colonial system. Colonial officials were well aware of the potential difficulties raised by expropriation of property, and so the interests of Muslims could be taken into account as a pragmatic measure to ensure the continuing loyalty of colonial subjects.

Most work on the economic dimensions of colonial rule in the Maghrib has concentrated on the seizure of collectively held tribal lands, often as punishment for rebellion, or the legally manipulated 'transfer' of Islamic endowments (habus or waqf) to serve the interests of newly arrived settlers. However, the 'legal' acquisition of agricultural land predated the protectorate. The 1861 constitution, although contested by many Tunisians as a grave violation of the shari'a, theoretically conferred property rights on some foreigners, mainly bourgeois European investors enjoying ties to local land-holding elites. Large-scale 'legal transfers' of land from Tunisian owners, usufruct holders, or tenant farmers, to settlers occurred around or after the turn of the century. As one historian argued:

> One of the most striking aspects of French policy in the domain of agriculture was the colonial rapacity for public and private habus lands... by undermining the habus administration, Protectorate officials struck a blow at the very symbol of Tunisian

[51] Author's interview with Madame Hasiba Agha, Carthage, Tunisia, 18 June 2009.
[52] Mohamed El Aziz Ben Achour, *Catégories de la société tunisoise dans la deuxième moitié du XIXème siècle* (Tunis, 1989), 203.

Islam, while removing from the *fallah* (peasant) the most productive farms in the country.[53]

Furthermore, it is clear that once protectorate authorities had, with great difficulty, sorted out the competing legal systems in Tunisia, they targeted Islamic courts in particular because 'Sharia magistrates frequently used their knowledge of Islamic law to frustrate European land developers and speculators'.[54] This was paralleled by an attack on both Italian and Tunisian property rights. Obsessions with the growing Italian farming community induced a dramatic shift in policies towards collectively held lands and Islamic endowments after 1900. To offset Italian agriculture, settler colonization was vigorously promoted by Paris, although big French landowners already established in Tunisia proved unenthusiastic about campaigns to lure fellow citizens across the sea. The influx of French farmers enjoying hefty subsidies brought unbearable pressures to bear on peasant and tribal producers to alienate or abandon properties, notably in grain-growing regions and the olive-producing Sahil, where indebtedness to absentee urban landholders was rampant. This in turn sparked violence against European estates, pauperization, and rural-to-urban peasant migrations which fueled the Tunisian anti-colonial movement by the First World War.[55]

The same tension was also evident in another sphere of colonial society: education. In fact, the issue of education for Muslims followed a similar dynamic to the conflicts over the law courts and the colonial economy: initial attempts to accommodate Muslim opinion could founder in the face of private interests and of a conflicted colonial attitude towards Islam.


## ISLAM AND EDUCATION


Colonial educators, such as Louis Machuel, greatly influenced early protectorate policies. According to Machuel, there existed in Tunisia 'a considerable intellectual life' whose pillars were the Zaytuna mosque and university and the Sadiqi College in which Tunisian Muslims (and those from other countries) rightfully 'took great pride'. Machuel argued, 'let us take care to avoid committing the same errors in Tunisia as were made in Algeria'.[56] Machuel did, however, regularize the statutes of the Sadiqi through a beylical decree issued in January 1886, which expanded pre-colonial regulations.

---

[53] Béchir Yazidi, *La politique coloniale et la domaine de l'état en Tunisie de 1881 jusqu'à la crise des années trente* (Tunis, 2005), 233.

[54] Yazidi, *La politique coloniale et la domaine de l'état en Tunisie*, 143–4 and 196–9; and Perkins, *History*, 47–61.

[55] Mohamed Ali Habachi, *Les Sahéliens: L'histoire: Documents inédits, archives beylicales et coloniales, 1574–1957* (Tunis, 2009), 110–49; and Yazidi, *La politique coloniale*, 233–66.

[56] Louis Machuel, 'L'Enseignement public en Tunisie', *Revue pédagogique* (nouvelle série), 7 (July–December 1885), 46–9, quotation on 46; and also Noureddine Sraieb, 'L'idéologie de l'école en Tunisie coloniale (1881-1945)', *Revue du monde musulman et de la Méditerranée*, 68–69 (1993), 239–54.

Prior to colonial rule, most students in Tunisia would have attended either a *kuttab* (Qur'anic primary school) or a Jewish institution. In addition, some Catholic, secular irredentist Italian, and French-Jewish (Alliance Israélite Universelle) schools had been established in the pre-colonial era. Traditionally, formal Islamic education was reserved for boys who memorized the Qur'an. The most gifted were accepted to the Zaytuna mosque-university for advanced studies.

Under Louis Machuel, the Directorate of Public Instruction created a more or less unified elementary school system for French and European nationals, but refrained from intervening too overtly in Muslim or Jewish schooling, preferring to oversee them from a distance and promote select reforms whose aim was gradual secularization.[57] A parallel and competing system of 'Franco-Arab' primary schools was set up for Muslim and Jewish Tunisians who, upon graduation, might enroll in French schools, including the prestigious Lycée Carnot where Bourguiba studied. An *école normale*, the Collège Alaoui founded in 1884 to train Muslim instructors for Franco-Arab schools, also enrolled the children of settlers and colonial officials. One of Machuel's goals in educating Muslims and Jews was to foster amicable relations between French and Tunisians in order to checkmate the Italians.[58] In 1908, Tunisian educators established a system for creating a style of 'reformed *kuttab*' which would combine religious studies with modern curriculum.

Muslims, like colonialists, might oppose colonial education. This was especially true in the provinces, such as the Qur'an instructor in Beja who declared his classroom off limits to pupils attending the local Franco-Arab institution. Nevertheless, schooling in the provinces and the *kuttab* sometimes led to foreign study. The noted Tunisian Orientalist scholar, Hasan 'Abd al-Wahhab (1884–1968), who was educated at a Qur'anic school in Mahdiya, entered the Sadiqi in 1899, and subsequently traveled to Paris, where he enrolled in 1902 in the Institut d'études politiques.[59]

By the eve of the First World War, Muslim intellectuals attended scholarly gatherings in Algiers or crossed the Mediterranean to address French audiences directly about their aspirations and grievances and solicit international support. This was manifest during the 1905 Congress of Orientalists in Algeria, which Hasan 'Abd al-Wahhab attended, the 1908 Congrès de l'Afrique du Nord in Paris, and the Colonial Congress held in Marseille in 1906, where the major complaint leveled

---

[57] Perkins, *Tunisia*, 61–70, quotation on 62; and Noureddine Sraieb, 'L'Idéologie de l'école en Tunisie coloniale', 239–54.

[58] A. Sebaut, *Dictionnaire de la legislation tunisienne* (Tunis, 1888), 157–9; Perkins, *History*, 61–4; and Julia Clancy-Smith, 'Algeria as *mère-patrie*: Algerian "Expatriates" in Pre-Colonial Tunisia', in Patricia Lorcin (ed.), *Identity, Memory and Nostalgia: France and Algeria, 1800–2000* (Syracuse, NY, 2006), 3–17; and Nishiyama Noriyuki, 'Les civilisés ont-ils besoin d'apprendre la langue des indigènes? La politique linguistique éducative de l'arabe chez Louis Machuel dans la Tunisie sous le protectorat français à la fin du XIXe siècle', *Revue japonaise de didactique du français*, 2/2 (2007), 23–42.

[59] Green, *Tunisian Ulama*, 158; Perkins, *Tunisia*, 62–63; and Sadok Zmerli, *Les figures tunisiennes* (Tunis, 1993), 133–40. A handful of Muslim girls in Tunis attended either Catholic missionary or French schools; the rest were channeled into technical education, particularly handicraft establishments or *ouvroirs*.

against the protectorate centered on the unmet demand for modern schooling for Muslim children that respected Islamic norms and culture.[60]

The mixed system of education in Tunisia demonstrates how colonial officials and advocates were divided on the issue of education for Muslims. Torn between the desire to create a pro-French Muslim elite and the fear of breeding a nationalist vanguard, opinions on educational policy differed widely. The polemic on this issue continued into the period after the First World War, when the Church in Tunisia backed by the clerical authorities in France and Rome assumed a much more muscular stance towards Islam.

## THE 1930 EUCHARISTIC CONGRESS AND THE END OF ACCOMMODATION

During the inter-war period, the protectorate faced multiple intersecting threats. In addition to entrenched worries over 'Muslim fanaticism' and the Italians, other menaces to colonial rule arose: socialism, communism, and fascism as well as nationalism, frequently intertwined with militant syndicalism.[61] In 1927, the Association des Etudiants Musulmans Nord-Africains formed in Paris, whose aspirations for independence sharpened due to contacts with the French Left.[62] That same year, Bourguiba left the French capital for Tunis with a newly minted law degree and began writing for the nationalist newspaper, *La Voix tunisienne*, associated with the Confédération Général des Travailleurs Tunisiens, created in 1924 and the second-oldest native labor union in Africa. Thus new and old, internal and international, fears haunted the colonial mind and were fully shared by the Church.

In 1922, the White Father Monsignor Lemaître, a disciple of Lavigerie's style of confrontational Catholicism, was appointed archbishop of Carthage. A soldier-priest who had served as chaplain to native troops during the First World War as well as a brigadier general in the reserves, in 1925 he provocatively erected a statue of Cardinal Lavigerie 'defiantly facing the medina of Tunis at the Porte de France'.[63] Under him, the Catholic presence rapidly expanded. New places of worship were constructed, vocations for the priesthood strongly promoted, and new religious orders arrived. Significantly, Lemaître ordered all missionary schools to reopen their doors immediately.[64] Clearly, Tunisia represented a place where the

---

[60] Perkins, *History*, 68–9; and Sraieb, 'L'Idéologie', 245–8.

[61] Martin Thomas, *Empires of Intelligence: Security Services and Colonial Disorder after 1914* (Berkeley, 2008), 90–106, quotation 90; and Jennifer Anne Boittin, *Colonial Metropolis: The Urban Grounds of Anti-Imperialism and Feminism in Interwar Paris* (Lincoln, NE, 2010), xiii.

[62] Clement H. Moore and Arlie R. Hochschild, 'Student Unions in North African Politics', *Daedalus*, 97/1 (1968), 21–50.

[63] Jacques Berque, *French North Africa: The Maghrib Between Two World Wars*, trans. Jean Stewart (London, 1967), 220. The work was originally published as *Le Maghreb entre deux guerres* (Paris, 1962).

[64] Dornier, *La Vie*.

wrongs of anti-clericalism could be righted, disestablishment nullified, and battle waged against an array of enemies. Reprising a well-worn dictum, *L'Afrique française* asserted that 'anti-clericalism is not for export'.[65]

Envisioned as a matching pair of colonial commemorations, significant differences nonetheless existed between the centenary celebrations of French Algeria and the 1930 Congress in Tunis. The former constituted more a grandiose display of imperial self-congratulation and tourist promotion than a celebration of Christianity in French North Africa, but religion was much less in evidence than in Tunisia.[66] The Carthage pilgrimage enjoyed the full support of Gaston Doumergue, president of France between 1924 and 1931, the only Protestant to hold that office, and of François Manceron, resident-general from 1929 until 1933. Both Paris and Tunis appeared comfortable with patronizing an event that violated the 1905 law.

Algerian writer and anti-Islamic polemicist Louis Bertrand had already in 1914 proposed Carthage for a future Congress in his *Le sens de l'ennemi*, where he stated that 'we are at home in Carthage where we have nothing to fear from Islamic susceptibilities'.[67] Preparations had begun in earnest three years prior to the Congress, when Pope Pius XI chose the site for the event.[68] For the Congress itself, a guidebook of over one hundred pages was published in Tunis and sold to delegates in advance. Profit considerations were also at work, as local French entrepreneurs anticipated financial windfalls from throngs of religious tourists.[69]

A major challenge was lodging the thousands of Catholics who came in delegations from Europe and the Americas. There was even a 'section orientale' comprised of Armenian, Syriac, and Melkite Catholics, then under French rule in the mandates of Syria and Lebanon. To house the multitude, Tunis families were implored to welcome the pilgrims. The shaykh of the municipality and other urban officials inventoried Muslim households willing to take in pilgrims. The princesses of the Husaynid family offered to put up visitors, both ordinary people and prelates, in their seaside palaces. One of the princes gave over his family residence and six Mediterranean villas to the members of the organizing committee. Tunisian Jews of means offered the same hospitality. The names of Muslim notables, mostly from old Tunis families, listed on various planning committees hints at feverish behind-the-scenes 'arm-twisting' by protectorate authorities. Both Shaykh al-Islam Sidi Ahmad Bayram and Sidi Tahar ibn al-'Ashur, the *bash mufti* (chief mufti), sat on such committees.[70]

---

[65] *L'Afrique française*, 47/4 (April 1937), 231.

[66] Indeed, the *Almanach illustré du 'Petit Parisien'* (Paris, 1930), carried a piece emblematic of Centenary promotion that vaunted the 'seductive nature of Algeria', secular and sensual; clearly not the religious tourism organized at the same time in Tunisia.

[67] Anonymous, *Carthage 1930: Actes et documents* (Tunis, 1930), 3–4.

[68] *Livre-guide à l'usage des congressistes* (Carthage, 7–11 May 1930) (Secrétariat du Congrès, Tunis); and Mahjoubi, 'Le Congrès'.

[69] Mahjoubi, 'Le Congrès', 111–13.

[70] Anonymous, *Carthage 1930*, 37–8 and 69–70; and *Livre-guide*, 15–22.

**Fig. 5** The Eucharistic Congress in Carthage, Tunisia, 1930 (Bettmann/Corbis).

The Congress made a serious ecumenical effort to involve Maltese and Italians in various rituals, even allowing the latter their own 'national section'. It drew upon archaeological excavations in Carthage carried out for several decades by the White Fathers that had brought to light buried Roman and Byzantine basilicas as well as the shrines of African Christian martyrs. Indeed, martyrdom was a major theme. In addition to solemn masses, processions in Tunis and Carthage, liturgical musical events, and an abundance of indulgences, posters went up across Tunis announcing that the crusades had returned. Thousands of European children, both residents and foreign pilgrims, were dressed in white robes emblazoned with large crosses (Fig. 5). Then during his official sermon, with the beylical family and Muslim dignitaries in the audience, papal legate Cardinal Lépicier characterized Islam in the Maghrib as 'fourteen centuries of ruin and death'.[71]

The response was swift and unequivocal. Students at the Zaytuna University and the Sadiqi College boycotted classes, taking to the streets. Many were arrested and brought before French magistrates. From Paris, the students in the Association des Etudiants Musulmans Nord-Africains dispatched telegrams denouncing the crusade against Islam. Petitions circulated throughout the country and the signatories published open letters of protest in the press. The outrage generated by the

---

[71] Anonymous, *Carthage 1930*, 192 has a photo of the child crusaders; Berque, *North Africa*, 220–1; Charles Diehl, *Les découvertes de l'archéologie française en Algérie et Tunisie* (Paris, 1982); and Mahjoubi, 'Le Congrès', quotation on 118.

Congress resulted in a drastic reorientation of older political alliances or compromises. One wing of the Tunisian 'ulama that had remained 'neutral' or accommodated in the protectorate now openly joined with the nationalist anti-colonial movement. Some of the old notables of Tunis, whose reputations were irrevocably tied to the Congress, were discredited after their names appeared in French and Arabic newspapers. They were soon shoved aside by a new generation of men from the Sahil, many of whom, like Bourguiba, had been educated in religious and Franco-Arab schools.[72]

Five days after the closure of the Congress, the Berber Dahir was proclaimed in Morocco, which further confirmed suspicions held by North African Muslims that Islam was under siege. The timing of the 1930 celebration could not have been more cruel. It followed years of drought, failing harvests, and massive land transfers to French colonists to compete with Italian agricultural investments. With the Great Depression, agrarian disaster and famine ravaged the country. Three years after the Congress, the nationalists and Neo-Dustur Party demanded total independence.[73]

For Resident-General Manceron and the archbishop of Carthage, the Eucharistic Congress proved professionally disastrous. The former was sacked in 1933 and replaced by Marcel Peyrouton. In August that year, the Algiers publication *L'Africain hebdomadaire illustré* noted that: 'Manceron has been powerless to put an end to fanatic nationalist agitation which for several years has shaken Tunisia. For months the Tunisians have dared to attack France and its representatives without fear of consequences.'[74] Monsignor Lemaître's maladroit international celebration of the Eucharist dismayed the Vatican; the cardinal's hat, that he had long coveted, would never be his.

Another set of relationships between Catholics and Muslims emerged from the crucible of disestablishment and the Eucharistic Congress, nurturing the anti-colonial movement during the inter-war period. In 1932, the White Fathers transformed the Centre d'Études Arabes, a school founded in 1926 to teach Arabic to missionaries, into something new. The Institut des Belles Lettres Arabes was situated near the casbah in the upper medina, where it still remains today. Dedicated to intellectual and artistic exchanges in French and Arabic, the Institut taught the history, cultures, languages, and folklore of Tunisia and North Africa for the first time. Indeed, its director, Père André Demeerseman, courageously opposed the Eucharistic Congress in a letter addressed to the archbishop in 1930. Several years later, he stated in writing that 'the hour has come for (France) to allow the Tunisian

---

[72] Mahjoubi, 'Le Congrès', 121–32.

[73] In May 1931, Habib Bourguiba published a series of articles on famine in *La Voix du Tunisien*, the organ of the nationalist party, in which he invoked international audiences interested in the 'Tunisian problem'—namely, the International Women's League for Peace, and the League of Human Rights—making a direct link between human rights and food security, see *Habib Bourguiba: Articles de presse, 1929–1934* (Tunis, 1967), 62–80.

[74] Anonymous,'La Tunisie sous l'égide de la France', *L'Africain hebdomadaire illustré* (27 August 1933), 2.

people to take destiny into their own hands', which earned him vicious attacks in the colonial press for being a Tunisian nationalist, which, in a sense, he was.[75]

A last-ditch effort was made in 1934 to develop a rational, uniform policy for France's Mediterranean empire, which by then governed Muslims from Syria to Morocco and West Africa. Organized in Paris, the Haut Comité Méditerranéen et de l'Afrique du Nord's membership roll constituted a 'who's who' of high-ranking colonial officials, ministers, and intellectuals. In 1935, the Haut Comité drew up security measures designed to suppress dissent, survey the native population, monitor the activities of North African students in French universities, curb freedom of the press in Algeria, undermine the trade unions (notably the Tunisian CGTT), forcibly transport Tunisian activists to French colonies, expel outside agitators from North Africa, and apply penal laws much more harshly to quell political crimes.[76] Devised to counter the after-shocks of the Tunisian Eucharistic Congress, the Moroccan Berber Dahir, and the Algerian Centenary, these measures, advanced from an assumed position of strength, demonstrated instead imperial frailty, above all, in the realm of religion and empire.


CONCLUSION

The previous pages have explored some of the ways in which colonial regimes in North Africa governed, legislated, and accommodated Islam and Muslims. Its approach illuminates the tortured—as imbricated—relationships between protectorate authorities, Muslims, missionaries, the Catholic Church in Europe and the colonies, and non-French communities. Together, triangulation and ethnography reveal that policies, postures, and laws aimed at Islam and Muslims were shaped to no small degree by the 'expatriate' non-Muslims as well as by ancient, bitter quarrels in France between church and state that eventually resonated in colonial possessions across the globe.

Tunisia offers a rich terrain for studying modern empire and religion in the *longue durée* because of the torque of the pre-colonial past with its unpredictable countervailing forces that circumscribed what officials could do, thereby forging the colonial state itself and, inevitably, resistance. As a method, triangulation supports the chapter's argument that colonial governance must take into account non-Muslims as well as the time before colonialism. The persistence of older bargains and pacts concluded between the Husaynid dynasty, resident Italians, and Catholic missionaries meant that policies for Muslim subjects entailed calculations regarding these others.

An ethnographic excavation of Islam and empire in the Tunisian protectorate reveals the dynamic and logic of struggles over courts, property, schools, and

---

[75] Dornier, *La vie*, 551. Born in Belgium, André Demeerseman (1901–93) began his missionary studies at the White Father novitiate in Maison Carrée in 1922, was sent to Carthage in 1927, and ordained in 1928.

[76] Hoisington, 'France and Islam', 80.

processions. As conflict zones, these disputed places were partially the product of pre-colonial migratory processes and politically astute dynastic patronage within the larger envelope of Tunisia's positioning in the Mediterranean. Outcomes were not always determined by the straightforward dialectic of race and religion. The Muslim Husaynid dynasty provided patronage and shelter for Catholic religious orders, while the colonial state turned on and attacked the church after disestablishment. Nevertheless, the protectorate was ultimately caught in the cleft stick of affirming and maintaining European superiority while simultaneously placating the religious sensibilities of its colonial subjects. The débâcle of the 1930 Eucharistic Congress is therefore emblematic of this inherent tension within the colonial project. Ironically, the authorities had by that time succeeded to a degree in their aim of suborning the Tunisian religious hierarchy. It was to be the graduates of the Franco-Arab schools—intended by the French to be a nursery of a pliant Muslim elite—who seized the initiative, militated against colonial rule, and went on to become the chief beneficiaries of the post-independence state.

# 5

# Islam and Imperialism in East Africa

*Felicitas Becker*

## INTRODUCTION

Both 'Islam' and 'empire' are, when applied to a particular time and place, deceptively coherent terms. In nineteenth- and twentieth-century East Africa, Islam both underpinned and opposed, profited and suffered from imperialism, as the region was shaped by different forms of imperialism and of Islam. Until very late in the nineteenth century, the dominant imperial frontier in the region was that of a Muslim power, the sultanate of Zanzibar, whose elites invoked their Islamic allegiance as a justification for their rule.[1] On the Swahili coast, the Bu Saidi sultanate of Zanzibar with its Omani roots was only the last in a succession of hegemons from across the sea that had included other Arab dynasties as well as the Portuguese.[2] When European imperialism superseded the Zanzibari power from 1885, the relationship between European (Christian) rulers and now-dependent Muslim ones became strongly hierarchical, but still remained ambivalent. Some Europeans appreciated Muslims' 'half-civilized' ways (*Halbkultur*), many found them somewhat more familiar than the newly defeated African empire-builders of the mainland such as Mkwawa of Iringa (*d.*1898) with their African religions, and most wanted to instrumentalize Islamic institutions in the pursuit of social control.

The internal diversity of Islam in East Africa, already evident at the onset of European rule, increased further in the colonial period. While the old Islamic congregations on the Swahili coast followed the Shafi'i legal school, the nineteenth-century immigrants from Oman were overwhelmingly Ibadhi. Many of the South Asian Muslims, important in the produce trade and in banking, were Shi'a. Moreover, the late nineteenth century saw the spread of various branches of the Shadhili and Qadiri Sufi orders.[3] These doctrinal and ritual differences can be mapped, albeit imperfectly, onto social ones. The established patricians of the Swahili towns, known as *waungwana*, were struggling to assert their leadership

---

[1] On this period in general, see John Iliffe, *A Modern History of Tanganyika* (Cambridge, 1979).
[2] Randall Pouwels, *Horn and Crescent: Cultural Change and Traditional Islam on the East African Coast, 800–1900* (Cambridge, 1987).
[3] B. G. Martin, *Muslim Brotherhoods in Nineteenth-Century Africa* (Cambridge, 2003).

against both aristocratic Omani immigrants and the rising Sufi leadership, whose rituals, in particular the ecstatic forms of *dhikr* some of them practiced, attracted many marginal, struggling townspeople.[4] Later, these Sufi communities provided resources for the spread of Islam beyond the coastal belt under imperial rule, where it again became a factor in the renegotiation of social relationships.[5]

The intensity of this dialogue within coastal society and with the African mainland helps explain the absence of a concerted response, in the name of Islam, to imperial encroachment. But it was not just coastal Islam that was 'pacific', but rather coastal society, which had long thrived on minimizing conflict with both African mainlanders and overseas contacts in the pursuit of exchange.[6] The apparent contrast between East Africa and both North and West Africa, where armed resistance to European rule under the banner of Islam occurred frequently, therefore does not point to an explicitly different interpretation of legal rules on jihad or Muslim–Christian relations.[7] Rather, it is indicative of the way Islam in East Africa was interwoven with a long-standing practice of exchange in the Indian Ocean setting.[8] These antecedents combined with the social tensions among the region's Muslims to ensure that the European imperial challenge did not unite them. In fact, an art form that has been described as intrinsically Islamic, Swahili poetry, produced some of the most striking evidence of discord in the face of colonization.[9]

Disunity among the Europeans present in the region in the run-up to colonialism meant that European intentions and capacities were hard to gauge for East Africans until they took formal control in 1884–90. After 1890, divisions were clear. Germany had obtained 'German East Africa', today's mainland Tanzania. Britain controlled the Uganda Protectorate and Kenya Colony, while the Zanzibar archipelago (now part of Tanzania) and the coastal strip of Kenya formed a British protectorate under the sultan of Zanzibar. But representatives of European imperial interests had been on the scene for some decades before then, expressing widely divergent stances on Islam. There were French, German, and British missionaries exasperated by Muslim 'competition' or intransigence; successive British consuls highly critical of slavery and slave trading; European trading firms that dealt

---

[4] Often glossed by Swahili-speakers as 'mentioning' or 'remembering' the name of God, the ecstatic *dhikr* practices that spread in the late nineteenth century focused on deep-breathing exercises whose rasping sound prompted distractors to describe this as a 'worship of coughing'. Their main proponent, Shaykh Uways al-Barawi, claimed to have learned them at the focal sites of the Qadiriyya in Iraq, see Martin, *Muslim Brotherhoods*, 152–76.

[5] Jonathon Glassman, *Feasts and Riot: Revelry, Rebellion and Popular Consciousness on the Swahili Coast, 1856–88* (Oxford, 1995); and Felicitas Becker, *Becoming Muslim in Mainland Tanzania, 1880–2000* (Oxford, 2008).

[6] 'Pacific' is Iliffe's term, see Iliffe, *Modern History*, 95; see also Pouwells, *Horn and Crescent*; and James de Vere Allen, *Swahili Origins: Swahili Culture and the Shungwaya Phenomenon* (Oxford, 1993).

[7] On West Africa, see Christopher Harrison, *France and Islam in West Africa, 1860–1960* (Cambridge, 1988). On North Africa, see Julia Clancy-Smith, *Rebel and Saint: Muslim Notables, Populist Protest, Colonial Encounters (Algeria and Tunisia, 1800–1904)* (Berkeley, 1994).

[8] For the Indian Ocean setting, see Edward Alpers, *East Africa and the Indian Ocean* (Princeton, 2009).

[9] Gudrun Miehe, Katrin Bromber, Said Khamis, and Ralf Grsserhode (eds), *Kala Shairi: German East Africa in Swahili Poems* (Cologne, 2002).

complacently in products implicated in slave trading and slavery; and, imperial travelers whose attitudes to Islam ranged from detached interest to vociferous contempt.[10] The disunity lived on in the diversity of opinions concerning how best to relate to Islam that prevailed among Europeans in the early colonial period. Colonial officialdom, missionaries, and government experts debated the merits and problems of Islamic influence without getting close to consensus. In German East Africa, in particular, missionaries were much exercised about the involvement of Muslims in local administration and government schools.[11]

After 1917, when all of East Africa became British, the pattern of interaction and accommodation between Muslim representatives and colonial authorities became more routinized and less contentious. At the same time, British rule presided over an expansion of Islam that saw it become the predominant religion in parts of the countryside hitherto dominated by African religions. Yet this expansion, far from being a function of the presence of Muslim elites, was allied with a communalist ethos that contrasted starkly with Islam's pre-colonial role in elaborating social hierarchies. The old Muslim towns on the coast, meanwhile, changed from pivots of commercial and cultural exchange into margins of territorial states seeking their economic well-being in peasant commodity production.[12] Ironically, accommodation with British rule mitigated the reality of social and political displacement for the old Muslim milieus of the coast. Decolonization would force them to confront the new realities and set the scene for uneasy accommodation into post-colonial polities and eventually the rise of political discontent and 'Islamism' in East Africa.[13]

The following pages explore further the diverse mutual perceptions of East African Muslims and European imperialists between *c.*1870 and the First World War. The chapter then examines the limited official interest in East African Islam during the inter-war period, and how British colonial administrations, their frequent cooperation with Christian missions notwithstanding, came to preside over a massive expansion of Muslim congregations in East Africa during this period.

[10] The diversity of opinion on different groups of Europeans is captured in Glassman, *Feasts and Riot*. For contemptuous treatment of East African Islam, see Richard Burton's writings, e.g. *Zanzibar: City, Island and Coast* (London, 1872); for more sympathetic observations on East African society at large, see Franz Stuhlmann, *Handwerk und Industrie in Ostafrika* (Hamburg, 1910).

[11] For the attitudes of linguists, see Katrin Bromber, 'Gustav Neuhaus: Mwalimu wa Kiswahili, Mhariri na Mtumishi wa Serikali ya Kikoloni', *Swahili Forum VI* (1999), 175–82; *and* Ludger Wimmelbuecker, *Mtoro bin Mwinyi Bakari (c.1869–1927): Swahili Lecturer and Author in Germany* (Dar es Salaam, 2009); for the lack of consensus, the records of the *Kolonialkongresse*, large-scale conferences held at irregular (at least biannual) intervals by different organizations involved in the German colonial project, especially *Verhandlungen des deutschen Kolonialkongresses 1910* (Berlin, 1910).

[12] A. I. Salim, *The Swahili-Speaking Peoples of Kenya's Coast, 1895–1965* (Nairobi, 1973), on the economic decline of the Kenyan coast; and Jonathon Glassman, *War of Words, War of Stones: Racial Thought and Violence in Colonial Zanzibar* (Bloomington, IN, 2011), ch. 1, for the decline of Zanzibar.

[13] Anne Bang, *Sufis and Scholars of the Sea* (London, 2003), on the relatively comfortable accommodation of coastal Muslim networks with colonialism; Kai Kresse, *Philosophising in Mombasa* (Edinburgh, 2007), on nostalgia for the colonial past; Becker, *Becoming Muslim*, ch. 7 and 8; and Roman Loimeier, 'Perceptions of Marginalization: Muslims in Contemporary Tanzania', in Benjamin Soares and René Otayek (eds), *Islam and Muslim Politics in Africa* (London, 2007), 136–56, on the rise of Islamism.

It concludes with a consideration of the paradoxical effect of decolonization in 'provincializing' East African Islamic congregations. In so doing, the chapter draws on a growing body of work by historians and anthropologists, which traces 'paths of accommodation' between Muslim milieus and imperial rulers, as well as persistent distrust and the great cultural distance between Christian rulers and Muslim ruled.[14] Much information on East African Islam, moreover, is contained in studies of Swahili society, effectively perpetuating the colonial notion that Islam (or at least 'genuine' Islam) in East Africa was limited to specific ethnic milieus with ties beyond the continent.[15]

## ISLAM IN THE TRANSFORMATION OF AN IMPERIAL FRONTIER

'If they blow a pipe in Zanzibar, they dance on the mainland all the way to the Great Lakes' goes a saying which characterizes the relationship between the predominantly Muslim coast and the mainland of East Africa in the mid- to late nineteenth century. It serves to highlight the informal character of Zanzibari hegemony which, beyond the coastal towns where the sultan collected customs, rested on the influence of Zanzibar's demand for slaves and ivory, and its ability to pay for them in goods that enabled both coercion and patronage.[16] It is misleading as it does not acknowledge the other factors that contributed to rapid and often disruptive social change on the mainland, such as internal migrations and the initiative of local rulers.[17] But it captures the fact that for many (though not all) people in mainland East Africa, the influence of trade with Zanzibar was inescapable. It might make them vulnerable to enslavement or provide them with cloth to share out among dependents, but it could not be ignored.

It is clear, too, that Islam played a major role in the way people in Zanzibar and on the Swahili coast construed their relations with the mainland. It lent a moral coloring to the widespread dismissal of the interior as a realm of barbarism and ignorance, and of slaves recently imported from the interior as (unbelieving)

[14] David Robinson, *Paths of Accommodation* (Athens, OH, 2000), for an influential West Africa-focused exploration of accommodation; for East Africa, see Salim, *Swahili-Speaking Peoples;* August Nimtz, *Islam and Politics in East Africa* (Minneapolis, 1981); Becker, *Becoming Muslim,* ch. 3 and 6; Janet McIntosh, *The Edge of Islam: Power, Personhood and Ethno-Religious Boundaries on the Kenya Coast* (Durham, NC, 2009), ch. 1; and Kresse, *Philosophising.*

[15] This is not to say that this work is unaware that coastal Muslims look both ways, to the ocean and the interior. See, for example, Roman Loimeier and Ruediger Seesemann (eds), *The Global Worlds of the Swahili* (Münster, 2006); John Middleton, *The World of the Swahili: an African Mercantile Civilization* (New Haven, 1992); and Stephen Headley and David Parkin, *Islamic Prayer Across the Indian Ocean* (London, 2000). On the 'Africanization' of Islam in Africa generally, see David Robinson, *Muslim Societies in African History* (Cambridge, 2004).

[16] Steven Feierman, *The Shambaa Kingdom* (Madison, WI, 1974); C. S. Nicholls, *The Swahili Coast* (London, 1971); Glassman, *Feasts and Riot;* and Iliffe, *Modern History.*

[17] Patrick Redmond, *The Politics of Power in Songea Ngoni Society* (Chicago, 1985); Shane Doyle and Christian Medard, *Slavery in the Great Lakes Region of East Africa* (Oxford, 2007); and Iliffe, *Modern History.*

brutes. The extent to which Islam became discernible to people beyond the coast as a distinctive ritual and social order, or a set of doctrines, is less clear. Some rulers of the Yao ethnic group, in control of much of the slave-trading networks running from present-day Malawi and northern Mozambique to the Swahili coast, were called 'sultan' and kept Arabic-language scribes; they observed Ramadan but did not abstain from alcohol.[18] Many minor strongmen practiced displays of 'coastal' goods such as Arabicate dress (black silk robes; turbans).[19] Islamic practices here appear as one of many ways to claim access to the resources of the coast; to be chosen as part of personal stratagems of power, not to be adopted as part of a religious reorientation.[20]

For the Omani planters and entrepreneurs pursuing their fortunes on the Swahili coast, and the indigenous patricians struggling to assert their dominance against them, invoking Islam to assert their status was an obvious but not a risk-free choice.[21] Marginal townspeople, including advantageously placed slaves, were also experimenting with Islamic identities. In a context of sometimes extreme social mobility, Islam was for established patricians an issue of hierarchy, while for the 'plebeians', as Jonathan Glassman has called them, it was about entitlement. It enabled these 'plebeians' to challenge their ascribed marginality. This was the origin of many new Sufi congregations, the Qadiri and Shadhili orders, that gathered people struggling for inclusion in town life around novel, often public, forms of worship. Amid these tense negotiations and intermittent struggles, European foreigners, present in gradually increasing but small numbers, occupied a liminal place.

The increase in the power of the European empires became evident in 1873, when the British consul in Zanzibar 'persuaded' the sultan to close the island's slave market and outlaw slave trading.[22] Between 1885, when the German government endorsed Carl Peters' German East Africa Company in what would become Tanzania, and 1896, when the British government enforced its choice of successor for the Zanzibari sultan's throne by bombarding Zanzibar town, the military and political dominance of European imperialism became abundantly clear.[23] During these years British military support ensured the victory of a Protestant faction over Catholic and Muslim ones in the kingdom of Buganda (now southern Uganda), leading to a political settlement that Ugandan Muslims still today identify as the origin of their political marginality.[24] Likewise, in both Kenya and Tanzania, British

---

[18] Edward Alpers, *Ivory and Slaves in East Central Africa* (Berkeley, 1975).

[19] I am taking inspiration from Marshall Hodgson's 'Islamicate', in using this term. I mean to suggest close kinship of cultural practices on the East African coast with precedents in Arab countries. It helps keep in mind the flexible and partial use of these 'cultural markers' even among people who did not try to project Arab ethnic identity and would have stood little chance of succeeding if they had, see Marshall Hodgson, *The Venture of Islam* (Chicago, 1974).

[20] Edward Alpers, 'Towards an Understanding of the Expansion of Islam in East Africa', in Terence Ranger and Isaria Kimambo (eds), *The Historical Study of African Religion* (Nairobi, 1972).

[21] Glassman, *Feasts and Riot*, 134–40.

[22] On this diplomatic process and the threat of blockade eventually used to obtain the sultan's consent, see Reginald Coupland, *The Exploitation of East Africa, 1856–1890* (London, 1939).

[23] For events in Kenya, see Salim, *Swahili-Speaking Peoples*.

[24] A. Kasozi, *The Spread of Islam in Uganda* (Nairobi, 1988), 49–55.

and German troops defeated military resistance, which was sponsored partly by coastal Muslim networks.

However, once established, the colonial administrations of German and British East Africa took some pains to cultivate amicable relations with the elites freshly displaced from political power. This included attempts to defer to their perceived 'Islamic' sensibilities, especially in the form of great reluctance to interfere with slavery where it overlapped with concubinage and marriage.[25] At the same time, officials, missionaries, settlers, and colonial enthusiasts began to debate the character, importance, and future role of Islam in the colonies. This debate took somewhat different forms in Tanzania and Kenya, shaped, as far as can be made out, by the larger scale of violence in Tanzania, differences in the legal form of colonialism, and differences in experience and mind-set among the colonizing powers involved.[26] Overall, British administrators appear more at ease in their relations with the Muslim intermediaries: more resigned to the fact that they might have agendas of their own, and more confident that they would nevertheless be useful.[27]

Both colonial powers retained the default assumption that Muslim religious and political representatives of coastal milieus made better intermediaries than other Africans (or, as they might say, in keeping with many coastal notables' view of themselves as unrelated to 'mainland' Africans, than 'Africans'). They considered Muslim patricians the most 'civilized' part of the population, and some of them, such as Mbarak bin Ali Hinawy (1896–1959) in Mombasa, had long careers in the colonial administration.[28] But the independent social influence of these patricians also caused concern among administrators and missionaries. As a consequence, the folders on 'religious movements' are among the most interesting of the slim archival holdings surviving in Tanzania from the German period.[29] German officials corresponded at great length about the potential political and security implications of increased interest in Sufism, of the overlap between Muslim scholarly networks and discontented coastal elites (all the more as these networks extended into British colonies), and of flurries of Islamic millenarianism that occurred in the first decade of the twentieth century.

[25] E.g. Gouverneur von Liebert, 'Runderlass', 5 March 1899, Dar es Salaam, Federal Archives Berlin (Bundesarchiv Berlin; hereafter BA), R 1001/1004, 194–7; and R 1001/1005, *passim*.

[26] Generally on comparisons and relations between British and German rule in East Africa, see Ulrike Lindner, *Koloniale Begegnungen* (Frankfurt M., 2011). For previous British experiences with Islam in their colonial possessions (whose influence on East Africa remains to be traced in detail), see Nile Green, *Bombay Islam: The Religious Economy of the West Indian Ocean, 1840–1915* (Cambridge, 2011); and Muhammad Qasim Zaman, *The Ulama in Contemporary Islam: Custodians of Change* (Princeton, 2007), ch. 1–2. Indian inspiration for policy on slavery makes Indian Office influence on policy on Islam likely, see Frederick Cooper, *From Slaves to Squatters* (New Haven, 1977). Elke Stockreiter has traced Indian influence on the policies on 'qadis' courts' in Zanzibar, see Elke Stockreiter, '"British *Kadhis*" and Muslim Judges": Modernisation, Inconsistencies and Accommodation in Zanzibar's Colonial Judiciary', *Journal of Eastern African Studies*, 4/3 (2010), 560–76.

[27] Arthur Hardinge, *A Diplomatist in the East* (London, 1924).

[28] On Hinawy, see Salim, *Swahili-Speaking Peoples*, 91 and 190–2.

[29] See the files 'Allgemein religioese Bewegungen', Tanzania National Archive, Dar es Salaam (Tanz.NA), German-era holdings, G 9/45-48.

These records are at times a study in paranoia, and this paranoia resulted in recurrent deportations and imprisonment of suspected Muslim 'fanatics'. But ultimately pragmatism won out. The level of prejudice against the practical and intellectual abilities of 'ordinary' Africans was very high, and Muslim intermediaries were indispensable in German and British East Africa.[30] The most influential adviser on Islamic questions to the German government, Orientalist Carl Heinrich Becker (1876–1933), was dismissive of the educational status of East African Muslims, but confident that they could be useful for the colonial administration.[31] His assessment prevailed over the objections of missionaries.[32] It was in keeping with the wider efforts of Imperial Germany before and during the First World War to position itself as a Muslim-friendly power; a benign alternative to Britain and France with their large colonial holdings in Muslim lands.[33] There is little evidence that Muslim public opinion in East Africa took these claims on board. The same political pragmatism, meanwhile, compounded the political marginalization of Muslims in the kingdom of Buganda, after the British instituted a political settlement that placed Buganda's Protestant converts at the heart of power.[34]

Throughout the colonial period, European missionaries remained anxious that official cooperation with Muslims would be seen as an endorsement of their faith, and they occasionally rehearsed arguments about the dangers of Muslim militancy and 'secret orders' that had their parallels in Francophone discussions of North and West Africa.[35] Yet, at the same time, the establishment of colonies in Kenya and Tanzania also opened new 'mission fields'. Large parts of the new colonial territories were inhabited by people practicing indigenous religions, and many missionaries chose to focus on 'unspoilt' (i.e. non-Muslim) Africans, initiating the growth of Christianity in twentieth-century East Africa.[36] Unlike other parts of the British empire, such as Northern Nigeria, the British did not seek to limit the missionary presence on the Muslim Swahili coast. It would have been politically difficult, as

[30] The dismissive tone on Africans can be sampled in F. O. Karstedt, 'Zur Beurteilung des Islam in Deutsch-Ostafrika', *Kolonial Rundschau*, 5 (1913), 728–36.

[31] C. H. Becker, 'Materials for the Understanding of Islam in German East Africa', *Tanganyika Notes and Records*, 68 (1968), 31–61; and C. H. Becker, 'Ist der Islam eine Gefahr fuer unsere Kolonien?', in C. H. Becker, *Islamstudien*, i (Leipzig 1924).

[32] A recurring topic in the *Verhandlungen des Deutschen Kolonialkongresses 1910* (Berlin, 1911); and also in the *Verhandlungen des Deutschen Kolonialkongresses 1902* (Berlin, 1903); *Verhandlungen des Deutschen Kolonialkongresses 1905* (Berlin, 1906); and *Verhandlungen des Deutschen Kolonialkongresses 1924* (Berlin, 1925).

[33] Tilman Lüdke, *Jihad Made in Germany: Ottoman and German Propaganda and Intelligence Operations in the First World War* (Münster, 2005).

[34] Arye Oded, *Islam in Uganda* (New York, 1974).

[35] Report by the Mission Benedictines on the potential for unrest in Lindi region, BA, R 1001/702, 49; Richard Reusch, *Der Islam in Ost-Afrika* (Berlin, n.d. (*c.*1930)); and Harrison, *France and Islam*, chs 2 and 3.

[36] Bengt Sundkler and Christopher Steed, *A History of the Church in Africa* (Cambridge, 2000), on the Church Missionary Society at Mombasa. Part of its attempt at 'interreligious dialogue' was one missionary's project to translate the Qur'an into Swahili, which raised a great deal of mistrust, see Justo Lacunza Balda, 'Translations of the Qur'an into Swahili, and Contemporary Islamic Revival in East Africa', in Eva E. Rosander and David Westerlund, *African Islam and Islam in Africa* (London, 1997), 95–127.

some missions had been established there since the pre-colonial period, and had strongly supported the imperialist agenda in the name of ending the slave trade. An Anglican cathedral rose on the site of the former slave market in thoroughly Muslim Zanzibar Town, and nearby Kiungani school trained future Anglican priests. Most of the trainees, though, originated from previously 'pagan' areas, where mission was more successful. Since British rulers, here as elsewhere in Africa, left formal education largely in the hands of missionaries, Muslim participation remained low, setting the scene for discontent over limited Muslim participation in post-colonial bureaucratic elites.

Surviving Swahili poems on the establishment of German rule in East Africa give some insight into the ambivalence and disunity prevailing on the coast in the face of imperial takeover. Many authors began their accounts with the Islamic invocations of God traditional in Swahili poetry, but their commentary on the new rulers ranged from deploring the decadence into which the coast had fallen to sycophancy for the German emperor.[37] By the First World War, coastal Muslims were effectively displaced from political power and the plantation economy was in steep decline.[38] But they retained a role as colonial intermediaries, and as a party in on-going negotiations about social status and belonging. Colonial endorsement of Muslim elites, defined partly in racial terms, even helped some coastal Muslims elaborate an account of themselves as separate from the African majority, with far-reaching political ramifications.

## ISLAM AND COLONIAL RULE IN INTER-WAR EAST AFRICA

There is limited official information on Islam in colonial East Africa during the inter-war period and even mission records are patchy. The records do not explain why the British were so little concerned about Islam in their East African possessions, despite the strong Muslim opposition they faced in the Horn and indeed other parts of their empire. Part of the explanation lies in a view of African Muslims, especially recent converts, as 'not really' Muslim, and in particular, largely untouched by the doctrines of jihad.[39] This dismissive view of Muslim Africans proved remarkably persistent, being repeated by a British observer as late as 1963.[40] Moreover, the British had long experience of political accommodation with the

---

[37] Miehe, Bromber, Khamis, and Grosserhode (eds), *Kala Shairi.*

[38] Salim, *Swahili-Speaking Peoples,* on the decline of the Kenya coast; and Glassman, *War of Words,* on Zanzibari planters' problems.

[39] The British in Africa never enunciated a doctrine as elaborate as the French notion of '*Islam noir*', which theorized the claim—in the face of much evidence to the contrary—that Black African Muslims were non-jihadist. Nevertheless, their view of African Muslims was quite similar, see Robinson, *Paths of Accommodation*; and Christopher Harrison, *France and Islam in West Africa, 1860– 1960* (Cambridge, 1988).

[40] J. K. Leslie, *A Survey of Dar es Salaam* (Oxford, 1963) deemed the majority of African Muslims in the city 'fundamentally irreligious' (p. 211). This contrasts sharply with oral recollections of Sufi activity in late-colonial Dar.

Muslim sultanate of Zanzibar, which served as a model for the Kenyan coast and, more haphazardly, Tanganyika. Lastly, due to over-attention to the recent history of Arab immigration on the coast, Muslim identity tended to become subsumed within racial identity. Following a diffusionist model of coastal history, officials identified Islam with Arab 'bringers of culture'. Exaggerating their Arab allegiances, British officials and their coastal Muslim intermediaries jointly elaborated notions of Muslim separateness, while largely ignoring, as inauthentic and politically irrelevant, those Muslims who were undeniably African.[41]

The official record thus fails to reflect the expansionary dynamism of Islam in the inter-war period. In Zanzibar, where Islam had been dominant since well before colonization, this period saw the further differentiation and entrenchment of Sufi practice. In Kenya, conversions to Islam occurred predominantly near its old centers on the coast, though there were under-studied Muslim congregations far inland, for instance in the capital Nairobi and in Kisumu in Western Kenya. In Tanzania, by contrast, substantial swathes of the countryside became predominantly Muslim, including in the far west of the country around Ujiji. At independence, the country had a substantial Muslim minority of thirty to forty percent. To the frustration of researchers, this religious demography led to the removal of the question of religious affiliation from census records so as to make it harder to instrumentalize religious difference for political ends.[42] This expansion occurred despite the demise of most of the Muslim-staffed government schools about which missionaries had been so exercised.

Missionaries deplored this development, blaming it partly on the interruption to their work during the First World War, while administrators mostly ignored it.[43] Nevertheless, to the extent that colonial officials commented on the shift, their views were revealing; for them, it was an unwelcome form of social change, reflecting the naïve ambitions of Africans. A district officer in the coastal town of Kilwa commented:

> Since the war...it is amazing to see the number of unsophisticated and uneducated natives who profess Mohammedanism...it is a sign of the times to see the amazing number of native converts, whose mode of life as untutored and unashamed pagans was infinitely preferable to the lip-serving, hypocritical attitude they have assumed since the war.[44]

---

[41] See especially the conflicts surrounding claims to 'Arab' status by populations near Mombasa: Justin Willis, *Mombasa, the Swahili, and the Making of the Mijikenda* (Oxford, 1993); and Kresse, *Philosophising*, ch. 1; and the discourse on the need for Arab leadership in Zanzibar: Jonathon Glassman, *War of Words*.

[42] The last census to include a question on religious affiliation was conducted in 1967, and the removal of the question since then has fed conspiracy theories that the state is unwilling to acknowledge a Muslim majority, see David Westerlund, *Ujamaa na Dini* (Stockholm, 1980), 8 and 15 (footnote 7). Some contemporary Muslim activists cite the 'suppression' of this information as an indication of the existence of a Muslim majority in Tanzania, so the hay-making has not really stopped, see Mohamed Said, *The Life and Times of Abdulwaheed Sykes (1924–68): The Untold Story of the Muslim Struggle Against British Colonialism in Tanganyika* (London, 1998).

[43] E.g. 'Letter from Nkowe', *Missionsblaetter*, 39 (May 1935), 137.

[44] Kilwa district annual report 1923, Tanz.NA, 1733/14.

Contempt for recent 'native' converts to Islam and their less educated rural teachers, as ambitious barbarians merely 'aping' coastal culture, was perhaps the single theme which united all parties to the conversation on Islam in the East African colonies—save for the objects of the scorn themselves.[45]

Historians of the twentieth century, meanwhile, have concentrated on three factors when seeking to explain the spread of Islam in inter-war East Africa, and for its differing extents. First, the expansion of Islam can be construed as an after-effect of the long-distance trade routes established in the nineteenth century and used by a large number of Muslims. As the trading network was more extensive in Tanzania than Kenya and most centers of rural Islam are indeed close to it, this reasoning goes some way towards explaining the geography of the spread of Islam.[46] Secondly, the far-reaching influence of Sufi leaders who took particular care to integrate marginal milieus into their congregations has been noted. The most famous among them is Habib Saleh of Lamu in northern Kenya. Mombasa had its version in Mwinyi Abudu, Bagamoyo in northern Tanzania had Shaykh Ramiyah (himself a former slave). Shaykh Hussein bin Mahmood in Kilwa and Shaykh Muhammad bin Yusuf, known as 'Shehe Badi', in Lindi, were similar figures.[47] Lastly, Alpers (for pre-colonial Mozambique) and Sperling (for colonial southern Kenya) have focused on the uses of Muslim allegiance in the efforts of local rulers or notables to reconstruct the bases of their authority.[48]

All these considerations remain useful; nevertheless, the oral sources collected since the 1960s suggest a different emphasis. The earliest oral accounts of Islamization in mainland Tanzania, collected by Joel Gallagher in the 1960s, contain the claim that 'only those who respected their neighbours could become Muslim'.[49] David Sperling found networks of local notables rather than proselytizers from the towns, undoubtedly patriarchal but with fairly flat internal hierarchies, leading villages in establishing mosques; a pattern also observed in rural Tanzania. In places as far apart as Pokomo, just off the northern Kenyan coast, and Tunduru, 200 miles inland from the southern Tanzanian coast, we have reports of (low-status) youth preceding their (high-status) elders in taking up Muslim allegiance.[50] Villagers in regions adjacent to the Southern Tanzanian coast acknowledged the role of teachers trained on the coast in establishing village Qur'an

---

[45] E.g. Bezirksamt Lindi to Dar es Salaam, 12 January 1909, report on a journey through Lindi district, starting 5 September 1908, Tanz.NA, G 9/47, 161.

[46] E.g. Francois Constantin, *Les voies de l'Islam* (Paris, 1987).

[47] For Lamu, see Abdul Hamid el Zein, *The Sacred Meadows* (Evanston, IL, 1974); and Patricia Romero, *Lamu: History, Society and Family in an East African Port City* (Princeton, 1987); for Mombasa, see Randall L. Pouwels, 'Sh. al-Amin B. Ali Mazrui and Islamic Modernism in East Africa, 1875–1947', *International Journal of Middle East Studies* 13, 3 (1981), 329–45; and for Bagamoyo, see Nimtz, *Islam and Politics*; for Lindi, Becker, *Becoming Muslim*, ch. 6.

[48] Alpers, 'Towards an Understanding'; David Sperling, 'The Growth of Islam among the Mijikenda of the Kenyan coast' (PhD, University of London, 1988).

[49] Joel Gallagher, 'Islam and the Emergence of the Ndendeuli' (PhD, Boston University, 1976).

[50] Ronald Bunger, *Islamisation Among the Upper Pokomo* (Syracuse, NY, 1978); and Kolumba Msigala, 'Autobiography', unpublished manuscript, Archive of the Universities Mission to Central Africa, 'box files', D1(2), Rhodes House Library, Oxford.

schools, but also described how they quickly achieved educational autarchy, relying on locally recruited and locally trained teachers.[51]

These oral sources, then, suggest that people who were junior not only in age but in status were deeply involved in expanding Islamic allegiance, and that villagers rather than townspeople often took the initiative to bring rural areas into the fold. These converts focused on equality rather than on the re-elaboration of the hierarchies of the pre-colonial period. It would be surprising if these implications of conversion were made very explicit; for many former slaves, especially in coastal communities, slave antecedents were a stigma to be covered up rather than addressed openly.[52] Yet the tone of ritual and congregational life in the new Muslim congregations was very different from that of the late pre-colonial period, when the display of tenets of Muslim (and hence coastal) allegiance was a privilege of the best connected—the 'big men' or warlord-traders. Rather than self-made individuals pursuing a very demonstrative practice of power, we find low-key negotiations among networks of notables.

After all, the colonial state provided conditions in which Islam could spread. Indeed, imperial rule was an essential part of this process. However, for the new up-country Muslim congregation, the colonial state was more noted for its neglect than its intervention. Outside the foci of British interest, above all Kenya's areas of European settlement (the 'White Highlands'), the kingdom of Buganda, and a handful of Tanzanian districts with exceptionally profitable agriculture and a settler presence, most of colonial East Africa was lightly administered. Imperial officials considered the African interior as 'pagan' by default and recognized so-called 'traditional' authorities, justified with reference to 'native law and custom'. By definition, 'natives' were not supposed to be Muslim, and little attention was paid to the social role of Islamic practices up-country. While mission-run schools were important as a source of literate clerical staff, Qur'anic education was regarded as irrelevant. But arguably this inattention did not detract from, and may actually have increased, the appeal of Islam in places where villagers expected little from their colonial overlords.

When choosing rural intermediaries, officials paid little explicit attention to local leaders' religious affiliations, which were increasingly either Muslim or Christian.[53] The extent of the intermediaries' legitimate or effective authority, and official satisfaction with them, varied greatly, due to factors that were not clearly aligned with religious affiliation. They included the antecedents of colonial appointees within their societies, the implications of on-going processes of social change in response to cash-cropping and migrant labor, and personal skill.[54] In some places oligarchies

---

[51] Interview with Bushiri Bakari Lipyoga, Rwangwa-Dodoma, 9 October 2003: he explains that when he studied the Qur'an in the countryside in the 1950s and 1960s, he had already studied with locally born and partly locally trained teachers.

[52] Some informants asserted that even today it would be inviting prosecution for libel to ascribe slave antecedents to anyone. Interview with Rajabu Feruzi Ismaili, Mingoyo, 11 August 2000.

[53] Iliffe, *Modern History*; and for Kenya, see John Lonsdale and Bruce Berman, *Unhappy Valley*, vol. 1 (Oxford, 1992).

[54] For an overview over these processes, see Thomas Spear, 'Neo-Traditionalism and the Limits of Invention in British Colonial Africa', *Journal of African History*, 44/1 (2003), 3–27.

came into being or were strengthened; in some, ruling lineages profited, and in others they found themselves reduced. But everywhere Africans grappled with the wider ramifications of colonial rule in their societies as much as, or more than, with the European rulers themselves. Religious change was part of this internal conversation.[55] Nevertheless, it had effects for the differential integration of rural regions into the developing states of colonial East Africa. Officials were more willing to recognize Christianization with the attendant expansion of mission schooling, as a sign of 'progress' among Africans, and were more willing to 'reward' such regions with attention to their needs.[56]

The salience of Islam in this context indicates the Janus-faced nature of societal change in colonial Africa. The problems were often local, even parochial, such as struggles within families, even if their causation stretched to far-away mines or markets. But the ways they were addressed drew on very large contexts and redeployed notions derived from many sources with equal readiness. In some regions, Muslim and Christian congregations grew in parallel.

On the coast, by contrast, British rule recognized Islamic institutions as an integral part of power structures it sought both to subordinate and preserve. Not all of them were equally politically relevant. Officials took very little interest in the limited numbers of hajj pilgrims (many of whom, as members of immigrant networks with Southern Arabian connections, were adept at moving through the colonial legal space).[57] Similarly, the running of mosques and the everyday activities of Sufi orders largely passed below the radar of colonial officials. By contrast, they took active interest in the administration of Islamic law through 'qadis' courts', under the aegis of the sultan of Zanzibar. They emphasized their commitment to respecting 'Muhammadan' law, but, as Elke Stockreiter and Hassan Mwakimako have shown, nevertheless marginalized Islamic law in the colonial legal system.[58] The 'qadis' courts' became subordinate to courts run by European magistrates and limited to dispensing personal status law. Inspired by the 'Anglo-Muhammadan law' of British India, British officials overall achieved a similar effect: a shift in emphasis from 'law as process' to 'law as structure', and a Europeanization of court proceedings.[59] Nevertheless, especially in more marginal regions, much dispensing of justice by local shaykhs in matters of personal status went unrecorded and unregulated by colonial authorities.

At the same time, the literate Muslim networks of the coast encountered and discussed new doctrinal stances, some of these critical of Sufism, through their

---

[55] This is true of Christianity as well as Islam, see, for example, Derek Peterson, *Creative Writing* (London, 2004).

[56] For the 'virtuous circle' of education, Christianization, and encouragement for 'progressive' Africans, see e.g. Iliffe, *Modern History*, on the Kilimanjaro region.

[57] Bang, *Sufis and Scholars*.

[58] Elke Stockreiter, 'British *"Kadhis"*'; and Hassan Mwakimako, 'Conflicts and Tensions in the Appointment of Chief Kadhi in Colonial Kenya' 1898–1960', in Shamil Jellie, Ebrahim Moosa, and Richard Roberts (eds), *Muslim Family Law in Sub-Saharan Africa* (Amsterdam, 2007), 109–34.

[59] Muhammad Qasim Zaman, *The Ulama in Contemporary Islam: Custodians of Change* (Princeton, 2007).

participation in scholarly networks connecting East Africa with southern Arabia and the Hadrami diaspora.[60] The sultan's court in Zanzibar subscribed to Rashid Rida's pan-Islamic journal *al-Manar*.[61] While these conversations occurred by and large very quietly in the colonial period, they would inform sometimes acrimonious disputes after independence. Yet, arguably the most important processes of Islamic history under imperial rule were, on one hand, the integration of ex-slave populations into Muslim congregations through Sufism, and, on the other, the subtle racialization of Islamic community politics. The two processes were related: the invocation of difference, conceived of variously in cultural, ethnic, or racial terms, bolstered the status claims of former slave-owners, while the growing Sufi congregations gave former slaves a stake in the towns.

But while colonial officials were mostly distant observers of the expansion of Sufism, colonial rule was deeply implicated in the elaboration of racialized group identities, with which Islam became entangled. Everywhere in Africa, colonial rule fostered the elaboration of ethnic identities for political claims-making.[62] The recognition of 'Arab' (alongside 'European' and 'South Asian') as a separate legal category in Zanzibar and coastal Kenya meant that the benefits of claiming this identity were particularly significant and clearly defined. It also created scope for conflict around groups with marginal claims to Arab allegiance, most notably Mombasa's Mijikenda people, and entrenched the perception of Arabs as outsiders.

Imperial agents elaborated the association between Arabness and Islam most explicitly in Zanzibar, where Islam was fully hegemonic. Here, Jonathon Glassman has traced the give-and-take between British educational officials, Arab patricians, and aspiring teachers that produced a narrative of Arabs as bringers of *Islamic* civilization, and hence natural leaders of the African majority.[63] This narrative was harder to sustain on the mainland, where the Christian alternative was more visible, and especially in mainland Tanzania, where Arabs did not have separate legal status. But here too, critics of innovative Sufi ritual rejected it as 'African' (even if the contrasting, more desirable category was defined as 'Swahili' or 'coastal' rather than 'Arab').[64] Ultimately, colonial officials were more interested in finding effective intermediaries than in sustaining the status of their patrician Muslim allies, or in the nuances of origins and social allegiance among them. In Mombasa, for example, they promoted the relatively plebeian but visibly popular Sufi shaykh Mwinyi Abudu to the office of chief qadi over contenders from the patrician Mazrui clan.[65] Still, the colonial identification of Islam with racial allegiances contributed to a cross-over between ways of being religious and racialized group identities that would help shape the politics of the end of empire and still faintly resonate today.[66]

---

[60] Bang, *Sufis and Scholars*; and Kresse, *Philosophising*.

[61] See the chapter by Umar Ryad in this volume.

[62] Spear, 'Neo-Traditionalism'; and for a classical statement of this point, see Leroy Vail and Landeg White, *The Creation of Tribalism in Southern Africa* (Oxford, 1989).

[63] Glassman, *War of Words*.          [64] Becker, *Becoming Muslim*, ch. 6.

[65] Mwakimako, 'Tensions'.

[66] McIntosh, *The Edge of Islam*, on what she calls 'ethno-religious' identities.

We can trace this entanglement further by considering the development of Sufism. Furthest north, in Lamu, the crucial figure in the growth of an inclusive Muslim community was Habib Saleh, a *sharif* (descendant of the Prophet) from the Comoros and member of the scholarly 'Alawiyya Sufi order also influential in Zanzibar. From 1901, Habib ('Beloved') Saleh's Riyadha Sufi lodge, a combination of mosque, Qur'an school, practice ground for Sufi ritual, and hostel for students and visitors, became a magnet for Muslims from the ex-slave quarters of Lamu. His introduction of new performance styles, in particular the use of a kind of tambourine, *duffu*, in Sufi ritual, provoked vitriolic criticism from other scholars as an unscriptural innovation and a concession to 'African' tastes. It did nothing to lessen his popularity, though, and his descendants still run the Riyadha as an influential site of learning.[67] In keeping with their general hands-off approach to religious institutions, British officials observed the Riyadha, but did not seek to regulate it. Such confrontations of ritually creative, popular Sufi leaders with more conservative and exclusivist critics repeated themselves, with variations, all along the Swahili coast. While the critics remained more influential in some places (especially Mombasa) than others, everywhere local people accommodated the Sufi newcomers.

Again, we can interpret the regional differences with reference to different elaborations of the way of thinking that Glassman has recently described as 'Arabocentrism': the valorization of all things Arab as markers of coastal civilization.[68] During colonial rule, accommodation between colonial agents and Muslim elites on the coast perpetuated these ideas, but did not prevent the elaboration of an alternative 'populist' account of Islam. In Mombasa and Lamu, different local formulations of Arabocentrism remained influential, bound up with the religious leadership of the Mazruis in Mombasa and Habib Saleh's Jamal al-Layl clan in Lamu. By contrast, Shaykh Ramiyah in Bagamoyo explicitly asserted that Arab identity was irrelevant to religious leadership. Similarly on the southern Tanzanian coast, informants flatly say that the Arabs have 'disappeared'.[69] The Sufi shaykhs here, Hussein bin Mahmood and Shehe Badi, barely referred to Arab allegiance at all, even while cultivating elements of Arabicate material culture.

Colonial officials looked on benignly, ignoring either actively or naively the overtones of status conflicts involving ex-slaves and ex-slave owners in popular Sufi practice. In Kilwa, the acting governor was guest of honor at the annual *mawlid* in 1934. Shaykh Hussein welcomed him, saying: 'There are many great cities with better people in them than this town ... we have to thank the Almighty God for the generosity he has shown us in bringing to us this eminent ruler, full of blessings and inspiring of trust.'[70] The district officer reporting the events, in his turn,

---

[67] El Zein, *Sacred Meadows,* on the early history of the Riyadha; Kresse, *Philosophising,* 82–9, for post-colonial debates on the Lamu *mawlid.*

[68] Glassman, *War of Words,* ch. 1.

[69] The only seemingly naive references to Arabs' 'disappearance' arguably form part of a long story, focused on descendants of former slaves and of former owners finding a modus vivendi together. It is intended that this will be the subject of a forthcoming article.

[70] 'E. W. M.' in Kilwa district book, sheet 11–12, 5 October 1934, Tanz.NA.

had high praise for the shaykh's school. Indeed, accommodation was working for both sides. Yet, even where colonial officials endorsed Muslim leaders who thrived on accommodating African converts, they did so while implicitly tying them into trans-oceanic Islamic history, emphasizing their Arab allegiance.[71]

The different fates of Arab identity in different locations are in part the outcomes of very local processes: the ascendancy of Ramiyah in Bagamoyo, for instance, and the success of the Mazruis in Mombasa in defending their social position. It is tempting and plausible to suggest that differences in colonial policy between Kenya and Tanzania, namely the legally separate status of the 'Arab-ruled' coast in Kenya, versus the classification of Arabs with other 'natives' in Tanzania, contributed to these different outcomes.[72] Still, this factor should not be over-stated. In Tanganyika too, Arabs answered to a different court system from Africans and, in conflicts with Africans, colonial racism worked in their favor.

Moreover, local negotiation of hierarchies between older settlers and newcomers, partly in terms of competing claims to Islamic knowledge, is also a long-standing part of the history of Swahili towns.[73] These 'community politics' were not shut down in the colonial period, but repositioned within the larger power structures of the colonial state. Arguably, this period marked a significant shift, when debates hitherto recognized as entirely political began to be recast as 'cultural', and hence safely compartmentalized away from contests for institutionalized power. In this form they have survived into the post-colonial period. The slippage between Arab and Muslim identity is a persistent feature of these community contests. Claims to privileged access to knowledge of Islam became unmoored, to a greater or lesser extent in different places, from their nineteenth-century association (always contested) with Arab antecedents. Both the Africans involved and colonial observers understood these contests as outcomes of the 'peripheral' status of East African Muslim congregations within the Islamic *umma*, as struggles to stay connected to an imagined universal orthodoxy. The politicization of education at large and religious learning in particular among recent Muslim reformists is thus in a sense a reintroduction of a long-standing concern into the public sphere.

## COLONIAL ACCOMMODATION AND POST-COLONIAL DISPLACEMENT

Anti-colonial nationalism dominated the political scene across East Africa in the 1950s, albeit with many country-specific features. Due to the very local identities and weak corporate organization of the new Islamic congregations, their representatives rarely came to the fore *qua* Muslims in nationalist politics. Their grassroots

---

[71] In his report on the performance, the District Officer commented on the use of boughs 'in place of the more traditional swords', implicitly comparing the performance he had seen to Arabicate precedents (there is no record of the use of ceremonial swords in Kilwa).

[72] On the Kenyan coast, see James Brennan, 'Lowering' the Sultan's Flag: Sovereignty and Decolonization in Coastal Kenya', *Comparative Studies in Society and History*, 50/4 (2008), 831–61.

[73] Pouwells, *Horn and Crescent*; see also the contributions in David Parkin and Stephen Headley (eds), *Islamic Prayer across the Indian Ocean: Inside and Outside the Mosque* (London, 2000).

networks nevertheless took up the cause of independence with enthusiasm.[74] By contrast, political stances that developed in the 1950s and 1960s among the old Muslim populations of the coast indicate their discomfort with the then-dominant form of anti-colonial nationalism. In both Tanzania and Kenya, movements expressing fears of (Christian) mainland political dominance were defeated at the ballot box.[75] Shaykh al-Amin Mazrui in Mombasa summed up these worries by asserting that if slavery returned now, coastal Muslims would find themselves bought and sold by up-country (now increasingly Christian) Africans.[76] But the colonial authorities, resigned to decolonization, now paid little heed to particularistic identities they had once cultivated: they had lost their political usefulness. Officials preferred to deal with formally educated (and thereby predominantly Christian) nationalist leaders.

In Zanzibar, the colonial-era elaboration of the association of Muslim with Arab identity fed into devastating social conflict. Here, the 1964 revolution overthrew a government friendly to Britain and drawn mostly from the old Arab elites which British rule had cultivated. More than elsewhere in East Africa, in the confined space of the islands, with their intense social stratification, ethnic and religious categories had become the lines of battle in conflicts over access to land, resources, and patronage.[77] The revolutionary government positioned itself as strongly pro-African, hence anti-Arab; early on it presided over pogroms against Arabs and for some years practiced active discrimination. This did not, of course, equate to a straightforward anti-Islamic platform; the revolutionaries were themselves Muslim. Nevertheless, due to the way in which religious markers of class and ethnicity had become attributed in Zanzibar, to be anti-Arab implied a challenge to the established ways of being Muslim. However, it was impossible to purge Islam in Zanzibar of those 'Arabizing' elements which the new rulers identified with past racial oppression without profound disruption to Islamic practice. The isolationism of the revolutionary government during its first decade, its anti-Arab measures, and interventions in the educational system ended Zanzibar's role as a platform for the part-ethnic, part-scholarly networks that had connected the old Muslim congregations of the coast to other Islamic centers of the Western Indian Ocean.[78]

These events contrasted with the strong support which the majority of East Africa's Muslims offered the project of independence. The communitarian overtones of the new Muslim congregations resonated with the populism of the independence movements. Some of the leading Sufi shaykhs were official guests at flag-raising ceremonies.[79] It would be mistaken to sort East African Muslims in the mid-twentieth century (or now) neatly into pro- and anti-nationalist, plebeian and patrician, 'Africanized' and 'Arabizing'. Rather, coastal Muslims fell victim to an irony of the end of empire. The elaboration of 'coastal Muslim' identity was

---

[74] Iliffe, *Modern History,* 550–2; Becker, *Becoming Muslim,* ch. 7; and Oded, *Islam in Uganda.*

[75] Brennan, 'Lowering'; and Iliffe, *Modern History*, 551–2.

[76] Al-Amin Mazrui, *Uwongozi (Guidance)* (Mombasa, 1944), 32–33, quoted in Randall Pouwels, 'Islamic modernism', 340.

[77] Glassman, *War of Words.*     [78] Loimeier, *Social Skills,* ch. 9.

[79] Becker, *Becoming Muslim,* ch. 7.

only one of many processes of the elaboration, assertion, and politicization of particular identities under colonial rule, and under colonial rule, it could sometimes be deployed to access privilege. But while many such identities, especially 'nativist' ones, retained or fully developed their character as political resources in the new nation-states, this trans-regional version of the widespread phenomenon became a liability.[80] Still, even in Zanzibar, the political polarization of the last years of colonialism separated people who had much in common, and who had to emphasize and de-emphasize different elements of their identity to approximate themselves to newly politicized stereotypes. In wider East Africa, where polarization was less intense, there was less pressure to choose one set of allegiances to the exclusion of all others.

## CONCLUSION

If East African Muslims today perceive the post-colonial states as the most important—and indeed most problematic—legacy of the colonial era, this is because the expansion of Islam during this period is regarded as an inevitable outcome of the universal spread of Islam. Recently, the antagonistic element in Muslims' relationship to these states has become the most visible one, but it coexists with a good deal of pragmatic accommodation, as well as continued commitment to the national project.[81] Traumatic moments notwithstanding, East African Islam has made the transition to a world of nation-states, though its political imagination is not limited to this model. Muslim congregations remain multi-polar, and perhaps their most striking feature is not so much the persistence of any particular Islamic-inspired political vision, as the ability of elements of these to disappear and reappear.

The history of East African Islam under colonial rule, then, is characterized by fundamental ambiguity. European rulers accommodated Islamic law and religious practice, but they also compartmentalized it politically, legally, and—through the elaboration of separate ethnic identities—socially. They oversaw an expansion of Muslim congregations, as well as an even greater expansion of Christian ones. They carefully elaborated elements of Muslim civilization, but also sneered at decadent 'Orientals'. Muslims' experience with colonialism highlights the disconnect between imperialists' aims and achieved outcomes. Where Islam was concerned, the aims themselves were far from clear, as officials' level of interest in, and assessment of the benefits of, cultural change in Africa differed greatly. But none of them would have listed the growth of Muslim congregations among their desired outcomes. That it nevertheless occurred is partly due to means—the need to project power through intermediaries—taking precedence over stated ends. It is also a function of the deep-seated ambivalence of colonization, which could give rise to change in colonized societies, but not direct it.

[80] Kresse, *Philosophising,* clearly describes the resulting sense of loss, especially in ch. 1.
[81] Westerlund, *Ujamaa na Dini*; Arye Oded, *Islam and Politics in Kenya* (London, 2000); and Becker, *Becoming Muslim,* ch. 8.

# PART II

# ISLAM AND ANTI-COLONIAL RESISTANCE

# 6

# Anti-Imperialism and the Pan-Islamic Movement

*Umar Ryad*

## INTRODUCTION

Much has been written about the role of pan-Islamism in confronting the European empires in the colonial era. In the late-nineteenth and early-twentieth centuries, this political ideology fueled an international movement that denounced the deterioration of the Muslim world in general, and of the Ottoman empire in particular. Muslim reformers associated with it were confronted with a twofold challenge—namely the yoke of European colonialism and the perceived Muslim decline itself. Historians still differ on exactly when in modern times the term 'pan-Islam' emerged in Muslim politics. It has been argued that the term was first used in German and English in late 1877 and early 1878. Yet the first extensive use of the word occurred in the 1880s due to the French journalist Gabriel Charmes, who became particularly interested in the Ottoman empire and its policy of mobilizing Muslim public opinion across the world against the French takeover of Tunisia.[1] It is clear that the term 'pan-Islamism' was of European coinage and was adopted in imitation of 'pan-Slavism' or 'pan-Germanism', which had become current in the 1870s.[2] However, it is obvious that Muslim pan-Islamic thinkers and propagandists did not develop terms such as *al-jami'a al-islamiyya* or *al-ittihad al-islami* ('pan-Islam' or 'Islamic unity') as a simple translation or projection of Western concepts without any traditional basis in Islam. In fact, although pan-Islamism had its origins in nineteenth-century Ottoman political thought, it emerged—connoting Muslim unity and brotherhood—as a historical moment only once it had become connected to the *salafiyya* movement, which powerfully called for an immediate return to the first generations of Muslims who had rallied themselves behind the Prophet.[3] It is therefore no coincidence that one of the earliest uses of

---

[1] Jacob M. Landau, *The Politics of Pan-Islam: Ideology and Organization* (Oxford, 1990), 1–2.

[2] Dwight E. Lee, 'The Origins of Pan-Islamism', *American Historical Review*, 47/2 (1942), 278–87, 280; and Nikki R. Keddie, 'Pan-Islam as Proto-Nationalism', *The Journal of Modern History*, 41/1 (1969), 17–28.

[3] Cemil Aydin, *The Politics of Anti-Westernism in Asia: Visions of World Order in Pan-Islamic and Pan-Asian Thought* (New York, 2007); and Azmi Özcan, *Pan-Islamism: Indian Muslims, the Ottomans and Britain, 1877–1924* (Leiden, 1997).

the Arabic term *al-jami'a al-islamiyya* (equivalent to 'pan-Islam') was made in one
of the articles in the magazine *al-'Urwa al-Wuthqa* (*The Firmest Bond*) by Jamal
al-Din al-Afghani and Muhammad 'Abduh in 1884. Al-Afghani and 'Abduh must
have been aware of the term 'pan-Islam', which was increasingly used in Europe by
Charmes and others.[4]

This chapter addresses pan-Islamism as a global movement for Muslim reform
and against European imperial domination. It focuses on anti-colonial discourse
and the activities of the leading pan-Islamic proponents, most notably the triad
of Jamal al-Din al-Afghani (1838–97), Muhammad 'Abduh (1849–1905), and
Muhammad Rashid Rida (1865–1935), who sought to strengthen Islamic unity
in order to confront the European penetration of Muslim lands. As one of the
most important pan-Islamic agitators of his generation, al-Afghani was troubled
by his experiences in British India, where Muslims were ruled by non-Muslims
even though the *dar al-Islam,* in his view, should only be governed by the faithful.
Islamic unity, he believed, was the strongest force to mobilize Muslims against
imperial domination, an idea that was carried on by various Muslim activists and
thinkers, most importantly by al-Afghani's follower Muhammad 'Abduh, who later
became Mufti of Egypt, and 'Abduh's disciple, Rashid Rida.

This chapter discusses al-Afghani's and 'Abduh's revolutionary journal *al-
'Urwa al-Wuthqa*, which promoted not only Islamic renewal but also Muslim
revolt against the British empire, and Rida's paper *al-Manar* (*The Lighthouse*). It
argues that the colonial experience of these revolutionaries, their disillusionment
with European intervention, and their varying visions of *Weltpolitik* determined
their anti-imperialist intellectual and activist strategies. The first agitator of the
three, al-Afghani, was shaped by his experience in colonial India, participation in
Masonic lodges, dissatisfaction with the traditional 'ulama, confrontations with
the Sublime Porte, and his exile in Paris. Al-Afghani advocated revolution from
above. 'Abduh developed different ideas regarding the reformation of Islam and
firmly believed in a revolution from below, brought about by a reform of religion
and religious education. Rida, on the other hand, called for a pan-Islamic project
on the twin basis of nostalgia for the Islamic caliphate and the reformation of
Muslim activism. The following pages emphasize the diversity of the pan-Islamic
movement. They also broach the question of the popular impact of their ideas and
of the extent to which pan-Islamic ideas inspired anti-imperial uprisings such as
the 'Urabi revolt in Egypt and the tobacco protests in Persia.


## REVOLUTION FROM ABOVE

The impact of Jamal al-Din al-Afghani's psychological, ethnic, and social background on pan-Islamism has long caused controversy among historians of the

---

[4] Landau, *The Politics of Pan-Islam*, 3–4.

Middle East (Fig. 6).[5] Although his reformist political and religious career has been extensively studied, many passages of al-Afghani's life are still obscure. Nevertheless, it remains undisputed that he was widely regarded as a fervent defender of Islamic unity in the face of the expansion of the European empires. Due to the limited space available, this chapter does not describe the multifaceted contours of his life, political journeys, and exiles between Afghanistan, Persia, Istanbul, British India, Ottoman Egypt, St Petersburg, London, and Paris. Instead, the chapter focuses on al-Afghani's understanding of pan-Islamism as a 'revolutionary' concept, which, once put into practice, could bring about radical change in Muslim societies by liberating them from the shackles of European empires. In that sense, it is an undeniable fact that his life and 'revolutionary pan-Islamism... touched and deeply affected the whole Islamic world in the last quarter of the nineteenth century', as Albert Hourani once put it.[6]

Pan-Islamism was not al-Afghani's invention. Throughout the 1870s, pan-Islamic notions became appealing for a good number of Muslim thinkers. It was a concept that was born in a specific historical and political context. Before his arrival in Egypt in 1871, we know that al-Afghani did not clearly defend an all-purpose anti-colonial policy based on religious pan-Islamism.[7] In his fiery speeches, he instead focused on local proto-nationalisms, especially in countries with mixed religious communities. In the late 1870s, for example, he stressed the significance of the Egyptian national unity by recalling the glories of Egypt's Pharaonic past.[8] Due to a significant decline in the social, economic, political, and administrative system of Egypt under Khedive Isma'il as associated with the increase of European power, al-Afghani later combined this sense of proto-nationalism with pan-Islamism on the Egyptian scene.[9] Combining religious zealotry with political activism, he saw religion as a powerful vehicle by which he could address the communal sentiments of Muslims everywhere beyond any ethnic or linguistic ties.

Al-Afghani's Egyptian years were the most fruitful in his career. In Egypt, he became involved in the intellectual and political discussions of his time and his influence was spreading across various parts of the Islamic world. During his time, he also established ties with Masonic lodges in Egypt. According to A. Albert Kudsi-Zadeh, al-Afghani used his Masonic activity 'as a ready-made agency for political mobilization and agitation against the Khedive Isma'il and the increasing

---

[5] See, for example, Nikki R. Keddie, *An Islamic Response to Imperialism: Political and Religious Writings of Sayyid Jamal ad-Din 'al-Afghani'* (Berkeley, 1968); Nikki R. Keddie, *Sayyid Jamal ad-Din 'al-Afghani': A Political Biography* (Berkeley, 1972); Elie Kedourie, *Afghani and 'Abduh: An Essay on Religious Unbelief and Political Activism in Modern Egypt* (London, 1966); Elie Kedourie, 'Further Light on Afghani', *Middle Eastern Studies*, 1 (1965), 187–202; Albert Kudsi-Zadeh, 'Islamic Reform in Egypt: Some Observations on the Role of Afghani', *The Muslim World*, 61/1 (1971), 1–12; Albert Kudsi-Zadeh, *Sayyid Jamal al-Din Al-Afghani: An Annotated Bibliography* (Leiden, 1970); and Anwar Moazzam, *Jamal al-Din al-Afghani: A Muslim Intellectual* (New Delhi, 1984).

[6] Albert Hourani, *Arabic Thought in the Liberal Age 1798–1939* (Cambridge, 1983), 128.

[7] Keddie, *Sayyid Jamal ad-Din 'al-Afghani'*, 84–5.

[8] Keddie, *Sayyid Jamal ad-Din 'al-Afghani'*, 109.

[9] Keddie, *Sayyid Jamal ad-Din 'al-Afghani'*, 139–42.

**Fig. 6** Jamal al-Din al-Afghani (1838–97)     **Fig. 7** Muhammad 'Abduh (1849–1905)
(Bodleian Library, Oxford).                       (Egyptophilia Books).

European intervention in the affairs of Egypt'.[10] Al-Afghani's spirit of revolution in Egypt was sometimes militant. Generally, he had two aims in mind: to remove Khedive Isma'il's authoritarian rule; and to oppose what he regarded as the superstition, ignorance, and lack of political awareness of the masses. This could only take place by means of mobilizing the crowd and organizing his followers to overthrow—and, if necessary, assassinate—the authoritarian khedive and establish a modern Islamic regime.[11] Wilfrid Scawen Blunt (1840–1922), a British poet and political writer, recounted that 'Abduh reported in 1903 that al-Afghani proposed to 'Abduh himself to assassinate Khedive Isma'il as he passed in his carriage daily over the Qasr al-Nil bridge in Cairo, and 'Abduh seemed to have approved.[12] On the other hand, al-Afghani was on good terms with Crown Prince (and later Khedive) Tawfiq, who was also a prominent member of the Star of the East lodge, headed by al-Afghani himself. But al-Afghani's confrontational political mass speeches coupled with complaints from conservative 'ulama and European consuls negatively affected his relations with Tawfiq when the latter succeeded his father as Khedive

---

[10] A. Albert Kudsi-Zadeh, 'Afghānī and Freemasonry in Egypt', *Journal of the American Oriental Society*, 92/1 (1972), 25–35.

[11] Ahmed Ali Salem, 'Challenging Authoritarianism, Colonialism, and Disunity: The Islamic Political Reform Movements of al-Afghani and Rida', *American Journal of Islamic Social Sciences*, 21/2 (2004), 25–54, 28.

[12] Quoted in Keddie, *Sayyid Jamal ad-Din 'al-Afghani'*, 114.

**Fig. 8** Muhammad Rashid Rida (1865–1935) (Rida Family Archive, Cairo).

**Fig. 9** Hasan al-Banna (1906–49) (Public Domain).

in June 1879. Al-Afghani and many Egyptian nationalists had high expectations of the reforms which Tawfiq had supported before his accession to the throne. They even put pressure on the new Khedive, and al-Afghani in particular urged him to keep foreigners out of the government and to get rid of his non-Egyptian entourage.[13] Foreign consuls, especially the British, considered al-Afghani a serious threat to their relations with the new ruler. Consul-General Frank C. Lascelles (1841–1920) noted that al-Afghani became:

> a man of considerable capacity and of great power as an orator, and he was gradually obtaining an amount of influence over his hearers which threatened to become dangerous. Last year [1878] he took an active part in stirring up ill feeling against the Europeans, and more especially the English, of whom he seems to entertain a profound hatred.[14]

Tawfiq became frightened, and al-Afghani was eventually seized by the police and deported to the Suez Canal. From Suez, he was sent to India, where he stayed till 1882. In the 1880s, Egypt was occupied by the British after the collapse of the 'Urabi revolt. Soon al-Afghani decided to move from India to France, which he saw as a suitable place to carry out his anti-British policies.

---

[13] Kudsi-Zadeh, 'Afghānī and Freemasonry in Egypt', 32–3.
[14] Quoted in Kudsi-Zadeh, 'Afghānī and Freemasonry in Egypt', 33.

Al-Afghani was able to change his places of exile into platforms for the dissemination of his revolutionary ideas. His utilization of pan-Islam as a weapon against
European encroachment became more significant in his short-lived, though influential, journal *al-ʿUrwa al-Wuthqa* (published from 13 March to 16 October
1884), which was closely connected to a secret society of the same name. This society and its journal recruited many Muslim scholars, political activists, and thinkers, such as the Egyptian revolutionary Saʿd Zaghlul (1857–1927) and the eminent
Egyptian journalist Ibrahim al-Muwaylihi (1846–1906), who had to take an oath
of seeking every way to strengthen the unity of Islam and Muslims.[15] Al-Afghani
invited his Egyptian disciple ʿAbduh to join him in Paris; ʿAbduh had been living
in exile in Beirut because of his active role in ʿUrabi's uprising. In a small room
on a roof situated in the Rue Martela in Paris, al-Afghani, assisted by ʿAbduh as
co-editor, penned many revolutionary articles for the journal, which was distributed free of charge across the Muslim world. Already during his time in Egypt,
al-Afghani had advocated the power of the press in disseminating religious reform
ideas and political resistance. He urged his Egyptian admirers to use journalism as
a medium for that purpose. Throughout *al-ʿUrwa*'s articles, the editors proclaimed
that the journal's program was to serve Orientals by dwelling on the causes of
their deterioration and how they would reclaim their progress and power. Its main
themes included hostility to British imperialism, advocacy of Islamic unity, and
interpretation of Islamic notions in the light of urgent contemporary needs.[16]

It is remarkable that al-Afghani remained silent about French imperialism in
North Africa. He tried to exploit Anglo-French rivalry by attempting to interest the
French government in his anti-British enterprise.[17] However, he was well aware that
his pan-Islamic project was doomed to failure as long as Western colonialism (especially the British empire) and Eastern despotism continued to exist. He had therefore
devoted most of his energy to confronting colonialism in all its intellectual, military,
economic, and political aspects. The removal of European domination, he was convinced, would be a significant prelude to a renaissance based on Islamic tenets. Egypt
occupied a central place in *al-ʿUrwa*. The deteriorating political state of the country
became 'painful' for all Muslims because they considered it as a 'holy land' due to its
central location as a gateway to the Holy Shrines in the Arabian peninsula.[18]

Furthermore, articles in *al-ʿUrwa* argued that Western military expansion was
against the 'peaceful' tenets of Christianity. In contrast to the Gospel's admonition
to leave personal, racial, and world conflicts aside, its Western adherents competed
in seizing power in new colonies and in inventing devastating military machines
and arms. Muslims, on the other hand, were urged by their Holy Scriptures to
take the lead not only in professional military studies and arms, but in all fields of

---

[15] Rashid Rida, 'Fatihat al-mujallad al-hadi wa al-thalathin' ('Preface to Volume 31'), *Al-Manar*,
31/1 (May 1930), 6–10.
[16] Keddie, *Sayyid Jamal ad-Din 'al-Afghani'*, 220.
[17] Elie Kedourie, 'Afghani in Paris: A Note', *Middle Eastern Studies*, 8/1 (1972), 103.
[18] Jamal al-Din al-Afghani, *Al-Athar al-kamila* (*Complete Works*), ed. Sayyid Hadi Khusrawshahi,
9 vols (Cairo, 2002), i: *Al-ʿUrwa al-wuthqa*, 98.

science and arts, such as physics, engineering, and chemistry.[19] The West accused the Orientals of 'religious fanaticism', but they wholeheartedly supported Christian missions in their spread of Christianity. *Al-'Urwa*, for example, pointed to William Ewart Gladstone, a British leader who, according to al-Afghani, should have been attached to the principles of Western 'liberty', but still 'breathes the spirit of St Paul' in his personal life and politics.[20]

In al-Afghani's rhetoric, British colonial authority was merely 'illusion'. European states did not oppose the British expansion into the Islamic world because of its military powers and navy. They perceived Great Britain as a 'pale monster' or a 'tapeworm' that, despite its weakness, spoils health and ruins the environment.[21] Elsewhere, al-Afghani called the Indian people to assemble their great number of millions and power against the British encroachment in their land:

> If you [turned] into flies,' he wrote, 'your buzzing would deafen the ears of Great Britain... And if God changed each one of you into a turtle, that would cross the sea and surround Great Britain, you could drag its islands to the depth [of water] and return back to your India being liberated.[22]

Facing increasing financial problems, *al-'Urwa* was finally suspended. Al-Afghani changed his political tactics, when he finally recognized that none of his political goals had been achieved. Already during his stay in Paris, he had become involved in direct political discussions with British policy-makers concerning the Sudanese Mahdi and his resistance movement.[23] Al-Afghani was sometimes ambivalent in his political positions. At times, he encouraged the British to declare war on Russia, but in 1887 he asked the tsarist government to declare war on Britain.[24] Finally he felt obliged to cooperate with the existing Muslim regimes, some of which he had previously deemed as authoritarian and corrupt. He was invited by Shah Nasir al-Din to Persia to propose a political reform program. Once there, his relationship with the shah soon completely deteriorated. Al-Afghani hoped to establish an Islamic consultative regime in Persia, but soon realized that the shah was allowing more and more British influence in his country. Disillusioned, he was finally expelled from Persia. As al-Afghani had gained support from religious scholars and the pious across Persia, he submitted a plea to the famous Persian cleric Mirza Hasan Shirazi Shaykh al-Ra'is to issue a fatwa boycotting the tobacco trade with the British Tobacco Régie during the so-called Tobacco Protest in 1890. This revolt is considered to be the first mass movement in modern Persia. During the upheaval, some of the most respected Persian religious scholars employed anti-colonial pan-Islamic slogans to mobilize the masses. It was also one of the first times in modern Persian history that the religious elites were able to force

---

[19] al-Afghani, *Al-Athar al-kamila*, i, 118.
[20] al-Afghani, *Al-Athar al-kamila*, i, 138–9.
[21] al-Afghani, *Al-Athar al-kamila*, i, 222.
[22] Quoted in al-Afghani, *Al-Athar al-kamila*, i, 46.
[23] Keddie, *Sayyid Jamal ad-Din 'al-Afghani'*, 229–46.
[24] Keddie, *Sayyid Jamal ad-Din 'al-Afghani'*, 251.

the government to withdraw their policies. The revolt was a decisive victory for al-Afghani's plans.[25]

In the end, al-Afghani succumbed to Sultan Abdülhamid II's invitation to Istanbul, where he stayed during the final years of his life under house arrest. Frustrated by the sultan's hesitancy towards his political ambition of establishing a Muslim league, al-Afghani harshly attacked him and renounced his allegiance to him as caliph because, according to al-Afghani, the sultan no longer deserved that title.[26] During al-Afghani's stay in Istanbul, Nasir al-Din Shah was assassinated by Mirza Riza Kirmani, a Babi sympathizer of al-Afghani. Although his real motives are not entirely known, during the interrogations Kirmani declared that he was enticed by al-Afghani's call to 'kill the tyrant'.[27] At this time, al-Afghani came to regret that he had abandoned his former revolutionary path by yielding to his new strategy of achieving pan-Islamism through the ruling Muslim leaders. In one of his final notes to the Persians, he plainly stated:

> Would that I had sown all the seeds of my ideas in the receptive ground of the people's thoughts! Well would it have been had I not wasted this fruitful and beneficent seed of mine in the salt and sterile soil of that effete Sovereignty!... Nature is your friend, and the Creator of Nature your ally. The stream of renovation flows quickly towards the East. The edifice of despotic government totters to its fall. Strive so far as you can to destroy the foundations of this despotism, not to pluck up and cast out its individual agents. Strive so far as in you lies to abolish those practices which stand between the Persians and their happiness, not to annihilate those who employ these practices. If you merely strive to oppose individuals, your time will only be lost. If you seek only to prevail against them, the evil practice will draw to itself others. Endeavour to remove those obstacles which prevent your friendship with other nations.[28]

A few years later, in 1897, al-Afghani died without achieving his plan of uniting Islam against the expansion of European empires, but he significantly popularized his pan-Islamic visions as well as other political, religious, and intellectual concepts for his followers.


## REFORM FROM BELOW

Muhammad 'Abduh (Fig. 7), al-Afghani's close friend, remained involved in the Egyptian political nationalist movement and took an important part in the 'Urabi

---

[25] Keddie, *Sayyid Jamal ad-Din 'al-Afghani'*, 355; on the Tobacco Protest, see also Nikki R. Keddie, *Religion and Rebellion in Iran: The Tobacco Protest of 1891–1892* (London, 1966); and Mansoor Moaddel, 'Shi'i Political Discourse and Class Mobilization in the Tobacco Movement of 1890–1892', *Sociological Forum*, 7/3 (1992), 447–68.

[26] Salem, 'Challenging Authoritarianism, Colonialism, and Disunity', 32.

[27] Abbas Amanat, *Pivot of the Universe: Nasir al-Din Shah Qajar and the Iranian Monarchy, 1831–1896* (London, 1997), 441–3.

[28] Moazzam, *Jamal al-Din al-Afghani, a Muslim Intellectual*, 131; also quoted in Ulrika Mårtensson, '"The One" Over "the Many": A Historical Perspective on the Pan-Islamic Salafiyyah', *Studies in Contemporary Islam*, 10/1–2 (2008), 43–88, 66–7.

revolt after al-Afghani's deportation from Egypt. He wrote numerous articles in the Egyptian daily *al-Ahram*, which reflected al-Afghani's political views. Khedive Tawfiq, who had earlier expelled al-Afghani from Egypt, put 'Abduh under house arrest in his village in northern Egypt because of his political opposition to British-controlled Egypt. In 1880, 'Abduh was appointed as one of the three editors of the Egyptian official journal, *al-Waqa'i' al-Misriyya* (*Egyptian Proceedings*), and later became its editor-in-chief.[29] Joining the 'Urabi revolt, he soon entered the political arena. In a number of articles, he expressed his views on constitutionalism and the importance of the rule of law in the Egyptian state as based on liberty and civil principles.[30] After the British occupation of Egypt, 'Abduh was arrested and maltreated in prison. Later, he was exiled for three years in Beirut before voluntarily joining al-Afghani in Paris. Their press collaboration in the French capital reveals that 'Abduh shared al-Afghani's revolutionary political attitudes during this period. Supporting al-Afghani's political ideas, 'Abduh visited the House of Commons in London in 1884 and discussed with the British Secretary of State for War, Lord Hartington, and others many political issues concerning British control over Egypt and Sudan, especially the mahdi uprising. It was reported that 'Abduh then entered Egypt in disguise, hoping to negotiate with the mahdi in Sudan at al-Afghani's request.[31]

Despite al-Afghani's tremendous influence on 'Abduh, the latter had already decided during his stay in Paris to distance himself from his mentor's political path by exerting more effort in the field of education, which he considered as a gradual, but more effective, instrument to reform religion and society.[32] He now became persuaded that the revolution of the Islamic countries should take place from below through good education. It was futile, he now argued, to push people to seize their political rights from their leaders by force if they were not 'educated' about these rights. Rashid Rida, 'Abduh's Syrian student, recalled that, at their first meeting in Cairo in 1897, 'Abduh criticized al-Afghani and other Muslim intellectuals and papers for their involvement in politics. If al-Afghani had exploited his unique power in education and learning instead, he argued, it would have been much more beneficial for all Muslims. In Paris, al-Afghani and 'Abduh had already argued fiercely; 'Abduh had suggested to al-Afghani that it would be better to abandon politics by leaving for a far-off location, away from government surveillance and where they could teach a select group of students their reformist views. After ten years, these students could later return to their countries and disseminate such ideas. Al-Afghani regularly accused 'Abduh of timidity and dispiritedness.[33] 'Abduh tried to convince his mentor that reforming corrupt rulers and

---

[29] Mark Sedgwick, *Muhammad Abduh* (Oxford, 2009), 29.

[30] Sedgwick, *Muhammad Abduh*, 33.

[31] Hourani, *Arabic Thought in the Liberal Age*, 134; see also Christopher Radler, *Eine Biographie als politisches Mittel: Muḥammad 'Abduh (1849–1905) und die Rebellion des Aḥmad 'Urābī in der Rezeption Ṭāhir aṭ-Ṭanāḥis (Muḏakkirāt al-Imām Muḥammad 'Abduh)* (Berlin, 2010).

[32] Keddie, *Sayyid Jamal ad-Din 'al-Afghani'*, 228.

[33] Rashid Rida, *Tarikh al-ustadh al-imam al-shaykh Muhammad Abduh* (*The Biography of the Imam Master Sheikh Muhammad 'Abduh*), 3 vols (Cairo, 2003), i, 894.

their entourages was impossible. It would have been better for al-Afghani, 'Abduh claimed, to have improved education and the quality of religious preaching in mosques even if it sometimes involved political concession and the avoidance of direct attacks on rulers.[34]

'Abduh openly argued that, since Muslim interests had become unavoidably interwoven with those of Europeans throughout the world, cooperation could prove more fruitful than confrontation and discord.[35] This easing of relations with existing rulers, including European politicians, proved tremendously beneficial to 'Abduh in his reform program. Although he had cooperated with the leaders of the 'Urabi revolt, his revolutionary ideas were more moderate than those of the military and populist leaders. Furthermore, he argued that 'the Orient could not improve unless it is led by a just dictator', which contradicted al-Afghani's saying that 'the leader should be just and powerful, not a dictator'.[36] Confronting al-Afghani's political position, 'Abduh was reported to have regularly said: 'when *al-siyasa* (politics) enters, it corrupts everything'. One of his most famous statements was: 'I totally agree with you, if you say that politics persecutes the intellect, science and religion. I seek refuge of God from...the word *"siyasa"*, [its] meaning, [all its] letters, any thoughts of [it], each land where [it] is mentioned, and everybody who speaks or learns...about politics.'[37]

In 1885, 'Abduh for the second time returned to Beirut, where he taught theology, history, and classical literature. His house became a center for scholars and writers, Christians, Druzes, and Muslims who visited him to discuss religious and literary issues.[38] In Beirut, 'Abduh evolved a systematic theoretical program for religious education in particular, which should be accessible to all strata of society. In his view, there should be a different type of education for each class in society. The ordinary people should be taught the broad principles of beliefs—but not the details of differences between religious sects—and Islamic history and Muslim global expansion. Government officials should be trained in logic and philosophy, doctrines with special emphasis on rational proofs, the avoidance of dissension between the different rites, ethics with the same emphasis on its rational basis and a study of the exemplary lives of the *salaf*, and religious history. Teachers and spiritual directors should master: the religious sciences; the Arabic language; the Qur'an with its commentary, which would take into account the customs, traditions, languages, and intellectual methodology of the Arabs at the time of the Revelation; the hadith sciences and the authentication of hadith; a complete system of ethics; theology and jurisprudence; the arts of persuasion and argument; and ancient and modern history.[39]

---

[34] Rida, *Tarikh al-ustadh al-imam al-shaykh Muhammad Abduh*, 896.

[35] Sedgwick, *Muhammad Abduh*, 8.

[36] Salem, 'Challenging Authoritarianism, Colonialism, and Disunity', 36.

[37] Rida, *Tarikh al-ustadh al-imam*, 891.

[38] Hourani, *Arabic Thought in the Liberal Age*, 134.

[39] Hourani, *Arabic Thought in the Liberal Age*, 154; see also David C. Kinsey, 'Efforts for Educational Synthesis under Colonial Rule: Egypt and Tunisia', *Comparative Education Review*, 15/2 (1971), 172–87.

In 1888, 'Abduh decided to return to his homeland. 'The Syrians', he wrote, 'are not like my own people, and a day spent here is not like a day spent at home.'[40] After his return, he did not resume teaching at al-Azhar as he had hoped, but started a career in public service as a judge in local Egyptian tribunals. A year later, he was appointed Mufti of Egypt, the highest religious office of the country, which enabled him to realize his hope for reform, not only in legal matters but also in religious education, law, and waqf endowments. The fame of Abduh's religious reformist views reached across the world and his ideas were soon discussed among Muslims in Africa, tsarist Russia, Southeast Asia, and East Asia. Besides his significant role in establishing private schools, 'Abduh convinced the Khedive in 1895 to set up an administrative council for al-Azhar. For almost ten years, he served as one of this council's prominent members and managed to achieve essential educational reforms in that ancient university.[41]

In order to achieve his agenda for reform, 'Abduh cooperated with the British authorities in Egypt. He remained on excellent terms with the British Commissioner in Egypt, Lord Cromer (1841–1917), who had earlier supported 'Abduh's return to Egypt from Beirut. In his *Modern Egypt*, Cromer described 'Abduh as:

> a very superior type...a man of broad and enlightened views...He recognised the necessity of European assistance in the work of reform. But he did not belong to the same category as the Europeanised Egyptian, whom he regarded as a bad copy of the original...In fact, Sheikh Mohammed Abdu was a somewhat dreamy and impractical but, nevertheless, genuine Egyptian patriot; it were perhaps well for the cause of Egyptian patriotism if there were more like him...[42]

'Abduh believed that one of the reasons behind the perceived Muslim decline was that they, unlike the majority of Western people, did not work for the sake of the public interest of their countries. On one of his journeys to Europe on board an English vessel, 'Abduh tried assessing the social and intellectual status of ordinary English fellow-passengers. During a conversation with an English coal miner, he was surprised that this Englishman's regard for his country was part of his ambition in his work. His utmost aspiration was that his government would succeed in managing the national consumption of coal so his country could enrich its treasury, which in turn would benefit himself and his family.[43]

'Abduh was impressed by Western science and technology, arguing in his writings that Muslims must not only be impressed by the outcome of European civilization and its benefits, but that they should also studiously search for Western sources of knowledge. Anxious about the 'dangers' of Westernization, 'Abduh struggled with the question of authenticity. Livingston correctly remarked that 'Abduh worried that unthinking importation of 'Western civilization' would lead to the opposite of the intended result: a restricted,

---

[40] Sedgwick, *Muhammad Abduh*, 71.
[41] Hourani, *Arabic Thought in the Liberal Age*, 135.
[42] Evelyn Baring, Earl of Cromer, *Modern Egypt*, 2 vols (New York, 1908), ii, 179.
[43] Umar Ryad, 'Islamic Reformism and Great Britain: Rashid Rida's Image as Reflected in the Journal Al-Manar in Cairo', *Islam and Christian-Muslim Relations*, 21/3 (2010), 263–85, 266.

artificial ideology far removed from the real objectives of the reformers. In other words:

> intellectual or institutional models had to be understood in their European context, then in their Islamic context, in order to achieve authenticity of the transformed versions. Otherwise, without radical critical analysis and cultural reconstitution, as it were, they would be alien transplants without roots, destined to wither in Muslim soil.[44]

During his time as the Mufti of Egypt, 'Abduh regularly visited Europe and attended seminars and conferences of Orientalists. At the age of 40, he started to learn French and thus gained first-hand access to major European works on religion, philosophy, education, and history. 'Abduh admired Herbert Spencer, whom he visited in Britain in 1903. The reason for his various trips to Europe was to 'refresh' his spirit and thoughts. Remarkably enough, 'Abduh's stays in Europe, the continent of the colonizers, were a source of motivation. Every time he went there, it gave him new hope that the deteriorating state of Muslims could be reformed. 'When I come to Europe,' 'Abduh told his disciple Rida in early 1900, 'and stay there for one or two months, such hopes return to me. It becomes easy for me to believe in [the success] of what I have already thought to be impossible. Do not ask me what the reason for that is, as I cannot exemplify it. But this what such trips do with me.'[45]

'Abduh believed that colonial expansion over the Islamic world meant the dissemination of Western values in place of Muslim traditions and values. In his eyes, blind imitation of the West would uproot Muslim morality, ethics, and values. European ideas should not be totally rejected, but were to be 'filtered, distilled and integrated in a society whose core is religious and whose religious leaders have their place in the intellectual *avant garde* creating the new from the old. This can be done without losing what is perceived as essentially Islamic.'[46]

## NOSTALGIA FOR THE CALIPHATE

While al-Afghani and 'Abduh had close personal contacts with a number of Europeans, and lived in Europe for years, their follower Rashid Rida (Fig. 8), in contrast, was a Muslim scholar, who, in the words of Albert Hourani, 'belonged to the last generation of those who could be fully educated and yet alive in a self-sufficient Islamic world of thought'.[47] In his influential journal *al-Manar*, Rida positioned himself as heir to their pan-Islamic thought. Within the realm of ideas regarding the caliphate and pan-Islamism, Rida raised a lengthy and complex array of questions related to Europe, its peoples, religion, ethics, and culture. Such views took various shapes throughout the years, primarily due to the changing political

---

[44] John W. Livingston, 'Muhammad Abduh on Science', *Muslim World*, 85/3–4 (1995), 215–34, 223–4.

[45] Rida, *Tarikh al-ustadh al-imam*, 846–7.        [46] Rida, *Tarikh al-ustadh al-imam*, 224.

[47] Hourani, *Arabic Thought in the Liberal Age*, 83.

situation and turmoil in the Muslim world during the first three decades of the twentieth century.[48]

In his early years in Cairo, Rida did not only have 'an accommodating stance' towards Britain, but also sketched an idealizing picture of it as a colonizer.[49] For Rida, if a Muslim country had to be ruled by a European power, it should preferably be Britain, since Muslims under British rule enjoyed freedom of religion. In these early years of his journal, Rida's tone was moderate, and he was sometimes even ready to defend the British empire against accusations. When many Eastern newspapers attacked the aggressive British policy during the Second Boer War (1899–1902), for example, he defended the British people as the nation furthest from cruelty in war, who always opted for peace. In his view, most of these journals blindly echoed the attacks made by the press in other 'jealous' European nations, whose aim was to denigrate the British as deviating from the common path of human virtue. Rida concluded that the British attitude was 'natural', and the Transvaal reaction was not 'surprising'. In his eyes, Britain did not commit any improper actions:

> All living bodies, animals or plants... demand nutrition from outside as long as they are alive. This nutrition allows their constitution to grow by preserving their existence and power from one stage to another. When the Maker of the universe allows the [body] to become dissolute and vanish, it will be unable to get sufficient food to preserve its existence. Factors of decomposition will assault it suddenly till it ends with its exhaustion and annihilation.[50]

Influenced by Edmond Demolins (1852–1907) and his views on the superiority of the Anglo-Saxons, Rida became impressed by 'the English independent way of upbringing and education'. He even argued that, despite the spread of its colonies over a quarter of the world, Great Britain was less interested in wars than any other state. If the empire had established an alliance with the United States, Rida asserted, the Anglo-Saxons would have dominated half the world. Although many contemporary nations might outmatch the Anglo-Saxons in many aspects of ethics and virtue, the Anglo-Saxons' increasing moral and material progress primarily arose from their combination of dignity and supremacy, together with fundamentals of knowledge, virtue, and ethics in society. In the early 1900s, Rida argued that the link between ethical habits and military power as intertwined with economic and political success was the secret behind British progress and superiority over other European states.[51]

After Queen Victoria's death in January 1901, Rida published a positive obituary of her cultured manner and zeal for religiosity. He praised Great Britain as a nation rich in great politicians, adding that Queen Victoria was fortunate to be

---

[48] Ryad, 'Islamic Reformism and Great Britain'.
[49] Mahmoud Haddad, 'Arab Religious Nationalism in the Colonial Era: Rereading Rashid Rida's Ideas on the Caliphate', *Journal of the American Oriental Society*, 117/2 (1997), 253–77, 255.
[50] Ryad, 'Islamic Reformism and Great Britain', 264.
[51] Ryad, 'Islamic Reformism and Great Britain', 265.

served by such great men as Lord Melbourne, Sir Robert Peel, Lord John Russell, the Earl of Derby, Gladstone, and Lord Salisbury. Rida defended the queen against critics who accused her of being a 'mute machine', who neither knew how to work on her own, nor was capable of administering her cabinet. Rida found that she used to look at things and express her views on issues as a whole. He was moreover impressed by her great influence within Europe, her age, and her strong family ties with other European rulers, namely the Russian tsar and the German kaiser. A hand-written letter from the queen, Rida wrote, would solve the most complicated political problems, which any men would fail to manage. 'Britain', he concluded, 'lost the sun of glory and the star of luck by losing her.'[52]

Rida believed that one of the secrets of the success of the British empire was its endurance and ability to combine 'comfort and luxury' with 'strength and power'. On his way to India in 1912 on the Royal Mail ship, for instance, he made a favorable remark regarding the keenness of Englishmen on physical fitness and their 'unforgettable high manners and behavior'. Observing their habitual physical fitness, Rida now understood the secret of how their rulers and soldiers could bear the 'burning heat [of the Indian climate] without weariness, boredom or harm'.[53]

On the other hand, like his pan-Islamic predecessors, Rida was absolutely convinced that there was a close connection between religion and European foreign policy. Europe would simply exploit religion as a political tool for mobilizing European Christians and for inflaming their 'fanatical' sentiments against Muslim countries. In Britain itself, religious strife between Catholics and Protestants was a symptom of deep-rooted fanaticism in Europe.[54] In his analysis of the linkage between Christian missionaries and colonial powers, Rida drew further historical parallels, such as the collaboration of the Church with the authorities in converting Muslims and Jews in medieval Spain. Like Afghani, he gave the example of Gladstone, who was deeply imbued with Christian theology and hatred for Islam. Another example was the English politician Lord Salisbury, who, according to Rida, was reported to have said: 'We should retrieve what the Crescent had taken from the Cross.'[55]

Following 'Abduh, Rida abandoned any involvement in politics early in his career. Before the First World War, he often stressed his loyalty to the Ottoman empire, which he saw as the necessary representative of Muslim political power. During the war, he took a different course by calling for the re-establishment of an Arab caliphate in order to achieve Islamic unity. As the downfall of the Ottoman empire was foreseeable, Rida proposed that the new caliphate should build up a commonwealth of Muslim states. In this period, Rida promoted an Anglo-Arab agreement that might guarantee Arab independence and save both the temporal and spiritual authority of Islam. With the war underway, Rida went even further by

---

[52] Ryad, 'Islamic Reformism and Great Britain', 265.
[53] Ryad, 'Islamic Reformism and Great Britain', 266.
[54] Ryad, 'Islamic Reformism and Great Britain', 267.
[55] Umar Ryad, *Islamic Reformism and Christianity: Critical Reading of the Works of Muhammad Rashid Rida and His Associates (1898–1935)* (Leiden, 2009), 130.

appealing for a complete restoration of an Arab caliphate to replace the Ottoman one.[56] He made several attempts to obtain support for his plans from European colonial authorities in Egypt. In July 1915, he told Sir Mark Sykes (1879–1919), assistant secretary to the British war cabinet, that it was necessary to 'set up another Mohammedan state to maintain Mohammedan prestige'.[57] He also tried to persuade the British intelligence department in Cairo that his new organization, the Decentralization Party, could influence Arab officers in the Ottoman army and encourage them to rebel against their Turkish and German commanders.[58] Rida also approached Gilbert Clayton (1875–1929), the director of British intelligence in Cairo for negotiations in this regard. Clayton observed that Rida realized that his scheme for an independent Arab empire was 'unlikely to be fulfilled in his lifetime'. Skeptical regarding Rida's ambitions, British officials in Egypt considered him 'rather a visionary'.[59] However, at least for the purposes of propaganda, London supported the idea of an Arab caliphate and that King Hussein of the Hijaz should assume the title of caliph.[60]

In 1911, Rida established the Society or Arab Association whose main objective was to unite the rulers of Arabia. His Arab nationalism was not meant to replace the Ottoman rule, but rather to integrate it within the Ottoman empire. In the eyes of European colonial officials and diplomats, though, it was apparent that Rida did not represent the opinions of the Arab world. Sir Mark Sykes (1879–1919) portrayed Rida after one of their meetings as 'a leader of Pan-Arab and Pan-Islamic thought. In conversation he talks as much as he writes. He is a hard uncompromising fanatical Moslem, the mainspring of whose ideas is the desire to eliminate Christian influence and to make Islam a political power in as wide a field as possible.'[61] Rida's political activism and his pro-caliphate tone irritated British authorities in Egypt, who discussed sending him into exile in Malta during the First World War.[62] In the end, as British officials in Egypt showed themselves increasingly uninterested in his plans, Rida's anti-British sentiments ran high. His above-mentioned tone of admiration regarding the tolerance in British colonial policy had now changed: 'England was trying to efface the Muhammedan authority and rule from the world.'[63]

Rida's support of Britain was largely opportunistic. In fact, he also attempted to contact other European diplomats in Cairo during the First World War. A few

[56] Haddad, 'Arab Religious Nationalism in the Colonial Era', 263.
[57] Haddad, 'Arab Religious Nationalism in the Colonial Era', 263.
[58] Eliezer Tauber, 'Rashid Rida's Political Attitudes During World War I', *The Muslim World*, 85/1–2 (1995), 107–22; and Eliezer Tauber, 'Rashid Rida and Faysal's Kingdom in Syria', *The Muslim World*, 85/3–4 (1995), 235–46.
[59] Eliezer Tauber, 'The Political Life of Rashid Rida', *Arabist: Budapest Studies in Arabic*, 19–20 (1998), 261–72, 265.
[60] S. O. Khan, 'The "Caliphate Question": British Views and Policy Toward Pan-Islamic Politics and the End of the Ottoman Caliphate', *American Journal of Social Sciences*, 24/4 (2007), 1–25.
[61] 'Select reports and telegrams from Sir Mark Sykes', report no. 14, quoted in Haddad, 'Arab Religious Nationalism in the Colonial Era', 268.
[62] Haddad, 'Arab Religious Nationalism in the Colonial Era', 268.
[63] Tauber, 'The Political Life of Rashid Rida', 265.

years earlier, in 1912 and 1913, the German consulate in Cairo reported to Berlin about the activities of Syrian exiles in Cairo led by Rida. It was reported that Rida met with the German emissary in Cairo and discussed the possibility of establishing an independent Arab caliphate under the Khedive of Egypt ruling Syria and Arabia. Rida asked for German diplomatic support in acquiring armaments to use against Britain and France—a request which was quickly refused.[64]

In Rida's eyes, the worst result of the First World War was the prospect that the European empires would make further efforts in the future to exert their military power.[65] For him, the war clearly demonstrated the 'beastly' and 'illusive' materialist character of European civilization which claimed to monopolize peace and justice.[66] Rida had anticipated that Britain was going to win the war, even though Germany was the foremost European nation in terms of its armaments and militarized order. Nevertheless, Rida believed that Britain was much cleverer in its 'political cunning', evident in its fueling of the sentiments of other governments against Germany.[67]

After the war, inspired by Woodrow Wilson's call for self-determination for all nations, Egyptian nationalists started to press the British for independence. On the eve of the Paris Peace Conference, they formed a *wafd* (delegation) under the leadership of Lutfi al-Sayyid, Sa'd Zaghlul, and others, to demand independence. When their request to travel to Paris was rejected, the American legation in Cairo received dozens of petitions against the British refusal and asking for Egyptian self-determination. In March 1919, Zaghlul and three other members of the *wafd* were arrested and were deported to Malta. This act provoked the popular uprising of spring 1919, which spread over the provincial cities of Lower and Upper Egypt.[68] At this point, Rida completely changed his views towards Britain. He declared that the Muslim world was sympathetic to Germany because of its alliance with the Ottoman empire, a symbol of Islamic sovereignty. He warned against the annexation of Iraq and Syria by Britain and France, warning that Great Britain should spare itself of the enmity of 300 million Muslims.[69] More than 50 years after the appointment of Gordon as the governor general of the Sudan, Rida cited Gordon as evidence of Britain's underhand dealings, claiming that Britain had sent a Christian clergyman on that mission purely in order to convert Muslims to Christianity and to monopolize their souls and bodies for the sake of its interests. Rida's former lofty rhetoric about religious freedom in British colonies had

---

[64] Donald M. McKale, *War by Revolution: Germany and Great Britain in the Middle East in the Era of World War I* (Kent, OH, 1998), 42–3.

[65] Rashid Rida, 'Al-haqq wa al-quwwa' ('Truth and Power'), *Al-Manar*, 18/2 (March 1915), 141–55.

[66] Rashid Rida, 'Harb al-madaniyya al-urubiyya' ('The War of European Civilization'), *Al-Manar*, 18/3 (April 1915), 182–92.

[67] Rashid Rida, 'Aqibat harb al-madaniyya al-urubiyya' ('Consequences of the War of European Civilization'), *Al-Manar*, 21/7 (April 1920), 337–44.

[68] Erez Manela, *The Wilsonian Moment: Self-Determination and the International Origins of Anticolonial Nationalism* (Oxford, 2007), 63–76.

[69] A. Tibawi, 'From Rashid Rida to Lloyd George', *Islamic Quarterly*, 20–2/1–2 (1978), 24–9, 26.

changed into a diatribe against the 'British plot to colonize nations, to enslave people and to destroy their religions'.[70]

Rida's antipathy towards European intervention in the Muslim world reached its peak in the 1920s when he formulated his comprehensive pan-Islamic thesis in his famous work *al-Khilafa aw al-Imama al-'Uzma (The Caliphate or the Exalted Imamate)*[71] in which he addressed the political problem of Islamic unity following the Turkish National Assembly's decision to strip the Ottoman caliphate of political power, and the failure of the Syrian Arab Kingdom.[72] Rida urged Muslims to make use of the international political changes after the war by creating a united political system on the basis of the bonds of their communal faith, rather than ethnicity and fragmented nationalism. Relying on a number of classical and medieval religious treatises, he argued the future caliph should be an independent *mujtahid* and an Arab Qurayshite by language and ethnicity.[73]

In his treatise, Rida stressed the role and supremacy of Arabs in unifying Islam. He also made a close connection between the Hijaz and Islam where, according to one hadith, two religions could never co-exist within the borders of the Arabian peninsula. British imperialist goals and European intervention in the Arabian peninsula should be therefore resisted by all means. He discredited the Hashemite Sharif Hussein Ibn 'Ali (1854–1931) as candidate for the caliphate, as he was too dependent on the British and was not an eligible *mujtahid*. His rule was above all repressive and personal.[74] The Saudis were the most appropriate nominees for taking up this task, not only because they were entitled to protect the holy cities from imperialism, but also due to their political power to bring stability and security to the Hijaz and to facilitate the purposes of the annual hajj. Rida refuted all 'rumors', which he ascribed to British propaganda, that the Wahhabis had desecrated shrines and corpses and slaughtered women and children in their conquest of Mecca. In reality, Rida assured his followers, they had restored Islamic rule to the holy city and ensured that it would not suffer the oppression of despotic rulers in the future.[75] His stance towards the Turks was somehow ambivalent. In 1932, he wrote to his close associate, the Druze Prince Shakib Arslan (1869–1946), that he would still prefer the rule of the Turks to the Europeans, despite the fact that the Turks had 'humiliated' the Arabs. He would even be ready to accept the rule of Turkish atheists, who primarily opposed the Arabic language and Salafi Islam, rather than be subject to European colonial rule.[76]

---

[70] Ryad, 'Islamic Reformism and Great Britain', 271.

[71] See, for example, Muhammad Rashid Rida, *Al-Khilafa aw al-imama al-'uzma (The Caliphate, or the Greatest Imamate)* (Cairo, 1934); and Henri Laoust, *Traduction annotée d'al-Hilâfa au al imâma al-'uzmâ (Le Califat ou l'imâma suprême)* (Paris, 1986).

[72] John Willis, 'Debating the Caliphate: Islam and Nation in the Work of Rashid Rida and Abul Kalam Azad', *International History Review*, 32/4 (2010), 711–32, 717.

[73] Willis, 'Debating the Caliphate', 717–19; see also Haddad, 'Arab Religious Nationalism in the Colonial Era', 273.

[74] Haddad, 'Arab Religious Nationalism in the Colonial Era', 275.

[75] Willis, 'Debating the Caliphate', 722.

[76] Quoted in Haddad, 'Arab Religious Nationalism in the Colonial Era', 276.

## CONCLUSION

This chapter has analyzed three different voices of pan-Islamism. Although al-Afghani, 'Abduh, and Rida represent a single school of thought, namely the *salafiyya* movement, their responses to the age of imperialism were anything but homogeneous. Each of them molded different solutions to the perceived malaise of Islam. Western powers made several attempts to exploit pan-Islamism when circumstances seemed to favor their policies. It is true that their interpretations and application of pan-Islamism in their reform plans should be 'linked with the whole problem of the reaction of the Islamic world to the impact of the Occident...and the international relations of the great powers toward one another'.[77]

The pan-Islamic ideologies we have discussed show the interplay between Islamic reformism, pan-Islam, and empire. They emerged in the period of the expansion of military and political colonialism on the one hand, and the social and intellectual transformation of the Muslim world on the other. The actors of pan-Islam theorized ideological instruments to challenge the imperial expansion of Europe. Above all, they stressed the significance of establishing a universal and central power, to which Muslims all over the world should owe loyalty and obedience. This central government would counteract the military, educational, political, and economic weakness of the Muslim world. In so doing, the spokesmen of this movement adopted a largely defensive tone in their emphasis on early Islam and its viability as a model for Muslim unity. Nevertheless, the '*Weltanschauung* of pan-Islam', as Jacob M. Landau put it, 'has been throughout a mixture (in various dosages) of utopian romanticism and modern pragmatism'.[78]

This chapter revolved around the actions and reactions of the three most eminent pan-Islamists who represent three different generations of global Muslim movements, networks, activists, and intellectuals who operated in the orbit of pan-Islam against imperialism. Many of these networks were entangled and had a transnational character. For example, in British India, the Khilafat Movement, which mobilized its pan-Islamic appeal for political gains in the broader context of the British policy towards Turkey and India, had solid connections with Rida in Egypt.[79] In the early twentieth century, pan-Islam was a crucial transitional moment of political nationalist resistance to imperialism in Morocco and North Africa.[80] As a zealous pan-Islamist Tatar intellectual, Abdurrashid Ibrahim (1857–1944) was able to establish direct contacts between pan-Islamist intellectuals and pan-Asianists in Asia and Japan.[81] In interwar Europe, Shakib Arslan (1869–1946),

---

[77]  Lee, 'The Origins of Pan-Islamism', 280.

[78]  Landau, *The Politics of Pan-Islam*, 307–8.

[79]  M. Naeem Qureshi, *Pan-Islam in British Indian Politics: A Study of the Khilafat Movement, 1918–1924* (Leiden, 1999).

[80]  Edmund Burke, 'Pan-Islam and Moroccan Resistance to French Colonial Penetration, 1900–1912', *Journal of African History*, 13/1 (1972), 97–118.

[81]  Sadia Sattar, 'Old Friendships: Exploring the Historic Relationship Between Pan-Islamism and Japanese Pan-Asianism' (MA, University of Pittsburgh, 2008); Mikhail Meyer, 'An Islamic Perspective in Russian Public Opinion: The Russian Tatar Thinker Abdurrashid Ibrahim (1857–1944)', *Archiv Orientální*, 80/2 (2012), 259–72; see also the chapter by Robert D. Crews in this volume.

one of 'Abduh's disciples and Rida's associate, made his place of exile Geneva 'the umbilical cord of the Islamic world'.[82] As a community of intellectual and activists beyond national boundaries, they therefore attempted to increase the ethos of transnational pan-Islamism in the face of colonial powers.

The influence of al-Afghani, 'Abduh, and Rida on many Muslim thinkers and activists of the twentieth century cannot be overestimated. In attempting to examine the interplay of complex socio-political forces that defined the major contours of pan-Islamism and its struggle against imperialism, one can look afresh at the contemporary scene without resorting to a neatly tailored or exaggerated hypothesis. Even at the grassroots level, the ideas of these great reformers and modernists became influential. Muslims in the contemporary age are still riding the crest of the same pan-Islamist waves. Pan-Islamic networks, in which Rashid Rida and his associates assumed a central position, were on the fault line of later developments in contemporary Islamic thought. Rida can be seen as the exemplary intermediate figure between classic and vernacular discourse and between secular rulers and masses, whose intellectual and journalistic pattern is being followed with the advent of digital technologies today.[83] The Muslim Brotherhood, one of the most influential reformist movements, was established in 1928 in Egypt. Their activities coincided with the flourishing of the worldwide pan-Islamist activities. Hasan al-Banna (1906–49) (Fig. 9), its founder, was a disciple of Rida and published the journal of *al-Manar* after the latter's death. After the Second World War, the heirs of this religious intellectual heritage developed their ideas into two extremes of Islam, namely, a reformist Islam open to external influences, and another variant which represents radical and rigid world views.[84]

---

[82] William L. Cleveland, *Islam Against the West: Shakib Arslan and the Campaign for Islamic Nationalism* (Austin, TX, 1985), 67; Raja Adal, 'Shakib Arslan's Imagining of Europe: The Colonizer, the Inquisitor, the Islamic, the Virtuous, and the Friend', in Nathalie Clayer and Eric Germain (eds), *Islam in Inter-War Europe* (London, 2008), 156–82; and Umar Ryad, 'New Episodes in Moroccan Nationalism under Colonial Role: Reconsideration of Shakīb Arslān's Centrality in Light of Unpublished Materials', *Journal of North African Studies*, 16/1 (2011), 117–42.

[83] Jon W. Anderson and Yves Gonzalez-Quijano, 'Technological Mediation and the Emergence of Transnational Muslim Publics', in Armando Salvatore and Dale F. Eickelman (eds), *Public Islam and the Common Good* (Leiden, 2004), 58–60.

[84] Jocelyne Cesari, 'Introduction', in Jocelyne Cesari et al. (eds), *European Muslims and the Secular State* (Aldershot, 2005), 1–9, 6.

# 7

# Islam and Resistance in the British Empire

*Benjamin D. Hopkins*

## INTRODUCTION

'Mad mullahs' in Somaliland, 'militant mahdis' in the Sudan, 'fanatical faqirs' on the Northwest Frontier: against such characters the might of the British empire was repeatedly thrown along the imperial peripheries and in to colonial backwaters. In the eyes of the colonial authorities, such spaces not only divided anarchy from order, barbarism from civilization, but also delineated rationalism from fanaticism. Frequently, the British found themselves embroiled in battles against tribesmen led by charismatic religious leaders who, from the perspective of the colonial administration, played on the ignorance and superstition of the locals, mobilizing them into rebellion against the colonial state, contrary to their best interests. Such violent opposition to the British empire and its 'civilizing mission', propelled by the narrative of religious resistance, often using the idiom of jihad, was not a one-off event of limited duration. Rather, it repeated itself time and again in these spaces, which ostensibly separated the modern from its antecedent world.

Arguably, the most important of such spaces of resistance was the Northwest Frontier of British India. During the entirety of imperial rule along the frontier, colonial authorities were regularly faced with what they regarded as outbreaks of religious 'fanaticism' and violence in opposition to British rule. Yet, this was not the only corner of the empire to succumb to such a fate. 'Mad mullahs' seemed almost ubiquitous along the outskirts of the imperial sphere, marking the edges where 'British civilization' lapped against the 'pre-modern'. The Northwest Frontier, Somaliland, the Sudan, northern Nigeria—all these regions succumbed to the forces of 'fanaticism' at roughly the same time. This was no accident. What the British saw as irrational and inexplicable—what they regarded as the symptoms of 'tribal' superstition and primitivism—were in fact locally conditioned responses to a commonly experienced peril: British imperialism. These 'mad mullahs', inhabiting similarly situated local milieus, responded to this challenge with a remarkably analogous vernacular.[1] Men of religious learning and authority were

---

[1] That vernacular consisted of a common Sufi lexicon which employed a corpus of highly portable Arabic terms circulating widely amongst the Muslim *umma*. I thank Michael Feener for this insight; see generally Nile Green, *Sufism: A Global History* (London, 2012).

well-positioned in these societies to straddle the disparate and often conflicting interests of local peoples. The protection of Islam became their rallying cry, providing a coherent narrative of and justification for resistance against the forces of colonialism, as well as a unifying force which superseded particularist tribal identities.

This chapter examines the role of Islam as an idiom of anti-colonial resistance in the British empire from the early nineteenth century through to the empire's dissolution in the mid-twentieth century. It takes a comparative approach, looking at the experience of 'Islamically informed' revolt on the frontiers of empire. It begins with the jihad of Sayyid Ahmed of Rai Barrielly on the Northwest Frontier of British India and traces the fortunes of the jihad's progeny, the so-called 'Hindustani fanatics'.[2] The 'fanatics', mostly plainsmen from northern India, represented a singular strain of anti-colonial resistance which employed Islam to justify and legitimate itself. The Frontier 'tribes' amongst whom the 'fanatics' lived also used the language of Islam during times of revolt against the Raj, most notably during the great uprising of 1897. Indeed, colonial administrators believed the Frontier to be full of 'mad mullahs' and 'fanatical faqirs' who continually stoked the embers of resistance amongst the tribesmen and who remained a source of particular concern. For both the 'fanatics' and the Frontier tribes, Islam provided a language of both unity and confrontation which adapted itself over time. The chapter then pivots its attention to similarly situated peripheries of the British empire where Islam played a key role in the development and expression of anti-colonial resistance.

There is a significant body of literature examining the role of religion in protest movements and rebellion against colonial authorities.[3] In many societies faced with the challenges of European colonialism, religion provided the central idiom of resistance to intrusive foreign authority, a role it historically played vis-à-vis indigenous political authority as well. Islam was by no means unique in this regard. But unlike many of the local religions employed in anti-colonial resistance movements, it was a global phenomenon with which colonial authorities engaged in the far reaches of their empires. Further, a shared experience of colonial subjugation by non-Muslim powers fomented a widespread discussion within the Muslim *umma*

---

[2] I use the term 'Hindustani fanatics' throughout this chapter as the term found in the colonial archives. There are obvious implications about the use of such language by colonial authorities, most prominently the way in which it denudes those described of 'rational' calculus. However, the archival story is more complicated than simply one of crass delegitimization and dehumanization of colonial subjects and opponents, through the use of derogative language. For a discussion of the use of the term 'Hindustani fanatic', see Magnus Marsden and Benjamin D. Hopkins, *Fragments of the Afghan Frontier* (London, 2012), 80–1. The so-called 'Hindustani fanatics' referred to themselves as 'mujahidin' in correspondence with the colonial state. The British adopted this nomenclature after 1890 to describe this particular colony of religious adherents, see, for example, A. Durand, Gilgit Agency: Official Dairy for week ending 2 June 1890, *Foreign Department, Secret F*, National Archives of India (henceforth NAI), No. 193.

[3] Richard Gott, *Britain's Empire: Resistance, Repression and Revolt* (London and New York, 2011), provides an overview of anti-colonial revolts; on the role of Islam in these anti-colonial movements, see Rudolph Peters, *Islam and Colonialism: The Doctrine of Jihad in Modern History* (The Hague, 1979), 39–104; and Nikki Keddie, 'The Revolt of Islam, 1700 to 1993: Comparative Considerations and Relations to Imperialism', *Comparative Studies in Society and History*, 36/3 (1994), 463–87, especially 481–5.

about the loss of temporal power and the right response to it. This discussion was facilitated by the very imperial regimes it opposed. Technological innovations introduced by colonial authorities, such as the telegraph and the steamship, as well as the *pax Britannica* which facilitated movement across previously fragmented spaces, most importantly in the form of the hajj, enabled Muslims to exchange ideas in ways hitherto unimaginable.[4] Imperial administrators in general, and British colonial officers in particular, thus found themselves faced with a seemingly global jihad contesting their authority.[5] The Northwest Frontier of British India provides an important, but by no means singular, example of such religious resistance to colonial rule. The Mahdist rebellion in the Sudan in the late nineteenth century, Muhammad 'Abd Allah Hasan (known to the British as the 'mad mullah') in Somaliland in the early twentieth century, and the fall of the Sokoto caliphate in northern Nigeria were not only contemporaries of the religiously inspired violence on India's famous Frontier, but also shared their origins in the dislocative effects of British imperialism. As imperial expansion destabilized indigenous polities, locals often turned to Islam as a common language of resistance against British incursions.

## BRITISH INDIA'S TROUBLESOME FRONTIER

Few places are as beholden to the myth of fanaticism as British India's Northwest Frontier abutting Afghanistan. From the inception of British authority there, following the annexation of the Punjab in 1849 up to the present day, the allegedly irrational and violent religion of the Frontier's inhabitants has been definitional of this space (Fig. 10). For all the language of religious fanaticism, past and present, there has been surprisingly little effort outside academe to understand the underlying causes of anti-colonial violence in this region.[6] When one subjects such simplistic caricatures to critical scrutiny, they quickly disintegrate and, in their place, much more interesting and nuanced stories emerge.

Though there is a long pedigree of religious revolt along the Frontier, the incipient rebellion at the beginning of the colonial period was that of Sayyid Ahmed

---

[4] This was by no means limited to the British imperial sphere, but was almost ubiquitous throughout the Muslim world and the European empires which occupied large swathes of it, see R. Michael Feener, 'New Networks and New Knowledge: Migrations, Communications and the Reconfiguration of the Muslim Community in the Nineteenth and Early Twentieth Centuries', in Robert W. Hefner (ed.), *The New Cambridge History of Islam*, 6 vols, vi: *Muslims and Modernity: Culture and Society Since 1800* (Cambridge, 2010) 39–68.

[5] Perhaps the most famous example espousing theories of widespread Muslim anti-colonial feeling and action is W. W. Hunter, *The Indian Musalmans: Are they Bound in Conscience to Rebel Against the Queen?* (London, 1871).

[6] Perhaps the worst example of popular history which has sought to detail this 'fanaticism of the frontier' is Charles Allen, *God's Terrorists: The Wahhabi Cult and the Hidden Roots of Modern Jihad* (Cambridge, MA, 2007). On the other hand, one of the best recent works of scholarship on the region and its religious history is Ayesha Jalal, *Partisans of Allah: Jihad in South Asia* (New Delhi, 2008). For a contemporary analysis of the idea of jihad and the Frontier, see Faisal Devji, *Landscapes of Jihad: Militancy, Morality and Modernity* (London, 2005).

**Fig. 10** European representation of Muslim rebels at the Northwest Frontier (Mary Evans Picture Library).

(1786–1831).[7] Sayyid Ahmed hailed from Rai Barrielly in modern-day Uttar Pradesh. This area, close to Rohilkand, a region home to a large population of Afghans who had migrated to the north Indian plain during the seventeenth and eighteenth centuries, long proved a hotbed of religious dissent against colonial authorities. Sayyid Ahmed's undoubted exposure to the Rohilla Afghans familiarized him with the cultural idioms of the Pashtuns, which would later facilitate his ingratiation and success amongst the tribesmen of the Northwest Frontier. He was a disciple of Shah Abdul Aziz (1726–1824), the famed religious scholar of Delhi and son of Shah Waliullah (1703–62), one of the most important reformers of Muslim political and intellectual life of the modern age. Through Shah Abdul Aziz, Sayyid Ahmed not only expanded his intellectual mastery of Islamic learning, but also was exposed to and participated in the Sufi strains of Muslim life long defining Islam on the Indian subcontinent. He undertook the hajj in the early 1820s, which later commentators insist was a transformational experience for Sayyid Ahmed, exposing him as it did to the ideas of the Wahhabis, whose legacy was very much alive in the Hijaz at the time.[8] On his return, he founded his own Sufi-like brotherhood, the *Muhammadiya-i tariqat*, and began to advocate a more militant understanding of jihad. Rather than 'spiritual' jihad (*jihad-i akbar*, or 'greater jihad') taught by Shah Abdul Aziz, and previously by his father, Sayyid Ahmed instead spoke in favor of a 'violent' jihad (*jihad-i ashgar*, or 'lesser jihad') against the non-Muslim rulers and authorities who succeeded the Mughal empire upon its disintegration. Sayyid Ahmed was prevented from pursuing this jihad in north India due to practical and theological impediments. Practically, he did not feel it propitious or possibly successful to launch a religious revolt in what was, essentially, the backyard of the British East India Company, the most important power on the Gangetic plain. Theologically, Shah Abdul Aziz's fatwa declaring Hindustan part of the *dar al-harb* ('house of war', lands ruled by non-Muslims), rather than the *dar al-Islam*, presented a legal injunction against launching a revolt within this realm.[9] Muslims were to respect the laws and orders of their rulers, even if those rulers were not themselves Muslims. In order to embark upon a sanctified revolt against infidel authority, Sayyid Ahmed and his followers would have to flee (hijra) to lands within the *dar al-Islam*, from where they could launch a theologically justified jihad against the infidel *sarkar*. This explains Sayyid Ahmed's decision to exile himself to India's Northwest Frontier, a Muslim area still within the *dar al-Islam*, albeit one under threat from the encroachments of the Sikh empire ruled by Ranjit Singh (1780–1839).

Sayyid Ahmed made his way to the Frontier via Sind, establishing himself in and around the Swat valley in 1827.[10] He immediately set about fomenting resistance

    [7] See generally Jalal, *Partisans of Allah*, ch. 3; and also Harlon O. Pearson, *Islamic Reform and Revival in Nineteenth-Century India: The Tariqah-i Muhammadiyah* (New Delhi, 2008).
    [8] Qeyamuddin Ahmad, *The Wahabi Movement in India* (Calcutta, 1966).
    [9] Sana Haroon, 'Reformism and Orthodox Practice in Early Nineteenth-Century Muslim North India: Sayyid Ahmed Shaheed Reconsidered', *Journal of the Royal Asiatic Society*, 21/2 (2011), 177–98.
    [10] Wade to C. T. Metcalfe, Delhi Resident, 30 March 1827, New Delhi, NAI, Foreign Department, Political Consultations, No. 32.

against the area's non-Muslim suzerains, the Sikhs, and their Muslim interlocutors. Sayyid Ahmed's ability to fashion a super-tribal confederacy reaching beyond the parochial interests of its individual tribes was largely based on his position outside the tribal universe in which he interceded.[11] As a charismatic religious leader whose authority derived simultaneously from his learning and lineage, he was able to broker alliances between disparate groups structurally predisposed to competition under different conditions. Further, his previous experience in Rohilkand equipped him with the cultural expertise necessary to navigate the Pashtun tribal universe. All this would have been for naught but for the circumstances in which Sayyid Ahmed found himself. The tribesmen's predisposition towards fragmentation was countered by the seemingly rapacious ambition and intervention of centralizing Sikh authorities who wished to subjugate the tribesmen to their rule.[12] Sayyid Ahmed thus hit on the winning combination of being the right man in the right place at the right time.

With the support of the tribesmen, Sayyid Ahmed and his followers, mostly Hindustanis from the plains of north India and many of whom had accompanied him in his hijra, quickly found success around the vale of Peshawar.[13] In 1829, they even occupied the city for a short time, before Sayyid Ahmed's strict demands of Islamic orthodoxy alienated his local allies.[14] With his success, the very reason for Sayyid Ahmed's leadership disappeared. By vanquishing the Sikhs, the incarnation of intrusive state authority, from the lives of the tribesmen, Sayyid Ahmed removed the threat, and thus the reason for their unity. The super-tribal confederacy at the heart of Sayyid Ahmed's power ultimately proved fleeting, much to his personal detriment. Sayyid Ahmed was betrayed by his Yusufzai Pashtun tribal allies, who killed a number of his followers and forced the survivors to flee Peshawar for the sanctuary of the hills. With the help of his former tribal allies, the Sikhs cornered and killed Sayyid Ahmed at the Battle of Balakot in May 1831.[15]

Sayyid Ahmed's ephemeral success had a number of important ramifications. Politically, his jihad was aimed ostensibly at the Sikhs ensconced in Peshawar, though many argue that it was more broadly aimed against all non-Muslim rulers of the South Asian subcontinent, most particularly the East India Company. Apart from the practical failure of his efforts, Sayyid Ahmed pioneered a new idiom

---

[11] This model of saintly leadership is perhaps best documented in Ernest Gellner, *Saints of the Atlas* (London, 1969).

[12] On Sikh rule of the vale of Peshawar, see B. D. Hopkins, *The Making of Modern Afghanistan* (Basingstoke, 2008/2012), 75–8; and Robert Nichols, *Settling the Frontier: Law, Land and Society in the Peshawar Valley, 1500–1900* (Karachi, 2001).

[13] 'Hindustanis' was the contemporary term denoting people from Hindustan or the Indian subcontinent.

[14] While this assessment is widely shared in much of the scholarship, it is also debatable. There is an obvious interest amongst many of the sources reporting this sense of discontent to delegitimize Sayyid Ahmed, see Marc Gaborieau, 'The *Jihad* of Sayyid Ahmed Barelwi on the North West Frontier: The Last Echo of the Middle Ages? Or a Prefiguration of Modern South Asia', in Mansura Haidar (ed.), *Sufis, Sultans and Feudal Orders: Professor Nurul Hasan Commemoration Volume* (New Delhi, 2004), 23–44; Jalal, *Partisans of Allah*; and Pearson, *Islamic Reform and Revival in Nineteenth-Century India*.

[15] For a detailed discussion of these events, see Haroon, 'Reformism and Orthodox Practice', 179–80; and Jalal, *Partisans of Allah*, 61–2.

of resistance. Using a well-established religious idea, namely jihad, he nonetheless imbued it with new meaning. This meaning was a combination of his own reformist thinking, best expressed in his writings such as the *Sirat-i-Mustaqim*, and carried on through his adherents in the *Muhammadiya-i tariqa*.[16] It included the Wahhabi strains of thought he encountered during his time in the Hijaz. Contrary to later colonial polemic, most notably W. W. Hunter's *The Indian Musalmans*, Sayyid Ahmed was not Wahhabi, at least not in any simple sense.[17] It is important, however, to note the intellectual lineages which informed his thinking and shaped his actions on the Frontier. He called both for opposition to non-Muslim rule, as well as reform within the Muslim community of South Asia.[18] Indeed, without the latter, the former had little hope of succeeding and virtually no purpose. Such thinking traces its intellectual genealogy back to Shah Waliullah, who argued that the implosion of Muslim political and temporal power he lived through on the subcontinent was an outcome of the *umma*'s moral decay. While Sayyid Ahmed inspired a new language of resistance against non-Muslims and, as Ayesha Jalal has argued, colonial authorities in South Asia, it was a language simultaneously familiar and alien to the Frontier tribesmen amongst whom he deployed it.[19] They proved a receptive audience during a period of external threat. Sayyid Ahmed's combination of religious legitimacy, learning, and lineage, as well as familiarity with the cultural milieu of the tribesmen, rendered him a singularly unique vessel for his message. However, with his success came his downfall as the once-familiar language of Islam, used to legitimate and activate resistance, became alien when turned to reforms of the *umma* itself.

Sayyid Ahmed's death in May 1831 marked the beginning, rather than the end, of his influence on the Frontier. Following his defeat at Balakot, his surviving supporters retreated deep into the mountain vastness of Swat. From there, over the course of the next century and a half, they periodically erupted into violence against the forces of central state authority. The British contemptuously referred to these supposed irredentists as 'Hindustani fanatics' and monitored their activity from the time the Raj assumed control of the Frontier in 1849 until the withdrawal from the Indian subcontinent in 1947.[20] This community of Hindustani Muslims maintained recurrent contact with supporters on the north Indian plain, and regularly received new 'recruits' who mimicked Sayyid Ahmed's original hijra to the Frontier. While these 'Hindustani fanatics' continued to play a role in the life of the Frontier, and in particular in violent contestation of colonial authority over this

---

[16] They would transform themselves into the *Ahl-i Hadith* of British India, see generally Pearson, *Islamic Reform and Revival in Nineteenth-Century India*. For a further discussion of the intellectual geneology of Sayyid Ahmed and his movement, see Marc Gaborieau, *Le Mahdi incompris: Sayyid Ahmad Barelvi (1786–1831) et le millénarisme en Inde* (Paris, 2010).

[17] Devji, *Landscapes of Jihad*, 36–41.

[18] Many movements of Muslim resistance and reform during the nineteenth century focused their efforts internally on the *umma*, see generally Keddie, 'The Revolt of Islam'.

[19] Jalal, *Partisans of Allah*, 58–114.

[20] For the complete history of this episode, see Marsden and Hopkins, *Fragments of the Afghan Frontier*, 75–100.

area, that role was, in the main, oddly circumscribed. Despite their long presence on the Frontier, the 'Hindustani fanatics' remained distinct from the tribal society in which they were embedded. Unincorporated, yet tolerated, with the ability in certain transitory moments to reconstruct the original super-tribal alliances Sayyid Ahmed had first built when circumstances permitted. After Sayyid Ahmed's failed fight against the Sikhs, religious resistance along the Frontier assumed a more local flavor, with indigenous holders of religious authority and men of piety taking the lead.

By the time the British assumed authority over the Frontier in 1849, there had been no major uprising of comparable size to Sayyid Ahmed's jihad since his death. The colony of 'Hindustani fanatics' largely limited itself to the occasional kidnapping of Hindu *bania* merchants.[21] Even during the great rebellion of 1857, the Frontier's inhabitants, including the 'fanatics' colony, refrained from hostile activity.[22] This quiescence may largely be accounted for by the fact that the British, overall, abstained from intervening too directly along the Frontier. Conscious of the violence intervention previously provoked, the colonial state thought discretion the better part of valor. This calculus changed, however, in 1863 with the Ambela campaign, a military expedition which turned into one of the largest Frontier operations of the nineteenth century.[23] Armed with supposedly seditious correspondence between the 'Hindustani fanatics' and their north Indian supporters, the Raj decided the time had come to extirpate this colony of religious dissent. To do so, however, required the British Indian army to transgress the territory of the Bunerwal tribesmen—the Chamla valley. Rather than negotiating passage, the command decided to risk a quick march through the Chamla valley, in the hope that British Indian troops would be clear before the tribesmen could mount any serious resistance. Unfortunately, this proved not to be the case. The sepoys became bogged down in their march, fomenting discontent amongst the Bunerwals and surrounding tribes. The Ambela campaign was notable not only for the violence it produced, but also for the transition in the leadership of religious revolt it represented. The British incursion along the Frontier was ostensibly to exterminate the colony of the 'Hindustani fanatics'. In doing so, however, they trespassed on the territories of Frontier tribesmen who lay outside the administrative control of the colonial state and who understood the colonial state's actions as an attempt to extend that control. It thus required little effort on the part of the 'Hindustani fanatics' to join their cause with that of the Bunerwals, and thereby provide religious sanction. In order to construct a larger alliance, drawing in not only those tribesmen directly affected but also those who saw in the treatment of

---

[21] *Banias* are a Hindu merchant caste prevalent throughout northern India. During the colonial period, they were strongly associated with money-lending, and often the focus of agrarian discontent.

[22] The exception was giving refuge to mutineers from Fifty-Fifth Native Infantry from Rawalpindi, see Marsden and Hopkins, *Fragments of the Afghan Frontier*, 85; and A. H. Mason and W. H. Paget, *A Record of the Expeditions Against the Northwest Frontier Tribes, since the Annexation of the Punjab* (n.p., 1884).

[23] For a colonial record of the Ambela campaign, see A. H. Mason and W. H. Paget, *A Record of the Expeditions Against the Northwest Frontier Tribes*.

the Bunerwals their own future fate, the antagonists looked to the leadership of a local man of piety and holder of religious authority, Abdul Ghaffar, the Akhund of Swat (1794–1877).[24]

Like Sayyid Ahmed, the Akhund's spiritual authority rested on his lineage and was augmented by hagiographic stories of his personal piety. The Akhund was able to leverage that spiritual authority into a position of temporal leadership. However, unlike Sayyid Ahmed, who served as an interlocutor facilitating tribal alliances and whose position was as fleeting as the alliances he brokered, Abdul Ghaffar's leadership had a more substantive and lasting place within Frontier society. Ghaffar could deploy not only his religious charisma, but also his social and economic status through the patron–client relations in which he was embedded, rather than being foreign to local power structures. His spiritual authority derived not from any particular accomplishment of learning, membership to the 'ulama, or feat of pilgrimage such as the hajj, but rather from his personal piety and his status as a Sufi *pir*, or saint. Indeed, it was this strain of personal piety and charisma, as well as the personal ties created through the *pir-murid* relationships at the heart of Sufi *tariqas* that proved the currency of religious authority along the Frontier. His assumption of leadership of religious dissent marks an important transition, where such leadership again became indigenous to local society. In truth this was the norm, rather than the historical aberration Sayyid Ahmed represented. But the reassertion of that norm occurred in an intellectual context redefined by Sayyid Ahmed through his frontier jihad.

Although the Akhund of Swat initially joined forces with the 'Hindustani fanatics' at the beginning of the Ambela campaign, the alliance proved short-lived. This was also true of the tribesmen who had rallied to the Hindustanis' defense. As the British expedition transformed from a quick strike to a drawn-out frontier campaign with mounting casualties on both sides, support for the Hindustanis' soured. In the end, the British negotiated the destruction of the 'fanatics' colony with local tribesmen, and the Akhund forced the now homeless Hindustanis into exile, declaring them Wahhabis and enemies of Islam. This ensured that future religious revolt would be in the hands of local men of piety and religious authority, rather than foreign interlocutors.

With the expulsion and exile of the 'Hindustani fanatics', opposition to British rule along the Frontier assumed more parochial dialects of dissent. Different communities and tribes reacted violently to the challenge posed by the colonial state to their autonomy and prerogatives, but most of these belligerent outbursts remained stubbornly local. The language of Islam, which had previously served as the glue binding disparate communities together in common antipathy, if not outright opposition to the Raj, lost its unifying force. This had much to do with British strategies of frontier management, which sought to divide the tribes into smaller, more localized units and emphasized ruling them through their own customs,

---

[24] On the Akhund of Swat, see Sultan-i-Rome, 'Abdul Ghaffur (Akhund) Saidu Baba of Swat: Life, Career and Role', *Journal of the Pakistan Historical Society*, 40/3 (1992), 299–308; and Muhammad Fahim, 'British Relations with the Akhund of Swat', *Islamic Studies*, 17/1 (1978), 57–66.

traditions, and institutions. Though there was the periodic outbreak of tribal violence, mainly in the form of raiding—an integral part of the Frontier economy—religiously inspired revolt was notable for its absence rather than its omnipresence in the years following the Ambela campaign. It was not until the 1890s that a series of uprisings erupted employing the language of Muslim militancy, namely jihad.

The great frontier uprising of 1897 was preceded two years beforehand by an outbreak of violence in Chitral. The Chitrali revolt is notable because, unlike the areas of the Frontier affected by the events of 1897, Chitral is not a Pashtun-majority area. Thus the dynamics of tribal alliances were absent. This indicates that, despite the assertions of some modern-day commentators, religious 'fundamentalism' and violence is not unique to the Pashtun or, more broadly, tribal societies.[25] The Chitrali rebels focused their ire on the local center of British authority, Chitral fort. Though they were suppressed in short order, the end of violence in Chitral did not dispel the spirit of dissent along the Frontier. A major rising occurred in 1897, engulfing much of the Frontier along the northern half of the recently agreed Durand line. The rebels of 1897 were led by a collection of local men of piety and holders of religious authority, including the Mullah of Hadda and Mullah Saidullah, whom the British referred to as the 'mad faqir'. These two men in particular represented two important types of religious leadership.[26] The Mullah of Hadda was an established presence in Frontier society whose authority was based in his religious learning; Saidullah, on the other hand, represented charismatic leadership. He rallied the tribesmen to his cause with tales of miracles which were a consequence of his piety.[27] Together, they combined many of the elements previously exhibited by Sayyid Ahmed, but unlike him, they were not handicapped by outsider status. To the British, the 'fanaticism' of the tribesmen who rallied to the call of these leaders was on all accounts impenetrable. The 1897 uprising left posterity with arguably the most striking colonial caricature of religious revolt in the writings of Winston Churchill, who regularly wired dispatches from the force sent to quell these disturbances.[28]

The likes of Saidullah and the Mullah of Hadda were joined in future years by other local men of piety and holders of religious authority. The Mullah Powindah, Haji Turangzai, and others remained a thorn in the side of the British Indian

---

[25] Thomas H. Johnson and M. Chris Mason, 'No Sign Until the Burst of Fire: Understanding the Pakistan–Afghanistan Frontier', *International Security*, 32/4 (2008), 41–77.

[26] It should be noted that the titles employed by and about many of these individuals were both multiple and fungible. In Frontier society, 'mullah' did not necessarily mean that the person was a graduate of a madrasa, or even attended one. Formal literate religious education was extremely limited along the Frontier. Amongst many of the tribes, the position of 'mullah' was a hereditary one and often lowly regarded. Mullahs were as much objects of ridicule as of leadership. Further, holders of religious authority might be, and indeed often were known by a number of titles. Thus a mullah could also be a *sayyid*, or a *pir*. The important point to remember is that, rather than delineating clear origins and lineages of religious authority, such titles were a recognition of piety and charisma, as well as some level of learning. See generally Asta Olesen, *Islam and Politics in Afghanistan* (London, 1995).

[27] On the memories of the miraculous escapes of Saidullah from the British, see David B. Edwards, *Heroes of the Age: Moral Fault Lines on the Afghan Frontier* (Berkeley, 1996), 172–219.

[28] Winston Churchill, *The Story of the Malakand Field Force: An Episode of Frontier War* (London, 1898).

empire during the first decades of the twentieth century. It was not until the outbreak of the revolt of the Faqir of Ipi in 1936 that the Frontier rose up on a scale
approaching that of the 1897 conflagration. However, in the interval, an interesting convergence between the language of religious resistance against the colonial
state and emergent strains and sensibilities of 'nationalisms' occurred. There was
a major outbreak of violence along the Frontier in the wake of the First World
War with the Third Afghan War (1919). And though the idiom of resistance was
once again that of religion—a jihad against the infidel *sarkar* ('government')—the
events of 1919 were clearly about the independence of the Afghan state rather
than the re-establishment of the *dar-al Islam* on the north Indian plain. This is
not to say the Afghan amir in some way 'fooled' the Frontier tribesmen into supporting a power-political ploy by feigning religious rhetoric. It is to acknowledge,
though, that Kabul used language, previously proven effective, with which to forge
and activate local alliances amongst the tribes inhabiting the Frontier with British
India.

Likewise, the revolt of the Faqir of Ipi Mirza Ali Khan (1897–1960), the last
great Frontier uprising which the British had to deal with, though couched in the
language of religious revolt, carried within it both old and new strains of local
grievance and identity formation.[29] The faqir's leadership position, like those of
his predecessors, was predicated on his charismatic authority, which allowed him
to facilitate the super-tribal alliances. These alliances are what made this revolt,
like that of 1897, more than simply a local event.[30] There were also reported connections between the Faqir of Ipi and the Axis powers, notably the Italian and
German legations in Kabul. These connections, however, were tenuous at best and
only instituted after the major part of the revolt had been suppressed. At issue was
not simply a perceived threat from the colonial state to the religious sensibilities,
and thus the identity of the Frontier tribesmen. There was also the threat to tribal
autonomy, physically represented by the colonial state's efforts to build roads into
the tribal areas. Moreover, there was a newly emerging sense of identity entangled
in the events of the 1930s, namely an incipient Pashtun ethnic identity.[31] This

[29] On the revolt, see Milan Hauner, 'One Man Against the Empire: The Faqir of Ipi and the British
in Central Asia on the Eve of and During the Second World War', *Journal of Contemporary History*,
16/1 (1981), 183–212; and Alan Warren, *Waziristan, the Faqir of Ipi, and the Indian Army: The
Northwest Frontier Revolt of 1936–7* (Oxford, 2000).

[30] The British were both aware and nervous about connections between religious dissenters
on the Frontier and Britain's European enemies. These fears were fed by German efforts during the
First World War to incite Muslims against British rule throughout the Middle East and South Asia.
They were also present during the 1930s, most notably with the incident of Shami Pir, whom the
British were convinced was an agent of a foreign power, see Hauner, 'One Man Against the Empire',
194–9; on Axis activities, see David Motadel, 'Germany's Policy Towards Islam, 1941–1945' (PhD,
University of Cambridge, 2010), 95–6; and on Soviet activities, see Peter Hopkirk, *Setting the East
Ablaze: On Secret Service in Bolshevik Asia* (London, 1997), 209–42.

[31] One of the most important political vessels of this emergent identity was the Khudai Khitmigar,
a Pashtun pseudo-nationalist political party which came to the fore during the 1930s, see Mukulika
Banerjee, *The Pathan Unarmed: Opposition and Memory in the North West Frontier* (Oxford, 2000).
While the Khudai Khitmigar was a largely secular political movement, recent scholarship has exam-
ined the role of the mullahs in Frontier politics during this period, see Sana Haroon, *Frontiers of
Faith: Islam in the Indo-Afghan Borderland* (London and New York, 2007).

Pashtun identity formulated claims similar to those of other contemporary communities within the realms of British India, most notably Indian Muslims. Just as
South Asian Muslims, under the contested leadership of Muhammad Ali Jinnah
(1876–1948) and the All-India Muslim League, called for their recognition as a
'nation' and consequently their right to a homeland, the Faqir of Ipi's revolt demonstrated a nascent claim for a Pashtun homeland, Pashtunistan.[32] Though this
claim fully bloomed in the wake of the transfer of power in 1947, the seeds were
planted earlier. Important here is the fact that at the same time, Mirza Ali Khan
employed a rhetoric of resistance, jihad, familiar to the Frontier tribesmen to forward well-known claims such as tribal autonomy, as well as new claims incumbent
in an emergent sense of social and political identity. Religious resistance provided
a stable form, but the substance proved dynamic.

## BEYOND BRITISH INDIA

The Northwest Frontier of India was not the only place where the British empire
faced resistance in the form of religious revolt. Indeed, within the borders of their
South Asian empire, there were innumerable examples of resistance to colonial
authority both justified and motivated by religious rhetoric and led by religious
figures.[33] What is remarkable, however, is how the story of resistance on the
Northwest Frontier repeated itself in multiple, geographically distant, and culturally distinct locales around the so-called periphery of Britain's global empire. Many
of these other incidents of resistance and revolt employed similar language as that
seen on the Northwest Frontier of British India. As importantly, they resulted
from similar circumstances and challenges which the advent of British imperialism
wrought in these spaces. It was no accident that these far-flung corners of empire
reacted in much the same way to the challenges they faced. Three examples are
representative of the trend of revolt along the periphery of empire which closely
mimicked the story of the Afghan Frontier: the Mahdist rebellion in the Sudan in
the 1880s and 1890s; the 'revolutionary' Mahdist uprising following the collapse
of the Sokoto caliphate at the beginning of the twentieth century; and the revolt
of Muhammad 'Abd Allah Hasan in Somaliland in the early years of the twentieth
century. By looking at each instance in turn, one can see the obvious similarities linking the outbreaks of violence both to one another and to the far-distant
Northwest Frontier.

---

[32] The development of the separatist politics of the Indian Muslim community is a long and complex story, see generally Ayesha Jalal, *The Sole Spokesman: Jinnah, the Muslim League, and the Demand
for Pakistan* (Cambridge, 1985).

[33] During the 1830s, for example, there was the Farzai movement as well as the so-called Wahhabi
revolt of Titu Mir in Bengal, see Dilip Kumar Chattopadhyay, 'The Ferazee and Wahabi Movements
of Bengal', *Social Scientist*, 6/2 (1977), 42–51; Abhijit Dutta, *Muslim Society in Transition: Titu Meer's
Revolt (1831)* (Calcutta, 1986); Narahari Kaviraj, *Wahabi and Farazi Rebels of Bengal* (New Delhi,
1982); and Ahmad, *The Wahabi Movement in India*.

In 1884, the death of General Charles Gordon in Khartoum at the hands of the forces of Muhammad Ahmad (1845–85), the self-proclaimed Mahdi of Sudan, shocked the British public (Fig. 11). Not only had a popular and highly regarded advocate of empire died, but also his death had been at the hands of 'uncivilized' Muslim *ghazis*, whose 'crazed' devotion to the Mahdi was regarded by the metropolitan public as fanatical.[34] While the rise of the Mahdi in the Sudan in the early 1880s resulted from a complex political and social story, the British press had little time for or interest in it.[35] Instead, the Sudan was depicted as a land of fundamentalism and Muhammadan bigotry, much like the Northwest Frontier of British India. The only way to properly deal with such crazed and fervent adherents of irrationality was with force; the British would have to subdue the Sudan the same way it forcefully suppressed the uprisings of the Pashtun tribesmen. Of course, the Sudan was different from the Northwest Frontier in that it was not itself a British colony, nor did it border one. Rather, it was an Ottoman-Egyptian colony and the British action against the Mahdi was in support of the Ottoman-Egyptian campaign to re-establish control of this recalcitrant backwater. While retaining its formal independence though, the paramount influence of the British cannot be underestimated.

Though the Mahdist state was contemporary with the great Frontier uprising of 1897, the more apt comparison with Muhammad Ahmad's movement is that of Sayyid Ahmed of Rai Barreilly, predating the Sudanese movement by nearly half a century. The personal biographies of the two men reveal important similarities, such as the fact that both were adherents of Sufi orders.[36] The men's claims of leadership employed religious traditions which resonated with a longer literate theological tradition, as well as local idioms and understandings. Muhammad Ahmad's proclamation of himself as the Mahdi was in keeping with a Mahdist tradition stretching back at least to the foundation of the Sokoto caliphate in modern-day northern Nigeria at the beginning of the nineteenth century.[37] Sayyid Ahmed, though he did not claim himself to be the Mahdi, assumed the title *amir*

---

[34] See, for example, 'The Soudan Campaign', *The Sunday Times* 3227 (15 February 1885), 6.

[35] P. M. Holt, *The Mahdist State in the Sudan, 1881–1898: A Study of its Origins, Development and Overthrow* (Oxford, 1970); Gabriel Warburg, *Islam, Sectarianism, and Politics in Sudan since the Mahdiyya* (London, 2003); A. B. Theobald, *The Mahdiya: A History of the Anglo-Egyptian Sudan, 1881–1899* (London, 1951); John Obert Voll, 'The Sudanese Mahdi: Frontier Fundamentalist', *International Journal of Middle East Studies*, 10 (1979), 145–66; and David Steele, 'Lord Salisbury, the "False Religion" of Islam, and the Reconquest of the Sudan', in Edward M. Spiers (ed.), *Sudan: The Reconquest Reappraised* (London, 1998), 11–34. On the roots of the Mahdiyya, see Alice Moore-Harell, *Gordon and the Sudan: Prologue to the Mahdiyya 1877–1880* (London and Portland, OR, 2001).

[36] Sayyid Ahmed established his own reformist order in the *Muhammdiya-i tariqat*, while Muhammad Ahmad was an adherent of the Sammaniyya order. Rather than subscribing to well-established traditional orders, these men participated in the reformist orders which blossomed during the nineteenth century. The Sammaniyya order itself arose out of the tumult of the latter part of the eighteenth century in the Yemen and the Hijaz. Many of these were overtly hostile to the established religious orders and instead integrated calls for reform and the abandonment of false accretions to religious practice as central parts of their platforms.

[37] Saburi Biobaku and Muhammad al-Hajj, 'The Sudanese Mahdiyya and the Niger-Chad Region', in I. M. Lewis (ed.), *Islam in Tropical Africa* (Bloomington, IN, 1980), 425–41.

**Fig. 11** Muhammad Ahmad (1844–85), self-proclaimed mahdi in Sudan (Getty Images).

*al-mu'minin*, 'Commander of the Faithful', during his lifetime. Following his martyrdom, he was said by many followers to have been the imam, a position not dissimilar to that of mahdi, though more familiar to the South Asian universe of Islam in which he lived.[38] There was a pronounced strain of millenarianism central to both men's movements and successes. Charismatic leadership in the form of theologically familiar and sanctified offices was thus central to their claims of authority.

The similarities between the movements led by Sayyid Ahmed and Muhammad Ahmad go beyond the men themselves. While neither fought against the British empire directly, instead facing off against local rulers, their revolts were caused by and in many ways targeted British imperial power. For both, the emasculation of Muslim authority by British imperialism lay at the heart of their protest. Sayyid Ahmed, though fighting the Sikhs, ultimately eyed re-establishing Muslim power on the north Indian plain. On the other hand, Muhammad Ahmad fought a Muslim power in the khedive, which he depicted as a corrupt and unjust and

[38] Jalal, *Partisans of Allah*, 58–113.

unduly swayed by European influence. The political moment these men inhabited was one of profound transition caused by the establishment of British power in their respective regions. British imperialism not only challenged and ultimately subverted the primacy of Muslim rule, but also led to fundamental reorderings of the political economies which in turn had widespread social and political ramifications. Both men rebelled in spaces which had formally been integrated in regional economic orders, but which increasingly found themselves either excluded by or subsumed into a new order of political economy based on a British imperial, industrial complex. The effect of this change was the impoverishment of these areas, which fed into a cycle of political instability difficult to break. The trade links which the Afghan tribesmen of the Frontier had exploited for plunder were destroyed by the new realities of the political economy of South Asia, as well as the later efforts of state construction by Afghan rulers.[39] Conversely, Nilotic Sudan found itself subjugated by the Egyptian khedive, which was itself being integrated into a global imperial economy in a position of subservience. Sayyid Ahmed and Muhammad Ahmad's calls for justice, though explicitly referring to the re-establishment of Muslim political hegemony, were also a protest against an unfair economic system to which these societies were being subjugated.

Yet the movements led by Sayyid Ahmed, Muhammad Ahmad, and a multitude of others across the Muslim world during the nineteenth century were not simply protests against the encroachments of European imperialism, formal or informal. They were also movements of reform within the Muslim *umma* itself.[40] These men were part of a larger discussion taking place across the Muslim world which sought to assess the reasons for the perceived multifaceted decline suffered contemporaneously by far-flung Islamic polities and communities. This discussion entailed a broader debate, not only considering why Muslims had lost power, but more importantly what to do about it. A wide array of movements of reform emerged over the course of the nineteenth century which sought to purify and thus rehabilitate Muslims as a social, religious, and political unit in the form of the *umma*. Somewhat ironically, this discussion was facilitated, practically and conceptually, by many of the globalizing elements of European imperialism which it was protesting. Far-removed thinkers were brought into contact with one another through an expanding Muslim public sphere not only based in a common print culture, but also in the imperial transportation networks that facilitated a boom in the hajj at this time.[41] Locating these men in the larger moment of Muslim reform

---

[39] On the changing nature of the South Asian political economy and its implications for Afghan state construction, see Hopkins, *The Making of Modern Afghanistan*, 90–8 and 110–62.

[40] These movements of reform arguably began with Muhammad ibn 'Abd al-Wahhab's iconoclasm of the eighteenth century. There were variants of movements of Muslim reform and revival throughout South and Southeast Asia, the Ottoman lands, as well as in North Africa, see, for example, John Voll, *Islam: Continuity and Change in the Modern World* (Syracuse, NY, 1994) 24–83; Francis Robinson, 'Islamic Reform and Modernities in South Asia', *Modern Asian Studies*, 42/2–3 (2008), 259–81; and Michael Laffan, *The Making of Indonesian Islam: Orientalism and the Narration of a Sufi Past* (Princeton, 2011) 40–64.

[41] See the chapters by Robert D. Crews, John Slight, and Eric Tagliacozzo in this volume.

in which they were participants draws our attention to the fact that their protests were directed as much at their fellow Muslims as European imperialists.

The doctrines of millenarianism and more specifically of Mahdism, which underpinned Muhammad Ahmad's successful revolt in the Sudan, were widely shared across northern Africa in the nineteenth century. Also, the Sokoto caliphate, established in the early years of the century in Northern Nigeria, was particularly influenced by and an important source of these ideas.[42] When the caliphate succumbed to the expansion of British colonial power up the Niger River as well as the concurrent expansion of French authority into the area at the beginning of the twentieth century, the inchoate strains of religious revolt coalesced into a violent contestation of colonial rule. The 'revolutionary Mahdism' which fueled revolts against the French and British in 1905 and 1906 can be distinguished from the doctrines seen most prominently in the Sudan.[43] However, the emphasis on justice, the language of Islam, and the undertones of millenarianism were common between the two movements, as well as with the revolts on the Northwest Frontier of India. Paul Lovejoy and J. S. Hogendom have argued that the key distinguishing feature of the 'revolutionary Mahdism' in the then former lands of the Sokoto caliphate was its class position. It appealed to and motivated not the aristocracy and elites who subscribed to the Mahdist doctrines translocated to the Sudan, but rather the peasantry and dispossessed. In this respect, the 'revolutionary Mahdism' of northern Nigeria was similar to the Frontier movement inspired by Sayyid Ahmed. Most of the recruits to Sayyid Ahmed's movement, the so-called 'Hindustani fanatics' were poor peasants from the northern Indian plains, coming especially from Bengal, Bihar, and the lands of the United Provinces (modern-day Uttar Pradesh).[44] Moreover, while the Frontier tribesmen who participated in his original jihad and those who later revolted against the Raj did so ostensibly in the name of religion, the impoverishment of the Frontier brought about by its incomplete integration into the colonial economy undoubtedly played into the tribesmen's sense of grievance.[45] This is not to say religious revolt was simply a stand-in for economic protest, but that in these circumstances they likely reinforced one another.

The final incident of revolt similar to those along British India's Northwest Frontier was that of the so-called 'mad mullah' of British Somaliland, Muhammad 'Abd Allah Hasan.[46] Hasan fiercely contested the establishment of British power in the Horn of Africa, remaining a continual thorn in the side of colonial authorities from the beginning of the twentieth century up until the early 1920s. However,

---

[42] Biobaku and al-Hajj, 'The Sudanese Mahdiyya and the Niger-Chad Region'.

[43] Paul Lovejoy and J. S. Hogendom, 'Revolutionary Mahdism and Resistance to Colonial Rule in the Sokoto Caliphate, 1905–6', *Journal of African History*, 31/2 (1990), 217–44.

[44] Marsden and Hopkins, *Fragments of the Afghan Frontier*, 78.

[45] On colonial 'development', see R. O. Christensen, 'Tribesmen, Government and Political Economy on the Northwest Frontier', in Clive Dewey (ed.), *Arrested Development in India: The Historical Dimension* (New Delhi, 1988), 226–34.

[46] Abdi Sheikh Abdi, *Divine Madness: Mohammed Abdullah Hassan (1856–1920)* (London, 1993).

like Sayyid Ahmed and Muhammad Ahmed, his jihad was as much about the reform of Islam and Muslim society as it was against a foreign (Christian) power. Indeed, his identification with the Salihiyya order, one of the so-called 'neo-Sufi' movements of the nineteenth century aimed at revival and reform, mirrored his predecessors' participation in similar orders.[47] He was influenced by the events in nearby Sudan, as well as the widely reported uprisings of Afghan frontiersmen in British India.[48] Hasan was able to successfully establish a polity in the interior of British Somaliland from whence he harassed British forces present on the coast. His ability to overcome parochial clan loyalties was at least in part based on his utilization of the hierarchical ordering of the Salihiyya brotherhood, much like Sayyid Ahmed was able to leverage the language of belonging in his own Sufi *tariqa* to facilitate his leadership amongst the Afghan tribesmen.[49] The position of his state, and British Somaliland more generally, was similar to that of the Afghan frontier in the sense that neither held much intrinsic value in the eyes of colonial authorities. Rather, their value lay in protecting more important parts of the empire, such as the port of Aden and the British Indian plains. As with the likes of the Mullah of Hadda and the Faqir of Ipi, Muhammad 'Abd Allah Hasan was able to rally local support to his cause through the idiom of Islam, though the cause of indigenous discontent was often broader than simply maligned religious sensibilities.[50] The attempts of British authorities to intervene into the interior of British Somaliland carried with them the dislocative effects seen previously when the colonial state intervened amongst the tribal societies of the Afghan frontier. Islam provided a source of unity for an otherwise highly fractious society, as well as a language of dissent against British colonialism.

## CONCLUSION

While the individual circumstances of each of these revolts was contextually and temporally unique, they shared a common set of values, common agenda, and common language of resistance against the incursions of British imperialism and the dislocative forces of globalization it represented. Each was a protest of the loss of Muslim political power and prestige. Equally important, they also represented dissent from the economic subjugation each of these areas experienced, although

---

[47] John P. Slight, 'British and Somali Views of Muhammad Abdullah Hassan's *Jihad*, 1899–1920', *Bildhaan: An International Journal of Somali Studies*, 10/7 (2010), 15–35, 25.

[48] Hasan was apparently exposed to news of these events during his hajj, see Robert L. Hess, 'The "Mad Mullah" and Northern Somalia', *Journal of African History*, 5/3 (1964), 415–33, 419. This simply underlines the point made earlier that the imperial structures which these men revolted against in many ways facilitated their revolts. The hajj, made safe by the advent of *pax Britannica* of the long nineteenth century, was a formative experience for both Hasan and Sayyid Ahmed. While there is no evidence these men necessarily knew of one another, they inhabited a Muslim intellectual universe made global through British imperialism.

[49] Slight, 'British and Somali views', 25.

[50] Also, like the latter, the British suspected Hasan of connections with the Germans and Ottomans during the First World War, see Slight, 'British and Somali Views', 23.

the understandings of that subjugation were far from clear, or even widely shared. They all employed a common idiom of resistance, namely that of millenarian Islam, which unified otherwise fragmented local political universes, but also provided a language with which to relate to a largely alien and unknown outside world. The British, though mischaracterizing that language as 'irrational' and 'fanatical', did, at minimum, have a basic recognition of the central tenets of Islam. While any direct connections between these movements were fleeting at best, they all firmly fit a larger pattern of resistance to colonial rule. Moreover, the similar circumstances of each of these instances, and similar situations on the periphery of empire, tie them together coherently as a category of resistance.

There are some reservations which necessarily need to be made about such a wide-ranging general assertion as that argued in this essay. The first is to acknowledge explicitly that resistance to colonial rule employing millenarian language was neither unique to the spaces of the periphery, nor to Islam, nor to the British empire. Indeed, as Michael Adas demonstrated in his classic work *Prophets of Rebellion*, such challenges were widespread.[51] Many of these revolts shared common cause in the dislocations brought about by an invasive colonial state. The revolts discussed here largely fit the model Adas constructs, but they also need to be recognized as constituting a distinct subset, defined by the choice of religious idiom and concurrent claims of participation in a wider Muslim community, as well as by their location on the physical periphery of colonial power. The revolts along the frontier of British India and across much of northern Africa affected and were affected by debates within the Muslim community sparked by the collapse of Islamic authority around the world. Consequently, they ignited an interesting dialectic which has yet to be fully explored.

The second caveat that needs to be recognized is the way Islam is framed in examining these revolts. In many ways, the argument that Islam provided an idiom of resistance reduces people's religious sensibilities to simply a functional aspect of their other 'real' concerns, most notably economics and political autonomy. Such a utilitarian approach gains one little and ignores the intellectual and emotional investment people earnestly make in their religious identities. The British themselves were guilty of ignoring subjects' religious sensibilities and conversely belittling them. There was widespread belief amongst colonial administrators that the mullahs of the Frontier played upon the religious ignorance of the local tribesmen. At the same time, they refused to believe the sincerity of the frontiersmen's religious discourse. In its place, they argued that the source of the tribesmen's anger was largely economic and cultural. To address the former, the colonial state put in place rudimentary development schemes, most of which revolved around security forces and the employment of tribesmen in them. With regard to the latter, the British pursued policies which governed the tribesmen by their own 'traditions'.[52]

---

[51] Michael Adas, *Prophets of Rebellion: Millenarian Protest Movements Against the European Colonial Order* (Chapel Hill, NC, 1979); and, more generally, Gott, *Britain's Empire*.
[52] The best example of this in South Asia was the so-called 'Sandeman system' of frontier governance, see Marsden and Hopkins, *Fragments of the Afghan Frontier*, 49–74.

In either case, the religious sensibilities were not taken seriously, but rather dismissed as irrational fanaticism.

Viewing Islam as simply providing an idiom of resistance, a language with which to relate to the outside world, runs the risk of replicating these colonial tropes.[53] The religious sensibilities of the leaders of the various revolts are important; however, of greater import—though also more difficult to access—are the sensibilities of the followers who rallied to the cries of jihad. For the Afghan experience, some scholars, most notably David B. Edwards, have worked to engage those religious sensibilities.[54] Yet more remains to be done. The work of Magnus Marsden, who wrote on the emotional religious life of inhabitants of the Frontier, is precisely the kind of work which needs to be replicated in the historical arena.[55] Such a focus is warranted by the fact that these charismatic religious leaders called not simply for resistance to the colonial state, but as importantly for reform within the Muslim community itself. The challenges, methodological and otherwise, to uncovering the sensibilities of participants in these revolts are daunting; many were not literate and did not leave a paper trial of their emotional lives.

As important is a consideration of the meaning of 'leadership'—religious and otherwise—in the contexts discussed, and in the space of the frontier more generally. The men examined here largely achieved their status through a combination of personal charisma and structural opportunity which created openings within local societies for their temporary ascendance. What was largely lacking was any sort of institutional basis on which to establish either their own authority or their movements. True, they all assumed some title of religious authority or learning. However, these were fungible and fluid in their meanings as well as their assignation. This raises the question then of the linkages between 'leader' and 'follower'. One wonders if the lines of differentiation, or indeed association were as clear as they appear in either the colonial records or subsequent hagiographies. At what point, for instance, did the *murid* become the *pir*? Questioning the presumed hierarchy these titles convey seems a potentially fruitful analytical avenue to better understand the emotional and social lives of these religious communities and their adherents.[56]

This essay has argued that the revolts which broke out along the frontiers of the British empire from the early nineteenth century to the early twentieth were not the result of nefarious musings of irrational 'mad mullahs' and their 'fanatical' followers. While such assessments made good imperial propaganda and good copy for the metropolitan press, they do little to reveal anything meaningful about these revolts. In their place, a serious consideration of the grievances of those who participated in the revolts, as well as an assessment of the structural limits and

---

[53] Akbar Ahmed makes this point about a language with which to relate to the world outside the tribal universe of the frontiersmen, see Akbar S. Ahmed, *Pukhtun Economy and Society: Traditional Structure and Economic Development in Tribal Society* (London, 1980).

[54] Edwards, *Heroes of the Age*.

[55] Magnus Marsden, *Living Islam: Muslim Religious Experience in Pakistan's Northwest Frontier* (Cambridge, 2005).

[56] I thank Michael Feener for raising this point.

opportunities which channeled their dissent provide a rich return. The charismatic leadership of a set of Muslim holy men, each speaking a local dialect of millenarianism, activated the disquiet of the inhabitants of an expanding imperial sphere. Those inhabitants responded due to feelings of dislocation and exclusion brought about by the new political, economic, and social structures created by British imperialism.

These men and their followers reacted in a markedly similar way to a markedly similar challenge. While the details of the individual incidents of revolt differ, the general outlines are largely shared. The fact that such geographically removed and culturally distinct locales produced a common reaction to colonialism is at one and the same time pedestrian and extraordinary. By juxtaposing these revolts, the 'mad mullahs' of the frontiers are rendered not so much idiosyncratic images of irrationality and rage as symbols of widespread disquiet and anger with the imperial global order.

# 8

# Religious Revolts in Colonial North Africa

*Knut S. Vikør*

## INTRODUCTION

It is one of the apparent incongruities of Islamic history that the religious strains that are Islam's most esoteric and inward-looking—those that aim to exclude the material world from the believer's consciousness—have often become the most potent revolutionary and political forces in times of crisis. There are many cases where stable political entities have been built around the framework of Sufi structures. The transformation of the Turkish-speaking Safavi brotherhood into the ruling dynasty and aristocracy of a new kingdom, Persia, in the fifteenth and sixteenth centuries is only one of many examples.[1]

There were many cases of such transformations from the esoteric to the exoteric in Muslim resistance to imperial rule in the nineteenth and twentieth centuries. Often, anti-colonial Sufi activism has been represented as a form of nationalist resistance, with its religious aspect downplayed, or even ignored altogether. Certainly, this was often how the brotherhoods were seen by their colonial opponents. This view was often restated in later political histories and popular commemorations in post-colonial states, in which the leaders of these movements appeared in the pantheon of heroes of national liberation. These histories tended to mask the fact that these movements had both religious and political dimensions, and that these were often clearly distinct. Certainly, militant movements were only a tiny minority compared with the vast number of purely religious Sufi brotherhoods, and those which became politically active usually did so through a form of transformation, often a reluctant one. The brotherhoods' political role may often have predominated during periods of crisis and was moreover regarded as crucial for the defense of the community; but, nevertheless, it was usually secondary to the religious objectives of the brotherhoods.

In North Africa, the two most famous cases of anti-colonial resistance led by Sufi shaykhs were that of 'Abd al-Qadir (1808–83) in western Algeria from 1832 to 1847, and that of the Sanusiyya brotherhood in eastern Libya and the Sahara from 1911 to 1931. Closer scrutiny shows that the relationship between religion

---

[1] Andrew J. Newman, *Safavid Iran: Rebirth of a Persian Empire* (London and New York, 2006); and Roger Savory, *Iran under the Safavids* (Cambridge, 1980).

and political resistance in their histories was highly complex. Both cases may indicate how the onset of colonial expansion made it possible, or necessary, to transgress pre-existing boundaries between the religious sphere and political affairs, so that religious structures and personal resources were redeployed in a novel form as required by the new situation.

The two examples cited here mark both the beginning and the end of the history of colonial expansion in North Africa. The French involvement in Algeria was the first and the Italian invasion of Libya, the last of the European military incursions in the region. During this time, Tunisia and Morocco came under French (or, in the case of northern Morocco, Spanish) control as protectorates. Yet, it was the regions that later became the present-day countries of Algeria and Libya which displayed many common features in their encounter with colonialism. While the establishment of the French protectorates were by and large accomplished with a comparatively small degree of violence, colonialism was imposed on Algeria and Libya through protracted warfare and, to a large extent, the destruction of traditional political and social structures.[2] It is therefore of particular interest to compare the anti-colonial resistance movements and, above all, the role of religion in these two colonial territories.

## 'ABD AL-QADIR AND FRENCH COLONIAL EXPANSION

It may be debatable whether it is reasonable to include 'Abd al-Qadir's movement under the heading of 'Sufi-based' resistance. 'Abd al-Qadir's political activity may be interpreted as standing at a crossroads between a traditional tribal alliance forged among the major tribes in the furthest west of the Ottoman empire's African domains, and a modernist tanzimat-inspired state that never quite covered a stable and coherent territory. Yet, it was 'Abd al-Qadir's religious background—his role as a shaykh of the Qadiriyya order—that led him to take leadership of the original tribal alliance in the first place. This role was inherited from his father, Muhyi al-Din and his grandfather Mustafa, who had reintroduced the order to the western Maghrib.[3] The largest Sufi brotherhood in the world, the Qadiriyya had nevertheless been dwarfed in this region for centuries by the dominant Shadhiliyya order. Mustafa had founded a center in the village of Guetna, not far from the Moroccan border. He was able to win over a number of local tribal and other leaders to the Qadiriyya, and his son Muhyi al-Din extended the support and was recognized as the leader of the Qadiriyya for all of the Ottoman far west (modern-day Algeria). Muhyi al-Din clearly also exerted a certain level of political authority in the region, although the reports of his eminence may have been exaggerated due to

---

    [2] Knut S. Vikør, *The Maghreb since 1800: A Short History* (London, 2012).
    [3] Raphael Danziger, *Abd al-Qadir and the Algerians: Resistance to the French and Internal Consolidation* (New York, 1977), 51–62; and Bruno Étienne, *Abdelkader: Isthme des isthmes (Barzakh al-barazikh)* (Paris, 1994), 21–85.

**Fig. 12** 'Abd al-Qadir (1808–83), taken around 1860 (Mideast Image).

**Fig. 13** Ahmad al-Sharif al-Sanusi (1873–1933) (Public Domain).

the later status of his son. His settlement at Guetna functioned as a religious and as an intellectual center of the region, and its autonomy, moreover, was recognized by the Ottoman authorities. It is reported that Muhyi al-Din, as a revered holy man, was asked to settle differences in tribal conflicts in a larger territory, in the traditional role of a religious leader or holy man who, as an outsider to the social structures, functioned as an impartial and authoritative arbitrator in nomadic societies. Muhyi al-Din may not have possessed executive political authority in the formal sense; it is more likely that his legitimacy and status depended on his personal charisma. In French colonial sources, he was also often portrayed as having had direct involvement in the political affairs of the region, but it is difficult to ascertain precisely the exact nature of this authority.

Born in 1808, 'Abd al-Qadir (Fig.12) was raised to take over this legacy as a scholarly leader and was trained in Sufism and other Islamic sciences. He spent some time in the urban center of Oran, but it seems that the most decisive influence for his later political activity came when he and his father went on the hajj in 1826.[4] During this trip, which lasted for more than a year, he spent some time in Cairo and was said to have been struck by the reforms of Muhammad 'Ali, which inspired some of the policies that he later pursued in his own state.

---

[4] Étienne, *Abdelkader*, 86–103.

The French invasion of Algiers in 1830, which led to the swift collapse of Ottoman authority in the western parts of the province, ushered in a period of confusion over the future control of the province. There were still Turkish troops in the region. The Moroccan sultan had his own interests, in particular in the town of Tlemcen close to the border, though he was not interested enough to confront the remaining Ottoman and *qulogli* (Turkish-Arab) soldiers who had dug in there.[5] The sultan withdrew and in 1831 instead asked local religious leader Muhyi al-Din to be his representative in the region. Although Muhyi al-Din had, according to some sources, previously refused several requests to call for jihad against the French, he did in the end accept the request from the Moroccan sultan.[6] It is, as always, difficult to say, however, what either of the parties actually meant by 'representative of the sultan'. Of advanced age, Muhyi al-Din remained reluctant to take on active leadership in the resistance. When he finally acceded to the demands from the Oran tribes to head the campaign, it was his son 'Abd al-Qadir who took charge of the fighting. Later in that year, in November 1832, the tribes accepted Muhyi al-Din's request to transfer their loyalties to his son and they swore an oath of allegiance to 'Abd al-Qadir as *amir al-mu'minin*, 'commander of the faithful'. From that point, it was 'Abd al-Qadir who became both the titular and actual leader of the anti-colonial resistance in Western Algeria, although he claimed whenever deemed useful that he was fighting on behalf of the sultan.[7]

Primarily because of the initial weakness of the French forces who were contained on the coast, and because of various French blunders when trying to venture inland, 'Abd al-Qadir was able to establish himself in the Oran region and lay the basis for a long struggle against French colonialists that lasted for fifteen years until his final surrender in 1847.[8] His relations with the enemy varied between a neutral truce, through two treaties of 1834 and 1837, and active conflict, in particular after 1839. 'Abd al-Qadir's main area of influence was always limited to Western Algeria, as the eastern regions were initially under the control of former Ottoman governor Ahmad Bey, in Constantine. During the struggle for the protection of the lands of Islam against the Christian invaders, 'Abd al-Qadir avoided challenging the authority of Ahmad Bey as another Muslim ruler. 'Abd al-Qadir even made it a condition for the truce with France that French colonial troops stayed away from Constantine.[9] When French officials ignored this and forced Ahmad Bey to flee, 'Abd al-Qadir again declared jihad and carried out an effective guerrilla war for a number of years more.[10]

In the periods between the campaigns, 'Abd al-Qadir began to establish the bases for a state structure. While Muhyi al-Din had played the role of leader for the people around his settlement at Guetna, his son created a polity on a different

---

[5] Amira K. Bennison, *Jihad and its Interpretations in Pre-Colonial Morocco: State–Society Relations during the French Conquest of Algeria* (London, 2002), 48–58.

[6] Danziger, *Abd al-Qadir and the Algerians*, 60–1.

[7] Danziger, *Abd al-Qadir and the Algerians*, 79.

[8] Danziger, *Abd al-Qadir and the Algerians*, 122.

[9] Except in the very last months of the struggle over Constantine, see Danziger, *Abd al-Qadir and the Algerians*, 159.

[10] For the text of the declaration, see Danziger, *Abd al-Qadir and the Algerians*, 170–1.

scale. In the first few years, he established his capital in the town of Mascara, set up a regularly structured army to complement his more unruly base of tribal fighters, and established an administration that levied taxes and provided services. Although the 'modernity' of this polity—which was created in a very short period of time and under wartime conditions—should not be exaggerated, it was a functioning independent state.[11] It appears that 'Abd al-Qadir always put great emphasis on the Islamic and religious nature of his polity. His leadership was couched in the terms of a classical Muslim ruler—as 'Commander of the Faithful', the title of a caliph—and he himself appeared as a pious ascetic not interested in material wealth or temporal glory. He had come to his position through his father's status as a leader of the Qadiriyya and emphasized this link by appointing 'marabouts', Qadiri shaykhs who worked as his closest aides and administrators. As time went on, however, the importance of these Sufi supporters seems to have been diluted into a larger number of *agha* (traditional leaders) and their associates with a tribal rather than Sufi background, although 'Abd al-Qadir did try to reinforce his Sufi support by establishing a number of Qadiri centers in his region. Nevertheless, when asking for allegiance to himself and his struggle, it was not his role as a Sufi shaykh, but his position as a caliph-amir, appropriate for the leader of a jihad, that was crucial.[12] It was clearly important that his war was considered a proper jihad. In fact, already Muhyi al-Din had first invited the French adversaries to join Islam before he had launched the initial campaign against them. Only when the French had ignored this call to the faith, could the war be a proper jihad.[13] Since the leadership of a jihad falls on the leader of the Muslim state under attack, 'Abd al-Qadir could fashion his actual state structures with considerable freedom as long as he was accepted as the legitimate head of his state. Looking at his fledgling state, inspirations from the tanzimat reforms of the great Muslim leaders of Cairo and Constantinople are obvious. Like most early Muslim reformers, the modernization effort was primarily focused on the military. Although it would be an overstatement to claim that his loose state had freed itself from the tribal structures of prior Ottoman rule, the drive towards a more modern, or at least 'Ottoman-inspired' political system is far more obvious than any great influence from his Qadriyya Sufi background.

However, after 1847, when he was finally forced to surrender and to go into exile—eventually ending up in Damascus, the global center of the Qadiriyya order—he returned to the life of a Sufi that he had perhaps never left privately, but

---

[11] Pessah Shinar, ' 'Abd al-Qadir and 'Abd al-Krim: Religious Influences on Their Thought and Action', *Asian and African Studies*, 1 (1965), 139–74; and Danziger, *Abd al-Qadir and the Algerians*, 180–218.

[12] Danziger, *Abd al-Qadir and the Algerians*, 195–6. It is however, arguable that Sufi affiliation was important in his conflict with the rival Tijaniyya order, which made him lay siege to and capture their center at 'Ayn Madi in 1838–39, although that was also a conflict over authority, see Jamil M. Abun-Nasr, *The Tijaniyya: A Sufi Order in the Modern World* (London, 1965), 62–8. For a comparative study on the relationship between Sufism and jihad, see Alexander Knysh, 'Sufism as an Explanatory Paradigm: The Issue of the Motivations of Sufi Resistance Movements in Western and Russian Scholarship', *Die Welt des Islams*, 42/2 (2002), 139–73.

[13] Danziger, *Abd al-Qadir and the Algerians*, 61, 73, 80, and 196.

had been eclipsed during his years of combat.[14] He devoted himself to religious and Sufi scholarship, and acquired a widespread reputation for his intellectual activities in the later years of his life.[15]

## THE SANUSIYYA AND ANTI-COLONIAL RESISTANCE IN NORTH AFRICA

Many aspects of the background to 'Abd al-Qadir's movement, such as its roots in his father's authority, were reflected in the later history of the Sanusiyya order in Cyrenaica. Muhammad ibn 'Ali al-Sanusi (1787–1859) was born not far from 'Abd al-Qadir's home place in western Algeria in 1787. He was raised in the Shadhiliyya tradition and later studied in Fez.[16] Although he was said to have met and had friendly contacts with 'Abd al-Qadir's family (a hagiographical story tells of 'Abd al-Qadir visiting al-Sanusi in Mecca in 1827), they were from different Sufi traditions, and there is nothing to indicate any particular relationship between them, except for the solidarity that comes from a shared home region.[17]

In 1826, al-Sanusi moved to Mecca, where he joined a well-known reformer of Sufi thought, Ahmad ibn Idris (1749–1837).[18] Al-Sanusi was, apart from his Sufi scholarship, also involved in Islamic law and wrote a number of scholarly works promoting new interpretations (*ijtihad*), giving examples of where it must be applied. He argued that a competent scholar should be open to seek the best solutions to a specific problem not just from the established opinion of his school of law, but also from the other schools and, if he was able, directly in the hadith itself.[19] When it came to practicable application of his theories, however, al-Sanusi almost exclusively referred to ritual, *'ibadat*, and in particular the correct practice of prayer. Although these theories were generally applicable and would also apply to more temporal or 'legal' aspects of the shari'a, it does not appear that these held any particular interest

---

[14] There is one reference to 'Abd al-Qadir in 1839, i.e. during the campaign, claiming to have held frequent conversations with the Prophet, a claim typical of the *tariqa Muhammadiyya* type of orders, to which the Sanusiyya and Tijaniyya, but not the Qadiriyya belonged. However, this is contradicted by other sources, and it seems that it was only after his capture that he could focus on his Sufi experiences, see Danziger, *Abd al-Qadir and the Algerians*, 181.

[15] Étienne, *Abdelkader*, 309–411; and Smaïl Aouli, Ramadane Redjala, and Philippe Zoummeroff, *Abd el-Kader* (Paris, 1994), 451–91; see also 'Abd al-Qadir's own writings from the period, such as *Kitab al-mawaqif* (*The Book of Halting-Places*), which has been translated in Abd el-Kader, *Écrits spirituels*, trans. Michel Chodkiewicz (Paris, 1982).

[16] K. S. Vikør, *Sufi and Scholar on the Desert Edge: Muhammad b. 'Ali al-Sanusi and his Brotherhood* (London, 1995).

[17] 'Abd al-Malik b. 'Abd al-Qadir al-Libi, *al-Fawa'id al-jaliyya fi ta'rikh al-'a'ila al-Sanusiyya al-hakima fi Libiya* (*The Manifest Lessons from the History of the Ruling Sanusi Family in Libya*) (Damascus, 1966), 43–4.

[18] R. S. O. Fahey, *Enigmatic Saint: Ahmad Ibn Idris and the Idrisi Tradition* (London, 1990); and Vikør, *Sufi and Scholar*, 100–31.

[19] See, for example, his main work in *usul al-fiqh, Iqaz al-wasnan fi al-'amal bi-l-hadith wa-l-Qur'an* (*The Awakening of the Somnolent to Labor through the Hadith and the Qur'an*) (Algiers, 1332/1914); see also K. S. Vikør, 'Opening the Maliki School: Muhammad b. 'Ali al-Sanusi's Views on the *madhhab*', *Journal of Libyan Studies*, 1/1 (2000), 5–17.

for al-Sanusi. In fact, it is impossible to find evidence of any particular interest in politics either in the writings of Ibn Idris or of his student al-Sanusi. Some aspects of their biography indicate that they had patrons among the governing classes in Mecca, and Ibn Idris's sudden departure from Mecca in 1827 may have been related to the changing political fortunes of his presumed patron, but if so, it did not have any effect on al-Sanusi's status in the town.[20] It was only when his master died in 1837 that al-Sanusi left to seek a place where he could organize his association.

Although the master, Ibn Idris never established any organized order, many of his students did. Apart from al Sanusi, Muhammad 'Uthman al-Mirghani founded the Khatmiyya in the Sudan and Ibrahim al-Rashid the Rashidiyya (later renamed the Dandarawiyya), in the Sudan and elsewhere. These brotherhoods appear to be more strictly organized and better structured than most Sufi orders that existed at the time.[21] This can be seen as the main feature of what some scholars have labeled the 'neo-Sufi' orders of the nineteenth century; they differed from older orders not so much in religious doctrine as in the superiority of their organization and perhaps the depth of their insertion into worldly life.[22]

On leaving Mecca, al-Sanusi actively sought out a region to strike roots. He was looking for a desert-side environment of Bedouin (he had already worked among Bedouin in the Hijaz), and found it in Cyrenaica (later to become part of eastern Libya), after a brief sojourn in western Tripolitania. Al-Sanusi had brought a number of Ibn Idris's students from Mecca, and quickly began spreading his order, traveling from one tribal group to the other, seeking out and befriending their leaders and dominant families, and acquiring an invitation to establish a lodge from each. He found fertile ground, and it did not take long before most of the major populated oases of the region had a Sanusi lodge.[23]

In view of the later relations between the Bedouin and the order, it is important to note the nature of these lodges. They did not aspire to any political authority over the Bedouin tribes, but inserted themselves into existing Bedouin structures by providing new services. Thus, in spite of the founder's legal interests, today there is no trace of Sanusi influence in the legal culture of the region, which has followed traditional Maliki interpretations.[24] The resolution of legal disputes within

[20] Bernd Radtke, John O'Kane, Knut S. Vikør, and R. S. O'Fahey, *The Exoteric Ahmad Ibn Idris: A Sufi's Critique of the Madhahib and the Wahhabis* (Leiden, 2000), 27–8.

[21] On the Khatmiyya, see primarily Ali Salih Karrar, *The Sufi Brotherhoods in the Sudan* (London, 1992); on the *Rashidiyya* and its derivations, see Mark Sedgwick, *Saints and Sons: The Making and Remaking of the Rashidi Ahmadi Sufi Order, 1799–2000* (Leiden, 2005); see also Yahya Muhammad Ibrahim, *Madrasat Ahmad b. Idris al-Maghribi wa-atharuha fi al-Sudan* (*The School of Ahmad b. Idris al-Maghribi and its Influence in Sudan*) (Beirut, 1994).

[22] On the debate over this term, see R. S. O'Fahey and Bernd Radtke, 'Neo-Sufism Reconsidered', *Der Islam*, 70/1 (1993), 52–87.

[23] Vikør, *Sufi and Scholar*, 132–60. The relationship between the Sanusis and the Bedouin tribes has been the topic of anthropological discussion on the 'structuralist' views of E. E. Evans-Pritchard, *The Sanusi of Cyrenaica* (Oxford, 1949), which was criticized by Emrys L. Peters, *The Bedouin of Cyrenaica: Studies in Personal and Corporate Power* (Cambridge, 1990), 10–28. For the purposes of this chapter, it is sufficient to state that there is clear agreement that the result was a close relationship between the order's lodges and the tribes and the tribal leaders.

[24] See, for example, the documentation in Aharon Layish, *Legal Documents on Libyan Tribal Society in Process of Sedentarization* (Wiesbaden, 1998).

the tribe was evidently an important aspect of a tribal shaykh's political authority and was not challenged by the brotherhood and the lodges. Instead, the lodges primarily provided religious learning and knowledge. Each lodge had a trained Sufi teacher, and all the major tribal families sent some of their younger sons to a lodge to receive a religious education. For most, this was probably not a very deep immersion, but more gifted students could be sent on to the order's central lodge at Jaghbub (on today's Egyptian–Libyan border) to receive further education. In addition to its purely religious and scholarly work, the brotherhood and the lodges also provided important services for the surrounding Bedouin. They cultivated 'gardens'—larger or smaller irrigated plots, depending on what the oasis could support—that fed the poor. Their religious and social work had political implications insofar as it created a focus of identity for the otherwise fractious nomadic groups. Only five years prior to al-Sanusi's arrival in Cyrenaica, the area had been ravaged by an intense tribal war.[25] After the order started to provide cohesion, there were no further conflicts of this intensity. This was not because the order imposed any superior political authority over the tribes—it clearly did not—but because it provided mechanisms to settle disputes. Also important in this respect was the increased economic development of the region. After the central Saharan trade route from Lake Chad to Tripoli dwindled in the latter half of the century, it was progressively replaced by a route for trans-Saharan goods passing through the Sanusi-influenced areas of Cyrenaica and crossing some extremely arid desert regions.[26] The brotherhood did not actively participate in the trade itself, but it worked actively to promote it. Clearly, the tribes that lived on this route benefitted considerably from the trade, both as participants and as protectors of the traders. Thus, while the order was consciously working for the spiritual betterment of the nomads and for the spreading of religious knowledge and piety, it also had some impact on Bedouin society. One reason for its success was clearly that the order did *not* challenge the existing political power structure of the tribes, but worked within the structures and between the tribes. Thus, the idea that Cyrenaica had 'come under Sanusi control', or that the Sanusis sought some sort of temporal kingdom and for this reason moved into the desert where the Ottomans 'could not reach them', does not stand up to scrutiny.[27] Everything seems to indicate that relations with the Ottoman authorities on the coast were perfectly amicable, and the order had an imperial firman to carry out its work. The Ottoman authority simply did not reach into the regions of the independent-minded tribes. Thus, it was the religious and not the political vacuum that the Sanusis sought to fill.

Nevertheless, in spite of the more or less apolitical nature of the order, the Sanusis aroused suspicion among the French colonial authorities in Algeria. They saw a possible threat in this remote order sitting far away in the desert with which

[25] Evans-Pritchard, *Sanusi*, 50.
[26] Glauco Ciammaichella, *Libyens et français au Tchad (1897–1914): La Confrérie senoussie et le commerce transsaharien* (Paris, 1987).
[27] See, for example, Michel Le Gall, 'The Ottoman Government and the Sanusiyya: A Reappraisal', *International Journal of Middle East Studies*, 21/1 (1989), 91–106; and documents in Ahmad Sidqi al-Dajjani, *Al-Haraka al-Sanusiyya: Nash'atuha wa-numuwuha fi al-qarn al-tasi' 'ashar (The Sanusi Movement: Its Formation and Growth in the Nineteenth Century)* (Beirut, 1967), 307–9.

Europeans had hardly any direct contact and only vague information.[28] Much of their knowledge about the Sanusis had been provided by members of the Tijani order in Algeria, to whom the Sanusis were potential rivals. Aided by an active and imaginative local agent, the French developed what has been called the 'black legend' of the Sanusiyya as a virulent anti-European and anti-French militant organization that was only waiting to strike at the Europeans.[29] When, for instance, three French missionaries were killed by Tuareg brigands in south-western Algeria in 1876, the French blamed the Sanusis, who were in fact not present in that area at all and apparently were not aware of the French suspicions.

This led to a confrontation at the turn of the century, as French colonial forces in West Africa advanced eastwards and northwards in what is now Niger and Chad.[30] Having taken control over the Sahelian regions around Lake Chad, they pressed eastwards towards Waday, the most powerful kingdom in what is today eastern Chad. The Sanusis by this time had expanded along the trade route across the Sahara. They had gained members in Waday and established a few lodges among the Teda and Daza nomads in northern Chad, although the influence of the order was fairly thin there and only extended to two or three lodges, the most southern being Bi'r Alali north-east of Lake Chad, established in the summer of 1900.[31] It was the first Sanusi lodge that the French forces came into contact with, only a year after it had been built. The Sanusis knew that French expansion would disrupt the peace, but seem not to have realized that they themselves would be the targets of French attacks. The French officials, on the other hand, saw the Sanusis as an element of the imagined 'fanatical anti-Christian' force, and attacked the lodge in December 1901. The brethren were caught by surprise. Although they had some arms for the general protection of the lodge, they were overpowered and hastily withdrew further north. The French could not pursue them into the desert, which provided them an escape. In response to the French attack on the Sanusis, the Teda tribes rose in resistance and chants of solidarity with the Sanusiyya quickly became their main slogan to mobilize support.[32] Now drawn into the conflict, the Sanusi leadership did send some shaykhs to assist, but it remained dependent on the will and the decisions of the local tribes who did the actual fighting. Thus, when the Sanusis suggested that the warriors should withdraw—referring to the religious concept of hijra—to lodges under Sanusi control to consolidate the strength, the tribal leaders rejected the idea.[33] The French in any case did not have the military capacity for an all-out attack on the desert strongholds. French colonial troops carried out raids into the desert in the following years, but mostly kept to its south.[34] A decade later though, they gave more attention to the north, and by 1913 had gained control over what are now the Saharan regions of Chad.

---

[28] Jean-Louis Triaud, *La Légende noire de la Sanûsiyya: Une confrérie musulmane saharienne sous le regard français (1840–1930)* (Paris, 1995).

[29] Triaud, *La Légende noire de la Sanûsiyya*.

[30] Jean-Louis Triaud, *Tchad 1900–1902: Une guerre franco-libyenne oubliée? Une confrérie musulmane, la Sanûsiyya, face à la France* (Paris, 1987), 13–36.

[31] Triaud, *Légende noire*, 516.          [32] Triaud, *Légende noire*, 669–90.

[33] Triaud, *Légende noire*, 683.

[34] Thus they briefly captured a lodge in Faya in Borkou in 1906, see Georges Djian, 'Étude sur les senoussistes et leur action dans le centre africain' (1916), *Islam et sociétés au sud du Sahara*, 6 (1992), 107–39, 123; and Djian, *Tchad et sa conquête: 1900–1914* (Paris, 1996), 128.

The French were helped in this by a new war that had started on the northern side of the desert and occupied the minds of their enemies. In October 1911, Italian forces invaded the Ottoman provinces of Tripolitania and Cyrenaica.[35] Rome had long wanted a colonial empire of its own, to emulate the French, British, and Germans in Africa. Since France had taken Tunisia, Italy's first choice, Italy's focus shifted slightly to the east and from the 1870s onwards, it began to develop interests in neighboring Tripolitania. This region had been de facto independent under a local dynasty until 1835, when Ottoman forces intervened and reimposed direct control. Ottoman authorities initiated a partial modernization of the administration in line with the tanzimat reforms.[36] In Cyrenaica, the less-populated region between Tripolitania and Egypt, the Ottomans established Benghazi—at the time no larger than a village—as their administrative center, but they had hardly any influence outside a few coastal towns. In the course of the century, Cyrenaica changed its administrative status several times between being a sub-province (*qa'im-maqam*ate) under Tripoli and a separate province (*mutasarrafiyya* or *wilaya*) ruled directly from Constantinople.[37] Ottoman interests in Cyrenaica were limited to the trans-Saharan trade through Benghazi. When the Italians came to these regions, they expected the local population to accept them as liberators from Ottoman rule and were surprised when the locals instead joined their former rulers in opposing the invasion. As the Ottomans soon became entangled in wars in the Balkans and elsewhere, they did not have sufficient forces in Tripolitania to stave off the Italians, and, in October 1912, following a year-long struggle, were forced to sign a treaty with Italy. Italy was recognized as temporal master of 'Libya', its name for the two provinces, while the sultan's religious authority as caliph of the Muslims was acknowledged.[38] Only a small number of Ottoman advisers remained, and it was left to the locals to respond to the new situation. Some leading notables accepted Italian overlordship, but the majority preferred resistance.

The most prominent anti-colonial leader was Sulayman al-Baruni, a Berber Ottoman politician based in the Jabal Nafusa mountains of western Tripolitania. Although his resistance kept the Italians in their coastal beachheads throughout most of 1912, a new Italian offensive in the spring of 1913 defeated al-Baruni's forces, and he was forced to flee. In the following year, the Italians gained the upper hand in Tripolitania, not least because of the internal rivalry between the various tribes, districts, and towns of the region. At times, the various militias spent as much time fighting each other as the enemy. But when, in 1914, the Italians tried to push southwards into the Fezzan region, they met with stiff resistance and

---

[35] John Wright, *Libya: A Modern History* (London, 1983), 25–41; Ali Abdullatif Ahmida, *The Making of Modern Libya: State Formation, Colonization and Resistance, 1830–1932* (Albany, NY, 1994), 103–40; Dirk Vandevalle, *A History of Modern Libya* (Cambridge, 2006), 24–42; and Anna Baldinetti, *The Origins of the Libyan Nation* (London 2010).

[36] Ettore Rossi, *Storia di Tripoli e della Tripolitania: Dalla conquista araba al 1911* (Rome, 1968), 297–352.

[37] Rossi, *Storia*, 322–3.

[38] Evans-Pritchard, *Sanusi*, 114–15; Nicola Ziadeh, *Muhadarat fi ta'rikh Libiya* (*Lectures on the History of Libya*) (Cairo, 1958), 83; and Vandevalle, *History of Modern Libya*, 26.

had to withdraw with great losses. In Cyrenaica, where they had taken the coastal towns, Italian attempts to move inland were widely unsuccessful. However, the Bedouin were also hampered here by a lack of coordination after the withdrawal of the Ottoman leadership. Unlike Tripolitania, Cyrenaica had a unifying force that could potentially guide the struggle. A number of tribal leaders approached Ahmad al-Sharif al-Sanusi (1873–1933), who had taken over the leadership of the order after his uncle Muhammad al-Mahdi's death in 1902 (Fig. 13). Al-Sharif consulted with the council of elders of the order in a meeting held in late 1911.[39] Several advised him to reject the tribal leaders' request for military leadership. However, the pressure from the Bedouin leaders was clear and al-Sharif was indeed motivated to take up the fight. He therefore decided to throw the order's resources and organization into the war. In late 1912, he met with the Ottoman envoy Enver Pasha, the Young Turk leader, and accepted the command of the struggle in his region.[40] Enver, in turn, promised the 'Tripolitanians' full autonomy. It remains contested whether al-Sharif was fighting formally as the 'representative of the sultan' or as an independent force. Al-Sharif now signed official documents with '*al-hukuma al-Sanusiyya*', the Sanusi government, although there was no such government at the time.[41] The phrase may, however, have been chosen to indicate that al-Sharif was fighting on behalf of religion and of the tribes in his region, not on behalf of the sultan or any other outside authority.

We can see more of the rationale behind this political stance in two public statements made by al-Sharif on his jihad. The first of these statements was published on 29 January 1912 in the Egyptian newspaper *al-Mu'ayyad*.[42] This four-page declaration (*bayan*) was published only three months after the initial Italian invasion of Tripolitania when the defence was still under Ottoman leadership. In this text, al-Sharif exhorts Muslims to join the struggle. He emphasizes the importance of self-defense for the community. For al-Sharif, the defence of the community is a collective duty (*fard kifa'i*), which obliges believers to join the struggle under any leadership (*imam*) that presents itself, without fear of being overwhelmed. Al-Sharif claims that, following the enemy's invasion of the land, the jihad becomes an individual (*mu'ayyan*) duty for each Muslim. Al-Sharif even states that any Muslim who shirks the duty of jihad has, in effect, left Islam and become an infidel—not to mention those who, he argues, had joined the enemy for money and fought against the Muslims!

Al-Sharif does not explicitly identify the leadership of the struggle in his declaration. It appears that he is calling on Muslims to join the Ottoman forces, but, in the absence of Ottoman military units, they should organize themselves independently.

---

[39] Abdulmola El-Horeir, 'Social and Economic Transformations in the Libyan Hinterland during the Second Half of the Nineteenth Century' (PhD, University of California, Los Angeles, CA, 1981), 224–6; and Triaud, *Légende noire*, 782–3; see also A. M. Hassanein Bey, *The Lost Oases* (London, 1925), 65–6.

[40] Ziadeh, *Muhadarat*, 84; Wright, *Libya*, 28–9; and Aghil M. al-Barbar, *Economics of Colonialism: The Italian Invasion of Libya and the Libyan Resistance 1911–1920* (Tripoli, 1992), 180–1.

[41] Evans-Pritchard, *Sanusi*, 116; and Ziadeh, *Muhadarat*, 84.

[42] Text in Erich Graefe, 'Der Aufruf des Scheichs der Senusija zum Heiligen Kriege', *Der Islam*, 3/1 (1912), 141–50.

Indeed, this seems to reflect the actual situation in Cyrenaica in the first few months. Bedouin flocked to the Ottoman units which were in the region, or attacked the Italian posts on their own initiative. The declaration does not refer specifically to a Sanusi leadership (except perhaps for ending, 'I will soon be with you'). To this extent, al-Sharif's stance may be seen as continuing the policy adopted by the founder of the order towards the French in Algeria half a century earlier. Al-Sanusi had, like any other concerned Muslim, apparently given tacit material support to those who fought in his native land. Nonetheless, al-Sanusi did not involve the brotherhood as an organization in the combat or make any public statement on the matter.[43] His successor al-Sharif, on the other hand, did go public. In calling on Muslims to do their duty, it is clear that he already envisioned a more active role, and was at least mentally preparing for the transformation that was to start later in the year when the Ottoman forces withdrew from Libya and someone had to 'take the banner', as he had intimated in his declaration. Nevertheless, al-Sharif was still primarily a scholar concerned with the religious and legal aspects and justifications of the anti-colonial struggle.

The second statement by al-Sharif was a more sophisticated, scholarly thesis on the legal issues of jihad, which was published in 1912 as a booklet, *al-Bughyat al-musa'id fi ahkam al-mujahid* (*The Desire of the Helper, concerning the Rules of the Mujahid*), in the following year.[44] In this work, al-Sharif returns to some of the same themes and emphasizes that, when the country is invaded, jihad becomes a duty for every individual Muslim. He discusses whether a Muslim should follow a Muslim ruler who abandons the jihad and makes peace with the enemy.[45] He quotes those scholars who argue that a negotiated peace is acceptable, provided that it improves the welfare of the Muslims. However, al-Sharif argues that jihad itself cannot be dispensed with and that it is wrong to follow a ruler who attempts to forbid jihad. A true imam, a just ruler, must lead Muslims into battle. It is unclear whether this was a veiled reference to the Ottoman sultan who had just signed the 1912 treaty with Italy; but it was certainly intended to prevent any propagandistic use of the treaty by the enemy. According to al-Sharif, if the enemy takes control over any region of the *dar al-Islam*—such as the Italian-held coastline—it becomes *dar al-harb*, a place where Islam cannot flourish, and which Muslims must leave in a hijra to Muslim-held lands. These sections can thus be seen as reflections of the situation at the time of writing.

Much of the work, however, is more academic and concerns issues traditionally discussed in jihad law, most importantly economic aspects. It is permissible for a Muslim to wage 'jihad with money', namely, to fulfill his religious duty by funding the war effort.[46] But is the ruler entitled to impose a tax for this purpose? And can he borrow money from unbelievers—or even hire infidel soldiers to fight for the just cause? Here, al-Sharif refers to differing opinions among the schools

---

[43] Vikør, *Sufi and Scholar*, 211–16.
[44] Ahmad al-Sharif al-Sanusi, *al-Bughyat al-musa'id fi ahkam al-mujahid: Risala fi al-hathth 'ala al-jihad* (*The Desire of the Helper, Concerning the Rules of the Mujahid: A Letter on the Urging of Jihad*) (Cairo, 1332/1913–14). For a more detailed discussion of this text, see Vikør, '*Jihad, 'ilm* and *tasawwuf*: Two Justifications of Action from the Idrisi Tradition', *Studia Islamica*, 90 (2000), 153–76.
[45] Al-Sanusi, *Bughya*, 15–18 and 37.     [46] Al-Sanusi, *Bughya*, 19–23.

of law, and concludes by supporting the Shafi'i view (in spite of his affiliation to Malikism). Al-Sharif concludes that such acts are permissible, assuming the presence of a superior non-Muslim force, with a single exception: it is not permitted to pay infidel soldiers, namely, to use non-Muslim mercenaries. It is difficult to see how this could be a relevant issue in the tribal guerrilla war in Cyrenaica at the time. It was, in fact, more of a legal discussion for its own sake. The same is probably largely true of al-Sharif's discussion on the division of booty between the ruler and his soldiers, and whether Muslims who are captured when fighting for the enemy should be regarded as enemies or apostates.[47] They are perhaps both, but the rules on how to treat them and their families differ depending on which status takes precedence. (Al-Sharif concludes that they are enemies, which means that their women are to be taken prisoners as well.)

Compared with other exhortations for jihad, this treatise reads as a rather dispassionate and scholarly piece. Certainly, it does include the expected appeals for the believer to do his duty and protect the homeland (which stretches from Egypt to Tunisia, that is including Tripolitania) with promises of heavenly reward for the fighter and hellfire for those who refuse but, nevertheless, it can be characterized as a scholarly text.[48] Al-Sharif had already written a handful of religious texts, primarily on Sufism. It seems clear that this publication was intended to link his religious and intellectual interests to his future role as the leader of a military struggle.[49] Al-Sharif knew that he would become a mujahid, but he remained the religious and scholarly leader of the Sufi order like his uncle and grandfather before him.

In 1915, the tide of war turned in Libya. Italy had joined the world war on the side of the Entente, and had to withdraw some of its forces from Libya. The Ottomans, now on the opposing side as an ally of Germany, asked all Muslims to join their jihad against the Entente and again came to the support of the resistance in Libya. Renewed fighting broke out in Tripolitania, centered on the town of Misurata under Ramadan Suwayhili, who set up a 'Tripolitanian Republic'. Even though the Tripolitanian resistance was still held back by internal rivalries and frictions, they were able to push the Italians back into a handful of coastal strongholds. However, Suwayhili was deeply suspicious of Sanusi intentions in Tripolitania, and vigorously resisted any cooperation with them in Cyrenaica. The anti-Italian resistance in Cyrenaica and Tripolitania thus took different paths, with violent battles taking place between them.[50] The Germans and Ottomans, for their part, gave material support to the Sanusi resistance and helped bolster their position, but also urged Ahmad al-Sharif to support their joint effort by attacking the British in neighboring Egypt.

---

[47] Al-Sanusi, *Bughya*, 39–42.

[48] Al-Sanusi, *Bughya*, 3.

[49] Ahmad al-Sharif al-Sanusi, *Al-Anwar al-qudsiyya fi muqaddimat al-tariqa al-Sanusiyya* (*The Sacred Lights in the Introduction to the Sanusi Order*) (Istanbul, 1339–42/1920–24); and Ahmad al-Sharif al-Sanusi, *Al-Fuyudat al-rabbaniyya fi ijazat al-tariqa al-Sanusiyya al-Ahmadiyya al-Idrisiyya* (*Emanations of Lordly Grace in the Degrees of the Ahmadi Idrisi Sanusiyya*) (Istanbul, 1342/1924–25); and others.

[50] Wright, *Libya*, 30; and Evans-Pritchard, *Sanusi*, 123.

The Sanusi had some support among the Bedouin in Egypt; and al-Sharif did accept the German request and sent a force across the border in 1916. This was, however, a major mistake. The British quickly overwhelmed the Sanusi guerrillas and, having been drawn into the Libyan conflict, intervened to put an end to the internal war there. The Ottoman and German advisors were forced to leave Libya, and the British insisted that Ahmad al-Sharif was deposed as leader of the Sanusiyya. He went into exile in Constantinople. After the fall of the empire two years later, al-Sharif moved to Mecca, where he spent the rest of his life.[51] Al-Sharif was replaced as head of the order by his younger cousin Muhammad Idris. Idris, as the son of the previous head of the order, Muhammad al-Mahdi, in fact had a stronger claim to religious authority than al-Sharif. On the other hand, the British were not able or willing to impose an Italian victory. Instead, they brokered a truce, the Akrama agreement of April 1917, which gave considerable concessions to the Tripolitanians and accorded virtually full autonomy to Cyrenaica behind the coastal strip. Two years later, Idris was recognized as 'amir' of that region. The religious order had become part of the political power structure, although still mostly as a nominal authority over a Bedouin tribal society.[52]

In the west, Tripolitania had by the early 1920s fallen into political chaos and was threatened by the renewed assertiveness of Italian colonialism. The most prominent leader of the resistance, Suwayhili, was in the end unable to secure his supremacy over the region. The Tripolitanians therefore swallowed their pride and asked Idris, who had established his position in the interior of Cyrenaica reasonably well, to extend his authority to Tripolitania. For the first time, the weak and thinly populated eastern region was asked to dominate their larger and richer neighbors in the west. Although Idris accepted the offer, a new Italian offensive pushed the Tripolitanian resistance aside, thereby rendering the new arrangement irrelevant. From 1922, all Libya had reverted to total war.

The Italians quickly subdued Tripolitania, but Cyrenaica remained indomitable. For the Italian authorities, the conflict may have begun as a war against the local 'rebels' in general, but it soon became a war on the Sanusiyya, whereby the order and anyone associated with it—which included most Bedouin in Cyrenaica—became targets. In return, the Bedouin fought for Islam and for the Sanusis. Although most of the Sanusi family may not have been involved in active warfighting—Ahmad al-Sharif being an exception—they still commanded the support of the Bedouin as symbols of Islamic religious leadership, from which the guerrilla commanders drew their legitimacy.[53]

---

[51] With his jihadist credentials, he was politically active in exile and several times mentioned as a potential king or even caliph, with more or less realism, but did on occasion play important roles as mediator between rival parties, both in Iraq and Yemen; Evans-Pritchard, *Sanusi*, 133; Nicola A. Ziadeh, *Sanusiyah: A Study of a Revivalist Movement in Islam* (Leiden, 1968), 71; and Anne K. Bang, *The Idrisi State in 'Asir, 1906–1934* (Bergen, 1996), 121–2; see also Claudia Gazzini, 'Jihad in Exile: Ahmad al-Sharif al-Sanusi 1918–1933' (MA, Princeton University, 2004).

[52] Evans-Pritchard, *Sanusi*, 141–4; and Vandevalle, *History of Modern Libya*, 28.

[53] Wright, *Libya*, 32.

Idris changed the political direction of the Sanusi entity by building ties with
the British in Egypt. Under Idris, the former alliance with the Ottomans was
replaced by close relations to Britain. From being part of a global conflict during
the First World War, the Sanusi anti-Italian war became a local, anti-colonial and,
later, an anti-fascist struggle. Idris was never closely involved in the actual conduct
of the war, and went into exile in Egypt when the active war began again in 1922.

Although many of the guerrilla leaders were tribal shaykhs lacking any status
within the order, a number of heads of Sanusi lodges now became war chiefs as
well and garnered authority both through their religious and their battle experience. The most dominant of them, a man soon to become the overall leader of the
resistance, was 'Umar al-Mukhtar, an elderly shaykh of a Sanusi lodge. As *na'ib al-
'amm*, the general representative of Idris, he united the tribal groups of Cyrenaica
under his command, in full understanding with Idris. Born in what would become
present-day Libya, 'Umar came from a client tribe of the coastal plains and had
served as shaykh of various Sanusi lodges when the war began, among other places
in Chad, where he had fought against the French.[54]

The relationship between the Sanusi shaykhs, the lodge heads, and the tribal
leadership had clearly evolved over the course of the century. Originally, the
founder had sought to keep the lodges 'external' to the tribes of their area by moving his shaykhs around from lodge to lodge at regular intervals, so that they did
not become too attached to a particular location. But under his successors, there
was much less circulation of shaykhs, and the distinction between the local tribal
leadership and the dominant religious families became less clear-cut, although the
distinction remained.[55] The guerrilla war helped to blur this distinction even further, so that people such as 'Umar, greatly respected for his piety and learning, also
gained respect for his qualities as an ostensibly 'tribal' and military leader. Thus, the
order became the political representative for the local Bedouin, although it never
became 'tribal' in the sense of directly representing one tribal section over another.

'Umar was able to organize effective guerrilla warfare by using local knowledge
of the terrain and by building on the close relations between the fighters and the
civilian population. Thus, although the Italians succeeded in subduing Tripolitania
and the Fezzan, Cyrenaica remained outside their control. Since the Sanusi order
was identified as their principal enemy, they targeted the lodges and infrastructure
of the order and destroyed most of them, including the central lodges in Kufra and
Jaghbub.[56] But it was only in the latter half of the 1920s, after the Italians had begun
to undercut the civilian support structure of the guerrillas, by destroying tribal settlements, erecting barbed wire fences, and eventually gathering civilian Bedouin into
concentration camps, that they began to gain the upper hand. In December 1931,
'Umar al-Mukhtar was captured. He was hanged the following month, and the
Sanusi resistance was finally, after nineteen years of struggle and diplomacy, crushed.

---

[54] Evans-Pritchard, *Sanusi*, 168.       [55] Vikør, *Sufi and Scholar*, 194–5.
[56] Evans-Pritchard sums up their attitude as 'delenda est Sanusiya', see Evans-Pritchard, *Sanusi*,
167.

The Italian period of full control was of short duration, lasting only from 1932 until the Allied invasion of Libya a decade later. The British allowed Idris to return from exile and installed him with his old title of 'amir' of Cyrenaica.[57] When the war was over, a proposal to partition Libya was narrowly defeated in the United Nations. For lack of a credible alternative, the reluctant and republican-minded Tripolitanians then accepted the UN proposal to make Libya a kingdom with the amir as the new king. Thus Idris, the Sufi shaykh, became king of a poor desert kingdom that only later came to glisten with oil wealth. Idris appears never to have been all that interested in politics.[58] An intellectual, he tried to revive the order as a scholarly organization, re-establishing lodges and using his royal patronage to promote studies on Sanusi history and theology and publications of his grandfather's works.

However, during the war against Italy, the religious side of the order had become less and less relevant. In fact, the order had basically ceased to exist as a religious structure as the rigors of the protracted war took precedence over Sufi intellectual activity.[59] Idris' attempts at renewal only succeeding in recreating the order as an aristocratic structure for Cyrenaican notables closely linked to the royal power. Thus, when Qadhafi ousted the old and weakened king in 1969, he had few problems in discarding these remnants of the Sanusiyya's history. Under his reign, 'Sanusi' became associated with royalty and 'British imperialism', while 'Umar al-Mukhtar was celebrated as a national anti-imperialist hero, an interpretation strangely divorced from the reality of his role as a shaykh of the Sufi order. The Sanusis, once so dominant in the central Sahara and North Africa, were reduced to a couple of lodges set up for the exiled royal family in Egypt and in Mecca.

## CONCLUSION

These two examples of Sufi-related anti-colonial resistance had features in common, but they also differed in many important respects. Both leaders gained their legitimacy and initial support from their leadership of a Sufi order, which in both cases was ultimately inherited from their grandfather. In both cases, the jihad leaders were committed Sufis who returned to scholarly and pious activity in exile, but during the war itself, they both became temporal leaders whose military activity overshadowed the religious aspects of their calling.

However, the differences are even more apparent. The Sanusis actively used their Sufi organization in the construction of the jihad: local lodges became centers of resistance, and lodge shaykhs led the tribal struggle. On the other hand, the

---

[57] Todd M. Thompson; 'Covert Operations, British Views of Islam and Anglo-Sanusi Relations in North Africa, 1940–45', *Journal of Imperial and Commonwealth History*, 37/2 (2009), 293–323; see also Wright, *Libya*, 44–59; and Vandevalle, *History of Modern Libya*, 38–40.

[58] Muhammad al-Tayyib al-Ashhab, *Idris al-Sanusi* (Cairo, 1957).

[59] Evans-Pritchard, *Sanusi*, 191–5.

Qadiri structures were hardly present in the Algerian case. Instead, unlike Ahmad al-Sharif or his successors, 'Abd al-Qadir established a rudimentary state that combined Islamic and modernist Ottoman models and used the caliphal title of 'Commander of the Faithful'. The Sanusis did eventually end up with an amirate and kingdom, but this was largely thrust upon them from outside, and does not seem to have originated in any such profound state-building ambitions during the struggle itself.

Both relied on tribal structures in their fighting, but the Sufi element was a much more important link between the leadership and the tribes in the Libyan case. This may have ensured the enduring cohesion of the Cyrenaican tribal resistance, compared with the more unstable Algerian resistance, which at several moments threatened to break apart. Clearly, this was related to the loose nature of Qadiri organization as opposed to the stricter structure of the Sanusi order.

The jihad was thus in no way a logical extension of Sufism. Rather, aspects of the organizational framework of some (but not all) Sufi orders, as well as the personal charisma of the Sufi leaders could be transformed from one existence to another, as required by historical and social circumstances. In some cases, this transformation was eminently successful, but the cost was that the original content and purpose for the brotherhood was lost—and it turned out to be impossible to regain it when the war was over and the brotherhood appeared to have won.

# 9

# Muslim Mobilization in Imperial Russia's Caucasus

*Michael A. Reynolds*

## INTRODUCTION

The theme of Muslim resistance to Imperial Russian rule has long defined the historiography of Russia and the Caucasus.[1] The Russian conquest of the Caucasus was a protracted struggle that began in the middle of the eighteenth century and concluded in 1864. Most famously, in the final phase of that struggle, a series of warrior imams staved off the Imperial Russian army for three decades by rallying the Muslim mountain peoples under the banner of Islam (Fig. 14). The Great Caucasus War produced figures such as Imam Shamil, who would become legendary in the Muslim world and it inspired some of the greatest authors of Russian literature, including Aleksandr Pushkin, Mikhail Lermontov, and Lev Tolstoy.[2] The conflict indelibly stamped the historical memories and imaginations of Muslims, Russians, and outside observers alike with the image of an Islamic Caucasus in perpetual defiance of Russian rule. Subsequent episodes of rebellion, deportation, and wars have only reinforced Muslim Caucasians' reputation for contumacy.

That Islam was a defining factor in the Great Caucasus War cannot be gainsaid. This is not to suggest that the conflict can be reduced to religion or that Islam suffices to explain the staunch resistance of the mountain peoples. Tsarist officials, like their British and French counterparts, found it convenient to ascribe the natives' resistance to religious fanaticism.[3] Imperial expansion, however, routinely generates violent conflict, regardless of the faiths involved. Highland peoples, for reasons unrelated to religion, are particularly predisposed to push back against aggrandizing states.[4] The highlanders' desire to defend their freedom against outside

[1] The author would like to thank Elizabeth Bospflug, Paul Bushkovitch, Laura Engelstein, Alan Mikhail, and members of Yale University's Modern Europe Colloquium, who commented on an early draft of this chapter.

[2] Susan Layton, *Russian Literature and Empire: Conquest of the Caucasus from Pushkin to Tolstoy* (Cambridge, 1994).

[3] Alexander Knysh, 'Sufism as an Explanatory Paradigm: The Issue of the Motivations of Sufi Resistance Movements in Western and Russian Scholarship', *Die Welt des Islams*, 42/2 (2002), 139–73.

[4] James C. Scott, *The Art of Not Being Governed: An Anarchist History of Upland Southeast Asia* (New Haven, 2009). Nikki R. Keddie has noted in passing that geography and the predominance of tribes and 'non-urban religious forms' have been among the factors informing Muslim resistance to

**Fig. 14** *Ordinary Feat of the 77th Infantry Regiment Tenghinka Arkhip Osipov, 22 March 1840* by Alexander Alexeyevich Kozlov, depicting Russian soldiers in battle with Muslim rebels in the North Caucasus (Public Domain).

domination reflects a universal human aspiration. Moreover, Islam in the Caucasus was far from monolithic. Interpretations of Islam in the Caucasus varied, and disagreements about the implications of religious doctrine for action were significant even among those who espoused identical theologies.

Nonetheless, religion did shape decisively the resistance and the course of the anti-imperial struggle. At the level of identity, Islam separated the Muslim mountain peoples from an empire closely tied to Orthodox Christianity. To be sure, identity never dictated conflict. The Russian empire often negotiated religious difference successfully, but it could never overcome the gulf, only bridge it.[5] At the level of ideas, a particular reading of Sunni Islam influenced by Salafi doctrines from Yemen helped channel and bolster the determination of the outmatched highlanders to resist the might of the vast Russian empire.

colonial powers, see Nikki R. Keddie, 'The Revolt of Islam, 1700 to 1993', *Comparative Studies in Society and History*, 36/3 (1994), 463–87, 482.

[5] For recent works on the Russian empire and Islam, see Paul Bushkovitch, 'Orthodoxy and Islam in Russia, 988–1725', in Ludwig Steindorff (ed.), *Religion und Integration im Moskauer Russland* (Wiesbaden, 2010), 117–44; Vladimir Bobrovnikov, 'Islam in the Russian Empire', in Dominic Lieven (ed.), *The Cambridge History of Russia*, 3 vols, iii: *Imperial Russia, 1689–1917* (Cambridge, 2006), 202–23; Robert D. Crews, *For Prophet and Tsar: Islam and Empire in Russia and Central Asia* (Cambridge, MA, 2006); Allen J. Frank, *Muslim Religious Institutions in Imperial Russia: The Islamic World of Novouzensk District and the Kazakh Inner Horde, 1780–1910* (Leiden, 2001); and Alexander Morrison, *Russian Rule in Samarkand 1868–1910: A Comparison with British India* (Oxford, 2008), especially 51–87.

## THE COMING STRUGGLE FOR THE
## NORTH CAUCASUS

The North Caucasus ranks among the very first lands touched by Islam. The conversion of the indigenous inhabitants of the northeast Caucasus, however, was not immediate, but unfolded over centuries in a gradual process as knowledge of Islam percolated from Derbent northward and up into the highlands. By the seventeenth century the majority of Dagestanis and their Chechen neighbors had become Muslims (the Ingush, the ethno-linguistic cousins of the Chechens, would complete their conversion only in the nineteenth century). During this process Dagestan, and in particular highland Dagestan, came to host a vibrant center of high Arabic-Islamic culture.[6] Arabic became the land's lingua franca of written communication and Dagestani scholars acquired fame throughout the Muslim world for their command of Arabic and the Islamic sciences.[7] The Muslims of the northeast Caucasus cultivated the Sunni Islam defined by the Shafi'i madhhab that they had learned from the Arabs. The Muslims of the southeast Caucasus in Azerbaijan, by contrast, followed the lead of Persia's Safavid dynasty and in the sixteenth century began embracing Shi'i Islam.

In the northwest Caucasus the process of Islamization unfolded differently. There it was not the early Arab Muslims coming from the south who brought Islam but rather later waves of Turkic Muslims. Sunni Islam of the Hanafi madhhab thus gradually became the dominant faith in the northwest Caucasus, but the region never witnessed the formation of an Islamic scholarly or cultural tradition as deep as that in Dagestan. In between the Muslims of the northeast and northwest Caucasus lay the Ossetians, an Indo-Iranian people who acquired a veneer of Orthodox Christianity that covered an indigenous animist culture. Their location would later have geopolitical consequences.

Although Tsars Ivan IV and Peter the Great made concerted efforts to project Russian power into the Caucasus in the sixteenth and eighteenth centuries respectively, it was under Catherine the Great (*r*.1762–96) that Imperial Russia established itself as a permanent influence in the North Caucasus.[8] In order to halt raids

---

[6] According to one count, in the sixteenth and seventeenth centuries, the highlands produced over ninety percent of Dagestan's manuscripts, see A. E. Krishtopa, 'Gornyi Dagestan nakanune prisoedineniia k Rossii: sotsioestestvennaia kharakteristika', in V. O. Bobrovnikov et al. (eds), *Severnyi Kavkaz v sostave Rossiiskoi imperii* (*The North Caucasus in the Russian Empire*) (Moscow, 2007), 333.

[7] Makhach Musayev and Diana Alkhasova, 'Daghestani Ulama in the Muslim World', in Moshe Gammer (ed.), *Islam and Sufism in Daghestan* (Helsinki, 2009), 43–56; see also Anna Zelkina, 'The Arabic Linguistic and Cultural Tradition in Daghestan: An Historical Overview', in Jonathan Owens, *Arabic as a Minority Language* (Berlin, 2000), 89–111.

[8] Moshe Gammer, *Muslim Resistance to the Tsar: Shamil and the Conquest of Chechnia and Daghestan* (London, 1994), 1–2; Michael Khodarkovsky, *Bitter Choices: Loyalty and Betrayal in the Russian Conquest of the North Caucasus* (Ithaca, NY, 2011), 8–10; see also Michael Khodarkovsky, 'Of Christianity, Enlightenment, and Colonialism: Russia in the North Caucasus, 1550–1800', *Journal of Modern History*, 71/2 (1999), 394–430. The Russian empire thereby displaced the Ottoman and Persian Safavid empires as the dominant outside power in the region. On the Ottomans and the Caucasus, see M. Sadık Belge, *Osmanlı Devleti ve Kafkasya: Osmanlı Varlığı Döneminde Kafkasya'nın Siyasi-Askeri Tarihi ve İdari Taksimatı* (*The Ottoman State and the Caucasus: The Political and Military History and Administrative Division of the Caucasus in the Ottoman Era*) (Istanbul, 2005).

from the south, the Russians built what became known as the 'Caucasus Line', a string of forts garrisoned by Cossacks and Russian soldiers and running east–west along the Caucasus.[9] Meanwhile, Russia vanquished its main regional rivals, the Ottomans and Persians, in a series of wars between 1768 and 1829. With each of its victories, Imperial Russia extended its territory, taking the Crimea, and then the lands of the South Caucasus under its control.

Tsarist Russia had isolated the North Caucasus, but it had not subdued it. The empire extended its writ over the low-lying areas of the Caucasus, including those in the south, before it asserted control over the highlands in the north. Taking and holding the lowlands was both easier and more important, because the lines of communication ran through the lowlands and because only the lowlands had significant agricultural value.[10]

Although the empire's policymakers refrained from projecting power into the interior of the North Caucasus as they redrew the map of the South Caucasus, the steady encroachment of tsarist power was felt in the highlands. Through the seventeenth and eighteenth centuries, Cossacks, Slavs, Germans, and Armenians had, with the encouragement of the tsars, taken to settling the lands just north of the Terek along the Caucasus Line.[11] The arriving settlers pushed natives into the highlands, while the forts of the Caucasus Line separated the highlanders from their winter pastures and easy access to salt, a vital necessity. The Caucasus had long been a center of slave trading, and tsarist efforts to stamp out the trade represented one more way in which the empire disrupted economic life in the mountains.[12]

The highlanders' harassment of lowland settlers, raids into Russia and Georgia, and the possibility that their truculence might assist outside invaders were chronic concerns for tsarist administrators.[13] The Russian state, with its regularized, hierarchical, and bureaucratic institutions, represented a form of organization wholly alien to the mountain communities. The North Caucasus had never known

[9] Sean Pollock, 'Empire by Invitation? Russian Empire-Building in the Caucasus in the Reign of Catherine II' (PhD, Harvard University, 2006), 71–198.

[10] Krishtopa, 'Gornyi Dagestan', 332; and Charles King, *The Ghost of Freedom: A History of the Caucasus* (New York, 2008), 38.

[11] A similar policy was followed in the South Caucasus, to where St Petersburg banished heterodox Christians. The belief was that in the periphery they would be less likely to unsettle the social order and would even contribute to the empire's stability by diluting the Muslim presence in the Caucasus, see Nicholas P. Breyfogle, *Heretics and Colonizers: Forging Russia's Empire in the South Caucasus* (Ithaca, NY, 2005).

[12] Gammer, *Muslim Resistance*, 40. Although tsarist officials were quick to combat and eventually stamp out the enslavement of Christians, they tolerated the enslavement of Muslims for a time even after Tsar Aleksander I outlawed slavery in 1805. The slave trade in the Caucasus remains woefully under-researched. For a rare study, see Liubov Kurtynova-D'Herlugnan, *The Tsar's Abolitionists: The Slave Trade in the Caucasus and Its Suppression* (Leiden, 2010).

[13] There exists some debate over the Caucasian highlanders' practice of raiding, with some scholars asserting that the rustling of livestock and stealing from neighbors had been an integral part of the way of life in the mountains. Others argue that raiding was a recent response to the economic disruption wrought by the Russian imperial expansion, see Vladimir Bobrovnikov, 'Bandits and the State: Designing a "Traditional" Culture of Violence in the Russian Caucasus', in Jane Burbank, Mark von Hagen, and Anatolyi Remnev (eds), *Russian Empire: Space, People, Power, 1700–1930* (Bloomington, IN, 2007), 239–45.

centralized rule. Its remote location and forbidding topography rendered it a ter-
tiary interest to major powers, including the Ottomans and Persians. Moreover,
the difficult terrain compelled the highlanders to live autonomously in small, isolated, but tightly knit communities. The individual mountain-dweller was highly
dependent for survival on his immediate community, and each community, absent
a central agent or guarantor of order, had to rely on itself to provide security.

Reflecting this, highland culture prized communal self-reliance and martial virtues. The mountain peoples developed a form of customary law they called *adat*,
from the Arabic word for custom, to distinguish it from the holy law of Islam,
shari'a. *Adat* varied in its particulars from village to village but reflected commonly
shared values in its fundamentals. In many villages, these laws evolved into codes
written down with the consensual approval of local elders.[14] The most vivid, and
arguably most significant, institution of *adat* was the blood feud, wherein the murder of an individual obliged the victim's clansmen to retaliate, initiating a cycle that
could last for generations. The idea was not to perpetuate conflict but rather to
use the threat of violence to impede the escalation of disputes and maintain social
order in the absence of a central enforcer.[15]

For its part, the bureaucratic machine of the Russian imperial state found itself
forced to deal with a bewildering multitude of communities. The Caucasus was
(and remains) host to an astonishing array of ethnic and linguistic groups. The
early Arab conquerors dubbed the Caucasus *Jabal al-alsun* or 'the mountain of languages' out of sheer awe at its linguistic diversity.[16] Moreover, these communities
embodied a variety of socio-political forms ranging from the comparatively complex aristocratic hierarchies of the Kabardians and other Adyghe people, through
the Avars with their khan and ruling family, to the fiercely egalitarian Chechens.
Thus not only did the ethnically variegated mountain peoples lack a unifying sovereign or institution, but the separate societies among them often lacked authoritative leaders who could speak for and command obedience from all the members
of the community. This structural asymmetry made negotiation inherently vexing.
The sheer number and variety of mountain communities overwhelmed the capacity of the tsarist bureaucracy to act with any nuance, let alone tailor policies to
particular communities. Along with the bureaucratic dominance of the military
over the civil administration, it helped propel Russian policy towards the lowest
common denominator of politics, force, to compel submission.

Still, it would be an error to conclude that these differences made unlimited
warfare inevitable. Tsarist administrators were heirs to a rich imperial tradition
composed of Mongol, Muscovite, and Byzantine strands that predated the comparatively recent assimilation of Western European forms and practices. They

---

[14] Michael Kemper, 'The North Caucasian Khâlidiyya and "Muridism": Historiographical
Problems', *Journal of the History of Sufism*, 1–2/5 (2007), 151–67, 160.

[15] Bobrovnikov, 'Bandits and the State', 239. These norms are not unusual among mountain
peoples; for comparison, see Margaret Hasluck, *The Unwritten Law in Albania* (Cambridge, 1954),
219–60.

[16] Abu al-Fida Isma'il ibn 'Ali, *Géographie d'Aboulféda*, trans. M. Reinaud and Mac Guckin de Slane
(Baghdad, 1963 (1840)), 71.

possessed considerable experience in dealing with and ruling over culturally diverse subjects, including Muslims, and had earlier integrated Circassian princes quite successfully.[17] Moreover, for the mountain peoples of the Caucasus, Russians and Cossacks were more than mortal enemies; they were also neighbors, partners in trading, occasional collaborators in raids, and spouses.[18]

## THE *GHAZAWAT* OF MANSUR

At the most fundamental level, however, the reality remained that the objectives of the Russian imperial state and the aspirations of the mountain peoples were irreconcilable. The aim of the tsar's servants was to place the whole of the Caucasus under the undisputed rule of their sovereign. The mountain peoples desired precisely to avoid such a fate. In 1779, formerly compliant Kabardian chiefs had grown disaffected. Joining together, they engaged tsarist units in pitched battle but were quickly vanquished.[19] As the failed uprising demonstrated, the highlanders had no chance of overcoming tsarist power through direct battle, and no single mountain community could have any hope of forcing a halt to the advance of that power.

A glimpse of the mountain peoples' potential for resistance, however, was revealed in 1785 when a Chechen named Ushurma or Shaykh Mansur (1732–94) mobilized a broad constituency of highlanders from Dagestan, Chechnya, and elsewhere. For six years Mansur managed to defy the Russians until the latter trapped and captured him at an Ottoman fort in Anapa in 1791. According to some, Mansur had been a shaykh of the Naqshbandiyya *tariqa* or Sufi brotherhood, a fact that, if true, would neatly foreshadow the pattern of resistance that emerged several decades later in the Great Caucasus War. No solid evidence supporting Mansur's alleged Naqshbandi affiliation has ever been found, however, and the claim was likely invented after his death. Nonetheless, it is clear that religion played a key role both in motivating Mansur and in enabling him to rally support. Mansur called on the highlanders to uphold the tenets of Islam, to pray zealously, to refrain from theft and blood feud, and to practice circumcision, in addition to waging *ghazawat*, or jihad.[20] Religious authorities joined his struggle, boosting the image Mansur cultivated of being a divinely blessed man.[21] Mansur's revolt marked a key moment. He succeeded, if for just a short time, in mobilizing the mountain

---

[17] Paul Bushkovitch, 'Princes Cherkasskii or Circassian Murzas: The Kabardians in the Russian Boyar Elite, 1560–1700', *Cahiers du monde russe*, 45/1–2 (2004), 9–30.

[18] Thomas M. Barrett, 'Lines of Uncertainty: The Frontiers of the North Caucasus', *Slavic Review*, 54/3 (1995), 578–601.

[19] Pollock, 'Empire by Invitation?', 177–93.

[20] An Arabic word meaning literally 'raid' or 'foray', *ghazwa* is often used as a synonym for jihad, and became widely used in the North Caucasus in its plural form, *ghazawat* (*gazavat*). The word *ghazi* (*gazi*) connotes a victorious commander of *ghazawat*.

[21] Julietta Meskhidze, 'Imam Shaykh Mansur: A Few Stanzas to a Familiar Portrait', *Central Asian Survey*, 21/3 (2002), 301–24, 305–8 and 312.

peoples across clan and tribal ties. The absence of an institutional structure, however, doomed the revolt to wither following the neutralization of its leader.

For the next three decades, small-scale raiding across the Caucasus Line remained endemic. Tsarist authorities had no obvious solution to the problem. The Russian army lacked the manpower to garrison the whole of the Caucasus Line in such a way as to repel any and all attacks. Due to the fractured and variegated nature of mountain society, the classic imperial tactic of co-opting local leaders was of little relevance to the North Caucasus. Moreover, when local rulers did utter an oath of loyalty to the distant tsar, they typically attached little meaning to it, if for no other reason but that past outside sovereigns had lacked the capability to impose their will. Finally, many local chiefs in the more egalitarian societies lacked the authority to compel obedience among their own nominal followers.

## THE EMPIRE STRIKES BACK

The imperial response to this problem was to apply a policy based on the lowest common denominator: brute coercion. If tsarist officials could not find a common language that would impress upon the natives the need to submit to the tsar's writ, they would let their guns—and axes—do the talking. In May 1816, General Aleksei Petrovich Ermolov (1754–1835), having proven himself on the battlefields of Europe against Napoleon, assumed the post of commander-in-chief of the Georgian (later Caucasian) Corps. His mission was to establish full political and military control over the whole of the North Caucasus.

The Imperial Russian army had bested Napoleon's armies, but in the Caucasus it found itself in an asymmetric conflict where it could not impose its will through decisive battle. Ermolov had roughly 60,000 men at his disposal. This number was more than ample to defeat any single force the mountain peoples might put together, but too few to garrison and defend every vulnerable point and settlement.[22] The general resolved that if the Russian army could not meet and repulse every raid, it would retaliate with such violence against the highlanders collectively that none would dare permit a fellow clansman to take up arms.[23] Ermolov had no intent to limit coercion to the battlefield. Impossible though it might be to destroy by combat a foe who refrained from pitched battle, he noted, 'everyone is subject to hunger and it [hunger] will cause them to submit'.[24] The way forward was clear: comprehensive struggle against the mountain peoples to compel the latter to submit or cease to exist.

---

[22] S. K. Bushuev, *Bor'ba gortsev za nezavisimost' pod rukovodstvom Shamilia (The Struggle for Independene of the Mountaineers under the Leadership of Shamil)* (Moscow, 1939), 98–9.

[23] As Ermolov famously summarized it in a letter to Tsar Alexander I, 'I desire that the terror of my name shall guard our frontiers more potently than chains or fortresses', see John F. Baddeley, *The Russian Conquest of the Caucasus* (Richmond, 1999 (1908)), 97.

[24] V. G. Gadzhiev (ed.), *Narodno-osvoboditel'naia bor'ba Dagestana i Chechni pod rukovodstvom Imama Shamilia: sbornik dokumentov (The Popular Liberation Struggle of Dagestan and Chechnya under the Leadership of Imam Shamil: Collected Documents)* (Moscow, 2005), 5.

Ermolov's approach was merciless by its very logic, but his personal contempt for Caucasians facilitated its application. He dismissed them as 'Asiatics', in his eyes beings ignorant of civilization and morals, capable of understanding only force. Even Tsars Alexander I (1777–1825) and Nicholas I (1798–1855) felt it necessary to criticize Ermolov's harshness. He remained unapologetic, 'Gentleness [*Sniskhozhdenie*] in the eyes of Asiatics is a sign of weakness, and out of pure humanity I am inexorably severe', adding:'One execution saves hundreds of Russians from destruction and thousands of Muslims from treason.'[25]

Ermolov may have been unusual in his willingness to defy his sovereigns with such sentiments, but he was by no means alone in holding them. His chief-of-staff Aleksei Aleksandrovich Vel'iaminov (1735–1838) shared them, and in fact was the author of the doctrine that later became known as the 'Ermolov system'. Likening the Caucasus to a 'mighty fortress', Vel'iaminov called for methodical campaigning to subdue the mountain peoples through comprehensive coercion, combining attrition by combat with the manipulation and destruction of the natural environment. If one could not beat the recalcitrant highlanders into submission with a handful of sharp blows, one could slowly but inexorably strangle and suffocate them.[26] Ermolov further believed that overturning the social order of the highlanders was essential to the region's long-term pacification. This required dislocating not just the shariʿa but also *adat*. Islamic law presented a threat because it was a rival to imperial law and a potential ideational font of resistance. In 1822, Russian officials disbanded the shariʿa courts in Kabarda that they had earlier permitted. *Adat* by its nature presented less of a doctrinal obstacle to imperial rule, but Ermolov initially sought to ban it in order to undercut the social status and authority of hostile highland elites.[27]

Ermolov decided to subdue the Chechens first and so moved the Caucasus Line forward by building new forts—Groznaia (1818), Vnezapnaia (1819), and Burnaia (1821)—inside Chechnya. The idea was to bottle up the Muslim mountain communities inside the valleys and settle Cossacks on the newly freed-up lands.[28] When the population responded with raids, Ermolov ordered retaliation, merciless and wholesale. Ermolov had his men regularly lay waste to whole villages, indiscriminately killing their inhabitants and destroying their dwellings, in order to drive home his message to submit unconditionally. The environment and ecology became his targets as well. The Russian army vastly expanded the road network in the Caucasus. By clearing trees along both sides of roads in order to deny cover to would-be ambushers it altered the landscape. Ermolov imposed blockades on rebel areas, targeted crops and farmland for destruction, and took to destroying whole swathes of forest in a bid to deny sustenance and cover to the population.[29]

---

[25] V.A. Pooto, *Kavkazskaia voina* vol. 2, *Ermolovskoe vremia* (St Petersburg, 1887), 15; John F. Baddeley, *The Russian Conquest of the Caucasus* (London, 1908), 97–99; and Gammer, *Muslim Resistance*, 34.

[26] Gammer, *Muslim Resistance*, 31, 34; and Baddeley, *Russian Conquest of the Caucasus*, 109.

[27] Bobrovnikov 'Bandits and the State', 253; and Bobrovnikov, *Severnyi Kavkaz*, 116.

[28] Bobrovnikov, *Severnyi Kavkaz*, 117.

[29] As Ermolov wrote, 'The enemy is absolutely dependent on his crops ... Let the standing corn be destroyed each autumn as it ripens and in five years they will be starved into submission', see Zelkina,

Poisoning water supplies was another tactic.[30] Deprived of their most productive lands, weakened by hunger, and forced up into the highlands, whole Chechen villages perished from disease. Other highlanders in Chechnya and even Dagestan despairingly drew the lesson Ermolov was trying to teach:'not the gun and cannon, but the axe will defeat them'.[31]

Given Ermolov's readiness to use all means at his disposal, the logic of his strategy to subdue the Muslim mountain peoples appeared unassailable. Yet pre-emptive punishments and pitiless reprisals failed to cow the resistance. In the early 1820s, Kabardians, Avars, Chechens, and Kumyks all mounted uprisings.[32] The revolts, however, were disconnected and local, and had no strategic impact. A Chechen named Beibulat Taimiev (Taimazov) (1779–1831) achieved a brief strategic effect in 1825 when he rallied Kumyks, Chechens, and others to join together in the name of Islam to fight the Russians. Beibulat himself was not a religious authority, but had spent time with a number of Kumyk mullahs who advocated more rigorous application of the shari'a and holy war against the 'cursed Russians'. At his direction, a mullah who had claimed to have received a message from God via an angel sparked a rebellion.[33] Beibulat himself declared it the duty of all believers to sacrifice themselves for the faith.[34] Yet his demands against the Russians—that they abandon Fort Groznaia (later the city of Grozny) and withdraw northward behind the Terek River—were concrete and rather worldly. Beibulat led his insurgents onto the Kumyk plain, where they overran a Russian fort—an unprecedented achievement for the resistance—before Ermolov arrived. The Russians attempted to impress the message of the insuperable might of the empire by arraigning several hundred local Kumyk men and compelling their leaders to surrender their personal *kinjals*, or daggers, in a ritual of humiliation. When one Kumyk instead drew his *kinjal* to kill a Russian general and wound another, the Russians promptly slayed the assembled Kumyks en masse.[35]

These harsh tactics were not wholly ineffective. Upon his return to Chechnya, Beibulat discovered that some of his lowland Chechens preferred not to challenge the Russians. He rebuked them, but then his mullah allies reproached him for dividing rather than unifying the mountain peoples. Now effectively confined to the Chechen highlands, however, Beibulat's movement began to implode. The rebels made an attempt to take Groznaia towards the end of 1825, but failed. The following January Ermolov marched along the Sunzha River, sacking villages,

'Islam and Society in Chechnia: From the Late Eighteenth Century to the Mid-Nineteenth Century', *Journal of Islamic Studies*, 7/2 (1996) 240–64, 253; and M. M. Bliev and V. V. Degoev, *Kavkazskaia voina (The Caucasian War)* (Moscow, 1994), 14.

[30] Gammer, *Muslim Resistance*, 187–8.

[31] N. F. Dubrovin, *Istoriia voiny i vladychestva russkikh na Kavkaze (The History of the War and Russian Rule in the Caucasus)*, 6 vols (St Petersburg, 1888), vi, 299 and 303.

[32] Khodarkovsky, *Bitter Choices*, 70–1.

[33] Baddeley, *Russian Conquest of the Caucasus*, 148.

[34] Bekovich-Cherkasskii to Sipiagin, n.p., 9 April 1828, in Gadzhiev, *Narodno-osvoboditel'naia or'ba Dagestana*, 29.

[35] Bobrovnikov, *Severnyi Kavkaz*, 117; N. I. Pokrovksii, *Kavkazskie voiny i imamat Shamilia (The Caucasus Wars and the Imamate of Shamil)* (Moscow, 2000 (1940)), 142–4; and Baddeley, *Conquest of the Caucasus*, 150.

cutting down forests, and taking hostages from settlements throughout Chechnya. These tactics suppressed rebellion, but only temporarily.[36]

Mansur's and Beibulat's revolts had provided glimpses of the potential of Islam to build unity across ethnic lines. The sudden collapse of both revolts, however, had revealed a weakness. Islam had mobilized a broad coalition for resistance, but it had not supplied an institutional base. That was about to change.

## THE BIRTH OF THE IMAMATE

Tsarist officers in the mid-1820s were aware that in the highlands of Dagestan a movement for religious reform was afoot. They knew that a young Avar named Ghazi Muhammad (1795–1832) was attracting crowds with his teachings on matters of Islam. But because he diligently avoided making any explicitly political statements, the officers declined to pay close attention to the preacher.[37]

Born in the early 1790s, Ghazi Muhammad ibn Isma'il al-Gimrawi al-Daghistani distinguished himself as a student first under the famous Avar *'alim* Said al-Harakani (*d.*1834) and then under another well-known Dagestani scholar, al-Shaykh al-Sayyid Jamal al-Din al-Ghazi-Ghumuqi. Jamal al-Din also initiated Ghazi Muhammad into the Naqshbandiyya *tariqa* and introduced him to his own mentor, the Lezgi al-Shaykh Muhammad al-Yaraghi. Accompanying Ghazi Muhammad in his studies was his closest friend Shamil (1797–1871), who also became a *murid* (Sufi adept) of Jamal al-Din.[38] Shamil joined Ghazi Muhammad when the latter struck out on his own as a preacher.

Ghazi Muhammad and Shamil concluded that the multi-dimensional crisis of mountain society was rooted in the mountain-dwellers' defective faith. The path out of the crisis therefore was to practice a more pristine Islam, one wholly in accord with the original sources of Islamic law: the Qur'an and the *sunna*. This would necessitate two distinct but linked struggles. The first and more fundamental would be an internal one against the un-Islamic practices of their communities. This would entail the wholesale repudiation of *adat* and the adoption across the board of properly Islamic practices such as abstention from alcohol, tobacco, dancing, usury, and un-Islamic forms of dress, particularly for women. The second struggle would be an external one against the Russian unbelievers.[39]

---

[36] Pokrovskii, *Kavkazskie voiny*, 145–7; and Khodarkovsky, *Bitter Choices*, 76–9.

[37] D. I. Romanovskii, *Kavkaz i Kavkazskaia voina* (*The Caucasus and the Caucasus War*) (Moscow, 2004 [1860]), 174 and 179–80.

[38] 'Abd al-Rahman al-Ghazi-Ghumuqi, *Abdurakhman iz Gazikumukha: Kniga vospominaniia* (*Abdurakhman of Gazikumukh: A Memoir*), A. R. Shikhsaidov and Kh. A. Omarov (eds), trans. M. S. Saidov (Makhachkala, 1997), 32; and M. A. Abdullaev, *Sufizm i ego raznovidnosti na Severo-Vostochnom Kavkaze* (*Sufism and its Varients in the Northwest Caucasus*) (Makhachkala, 2003), 28, 43.

[39] This worldview is readily evident in the account of Shamil's chronicler, Muhammad Tahir al-Qarakhi, see Ernest Tucker and Thomas Sanders (eds and trans.), 'The Shining of Daghestani Swords in Certain Campaigns of Shamil', in Thomas Sanders, Ernest Tucker, and Gary Hamburg (eds), *Russian-Muslim Confrontation in the Caucasus: Alternative Visions of the Conflict Between Imam Shamil and the Russians, 1830–1859* (New York, 2010), 11–74.

Significantly, Ghazi Muhammad and Shamil launched their campaign by preaching not armed jihad but temperance. Alcohol, of course, was in no way foreign to the Caucasus, but one of the effects of Russian influence had been the spread of hard liquor, and vodka in particular, thereby facilitating alcoholism among the mountain peoples and destabilizing family life. Shamil's own father had been a drunkard, and this almost certainly hardened the future imam's determination to bring mountain society into line with his understanding of Islamic norms. To underscore their seriousness, Ghazi Muhammad and Shamil lashed each other forty times in public for having tasted wine before understanding the gravity of the sin.[40] Their condemnation of alcohol was not without controversy, however, even among 'ulama. Al-Harakani, for example, interpreted the Qur'anic injunction against wine as applying only to alcoholic beverages made from grapes. Thus the consumption of vodka and *boza* (a fermented malt beverage) was acceptable. He also argued that smoking did not violate the shari'a. These opinions caused Ghazi Muhammad to break with his former teacher.[41]

By 1828, Ghazi Muhammad had attracted a following in the highlands, particularly from among the Avar youth. It was time to take more forceful action. That year he penned a treatise entitled, 'The Establishment of Proof of the Apostasy of the Rulers and Judges'. In it, he described *adat* as counter to God's will and Islam. Notably, he highlighted *adat*'s arbitrary, and hence oppressive, nature—a point that likely resonated with all those dissatisfied with the prerogative of village elders both to make law and interpret it. Ghazi Muhammad declared all rulers and judges who followed *adat* to be apostates. Apostasy had negative consequences, he warned, explaining that 'according to the principles of Islam' apostasy meant that their prayers, fasts, pilgrimages, marriages, religious endowments, and witness statements were illegitimate. Most ominously, he wrote that their apostasy made shedding their blood permissible.[42]

In December of the following year, a gathering of highland 'ulama and notables proclaimed Ghazi Muhammad as imam of Dagestan. Ghazi Muhammad promptly warned all locals to obey the shari'a or face retribution, and then began executing his jihad in earnest. Condemning *adat* as 'man-made' and contrary to 'what God has sent down', he had his followers burn the *adat* books maintained by many villages. They also beat and sometimes killed those who objected to their program.[43] Ghazi Muhammad's vision of a properly Islamic society had no place for

---

[40] Baddeley, *Conquest of the Caucasus*, 241.

[41] Pokrovskii, *Kavkazskie voiny*, 177; and Moshe Gammer, 'Collective Memory and Politics: Remarks on Some Competing Historical Narratives in the Caucasus and Russia and their Use of a "National Hero"', *Caucasian Regional Studies*, 4/1 (1999), n. 50.

[42] A photocopy of the original treatise is reproduced along with a translation into Russian in Iasin Rasulov, *Dzhikhad na Severnom Kavkaze: storoniki i protivniki* (*Jihad in the North Caucasus: Supporters and Opponents*), 76–8. This undated monograph was written sometime between August 2004 and the author's death in April 2006. It is banned in the Russian Federation due to its advocacy of armed jihad, but is widely available on the internet. Kemper provides an English translation of a very similar but not identical text, see Michael Kemper, 'Ghazi Muhammad's Treatise Against Daghestani Customary Law', in Moshe Gammer (ed.), *Islam and Sufism in Daghestan* (Helsinki, 2009), 94–100.

[43] Kemper, 'Ghazi Muhammad's Treatise Against Customary Law', 86.

the highlander nobility, who were in any event dependent on *adat*. He targeted the class for dismantlement, and over the course of the next two years would behead thirty noblemen (*bek*s).[44] Not content merely to enjoin un-Islamic behavior, Ghazi Muhammad also insisted that every highlander should possess a basic knowledge of Islamic precepts, and he was known to punish those who remained ignorant of their faith's fundamentals.[45]

Ghazi Muhammad's comprehensive jihad to uproot *adat* and 'Islamize' mountain society represented a radical break with precedent, but the ideational origins of this break are still not fully understood. Formerly, scholars assigned great importance to Ghazi Muhammad's, and Shamil's, affiliation with the Naqshbandiyya. That consensus held that the activist doctrines of Ahmad Sirhindi (1564–1624), an influential Punjabi Naqshbandi shaykh, who championed a militant Sunni orthodoxy against religious syncretism in Mughal India, migrated to the Caucasus via Naqshbandi networks around the beginning of the nineteenth century.[46]

This genealogical explanation is attractive, but recent research has called it into question. There is little to no mention or discussion of Sufism in the documentation left by Ghazi Muhammad or Shamil, and it appears that the links of the North Caucasian Naqshbandiyya with outside Naqshbandi circles were tenuous at best.[47] The North Caucasian Naqshbandiyya itself was split on the question of jihad against the Russians. Although al-Yaraghi came round to support it, Ghazi Muhammad and Shamil's own mentor, Jamal al-Din Ghazi-Ghumuqi, steadfastly objected to it. When Ghazi Muhammad broached the idea of armed struggle against the Russians, Jamal al-Din replied that a proper *murid* would practice *dhikr*, the prayerful remembrance of God, and not lead people to 'confusion and ruin'.[48] Indeed, contrary to the image of Caucasian Sufis bound by 'iron discipline' to their shaykhs, Jamal al-Din complained that after he told Ghazi Muhammad to 'sit quietly at home and study' rather than take up arms, the latter not only ignored his advice, 'but even began to reprimand and abuse me, writing a letter to me using the most vile expressions'.[49]

Shamil was more respectful than Ghazi Muhammad, but no more obedient. Speaking in 1843, Jamal al-Din upbraided Shamil's fighters for looting Muslims living on 'pacified' territory under the pretext that acceptance of infidel rule rendered Muslims fair targets. He reminded Shamil that from the beginning he had forbidden him from taking up arms and once again called upon the imam to stop

[44] Bobrovnikov, *Severnyi Kavkaz*, 119.   [45] Kemper, 'Ghazi Muhammad's Treatise', 89.

[46] Hamid Algar, 'A Brief History of the Naqshbandi Order', in Marc Gaborieau, Alexandre Popovic, and Thierry Zarcone (eds), *Naqshbandis: Cheminements et situation actuelle d'un ordre mystique musulman* (Paris, 1990), 34–36; Gammer, *Muslim Resistance*, 39–46; and Albert Hourani, 'Sufism and Modern Islam: Maulana Khalid and the Naqshbandi Order', in Hourani (ed.), *The Emergence of the Modern Middle East* (London, 1981), 75–89; and Zelkina, *In Quest for God and Freedom*, 75–99.

[47] Kemper, 'The North Caucasian Khalidiyya and "Muridism"'; and Knysh, 'Sufism as an Explanatory Paradigm'.

[48] 'Abd al-Rahman al-Ghazi-Ghumuqi, *Abdurakhman iz Gazikumukha*, 140; and Michael Kemper, 'The Daghestani Legal Discourse on the Imamate', *Central Asian Survey*, 21/3 (2002), 265–78, 265–6.

[49] M. G. Gadzhiev and A. I. Osmanov (eds), *Istoriia Dagestana s drevneishikh vremen do nashikh dnei* (*The History of Dagestan from Ancient Times to Our Era*), 2 vols (Moscow, 2005), i, 514–15, n. 23.

fighting.[50] Although Shamil continued to pay respect to his teacher, he rejected his advice.[51]

Perhaps unsurprisingly, there was also considerable criticism of the jihad among 'ulama outside Naqshbandi circles. The teacher of both Ghazi Muhammad and Shamil, al-Harakani, opposed fighting the Russians. Notably, in 1819 al-Harakani had called for a jihad against the Russian unbelievers in support of the Avar Khan. Al-Harakani's even wrote to the Ottoman sultan to request aid in the name of Islamic solidarity. After the Avar Khan made peace with the Russians, however, al-Harakani ceased his advocacy of jihad. In fact, he became a paid agent supporting the Russians as an informant and as a public critic of resistance to them. In his religious teachings he emphasized the necessity of cultivating the inner moral virtues in contrast to the legalism of the imams.[52]

As an alternative to the emphasis on the Naqshandiyya, Michael Kemper has suggested that the jihad be understood as the product of a native discourse devoid of outside influence.[53] Iasin Rasulov, a young Dagestani scholar, however, has contended that outside theological currents, in fact, did provide the ideational underpinning for Ghazi Muhammad's jihad movement.[54] These currents were not Sufi, but Salafi. Rasulov, a self-described Salafi and an advocate of armed jihad, had a clear agenda in making his argument that contemporary Islamist insurgents by virtue of their Salafi doctrine are the true heirs of the nineteenth-century jihad movement. His claims must therefore be treated with caution, but they merit attention. Indeed, Ghazi Muhammad's (and later Shamil's) rejection of conventional or traditional forms of authority in favor of the original sources of Islam, uncompromising condemnation of *adat*, insistence on strict application of a literalist and rather puritanical reading of shari'a, and readiness to wield the charge of apostasy, are all hallmarks of Salafism, albeit not exclusively so.[55] However, in the aforementioned treatise of Ghazi Muhammad we do find direct evidence of Salafi influence. In the course of making his argument, Ghazi Muhammad makes several references to Muhammad al-Quduki (1652–1717), an influential Dagestani whom Kemper describes as the 'initiator of a "sharia movement" long before the jihad of Ghazi Muhammad and Shamil'.[56] Quduki did not, however, develop his ideas in isolation in Dagestan. He spent seven years in Yemen studying with Salih bin Mahdi

---

[50] V. G. Gadzhiev, Kh. Kh. Ramazanov, and A. D. Daniialov (eds), *Dvizhenie gortsev severo-vostochnogo Kavkaza v 20–50 gg. XIX veka: sbornik dokumentov* (*The Movement of the Highlanders of the North Caucasus in the 1820s through 1850s: Collected Documents*) (Makhachkala, 1959), 419.

[51] Abdullaev, *Sufizm*, 179.

[52] Kemper, 'Daghestani Legal Discourse', 366; see also Michael Kemper, *Herrschaft, Recht, und Islam in Daghestan: Von den Khanaten und Gemeindebünden zum ğihad-Staat* (Wiesbaden, 2005), 382–92.

[53] Kemper, 'Ghazi Muhammad's Treatise', 92.

[54] Rasulov was killed in April 2006; see also n. 42.

[55] For an exposition of the concept of Salafism that underscores the pre-modern origins of this interpretation of Islam, see Bernard Haykel, 'On the Nature of Salafi Thought and Action', in Roel Meijer (ed.), *Global Salafism: Islam's New Religious Movement* (New York, 2009), 33–51.

[56] Kemper, 'Ghazi Muhammad's Treatise', 91.

al-Maqbali 'al-Yamani' (*d*.1696), a key figure in the development of Salafism.[57] Quduki ultimately quit Dagestan in disgust over the locals' refusal to forego *adat*.[58] We know from another Yemeni Salafi authority, Muhammad al-Shawkani, that Dagestanis after Quduki continued to actively debate al-Maqbali's ideas.[59] Notably, Ghazi Muhammad cites al-Maqbali as well.[60] It seems safe to conclude that the jihad movement had a partly Yemeni pedigree, although for reasons to be noted later on, it would be misleading to describe the movement as Salafi.

In 1830, Ghazi Muhammad made a bid to vanquish the Avar elite by seizing their seat, the village of Khunzakh.[61] He failed, and thereupon turned his attention against the tsarist forces in the lowlands, and scored some initial victories. The Russians, however, tracked and killed him in his home village of Gimry in 1832. Although his term as imam had been brief, Ghazi Muhammad had laid the foundation of an enduring movement. He had mobilized a large number of mountain-dwellers, especially among the youth. Not least important, his creation of the position of Imam of Dagestan gave the resistance an institutional basis that could survive him. Ghazi Muhammad was blessed with strategic vision. He had correctly grasped that the war against the Russians would necessarily be a drawn-out and extended affair. In order to prevail, the mountain peoples would have to reform their way of life to accommodate strategic and material demands, not only religious ones. Thus he urged the highland-dwelling Chechens to begin relocating to the forests, where the thick woods would hide and shield them. Although the Russians might destroy wooden huts in the forests more easily than stone dwellings in the highlands, the Chechens could rebuild those huts more quickly. In the same way, he advised the Chechens to cultivate maize rather than wheat, as the former brought much higher yields per acre, making it possible to minimize the territory for cultivation. One Russian officer concluded disconsolately that Ghazi Muhammad had put in place a 'well-conceived system of popular war' which 'could not be better suited to the local conditions and the primeval way of life of the Chechen tribes'.[62] The measures he implemented had made the Chechens 'vigilant, always ready to fight or run, and little sensitive to destruction'. Nonetheless, believing on the strength of precedent that the death of Ghazi Muhammad would suffice to finish off the movement, Russian commanders refrained from pressing their advantage.

[57] Bernard Haykel, *Revival and Reform in Islam: The Legacy of Muhammad al-Shawkani* (Cambridge, 2003), 10 and 120–1.
[58] Kemper, *Herrschaft, Recht, und Islam in Daghestan*, 357.
[59] I. Iu Krachkovskii, 'Dagestan i Iemen' ('Dagestan and Yemen'), in Ignatii Iu. Krachkovskii, *Izbrannye Sochineniia* (*Selected Essays*), ed. V. A. Gordlevski et al.; 6 vols, (Moscow, 1960), vi, 579–82.
[60] Rasulov, *Dzhikhad na Severnom Kavkaze*, 77. The copy Rasulov reproduces reads 'al-Yamani', i.e. al-Maqbali. Kemper's translation of his copy has 'Aymak' in place of 'al-Yamani'.
[61] 'Pokazanie osvobozhdennykh iz plena u gortsev gruzin o polozhenii del v Dagestane' ('Testimony of Georgian Highlanders Recently Released from Captivity on the State of Affairs in Dagestan'), n.p., 25 April 1830, in Sh. V. Tsagareishvili (ed.), *Shamil': Stavlennik sultanskoi Turtsii i angliiskikh kolonizatorov* (*Shamil: Protégé of Sultanic Turkey and English Colonizers*), (Tbilisi, 1953), 12–13.
[62] Gammer, *Muslim Resistance*, 64. It is worth noting the parallel adaptations made by other highlanders fighting to stave off predatory states, see Scott, *The Art of Not Being Governed*, 178–219.

Fig. 15 *Battle for Aul Gimry* by Franz Roubaud (1891) (Public Domain).

Shamil was the obvious successor to the post of imam, but had been badly wounded in the battle at Gimry (Fig. 15). Instead, a deputy of Ghazi Muhammad named Hamza Bek (1789–1834) was elected as the second imam. Hamza Bek was neither a Naqshbandi shaykh nor a religious scholar, but was from an Avar noble family. In his youth he had spent several years in the household of the Avar khan's widow, Pakhu Bike, who provided for his education. But after meeting Ghazi Muhammad, Hamza Bek swore off drink, embraced Islam, and became a stalwart supporter of his. This commitment necessarily put Hamza Bek at odds with the Avar ruling house. Moreover, the Russians were backing the Avar nobility as part of their strategy to snuff out the imamate. In the summer of 1834, Hamza Bek and his men laid siege to the ruling house in Khunzakh. During a parley between the two sides, a fight erupted in which the imam's brother and others were killed. In response, Hamza had the ruling household, including Pakhu Bike and all the women but for one who was pregnant, put to death.

The slaughter of the Avar ruling house was a watershed. It represented a stark transgression against highland tradition and laid bare what was at stake in the imamate's struggle. The elimination of the Avar ruling house removed the one local institution that, with Russian backing, might have contained the jihad movement. It also created a vacuum that only the imamate could fill and guaranteed that the clash between the empire and the imamate would be a direct one.[63]

Hamza Bek consolidated his power in Avaristan and from Chechnya received a pledge of loyalty from Tasho Hajji, a disciple of Shaykh al-Yaraghi and companion

---

[63] Gammer, *Muslim Resistance*, 61–3.

of Ghazi Muhammad and Shamil.[64] The jihad movement was expanding. Several weeks later, however, Hamza Bek met his end when in 1834 the Avar khan's milk brothers killed him in an act of vengeance as he entered a mosque to pray.

The 'ulama now elected Shamil as imam. Shamil was an extraordinary individual. He combined high natural intelligence, thorough training in the Islamic sciences, and a superb command of Arabic with charisma and athleticism. Using the legal and organizational infrastructure offered by Islam and drawing on mystical aspects of Islam to amplify his personal talents, Shamil would rally the impoverished and outnumbered mountain peoples and hold off the Russian empire for a full quarter-century.

## SHAMIL AND THE IMAMATE

In his efforts to counter the Russian imperial state and to transform mountain society, Shamil achieved a level of political centralization unprecedented for the North Caucasus. Given the vast imbalance in size between the combatants, it was imperative for the imamate to maximize what manpower and resources it had. One means was to expand the amount of territory under its control. Starting with a base in the Avar highlands and a foothold in Chechnya, Shamil extended the imamate's territory through most of Dagestan and Chechnya. At its peak, the circumference of the territory under Shamil's control measured some 900 kilometers. Essential to this expansion was Shamil's ability to appeal to a shared religious identity in order to mobilize mountain peoples against the Russians and accept the primacy of the shari'a. Shamil dispatched messengers to Sunni Muslims throughout the Caucasus to incite rebellion.[65] Where Sunni identity and institutions were strong, Shamil had success. Where they were weaker, his message of religious solidarity and resistance had profoundly less appeal. The nominally Sunni Circassians, although keen to fight the Russians, were less receptive to the idea of following Islamic law, pooling their resources, and coordinating their efforts with Shamil and his followers. In Azerbaijan, the Shi'i majority remained largely unresponsive, even hostile to Shamil's message.

The path Shamil followed resembled the classic one of state formation identified by Charles Tilly, whereby the demands of waging war stimulated the development of an increasingly centralized polity.[66] If the first order of business in waging war was the formation of a standing armed force that could be ready to go into battle as circumstance dictated, the second order of business was paying for it, and the third

[64] Hajj Tasho, known also as Tashu Hajji, is revered today by many Chechens as a religious leader as well as military hero, see Mairbek Vachagaev, *Chechnia v Kavkazskoi voine: sobytiia i sud'by* (*Chechnya in the Caucasus War: Events and Fates*) (Paris, 2003), 102.

[65] Gammer, *Muslim Resistance*, 248.

[66] Charles Tilly, 'Reflections on the History of European State-Making', in Charles Tilly (ed.), *The Formation of National States in Western Europe* (Princeton, 1975), 3–83. The North Caucasian case on this crucial point contradicts Scott's thesis about highlanders' principled rejection of centralized political power.

was compensating and looking after those who bore some of the greatest burdens of the struggle, such as the widows and orphans of the slain fighters. To coordinate these functions and ensure that they were replicated regularly, Shamil developed a legal administrative code of his own known by the Arabic *nizam*, or 'order', as well as a bureaucratic apparatus to enforce it.

Islam was foundational to Shamil's project. The imamate drew its legitimacy and legislation from religious sources. Shamil adopted the title of 'Commander of the Faithful', *amir al-mu'minin*, and portrayed himself as the successor, or 'Caliph', to the Prophet Muhammad. Ensuring proper religious observance was a constant concern of his and his administration.[67] It was no less important than the fight against the Russian empire. In this regard it is telling that the mountain peoples recalled the period of Shamil's rule as the 'time of the shari'a'.[68]

Yet although Islamic law provided the basis for the *nizam*, Shamil, like virtually all Muslim rulers, found himself confronted with issues on which Islamic jurisprudence offered no clear guidance and so he often had to make law on his own authority. In other instances, Shamil could and did deliberately depart from conventional interpretations of the shari'a when he felt circumstances dictated it by invoking *maslaha*, or 'public interest'. This was no deviation or innovation on the part of Shamil. Rather, it was an established principle in Islamic law known as *istislah*, by which it is acceptable to amend or dispense with the normal strictures of the shari'a where the public interest demands it.[69]

Thus, for example, Shamil, preferred to forego the prescribed punishment for stealing—amputation—reasoning that amputation ensured only that the criminal amputee could never be rehabilitated as a warrior and that he would become a burden on the community. Under Shamil the first two instances of stealing were punished with three-month terms of imprisonment, and the third was punished by death.[70] Other areas where he deviated from the norms of Islamic law were in the use of torture and the use of unrestricted violence against apostates. His supporters among the 'ulama cited *maslaha* to justify Shamil's wide authority to engage in these and other acts that were questionable from the standpoint of the shari'a.[71]

For the purposes of fielding a fighting force, mountain society offered a small but deep pool. Mountain culture esteemed warrior virtues, and men were expected to bear arms as a matter of course. Thus the *nizam*'s requirement that all men between the ages of 15 and 50 have at the ready arms, ammunition, provisions, and

---

[67] See, for example, Imam Shamil's instructions to the 'ulama and qadis (1844), in V.G. Gadzhiev, *Narodno-osvoboditel'naia bor'ba Dagestana i Chechni*, 330–1.

[68] 'Uchenie "zikr" i ego posledovateli v Chechne i Argunskom okruge' ('The Doctrine of "dhikr" and its Followers in Chechnya and the Argun District'), in V. Kh. Kokoshvili (ed.), *Sbornik svedenii kavkazskikh gortsakh* (*Collected Reports on the Caucasian Highlanders*), 10 vols (Tiflis, 1869; reprint Moscow, 1992), ii, 4.

[69] M. Khadduri, 'Maslaha', in *Encyclopedia of Islam*, ed. P. Bearman, Th. Bianquis, C. E. Bosworth, E. van Donzel, and W. P. Heinrichs (Leiden, 2012).

[70] Khadzhi Murad Donogo, *Sotsial'naia politika v Imamate Shamilia* (*Social Policy in the Imamate of Shamil*) (Makhachkala, 2001), 5.

[71] Kemper, 'Daghestani Legal Discourse', 273–4.

appropriate clothing was not too onerous. Improvised raiding parties and tempo-rary levies were not sufficient for long-term warfare, however, and so Shamil estab-lished two permanent military formations. One was a small elite force of especially fearless and loyal *murid*s who served the imam and his deputies as bodyguards and special operators. Ghazi Muhammad had pioneered this class of warrior and Shamil maintained it, expanding its ranks to roughly 400 and dubbing them *naibi murid*s. In the early 1840s, Shamil established a regular guard of mounted warriors, called the *murtaziq*s or 'the hired'. As their name implied, these horsemen were freed from all work but that of fighting, and deployed in units separate from levies. Every ten households had to provide one horseman to the guard. Soon thereafter Shamil formed a body of infantry, perhaps modeled on the new European-style armies of the Ottomans and Muhammad 'Ali. This corps, however, served under his direct command alone. Shamil further set up factories for making gunpowder and even foundries for casting cannon, using both technologically skilled defectors from the Russian army and some locals trained by the Ottomans.[72]

To manage his realm, Shamil relied on his deputies, or *naibs*, who were each assigned a territorially defined district to administer according to the *nizam*. In 1840, Shamil had four *naibs*. By 1856, this number had expanded to thirty-three.[73] A trained judge in Islamic law, or *qadi*, assisted each *naib* in applying the law. The religious origin of the law lent it legitimacy and facilitated its acceptance by mountain society. Nonetheless, the fiercely independent communities often did resist both Shamil's efforts to govern them and the constraints of the shari'a. The Chechens, in particular, were known periodically to reject Shamil's efforts to regu-late their internal affairs. In 1841, they actually rose against and killed the deputy he had sent to rule over them, giving the 'Commander of the Faithful' little choice but to reinstate their revered co-ethnic Tasho Hajji as *naib*.[74]

The bans on alcohol, tobacco, mixing of the sexes, and most forms of music and dancing were not popular. Most mountain communities had limited experience of conforming to these rigorous standards. Rigid separation of the sexes, for example, was foreign to mountain village life. Shamil's strenuous efforts to put an end to blood feud—a practice that was simultaneously contrary to Islam and damaging to the unity of the imamate—ran up against deeply engrained attitudes.[75] Religious orthodoxy was not the sole motive behind Shamil's effort to manipulate and alter mountain customs. A desire to bolster the social fabric and demographic health of the highland communities was another. Thus, for example, in addition to provid-ing subsidies to the widows of his *naibs* and *murtaziq*s, he also put a ceiling on bride prices (*kalym*), making the maximum amounts twenty silver rubles for vir-gins and ten for widows and divorced women.[76] Desertion from the Russian army, particularly by Poles, was relatively frequent. Deserters were potentially a valuable

[72] Gammer, *Muslim Resistance*, 228–9.     [73] Bobrovnikov, *Severnyi Kavkaz*, 122.
[74] Zelkina, *In Quest*, 222.     [75] Zelkina, *In Quest*, 218.
[76] Donogo, *Sotsial'naia politika*, 4.

source of manpower and technological know-how, but they could have become a drain on resources and a destabilizing presence in the villages. In order to promote the assimilation of the deserters and to strengthen mountain communities, Shamil encouraged widows and women who had engaged in premarital sex and would therefore have had dim marriage prospects, to marry deserters who converted to Islam.[77] Shamil permitted those who did not convert to build a church on his territory in accord with the principle that Christians as 'people of the Book' possessed a right to practice their faith under Muslim rule.[78]

There is little evidence of Sufi concepts either in the doctrines that undergirded the imamate or in Shamil's missives and writings. Indeed, it appears that Shamil himself never actually attained the rank of shaykh.[79] Yet it would be wrong to dismiss entirely the role of Sufism in the imamate. The Sufi term *murid* was used to denote a supporter of the imamate. To distinguish those who fought from those who followed the Naqshbandi spiritual path he dubbed the latter '*tariqa murids*', and exempted them from the requirement to fight so that they might focus on prayer and spiritual development. The fighters, the *naibi murids*, looked askance at the *tariqa murids*' avoidance of combat, yet Shamil steadfastly supported the latter, seeing their pursuit of spiritual development as both divinely mandated and a positive influence on mountain society overall.[80]

Although Shamil may not have been formally initiated as a shaykh, he would feign having the sorts of supernatural abilities that shaykhs are said to possess, such as the ability to be in two places at one time, to receive divine instruction through dreams, and to have foreknowledge of visitors. In order to heighten the dramatic effect of some pronouncements on important matters, Shamil would sometimes go into contemplative seclusion (*khalwa*) for several days to fast and pray until he lost consciousness. On awakening he would announce his decision as if having received divine guidance.[81] Sufism may not have defined the imamate, but it did influence the way in which it functioned.[82] Given that a hallmark of Salafism is opposition to Sufism, it would be erroneous to describe Shamil or the imamate as Salafi, even if, as it appears, Salafi thought helped frame highlander dissatisfaction and spur the jihad movement.[83]

---

[77] Gammer, *Muslim Resistance*, 253.

[78] While Shamil's treatment of deserters and prisoners of war was at times exemplary, it was not consistently so, see Baddeley, *Russian Conquest*, 396–7 (n. 1) and 455; see also 'Abd al-Rahman al-Ghazi-Ghumuqi, *Abdurakhman iz Gazikumukha*, 100–4.

[79] Kemper, 'The North Caucasian Khalidiyya', 163.          [80] Zelkina, *In Quest*, 212.

[81] Gammer, *Muslim Resistance*, 239–40.

[82] Clemens Sidorko, *Dschihad im Kaukasus: Antikolonialer Widerstand der Dagestener und Tschetshenen gegen das Zarenreich (18. Jahrhundert bis 1859)* (Wiesbaden, 2007), 403.

[83] A basic contention of Rasulov's is that the jihad movement of the nineteenth century was a Salafi enterprise.

## TSARIST POLICIES TOWARDS ISLAM AND THE WAR AGAINST SHAMIL

The willingness of tsarist officers and officials to embrace brute force and scorched-earth tactics did not mean that they were oblivious to more subtle methods of challenging the imamate. They were well aware that their status as non-Muslims made it more difficult for the highlanders to submit. Against the imamate's message that they were inveterate enemies of Islam, the Russians emphasized that they had no intention to eradicate the highlanders' faith. They insisted that they were interested only in punishing Shamil, a 'deceiver' who, the Russians warned, called for 'equality and the destruction of all hereditary authorities with the singular purpose of taking (personal) control of the inheritances of the khans and beks'. Their propaganda called Shamil's *murtaziqs* 'hated and cruel'; a description that likely resonated with at least some mountain dwellers who found their property requisitioned by the horsemen.[84] To underscore their empire's tolerance for religions, the Russians sponsored visits to the Caucasus by Muslim preachers sympathetic to the Tsarist state, provided an official institutional structure for Muslims, and published a calendar that marked Sunni and Shi'a Muslim religious festivals alongside Orthodox Christian ones.[85]

Tsarist officials likewise recognized that the imamate's project of displacing *adat* with shari'a was alienating many of the natives, and so offered support to advocates of *adat*. Some officials rationalized endorsement of *adat* by arguing that it would lead to the ultimate triumph of Russian civil law. *Adat* would first undermine the shari'a and the imamate. Thereafter, it would be juxtaposed to Russian civil law, whereupon its own arbitrary nature would discredit it.[86]

The fissiparous forces generated by clan loyalties and blood feud were persistent strains for the imamate. Tsarist officials could spot emerging fault lines but were usually too clumsy to exploit them fully. The most famous renegade was Hajji Murad (1790s–1852), whose story Leo Tolstoy (1828–1910) told in his eponymous novel. An Avar noble once close to the Avar ruling house and a participant in the vengeance killing of Hamza Bek, Hajji Murad was a natural ally of the Russians until the intrigues of a rival dissolved the Russians' trust in him and thereby drove him into Shamil's camp. After angering Shamil by objecting to the imam's plan to name his son as his successor, Hajji Murad fled back to the Russian side. When he subsequently attempted to break yet again from the Russians to rescue his family from Shamil's custody, a rival killed him.

---

[84] 'Obrashchenie komandira Otdel'nogo Kavkazskogo korpusa generala-ad"iutanta A. I. Neidgarta k lideram chechenskogo i dagestanskogo naroda' ('Address of the Commander of the Detached Caucasus Corp Adjutant General A. I. Neidgart to the Leaders of the Chechen and Dagestani People'), n.p., 2 April 1844, in V. A. Kozlov et al. (eds), *Vainakhi i imperskaia vlast': problema Chechni i Ingushetii vo vnutrennei politike Rossii i SSSR* (*The Vainakhs and Imperial Power: The Problem of Chechnya and Ingushetiia in the Domestic Policy of Russia and the USSR*) (Moscow, 2011), 70–2.

[85] Gary Hamburg, 'War of Worlds: A Commentary on the Two Texts in their Historical Context', in Sanders, Tucker, and Hamburg (eds), *Russian-Muslim Confrontation*, 184–5.

[86] Firouzeh Mostashari, *On the Religious Frontier: Tsarist Islam in Russia and the Caucasus* (London, 2006), 58.

Tsarist officials understood, too, that Shamil's movement threatened not just the tsar's power but also that of other religious authorities. In the 1840s, they began cultivating ties to local 'ulama and, in a bid to create a class of 'loyal' clergy, allowed them to apply the shari'a in family law and matters of ritual.[87] Through such methods tsarist administrators did manage to win loyalty, or at least compliance from a considerable number. Over time, however, the population in the Caucasus tended to become alienated from this 'official' co-opted clergy.[88] Another tactic was to import to the Caucasus loyal Sunni preachers from outside, particularly from among the Volga Tatars. The ranks of these preachers even included Naqshbandi shaykhs.[89] None of these outside figures, though, lasted for long or had much impact. More significant were Shamil's local religious critics. One such individual took up work as a qadi for the Russians and penned Arabic satires against Shamil. He even wrote to an authoritative scholar in Mecca to ask that the imamate be declared illegitimate. Since, he contended in his letter, the Qur'an made allowance for Muslims to live under infidel rule as long as they suffered no direct interference, Shamil's declaration of those who failed to migrate to the imamate's territory as apostates and his practice of killing them had no basis in Islam. The attempt backfired, however, when from Mecca the response came that jihad was obligatory for all Muslims under infidel rule, regardless of the character of the imam leading the jihad.[90]

Imperial authorities began thinking about how they might gain more permanent control over the spiritual lives of the mountain peoples from the beginning of the Great Caucasus War. Ermolov believed that over the long term the 'ulama would be the greatest impediment to Russian rule. He therefore sought to suppress their numbers through tight regulation and to weaken them economically by confiscating some of the alms and donations made to them by the faithful. In the South Caucasus, Russian administrators began erecting a structure through which to control and administer Muslims of the Caucasus when they established first the post of 'Shaykh al-Islam of the Caucasus' in 1823 and then that of 'Mufti of the Caucasus' nine years later. The former position was given to a Shi'i, and the latter to a Sunni. The mufti was originally placed in Kazan but soon thereafter brought to Tiflis, the tsarist administrative center for the Caucasus and the place where the shaykh al-Islam had been stationed.[91] The commander of forces of the Caucasus Line in the 1830s, Vel'iaminov, envisioned a Muslim spiritual hierarchy with three rungs: senior mufti, mufti, and, at the local level, mullah. Realizing these ambitions to regulate religious authorities took significantly more time at the local level. Only in 1872 did the empire introduce a system for administering local clergy in the South Caucasus, although they never dared to follow through in the North

---

[87] Mostashari, *On the Religious Frontier*, 86–7.

[88] Mostashari, *On the Religious Frontier*, 90.

[89] Kemper, 'Daghestani Legal Discourse', 266–7.

[90] Kemper, 'Daghestani Legal Discourse', 268.

[91] Rəsul Hüseynli, *Azərbaycan Ruhaniliyi: Xanlıqlar çağından sovet işğalınadek olan dövrdə* (*The Azerbaijani Clergy: From the Era of the Khanates to Soviet Occupation*) (Baku, 2002), 38–42. On the institutions of Islam in tsarist Russia, see also Robert D. Crews' chapter in this volume.

Caucasus. Officials there felt their control to be too tentative and the clergy too popular among the local populations to risk imposing regulation on the clergy.[92]

## THE FALL OF THE IMAMATE

The imamate's peak came in the 1840s. An impatient Tsar Nicholas I provoked his commanders to drop Ermolov's systematic approach and instead act recklessly on the battlefield and suffer defeats.[93] The emphasis on coercion generated a brooding hatred for the empire, even among pacified populations.[94] Nonetheless, Shamil's attempts to incite rebellions outside the northeast Caucasus and extend the imamate ultimately failed. During the 1830s, his defiance of the Russians did ripple southward to Azerbaijan, where it helped spark four rebellions. A letter of his to the Muslims living in and around Kuba in the north touched off the largest uprising in Azerbaijan in the nineteenth century. The uprising, however, was at least as anti-feudal as it was anti-Russian, and the land-owning *bek*s of Shirvan and southern Dagestan collaborated in suppressing it.[95] In 1844, a local Azerbaijani qadi who, unusually, urged Sunnis and Shi'a to cooperate against the Russian infidels and exploit the opportunity created by Shamil's success, roused the Muslims of Shusha to revolt, but this rebellion burned out before it could spread.[96]

The explanation for the comparative lack of sustained resistance to tsarist rule in Azerbaijan perhaps resides in a combination of Azerbaijan's lesser proportion of highlands and highlanders, the absence of an Islamic tradition as strong as that among the Dagestanis, and the Sunni–Shi'i rift, exacerbated by the history of Persian invasions of Dagestan. The Shi'a played a prominent role in suppressing most of Azerbaijan's anti-Russian rebellions.[97] Unsurprisingly, the Sunni imamate never derived substantial support from Azerbaijan.

Shamil attempted to rouse the peoples of Georgia, even sending emissaries to the Christian Khevsurs to convince them to follow the example of the Muslim Kists (ethnic relatives of the Chechens), and to reject Russian authority.[98] According to

[92] D. Iu. Arapov, 'Imperskaia politika v oblasti gosudarstvennogo regulirovaniia islama na Severnom Kavkaze v XIX-nachale XXV' ('Imperial Policy in the Area of State Regulation of Islam in the North Caucasus in the 19th and Beginning of the 20th Centuries'), in I. L. Babich and L. T. Solov'eva (eds), *Islam i pravo v Rossii* (*Islam and Law in Russia*) (Moscow, 2004), 23–6.

[93] William C. Fuller, *Strategy and Power in Russia, 1600–1914* (New York, 1992), 251–2.

[94] 'Zapiska Kapitana Brankena o prichinakh yspekhov Imama Shamilia i merakh borby s nim' ('Memorandum of Captain Branken on the Reasons for Shamil's Success and Measures for Fighting Him'), n.p., n.d. (1843), in V.G. Gadzhiev, *Narodno-osvoboditel'naia bor'ba Dagestana i Chechni*, 277–81.

[95] A. S. Sumbatzade, *Kubinskoe vosstanie 1837 g* (*The Kuba Uprising of 1837*) (Baku, 1961), 72–3 and 119–21.

[96] Hüseynli, *Azərbaycan Ruhaniliyi*, 72–7.

[97] Tadeusz Swietochowski, *Russian Azerbaijan: The Shaping of National Identity in a Muslim Community* (Cambridge, 1985), 9.

[98] 'Raport general-maiora Shvartsa Nachal'niku Glavnogo shtaba voisk na Kavkaze' ('Report of Major General Schwartz to the Chief of Staff of the Army in the Caucasus'), 2 July 1841; and 'Raport Telavskogo uezdnogo nachal'nika Gruzino-imeretinskomu grazhdanskomu gubernatoru' ('Report of the Chief of Telavi County to the Civilian Governor of Georgia-Imereti'), 13 May 1842, in Tsagareishvili (ed.), *Shamil'*, 200–1 and 214.

rumors, Shamil claimed to be the son of the Georgian heir Aleksandr as a gambit to attract Georgian support.[99] The Georgians' long experience with raids by Dagestanis, however, inclined them skeptically towards Shamil, and the imam's entreaties came to naught. Indeed, in 1854 when Shamil rode into Georgia and kidnapped two Georgian princesses in a bold (and ultimately successful) move to obtain the release of his son from the Russians, he lost much public favor in Europe and whatever sympathy he had possessed in Georgia.[100]

Shamil's efforts to expand his imamate to the west—as both Mansur and Ghazi Muhammad had tried to do—represented his best chance to widen his support-base. The prospects would seem to have been favorable, since the Sunni Circassian peoples were waging their own struggle against the Russians. In the 1840s, as Shamil's power was waxing, several Kabardians reached out and requested aid from the imam. Yet when Shamil entered Kabarda in 1846, the chiefs told him he was 'too late'. Over-extended, he had to withdraw without having secured any strategic benefit.[101] Two years later, the Kabardians requested that Shamil send a *naib* to them. Shamil's message on the need for compliance with the shari'a, however, failed to inspire the Kabardians, whose familiarity with Islamic doctrine was slight, and they remained outside the imamate. Similarly, the Ingush, who were geographically closer to the imamate's center and ethno-linguistically quite close to the Chechens, also never joined the imamate. The Ingush in the nineteenth century were still in the process of converting to Islam and were not receptive toShamil's message of religious struggle.

One way that Shamil sought to boost morale among his outnumbered followers was to play up the possibility of Ottoman intervention. Shamil wrote to the sultan on numerous occasions to request aid. In his correspondence, Shamil expressed his belief that the Ottoman sultan was legitimately the caliph, the successor to the Prophet, and head of the Sunni world, and thus a figure obliged to come to the aid of his co-religionists in the Caucasus. In 1843, Shamil spread a rumor that the Ottoman sultan would be arriving for a visit, and even instructed his guard that they should have dress uniform ready for the occasion.[102] The reality, however, was that the Ottomans had enough problems holding on to their own lands and were in no position to bail out Shamil.[103]

---

[99] 'Otryvok zapiski polkovnika Viktorova o politicheskom sostoianii Zakavkaz'ia' ('A Passage From the Notes of Colonel Viktorov on the Political State of Transcaucasia'), 1844, in Tsagareishvili, *Shamil'*, 236.

[100] The incident attracted media attention in Western Europe as well as Russia, and was the subject of a book by E. A. Verderevskii entitled *Captivity of Two Russian Princesses: Including a Seven Months' Residence in Shamil's Seraglio*, trans. Henry Sutherland Edwards (London, 1857).

[101] Gammer, *Muslim Resistance*, 162–71.

[102] 'Raport komanduiushchego voiskami v Severnom i Nagornom Dagestane—general-maiora Kliuki fon Klugenau—komandiru korpusa generalu Neigartu' ('Report of the Commander of Forces in Northern and Highland Dagestan Klüge von Klugenau to the Corps Commander General Neigart'), 22 March 1843, in Tsagareishvili, *Shamil'*, 220.

[103] This is readily apparent in Ottoman correspondence on Shamil and his movement, see, for example, Ismet Binark, (ed.), *Osmanlı Devleti ile Kafkasya, Türkistan ve Kırım hanlıkları arasındaki münâsebetlere dâir arşiv belgeleri (1687–1908 yılları arası)* (*Archival Documents on Relations Between the Ottoman State and the Caucasian, Turkistani, and Crimean Khanates (1687–1908)*) (Ankara, 1992).

By the 1850s, two decades of relentless war had ground down the mountain peoples. At this time a young, unschooled Chechen shepherd named Kunta Hajji (*d.*1862), emerged to pose the most formidable internal challenge yet to the legitimacy of Shamil and the imamate. Initiated into the Qadiriyya Sufi brotherhood while on the pilgrimage to Mecca, he returned home to preach an interpretation of Islam sharply at odds with Shamil's doctrines. Where Shamil asserted that it was the duty of every Muslim to wage jihad against the unbelievers, Kunta Hajji counseled that war and politics distracted the believer from God and that participating in Shamil's jihad was in fact a sin. Non-violent defiance, he taught, was the proper response to the Russians. The Chechen similarly contested Shamil's program of Islamization. For example, whereas Shamil sought to enforce a strict segregation of the sexes, Kunta Hajji taught that when passing an unfamiliar woman it was better to talk to her than to ignore and thereby sadden her.[104] This message of personal piety and political quietism appealed to many weary highlanders, and so Shamil exiled the Chechen from the Caucasus lest his teaching further sap the mountain peoples' will to fight.[105]

The Crimean War (1853–56) provided Shamil a last hope for foreign intervention. With the British and French taking the side of the Ottomans and British agents reconnoitering the region, Shamil and his *naib* among the Kabardians made plans to exploit the opportunity to join forces with an Ottoman force invading from the West. Ultimately, however, these plans came to naught. No Western force ever arrived and the war ended. The recognition that no substantial help would be forthcoming from the Ottomans dealt a severe blow to the morale of the mountain peoples. In desperation, Shamil appealed directly to the French and British, but to no avail.[106] Although the British sent some aid to the Circassians, Shamil received no support from London. For Russia, one positive consequence of a Crimean War that otherwise had been a fiasco was the deployment of a vast army in the vicinity of the Caucasus. Now with roughly a quarter of a million soldiers under him, the commander of Russian forces in the Caucasus, General Aleksandr Bariatinskii, pressed in on Shamil and his dwindling supporters. In 1859, Bariatinskii had Shamil surrounded in the high mountain village of Akhulgo. With just 400 hard-core supporters left, Shamil surrendered (Fig. 16). Held in exile outside Moscow in Kaluga and later Kiev, he was permitted to make the hajj to Mecca in 1869, on which trip he met another famed Muslim resistance leader, Algeria's 'Abd al-Qadir. While in Medina, Shamil died and was buried in that holy city in 1871.

---

[104] Anna Zelkina, 'Some Aspects of the Teaching of Kunta Hajji: On the Basis of a Manuscript by 'Abd al-Salam, written in 1852 AD', *Journal of the History of Sufism*, 1/2 (2000), 483–507, 492–4 and 502.

[105] V. Kh. Akaev, *Sheikh Kunta Khadzhi* (*Shaykh Kunta Hajji*) (Groznyi, 1994).

[106] Gammer, *Muslim Resistance*, 285.

**Fig. 16** *Imam Shamil surrendered to Count Baryatinsky on 25 August 1859* by Alexei Danilovich Kivshenko (1880) (Public Domain).

## CONCLUSION

Shamil's surrender did not end the fighting. Adyghe fighters in the northwest Caucasus held out for another five years until finally capitulating in 1864. To ensure that the Adyghe could never again pose a significant threat along Russia's vulnerable Black Sea coast, tsarist authorities expelled them en masse to the Ottoman empire.[107] The surrender of Shamil made possible the return of Kunta Hajji, and in Chechnya the Qadiriyya quickly displaced the Naqshbandiyya. Despite Kunta Hajji's quietist theology, tsarist officials nurtured deep suspicions about him and arrested him in 1862. Five years later he died in captivity.

In 1878, seven years after Shamil's death, the North Caucasus was again the scene of a major rebellion against Russian rule. This time it was the Qadiris of Chechnya who were in the forefront of the rebellion. Religion was again a key factor, but the transformation of the Qadiriyya from a quietist order to an organ of rebellion highlights the indeterminacy of theological perspectives alone.

---

[107] S. D. Shenfield, 'The Circassians: A Forgotten Genocide?' in M. Levene and P. Roberts (eds), *The Massacre in History* (New York, 1999), 149–62; see also Dana Sherry, 'Social Alchemy on the Black Sea Coast, 1860–65', *Kritika*, 10/1 (2009), 7–30.

The imamate left a profound stamp on mountain society. The decades-long struggle reinforced the Muslim identity of the Chechens and Dagestanis and provided an example of the potential of highland unity. Shamil would become and remains even today a popular hero and symbol of the North Caucasus and its peoples. Indeed, even the Soviet regime would have to pay homage to the imam who fought off Russian rule in the name of Islam, as uncomfortable as that could be.[108]

Yet, the legacy of the imamate should not be exaggerated. In the wake of the first Russian Revolution of March 1917, natives across the North Caucasus invoked the memory of Shamil for inspiration when they formed the Union of Allied Highlanders and then a state of their own. However, they deliberately overlooked Shamil's insistence on a severe interpretation of Islamic law and his opposition to Russia. After Bolshevik pressure fractured that attempt to unite the mountain peoples, a small coalition of Chechens and Dagestani highlanders made a bid to re-establish the imamate, but they were isolated and soon crushed.[109] In the post-Soviet Caucasus, marked by major war in Chechnya and chronic Islamist insurgencies in Dagestan and elsewhere, the imamate has proven inassimilable to all. Today's Islamists find its association with the Naqshbandiyya objectionable, ethno-nationalists dismiss its example of pan-highlander unity, and advocates of 'traditional' Islam are uncomfortable with its militantly pro-shari'a and anti-Russian essence. Nonetheless, the imamate's remarkable success in mobilizing a collection of small and impoverished mountain peoples to hold off one of history's greatest empires for three decades will long serve as a prime illustration of the power of religion to mobilize communities.

[108] Moshe Gammer, 'Shamil in Soviet Historiography', *Middle Eastern Studies*, 28/4 (1992), 729–77.

[109] Michael A. Reynolds, 'Native Sons: Post-Imperial Politics, Islam, and Identity in the North Caucasus, 1917–1918', *Jahrbücher für Geschichte Osteuropas*, 56 (2008), 221–47; see also Altay Göyüshov, *1917–1920-chi illärdä Shimali Gafgaz daghlïlarïnïn azadlïg ughrunda mubarizäsi* (*The North Caucasian Highlanders' Struggle for Freedom, 1917–1920*) (Baku, 2000).

# 10

# Islamic Resistance in the Dutch Colonial Empire

*Gerrit Knaap*

## INTRODUCTION

The relationship between the Dutch empire and the Muslim-majority population in Indonesia was often troublesome.[1] The colonial presence of the Netherlands in Southeast Asia lasted for more than three centuries. Territorial rule commenced in 1605, with the seizure of Amboina from the Portuguese by the Dutch East India Company, and ended in 1962, with the temporary transfer of power in West New Guinea from the Kingdom of the Netherlands to the United Nations, pending the definitive takeover of the area by the Republic of Indonesia. Over this long period, Dutch colonialism was challenged by many upheavals and the intervention of other empires, including the English Interregnum from 1811 to 1816, the Japanese occupation in the Second World War, and, finally, the Indonesian Revolution from 1945 to 1949, which ended Dutch rule in most of the archipelago.

Throughout the centuries, Islam played an important role in the resistance against Dutch colonial intrusion and hegemony. Essentially, this resistance presented itself in three forms: Islamic rulers and states; Islamic groups inside the colonial state and its indigenous satellite states; and, finally, Islamic organizations within the broader movement of Indonesian nationalism. Accordingly, actual conflict occurred in the form of: open wars with Islamic rulers; protracted guerrilla resistance, rebellions, disturbances, and non-violent mass movements; and, finally, party politics. The difference of religious identity between the colonial masters and the subject populations facilitated the inclusion of Islamic arguments into the motives and rhetoric of resistance. Fighting the colonial overlords and their indigenous allies was regularly interpreted as a struggle against the 'non-believer'.

This chapter traces the development of Islamic resistance against Dutch colonial rule in Indonesia, considering both transformations within Indonesian Islam, from traditional heterodox to modern orthodox forms, and attempts by

[1] This chapter has been inspired by the project 'Religious Policy of the Netherlands Indies, in particular with regard to Islam, *c.*1800–*c.*1940', which is underway in the author's institute. The author wishes to express his gratitude to Rosemary Robson for correcting his English.

the Dutch administration to lessen the potential conflict between 'believers' and 'non-believers' during this period. Before turning to the history of Islamic resistance to colonial rule, a brief section on the historical development of Indonesian Islam will set the scene.

## INDONESIAN ISLAM

Scholars have conventionally dated the beginnings of Indonesian Islam to the end of the thirteenth century; however, this narrative faces three major problems. First, Muslim groups frequented the region much earlier. By stating that Islam arrived in the last decades of the thirteenth century, the coming of Islam is equated solely with its adoption by particular indigenous rulers. Secondly, the concept of 'Indonesia' did not exist at the time. Southeast Asia was a geographical space, which was home to many ethnicities and early state formations—the latter are sometimes still hardly known to us because of the dearth of surviving source material. The term 'Indonesia' itself dates from the middle of the nineteenth century and only acquired political meaning at the beginning of the twentieth. Thirdly, the meaning of 'Islam' in the late thirteenth century was quite diverse and ambiguous. Throughout history, Southeast Asia, and even the Middle East itself, has experienced many variations of Islam. Southeast Asia and the area now known as Indonesia have been subject to different 'traditions' of Islam. For the historian, it is often difficult to decide with which tradition he or she is dealing, again because of insufficient information in the sources.

One of the best-known attempts to describe the multifaceted nature of Islam in Indonesia was by anthropologist Clifford Geertz in his work, *The Religion of Java*. However, as suggested by the title of this book, Geertz dealt only with Java, particularly Central and East Java, and focused only on the late nineteenth and twentieth centuries. He discerned three forms of Javanese Islam: the orthodox scriptural branch, which he labeled *santri* or *putihan*; the heterodox, ritualistic, and syncretistic branch, designated *abangan*; and, a third, less explicit form, observed by the local power-holders, which he called *priyayi*, after the administrative, sometimes hereditary 'gentry' class, who often implicitly also confessed to heterodoxy. The frame of reference for the *santri/putihan* variety was the *ummat Islam*, the cosmopolitan community of believers. For the *abangan*, it was the village community consisting of several families or clans, while the *priyayi* positioned themselves somewhere between the local and the universal, especially those families who considered themselves by nature to be superior to the rest of society.[2]

To some extent, the paradigm set out in Geertz's *Religion of Java* is also applicable to the other islands and regions of Indonesia, particularly in terms of the opposition between orthodox-scriptural and heterodox-syncretistic; the latter, sometimes including the local elites, was found in many other places. In Sumatra,

---

[2] Clifford Geertz, *The Religion of Java* (Glencoe, IL, 1960), 125–30, 228–9, and 231–5.

people often spoke about *kaum kuno* and *kaum muda*, meaning the 'old ones' and the 'young ones' for the heterodox and the orthodox. Consequently, Geertz's model is applicable insofar as it relates to a dichotomy, namely *putihan* and *abangan*, to speak in Javanese terms. The tripartite division, with a special place for an elitist *priyayi* version of Islam, seems more problematic. It goes without saying that a thick description of local conditions would bring to light additional varieties, which would not necessarily conform to the types described in Java. Furthermore, Geertz's suggestion that the dichotomy orthodox–syncretistic only existed from the nineteenth century and, in some areas, from the very beginning of that century, is questionable. Recent studies by Azyumardi Azra and Leonard Andaya have shown that the drive towards a more puritanical form of Islam was already being fueled by Malay-Indonesian 'ulama studying in the Middle East in about the middle of the seventeenth century. This 'ulama propagated 'neo-Sufism', a combination of Sufi mysticism and obedience to the shari'a, as the normative way of life for a Muslim belonging to a mystical brotherhood, the *tariqa*, thereby opposing the heterodox 'old' Sufism, which had allowed the persistence of a whole body of pre-Islamic beliefs.[3]

In the case of Java, Merle Ricklefs, in his thorough works on its political and cultural history, generally agrees with Geertz's *putihan–abangan* model, stating that it dated from the middle of the nineteenth century and that it 'hardened and became politicized' at the beginning of the twentieth in the context of anti-colonial resistance movements. Before the advent of the *putihan–abangan* dichotomy, Java had witnessed a process of adjustment within Islam and Javanese culture, resulting, as Ricklefs argues, in a 'mystic synthesis'. Sufism was a key element in this process. It was not before the beginning of the sixteenth century that Java, at least Central and East Java, could properly be regarded as an Islamic country and it took another century before rulers in Java began to use the title of 'sultan'. By the end of the eighteenth century, the mystic synthesis among the elite had resulted in an identity which was 'self-consciously Islamic', but 'yet recognized indigenous spiritual forces', such as local deities and spirits. Consequently, 'Javanese identity was a subset of Islamic identity'. In the course of the nineteenth century, the mystic synthesis was attacked by the devout *santri*, inspired by the increasing presence of Arab *sayyid*s in Java and better contacts through the hajj pilgrimage with the Middle East. Within a few decades, this resulted in the split between *putihan* and *abangan*, the former the 'pious and purifying' Muslims and the latter the 'impure' or 'nominal' Muslims. The *priyayi* class, caught in the dilemma of loyalty to 'modern' Dutch culture and colonial rule and growing antipathy towards the Dutch in *putihan* circles, became increasingly *abangan*.[4]

---

[3] Azyumardi Azra, *The Origins of Islamic Reformism in Southeast Asia: Networks of Malay-Indonesian and Middle Eastern Ulama in the Seventeenth and Eighteenth Centuries* (Canberra, 2004), 53, 59, 62, 66, 70, 84–5, 87–8, and 105; and Leonard Y. Andaya, *Leaves of the Same Tree: Trade and Ethnicity in the Straits of Melaka* (Honolulu, 2008), 125–31 and 144–5.

[4] M. C. Ricklefs, *Mystic Synthesis in Java: A History of Islamization from the Fourteenth to the Early Nineteenth Centuries* (Norwalk, CT, 2006), 6–8, 17–18, 34, 50–1, 186–7, and 221; and M. C. Ricklefs, *Polarising Javanese Society: Islamic and Other Visions c. 1830–1930* (Leiden, 2007), 52–8, 89–92, 95–103, 126–9, and 171–3.

Besides the tendency of Indonesian Islam to conform increasingly to a 'pure' Middle Eastern Islam, its political role was changing as well. The political significance of Islam was greatly enhanced when rulers declared themselves to be Muslims, usually taking the title of sultan. Along the coasts of Sumatra this happened in the fourteenth and fifteenth centuries, and in Java and the rest of the archipelago this was adopted mostly from the late fifteenth century to the early seventeenth century. The rulers saw it as their role to fashion themselves as leaders of Islam and to encourage Islamic practices. Amongst their functions were the protection of believers and Islamic doctrine, as well as the Islamization of the institutions of the state. Muslims would follow rulers who supported their religion; in this respect, colonial rule exercised by non-Muslims, 'infidels', could not be seen as anything other than a caesura.

## ISLAM AND THE DUTCH EAST INDIA COMPANY, *C.*1600–1800

The traders and sailors of the Dutch East India Company ('Verenigde Oost-Indische Compagnie', hereafter abbreviated to VOC), were not the first Europeans active in the archipelago. They were preceded by the Portuguese and, to a lesser extent, the Spanish. The Portuguese had conquered the mighty sultanate of Melaka in 1511 and soon became involved in the Spice Islands, particularly in the islands of Maluku (the area around Halmahera) and Amboina in the south. They were also present in the eastern part of Nusa Tenggara, specifically in Solor from 1561. In 1580, the Crown of Portugal was united with that of Spain. The Iberians were not in Southeast Asia just to conquer the riches of the East, but were also driven by a missionary zeal to propagate Roman Catholicism. This was quite obvious in the eastern part of the archipelago, where they facilitated Jesuits and other missionaries in their conversion of indigenous populations; one of the sultans of Ternate even became Catholic, albeit very briefly. Yet, the interventions in Ternate were short-lived and, in due course, armed conflict raged throughout the region. The conflicts fought by the sultans of Ternate, their Islamic subjects, and allies in opposition to the Europeans gradually turned into full-scale religious wars similar to those in sixteenth- and seventeenth-century Europe. Thus, from the very outset, the antagonism between Christianity and Islam was an inherent part of the encounter between Europeans and Southeast Asians, no matter how superficially the different religions had taken root among the followers of either party.[5]

When the first Dutch fleet arrived in the waters of Banten in West Java in 1596, the VOC had not yet been established. For the first seven years, Dutch navigation to the Indian Ocean basin was the concern of private companies. In 1602, in order

---

[5] Leonard Y. Andaya, *The World of Maluku: Eastern Indonesia in the Early Modern Period* (Honolulu, 1993), 114–43; Arend de Roever, *De jacht op sandelhout: De VOC en de tweedeling van Timor in de zeventiende eeuw* (Zutphen, 2002), 101–3; and Gerrit Knaap, *Kruidnagelen en Christenen: De Verenigde Oost-Indische Compagnie en de bevolking van Ambon 1656–1696* (Leiden, 2004), 15–21.

to strengthen the whole endeavor so that it could withstand the economic and political risks challenging its structural survival, the government of the Republic of the United Netherlands finally established a chartered company, the VOC. All companies that had previously been active in the region were expected to merge into the new organization, which was given the monopoly on all Dutch trade between the Cape of Good Hope and the Straits of Magellan. In the absence of representatives of the Republic in the East, the VOC was granted judicial, political, diplomatic, and military powers, as if it was acting on behalf of the Republic. However, the Republic of the United Netherlands itself was a young state, the product of a rebellion under the banner of Calvinist Protestantism against the Spanish Habsburg King Philip II (1556–98). Since the king of Spain had still not recognized Dutch independence by 1600, the two countries were locked in bitter warfare. Furthermore, as the Spanish Habsburgs had also been sovereigns of Portugal since 1580, any Dutch ship entering Asian waters was seen as an enemy vessel and ran the risk of being attacked by Portuguese forces. Threatened by Iberian enmity, all Dutch ships sailing to the East were heavily armed. In principle, VOC authorities hoped that a shared hostility towards the Catholic Portuguese would automatically ally them with indigenous Islamic rulers. This assumption had already proved fairly limited in 1596, when the ships of the first Dutch fleet were embroiled in violent incidents with indigenous leaders and groups in Banten and later in the roadstead of Sidayu in East Java and Arosbaya in Madura.[6]

The VOC scored its first success in its anti-Iberian campaign when it occupied the Portuguese fort and territory in the Amboina Islands in 1605. To the north, in Maluku, the VOC found an ally in the defeated sultan of Ternate. Although the VOC had no religious or missionary goals, it was soon drawn into taking a religious position. This first happened in Amboina in 1607, where the Christian indigenous leadership requested religious instruction after Catholic missionaries had been banned from the islands. The VOC decided that their instruction should be Calvinist Protestant. Moreover, the VOC's treaties with the sultan of Ternate and other Islamic rulers in the eastern part of the archipelago required stipulations to be made about each other's jurisdiction, particularly when individuals sought to change boundaries. The solution was that a Muslim was not supposed to become a Christian and vice versa. Both sides intended to keep this promise. In a sense, this meant an application of the principle of *cuius regio, eius religio* (literally, 'whose kingdom, his religion'), the concept used to end the European wars of religion. This implied that, in those areas where it exercised full sovereignty, the VOC was entitled to decide to which religion its subjects would adhere. Unsurprisingly, in such areas, Calvinist Protestantism was declared the official religion. This was legitimized in the second charter of the VOC in 1622, in which the Company was made responsible for the religious well-being of its subjects, clearing the way for the appointment of Protestant clerics among its salaried servants. In Amboina, this

---

[6] H. Terpstra, 'De Nederlandsche Voorcompagnieën', in F. W. Stapel (ed.), *Geschiedenis van Nederlandsch-Indië*, 5 vols (Amsterdam, 1938), ii, 321–52; and Femme S. Gaastra, *De geschiedenis van de VOC* (Zutphen, 2002), 20–4.

settlement worked for the first two decades but, from 1625 until about 1658, the Dutch waged the so-called Amboinese Wars to seal their monopoly on the export of cloves. These wars were basically fought by the VOC and its Christian subjects against Muslim Amboinese forces and their allies from elsewhere. On both sides religion functioned as a vehicle to cement a sense of solidarity, which helped to mobilize forces. Eventually, all Amboina, its Muslims included, fell under VOC sovereignty by right of conquest. Nevertheless, the principle of *cuius regio, eius religio* was not fully employed, as the attempt to convert Muslim subjects was more honored in the breach than the observance. The VOC limited its missionary zeal to animistic and polytheistic 'heathens' rather than Muslims, since its leaders were convinced that Muslims adhered firmly to their creed. Trying to convert them was believed difficult and would have posed a constant threat to political stability, the so-called *Pax Neerlandica*.[7]

This pragmatic policy was upheld, in spite of the Dutch distrust of Muslims, during the seventeenth century. The tension between pragmatism and distrust was very obvious during conflicts in the Banda Islands and with Banten and Mataram in Java, leading to dramatic consequences in the first and accommodation in the second. The conflict with the Bandanese eventually led to the annihilation of Bandanese society in 1621. This conflict was provoked by the killing of a Dutch admiral during negotiations. Moreover, the Bandanese did not observe the treaties, not only because these were to their disadvantage, but also because they adhered to the principle that a Muslim was not obliged to honor an agreement with a kafir. The distrust in Java originated from the initial refusal of the authorities in Banten and Mataram to grant the Dutch special trade privileges and the subsequent bad treatment of the Company trading personnel. In the end, this resulted in scheduled attacks and threatening sieges on VOC headquarters at Batavia towards the end of the 1620s. In these cases, compromise, rather than victory, was the best result the VOC could hope to achieve. Therefore, despite its mistrust of Muslims and its confidence in the truth of the Christian faith, particularly Protestantism, the VOC never openly presented itself as a Christian force. This was a matter of *realpolitik*: the religious feelings of the opposite party should not be aroused, because to do so might threaten the *Pax Neerlandica*, the Dutch guarantee of favorable terms of trade with the indigenous rulers of the islands of Southeast Asia in order to tap the riches of the region. The principle of not openly antagonizing Muslims remained immutable right to the end of Dutch colonial rule.[8]

As the seventeenth century progressed, the military and political power of the VOC steadily increased and the Dutch became an important power in the Malay-Indonesian archipelago. To safeguard its economic and political interests,

[7] Knaap, *Kruidnagelen en Christenen*, 23, 25–30, 99–101, 105–8, and 113–15.

[8] H. T. Colenbrander, *Jan Pietersz. Coen: Levensbeschrijving* ('s-Gravenhage, 1934), 403–4, 415–18, and 430–1; L. Kiers, *Coen op Banda: De conqueste getoetst aan het recht van den tijd* (Utrecht, 1943), 238–40; and H. J. de Graaf, *De regering van Sultan Agung, vorst van Mataram, 1613–1645, en die van zijn voorganger Panembahan Seda-ing-Krapjak 1601–1613* ('s-Gravenhage, 1958), 56, 58–63, 146–51, 178–91, and 233–41.

the VOC sometimes took the decision to become involved in struggles for power among local princes and pretenders, most notably in South Celebes, Java, and in the eighteenth century, around the Melaka Straits. One of the parties in these struggles usually became an ally of the VOC. Unsurprisingly, such an ally, whether devoutly Muslim or not, did not employ Islam in the conflict. Those who opposed the VOC would use religious slogans, though not consistently. During the wars of 1660s, for instance, the rulers of Makassar, in conflict with the VOC and its ally Arung Palakka of Bone, did not appeal to Islamic solidarity, despite the fact that the same Makassar had forced the other rulers of South Celebes to become Muslim less than 75 years earlier. When Mataram in Java endured Dutch intervention in its realm from 1677, the pretenders for the throne and enemies of the VOC, Trunajaya and Puger, were strongly opposed to a kingship reliant on support of Christians. Yet, almost thirty years later, that same Puger, alias Pakubuwana I, solicited VOC support to conquer the crown of Mataram for himself. Such ambivalence shown by the ruling dynasty towards the powerful kafir became a structural fact in the history of Mataram, even after its division into three successor states between 1755 and 1757. Whatever their objections to the Dutch, in the end they usually decided not to put the alliance to the test. However, those contesting the authority of a VOC-supported monarch usually resorted to Islamic arguments, sometimes couched in the rhetoric of jihad—proclaiming holy war against the kafir—to bolster their claims. The history of the sultanate of Banten reveals a similar experience, most obviously in the changing alliances of the crown prince Abdul Kahar who, with the support of the VOC, ascended to the throne as Sultan Haji in 1682. In the meantime, there were religiously charged appeals across the archipelago to forge coalitions against the intervention of the kafir. Such appeals to drive out the Dutch infidels, some issued by scholars in far-away Mecca, such as 'Abd al-Samad al-Palimbani, led to religious and diplomatic exchanges, but almost never to effective military cooperation.[9]

In order to maintain its control, the VOC refrained from initiatives to propagate Christianity among Muslims in areas under its rule. As time passed, Amboina was not the only Muslim region of the VOC. Muslim migrants, some of them former slaves, increasingly settled around Batavia. More significant, however, was the gradual expansion along the coast of Central and East Java from the end of the 1670s. By 1746, the VOC was virtually in control of all coastal districts. The population in this area, called the Province of Java's Northeast Coast, was Muslim.

---

[9] J. Kathirithamby-Wells, 'Ahmad Shah Ibn Iskandar and the Late 17th Century "Holy War" in Indonesia', *Journal of the Malaysian Branch of the Royal Asiatic Society*, 43/1 (1970), 48–63, 50–1, 53–7, and 62–3; Leonard Y. Andaya, *The Heritage of Arung Palakka: A History of South Sulawesi (Celebes) in the Seventeenth Century* (The Hague, 1981), 32–5, 211–13, and 215–16; Barbara Watson Andaya, *To Live as Brothers: Southeast Sumatra in the Seventeenth and Eighteenth Centuries* (Honolulu, 1993), 130–3; Johan Talens, *Een feodale samenleving in koloniaal vaarwater: Staatsvorming, koloniale expansie en economische onderontwikkeling in Banten, West-Java (1600–1750)* (Hilversum, 1999), 154–7; Willem Remmelink, 'De worsteling om Java', in Gerrit Knaap and Ger Teitler (eds), *De Verenigde Oost-Indische Compagnie tussen oorlog en diplomatie* (Leiden, 2002), 348–50; Azra, *The Origins of Islamic Reformism*, 117 and 140–2; and Ricklefs, *Mystic Synthesis in Java*, 59, 62–3, 65–7, 74–7, 87–90, 93, 132–3, and 172–6.

The Javanese administrators of the districts—*bupati* in Javanese and *regent* in Dutch—now governed their subjects in the name of the governor general, rather than the king of Mataram. Yet, neither in Batavia nor on Java's Northeast Coast did the VOC attempt to convert Muslims to Christianity. The VOC respected the Islamic legal system, with the exception of crimes requiring the death penalty, and even facilitated its continued existence, for instance, by issuing a compendium of the most important laws for Muslims in 1754.[10]

## ISLAMIC RESISTANCE AND THE COLONIAL GOVERNMENT IN THE NINETEENTH CENTURY

At the turn of the year 1799–1800, the debt-ridden VOC was liquidated and nationalized by the Dutch Republic. During this era of global wars of the French Revolution and of Napoleon, when the Dutch state was a satellite of France, contacts between the Netherlands and its colonies were often blockaded by the British. In 1810, the Netherlands were annexed by France, and Java, the last Dutch territory in the East, fell to Britain in 1811. After Napoleon's defeat, the Netherlands regained independence as a kingdom and its authority in the Malay-Indonesian archipelago was restored in 1816. It would last until 1942. With respect to Dutch policies towards religion, there were a few changes compared with the situation during the VOC era. As the French revolutionaries preached freedom of religion, the Roman Catholic Church was officially recognized alongside the Protestant Reformed Church in the first decade of the nineteenth century. More importantly, colonial officials continued the pragmatic approach with regard to Muslim subjects in territories directly ruled by the Dutch. Matters concerning the Islamic religion in Java were supposed to be the concern of the Javanese aristocratic bureaucrats, the *bupati*, administrating their areas in the name of the Dutch. As long as *Pax Neerlandica* was not endangered, the Dutch did not intervene. According to official regulations, colonial policy was to leave unchanged the religious status quo. Whenever this principle was imperiled, the colonial government took extra measures, for instance with Protestant and Roman Catholic missionaries, who usually operated outside the aegis of the official church hierarchy. In order not to upset the feelings of Islamic populations, the missionaries' entry to a region was subject to a rigorous policy of obtaining government permission.[11]

Nevertheless, at the beginning of the nineteenth century, gradual changes in patterns of resistance to colonial intrusion emerged. As the territory under Dutch rule expanded into indigenous Islamic states, the power of their rulers

---

[10] Karel Steenbrink, *Dutch Colonialism and Indonesian Islam: Contacts and Conflicts 1596–1950* (Amsterdam, 2006), 71–2; and Kwee Hui Kian, *The Political Economy of Java's Northeast Coast c. 1740–1800: Elite Synergy* (Leiden, 2006), 28–9, 34–5, 40–1, and 141.

[11] Ph. Kleintjes, *Staatsinstellingen van Nederlandsch-Indië*, 2 vols (Amsterdam, 1933), ii, 500–3, 506–9, 512, and 516–18.

and courtiers declined. Most sultans in the archipelago had become vassals of the Dutch. Anti-colonial resistance now emerged in Islamic movements from within society and was no longer led by the courts. Many of these movements were fueled by Islamic revivalist groups, which, over the course of the nineteenth century, reached an ever-increasing audience. This was very obvious in Minangkabau on Sumatra's western coast, where revivalism and the movement for the strict implementation of the shari'a had been growing since 1784. Azyumardi Azra has argued that at this time Islamic revivalism was still largely 'neo-Sufi'. However, in the first decade of the nineteenth century, revivalism in Minangkabau, known as the Padri movement, took a violent jihadi turn under the influence of Wahhabi concepts from the Middle East, which advocated a return to the way of life of the Prophet. These concepts were first introduced by three pilgrims returning from Mecca after 1803. Sufism was labeled a false doctrine. Gradually Minangkabau was riven by civil war between those advocating strict reform according to the shari'a and those, mostly the old elite, who wanted to retain the *adat*, the traditional customary law and a Minangkabau lifestyle centering on a matrilineal order. By 1815, the old royal line of Minangkabau had suffered many defeats at the hands of the Padri, and radical Islamic reformers even begun to attack moderates. When, in 1821, the remaining members of the royal line became subjects of the Dutch, they were able to involve Dutch troops in their struggle against the Padri. The Padri Wars lasted until 1837 with the fall of Bonjol, the last Padri stronghold. After the defeat of the Padri, it took another eighty years before the Muslims of Minangkabau rose again to confront Dutch colonial rule.[12]

In Java, resistance by independent heads of state ended at the beginning of the nineteenth century. The colonial overlords put an end to the sultanate of Banten in the years between 1810 and 1813. The successor states to the sultanate of Mataram, namely Surakarta, Yogyakarta, and the principalities of Mangkunagara and Pakualam, lasted until the end of colonial rule. The last significant resistance by a ruling monarch in Java was in 1812 in Yogyakarta and in 1815 in Surakarta. In both cases, this resistance was directed against the British empire, which had temporarily occupied the island of Java. Not long afterwards the last full-scale war was fought in Java, specifically Central Java. Waged between 1825 and 1830, it was called the Java War by the Dutch and the Dipanagara War by the Indonesians. Opponent of the Dutch and member of the royal dynasty of Yogyakarta, Prince Dipanagara was deeply grieved by the decay of the once-powerful state of Mataram and the subsequent intrusion of the kafir Dutch. From his early youth, Dipanagara had been in touch with Muslim scholars, inclining towards a Sufi way of Islam. He and his circle employed references to Islamic doctrine to spur the Javanese to wage war. On the other hand, Dipanagara also appealed to typically pre-Islamic concepts to mobilize his followers, namely the coming of the *ratu adil*, the 'just

---

[12] Christine Dobbin, *Islamic Revivalism in a Changing Peasant Economy: Central Sumatra 1784–1847* (London, 1983), 125–37, 143–9, 193, and 205; Azra, *Origins of Islamic Reformism*, 145–7; and Jeffrey Hadler, *Muslims and Matriarchs: Cultural Resilience in Indonesia through Jihad and Colonialism* (Ithaca, NY, 2008), 19–30.

**Fig. 17** *The Submission of Prince Diponegoro to General De Kock* by Nicolaas Pieneman (1835), depicting the arrest of Dipanagara by the Dutch on 28 March 1830, which marked the end of the Java War (Public Domain).

king' in Javanese prophecies, who was expected to expel enemies and to restore a righteous moral order. Dipanagara saw himself as a 'priest-king' and an Islamic ruler. In battle, Islamic scholars chanted phrases from the Qur'an to enhance the morale of Dipanagara's troops. Nevertheless, after five years of fierce fighting with the Dutch and the defection of a large number of his followers, including Muslims, Dipanagara's guerrillas were defeated and he was exiled (Fig. 17).[13]

During the nineteenth and early twentieth centuries, the colonial state increasingly intervened in indigenous society, including in Islamic issues. The Dutch authorities introduced specific policies on the administration of Islamic law, the pilgrimage to Mecca, and religious education. The Javanese administrative elite, the *bupati* and other, lesser members of the *priyayi* class, usually showed themselves accommodating towards the colonial authorities. After the Dipanagara War, Java saw only irregular and small-scale resistance to colonial intrusion. The colonial authorities called these outbreaks of violence 'disturbances'; when they

[13] Ota Atsushi, *Changes of Regime and Social Dynamics in West Java: Society, State and the Outer World of Banten 1750–1830* (Leiden, 2006), 143–6; Ricklefs, *Mystic Synthesis in Java,* 208–11; and Peter Carey, *The Power of Prophecy: Prince Dipanagara and the End of an Old Order in Java 1785–1855* (Leiden, 2008), 88–90, 102–4, 110–14, 331–42, 415–28, 483–5, 584–9, 597–602, and 626–39.

became more dangerous, the outbreaks were termed 'affairs' or 'uprisings'. Sartono Kartodirdjo labeled these 'agrarian' or 'peasant unrest', often of an endemic character. Now the concept of the *ratu adil* was exploited by local and lesser political and religious leaders, including ascetics. A spiritually potent savior king, the *ratu adil*, would use extraordinary powers to expel the evil forces responsible for all that was wrong in the present world and to establish a prosperous, righteous future; in short 'a heaven on earth'. The concept, imbued with messianic and millenarian features, had existed for centuries in legend in Javanese culture, centering on the mythical figure of Erucakra. These prophecies were ascribed to the semi-mythical pre-Islamic Javanese King Jayabaya. Sometimes they were mingled with Islamic elements from Sufi strands. Then the *ratu adil* became a sort of Mahdi, the savior king of the Muslim tradition, or an incarnation of a *wali*, an apostle known to have been one of those who converted Java to Islam. Usually, *ratu adil* movements coincided with periods of hardship caused by famine, disease, or natural disaster, such as volcanic eruptions and earthquakes. The geographic space in which these short-lived uprisings occurred was usually small and limited to one settlement, a cluster of villages, or, at the most, a small town. The uprising in Pekalongan in 1871 took place in just one village; the Banten uprising of 1888 had the district town of Cilegon at its center, spreading from there to the surrounding countryside.[14]

During the nineteenth century, the Dutch conquered many regions outside Java. Sometimes the groups organizing the resistance to the intrusion called for Islamic solidarity and jihad. Although this could prolong the conflict, it could not prevent defeat by the well-equipped colonial troops. A major example is the Aceh War, arguably the best-known Dutch colonial war in the nineteenth century, which lasted from 1873 to 1914. For centuries, Aceh, the northernmost part of Sumatra, was regarded as the most Islamic state in Southeast Asia. As it was nearest to the heartlands of Islam, it considered itself 'the veranda of Mecca'. Throughout the war, the Acehnese side, particularly the 'ulama, promoted the conflict as a struggle against the infidel in defense of Islam, a true jihad. Many warriors on the Acehnese side hoped to earn paradise. They were inspired by religious slogans and armed themselves with amulets to become invulnerable in battle. After a year, in 1874 the Dutch army conquered the sultan's capital, Koetaradja, only to discover that the actual authority in the country rested not in the sultan's court but with the *hulubalang*, the regional lords, who continued the fight after the fall of the court. These local warlords were supported by the 'ulama, who formed the backbone of resistance. The war dragged on for decades, and the Acehnese also tried

[14] Sartono Kartodirdjo, *The Peasants' Revolt of Banten in 1888: Its Conditions, Course and Sequel: A Case Study of Social Movements in Indonesia* ('s-Gravenhage, 1966), 1–4, 165–4, and 209–36; Sartono Kartodirdjo, *Protest Movements in Rural Java: A Study of Agrarian Unrest in the Nineteenth and Early Twentieth Centuries* (Singapore, 1973), 1, 8–12, 64–7, 77–9, and 107–10; Michael Adas, *Prophets of Rebellion: Millenarian Protest Movements Against the European Colonial Order* (Chapel Hill, NC, 1979), 98–9; Karel A. Steenbrink, *Beberapa aspek tentang Islam di Indonesia abad ke-19* (Jakarta, 1984), 152–4, 174–6, 219–23, and 236–40; Carey, *The Power of Prophecy*, 414–15, 480–5, and 489–93; and Gerrit Knaap, 'Millenarianism in Mountainous Central Java: The Case of Pekalongan 1871', *Archipel*, 76 (2008), 37–64, 40–5 and 48–54.

to rally pan-Islamic support outside the archipelago. The Acehnese even sent an embassy to Constantinople to ask for support. Pressured by European powers, the Ottoman Porte rejected the request. In order to limit the military and financial cost of the war, the Dutch for some time retreated to Koetaradja (today's Banda Aceh) and tried to ease the pressure by pursuing a divide-and-rule policy to quell the *hulubalang*. Eventually, these tactics proved futile. In around 1900, by stepping up the military campaigns and relentlessly tracking down the remaining guerrillas, most of them followers of the 'ulama, the Dutch finally crushed the resistance.[15]

## ISLAMIC RESISTANCE AND THE COLONIAL GOVERNMENT IN THE TWENTIETH CENTURY

In the first decades of the twentieth century, Dutch colonial power in the East Indies reached its zenith. Practically all the indigenous states or proto-states in the archipelago had been subjugated and the small-scale outbursts of resistance from below usually ended in defeat. Now others continued the resistance—not princes, aristocrats, or local religious leaders with their peasant following. Muslim politicians, active in the broader framework of Indonesian nationalism, entered the scene. The first mass movement among the anti-colonial nationalists, the Sarekat Islam established in 1911, was distinctively Islamic. It had grown out of local organizations of Muslim entrepreneurs opposed to Chinese businessmen. Its aim was to 'create harmony and mutual assistance amongst all Muslims' in order to promote the 'welfare, prosperity, and greatness of the country'. The organization was aligned with the *putihan* or *kaum muda*, but few among its leadership had any role in the mosques or the scholarly life of Islam; most of its early leaders had some sort of Dutch educational background. In its first years, the objectives of Sarekat Islam were moderate, thereby gaining recognition from the Dutch colonial government, a prerequisite for any public activities in the colonial state. After 1916, its aims became more politicized and anti-colonial, openly calling for the liberation of the indigenous population from Dutch rule. This shift indicated the faultlines among the party leadership regarding the tactics necessary to achieve its goals, including the desirability—or not—of cooperation with the colonial authorities. Nascent factionalism was aggravated by communists active in the organization. By 1921, however, the communists had been ousted from Sarekat Islam, which by that time was rapidly losing its mass base. Nevertheless, until the arrival of the Japanese in 1942, the party remained the most important political organization in the deeply divided Islamic community.[16]

[15] Anthony Reid, *The Contest for North Sumatra: Atjeh, the Netherlands and Britain 1858–1898* (Kuala Lumpur, 1969), 108–9 and 148–52; Paul-van 't Veer, *De Atjeh-oorlog* (Amsterdam, 1980), 52, 77–8, 96, 111–17, 119–21, 174–5, 177–9, 199–202, 237, and 260–6; and Helius Sjamsuddin, *Fighting Dutch Rule in the Nineteenth and Early Twentieth Centuries: The Social, Political, Ethnic and Dynastic Roots of Resistance in South and Central Kalimantan 1859–1906* (Melbourne, 1989), 229–41.

[16] Deliar Noer, *The Modernist Muslim Movement in Indonesia 1900–1942* (Singapore, 1973), 102–21, 125, 137–40, and 145–50; A. P. E. Korver, *Sarekat Islam 1912–1916: Opkomst, bloei en structuur*

Muslim nationalist politicians usually operated within the boundaries of the law. They knew that violence against colonial rule was too great a risk to their long-term prospects. Yet, such rationales could be absent at the lower levels of the organization, where local leaders of the Sarekat Islam employed messianic expectations described earlier. The national Sarekat Islam leadership warned against such sentiments, which in Java and elsewhere led to violence in the party's name. In 1916, full-scale rebellion in which Sarekat Islam members actively participated, broke out in Jambi in eastern Sumatra. It took the colonial government several months to restore peace. A number of significant revolts followed, carried out under the banners of both communism and Islam. Overall, however, violent resistance in the name of Islam faded after the First World War and only re-emerged after the invasion of Japanese troops in the beginning of 1942.[17]

The Japanese invasion and subsequent conquest of the Netherlands Indies in the first months of 1942 was such a quick operation that many, including the Indonesian nationalists, were taken by surprise. Between May 1940, when the Netherlands was occupied by Nazi Germany, and December 1941, the month of the attack on Pearl Harbor and the following Dutch declaration of war on Japan, the mood of the Indonesian nationalists, including its Islamic fractions, had been quite cooperative. The expectation was that, given the prevailing circumstances, the Netherlands Indies government would make political concessions. By December 1941, their hopes appeared futile and some Indonesians greeted the Japanese as 'liberators'. Since the beginning of the 1930s, officials in Tokyo had styled Japan as a 'protector of Islam', and the first formal contacts between Japanese representatives and Indonesian Muslims were established in 1939. Nevertheless, during the Japanese invasion, rebellions against the Dutch authorities were relatively rare. The most significant anti-Dutch uprising was the rebellion in Aceh, in which Islam played a central role. One of its fomenters was, in fact, the Persatuan Ulama Seluruh Aceh, an organization of influential 'ulama with a militant youth following. Anti-kafir and pro-jihad sentiments fueled the uprising. Sabotage and attacks on the Dutch presence, to some extent fueled by the propaganda of Radio Penang in occupied Malaya, had already occurred before the Japanese invasion. On 8 March 1942, after the Dutch colonial military headquarters in Java had capitulated, the Japanese troops still had to enter Aceh.[18]

*van Indonesië's eerste massabeweging* (Amsterdam, 1982), 15–17, 23–6, and 33–5; and Michael Francis Laffan, *Islamic Nationhood and Colonial Indonesia: The Umma Below the Winds* (London, 2003), 166–9.

[17] Kartodirdjo, *Protest Movements in Rural Java*, 150 and 163–82; Korver, *Sarekat Islam 1912–1916*, 79–91 and 139–43; Shiraishi Takashi, *An Age in Motion: Popular Radicalism in Java 1912–1926* (Ithaca, NY, 1990), 113–14, 251, and 261; Michael Charles Williams, *Communism, Religion and Revolt in Banten* (Athens, OH, 1990), 156–7, 167, 171, 181–8, 220–8, and 233–4; and Audrey R. Kahin, 'The 1927 Communist Uprising in Sumatra: A Reappraisal', *Indonesia*, 62 (1996), 19–36, 19, 22–7, and 31–4.

[18] A. J. Piekaar, *Atjeh en de oorlog met Japan* ('s-Gravenhage, 1949), 18–23, 43, 50, 57, 94–5, 108, and 173–4; Harry J. Benda, *The Crescent and the Rising Sun: Indonesian Islam under Japanese Occupation 1942–1945* (Dordrecht, 1983, reprint), 103–5; and E. Touwen-Bouwsma, 'De Indonesische nationalisten en de oorlog met Japan: Houding en reacties', in Petra Groen and Elly Touwen-Bouwsma (eds), *Nederlands-Indië 1942: Illusie en ontgoocheling* ('s-Gravenhage, 1992), 57–75, 57–61, and 64–5.

Initial hopes for 'liberation' were soon shattered. Those who had rebelled against the Dutch quickly discovered that the Japanese military authorities had no interest in Indonesian independence. Their aim was to mobilize Indonesian natural resources and, later, Indonesian labor to bolster the Japanese war effort. As the tide turned against the Japanese, they tried to mobilize the population, using nationalist and Islamic leaders as propagandists. Only when Japan grew more desperate was the future independence of Indonesia hinted at in September 1944. Between then and the August 1945 capitulation of Japan, the nationalist leadership, including its Islamic elements, began to pave the way for independence. By the end of 1944, a small Muslim paramilitary force called Hizbullah, had been established. The sudden capitulation of the Japanese forces on 15 August 1945 took everybody by surprise. Two days later, on 17 August 1945, the Republic of Indonesia was proclaimed. As the Dutch government refused to recognize this new state, a protracted and bitter war of independence was fought between the end of 1945 and the moment the Netherlands transferred sovereignty to the United States of Indonesia on 27 December 1949. During this period, the Islamic parties and their paramilitary groups, such as Hizbullah and the post-independence Sabilillah, fought against the Dutch. A few months after the proclamation of independence, in November 1945, Nahdlatul Ulama (the leading organization of 'ulama in Java) issued a decree calling for a jihad against the Dutch and their allies. In August 1949 in the mountainous part of West Java, with the backing of former local units of paramilitary Islamic groups, Sekarmadji Maridjan Kartosuwirjo proclaimed the Negara Islam Indonesia, the Islamic State of Indonesia, otherwise known as Darul Islam, which fought the Republic of Indonesia after the transfer of sovereignty until its suppression in 1962. However, Kartosuwirjo's struggle was not supported by the traditional Muslim parties, which remained within the apparatus of the new independent state.[19]

## CONCLUSION

Reviewing the three-and-a-half centuries of contact between the Dutch colonial empire and Indonesian Islam, it is not surprising the relationship was largely antithetical. Non-Muslim rule over Muslims certainly spawned animosity among the population. However, this opposition alone does not seem to be a sufficient explanation for the escalation into full-fledged conflict. A comparison of the Dutch policy towards Islam with that of the Portuguese, who had openly promoted themselves as a Christian power in the East Indies, shows quite unequivocally that the Dutch were particularly cautious to avoid irritating Muslim religious sentiment.

---

[19] C. van Dijk, *Rebellion Under the Banner of Islam: The Darul Islam in Indonesia* (The Hague, 1981), 19–20, 43, 73–7, 92–3, and 125–6; Benda, *The Crescent and the Rising Sun*, 133–4, 150–2, 178–9, and 184; Touwen-Bouwsma, 'De Indonesische nationalisten en de oorlog met Japan', 67–9; and Faisal Isma'il, *Islamic Traditionalism in Indonesia: A Study of the Nahdlatul Ulama's Early History and Religious Ideology (1926–1950)* (Jakarta, 2003), 54–7.

Christianity was hardly ever aggressively promoted. It would be easy to draw the conclusion that over the centuries such a policy of accommodation succeeded.

Another conclusion is that the argument of the defense of Islam alone was never strong enough for the majority of Muslims to cross the line from non-violent to violent opposition to the empire. The examples given in this chapter show that the full potential of Islam to motivate anti-colonial resistance was seldom mobilized. Conflicts, in particular armed revolts, always arose from a combination of con-tested power, wealth, and ideology. Indonesian Islam did play a major part in the domain of ideology. An individual self-identifying as a Muslim was, like any human being, the bearer of multiple identities and, hence, had different roles to play in society. A Muslim could be a Javanese, a Malay, a Makassarese, or an Indonesian, and at the same time a prince, a peasant, an administrator, or a journalist. As a Muslim and an Indonesian, he might become convinced that Dutch empire was injurious for Islam, but as an administrator, he may have decided that resistance was a personal risk. Such calculations must have been made continuously by those who were capable of mobilizing support in indigenous society. Certainly, persons who considered themselves members of the *ummat Islam* were not automatically the enemy of the kafir colonial Dutch. Nevertheless, being Muslim could at times stimulate anti-Dutch resentment, and anti-Dutch rhetoric could win Muslim leaders—in particular, those advocating a reformed, revived, and more scriptural Islam—a substantial audience and greater authority in their societies, especially in times of crisis.

Changing power relations also influenced perceptions of the Dutch–Muslim relationship and—in particular circumstances—may have led to the belief that armed conflict was unavoidable. Initially, the Dutch were allies of Muslim Indonesian states but, as the Dutch stepped up their demands and the balance of power, expressed in military terms, changed in favor of colonial empire, the Dutch evolved from allies into sovereigns. This evolution also explains why initial clashes with the Dutch were led by sultans and princes. Later, in order to survive, this class of people had to drop their oppositional role and adopt a collaborative course with the colonial authorities. In East Indonesia, this had already occurred by the seventeenth century; in Java, during the late eighteenth and early nine-teenth centuries; and in the other islands, over the course of the nineteenth century. Thereafter, Islamic opposition became a matter of men in less exalted locations, such as self-proclaimed *ratu adils* and local 'ulama in Java and the other islands, with the exception of East Indonesia, where Muslims were not in the majority everywhere. At the beginning of the twentieth century, however, the influence of such individuals ceased, not only due to the success of Dutch military repression, but also because Indonesian Islam embarked on a new stage of reform, and local charismatic leaders had to cede power. Increasingly, the Islamic opposition used non-violent means and acted in the framework of nationalist political parties and newspapers, in which Indonesian Muslims were enthusiastic participants.

# PART III

# ISLAM AND COLONIAL KNOWLEDGE

# 11

# Debates on Islam in Imperial Germany

*Rebekka Habermas*

## INTRODUCTION

It is now generally acknowledged that the German empire took a far greater interest in questions of religion than was hitherto believed, despite the activity of contemporaries such as Max Weber, who focused so intently on secularization.[1] Indeed, religion played such an important role that at certain times it even took center stage, as in the 'culture wars' referred to collectively—and inadequately—as the *Kulturkampf* in earlier research. Those conflicts included debates on anti-Semitic articles published by prominent historians, disputes about very popular Catholic pilgrimages, arguments over new legal restrictions concerning Catholic schools, and accusations against ostensibly sexually crazed Jesuits.[2] A considerable body of research now exists about these battles, whether large or small, between Protestant, Catholic, and Jewish interests.[3] However, it has been largely overlooked that Imperial Germany engaged in disputes not only about Catholicism, Protestantism, and Judaism, but also about Islam.[4] As the

---

[1] This chapter is an abbreviated and revised version of Rebekka Habermas, 'Islam Debates Around 1900: Colonies in Africa, Muslims in Berlin, and the Role of Missionaries and Orientalists', *Chloe: Beihefte zum Daphnis*, 46 (2012), 123–54. The text was translated by Elizabeth Bredeck. I would like to thank Roman Loimeier (Göttingen) for his reading and suggestions and Tobias Mertke, Lisa Schneider, and Karolin Wetjen for many corrections.

[2] David Blackbourn, *Marpingen: Apparitions of the Virgin Mary in Bismarckian Germany* (Oxford, 1993); Helmut Walser Smith, *German Nationalism and Religious Conflict: Culture, Ideology, Politics, 1870–1914* (Princeton, 1995); articles in Christopher Clark and Wolfram Kaiser (eds), *Culture Wars: Secular–Catholic Conflict in Nineteenth-Century Europe* (Cambridge, 2003); Uffa Jensen, *Gebildete Doppelgänger: Bürgerliche Juden und Protestanten im 19. Jahrhundert* (Göttingen, 2005); and Michael B. Gross, *The War Against Catholicism: Liberalism and the Anti-Catholic Imagination in Nineteenth-Century Germany* (Ann Arbor, MI, 2004).

[3] Manuel Borutta, 'Der innere Orient: Antikatholizismus als Orientalismus in Deutschland, 1781–1924', in Monica Juneja and Margrit Pernau (eds), *Religion und Grenzen in Indien und Deutschland: Auf dem Weg zu einer transnationalen Historiographie* (Göttingen, 2008), 245–73; Manuel Borutta, 'Genealogie der Säkularisierungstheorie: Zur Historisierung einer großen Erzählung der Moderne', *Geschichte und Gesellschaft*, 36/3 (2010), 347–76. See the standard work by Gross, *War Against Catholicism*; and also the overview by Rebekka Habermas, 'Piety, Power, and Powerlessness: Religion and Religious Groups in Germany 1870–1945', in Helmut Walser Smith (ed.), *Oxford Handbook of Modern German History* (Oxford, 2011), 457–84.

[4] Recent literature on the debates on Islam in Imperial Germany includes Holger Weiss, 'German Images of Islam in West Africa', *Sudanic Africa*, 11 (2000), 53–93; and Holger Weiss, 'Variations in the Colonial Representation of Islam and Muslims in Northern Ghana, *ca.* 1900–1930', *Journal of*

following pages will show, Germany's empire was instrumental in inspiring German interest in Islam and, indeed, the first debates about Islam focused on the role of Islam within the empire. Perhaps the most important of these debates took place in the first decade of the twentieth century. Focusing primarily on the possible dangers Islam might pose, the potential for violence in Islam was at the heart of the debate.

The first part of this chapter explores the debate about Islam in Imperial Germany around 1900, examining the scholars and practitioners who took sides on the issue, and who thereby shaped German discourse on Islam and Muslims, despite the lack of precise or empirical investigation into the question. This chapter argues that these debates were rooted in a fundamental consensus regarding many classic tropes of Orientalism, but also struck new ground in their focus on religion. The second part of the chapter demonstrates that this new focus on religion was largely due to the impact of missionaries. The third part analyzes in detail a number of large-scale and survey-based projects about Islam, initiated in the first decade of the twentieth century and carried out by missionaries as well as by scholars in the German colonies. But, it is argued, even these new empirical investigations did not lead to a crucial shift in views on the main features of Islam. The fourth part explores the background to some of these new research projects. It argues that they were mainly grounded in colonial policies or, to be more precise, in colonial fantasies about the presumed danger of Muslim 'fanatics'. Debates on Islam at the beginning of the twentieth century owed much to Germany's specific colonial situation and less to other areas of foreign affairs. The final part of the chapter discusses continuity and change in the German discourse on Islam after 1914.

## DEBATES ABOUT ISLAM

The debate on Islam in the German empire reached its first critical point in 1905 for a number of reasons. Royal visits from representatives of Muslim countries, the growing economic and political interest in the Ottoman empire, and reports

*Muslim Minority Affairs*, 25/1 (2005), 73–95; see also Per Hassing, 'Islam at the German Colonial Congresses', *The Muslim World*, 67/3 (1977), 165–74. Hassing admittedly does not explore the role of the debate in the history of the German empire, but rather colonial representations of Islam. Suzanne L. Marchand, *German Orientalism in the Age of Empire: Religion, Race, and Scholarship* (Washington, DC, 2009), touches on this in her discussion of the Orientalists Hartmann and Becker; see also Sabine Mangold, *Eine 'weltbürgerliche Wissenschaft': Die deutsche Orientalistik im 19. Jahrhundert* (Stuttgart, 2004); and Andrew F. Walls, 'Africa as the Theatre of Christian Engagement with Islam in the Nineteenth Century', *Journal of Religion in Africa*, 29/2 (1999), 155–74, on debates about Islam in nineteenth-century England. See also Roman Loimeier, 'Afrika in der deutschen Islamwissenschaft', in Abbas Poya and Maurus Reinkowski (eds), *Das Unbehagen in der Islamwissenschaft: Ein klassisches Fach im Scheinwerferlicht der Politik und der Medien* (Bielefeld, 2008), 119–35; and Alexander Haridi, *Das Paradigma der 'islamischen Zivilisation'—oder die Begründung der deutschen Islamwissenschaft durch Carl Heinrich Becker (1876–1933): Eine wissenschaftsgeschichtliche Untersuchung* (Würzburg, 2005). Studies exploring contemporary ethnological or sociological discourses on Islam are rare. For an excellent analysis of Max Weber's studies of Islam, see Gudrun Krämer, 'Islam, Kapitalismus und die protestantische Ethik', in Gunilla Budde (ed.), *Kapitalismus: Historische Annäherungen* (Göttingen, 2011), 116–46.

of exciting new excavations in Egypt led by German archaeologists, all played a role. However, of crucial importance was—as I want to argue—the fact that colonial officers, settlers, and, perhaps most of all, missionaries were confronted by the so-called 'Islamic question' (*Islamfrage*) in the German colonies.[5] It was from around 1900 that the German public became more aware of the fact that German East Africa, Cameroon, and Togo were not entirely dominated by so-called 'heathens' but that Muslims sometimes played a crucial role in these regions.[6] The first critical point of the central debate about Islam was reached in 1905 at the Colonial Congress, an important forum for the discussion of colonial issues, where the topic 'Islam as a Problem' was addressed.[7] Julius Richter, a representative of the Berlin Missionary Society, delivered a lecture on 'Islam as a danger for our African colonies' and Dr Froberger, the provincial superior of the White Fathers from Trier, asked: 'What cultural value does Islam have for colonial development?'[8]

The Colonial Congress convened for the first time in 1902 as a meeting of citizens interested in colonial affairs, and was so successful that additional meetings were scheduled for 1905 and 1910. In 1905, more than 2,000 men and women gathered in the Berlin Reichstag, where scholars, colonial public officials, missionaries, and members of associations devoted to colonial matters delivered speeches about pertinent colonial topics. In attendance were prominent members of the German Colonial Society, headed by its chairman Johann Albrecht zu Mecklenburg (1857–1920), together with representatives of the high nobility and the cultural and political elite of the German empire, and the most important business people and bankers in colonial trade.[9] A total of some 100 organizations and associations took part in the event, including various missionary societies and representatives of missionary orders.

Islam remained an important topic after this Congress. In 1906, several missionaries published articles in national daily newspapers on the pressing issue of how to gain control over the dangers posed by 'Mohammedanism', which appeared to be spreading in the German colonies.[10] The debate reached a second critical point

---

[5] David Motadel, 'Qajar Shahs in Imperial Germany', *Past and Present*, 213/1 (2011), 191–235; and Salvador Oberhaus, '"*Zum wilden Aufstande entflammen*": *Die deutsche Ägyptenpolitik 1914–1918: Ein Beitrag zur Propagandageschichte des Ersten Weltkrieges*' (DPhil, University of Düsseldorf, 2006), 56.

[6] Carl Heinrich Becker, 'Islam', in Heinrich Schnee (ed.), *Deutsches Kolonial-Lexikon*, 3 vols (Leipzig, 1920), ii, 106–14.

[7] In 1910, Becker published an essay with this title, which also served as an editorial in his new journal, see Carl H. Becker, 'Der Islam als Problem', *Der Islam*, 1 (1910), 1–21.

[8] Julius Richter, 'Der Islam: Eine Gefahr für unsere afrikanischen Kolonien', in *Verhandlungen des Deutschen Kolonialkongresses 1905 in Berlin am 5., 6. und 7. Oktober 1905* (Berlin, 1906), 510–27, 519; and Josef Froberger, 'Welches ist der Kulturwert des Islam für koloniale Entwicklung? (Koreferat.)', in *Verhandlungen des Deutschen Kolonialkongresses 1905 zu Berlin am 5., 6. und 7. Oktober 1905* (Berlin, 1906), 527–38, 531.

[9] Hassing, 'Islam at the German Colonial Congresses'; and Weiss, 'German Images of Islam in West Africa', 60ff. On the Colonial Congresses generally, see Rathgen, 'Deutsche Kolonialkongresse', in Heinrich Schnee (ed.), *Deutsches Kolonial-Lexikon*, 3 vols (Leipzig, 1920), i, 309–10, 309.

[10] Anonymous, 'Die Haussa in den Schutzgebieten Kamerun und Togo', *Deutsche Reichszeitung: Bonner Stadtanzeiger* (9 October 1906).

in 1910 when, together with various missionaries, the most prominent German Orientalist at the time, Carl Heinrich Becker (1876–1933), used the Colonial Congress as a platform for a lecture about the 'Spread of Islam'. At the Congress Becker also proposed a resolution in which he evoked the 'serious danger' of an increasingly aggressive Islam. At the same time—and probably influenced by precisely these debates—Max Weber (1864–1920) started becoming interested in Islam.[11] Other German scholars also published some initial ideas on how to use surveys as the basis for larger-scale research projects on the contemporary situation in the Muslim world.[12] In addition, a growing number of newspapers focused on 'Mohammedans', as they were called at the time. In short, it was not only scholars and representatives of colonial or missionary associations who began to develop an interest in Islam; increasingly, it also became the focus of broader public attention.

What exactly were these debates about and who shaped them? Holger Weiss has contended that the discussions were dominated by two clearly delineated positions: on the one hand, missionaries who underscored primarily the negative implications of Islam; and on the other hand, researchers such as Carl Heinrich Becker, who emphasized the positive effects of Islam.[13] Indeed, at least at first glance, it does appear that two different basic perspectives on Islam had developed in the debates. Missionaries often equated Islam with enslavement, the slave trade, slave traders, and polygamy[14]—a line of argument frequently and vigorously pursued in the 1880s, and enforced by the campaign of Cardinal Lavigerie (1825–92), the founder of the White Fathers. Missionaries further claimed that Muslims were particularly fanatical 'anti-colonial, politically destructive vermin' who were also quite gullible as well.[15] Finally, Muslims were represented as unreliable workers

---

[11] Wolfgang Schluchter (ed.), *Max Webers Sicht des Islams: Interpretation und Kritik* (Frankfurt M., 1987). Weber plays a role here insofar as Becker belonged to the circle of friends around Max Weber.

[12] Weiss, 'German Images of Islam in West Africa', 92, looks at Becker's studies from 1908, and also at empirical studies by Martin Hartmann that are based on a survey reprinted in the 1911 announcements of the Seminar for Oriental Languages and entitled 'Zur Islamausbreitung in Afrika'.

[13] Weiss, 'German Images of Islam in West Africa'.

[14] See, for example, Amandus Acker, 'Über einige Mittel zur allmählichen Abschaffung der Sklaverei', in *Verhandlungen des Deutschen Kolonialkongresses 1902 zu Berlin am 10. und 11. Oktober 1902* (Berlin, 1903), 452–9, 456; P. W. Schmidt, 'Die Behandlung der Polygamie in unseren Kolonien', in *Verhandlungen des Deutschen Kolonialkongresses 1902 zu Berlin am 10. und 11. Oktober 1902* (Berlin, 1903), 467–79, 467; and Erich Schultze, *Soll Deutsch-Ostafrika christlich oder mohammedanisch werden? Eine Frage an das deutsche Volk, zugleich ein Wort der Aufklärung über die Gefahr der Islamisierung unserer größten Kolonie und den einzigen Weg zu ihrer Rettung* (Berlin, 1913), 52–6; see also William G. Clarence Smith, *Islam and the Abolition of Slavery* (London, 2006).

[15] Catholic Hubert Hansen used this phrasing in one of his articles. See Hubert Hansen, 'Welche Aufgaben stellt die Ausbreitung des Islam den Missionen und Ansiedlern in den deutschen Kolonien? (mit anschließender Diskussion)', in *Verhandlungen des Deutschen Kolonialkongresses 1910 zu Berlin am 6., 7. und 8. Oktober 1910* (Berlin, 1910), 652–73, 659. On this kind of rhetoric, see also Schmidt, 'Die Behandlung der Polygamie in unseren Kolonien', 471; Richter, 'Der Islam', 519: 'An Islamic Africa is therefore a permanent danger…'; and Karl Axenfeld, 'Die Ausbreitung des Islam in Afrika und ihre Bedeutung für die deutschen Kolonien', in *Verhandlungen des Deutschen Kolonialkongresses 1910 zu Berlin am 6., 7. und 8. Oktober 1910* (Berlin, 1910), 629–38, 635: 'Even the riot that took place in East Africa in 1905 was—though hidden—strongly influenced by Islam.' The same negative argument concerning Islam and its effect on the business world can be found in Martin Hartmann, *Islam, Mission, Politik* (Leipzig, 1912), 30–1.

and 'brake shoes' on economic development.[16] Finally, missionaries warned that the German nation had reason to fear the rapid spread of Islam in at least three of its colonies: first and foremost in German East Africa, but also in Togo and Cameroon.[17] In contrast to these primarily negative attributions, Orientalists such as Carl Heinrich Becker stressed that Islam had made 'a considerable cultural contribution in Africa'.[18] Becker wrote, for example, that Islam had helped transform 'savages' into 'human beings', in that 'it has led them out of an ethnic collectivism into individualism',[19] especially since Arabs were 'superior to the black population as a race and a culture'.[20]

However, although missionaries and Orientalists did evaluate some things differently, they nonetheless had more in common than appeared at first glance.[21] Moreover—and this is my second point—unlike Holger Weiss, I contend that the importance of this debate cannot be reduced to the notion that one side emphasized the positive effects and the other the potential dangers of Islam.[22] Instead, the real significance of the debate consisted in the fact that Islam itself was put on the agenda. Prior to this debate, Islam had received no special attention in either relevant travel reports or in adventure stories (most notably of the popular German novelist Karl May (1842–1912) nor in high-profile public debates, let alone as a controversial topic outside scholarly circles. Up until this time, the general public had encountered the 'Orient' primarily in the form of harem descriptions, reports

[16] See, for example, Hansen, 'Welche Aufgaben stellt die Ausbreitung des Islam den Missionen und Ansiedlern in den deutschen Kolonien?', 658.

[17] Axenfeld, 'Die Ausbreitung des Islam in Afrika und ihre Bedeutung für die deutschen Kolonien', 629, writes of an 'unsystematic, but all in all very successful expansion of North African Islam'; Richter, 'Der Islam', 512, likewise postulates the danger of an 'Arabic conquest'.

[18] Carl H. Becker, 'Staat und Mission in der Islampolitik', in *Verhandlungen des Deutschen Kolonialkongresses 1910 zu Berlin am 6., 7. und 8. Oktober 1910* (Berlin, 1910), 639–51, 645.

[19] Becker, 'Staat und Mission in der Islampolitik'.

[20] Becker, 'Staat und Mission in der Islampolitik', 647; also Becker, 'Der Islam und die Kolonialisierung Afrikas', *Internationale Wochenschrift für Kunst und Technik*, 4 (1910), 227–51, 246: 'There is no doubt that Islamic civilization is superior to that of the Negroes' but inferior to ours.' On Becker's ideas about 'Islamic civilization', see Haridi, *Das Paradigma der 'islamischen Zivilisation'*, 30–79.

[21] Scholars claimed in particular that their knowledge was objective and therefore true: 'I speak as a scholar, as a researcher, not as a lawyer for the mission', was Becker's response to the accusations of a mission representative in a debate at the Colonial Congress of 1910, see Hansen, 'Welche Aufgaben stellt die Ausbreitung des Islam den Missionen und Ansiedlern in den deutschen Kolonien?', 671.

[22] In their style of argumentation and professional identity, academic Orientalists did not fail to underscore the difficulties involved in analysis. The few researchers who were interested in contemporary phenomena at all worked more in non-religious areas such as economic or social aspects of the 'Arab world'. In contrast to the missionaries, they also took an interest in diverse political, social, and religious structures. First and foremost, they tried to take into account the 'infinitely complex relations' which existed in Islamic countries that were 'defined only in part by religion', to use Hartmann's words, see Hartmann, *Islam, Mission, Politik*, 37. For this reason, their explanations also differed; Becker, for instance, frequently cited economic interests. In Carl H. Becker's 'Materialien zur Kenntnis des Islam in Deutsch-Ostafrika' (*Der Islam*, 2 (1911), 1–48), for example, he claimed that Indians were interested in the spread of Islam for economic reasons, so that, as cloth merchants, they might sell more fabric. After all, he pointed out, Islam has strict clothing requirements, and the Islamic population would therefore need a great deal of fabric, see Carl H. Becker, *Islamstudien: Vom Werden und Wesen der islamischen Welt*, 2 vols (Hildesheim, 1967 (Leipzig, 1932)), ii, 71.

of lazy or selectively lascivious Orientals, or high cultures long since in decline, and Islam had rarely been the focus of intensive study beyond academic circles.

There were commonalities between the scholarly and the missionary viewpoints. First, researchers and missionaries alike equated Islam with slavery and the slave trade, just as in the discussions of the 1880s that were shaped so decisively by Cardinal Lavigerie.[23] Both missionaries and scholars such as Carl Heinrich Becker claimed that the East African slave trade was in the firm grip of Arab hands.[24] It is evident that both groups were morally outraged over this alleged fact, since slavery—in the picture they painted of themselves—was alien to the very core of civilized societies; a view that conveniently overlooked not only the past, but contemporary European practices as well.[25]

Both groups also shared the idea that, particularly in Africa, Islam was a superficial religion for gullible people with a proclivity for magical practices. Like the missionaries, Becker and other Orientalists never tired of stressing the importance of amulets and other magic objects, and worked diligently to describe as precisely as possible different forms of witchcraft, which they understood to be phenomena typical of African Islam.[26] A third shared assumption—and one that carried a menacing undertone whenever it was evoked—concerned the supposedly ubiquitous impulse of Islam to spread throughout all of Africa, but especially in German East Africa and in northern Togo.[27] Thus Carl Heinrich Becker writes that 'the fact—the spread of Islam—is irrefutable'. This putative spread seemed particularly threatening because it was felt to increase the chance of uprisings. Behind this belief was the notion that anti-colonial uprisings could be traced directly to Islamic

---

[23] Gustav Warneck, *Die Stellung der evangelischen Mission zur Sklavenfrage* (Gütersloh, 1889); and the study by Rebekka Habermas, 'Wissenstransfer und Mission: Sklavenhändler, Missionare und Religionswissenschaftler', *Geschichte und Gesellschaft*, 36/2 (2010), 257–84. On the actual elimination of slavery in German East Africa and the less-than-honorable role played by the German government, see Jan-Georg Deutsch, *Emancipation without Abolition in German East Africa, c. 1884–1914* (Oxford, 2006). A more detailed differentiation of various positions within the developing field of Islamic Studies around 1900 would doubtless reveal important differences between individual scholars, see, for example, Haridi, *Das Paradigma der 'islamischen Zivilisation'*, 69–79. Without wishing to deny these differences, even a more detailed investigation would still show that Hartmann and Becker share the same basic axioms of an 'Islam' that is distinguished by being 'fanatic, primitive, despotic and lazy' (Haridi, *Das Paradigma der 'islamischen Zivilisation'*, 78); see also Clarence Smith, *Islam and the Abolition of Slavery*.

[24] Becker, 'Materialien zur Kenntnis'; and Becker, *Islamstudien*, 73.

[25] See the impressive work by Deutsch, *Emancipation without Abolition*, 19, who juxtaposes the Reichstag debates with the current practices in German East Africa. Deutsch also shows how tightly the German colonial government and to some extent also the missions clung to slavery; and, most importantly, that the end of slavery was by no means the outcome of German or European policies, but 'a result of the prolonged struggle between owners and slaves, in which slaves tried to make the best of the limited choices and opportunities available to them' (p. 242).

[26] Becker, *Islamstudien*, 97. A different debate concerns the emphasis that Becker and others placed on the idea that in Africa there was no form of Islam like that found in the Qur'an. They stress the diversity of different practices and the idea that nowhere do these adhere strictly to the Qur'an, see Schultze, *Soll Deutsch-Ostafrika christlich oder mohammedanisch werden?*, 9–13.

[27] Schultze, *Soll Deutsch-Ostafrika christlich oder mohammedanisch werden?*, 15. Becker, *Islamstudien*, 71, is also a good example, in that his second question already addresses the 'spread and character' of Islam, and its spread is affirmed.

propaganda.[28] Again, this conviction was shared by missionaries[29] and scholars alike.[30]

Additional shared basic assumptions also existed, and while these may be less obvious at first glance, they are certainly no less important for the argument as a whole. There was general agreement, for instance, that African 'heathens' should be regarded as inferior not only to European Christians, but also to the African Muslim population. Missionaries and researchers on Islam agreed on this point, since both groups used a model of civilization in which the categories of race and religious belief were linked.[31] At work here was the notion that, on the one hand, Islam was just as superior to animistic religions as 'Arabs' were to 'Africans'. On the other hand, it also becomes clear that Africans per se were presumed not to be Muslims, and that Islam was a non-African religion. In doing so, German missionaries and scholars relied on assumptions made in other contemporary debates in Britain and France. Here as well, distinguished experts such as Emile Durkheim (1858–1917) pretended to be able to draw a clear line between a 'pure' Arab Islam and an *Islam noir*.[32] Finally, missionaries and researchers were in agreement insofar as they both ascribed to Muslims an extremely restricted agency: Muslims, it was assumed, acted either almost reflexively out of economic motives, or because they had fallen prey to a magical form of religious belief, not because they as Muslims were human beings endowed with intelligence and the ability to act rationally, or even analytically.[33]

---

[28] The quotation is from Becker, 'Materialien zur Kenntnis', 10. Becker, *Islamstudien*, 108ff., stressed on the one hand that Islam had played no role in the 1905 uprising in German East Africa, yet then went on to present a document *in extenso* that establishes precisely that connection. Becker argued in a similarly slippery fashion in an article in the *Koloniale Rundschau*, Carl H. Becker, 'Ist der Islam eine Gefahr für unsere Kolonien?' *Koloniale Rundschau*, 1 (1909), 266–93: 'Locally, e.g. in West Africa, Islam poses an imminent danger.' (p. 284) 'All in all Islam in terms of an Islamic state-ideal is politically dangerous neither in western nor in eastern Africa. It is not a danger to German possessions. Nevertheless, Islam can become a local danger. This can only be dealt with by respecting religious feelings and by carefully observing religious life and the leading Muslims' (p. 285).

[29] Hansen, 'Welche Aufgaben stellt die Ausbreitung des Islam den Missionen und Ansiedlern in den deutschen Kolonien?', 655. Hansen postulates that 'Islamic propaganda is mainly political and shows strong tendencies against Europe.'

[30] Hartmann, *Islam, Mission, Politik*, 34: 'Islam preaches hostility and hatred against all heretics' and 'Islam is an ecclesia militans and therewith a political danger' (p. 44).

[31] See Hansen, 'Welche Aufgaben stellt die Ausbreitung des Islam den Missionen und Ansiedlern in den deutschen Kolonien?', 655; Becker, 'Der Islam und die Kolonialisierung Afrikas': 'One may not say that it was foolish superstition which is to be exterminated: it is the Negroes' way of thinking... The Muslim faith, that has neither symbols nor sacraments, leads to a magical sight on words... This is why the Negro opens his mind naturally to Islam' (p. 236). 'But Islam offers the Negroes other advantages. It spreads by adjusting to their customs... The Negro copies everything he sees people doing whom he thinks to be superior to him' (p. 238); Schultze, *Soll Deutsch-Ostafrika christlich oder mohammedanisch werden?*, 13: 'The Negro, whose animism crumbled down like a mummy being exposed to draught before the intrusion of the Western mind, is looking for a new theoretical basis for his disoriented existence and Islam offers him that.'

[32] For an overview, see David Motadel, 'Islam and the European Empires', *Historical Journal*, 55/3 (2012), 831–56, 852–6.

[33] In this connection an interesting comparison can be made with English and French research at that time, which took a very different approach. Also noteworthy is an article by the missionary Klamroth, in which he recounts a religious discussion with a black 'Mohammedan', and at least allows him to speak as a theological conversation partner, see Martin Klamroth, 'Religionsgespräche mit

To conclude, aside from some minor differences that will be discussed shortly, especially concerning the issue of fanaticism, the debate on Islam was not so much a dispute between scholars and missionaries as a debate informed by a consensus that an ontological and essentialist difference existed between the Muslim and the Christian world.[34] According to this consensus, the Muslim world was defined by the slave trade, superficial and magic elements of faith, polygamous practices, the complete absence of agency, and the fact that Islam threatened first to overrun the African colonies and then all of Europe. At the same time, it was presumed that Africans by definition were inferior to Islam, and therefore could not really be Muslims themselves. This also helped solidify a particular image of European civilization, one that did not include slavery, polygamy, and superstition.[35] Moreover— and this confirms the importance of the debate—the religious dimensions of issues addressed in debates within Orientalism now came to the fore.

## ORIENTALISMS AND THE ROLE OF MISSIONARIES

The debate on Islam at the beginning of the twentieth century was thus part of the long and unique tradition of Orientalism as described by Edward Said; a tradition characterized first and foremost by its ontological and epistemological differentiation between Orient and Occident. This tradition gave rise to a discourse of 'dominating, restructuring, and having authority over the Orient',[36] but Said

---

einem Führer der Daressalamer Mohammedaner', *Allgemeine Missionszeitschrift: Beiblatt*, 40 (1913), 65–80.

[34] Unlike missionaries, scholars of Islam deemed it necessary to make frequent claims that the 'Mohammedan' could quickly turn toward fanaticism, see, for example, Becker, 'Ist der Islam eine Gefahr für unsere Kolonien?' 287: he argues that everything possible must be done 'that it does not become fanatic'. On Hartmann's ideas about fanaticism, see Haridi, *Das Paradigma der 'islamischen Zivilisation'*, 75.

[35] Concerning slavery, see Deutsch, *Emancipation Without Abolition*, which sketches the importance of German colonial rule in upholding slavery.

[36] Gottfried Hagen, 'German Heralds of Holy War: Orientalists and Applied Oriental Studies', *Comparative Studies of South Asia, Africa and the Middle East*, 24/2 (2004), 145–62, 146. For a critique of Said's failure to appreciate fully the German tradition, see Nina Berman, *Orientalismus, Kolonialismus und Moderne: Zum Bild des Orients in der deutschsprachigen Kultur um 1900* (Stuttgart, 1997). Berman takes issue with Said's claim that the German Orient was an almost entirely scholarly and classic one; she emphasizes the importance of Karl May, for example, and the scope of the public debate about the 'Oriental question', as does Marchand, *German Orientalism in the Age of Empire*. On Said's lack of resonance in German-language Arab Studies, see Roman Loimeier, 'Edward Said und der Deutschsprachige Orientalismus: Eine kritische Würdigung', *Wiener Zeitschrift für kritische Afrikastudien*, 1/2 (2001), 63–85. On the continuation and critical discussion of Said's work from a German perspective, see Hagen, 'German Heralds of Holy War'; Jennifer Jenkins, 'German Orientalism: Introduction', *Comparative Studies of South Asia, Africa and the Middle East*, 24/2 (2004), 97–100; and Suzanne Marchand, 'German Orientalism and the Decline of the West', *Proceedings of the American Philosophical Society*, 145/4 (2001), 465–73, 465: '…focused on the languages of the ancient world. German Orientalism helped to destroy Western self-satisfaction, and to provoke a momentous change in the culture of the West: the relinquishing of Christianity and classical antiquity as universal norms.'

also underscored another side of Orientalism, namely, 'that European culture gained in strength and identity by setting itself off against the Orient as a sort of surrogate and even underground self'.[37] In contrast to what Said wrote in 1978, we know today that this form of Orientalism existed not only in England and France, but also in Germany. Here, too, we can trace a growing fascination with the exotic world of barbarous, fanatical, irrational, and lascivious men and women of the Orient. At the same time, the Orient was widely admired because of its long and venerable cultural traditions. The educated middle class broadened its horizons, which had previously stopped with ancient Greece and Rome, discovered the *Arabian Nights*, examined the life of Christ, and started archaeological digs in Troy, and later in Baalbek in present-day Lebanon.[38] In the newly established field of *Arabistik*, scholars began to collect and translate Arabic manuscripts, and even the eminent Social Democrat August Bebel (1840–1913) devoted himself to the study of the 'Mohammedan-Arabic Cultural Period'.[39] Travelers including Duchess Hahn-Hahn (1805–80) discovered the world of the Ottoman harem,[40] and almost every young person in the German empire—together with more than a few adults—followed the battles that Karl May's Kara ben Nemsi Effendi waged against Bedouins, Arab soldiers, and the 'savages' of the North African deserts.[41]

As influential as these forms of Orientalism were, and although the debate on Islam was certainly part of this tradition, the debate also marked an important shift in emphasis, since its focus was limited to the religious aspect of what was understood to be the 'Orient', namely Islam. Unlike the stories of Karl May, the *Arabian Nights*, or the popular Oriental motifs of contemporary paintings, this discussion was not about harems, Bedouin chiefs, the desert, or pyramids; it was exclusively about Islam, which now assumed central importance. There were many different reasons for this new focus on religion. In addition to the increased importance of religion in general in debates within the German empire, we need to highlight first and foremost the importance of missionaries in all extra-European matters, an influence which has often been underestimated.[42]

---

[37] Edward Said, *Orientalism* (New York, 1994 (1978)), 3.

[38] On German Orientalism, see Marchand, *German Orientalism*; and Charlotte Trümpler (ed.), *Das große Spiel: Archäologie und Politik zur Zeit des Kolonialismus (1860–1940) (Ein Ausstellungsprojekt des Ruhrlandmuseums auf Zeche Zollverein, Mai–August 2008)* (Cologne, 2010).

[39] August Bebel, *Die mohammedanisch-arabische Kulturperiode* (Stuttgart, 1889). The work was republished in 1999 by Wolfgang G. Schwanitz in Berlin.

[40] On German female travelers to the Orient, see Annegret Pelz, *Reisen durch die eigene Fremde: Reiseliteratur von Frauen als autogeographische Schriften* (Cologne, 1933); and Annette Deeken and Monika Bösel, *An den 'süßen Wassern Asiens': Frauenreisen in den Orient* (Frankfurt M., 1996).

[41] Berman, *Orientalismus, Kolonialismus und Moderne*. May's 'Orient cycle' appeared in 1881–88, see Andrea Polaschegg, *Der andere Orientalismus: Regeln deutsch-morgenländischer Imagination im 19. Jahrhundert* (Berlin, 2005).

[42] On this topic, see Habermas, 'Wissenstransfer und Mission'. Islam had been put on the agenda by the 1880s by the French Cardinal Lavigerie, who was also the founder of the Catholic White Fathers missionary order. Lavigerie initiated a campaign against slavery and called for a holy war against Muslim Arabs, who were charged with involvement in the African slave trade. He and an entire missionary propaganda apparatus argued that Islam as a religion permitted and supported slavery, and that the entire slave trade in Africa was dominated by Arabs. The logical conclusion of this line of argument was a holy war against Islam.

What enabled missionaries to play such a prominent role, and thereby effect a shift in focus toward religious topics in the long tradition of Orientalist debates? One reason is as obvious as it is important: in Imperial Germany, missionaries were often the most crucial 'men on the spot', the only people with empirical expertise in religious practices in areas outside Europe. From time to time colonial civil servants also pursued amateur scholarly studies, but academic scholars of Islam only rarely arrived on the scene to collect material. German researchers, in particular, seldom left their armchairs prior to the First World War.[43] Aside from Carl Heinrich Becker, who traveled to Egypt and the Near East,[44] and Martin Hartmann (1851–1918), who visited China and Russia,[45] German scholars of Islam who left Europe remained the exception. As a result, those who were interested in the current situation around 1900 had to rely on books by their Dutch, British, and French colleagues[46] or studies done by missionaries[47] and perhaps the occasional work of individual colonial civil servants and other amateur scholars. In contrast to French and English researchers, German scholars devoted themselves almost exclusively to investigating the extra-European past. In Göttingen, Marburg, and Tübingen—the universities with the main professorships in Oriental Studies—they studied ancient and medieval manuscripts, searching for similarities and differences; they compared Arabic poems with Greek inscriptions or worked on linguistic analyses of preferably dead languages.[48] German professors had a particular fondness for ancient textual sources, and as a rule knew almost nothing about the contemporary Muslim world.

Because of this concentration on the past, most German Orientalists had no empirical experience whatsoever of contemporary societies and were correspondingly dependent on missionary expertise if they wished to address contemporary issues. The focus on the past also had other, epistemological consequences. Not only were contemporary societies by and large ignored, the past itself was studied

---

[43] Becker's 'Materialien zur Kenntnis des Islam in Deutsch-Ostafrika' is a notable example. An examination of the footnotes, and the fact that Becker himself conducted no research in German East Africa, shows how much he benefited from the work of the mission. See also Becker, 'Staat und Mission in der Islampolitik', 639: 'until recently in our colonies only missionaries were interested in Islam. Mission fed not only scholars with information about the huge expansion of Islam in Africa, but also drew politicians' attention to the dangers of this expansion and its reasons.' On this issue, see Schultze, *Soll Deutsch-Ostafrika christlich oder mohammedanisch werden?*, 17.

[44] Cornelia Essner and Gerd Winkelhane, 'Carl Heinrich Becker (1876–1933): Orientalist und Kulturpolitiker', *Die Welt des Islams*, 28 (1988), 154–77.

[45] Marchand, *German Orientalism*, 356ff.

[46] Hartmann, for example, was heavily influenced by French research of the time, see Hartmann, *Islam, Mission, Politik*, 101ff.

[47] Hartmann made repeated references to his disputes with representatives of the mission (Mirbt, Richter, and Simon). He also referred to works by the missionary Klamroth, whose publications included a 1910 study of East African Islam in the *Allgemeine Missionszeitschrift*, and a 1913 article entitled 'Religionsgespräche mit einem Führer der Daressalamer Mohammedaner' in the *Beiblatt der Allgemeinen Missionszeitschrift*. See Martin Klamroth, 'Ostafrikanischer Islam', *Allgemeine Missionszeitschrift*, 37 (1910), 477–93; and Klamroth, 'Religionsgespräche mit einem Führer der Daressalamer Mohammedaner'.

[48] Mangold, *Eine 'weltbürgerliche Wissenschaft'*, on the history of German Orientalism; Marchand, *German Orientalism*; and Polaschegg, *Der andere Orientalismus*.

only through a very selective body of texts, namely, texts with a particular theological, literary, or philological quality that had been carefully defined in advance according to the standards of nineteenth-century European philology. Those parts of the Muslim world that stood outside this particular written tradition were deemed unworthy of serious research. This meant that many parts of Africa whose recorded written traditions did not meet the standards of European philology never entered the purview of Oriental Studies.

Though often lamented,[49] the almost complete lack of information about African Islam in the past or present did not deter people from writing long articles and even books about Islam, or from claiming to understand complex interconnections better than the local missionary experts, even though the sole sources of information came from these very missionaries.

In summary, the new focus on Islam was due in part to a growing interest in religious topics within German society itself, but was also largely due to the prominent role that missionaries played in German Orientalism. Missionaries were often the only people who collected material on site and reported on the contemporary situation outside Europe on the basis of this empirical material.[50] This unique position of the missionaries also explains why Orientalists working on contemporary topics and missionaries agreed on fundamental points in their evaluations: the analyses of both groups were based on the very same empirical material.

## NEW RESEARCH PROJECTS AND OLD IDEAS

The German academic community long viewed this division of labor—missionaries on location and scholars of Islamic studies in their armchairs—as unproblematic, since only a handful of researchers even worked on contemporary societies and used the empirical material of the missionaries, but at the beginning of the twentieth century this changed. By 1900, an increasing number of voices began to openly criticize the practice of 'armchair scholarship' and to argue for increased attention to the contemporary situation.[51] At the same time, a number of researchers called for new and modern methods of investigation, such as surveys that

---

[49] Becker, *Islamstudien*, 74; compare Becker, 'Ist der Islam eine Gefahr für unsere Kolonien?', 293: 'We do not have statistical information, even an attempt to gather statistical information is missing. Numbers from particular districts, preliminary as they might be, are also lacking as we don't have precise information concerning the number of mosques or Qur'an Schools. It's hard going to gather hints from missionary articles and own impressions and put them together into a more or less incomplete picture.'

[50] Another important factor is that the very concept of world religions developed at the beginning of the nineteenth century, and with it the effort to describe these respective religions accurately as self-contained entities. This development occurred in, of all places, Oriental Studies, see Tomoko Masuzawa, *The Invention of World Religions: or, how European Universalism was Preserved in the Language of Pluralism* (Chicago, 2005).

[51] Marchand, *German Orientalism*, 333ff., writes that, toward the end of the nineteenth century, the concentration on philological methods decreased. Then in 1913 the journal *Welt des Islam* was founded, the first journal to address the contemporary situation, see Mangold, *Eine 'weltbürgerliche Wissenschaft'*.

would allow them to make detailed inquiries on-site, with the expectation that these would produce more reliable data than had been possible with the missionaries. At the time, surveys were considered the most reliable method possible of collecting data not only in the developing social sciences, but also among national economists, and even jurists. Surveys were felt to be invested with great scientific authority because their standards were believed to reflect the same notion of objectivity as the natural sciences.[52]

These demands for new research methods did not fall on deaf ears. Around 1910, at least four research projects were initiated, all concentrating on Islam in the African colonies of the German empire and working consistently with surveys. Becker started his investigation in 1908, and in 1911 Hartmann followed by sending surveys to colonial administrators in Togo, Cameroon, and German East Africa. Several years before Becker, Protestant missionary Martin Klamroth (1855–1918) had begun his own research in German East Africa;[53] and in 1910 the World Missionary Conference commissioned Diedrich Westermann (1875–1956), a former missionary of the North German Mission, to undertake a similar project using surveys,[54] which he began in 1913.[55]

How useful were these survey-based projects to scholars of Islam who hoped these would enable them to gain their first scientifically grounded insights into contemporary Islam? Did they unearth new results that altered the debate? Was it really possible to cast the practices, ideas, and rites of the different facets of African Islam in a new light? Did the research yield results that called into question previously held essentialist and ontological assumptions? Did this research dismantle the usual equation of Islam with the slave trade, fanaticism, and superficial religious practices to reveal different connections, or did it only serve to reinforce existing fears about unrest fueled by Islam and about the further spread of Islam in Africa?

First, we need to note that neither Becker nor Hartmann's research was ever published. Thus although it is possible that they gained some new insights, these had no effect whatsoever. The only studies ever published were those done by the

[52] Irmela Gorges, 'The Social Survey in Germany Before 1933', in Martin Bulmer, Kevin Bales, and Kathryn Kish Sklar (eds), *The Social Survey in Historical Perspective, 1880–1914* (Cambridge, 1991), 316–39; Andrew Zimmermann, *Anthropology and Antihumanism in Imperial Germany* (Chicago, 2001); and Rebekka Habermas, 'Die deutschen Großforschungsprojekte zum „Eingeborenenrecht" um 1900 und ihre Folgen', *Zeitschrift der Savigny-Stiftung für Rechtsgeschichte: Germanistische Abteilung*, 128 (2012), 150–82.

[53] Schultze, *Soll Deutsch-Ostafrika christlich oder mohammedanisch werden?*, 17; Becker, *Islamstudien*, chapter entitled 'Ein Missionar über den Islam in Deutsch-Ostafrika', 116–21; and also Martin Klamroth, *Der Islam in Deutschostafrika* (Berlin, 1912). His work is based on both his own observations and on surveys he distributed.

[54] The World Missionary Conference convened in Edinburgh in 1910. 1,200 delegates from Europe, the USA, and several non-Western countries—all associated with Protestant missions—met here to discuss mission-related matters, see Brian Stanley, *The World Missionary Conference, Edinburgh 1910* (Grand Rapids, MI, 2009). See also Westermann's contemporary report on the conference: Diedrich Westermann, 'Die Edinburgher Weltmissionskonferenz in ihrer Bedeutung für die Mission in den deutschen Kolonien', *Jahrbuch über die deutschen Kolonien*, 4 (1911), 128–33.

[55] All of the projects were based on surveys sent to missionaries and colonial officials in Africa, whose task it was to collect new data about Islam in the colonies; Weiss, 'German Images of Islam in West Africa', 73ff.

two missionaries, Klamroth and Westermann, though it should be mentioned that Westermann made use of Hartmann's material. Secondly, it is clear that while the individual surveys differed greatly in length and sometimes thematic focus (Westermann's survey contained almost a hundred questions, Becker's in contrast only three, and Hartmann's ten), the basic line of questioning in all the surveys barely deviated from the one taken in earlier articles that had been written without the help of detailed surveys. All researchers concentrated on precisely those issues that had been on the agenda since the Colonial Congress of 1905 at the latest: of primary interest were the spread of Islam and its propaganda mechanisms.[56] Hartmann's choice of title for his work conveys the importance of these questions about the spread of Islam, and with it the spread of threat and fear. Likewise, one of Westermann's studies is called 'A Questionnaire on the Spread of Islam', and the other 'A Survey Concerning the Spread of Islam in West Africa'.[57] Admittedly, Westermann took a far keener interest in the organization of Islamic rituals, and he wished to learn more about daily life under Islam and about Muslim views of the Christian mission.[58] His work also had certain aspects that we look for in vain in Hartmann or Becker: he wished to know, for example, how the colonial government helped support Muslims. Ultimately, however, the surveys show no essential differences. All researchers hoped to discover more about the most important Islamic practices and about how Islam was spreading. Moreover, and more importantly, the surveys reveal the same basic assumptions that we find present in the debates of earlier years. Instead of questioning these assumptions in order to gain new insights and knowledge about the contemporary situation of Islam, the studies were organized in such a way that questions about the spread of Islam and/ or how to stop it clearly dominated.[59]

It therefore comes as no surprise that for all their presumed scientific authority, these new studies tended merely to confirm assertions that had already been made about the character and status of Islam. Westermann reinforced the notion found in earlier debates that Islam tends towards superficiality,[60] and then emphasized

[56] Martin Hartmann, 'Zur Islamausbreitung in Afrika', *Mitteilungen des Seminars für orientalische Sprachen*, 14 (1911), 159–62, on question 5 about propaganda; also Becker's survey, which is reprinted in Weiss, 'German Images of Islam in West Africa', 92–3. Here, two of the three questions refer to propaganda and its spread. The third question even posits a connection with 'Muslim unrest'.

[57] Hartmann, 'Zur Islamausbreitung in Afrika', 162; question 10 in the survey refers specifically to this connection.

[58] See the unpublished survey, 'Fragebogen über die Ausbreitung des Islams in Westafrika' by Westermann, 'Mitteilungen', *Die Welt des Islam*, 1/1 (1913), 45–6. Under the rubric '3. moral, religious' the following questions are posed: '18. What do Muslims think about Christian mission? 19. What do Muslims mainly criticize about Christianity?...21. Do Muslims circulate rumours on Christians or Christian habits?'

[59] Diedrich Westermann, 'Die Verbreitung des Islams in Togo und Kamerun: Ergebnisse einer Umfrage', *Die Welt des Islams*, 2/2–4 (1914), 188–276, 244: 'For understanding future expansion of Islam one should concentrate on aspects that caused Islamic expansion until now.'

[60] His inquiries revealed that the Hausa, a 'tribe' of northern Togo known for its economic power, were also a people who merely imitated a few religious customs, and therefore only nominally supported the character of Islam, see Westermann, 'Die Verbreitung des Islams in Togo und Kamerun', 190.

that the religion was spreading, though he admitted this could not be claimed for each and every region.[61] He also voiced a 'suspicion of human trafficking' connected with Islam.[62] Finally, he wrote about the possibility that uprisings could occur, though he acknowledged that an 'attempt to shake off one's yoke... is not yet an Islamic uprising'.[63]

Aside from this admittedly surprising rejection of a direct link between Islam and fanaticism, the new survey-based projects failed to produce any actual new insights. Even if at that time the research methods were felt to reflect great scientific dignity, we can hardly claim that knowledge was advanced. Instead, these studies provided only variations on themes that—even without the help of empirical studies—had already been discussed years earlier.[64]

## CONTRIBUTING FACTORS

Here at the very least, this aspect of the discussions about Islam in the German empire raises a series of questions. Why did a debate take place at all at this time? When and why did it end, or rather: when did the key topics shift enough that it becomes necessary to speak of a new discussion? Or did the debate remain by and large the same as when it began around 1900, and as it continued after 1910 despite new research—still characterized by the same essentializing and ontologizing, and by the familiar equation of Islam with the slave trade and superficial belief?

Around 1900, numerous factors contributed to the interest in Islam. Only two years earlier, Kaiser Wilhelm II (1859–1941) had traveled to the so-called Holy Land, accompanied by great media fanfare, to present himself there as the flesh-and-blood successor to the crusaders and, as such, a Christian and a pilgrim (Fig. 18). This image also helped serve as a reminder that Christianity must defend itself against Islam.[65] On that same journey, Kaiser Wilhelm II

---

[61] Westermann, 'Die Verbreitung des Islams in Togo und Kamerun', 207: 'There is no Islamic propaganda.' The same was claimed for Lomé and Atakpame; likewise, in Mangu-Jensi no 'actual propaganda activity' ('eigentliche Propagandatätigkeit', p. 213) could be observed. In Cameroon, however, there were ostensibly areas in which Islam had slowly spread (see, for example, p. 233).

[62] Westermann, 'Die Verbreitung des Islams in Togo und Kamerun', 241.

[63] Westermann, 'Die Verbreitung des Islams in Togo und Kamerun', 244–5.

[64] 64 Weiss, 'German Images of Islam in West Africa', 89, came to the opposite conclusion, and claimed that this research had only 'scratched the surface' ('nur die Oberfläche') of the respective societies.

[65] For a detailed study of this trip to the Orient, including the role of the media, see Jan Stefan Richter, *Die Orientreise Kaiser Wilhelms II. 1898: Eine Studie zur deutschen Außenpolitik an der Wende zum 20. Jahrhundert* (Hamburg, 1997); see also Bebel, *Die mohammedanisch-arabische Kulturperiode*; and Horst Gründer, 'Die Kaiserfahrt Wilhelms II. ins Heilige Land 1898: Aspekte deutscher Palästinapolitik im Zeitalter des Imperialismus', in Heinz Dolliner, Horst Gründer, and Alwin Hanschmidt (eds), *Weltpolitik, Europagedanke, Regionalismus: Festschrift für Heinz Gollwitzer zum 65. Geburtstag am 30. Januar 1982* (Münster, 1982), 363–88; see also Nicolas Bilo, 'Der "Kreuzzug der Liebe": Palästinabilder in Reiseberichten anlässlich der Kaiserreise 1898' (MA, University of Göttingen, 2011).

**Fig. 18** German representation of the entry of Wilhelm II into Ottoman Damascus on 7 November 1898 (Topfoto).

had also described himself to great public effect as the 'friend' of the '300 million Mohammedans'.[66] In addition, towards the end of the nineteenth century, the Armenian massacres gained an increasing amount of attention; Pietists in

---

[66] This was the wording of a speech given after a visit to Saladin's grave in Damascus, or at least was quoted this way by the European press, see Richter, *Die Orientreise Kaiser Wilhelms II*, 86.

particular, but later also Catholic commentators were eager to interpret them as the result of Islamic aggression.[67]

At least until the end of the Bismarck period, the German empire had maintained friendly relations with the Ottoman empire, repeatedly sending them financial and military advisors, but events in the Ottoman empire did not trigger the German debates about Islam. Nor did events in Persia (despite the presence of German military advisors) have any influence on German debates about Islam.[68] Rather, the sudden interest in Islam was due primarily to events in the colonies, starting with numerous uprisings in African colonies that could be traced back to Islam. Already in the mid-nineteenth century, Great Britain had been shaken by uprisings in India that were alleged to have been provoked by Muslims, but it was not until the late 1880s that comparable threats were felt in the German empire.[69] In August 1888, the violent conflicts that broke out in the protectorate of German East Africa were allegedly started by fanaticized 'Mohammedans'. In October of 1888, at the first People's Assembly in Cologne, 'holy war' was declared against Islam[70] so that Africa would not fall victim to the 'crescent moon'.[71] Sparked by events in the colonies and initiated primarily by Catholic Cardinal Lavigerie, the first major debate on Islam had begun.[72] In 1906, rumors circulated in the German colony of Togo about a Mahdi named Malam Musa, who was believed to possess supernatural powers, a redeemer bringing salvation. And some Muslims believed he was capable of liberating Muslims from the domination of non-Muslims, thereby ending an unjust regime. In Togo, the German colonial government was able to render Mahdi Malam Musa 'harmless', but in 1907 conflicts between German colonial troops and rebels of another Mahdi were reported in northern Cameroon.[73] In 1908, reports

---

[67] The German public, however, remained noticeably quiet about the Armenian massacres, and unlike England, for example, did not use them as an opportunity to decry Turkish Muslims as fanatical religious warriors. Margaret Lavinia Anderson, '"Down in Turkey, Far Away": Human Rights, the Armenian Massacres, and Orientalism in Wilhelmine Germany', *Journal of Modern History*, 79/1 (2007), 80–111, explains this reticence by noting that the Armenians had received most of their support from Catholics (if we leave aside Pietist initiatives); the lack of protest against the massacres was thus related to the denominational dispute in Wilhelmine Germany.

[68] On German relations to Persia, see Motadel, 'Qajar Shahs'.

[69] Mervyn Hiskett, *The Development of Islam in West Africa* (London, 1984), 208. For an overview of English and French policies concerning Islam, see Rüdiger Sesemann, '"Ein Dialog der Taubstummen": Französische vs. britische Wahrnehmungen des Islam im spätkolonialen Westafrika', *Africa Spectrum*, 37/2 (2002), 109–39.

[70] Heinrich Loth, *Kolonialismus und 'Humanitätsintervention': Kritische Untersuchung der Politik Deutschlands gegenüber dem Kongostaat (1884–1908)* (Berlin, 1966), 47.

[71] Alexander Merensky, 'Mohammedanismus und Christentum im Kampf um die Negerländer Afrikas', *Allgemeine Missionszeitschrift*, 21 (1894), 145–62, 153.

[72] Friederike Szamborzki, 'Die armen Schwarzen und ihre schlimmsten Feinde: Die "Araber" Debatten der deutschen Antisklavereibewegung im ausgehenden 19. Jahrhundert' (MA, University of Göttingen, 2009). On contributing factors, see Habermas, 'Wissenstransfer und Mission'.

[73] Peter Sebald, *Togo 1884–1914: Eine Geschichte der deutschen "Musterkolonie" auf der Grundlage amtlicher Quellen; Mit einem Dokumentenanhang* (Berlin, 1988), 468; and also Thea Büttner, 'Die Mahdi-Erhebungen 1907 in Nordkamerun im Vergleich mit antikolonialen islamischen Bewegungen in anderen Regionen West- und Zentralafrikas', in Peter Heine and Ulrich van der Heyden (eds), *Studien zur Geschichte des deutschen Kolonialismus in Afrika: Festschrift zum 60. Geburtstag von Peter Sebald* (Pfaffenweiler, 1995), 147–59, 148.

spread about dangerous Muslims from German East Africa who, spurred on by letters from Mecca, threatened to band together. German newspapers were soon full of the so-called 'Mecca Letter Affair', fueling discussions about the importance of Islam. It was assumed that the Maji-Maji uprisings in German East Africa, which were clearly directed against colonial rule, had a direct connection to the Mecca Letter Affair, so attention now focused once again on the ostensibly fanatical character of Islam.[74]

The effectiveness of this paradigm based on the equation of Islam with fanaticism and uprising can be seen in a whole series of measures taken in those regions of the African colonies with particularly large Muslim populations. In northern Togo, for instance, Governor Zech (1868–1914) instituted a so-called 'backcountry blockade', which meant nothing more than that Muslims living in the region were not to be bothered by missionaries.[75] The blockade was not lifted until 1912. It was thought that the local population needed protection from Christian missionaries, lest the efforts of those missionaries provoke a violent backlash among Muslims.[76] The colonial government, of course, wanted no such thing. Aware that the stability of the colonies depended not only on suppressing possible uprisings, but on effective governance, economic well-being, and a contented population, the colonial government also realized that these things could be achieved only by working with, not against, the Muslims. Moreover, German district offices and governors depended on Muslims, since a stable government and large segments of the colonial economy were heavily dependent on Muslims. They were indispensible as translators and middlemen, since oftentimes they could read and write while non-Muslims could not.[77] In addition,

---

[74] Several uprisings that took place in English and French West African colonies were likewise interpreted as anti-colonial rebellions inspired by an increasingly dangerous Islam. Michael Pesek, 'Kreuz oder Halbmond. Die Deutsche Kolonialpolitik zwischen Pragmatismus und Paranoia in Deutsch-Ostafrika 1908–1914', in Ulrich van der Heyden (ed.), *Mission und Gewalt: Der Umgang christlicher Missionen mit Gewalt und die Ausbreitung des Christentums in Afrika und Asien in der Zeit von 1792 bis 1918/19* (Stuttgart, 2000), 97–112, sees a direct connection here to the debate about Islam; see also the connections to the uprisings drawn by Weiss, 'German Images of Islam in West Africa', and also Holger Weiss, 'Islam, Missionaries and Residents: The Attempt to the Basel Missionary Society to Establish a Mission in Yendi (German Togo) before WWI', in Ulrich van der Heyden and Holger Stoecker (eds), *Mission und Macht im Wandel politischer Orientierungen: Europäische Missionsgesellschaften in politischen Spannungsfeldern in Afrika und Asien zwischen 1800 und 1945* (Stuttgart, 2005), 173–86.

[75] Julius Graf von Zech seems to be closely related to Max von Oppenheim, an important amateur Orientalist, who was of leading importance in the establishment of the 'Intelligence Office for the East' in 1914. They traveled together in the late 1890s in Africa, see Oberhaus, *'Zum wilden Aufstande entflammen'*, 56.

[76] Both the Catholic and Protestant missions protested vehemently against this restriction of the area where they might work. They had some success in taking their concerns to the German press, which reported on how strongly the policies of the district leaders worked against the Christianization of Africa, see, for example, the *Deutsche Reichszeitung: Bonner Stadtanzeiger*, 9 October 1906, where an article entitled 'Die Haussa in den Schutzgebieten Kamerun und Togo' reports on how missionaries were stopped from traveling into the backcountry.

[77] It was also believed that Muslims were more polyglot and therefore mastered not just one but a number of different local languages. Without them, neither a station leader nor a governor could communicate with the local population, nor could court sessions be held, tolls be collected, or chiefs controlled. On the importance of these intermediaries, see Trutz von Trotha, *Koloniale Herrschaft: Zur*

they dominated important branches of trade and trade routes such as the important connection between East and West Africa.[78] In some regions, such as northern Togo, they dominated the entire economy.

Which threats were actually posed by Muslims and which were posed by Protestants or other religious groups in the local population is a different question. What was really at stake in these and numerous other uprisings in the colonies, and what role religion played in them, is, no doubt, also more complicated.[79] It is clear, however, that even if religion did play an important part in anti-colonial movements, no simple causal relationship existed in which the spread of Islam cor-related directly to the proliferation of anti-colonial revolts. The fact that African colonies were characterized by religious plurality that included numerous Islamic, Christian, and other local groups means that we can draw no simple conclusions. Moreover, colonial systems of power varied greatly from region to region, and at times relied on local chiefs, the local population, and the governors.[80] All we know for certain is that the relationship between Islam and anti-colonial uprisings was not the same in any two regions.

## THE FIRST WORLD WAR AND *EL DSCHIHAD*

The situation may have varied widely from one African colony to the next, but London, Paris, and Berlin feared all these uprisings equally, and all three colo-nial powers repeatedly saw them as directly related to Islamic propaganda.[81] While

---

*soziologischen Theorie der Staatsentstehung am Beispiel des 'Schutzgebietes Togo'* (Tübingen, 1994), 176ff.; and on the individual case of district official Hans Gruner and his administrative activity, see Gesa Hollermann, 'Kolonialer Alltag eines Bezirksbeamten: Dargestellt anhand eines Tagebuches des Kolonialbeamten Dr. Hans Gruner in der Zeit von 01.04.1910-31.07.1910' (MA, University of Hannover, 2000).

[78] Viera Pawlikova-Vilhanova, 'Crescent or Cross? Islam and Christian Missions in Nineteenth-Century East and Central Africa', in Ulrich van der Heyden (ed.), *Mission und Gewalt: Der Umgang christlicher Missionen mit Gewalt und die Ausbreitung des Christentums in Afrika und Asien in der Zeit von 1792 bis 1918/19* (Stuttgart, 2000), 79–95.

[79] See the excellent overview by Motadel, 'Islam and the European Empires'; and Paul E. Lovejoy and J. S. Hogendorn, 'Revolutionary Mahdism and Resistance to Colonial Rule in the Sokoto Caliphate, 1905–6', *Journal of African History*, 31/2 (1990), 217–44; on revolutionary Mahdism, see also Klaus Hock, 'Jihâd—Mahdismus—Sklaverei: Eine islamische Tradition der Gewalt im Zentralsudan?', in Ulrich van der Heyden (ed.), *Mission und Gewalt: Der Umgang christlicher Missionen mit Gewalt und die Ausbreitung des Christentums in Afrika und Asien in der Zeit von 1792 bis 1918/19* (Stuttgart, 2000), 67–77.

[80] Some of the uprisings learned from Mahdism a universal language that transcended blood rela-tions, locality, and pre-colonial government structures which could provide a revolutionary impulse, while other uprisings developed it out of class structures and other religious traditions. Pluralistic religious traditions were quite diverse, both from one colony to the next, and within individual col-onies. Some indigenous groups allowed Muslims to hold positions of honor even if they were excluded from affairs of state, while others privileged the Catholic missions, see Patrick J. Ryan, 'Ariadne auf Naxos: Islam and Politics in a Religiously Pluralistic African Society', *Journal of African Religion*, 26/3 (1996), 308–29, on the role of Islam in multi-religious societies in Africa.

[81] In addition, since colonial borders had been drawn cutting directly across historical borders, and since different regions were connected by numerous transportation routes (caravan routes), uprisings frequently affected more than one colonial government.

reports from the African colonies thus provided a starting point for the debate on Islam in Imperial Germany, it was the specific constellation at the start of the First World War that marked a decisive shift in that debate, though not an end to it. This turning point occurred with the First World War. The familiar equation of Islam with grotesquery, slave traders, dull-wittedness, and fanaticism by no means disappeared from the debate in 1914, but now it was judged differently. In October 1914, Max von Oppenheim (1860–1946), an amateur Orientalist and student of Michael Hartmann, wrote a memorandum in which he combined some of the pan-Islamic ideas then circulating in Muslim countries in a way that appealed to German and Ottoman interests alike.[82] He took up pan-Islamic topics and developed the idea that Islam might be used to incite Muslims against the British, French, and Russians.[83] The main idea was that Germany could benefit from pan-Islamic mobilization to foment Muslim disobedience against the Christian colonizing allies France, Britain, and Russia. In concrete terms, he proposed that, first, all Muslim prisoners of war—primarily those Muslims from Algeria and Morocco who were fighting for France, Indians fighting for England, and Tatars from the Russian army[84]—be placed in camps near Berlin built especially for them, and cared for so well that they developed a positive image of Germany. Secondly, in the camps they would be provided with relevant propaganda materials that cast the war against the French, British, and Russians as a jihad, just as the Sultan-Caliph Mehmed V Reshad had stated in a number of fatwas of 14 November 1914.[85] In these fatwas the caliph had called for a 'holy war' against the Entente, which clearly played to Ottoman interests, but suited German interests as well. Oppenheim reasoned that as soon as the prisoners of war realized the necessity of jihad, they could be sent back into the war—but this time on the side of the Ottoman empire. In addition, they could be dispatched to the British and French colonies in their home countries to instigate jihad against the colonial powers.

The German military command actually did open such so-called 'crescent moon' camps in Brandenburg, where they housed some 12,000 prisoners of the Muslim faith during the war, and using newspapers the militiary wrote themselves with the aid of some Orientalist scholarly expertise, tried to convince the prisoners of the necessity of jihad. Prisoners heard lectures on the topic 'What afflicts the Islamic

---

[82] Oppenheim's role is a controversial issue, see Oberhaus, *'Zum wilden Aufstande entflammen'*, 131–35; and Tilman Lüdke, *Jihad Made in Germany: Ottoman and German Propaganda and Intelligence Operations in the First World War* (Münster, 2005), 70–5.

[83] In contrast to other interpretations, Marchand, *German Orientalism*, 438ff., stresses that Max von Oppenheim and the German side were by no means the only ones to develop this policy. She emphasizes that Turkey tried just as hard to promote its interests. On the Ottoman and German propaganda and intelligence operations in the First World War, see the recent studies of Lüdke, *Jihad made in Germany*; and Oberhaus, *'Zum wilden Aufstande entflammen'*.

[84] These Muslims came primarily from the French colonies of Algeria and Tunisia, from West Africa and India, and from Russian areas that had fought for the Entente. For their numbers, see Gerhard Höpp, *Muslime in der Mark: Als Kriegsgefangene und Internierte in Wünsdorf und Zossen, 1914–1924* (Berlin, 1997).

[85] Original wording republished in Margot Kahleyss, *Muslime in Brandenburg—Kriegsgefangene im 1. Weltkrieg: Ansichten und Absichten* (Berlin, 2000), 15.

people?',[86] and the camp newspaper *El Dschihad* defamed British and French colonial rule in Arabic, Tatar, and Russian.[87] At the hastily established 'Intelligence Office for the East' in the Foreign Office, scholars of Islam wrote propaganda poems and appeals intended to show both the greatness of Islam on the one hand and the ignominy of the Entente on the other. More than two million leaflets were printed in eleven Asian and African languages, to be dropped by balloon on enemy troops.[88]

In what way did this large-scale propaganda offensive alter attitudes toward Islam? We can trace two distinct and at first glance contradictory shifts in conceptions of Islam, together with one very clear difference affecting the participants in the debate on Islam. The new tenor in terms of content is easy to see: it was only logical that if—as the relevant literature of German agencies put it—the 'sympathies and interest of the people for Germany' were to be awakened in Muslims, it was necessary to move away from the traditional, negatively charged, essentializing view of Islam as a religion of cruelty.[89] And it was easy to find these new pro-Islamic arguments in the broad pan-Islamic literature which had emerged in the Ottoman empire several decades previously and which was all but unknown in diplomatic German circles. Comments about the gullibility of Muslims and their affinity for the slave trade, about their lack of civilization, and fundamental inferiority were no longer voiced. On the other hand, Max von Oppenheim's suggestions could also draw on convictions that had been forged in the German debate on Islam prior to the First World War.[90] Becker's work on the topic, 'Germany and Islam', was relevant in this regard,[91] as were other pre-war publications[92] by scholars who had linked Islam with fanaticism but who had nevertheless called for a positive approach to the religion, not least because they felt it necessary to cooperate with Muslims in the colonies if uprisings were to be avoided. Thus, von Oppenheim's memorandum took up a line of argument from the debate after 1900 that characterized Islam as barbarous, but nevertheless—or perhaps for this very reason—called for a conciliatory attitude towards Muslims and combined

---

[86] Höpp, *Muslime in der Mark*, 73; see also Christian Koller, *Von Wilden aller Rassen niedergemetzelt: Die Diskussion um die Verwendung von Kolonialtruppen in Europa zwischen Rassismus, Kolonial- und Militärpolitik (1914–1930)* (Stuttgart, 2001), 125ff.

[87] Kahleyss, *Muslime in Brandenburg*, 19.

[88] Oberhaus, '*Zum wilden Aufstande entflammen*', 167; Höpp, *Muslime in der Mark*, 22. Various studies show that this propaganda was far from successful, see Hagen, 'German Heralds of Holy War', 150ff; and also Höpp, *Muslime in der Mark*, and Kahleyss, *Muslime in Brandenburg*.

[89] Nadolny, Instruktion für die Propagandalager, 12 July 1915, Political Archives of the German Foreign Office (Politisches Archiv des Auswärtigen Amtes), Berlin, R 21252, quoted in Höpp, *Muslime in der Mark*, 70.

[90] Hagen, 'German Heralds of Holy War', 150.

[91] Carl H. Becker, *Deutschland und der Islam* (Stuttgart, 1914); see also Hagen, 'German Heralds of Holy War', 154. On the dispute between Becker and the renowned Dutch Orientalist Christian Snouck Hurgronje, see Marchand, *German Orientalism*, 443.

[92] Hagen, 'German Heralds of Holy War', 154, notes that although academic Orientalists did not devise the idea of jihad, they had been quite compliant in helping put it into practice. Höpp, *Muslime in der Mark*, 31, explicitly mentions several of its opponents: Georg Kampffmeyer and the journalist Harry Stuermer, and also the Dutch Orientalist Christian Snouck Hurgronje.

this with pan-Islamic arguments.[93] The propaganda offensive of 1914 thus did not signal a complete break with pre-war argumentation, but it did mark a noticeable shift towards a less disparaging assessment of Islam. This change in terms of content becomes even more apparent when we take another factor into account: that the second and most important group, the missionaries, who had shaped the debates of the pre-war years and whose judgments had been even more explicitly negative than those of researchers, now fell silent. Their silence was a result of the fact that in this new propaganda apparatus there was no place for the mission.[94] The reasons are obvious: Christian missionaries were by definition completely unsuitable candidates for legitimizing jihad; further, because of the government's sometimes pro-Muslim colonial policies in the years before the First World War, missionaries had little desire to act on behalf of the state in this matter.[95] On the contrary, at least as early as the backcountry blockade in Togo, open conflicts about policies concerning Islam had developed between the missions and the colonial government. Missionaries who were suspected of working primarily for the 'arousal of Muslims, which could lead to political unrest',[96] could hardly have been won over to the idea of jihad, even if it was in the name of weakening the wartime enemy.[97] In short, the missions, that to some extent

---

[93] There were ostensibly good reasons for this view, and not just in the German colonial government that depended on the Muslim population in the colonies. Many scholars of Islam had close ties to the government and therefore took colonial interests into account, sometimes offering massive support. Even before 1914, many of these scholars also worked at state-supported educational institutions. Hartmann, for instance, was at the Seminar for Oriental Languages in Berlin, and Becker taught at the Hamburg Colonial Institute, a newly founded institute with close connections to colonial interests. Carl Heinrich Becker later became State Secretary and finally Prussian Minister of Science, Art, and National Education (*Volksbildung*); he, like many others, had close ties to the News Agency for the Orient. On Martin Hartmann and Carl Heinrich Becker, see Marchand, *German Orientalism*, 353ff. See also Mangold, *Eine 'weltbürgerliche Wissenschaft'*, 254. On the close relationship between Islamic Studies and colonial institutions and interests, see also Haridi, *Das Paradigma der 'islamischen Zivilisation'*, 79–84.

[94] We search in vain for missionaries in the propaganda apparatus or news agency, or among the scholars who undertook projects in the camps beginning in 1915. There was only one missionary in the 'Intelligence Office for the East': Ferdinand Grätsch, who was head of the department for India, see Oberhaus, *'Zum wilden Aufstande entflammen'*, 318. On the research done in the 'crescent moon camps', see Kahleyss, *Muslime in Brandenburg*, 33ff. Research was conducted there by Frobenius and the Viennese anthropologist Rudolf Pöch, but also by legal ethnologists. Carl Stumpf also recorded the songs and music of the prisoners for scholarly purposes.

[95] Though the missionaries did not maintain their distance from colonial governments as a matter of principle, they did take a decidedly different position concerning Islam. Here, once again, it is necessary to distinguish very carefully between individual missionary societies, and also between missionary orders and missionary societies. For an overview, see Klaus J. Bade, 'Antisklavereibewegung in Deutschland und Kolonialkriege in Deutsch-Ostafrika 1888–1890: Bismarck und Friedrich Fabri', *Geschichte und Gesellschaft*, 3/1 (1977), 31–58. The positions taken ranged from sometimes open criticism—of individual officials' sexual behavior, for example—to full support, as in the case of the North German Mission, which helped establish a cotton project in Togo based on the concept of folk culture (*Volkskultur*), see Zimmermann, *Anthropology and Antihumanism*.

[96] Westermann, 'Die Verbreitung des Islam in Togo und Kamerun', 246.

[97] Seen against this background, it comes as no surprise that the paradigm 'fanaticism equals Islam' had led to a difference between the positions of missionaries and scholars even before the war. Precisely because the 'fanaticism' argument had prompted colonial governments to adopt a policy of conciliation toward Muslims in the colonies, missionaries were unable to share the government's point of view: Islam posed the most difficult challenge to their missionary work, since they saw in Islam an opponent which was almost impossible to convert. To them, peaceful coexistence with Muslims seemed almost inconceivable. The mission's sometimes openly hostile attitude towards Islam intensified even

had written far more disparagingly about Islam and had openly opposed conciliatory tendencies in the colonial government, even writing a letter of protest against the idea of peaceful coexistence, no longer had a voice in the debate on Islam during the First World War. This in turn reinforced tendencies in the direction of an upward re-evaluation of Islam. However, this upward re-evaluation of Islam was also due to concrete political and military interests and broader foreign-policy concerns, closely related to war aims. This re-evaluation benefited from pan-Islamic arguments, which had been put forward neither in Berlin nor in Africa, neither by scholars nor by missionaries, but by the Westernized intellectuals of the Ottoman empire.

## CONCLUSION

The debate on Islam was triggered by events in the colonies and shifted during the First World War as a result of the changing priorities of German foreign policy. Both in terms of content and the circumstances surrounding its origins, the debate on Islam thus provides yet another indication that Imperial Germany—and its culture of debate—had transnational connections. Moreover, the discussions about Islam show that religious issues remained on the agenda after 1900, and that religious figures were deeply involved in formulating these topics. The First World War itself was framed by religious issues. Finally, the debate demonstrates that Imperial Germany engaged not only in negotiation with Protestants and Catholics, but also with the question of how to judge Islam.[98]

---

further with the introduction of measures such as the backcountry blockade in northern Togo. By imposing this blockade, the general governor of Togo Zech acted just as the British colonial government had done in northern Nigeria and parts of Sudan. In order to counter the idea that mission activity might be encouraging agitation among Muslims, missionaries had always been careful in their journal contributions to claim that 'Mohammedans' already had an inherent tendency towards fanaticism. By way of contrast, the backcountry blockade also helps to explain why missionaries such as Westermann, a member of the North German Missionary Society which was quite active in Togo; had no interest in characterizing Muslims as fanatics, since it was this very attribution that the colonial agencies had used as an argument to keep missionaries out of northern Togo, see Weiss, 'German Images of Islam in West Africa', 60ff., on these connections.

   [98] It also became clear that in this debate Catholicism and Protestantism had more in common than expected, even though arguments and metaphors were used in the debate on Islam that Protestants had used against Catholics in the earlier *Kulturkampf*. In the *Kulturkampf*, too, one denomination had been defamed as having particularly strong tendencies toward fanaticism and superstition (Catholic) and the other (Protestant), had tried to present itself as a rational force. Gross (see n. 2) has done an excellent job of showing what a key role these attributions, and with them an anti-Catholic line of argument, played in public discourse in the German Empire. Borutta, 'Der innere Orient', proposed the thesis that Catholicism had become 'orientalized' at the end of the nineteenth century, i.e. that anti-Catholic rhetoric had used orientalized stereotypes. The same cannot be said of the Islam debate, insofar as Catholics used the same negative ascriptions as Protestants in reference to the 'Orient'. I take issue with Borutta's view of the *Kulturkampf* as a dispute only between two Christian denominations, since it obscures two crucial aspects of the *Kulturkampf*. First, it overlooks the fact that battles were also fought from within the respective denominations. In the debate on Islam we thus find anti-Catholic elements even in the arguments of Catholic missionaries. Second, Borutta overlooks the fact that the *Kulturkampf* also involved battles over the definitions of 'sacred' and 'secular' and the boundaries of different denominations. Similarly, in the Islam debate we have a dispute that also

Discussion of Islam continues in the twenty-first century with some of the same, or similar, tendencies found in the debates of 1900. For example, the equation of violence with Islam, as well as the idea that Islam poses a threat are very common in popular television programs, books, and newspapers.[99] Noticeably missing today, compared with the debate around 1900, is only the third equation of Islam with slavery.[100] Instead, today we often read about a connection between Islam and the repression of women. The headscarf, it is argued, is a specifically Muslim expression of a misogynist attitude and an assault on civil rights, and therefore Muslim women must be freed of this yoke, a narrative of liberation which recalls the imputations of slavery made against Islam.

Even so, this is not a simple case of continuity. The situation is far more complex since, in addition to similarities, there are also obvious differences between the debates of 1900 and those of today. These obvious and important differences between 1900 and the present day notwithstanding, we must also acknowledge that connections exist—connections I would like to mention in the form of two contradictory concluding remarks. First, numerous arguments still made today can be traced back to the missionaries and Orientalist scholars of the late nineteenth and early twentieth centuries. It was they who decisively shaped the debate on Islam over a hundred years ago with strongly held views about the attributes of Islam; these same attributions continue to be of key importance in present-day debates. This also means that contemporary society, which views itself as secular, employs more religiously motivated modes of argumentation than its secular self-image might lead us to believe. Secondly, these lines of argument have their origin in a surprisingly close and enduring connection between the German empire and Africa, something long overlooked by historians. This, in turn, means that global interconnections have a variety of different religious aspects, and that even in self-proclaimed secular societies these aspects exert influence and help to shape the society's debates—in Imperial Germany and today.

---

involves a struggle from within Catholic circles over the position of the Church; in other words, more was involved than purely anti-Catholic propaganda.

[99] See the brilliant overview on anti-Islamic stereotypes by Patrick Bahners, *Panikmacher: Die deutsche Angst vor dem Islam; Eine Streitschrift* (Munich, 2011).

[100] Egon Flaig, *Weltgeschichte der Sklaverei* (Munich, 2009), is an exception.

# 12

# Islam and British Imperial Thought

*Faisal Devji*

## INTRODUCTION

This chapter deals with the complexity of the way in which Islam was perceived in the British empire. It focuses on the ambiguous fear of pan-Islam, but also on the inability of British commentators to turn Islam into an alien object. From the late nineteenth until at least the second decade of the twentieth century, a variety of British imperial officials, experts, and scholars took to describing their empire as a Muslim power. Although it never became the dominant way in which it was seen, identifying the empire in this way had important intellectual and political consequences, both for Britain and for parts of what was coming to be known as the Muslim world during this period.[1] Going well beyond a merely instrumental function, namely appealing to the loyalty of Muslims in the empire, the following pages will show how this identification of Britain as the 'greatest Mohammedan power' not only went on to shape Muslim politics in India, but also allows us to think more critically about Orientalism as a 'Western' discourse. By looking at this theme, this chapter seeks to demonstrate that Orientalism operated in a thoroughly ambiguous and even contradictory way as far as modern or colonial forms of domination are concerned.

Orientalism, argued Edward Said in his famous book of that name, is a discourse characteristic and indeed constitutive of the 'West', which distinguishes it from the 'East', and more particularly the Islamic Middle East, in a generally hierarchical and often violent way.[2] With its thematic roots going back to ancient Greece, Orientalism, Said contended, eventually came to define the way in which colonial powers understood and controlled their Asian and African possessions, starting in the eighteenth century, and it continues to be deployed in American and European political and popular life to this day. While it is a defining narrative for the 'West', Orientalism is also said to have deformed and lent a spurious reality to Muslim perceptions of their own past and present, especially among those who had been subjugated to colonial rule, and thus it remains a deeply influential, if traumatic, discourse in Orient and Occident alike.

---

[1] Cemil Aydin, 'Globalizing the intellectual history of the idea if the "Muslim World"', in Samuel Moyn and Andrew Sartori (eds), Global Intellectual History (New York, 2013), 159–86.
[2] Edward Said, *Orientalism* (London, 2003 (1978)).

One of the marks of Said's success is that it has become impossible, even for those who disagree with him, to discuss the mutual relations of Europeans and Asians or Africans, especially from the age of empire, without referring to his work on Orientalism. This scholarly hegemony exists only because his critics have been unable to proffer an alternative theory to Said's own, one capable of resituating his evidence, and can only cavil at *Orientalism*'s factual inaccuracies, lack of causal connections, and apparently trans-historical claims. But however serious these failings, they do little to tackle the force of Said's argument, which can merely be adjusted here and there to accommodate them. Thus, Robert Irwin, *Orientalism*'s chief critic, can only follow up his revelation of Said's many errors by attributing the fascination that the 'East' held for 'Western' scholars to a 'lust of knowing', the suggestive title of his book on the Orientalists.[3]

It is possible, of course, to contest Said's argument by objecting to large historical narratives in general, but this, too, would require making the case for a disaggregated history in theoretical terms. More productive, perhaps, is an immanent critique that might allow us to gain a more complex understanding of Orientalism, one that is very different from Said's own. And this, I think, is important not least because Said's conception of the 'West's' sempiternal self-making comes uncomfortably close to the visions of those who would glorify its universality and absolute distinction from any other 'culture' or 'civilization'. Indeed, this was noted years ago by Aijaz Ahmad, one of Said's most sophisticated critics, who, unhelpfully for those who are not persuaded by Marxist polemics, attributed what he took to be Said's culturalist argument to his 'cosmopolitan' class position as part of an immigrant elite in the United States.[4]

Ahmad had also recognized Said's divergence from his intellectual role model, Michel Foucault, and this analysis will begin with this point. Using Foucault's category of discourse to describe the simultaneous development of similar themes in all manner of fields, from art and literature to scholarship and diplomacy, Said was able to define Orientalism as a collective project without predicating it to the plan or intentionality of any individual or group. The consequences of Orientalism, in other words, were structural as much, if not more than they were intentional, which might account for its strength. Unlike Foucault, however, Said did not trace the modernity of this discourse by attaching it to any process of institutional regulation or individual discipline, as the former had done with his histories of the clinic or prison. Instead, he claimed that Orientalism, which itself never became a modern discipline, forms a part of many regimes of order, including fields such as history or anthropology, without dominating any single field—apart, perhaps, from Islamic or Middle Eastern Studies.[5]

Like his view of Orientalism, then, Said's critique was also fragmented, since the discourse he professed to analyze could not be said to constitute a disciplinary

---

[3] Robert Irwin, *For Lust of Knowing: The Orientalists and their Enemies* (London, 2007).

[4] Aijaz Ahmad, 'Orientalism and After: Ambivalence and Metropolitan Location in the Work of Edward Said', in Aijaz Ahmad (ed.), *In Theory: Classes, Nations, Literatures* (London, 1992), 159–219.

[5] Said, *Orientalism*, 2.

subject in its own right, and thus remained curiously non-modern. For even in the world of contemporary scholarship, Orientalism, in Said's view, is peculiarly old-fashioned, bringing together philosophical speculation, moral reflection, and amateur ethnography in an almost eighteenth-century fashion. And in this way Orientalism represents not the disciplinary 'invention' of the Middle East, as Said would have it, but rather works to interrupt and even prevent such regimes of knowledge and power. In other words, Orientalism as a 'non-modern' phenomenon may play the opposite role that Said thought it did, and the ubiquity of its themes might serve to illustrate its undisciplined character.

It is clear from Said's very triumph, inspiring as it did the subsequent and often ridiculous 'discovery' of Orientalism in almost every subject of study, that it possesses no historical, geographical, or disciplinary limits. Its lengthy survival, then, is in the nature of a set of literary themes more than institutional processes, as is only appropriate for an essentially non-modern phenomenon. Orientalism's power, therefore, resides precisely in its speculative and fantastical character, one that is capable both of interrupting and supplementing institutional forms of discipline and regulation, if only from outside their demesne. With neither a methodology nor indeed an ontology of its own, then, Orientalism may allow for the interaction and self-transcendence of such institutional forms. And it is in this sense resolutely non-Foucauldian.

If it is neither an art nor a science, Orientalism is incapable of constituting its subjects or objects in any institutional sense, with its themes always available for reversal in the way they had been with figures such as Montesquieu in the eighteenth century. But this entails more than being able to see Persia as a version of France, or, in the nineteenth-century way, of the contemporary Middle East as a version of Europe's past. Instead, the possibility of reversal means that the famous 'otherness', which Said describes as being fundamental to the Orientalist project, remains something transient and threatens, in fact, to lapse into identification. This probably accounts for the Orient's celebrated fascination, which should not be reduced merely to a form of instrumentality, or divided into 'good' and 'bad' versions, as Said regrettably does.

## PATRONIZING ISLAM

One of Said's principal claims is that Islam as an Orientalist subject is grounded in a 'Western' understanding and eventually control of the Middle East. But there is another narrative here, one in which the Middle East turns out to be a false ground for Islam, at least in English-language texts. In fact, the British discourse on Islam was shaped politically as well as conceptually by India, which was not only recognized from the nineteenth century as possessing the world's largest Muslim population, but was also of far greater political and strategic importance to Britain than the Middle East. Until its partition and independence in 1947, then, India defined the Middle East's role in British political and intellectual life, not only because the latter stood on the route between Britain and its Raj, but, more importantly, because India served as a military base and the source of troops used to control large parts of Asia, Africa, and, eventually, even Europe during the two world wars. And as a source of labor, free or indentured, India also made British rule possible well beyond its military needs. After 1947 and India's retreat into a largely domestic military and economic role, the two regions become separated, and Islam was transformed into a different kind of object for American policy.

But in the early nineteenth century, Britain's victory over the French empire under Napoleon, as well as its economic and diplomatic subordination of the Ottomans, meant that invocations of Islam in the English language inevitably possessed an Indian reference, even when it was the Middle East that was being described as that religion's true home. Indeed, we might claim that India played the role of a (false) supplement, as Jacques Derrida might say, one that in reality offered Islam an intellectual and political foundation that its own lands of origin and supposed purity were unable to. Although Said might be right in saying that the Middle East was conceptualized in the name of Islam, we might also argue that Islam was imagined in the name of India, which provided its analytical categories, objects of study, and sense of importance. This was true even at what Said identifies as the founding moment of Orientalism, when Napoleon invaded Egypt, famously accompanied by a team of scholars.

We know from his correspondence and attempted alliance with the Indian ruler Tipu Sultan (1750–99), at that time the scourge of the East India Company, that Napoleon's Egyptian campaign was neither about the Middle East, nor indeed about Islam, so much as it was about France's worldwide competition with the British empire.[6] And we shall soon see that his British enemies represented Napoleon's Egyptian conquest as a threat precisely to their Indian empire, rushing therefore to support the Ottomans against him in possibly their earliest effort to claim the status of Islam's true protectors, something that would become a standard rhetorical gesture, at least in India.

But in doing so, of course, the British were only competing with Napoleon, who spread rumors about his own conversion to Islam and thus set in place a crucial theme in the narrative of imperial Orientalism. For the identification with Islam was at the same time a rejection of a European rival, making it difficult to distinguish who or what was the object of this Orientalist narrative. The French ruler was responsible for establishing religion as the most significant subject for understanding the Middle East.[7] This he did by focusing on the authority of the Prophet rather than that of the ruler, trying to delegitimize both the Ottoman sultan and Egypt's Mamluk rulers in the process. In other words, by asserting his friendship for and even conversion to Islam, Napoleon dealt with Islam in a newly instrumental way as an autonomous object of knowledge, drawing on the writings of important Enlightenment figures such as Voltaire and Rousseau

---

[6] Juan Cole, *Napoleon's Egypt: Invading the Middle East* (New York, 2007).
[7] Cole, *Napoleon's Egypt*, see especially ch. 7.

to do so. Rejecting the old Christian stereotype of Muhammad as an impostor, Napoleon saw him as representing a peculiarly modern form of political 'genius'. And such views, shared by eighteenth-century British writers such as Gibbon and nineteenth-century ones such as Carlyle, ended up informing modern biographies of the Prophet by European and Muslim authors alike.

These Enlightenment thinkers and their descendants located Islam's truth not in any metaphysical or juridical category, such as the Muslim *umma* (community) or the *dar al-Islam* (Islamdom), but in the sheer number of its worldwide following. The new kind of statistical truth represented by Muslim numbers was also invoked by British scholars and statesmen, who started claiming for their empire the status of the world's 'greatest Mohammedan power'. In large measure an attempt to controvert the sources of authority of the Ottoman caliphate, this claim was only possible because of the number of Muslims who lived under British rule in India, and its plausibility became greater as Islam came to be seen in statistical rather than metaphysical terms, as for instance in the category of 'the Muslim world'.

More than a demographic notion, however, Islam, or rather what would come to be known as pan-Islam, represented for European statesmen a way of thinking about the new, world-encompassing politics created by the rivalry of the Great Powers, which after all occurred outside the bounds of traditional European categories and institutions. And this epistemological as much as instrumental manner of considering Islam has re-emerged in our own day, as the global arena coming to light after the Cold War allows Muslims and others to define its still inchoate character in religious terms. Pan-Islamism has always been a shared enterprise, bringing together, even if unequally, Muslims with European scholars, statesmen, and others who sought to understand or control them in joint projects, one that constantly escapes both the systematic and instrumental character that Edward Said attributed to Orientalism.

This project is one in which Islam and the Middle East constitute, at best, ambiguous objects of knowledge, and where the distinction between Occident and Orient is constantly being lost. British officials and experts on Islam such as T. W. Arnold, for instance, were aware that the stirrings of pan-Islamism as an Ottoman policy had its origins in the Treaty of Kuchuk-Kainarji.[8] Signed between the Russian and Turkish empires in 1774, this treaty had given Catherine the Great the right to 'protect' the sultan's Orthodox subjects, and, by a reciprocal arrangement, turned the Ottoman emperor into a religious authority for Muslims outside his dominions in a way that had never before been the case. In its earliest incarnation, however, British concern with pan-Islamism was expressed as an anxiety about an alliance between Napoleon and Muslim rulers such as Tipu Sultan, who represented, in their collective demographic authority, an alternative vision of politics as a world-encompassing practice.

---

[8] See, for instance, T. W. Arnold's mention of this well-known fact in T. W. Arnold, *The Caliphate* (Oxford, 1924), 165–6.

Wilfred Scawen Blunt (1840–1922), an influential British commentator on Islam who advised both Randolph and Winston Churchill, provides a good example of the way in which British political writers were able to think about Islam both as joint project and a site of imperial identification.[9] He described the emergence of pan-Islam as a political problem in two lengthy articles published in 1881 and 1882 in the *Fortnightly Review* and put together as a book later that year. Both articles and book bore the title *The Future of Islam*, and in them Blunt identified Napoleon as the progenitor of pan-Islam, seeing in his invasion of Egypt not simply an effort to cut Britain's route to India and even rouse its inhabitants to rebellion, as British accounts of the time held, but also to claim the caliphate in the same way as the Ottomans had centuries before.[10] Recognizing the crucial role that India played in British anxieties about pan-Islam from the very beginning, Blunt went on to derive Napoleon's politics from Ottoman precedents, rather than opposing the two. Moreover, to make the difference between Islam and Christendom even more indistinct, he proceeded to make Napoleon into the founding figure of pan-Islamic ambition for Muslim monarchs as well, identifying Muhammad 'Ali (1769–1849), who had undertaken the governance of Egypt once Napoleon had been defeated, as the latter's disciple in politics.[11]

Having traced the modern emergence of pan-Islam to Napoleon and Muhammad 'Ali, Blunt described Ottoman attempts to deploy it as a diplomatic instrument, which he thought were unlikely to succeed or prevent the empire's dissolution, eventually, he concluded recommending that Britain in effect take up Islam's protection in an imagined future when North Africa had been colonized by France, Italy, and Spain, and the European and Central Asian territories of the Turks had been taken by Austria-Hungary and tsarist Russia. Islam, thought Blunt, would in this worst-case scenario find a new and more suitable world for its expansion in Africa and Asia, in the process taking over Buddhism's following, while the Royal Navy would guarantee the newly spiritual sovereignty of an Arab caliph based in Mecca, and spearheading a worldwide Islamic revival:

> Islam, if she relies only on the sword, must in the end perish by it, for her forces, vast as they are, are without physical cohesion, being scattered widely over the surface of three continents and divided by insuperable accidents of seas and deserts; and the enemy she would have to face is intelligent as well as strong, and would not let her rest…If she would not be strangled by these influences, she must use other arms than those of the flesh, and meet the intellectual invasion of her frontiers with a corresponding intelligence. Otherwise she has nothing to look forward to but a gradual decay, spiritual as well as political. Her law must become little by little a dead letter, her Caliphate an obsolete survival, and her creed a mere opinion. Islam as a living and controlling moral force in the world would then gradually cease.[12]

[9] Warren Dockter, 'The Influence of a Poet: Wilfrid S. Blunt and the Churchills', *Journal of Historical Biography*, 10 (2011), 70–102.

[10] Wilfred Scawen Blunt, 'The Future of Islam', *Fortnightly Review*, 36 (1881), 326.

[11] Blunt, 'The Future of Islam', 327.     [12] Blunt, 'The Future of Islam', 585.

Blunt's description of Islam's lack of 'physical cohesion' suggested that of Britain's own empire, whose defense depended more on controlling the sea-lanes and canals that connected its various parts than any merely territorial governance. Britain's empire, in other words, could be seen as a homologue or even successor to an Islamic empire, and Blunt was one of the first to suggest in his book that it be seen as the 'world's greatest Mohammedan power', precisely because of the demographic weight that India's Muslims possessed within its realms:

> With the disappearance of the Ottoman Sultan there will no longer be any great Mussulman sovereignty in the world, and the Mohammedan population of India, already the wealthiest and most numerous, will then assume its full importance in the counsels of believers. It will also assuredly be expected of the English Crown that it should then justify its assumption of the old Mohammedan title of the Moguls, by making itself in some sort the political head of Islam.[13]

The characterization of Britain's empire as the world's 'greatest Mohammedan power' would become an abiding trope of imperial rule, with the very distinctiveness of Blunt's analysis flowing easily into a general and even stereotyped account of pan-Islam as a joint enterprise with Christendom. Thus, he invoked what would come to be two familiar themes in closing his article: the world-encompassing nature of a politics that might be conceptualized in the vocabulary of Islam; and, Britain's duty to the Muslims over whom it ruled:

> The Caliphate is a weapon forged for any hand—for Russia's at Bagdad, for France's at Damascus, or for Holland's (call it one day Germany's) in our stead at Mecca. Protected by any of these nations the Caliphate might make our position intolerable in India, filling up for us the measure of Mussulman bitterness, of which we already are having a foretaste in the pan-Islamic intrigues at Constantinople. But enough of this line of reasoning, which after all is selfish and unworthy. The main point is, that England should fulfill the trust she has accepted of developing, not destroying, the existing elements of good in Asia. She cannot destroy Islam, nor dissolve her own connection with her. Therefore, in God's name, let her take Islam by the hand and encourage her boldly in the path of virtue. This is the only worthy course, and the only wise one, wiser and worthier, I venture to assert, than a whole century of crusade.[14]

However cynical it may at times appear, Blunt's narrative was also full of fantasies about Britain's identification and even inter-changeability with Islam, which, in an unusual appeal to Muslims themselves, he described in terms of their religion's final inheritance from the dominance of Europe.[15] Blunt's fantasy of an Anglo-Muslim alliance to govern half the globe was premised on the decline of the Ottoman empire, whose Turkish character was ironically seen as being more foreign to the genius of Islam than Britain's religiously neutral empire. This latter had been formally declared after the suppression of the Indian Mutiny in the Queen's Proclamation of 1858, making the Raj a 'secular' polity even before Britain itself. Although he might have been unusual in mounting such a strong defense of Islam,

---

[13] Wilfred Scawen Blunt, 'The Future of Islam: Conclusion', *Fortnightly Review*, 37 (1882), 40.
[14] Blunt, 'The Future of Islam', 48.        [15] Blunt, 'The Future of Islam', 48.

Blunt was entirely typical of European writers in his desire to save some of Islam's glory, and his vision of Britain as a Muslim power was by no means untypical. Another writer who famously devoted himself to this identification was R. G. Corbet in his 1902 book *Mohammedanism and the British Empire*.[16] And in this they were only the forerunners of a long-standing British narrative, culminating perhaps with the writing and propaganda of T. E. Lawrence, for which the genuinely 'Arab' nature of Islam had to be rescued from Turkish misrule.

Yet, these desires to replace the Ottomans were constantly paired with efforts at convincing India's Muslims in particular that Britain had no intention of interfering with the caliphate. This had the inadvertent consequence of increasing the importance of Ottoman claims for Indian Muslims. Thus, during the Indian Mutiny of 1857, the East India Company secured a decree from the Ottomans legitimizing its rule over Muslims, despite the fact that none of the mutineers seem to have given the Turks any thought at all. Indeed, the major slogans of the rebels drew on themes from the Mughals, for whom the Ottomans were not recognized as constituting any kind of religious authority. Of more consequence were Mughal concepts of sacred kingship that had as their reference Safavid Persia, a rival of the Turks.[17] Even so, and following the precedent set by the Napoleonic Wars, it was not the Ottoman empire or even Persia that presented the British with their imagined enemy, but rather another European power, tsarist Russia, which took the place of France here, one that it would eventually give up to Germany. What kind of object was Islam in this narrative, apart from a thoroughly ambiguous instrument of European conflict, one that could therefore be opposed and identified with at will?

Although some Indian Muslims were concerned with the fate of the Ottomans from late in the nineteenth century, just as they were with that of the Persians or North Africans, it was not until the second decade of the twentieth century, and at least in part because of British concerns about the Turks, that large numbers of them started seeing the Ottomans as the protectors of their religion. But the Mutiny, which represented the most serious military threat faced by any European empire in the whole course of the nineteenth century, quickly came to constitute the single most important illustration of the danger that Islam posed to British power. Indeed, British writers were quick to see 'Wahhabis' playing a role in the Mutiny and Muslim militancy in India for decades afterwards, even if these Arabian puritans posed no danger to them in their own lands. The Middle East, in other words, took both its meaning and its threat from the Indian movements it was meant to influence, thus making for a complex relationship between Islam's lands of origin or 'purity' and its Indian frontier. Indeed, it was precisely this conceptual as much as geographical distance between its origins in Arabia and political importance in India that made it possible for pan-Islamism to become a threat in the first place.

---

[16] R. G. Corbet, *Mohammedanism and the British Empire* (London, 1902).
[17] F. W. Buckler, 'The Political Theory of the Indian Mutiny', *Transactions of the Royal Historical Society*, Fourth Series, v (1922), 71–100.

Yet, this way of thinking about Islam was not instinctual, but had to be put into place gradually. So the earliest reports of the rebellion in India were explicit in identifying its movers as Hindus, with Muslims and Sikhs seen as being loyal to the East India Company. However, once the puppet Mughal emperor had been put at its head, it became possible to conceive of the revolt in Muslim terms, even though the larger number of Hindus involved posed a conceptual problem for British observers, who could only account for it by accusing Muslim conspirators of playing upon the Hindus' superstitious credulity. It was Hindu rather than Muslim 'fanaticism', in other words, that occupied pride of place in such accounts. Given the British concern with demographic threats, however, what kind of danger did Islam pose to British rule in India, where Hindu numbers were so much larger? The next section will look at the subterranean but essential role that Hindu numbers played in colonial fears of pan-Islamism.

## THE FEAR AND SEDUCTION OF PAN-ISLAMISM

In India, as elsewhere in the empire, British concerns with pan-Islamism possessed their own politics; a politics that was as much about positing a special relationship with the country's Muslims and thus leaving the more numerous Hindus out, as it was about constituting Islam as an object of knowledge and rule. We can see how this relationship worked in the nineteenth century by looking at one of the most famous books on the so-called 'Indian Wahhabis' published in 1871 by the colonial administrator W. W. Hunter. This work, which became a textbook for those entering the Indian Civil Service, was titled *The Indian Musalmans: Are They Bound in Conscience to Rebel Against the Queen?* The question it posed was taken from one asked by the viceroy, Lord Mayo (1822–72). Hunter's book assembled what appear to be a few well-worn Orientalist themes about the rebellious nature of Islam, the inherent disposition of Muslims toward fanaticism, and the threat of pan-Islamism into an argument that is itself rather ambiguous. Hunter concluded that although the colonial state was not *dar al-Islam,* the Abode of Islam, Muslim rebels were still not obliged to rise against it. *The Indian Musalmans,* in other words, represented a certain way of considering the Indian Muslim. Did he feel obliged to dissent in a Christian sense? Was his conquering spirit comparable to the civilizing mission of colonialism?

Hunter began by claiming that he was concerned exclusively with Islamic revivalism in Bengal, primarily the Faraizi movement.[18] Over the course of the book, however, he went on to consider Sayyid Ahmad Barelwi's jihad on the Northwest Frontier, and indeed Muslim agitation across India. This mysterious expansion of his subject suggested two things. First, that Muslims were everywhere the

---

[18] W. W. Hunter, *The Indian Musalmans: Are They Bound in Conscience to Rebel Against the Queen?* (Delhi, 1969 (London and Edinburgh, 1871)), 1.

same because Islam was some kind of trans-historical force that determines their thoughts and actions; and secondly, that Islam posed a trans-regional threat:

> It is not the Traitors themselves whom we have to fear, but the seditious masses in the heart of our Empire, and the superstitious tribes on our Frontier, both of whom the Fanatics have again and again combined in a Religious War against us. During nine centuries the Indian people have been accustomed to look for invasion from the north; and no one can predict the proportions to which this Rebel Camp, backed by the Musalman hordes from the westward, might attain, under a leader who knew how to weld the nations of Asia in a Crescentade.[19]

By emphasizing a specifically Muslim menace, namely the threat of a minority concentrated on the borders of the Raj, Hunter permitted himself to ignore or repress the possible danger of a Hindu majority in the heartland. Indeed, the artificiality of this threat was made clear in Hunter's examples of Muslim dissent, which were all insignificant, for no Islamic movement posed a serious threat to the empire until well into the twentieth century. And, in fact, the slightly ludicrous character of Britain's Muslim bogey was apparent to many of Hunter's contemporaries, including even Wilfred Scawen Blunt, who in an account of a visit to India recalled a conversation with Muslim leaders there:

> I told them, if the Mohammedans only knew their power they would not be neglected and ill-treated by the Government, as they now were. In England we were perpetually scared at the idea of a Mohammedan rising in India, and any word uttered by the Mohammedans was paid more attention than that of twenty Hindus.[20]

Considering only the threat of outside agitators and their foreign supporters, of course, permitted Hunter to suppress the possibility of a rebellion inside the minority Muslim community and claiming the majority's loyalty. His denial of real responsibility to Indian Muslims made possible and justified a strategy of policing borders to stop the spread of foreign subversion. Indeed, a belief in the effectiveness of this form of surveillance, which vastly reduced the number of people who had to be dealt with, was important enough to make Hunter stress repeatedly the global dimension of Islamic revivalism, when for instance commenting on the importance of Islam's Middle Eastern source: 'The obligation of the Indian Musalmans to rebel or not rebel, hung for some months on the deliberations of three priests in the Holy City of Arabia.'[21]

Hunter's preoccupation with the threat of pan-Islamism also allowed him to repress any discussion of historical Indian revolts, such as the Mutiny of 1857, which might have indicated a rational dissatisfaction with colonialism and forced him to think about the possibility of Hindu disloyalty. And his use of the term 'Crescentade', which of course evoked the idea of a crusade, took the issue out of the historical present altogether. Moreover his consideration of Islamic revivalism in terms of an exclusive Christian–Muslim relationship did more than simply

---

[19] Hunter, *The Indian Musalmans*, 34–5.
[20] Wilfred Scawen Blunt, *India Under Ripon* (London, 1909), 103–4.
[21] Hunter, *The Indian Musalmans*, 3.

exclude a third, dangerous element: the Hindu. It also allowed the Christian and the Muslim to trade places, for Hunter had a Muslim revivalist take the Christian's place both as crusader and as puritan. Thus, his work was sprinkled with words of praise and admiration for these Islamic puritans, whom he compared to the reformers of the Catholic Church.[22]

Hunter's views provoked sharp criticism from Muslim intellectuals and political leaders. So the famous 'reformer' Sayyid Ahmad Khan (1817–98), in his review of Hunter's *Indian Musalmans,* began by warning the English to censor their views on Muslims, as 'natives anxiously con all articles bearing upon the feelings with which their rulers regard them'.[23] On the one hand, this interesting advocacy of secrecy no doubt reflected on Ahmad Khan's efforts to represent the English in a good light, efforts that were defeated by books such as Hunter's. On the other hand, Ahmad Khan's call for censorship simply allowed him to put his constituency of loyal and educated Muslims forward as brokers between the British and India's Muslims as a whole by playing on the former's fear of Islamic puritanism:

> The evils that now exist, however, owe their origin greatly to the want of union and sympathy between the rulers and the ruled, and ideas like Dr. Hunter's only tend to widen the gap. I admit that owing to the difference in the mode of life, there is but a limited number of native gentlemen with whom European gentlemen can have cordial intercourse; but this number will, I trust, increase largely every year.[24]

In order to achieve this brokering ambition Ahmad Khan had to raise insistently the possibility of a Muslim threat in a work, and indeed a career, that was ostensibly devoted to proving the loyalty of India's Muslims. And he used this threat quite consciously to obtain the maximum advantage, as in the following passage:

> I cannot, however, predict what the actual conduct of the Musalmans would be in the event of an invasion of India by a Mahomedan or any other power. He would be a bold man indeed who would answer for more than his intimate friends and relations, perhaps not even for them. The civil wars in England saw fathers fighting against sons, and brothers against brothers; and no one can tell what the conduct of the whole community would be in any great political convulsion. I have no doubt, but that the Musalmans would do what their political status—favorable or the contrary—would prompt them to do.[25]

This barely veiled threat raised two more themes in the English fear of Islam: pan-Islamism and Protestant iconoclasm (the latter implied in Sir Sayyid's reference to the English Civil War). Again, Sir Sayyid played on these fears while simultaneously using them to tie the English and Muslims together historically in a special relationship. So he said about Hunter's 'Mahomedan Puritans' that 'In

---

[22] Hunter, *The Indian Musalmans,* 51, 67, and 100.
[23] Sayyid Ahmad Khan, *Review on Dr Hunter's Indian Musalmans: Are They Bound in Conscience to Rebel Against the Queen?* (Lahore, n.d.), 5–6.
[24] Ahmad Khan, *Review on Dr Hunter's Indian Musalmans,* 50.
[25] Ahmad Khan, *Review on Dr Hunter's Indian Musalmans,* 45.

my opinion, what the Protestant is to the Roman Catholic, so is the Wahabi to the other Mahomedan creeds.'[26] It appears that the Muslim reformer here was the one making a political career out of British superstition rather than the reverse. After all, Hunter's fear of pan-Islamism, familiar enough as a classic Orientalist trope, was nevertheless disturbed by his equally strong identification with it.[27]

## MUSLIM RECEPTIONS

The First World War marked the apogee as well as the destruction of such an imperial model of pan-Islamism, with India's Muslims being at the forefront of an agitation for the protection of Turkey's suzerainty of Islam's holy places after its defeat. This defeat, of course, had been accomplished with the support of Muslim troops in the Indian army, and the British, worried as they always were about the loyalty of these soldiers, had pledged not to interfere with the great sites of Muslim pilgrimage in Iraq and Arabia.[28] While they fought a propaganda battle with the caliph's German allies, who claimed to be acting in the name of Islam, and kept close watch on pan-Islamic plots, of which there were several, the British could not have imagined that the threat they so feared would end up taking the form it did.[29] For the Khilafat movement's massive agitations between 1919 and 1922 brought Hindus and Muslims together to contest British authority for the first time since the Mutiny of 1857.

F. W. Buckler, a British expert on Islam in India, was not the only Englishman of the time who commented on the similarity between the Mutiny and the Khilafat movement, and in an article for the *Contemporary Review* went on to argue that the latter had been made possible by Britain's betrayal of its obligations as a Muslim power. Tracing the history of British rule in India from the East India Company's acceptance of the suzerainty of a Muslim monarch, which, he held, was reinforced by its repeated deployment of Islamic idioms of loyalty subsequently, Buckler concluded that only by reasserting her long-standing admission of a specifically Muslim authority might Britain regain legitimacy in India. In the following passage, for instance, he accuses the Company of trying to subvert both the British and Mughal monarchies, and, having succeeded in the latter, being removed from power by the former in the person of Queen Victoria, who was then seen by Indians

[26] Ahmad Khan, *Review on Dr Hunter's Indian Musalmans*, 7.
[27] For more examples of this fear among British politicians, see David B. Edwards, 'Mad Mullahs and Englishmen: Discourse in the Colonial Encounter', *Comparative Studies in Society and History*, 31/4 (1989), 649–70; David Steele, 'Lord Salisbury, the "False Religion" of Islam, and the Reconquest of the Sudan', in Edward M. Spiers (ed.), *Sudan: The Reconquest Reappraised* (London, 1998), 11–34; and Alex Padamsee, *Representations of Indian Muslims in British Colonial Discourse* (New York, 2005).
[28] See the chapter by John Slight in this volume.
[29] For accounts of some of these conspiracies, see Kris K. Manjapra, 'The Illusions of Encounter: Muslim "Minds" and Hindu Revolutionaries in First World War Germany and After', *Journal of Global History*, 1/3 (2006), 363–82; and Majid Hayat Siddiqi, 'Bluff, Doubt and Fear: The Kheiry Brothers and the Colonial State, 1904–45', *Indian Economic and Social History Review*, 24/3 (1987), 233–63.

to assume the protection of Islam (and Hinduism) from it. But the removal of the Mughal emperor had as its consequence a turn to the Ottoman caliphate, given Britain's inability to lay full claim to her Islamic role:

> The root of the trouble, then, would appear to lie in the falsehood of the East India Company, which misinterpreted the East to the West, and belittled the religious feeling which centred upon Muslim Monarchy in general, and the Mughal Emperor in particular, as *Khalifah*. It is the *damnosa hereditas* of the practical man's *régime*. The Company's policy was to enslave two monarchies—the Mughal and the British—the former, by the capture of offices, the latter, by means of 'placemen' in Parliament. The Reform Act of 1832 stopped the progress of corruption in Britain, but not before the Mughal *jagir* (fief) had been turned, in the West, into 'British Territory' by the British retort to the Company's impossible claim of 1812. His Majesty's Opposition could fight its battles in Parliament, while Sindia had only the field of battle on which to argue, for whenever he attempted to assert his Master's rights in discussion, the Company's Resident at Delhi used, as his ultimate argument, the threat of hostilities. Therefore, the Company failed in England, but in India it succeeded, and Bahadur Shah II was deposed in 1858. His own *Khalifah* had gone, and so the Indian Muslim looked to Rum. Whatever criticism in detail may be advanced against the technical qualifications of the Sultan of Turkey's claim to be the *Khalifah* of the Prophet and Leader of the Faithful, it sinks into insignificance before the title of recognition by the unanimous voice of the Faithful.[30]

Having laid out an alternative history of British rule in India from the perspective of Islamic political concepts of authority, in which it no longer possessed the grandiosity of a writer like Blunt's vision, Buckler proceeded to recommend that only a recognition of its Islamic character might save the Raj:

> A diagnosis, if sound, should of itself suggest some possible line of treatment, if the case be not already hopeless. By this time it may be; but, if not, the clue would seem to lie in going behind the false position set up by the Company—behind 1773, by recognising that the English in India, in accepting tokens of Mughal suzerainty and presenting symbols of allegiance, had entered the *Respublica Moslemica* as loyal members; by claiming a *Muslim* motive in the stoppage of revenue (1773), the Wars against Tipu and against the Mahrattas; by acknowledging that the action of the Queen of England in 1857–8 was that of an *external power*, protecting the lives of its *natural* subjects, the servants of the Company, and not as a suzerain reducing a rebellious vassal; that the deposition of Bahadur Shah II was by right of victory in that war, which his miscarriage of justice and its awful consequences had rendered inevitable; that her Government did punish the true culprit—the East India Company—by sentence of suppression. That acknowledgement involves the identity of Great Britain with the *Respublica Moslemica*, and it will force her to reconsider her view on the subjects of Persia, Turkey, Egypt, Palestine and the Hedjaz—to mention only the chief non-Indian problems, which affect Indian opinion, but where her intervention could be effective.[31]

---

[30] F. W. Buckler, 'The Historical Antecedents of the Khilafat Movement', *Contemporary Review*, 121 (1922), 610.

[31] Buckler, 'The Historical Antecedents of the Khilafat Movement', 610–11.

Whatever the reality of its links with Islamic political thought, it is interesting to note that Buckler's argument, probably the most sophisticated narrative of Britain as a Muslim power, did in fact have some resonance among the Indians agitating for the caliphate's protection by Britain. So when Gandhi, who was formally invested by India's Muslim prelates and politicians as the movement's leader, justified Muslim resentment at Turkey's dismemberment after its defeat, he could draw upon a common understanding of pan-Islam as an element of British as much as Muslim politics. This he did when citing the following words of Prime Minister David Lloyd George, referring to his wartime pledge to India that the sacred sites of Islam would not be taken away from Ottoman control:

It is too often forgotten that we are the greatest Mahomedan power in the world and one-fourth of the population of the British Empire is Mahomedan. There have been no more loyal adherents to the throne and no more effective and loyal supporters of the Empire in its hour of trial. We gave a solemn pledge and they accepted it. They are disturbed by the prospect of our not abiding by it.[32]

Only much later and indeed after her independence would factors such as socialism, anti-colonialism, non-alignment, and finally nuclear capability and economic prowess permit India to play as important a *political* role in the world as pan-Islam, which thus signified an effort to imagine the contours of a new world emerging from the dissolution of the old one which had been defined by the Congress of Vienna. But it is also important to remember that the Khilafat movement, so often and contradictorily judged as nationalist or pan-Islamic in its politics, was nevertheless loyal because it petitioned the colonial government not as potential Ottoman subjects but British ones:

What is this British Empire? It is as much Mahomedan and Hindu as it is Christian. Its religious neutrality is not a virtue, or if it is, it is a virtue of necessity. Such a mighty Empire could not be held together on any other terms. British ministers are, therefore, bound to protect Mahomedan interests as any other.[33]

And it was because he sought to fulfill the universality of this empire as the world's greatest 'Mohammedan power' that Gandhi argued with the British on the basis of their own political rhetoric, thus exposing its hollowness:

If India is to remain equal partner with every other member of the Empire, India's voting strength must be infinitely superior to that of any other member... Thus, the centre of equilibrium must shift to India rather than remain in England, when India has come into her own. That is my meaning of Swaraj within the Empire... To-day we are striving for Swaraj within the Empire in the hope that England will in the end prove true, and for independence if she fails. But when it is incontestably proved that Britain seeks to destroy Turkey, India's only choice must be independence.[34]

---

[32] M. K. Gandhi, 'Mr Candler's Open Letter', *Young India* (26 May 1920), 3.
[33] Gandhi, 'Mr Candler's Open Letter', 3.
[34] M. K. Gandhi, 'The Turkish Question', *Young India* (29 June 1921), 1.

Given its reliance on the force of arms, in other words, only the force of truth or *Satyagraha* was capable of doing justice to the British empire by compelling it to be true to itself. And this, in Gandhi's view, was the essence of loyalty, seen as the desire to save Britain, alien though its soul was, from an inner disintegration wrought by the lust for power.

## CONCLUSION

This chapter has explored a number of British conceptions about the place of Islam in the empire. It has enquired into the notion of Britain as a 'Mohammedan power' for which India was crucial, not only because of its enormous Muslim population and important role in making possible Britain's rule over large parts of Asia and Africa, but also because it seemed to have a mysterious and even mystical relationship with the Middle East. And yet, this anxiety, which we have seen expressed in British accounts hostile to Islam, never led pan-Islamism to be taken for an object of knowledge or control in its own right, but only as part of an intra-European struggle in which Muslims occupied a most ambiguous status as possible friends as much as enemies. Rather than British views of Islam representing 'good' and 'bad' versions of Orientalism, then, as Edward Said would have it, even negative accounts of the religion dealt with it in ambiguous ways that never managed to escape the seduction of identification with the Prophet's followers.

Eventually, however, the Muslim and Hindu subjects of Britain's empire came to inhabit, appropriate, and transform its characterization as the world's greatest Mohammedan power, making an anti-colonial category out of it. But because this Orientalist narrative was never fully institutionalized or constrained by the kinds of disciplinary and regulative measures that might make it part of a discourse in Foucault's sense of that word, it always managed to float free of such forms and was incapable, therefore of 'constructing' either a self-identity or one belonging to another. On the contrary, as a non-discursive or even non-modern form of thought, it served to interrupt and limit the disciplinary and regulative measures on which colonial rule increasingly depended, and in this way described it in some sense from outside their reach.

# 13

# French Colonial Knowledge of Maraboutism

*George R. Trumbull IV*

## INTRODUCTION

'God knows Maymunia, and Maymunia knows God.' With this gnomic pronouncement, a wandering saint welcomed an influential French scholar, translator, and bureaucrat to Fez at the turn of the twentieth century. Opaque though her statement was, it nonetheless situated her in a clear religious context: that of local traditions of sainthood, personal mysticism, and piety on the boundaries of ecstasy and apparent madness. Often referred to in colonial texts as maraboutism, such local practices occurred throughout the Maghrib. Faced with the not unrepresentative impenetrability of statements such as that of Maymunia, colonial writers on Islam never articulated an exclusive definition of the marabout or agreed on an ultimate import for maraboutism itself. Nevertheless, marabouts attracted much attention from colonial bureaucrats as a potential source of political disruption in the colony. However vague the definition of the term, administrators largely concurred that maraboutism played a major political role.

French policies towards Islam emerged out of more generalized anxieties about the role of religion in the colonial state.[1] Missionaries, resurgent indigenous religions, transnational religious organizations, and local practices occupied administrators throughout the empire. Moreover, Islam posed a particularly challenging epistemological problem for colonial administrators, as the faith's textual emphasis on its universal mission and the unity of the *umma* often did not correspond exactly to the myriad local practices of Muslims in North and West Africa. Although colonial writers tried to take diversity into account, French generalizations about Islamic diversity rarely corresponded to the experiences of Muslims themselves. Most notably, the racialization of Islam through the articulation of spurious concepts of an *Islam noir* attempted to divide Muslim belief, practice, and politics according to imposed divisions of black and white. These patterns of

[1] J. P. Daughton, *An Empire Divided: Religion, Republicanism, and the Making of French Colonialism, 1880–1914* (Oxford, 2006); and Charles P. Keith, 'Catholicisme, bouddhisme, et lois laïques au Tonkin (1899–1914)', *Vingtième siècle*, 87/3 (2005), 113–28.

religiosity did not map cleanly on to colonial politics, nor less to skin color.[2] Even in Algeria, where purportedly 'racial' differences in Islam attracted little attention, colonial administrators and scholars attempted to categorize the politics of individual Muslims according to identity as Kabyle or Arab.[3]

Administering France's longest-held and most intensively controlled colony, bureaucrats in Algeria produced the preponderance of texts on the politics of maraboutism. Mystical practices dominated French colonial texts on Algerian Islam. In particular, Sufi orders, with their wide geographic spread, organized structure, and often secretive practices, obsessed colonial administrators and the experts so closely linked with their work. Indeed, Sufi leaders, most notably those of the Rahmaniyya, Sanusiyya, and Tijaniyya, played major political roles in Mauritania, Algeria, and throughout the Sahara. Scholars have traced these varying colonial perceptions and interpretations of Sufi orders and their politics in a wide variety of important works.[4] Other mystical practices, associated though not coterminous with Sufism, have received less attention, however.

The construction of French expertise about Algerian Islam revolved around demonstrating mastery over its popular forms. The most able colonial administrators and the scholars with easiest access to governmental resources conducted detailed fieldwork, in specific locales in Algeria. In particular, by the late nineteenth century, the colonial state in Algeria developed a mutually reinforcing apparatus of scholarly publishing and bureaucratic promotion.[5] French scholars and administrators of empire concentrated on mystical, popular, and less-institutionalized forms of Islam, largely out of fear that they escaped the strict surveillance to which they subjected the urban 'ulama.[6] They disaggregated from Sufism the veneration of local holy people and sites of pilgrimage. Labeled 'maraboutism', these forms of mysticism embodied a locally situated piety. Although scholars on West and Sahelian Africa have long acknowledged the importance of marabouts, of their local influence, and of their local spatial contexts, France's experience in Algeria, its first sustained encounter with local forms of mysticism outside the Catholic tradition, produced a rich variety of texts attempting to define and come to terms with the religious, social, and political meanings of local piety. Indeed, the Algerian colonial bureaucracy institutionalized the production of knowledge about marabouts not

---

[2] Christopher Harrison, *France and Islam in West Africa, 1860–1960* (Cambridge, 1988); and David A. Robinson, *Paths of Accommodation: Muslim Societies and French Colonial Authorities in Senegal and Mauritania, 1880–1920* (Athens, OH, 2000).

[3] Patricia Lorcin, *Imperial Identities: Stereotyping, Prejudice and Race in Colonial Algeria* (London, 1999).

[4] Jamil Abun-Nasr, *The Tijaniyya: A Sufi Order in the Modern World* (Oxford, 1965); Julia Clancy-Smith, *Rebel and Saint: Muslim Notables, Populist Protest, Colonial Encounters (Algeria and Tunisia, 1800–1904)* (Berkeley, 1997); Harrison, *France and Islam in West Africa*; Robinson, *Paths of Accommodation*; Jean-Louis Triaud, *La légende noire de la Sanusiyya: Une confrérie musulmane saharienne sous le regard français (1840–1930)*, 2 vols (Paris, 1995); Jean-Louis Triaud and David A. Robinson, *La Tijaniyya: Une confrérie musulmane à la conquête de l'Afrique* (Paris, 2000); and George R. Trumbull IV, *An Empire of Facts: Colonial Power, Cultural Knowledge, and Islam in Algeria (1870–1914)* (Cambridge, 2009), ch. 3.

[5] Lorcin, *Imperial Identities*; and Trumbull, *An Empire of Facts*, ch. 1.

[6] Allan Christelow, *Muslim Law Courts and the French Colonial State in Algeria* (Princeton, 1985).

solely for intellectual purposes, but more expressly to attempt to control the influence of the marabouts and to ascertain their political views on the colonial project.

## EXPERTISE AND THE POLITICAL DEFINITION OF THE 'MARABOUT'

The term 'marabout' derives from the root r-b-t, denoting connection, attachment, garrisoning. In the Maghribi context, however, it denotes a range of attributes, some attached to Islamic notions of the saint (*wali*) and some, such as the veneration of *dead* holy people and specific, physical locales, transcending them. The attribute of holiness conferred through divine blessing (*baraka*) is heritable, in contrast to Sufi orders, which any Muslim may join. For administrators, maraboutism referred to practices honoring local holy people (living or dead), their families, and the places associated with them, as distinct from Sufi mysticism. Although it often implied an inherited component, at times this aspect was more notional or professed than strictly genealogical. Though maraboutism and Sufism are distinct phenomena, they are overlapping, and not mutually exclusive. The distinction between marabout and Sufi frequently mattered more to non-Muslim administrators than it did to Maghribi Muslims, especially as many members of maraboutic families affiliated with Sufi orders, and the prestige of particular orders often took root from connections with maraboutic *baraka*.

Nevertheless, French administrators and scholars devoted much attention to defining maraboutism with the goal of better bringing local mystics to heal. Louis Rinn (1838–1905), administrator, scholar, and deeply knowledgeable about Algerian Islam, distinguished the two varieties of mysticism in his landmark *Marabouts et khouan* (1884), both from each other and from the 'ulama, whom he incorrectly labeled the 'clergy'.[7] Indeed, Rinn pursued this analogy with Christian mysticism, categorizing Islamic practices by their relationship to a notional official hierarchy owing more to Catholicism than to the decidedly more decentralized operations of Muslim clerics or mystics. 'The first category', contended Rinn, 'comprises the Muslim clergy, invested and salaried under the same title as the other religions recognized by French laws. The second category is composed of *local marabouts*, free religious figures exercising the rights of the priesthood or of Islamic teaching.' He concluded, 'the third and last category includes the congregant religious orders'. For Rinn more so than for the Algerians he purported to describe, 'these three categories are almost always absolutely distinct and separate'.[8] Thus, Rinn categorized each division of Muslim forms of piety by associating them

---

[7] *Khouan* (literally, 'brothers'; *ikhwan* in classical Arabic) denoted members of a Sufi order. On Rinn, see Trumbull, *An Empire of Facts*, 21–5; and John Strachan, 'Murder in the Desert: Soldiers, Settlers and the Flatters Expedition in the Politics and Historical Memory of European Colonial Algeria, 1830–1881', *French History and Civilization*, 4 (2011), 217–20.

[8] Louis Rinn, *Marabouts et khouan: Étude sur l'Islam en Algérie* (Algiers, 1884), 6.

with *social*, as opposed to religious, functions: the 'official' clergy; the congregationalist Sufis, and the free, *local* marabouts.

Moreover, Rinn locally contextualized the marabout, not merely through his use of italics, but in detailing the specific bonds that connected marabout to community. Marabouts undertook their religious offices, he noted, 'in edifices that belong to them, or constructed and maintained by the piety of the faithful (zaouïa,...djama, mesdjed, kobba, etc.)'.[9] These physical locations testify to the embodied nature of holiness: *jami'* and *masjid* refer to mosques, and *qubba* to the memorial shrines that mark the tombs of holy people and that serve as sites of pilgrimage. *Zawiya*, however, attests to the ambiguity of the categories whose fixity Rinn avowed: the term can refer to a small mosque associated with a saint but, in the context of nineteenth-century Algeria, denoted almost exclusively private quarters for prayer and communal gathering, as often that of a Sufi order as of a marabout. The term indicates the overlap among categories Rinn portrayed, incorrectly, as discrete.

Rinn exercised a preponderant influence on the genesis of official *policy* on the marabouts. Simply put, *Marabouts et khouan* functioned not merely as a codification of French knowledge about Islamic mysticism, but also as a manual for practice. The colonial administration insisted that every local administrative library had a copy, expressing dismay at its occasional absence. *Marabouts et khouan* was quickly transformed from a text into a category of knowledge itself; the phrase '*marabouts et khouan*' became used as on the title for files of surveillance documents produced by even the most petty of colonial bureaucrats regarding Muslim notables in their jurisdictions. Rinn created marabouts as a codified object of surveillance, an object of political intervention policing religious behavior as a subset of politics. After *Marabouts et khouan*, the surveillance of both marabouts and Sufi mystics became one of the most basic and certainly the best attested tasks of colonial bureaucrats.[10]

Indeed, the very opacity of the marabout attracted the attention of other scholar-administrators, many of whom attempted categorizations through more functional rubrics than those of Louis Rinn. Edmond Doutté, ethnographer, scholar, administrator, and expert on Algerian and Moroccan Islam, who had started out teaching administrators about Islam, and was later employed in the colonial bureaucracy to codify and implement a more systematized means of producing knowledge about Algerian Islam, analyzed the centrality of *baraka* to the definition of the marabout:[11]

---

[9]  Rinn, *Marabouts et khouan*, 6.

[10]  Following the publication of *Marabouts et khouan*, the voluminous AGGA, série H recorded in minute and often mundane detail the operations of local mystics under the rubric 'marabouts et khouan'.

[11]  On Doutté, see Trumbull, *An Empire of Facts*; Abdellah Hammoudi, *The Victim and its Masks: An Essay on Sacrifice and Masquerade in the Maghreb* (Chicago, 1993), 26; and Edmond Doutté, 'Au pays des Moulaye Hafid', *Revue de Paris* (1 October 1907), 481–508.

How does one become a marabout?...science [i.e., in the Islamic sense of knowledge of the Qur'an], good works, reputation for justice, asceticism, mystical practices, insanity and even imbecility can result in the dignity of a marabout. Once acquired, the quality is hereditary: it assures moreover to its possessor such privileges that it is rare that his descendants let it be lost...If the son of a marabout neglects to exercise the influence that they hold from their ancestors, the traditions that attribute *baraka* to them end up vanishing, unless a more gifted descendant knows how to recall the faithful to him.[12]

Doutté's last sentence introduced an instability into his own definition, allowing for the strategic resuscitation of maraboutic stature. Moreover, Doutté hinted that such a recovery might arise for less than pious reasons; the social privilege of *baraka* defined maraboutism at least as much as piety.

In a synthetic work aimed at introducing Islam to the fairgoers at the Exposition Universelle of 1900, Doutté elaborated on his definition of maraboutism, culled from his conversations with holy people. Rich, poor, filthy, cultivated, virtuous, greedy, male, female, learned, pious, insane, ascetic, sybaritic—in a dazzling variety of forms and personae the marabout emerged from Doutté's text.[13] Once again, Doutté traced out a definition as much social as religious, more bound up in communal behaviors such as clothing, diet, and comportment than in specific religious practices.

Doutté exemplified the imbrication of scholarship, administration, and policy. An instructor in Tlemcen and later Algiers, he focused specifically on training future colonial administrators in the study of Islam and the ethnographic methods he used in his own work. When illness menaced Doutté with poverty, and hence also threatened to limit his continued production of useful texts, the administration in Algiers hired him expressly to continue the codification of knowledge about mystical Islam. His seemless transition from scholar to administrator reflects the influence scholarship had on policy; the production of texts about mystical Islam represented, for higher administrators, enough of a central element to the formation of policy to hire Doutté, and others like him, rather than risk the cessation of their work.[14]

---

[12] Edmond Doutté, *Les Marabouts: Notes sur l'Islam maghribin* (Paris, 1900), 73; A. Hanoteau and A. Letourneux, *La Kabylie et les coutumes kabyles*, 2 vols (Paris, 1893), ii, 83 and 93; Fernand Hugonnet, *Souvenirs d'un chef de bureau arabe* (Paris, 1858), 46; Paul Lapie, *Les civilisations tunisiennes: Musulmans, Israélites, Européens* (Paris, 1898), 246; and Rinn, *Marabouts et khouan*, 15.

[13] Edmond Doutté, *L'Islam algérien en l'an 1900* (Algiers, 1900), 45–7.

[14] 'Rapport à Moniseur le Gouverneur Général: Au sujet de M. Doutté', Algiers, 3 June 1901; Governor General, 'Note pour le Secrétaire Général du Gouvernement', n.d, Archives Nationales d'Outre Mer (hereafter ANOM), Archives du Gouvernement Général de l'Algérie (hereafter AGGA), 4H/32; see 'Note pour Monsieur le Sécrétaire Général du Gouvernement', 26 Feburary 1901, Algiers; Edmond Doutté, *L'Islam algérien en 1900, Exposition Universelle de 1900, Algérie* (Algiers-Mustapha, 1900); Edmond Doutté to Governor General, 17 June 1901, Rabat, AGGA, 4H/32; Edmond Doutté to Governor General, 16 July1901, Tangier, cf. 'Programme des études qui seront pourvsuivies par M. Doutté dans sa mission au Maroc', n.d., AGGA, 4H/32; Edmond Doutté to Governor General, Marrakesh, 26 April 1902, AGGA, 4H/32; Edmond Doutté to Governor General, Mogador, 18 May 1901, AGGA, 4H/32; Governor General to the General Commanding the Division of Constantine, 12 March 1902, Algiers, AGGA, 1K/288; Colonel Rougon, Commander of the 3rd Regiment of Spahis, to General Commanding the Division of Constantine, Batna, 28 March 1901; Edmond Doutté,

## THE POLITICS OF MIRACLES

The miracles of the marabouts tied their social and religious roles together. Effected by those endowed with *baraka*, these acts of faith and for the faithful cemented the role of a marabout as an active participant in daily lives. The ambiguity of belief in divine intervention and miraculous intermediaries permeated French understandings of such events and catalyzed a deep fascination with their forms and outcomes. In his ambitiously named study of local practices and folklore, *L'Arabe tel qu'il est* (*The Arab As He Is*) (1900), the erstwhile administrator Achille Robert scornfully cataloged the purported miracles of marabouts as evidence of Muslim credulity and backwardness. In 1866, in the mountains of north-central Algeria, one Ali ben el Akhdar ('Ali bin al-Akhdar), convinced of his divinely granted invulnerability to bullets and 'whose religious exaltation was at its height', successfully goaded his half-brother into killing him, while another mystic changed himself into a lion to protest the laxity of Muslims in his community.[15] According to Robert, such events evinced, not personal spirituality, but an unparalleled credulity. 'The Arab people', he claimed, 'is one of the most superstitious in the world. There is no marvelous fact, a miracle that does not immediately gain credence among them.'[16] 'Credence' in the powers of holy people had, after all, a long history of fomenting rebellion in colonial Algeria.[17]

Achille Robert demonstrated the inseparability of scholarly texts, administrative expertise, and popular publications. The colonial administration encouraged its employees to publish texts drawing on their experiences *in situ*, and frequently rewarded them with promotion, subventions, access to publishers, and large-scale purchases of the resulting texts.[18] He dedicated *L'Arabe tel qu'il est* to René Basset, a foundational figure in Islamic studies in the twentieth century, major interlocutor of the colonial government, and Robert's teacher, but his handwritten, personal dedication to the director of the governor general's office offered 'the homage of the author, A. Robert, administrator'.[19] Robert, like Rinn, Doutté, and almost all those publishing on marabouts, did not separate his role as expert and bureaucrat, as author and administrator.

In 1913, Lucien Bertholon and Ernest Chantre published a major work on Berber identity, *Recherches anthropologiques dans la Berbérie orientale: Tripolitaine, Tunisie, Algérie*. In comparison to Robert, Chantre had only scholarly connections with the colonial administration, working in a provincial museum in Lyons. The

'A Rabat, chez Abdelaziz: Notes prises en 1907', *Bulletin de la Société de Géographie et d'Archéologie d'Oran*, 33/1 (1910), 21–68; Brives, *Voyages au Maroc*, 358–60; and Ch. René-Leclerc, 'Bibliographie: Le Maroc connu', *Bulletin de la Société de Géographie et d'Archéologie de la Province d'Oran*, 23 (1903), 359–66.

[15] Achille Robert, *L'Arabe tel qu'il est: Études algériennes et tunisiennes* (Algiers, 1900), 50–2; see also Division d'Alger, Etat-Major de la Première Division, Section des Affaires indigènes, no. 119: 'Au sujet des agissements du nommé Abdallah ben Mebrouk', General commanding the division of Constantine to Governor General of Algeria, 19 February 1877, ANOM, AGGA 16H/1.

[16] Robert, *L'Arabe tel qu'il est*, 50.          [17] Clancy-Smith, *Rebel and Saint*, 91–125.

[18] Trumbull, *An Empire of Facts*, ch. 1.

[19] Robert, *L'Arabe tel qu'il est*, title page, ANOM, AGGA, Bibliothèque.

primary author, Lucien Bertholon, had risen through the ranks as an army doctor and general secretary of the *Institut de Carthage* in Tunis. Their collaboration proved fruitful, 'honored with subventions from the Tunisian and Algerian governments, by the Academy of Sciences, Belles-Lettres and Arts of Lyons, and the French Association for the Advancement of Sciences'.[20] The very publication of their work both exemplified and profited from the close association of colonial governance and intellectual production.

Like Robert, they focused on miracles as evidence of larger principles about Muslim belief and practice. The two traced multiple maraboutic traditions among Berbers, most notably healing, the ability to create wells and streams, the ability to remedy sterility, and the punishment of false testifiers. Such practices mitigated the uncertainty of daily life and provided succor to the ill, disquieted, or calumnied. For the two scholars, however, these beliefs testified to the fundamentally different nature of Islam among Berbers.[21] 'A survey of the cult of marabouts...will make known an example of this indigenous pantheism.'[22] Islam explicitly disavows pantheism as equivalent to *shirk* or polytheism. Bertholon and Chantre, erring in identifying maraboutism as especially Berber, used popular practices to erect arbitrary and spurious distinctions of Muslimness among ethnic groups, distinctions that in turn contributed to the creation of policies that treated the religious politics of Berbers and Arabs differently.[23]

Similarly, the scholar Alfred Bel, reviewing a work by Edmond Doutté, interpreted the importance of maraboutic *baraka* as transmitted through physical locations and bodily fluids and remnants (saliva, blood, hair, nails) as religious atavism. 'The theory of these ex-voto, so widespread among other people than Muslims, and particularly in modern Catholicism, has no other base than the primitive belief in the expulsion of evil and the acquisition of good.'[24] However, while Bertholon and Chantre and Robert dismissed the actual beliefs themselves as fantastical evidence of credulity and naïveté, Bel, instead posited a more general interpretive framework about sainthood as a general category in religious practice. For Bel, maraboutic miracles evinced, not a specifically Muslim form of credulity or superstition, but a 'primitive' intellectual apparatus common to nearly all religions.

Doutté highlighted the tensions between Islamic orthodoxy and maraboutic belief. He envisioned maraboutism as embedded in perceived 'flaws' within Islam itself, in its entirety, not as a mark of the meaningful personal experiences the cult of saints provided. 'The cult of saints...is explained [by the fact] that pure Islam, which scarcely admits this cult, has not sufficiently contented its followers: Allah is too distant from the faithful; he is separated by an abyss and the Muslim seems a tool in the hands of his God.'[25] The vast majority of practitioners in North

---

[20] L. Bertholon and E. Chantre, *Recherches anthropologiques dans la Berbérie orientale: Tripolitaine, Tunisie, Algérie*, 2 vols (Lyons, 1913), i: *Anthropométrie, craniométrie, ethnographie*, title page.

[21] On the Kabyle myth, see Lorcin, *Imperial Identities*.

[22] Bertholon and Chantre, *Recherches anthropologiques*, 605.

[23] Lorcin, *Imperial Identities*, 156 and 210.

[24] Alfred Bel, 'Bibliographie: Edmond Doutté, *Magie et religion dans l'Afrique du Nord*', *Bulletin de la Société de Géographie de la Province d'Oran*, 29 (1909), 129.

[25] Doutté, *Islam algérien*, 39–40; and Hammoudi, *Victim and its Masks*, 19 and 49.

Africa saw no friction between 'pure Islam' and maraboutic veneration, but Doutté admitted only philosophical conflict. Moreover, he contended that 'this cult in the Maghreb has the character of a veritable adoration of man, of an anthropolatry...practiced from high antiquity'.[26] Equally knowledgeable about Islam in both its legalistic and its mystical incarnations, Doutté expressly established maraboutism as anti-Islamic, as dating to the *jahiliyya* and as worshipping humans. It was, then, precisely the social role of maraboutism that, for Doutté, marked its incompability with what he described as 'pure Islam'.

## REGULATING HOLY INTERVENTIONS

The social and economic, and hence potentially political roles of local holy people attracted interest among French colonial scholars and bureaucrats, writers little concerned with the spiritual state or solace of Muslim souls. Throughout North Africa, marabouts played vital roles as arbiters of local disputes, provisioners of the needy, and places of refuge for the guilty and falsely accused alike. In a cultural context that valorized Islam's insistence on the coterminous nature of justice and the just, local men and women invested with *baraka* took on an authority both regulatory and admonitory.[27] One military interpreter surnamed Torré offered an extremely detailed study on a local *zawiya* deep in the Algerian Sahara, informed by his personal research with the shaykh, Moulay Hasan ben Abdelkader (Hasan bin 'Abd al-Qadir), and his intimate knowledge of the physical plant of the holy site. He traced the *baraka* of an earlier shaykh, Moulay Abdelmalik, renowned for his piety, kindness, purity, and virtue. An accomplished mind-reader, Abdelmalik also advocated for the downtrodden of his community: '"Keep yourself from committing injustices, for I will always show myself on the side of the oppressed".'[28] The founder himself, Erragani (al-Ragani, a Berber name spelled with three dots over a *qaf*), was said to battle demons, strike dead oath-breakers from a distance, vanish into thin air, and fly.[29] Unlike many of his contemporaries, Torré expressed no doubt about or interest in the veracity of such accounts, their import for theories of religion, or their indications about the purported evolutionary states of the minds of the Muslims in the region. He offered such miracles, instead, in much the same way as Moulay Hasan would have interpreted them, and perhaps as Hasan may have presented them to Torré: as evidence of *baraka* and of the spiritual import of the lineage of the *zawiya*.

The spiritual aspect of *baraka* mattered little to Torré, except insofar as it provided legitimacy to a man he viewed as a valuable French ally. Hasan, 'very corpulent,

---

[26] Doutté, *Islam algérien*, 39–40; and Hammoudi, *Victim and its Masks*, 19, 49.

[27] Henri Duveyrier, *Les Touareg du Nord: Exploration du Sahara* (Paris, 1864), 332–4 and 362.

[28] Torré, 'Notes sur la Zaouiat Erregania: son fondateur, ses miracles, le cheikh actuel de la zaouiat', *Bulletin de la Société de Géographie d'Alger*, 8/1 (1903), 50–1. The *zawiya* itself may have had loose affiliations with Sufi organizations, but its importance, according to Torré, came exclusively from its maraboutic lineage, see p. 58.

[29] Torré, 'Notes', 54–6.

tanned...of a sympathetic aspect and exterior...is the object of a profound veneration he is universally revered in Touat...He has a real influence that comes to him above all from his ancestors.'[30] As a result, he limited the depredations of local Tuareg raiders, providing security to the caravan trade. Most importantly, 'his deference to authority, his haste to respond to its desires, the good welcome that officers receive with him, are enough proof that testify in his favor'.[31] His local stature enabled Hasan 'to render the greatest services to local French authorities', and indeed, 'to the French cause'.[32] Torré's 'Notes sur la Zaouiat Errgania' cataloged miracles, *baraka*, and maraboutic tales to establish the local political role of the marabout himself. An influential local mediator, his political importance came from his religious role, and Torré could only fully understand the political landscape of his circumscription by analyzing the social and cultural context of Hasan himself.

A 1909 report from Sersou in northwest Algeria indicated the social importance and political disengagement of local marabouts. The administrator, de Chelly, de-emphasized the Sufi connections of local holy people. They shared nothing 'of this homogeneity, so powerful, of the Muslim religious brotherhoods', and 'their attitude is not at all that of the intolerant fanatics...and most appear rather disposed to enter into relation with' European settlers.[33] Demolishing Rinn's neat division between Sufi and marabout, de Chelly nevertheless saw these holy people as intentionally emphasizing their local roots and downplaying their wider connections, without entirely disavowing them. Unaffiliated marabouts loomed more as locally embedded social figures than as unruly religious ones: 'Their role, outside of the example they give of more or less rigorous observation of religious rites, is limited to that of conciliators between Muslim subjects.'[34] Expressly setting aside their religious role and its 'more or less' rigorous nature, de Chelly accorded primacy to marabouts as local mediators. He portrayed a religious landscape that, while contextualized in the larger politics of Islam in colonial Algeria, remained inescapably local, bound to the specific community of Sersou and its—according to the administrator—ostensibly rather harmonious local relations. The administrator subordinated the religious role of marabouts to their roles as potentially useful pillars of this changing community. The individual marabout in places such as Sersou could, de Chelly hoped, provide a vital agent for French political control in the smallest circumscriptions of empire. De Chelly, like many of his colleagues, saw in the role of marabout as mediator between Muslims the ultimately ill-founded hopes for their use as political mediators between colonizer and colonized.

Charitable tribute, known as *ziyara*, attracted a different kind of attention.[35] This transfer and concentration of wealth in the hands of religiously prominent

---

[30] Torré, 'Notes', 46.    [31] Torré, 'Notes', 47.    [32] Torré, 'Notes', 46 and 57.

[33] Département d'Alger, Arrondissement de Miliana, Commune-mixte de Sersou, Administrator de Chelly, 'Rapport semestriel sur les confréries religieuses musulmanes', Trailar, 30 January 1909, ANOM, Archives du département d'Alger (hereafter ADA), 2U/21.

[34] Département d'Alger, Arrondissement de Miliana, Commune-mixte de Sersou, Administrator de Chelly, 'Rapport semestriel sur les confréries religieuses musulmanes', Trailar, 30 January 1909, ANOM, ADA, 2U/21.

[35] On *ziyara*, see also Clancy-Smith, *Rebel and Saint*, 29 and 36–8.

individuals, combined with the pilgrimages undertaken to transport the tribute, struck colonial administrators as dangerous. Local bureaucrats emphasized their importance and the difficulty of their tabulation.[36] In a moment of 'economic crisis' in 1893, Governor General Jules Cambon temporarily suspended the prohibition on *ziyara* in place since 1876. At the same time, he recalled the necessity of strict control over any wandering religious figures and the near-impossibility of completely banning *ziyara*.[37] Cambon reiterated that official policy had to acknowledge the threat posed by tribute and pilgrimage, even if it also admitted a social role. Official policy resulted from two contradictory bases: first, the conviction that mobile, wealthy Islam could only be political; and, secondly, that far from preying upon the poor, *ziyara* often played a vital role in providing to the indigent social succor that the colonial state would or could not.[38]

More commonly, administrators viewed marabouts with more of a jaundiced eye. After all, as Lawrence Rosen has written about contemporary Morocco, 'Moroccans refer to the white egrets that follow a plowman as *mrabtin* (marabouts, saints) because, they say, they appear elegant and untouched by the dirt but are actually benefiting from the hard labor done by others in turning up food for them.'[39] Texts from colonial Algeria do reveal a more cynical interpretation of marabouts in their communities. In a 1911 monograph on Oudjda on the Moroccan border with Algeria, the colonel and geographer Louis Voinot painted a seemingly idyllic shrine with a spring shaded by date palms, poplars, and terebinths, the fish and tortoises paddling about placidly, the fowl repairing to the nearby jujube trees or the calm of the cemetery near the mosque.[40] The reputation of the departed saint protected animal, plant, and edifice from harm or from scavenging. It also sheltered, however, a decidedly less savory and no doubt less placid menagerie in its midst. The marabout's 'domain is a place of asylum considered inviolable', he wrote, adding: 'Thieves, murderers, and other criminals who took refuge there were not pursued; also, even up to most recent years, it was a

[36] 'Notice concernant Si Mohamed Saghir ben Cheikh Mokhtar, marabout de la Zaouïa des Ouled-Djellal', Division de Constantine, Cercle du Biskra, 16 January 1903, AGGA, 16H/2; 'Tableau indiquant les Mokaddim des Ordres religieux qui résident sur le territoire de l'annexe de Barika, leur Khouans, leur influence, etc.', 9 January 1903, Barika, ANOM, AGGA, 16H/2; 'Rapport sur la situation des Ordres religieux. 2e Semestre 1905', 6 January 1906, Tiaret, ANOM, Archives du département d'Oran (hereafter ADO), 2U/4; Gouvernement Générale de l'Algérie, Affaires indigènes, no. 3573, 'Au sujet de deux européens qui ont embrassé la religion musulmane', Governor General to the General Commanding the Division of Algiers, 31 December 1892, Algiers, AGGA, 1I/151; 'Note historique sur l'Ordre de Mouley-Tayeb', n.d. (after 1864), AGGA, 10H/38.

[37] Governor General Jules Cambon to General and Prefects of Algiers, Constantine, and Oran, 7 April 1893, ANOM, AGGA, 9H/9. ANOM, AGGA, Carton 16H/7 details exceptions granted to political allies permitting the collection of *ziyara*.

[38] Département d'Oran, Arrondissement de Mascara, Commune-Mixte de Saïda. Surveillance des Personnages religieux. Extrait du Registre tenu en suite des prescriptions de la Circulaire Gouvernementale du 24 Novembre 1903, no. 8996, 28 February 1904, Saïda, ANOM, AGGA, 16H/5.

[39] Lawrence Rosen, *The Culture of Islam: Changing Aspects of Contemporary Muslim Life* (Chicago, 2003), 33.

[40] Louis Voinot, 'Oudjda et l'Amalat', *Bulletin Trimestriel de la Société de Géographie et d'Archéologie d'Oran*, 31/127 (1911), 93–200, 175.

veritable refuge for bandits', some of whom may even have helped themselves to fish or fowl.[41]

Edmond Doutté's fieldwork in Morocco elucidated the marabout as a marker of social ossification. Among the Haha, a Chleuh people on the Atlantic Coast, Doutté perceived a rigid class system. 'The marabouts', he contended, 'are the aristocracy the most respected', even more than the descendants of the prophet. 'The quality of *marabout* (chelh'a: *agourram*) is essentially hereditary [and] assures much consideration and a large amount of... privileges.'[42] Moreover, he noted no sense of inherited responsibility. Instead, rigid class lines divided the community; slaves had a particularly difficult time, and even the very few freed slaves lived in a state of precarious freedom. Slavery was racialized in Morocco, though not entirely rigidly.[43] Doutté himself remarked on the existence of dark-skinned *sharifs* (descendants of the prophet), aristocrats second only to the marabouts, alongside the poorest of impoverished slaves and their descendants. The latter, the most marginalized members of society, 'as scorned as the marabouts are honored',[44] expected little aid from the marabouts, or so little that Doutté did not mention it. For Doutté, his deep knowledge and, indeed, experience of the different local roles of individual marabouts, whether among the Haha or elsewhere, prevented him from formulating a single recommendation about their potential political use.

## INSANITY, DEVIANCE, AND DESTABILIZATION

In colonial texts, scholars acknowledged the accommodation of maraboutism with madness and the deviant. The equation of mental difference with holiness provided communities with a means of coming to terms with individuals who, though deemed deviant, remained embedded in a web of familial and social ties, affections, and obligations.[45] Indeed, the very notion of the 'credulous' or the 'miraculous' at times courted the definition of insanity. In their *La Kabylie et les coutumes kabyles*, Hanoteau and Letourneux included madness as part of the very definition of a marabout. In addition to inheritance, they delineated two other methods to become one: first, the diligent study of religious texts; or, secondly, 'to be mad or feign madness and prophesize the future'.[46] The authors introduced a complex system of identification whereby holiness, madness, and deception graded into each other in the mind of the marabout, and, indeed, in the body, too, 'covered in

---

[41] Voinot, 'Oudjda et l'Amalat', 175.

[42] Edmond Doutté, 'Quatrième voyage d'études au Maroc: rapport au Comité du Maroc: L'organisation domestique et sociale chez les H'ah'a', *Renseignements Coloniaux et Documents publiés par le Comité de l'Afrique Française et le Comité du Maroc*, 1 (1905), 1–16, 12.

[43] Chouki el Hamel, '"Race", Slavery, and Islam in Maghribi Thought: The Question of the Haratin in Morocco', *Journal of North African Studies*, 2/3 (2002), 29–52.

[44] Doutté, 'Quatrième Voyage', 13.

[45] Marius Bernard, *L'Algérie qui s'en va* (Paris, 1887), 43; and Camille Brunel, *La Question indigène en Algérie: L'affaire de Margueritte devant la cour d'assises de l'Hérault* (Paris, 1906), 96.

[46] Hanoteau and Letourneux, *Kabylie*, ii, 94.

rags'.[47] Hanoteau and Letourneux declined to distinguish in any clear way among the holy fool, the madman, and the trickster, merely noting that whatever the motives of the performer, the costume remained the same. The anxieties about religious madness in colonial Algeria focused almost exclusively on *feigned* madness, and in particular on the notion that feigned insanity could provide cover for nascent anti-colonial insurgencies.

Edmond Doutté similarly concentrated on madness as a path to sanctity. In attempting to define the proliferation of Arabic terms associated with maraboutism and the *wali* (saint), he began by explicating madness as a primary category. 'A *bahloul* [literally, a buffoon or clown, but from the root b-h-l, to curse, and related to *ibtahala*, to supplicate or ask of God] is a simpleton, everywhere regarded as one favored by God, as with the madman or the epileptic', he wrote, explaining: 'The bahloul is naturally predisposed to be *medjdzoub* [insane, possessed; a lunatic; literally, one who is drawn out of oneself], that is to say 'ravished in ecstacy' by God, illuminated.'[48] It was, moreover, 'the saint who is continually *medjzoub, ravi*, [who] become[s] a *ouali* [wali], that is to say a friend, a familiar of God'.[49]

Nevertheless, Doutté himself evinced doubt about the veracity of the holy fool. Like Hanoteau and Letourneux, he speculated about the possibility of deceit, or at least dissemblance. The surest path to holiness, he noted, was for 'the *bahloul*, the *medjzoub*, idiots, madmen, more or less sincere, to whom all is permitted', even insulting persons of high social, political, or religious standing, 'and who pass for favored with divine grace'.[50] Doutté did not explicitly cast these 'idiots' as charlatans or wily tricksters, but merely introduced the possibility. His 'more or less' indicated a real ambiguity for Doutté. For many colonial writers, madness and sanctity loomed by definition as wholly separate categories and their permeability in the maraboutic tradition destabilized assumptions about such discrete, 'rational' divisions. In that destabilization, scholars such as Bertholon and Chantre and Doutté found room for prevarication on the part of the holy fool. In the absence of any means to ascertain the legitimacy or even sanity of the marabout, no possible unitary political recommendation emerged for those who, like Doutté, acknowledged such ambiguity. The generalizations of scholar-administrators such as Louis Rinn provided for easier use in formulating policy, but ultimately proved far less accurate as descriptions of the myriad roles of the marabouts in various communities.

In his memoir of his time as a military doctor, Dr Bonnafont recounted his own unsettling encounters in Milah in 1838. This young saint openly flouted conventional boundaries of gendered propriety. Roughly 17 years old, she promenaded naked; 'her principal nourishment consisted of going to drink the blood of animals killed at the abattoir'. Bonnafont himself 'saw her delighting in this hot and liquid food', and occasionally raw meat.[51] Her daily comportment marked her as

---

[47] Hanoteau and Letourneux, *Kabylie*, ii, 94.    [48] Doutté, *Islam algérien*, 43.
[49] Doutté, *Islam algérien*, 43; and Doutté, *Les Marabouts*, 32–3.
[50] Doutté, *Islam algérien*, 43–4; and Doutté, *Les Marabouts*, 75–6 and 82–5.
[51] Dr Bonnafont, *Pérégrinations en Algérie: 1830 à 1842: Histoire, éthnographie, anecdotes* (Paris, 1884), 202–3.

inescapably and unreachably alien, a familiar stranger who heeded no custom or laws. This potential isolation, and above all her nudity, placed her at no small risk upon the arrival of the soldiers with whom Bonnafont arrived. No lesser a figure than the shaykh of Milah recognized this and undertook her protection. 'All the inhabitants having for her the greatest veneration, he asked the general to make the entire army respect her', observed Bonnafont.[52] The general and his troops complied, even when 'this girl came to the camp and promenaded herself amongst the soldiers' or imitated them hunched over their meal.[53] If true, this account of their encounters provides an all-too-rare instance of accommodation, if an uneasy one, between local notables and the army in the early days of the conquest. Bonnafont himself, however, found nothing edifying in such scenes, even cautioning against, as if warding off, any positive interpretation. The conflation of madness and holiness, according to the doctor, marked Algerians as inalterably lesser, a testament to a disorder, not individual or mental, but general and cultural. 'Many people, reading these details, will perhaps see only the pleasing side of Arab mores; but, upon reflecting and studying them seriously, as I have done, the episodes that I have recounted here and elsewhere justify' a different interpretation 'of these people, among whom ignorance and superstition ... cause the elevation of the mad to the height of divinities whom they adore'.[54] Invoking of his own study and reflection, his association of holiness and madness reinscribed maraboutism as a marker of ignorance. What seemed, after all, a rather compassionate manner of accommodating a vulnerable member of the community became, in Bonnafont's eyes, an object-lesson in moral difference. His admonition against reading 'the pleasing side of Arab mores' explicitly attempted to foreclose other possible readings of the moral construction of madness.

Even in unambiguously tragic circumstances, the conflation of religion and madness unfolded on the stage of the body. A Prefect of Constantine equated piety, at least in its more excessive forms, and madness. On 29 May 1908, he observed: 'Ayoug Muhammad ben 'Ali—sweeper of the Mosque of Bougie, aged forty-one...after the morning prayer, in a fit of madness, climbed over the parapet of the minaret and threw himself into the void from a height of fifteen meters. Death was instantaneous.'[55] Ben 'Ali was probably not a marabout, occupying as he did a low-status job at the mosque and dying without mention of any claim to a lineage. Nevertheless, the prefect's interpretation of the suicide firmly situated it within the context of pathological religiosity associated with maraboutism itself. 'One gets lost in conjecture on the motive of this suicide. However this man for several years was manifesting exaggerated sentiments of piety and continued this year, since last Ramadan, the fast every day. It would not be improbable that this

---

[52] Bonnafont, *Pérégrinations*, 202.     [53] Bonnafont, *Pérégrinations*, 203.
[54] Bonnafont, *Pérégrinations*, 203.
[55] Préfecture de Constantine, Secrétariat Général des Affaires indigènes et de la Police Générale, 1⁰ Section, no. 15047. Mosquée de Bougie. Suicide du balayeur. Le Préfet du Département de Constantine to Monsieur le Gouverneur Général (Police et Sûreté), 6 June 1908, Alger, Constantine, ANOM, AGGA, 16H/78.

suicide might be due to a religious hallucination.'[56] The continuation of the grueling fast long past Ramadan might itself indicate a kind of imbalance, but religiosity would represent merely its form, not its content.

Ultimately, however, philosophical questions doomed any attempt to firmly distinguish faith and madness. When Auguste Mouliéras, government translator, ethnographer, and professor of Arab Studies in Oran, traveled to Fez on a research mission on behalf of the Ministère de l'Instruction Public, he encountered numerous holy people. One 'Lella Maïmounia Tagnaout... half ecstatic, half lucid... went through the paths of her tribe repeating to satiety these simple words: "Rebbi iaaref Meïmounia ou Meïmounia taaref Rebbi ['God knows Maymunia, and Maymunia knows God']".'[57] Nonsense, tautology, or profundity? Her words, her claims that God knew her and she him, remain as uninterpretable as uncontestable.

Overall, colonial interpretations of Algerian maraboutism frequently took the form of anxieties over such practices as potentially destabilizing. In particular, marabouts, like the young woman Bonnafont met in Milah, exempted themselves from more rigidly gendered structuring of social organization. For colonial scholars, bureaucrats, and other writers who often defined Islam through its gendered hierarchies, their undermining by religious individuals threatened to upend conventional, inscribed knowledge about Islam as a whole. Doutté called attention to the considerable number of female marabouts.[58] In particular, he emphasized the importance of virginity and the transgressive nature of their comportment, namely their masculine dress that facilitated their free movement.[59] Mouliéras noted the opposite: male marabouts attired as women.[60] Auguste Mouliéras also, however, found in Fez 'a holy sinner who...addressed us with *vœux* that my Muslims listened to religiously'.[61] Mouliéras played off the juxtaposition of holiness and sinning to call attention to the unexpected, indeed frankly transgressive aspect of the woman. As Mouliéras's companion, Jilali, explained, 'these women...are maraboutes [i.e., in the feminine] of easy morals. Before death, their holy ancestor recommended to the female population of his tribe to deliver themselves to prostitution and to predict the future.'[62] While Doutté limited the transgressive aspect of female marabouts to cross-dressing, Mouliéras himself depicted some as prostitutes. Moreover, his insistence that '[his] Muslims listened *religiously*' (emphasis added) underlined both the incongruity and the potentially destabilizing influence of a holy prostitute.

[56] Préfet du Constantine to Monsieur le Gouverneur Général, 6 June1908, ANOM, AGGA, 16H/78.

[57] *Rabbi ya'arif Maymunia wa Maymunia ta'arif rabbi*, see Auguste Mouliéras, *Fez* (Paris, 1902), 67–8. *Lella* is a Moroccan term of respect for a woman, *Maymunia* a personal name, and *Tagnaout* indicates some connection with Berber identity.

[58] Doutté, *Marabouts*, 93, 95, and 96.

[59] Doutté, *Marabouts*, 100; Doutté, *Islam algérien*, 45–7; and Auguste Mouliéras, 'Hagiologie', in *Bulletin de la Société de Géographie et d'Archéologie de la Province d'Oran*, 19 (1899), 374–6.

[60] Mouliéras, 'Hagiologie', 374–6.      [61] Mouliéras, *Fez*, 75.

[62] Mouliéras, *Fez*, 76.

Gender among marabouts unsettled colonial expectations about Muslim masculinity and feminine seclusion. The importance of female saints, their veneration, and the freedoms allowed them in multiple communities threatened to erode the strict gendered hierarchies that undergirded colonial fantasies of Islam. Holy sinner, sinning saint, prostitute, and preacher, man-as-woman, or woman-as-man, the marabouts destabilized gender categories, more to the consternation of colonial observers than of her fellow Muslims.

## THE THREAT OF THE MARABOUT

If scholars and bureaucrats in their published texts carefully teased out the complexities of maraboutic definitions and actions, administrative documents focused rather more narrowly on the potential threat marabouts might pose to colonial control in Algeria. Indeed, colonial observers scrutinized marabouts, male and female, for any indication of subversion or rebellion. Many feared that, unlike Sufi orders, a lone and unaffiliated marabout, whose geographic extent and multiple geographic locations made surveillance, at least from a physical standpoint, somewhat easier, might exert great and disruptive influence without calling attention to him-or herself.

It was precisely such fears that led to the imprisonment and eventual deportation to Corsica of Kouider ben Amar (Kouider bin Amar) in 1882. Deemed a 'very influential marabout', Kouider found himself accused of propagating doctrines hostile to French control, probably unavoidable in his capacity as instructor of students at a Qur'anic school in Kabylie.[63] His internment in Corsica and the shuttering of his *zawiya* represented a rather severe punishment for anti-French propaganda ultimately more bruited than attested in the official records of his case. His internment came at the end of a tortuous series of interpretive leaps and ill-founded conclusions about the nature of his maraboutic activity as the leader of a *zawiya*. After noting the near-impossibility of gathering information about Kouider and his followers, one administrator noted that 'he had up until this point provoked no complaint and his attitude appeared absolutely correct'. Nonetheless, the secretary of the subprefecture of Tizi-Ouzou, like his colleagues in other jurisdictions, 'did not doubt the hostile tendencies' of Kouider and his followers. The actual source of such doubts came from an apparent echo chamber. In fact, the secretary merely repeated the accusations of his colleagues, which 'he could not but share', without any motivation. He himself remarked that the marabout gave no cause of suspicion. The only source of the secretary's suspicion was, ultimately, the suspicion of his colleagues, and Kouider's quality as an influential marabout.[64]

---

[63] Affaires indigènes, no. 1588, Secretary General of the Government for the Governor General to the Prefect of Algiers, 18 March 1882, ANOM, ADA, 2U/23.

[64] 'Au Sujet du Si Kouider ben Amar', no. 8971, Secretary of the Sub-Prefecture of Tizi-Ouzou to Prefect of the Department of Algiers, 26 January 1882, Tizi-Ouzou, ANOM, ADA, 2U/23.

Other administrators' aspersions on Kouider were scarcely better founded. The subprefect in Palestro whose suspicions so influenced the secretary in Tizi-Ouzou accused Kouider of unauthorized visits to his circumscription. The marabout's marriage to a local woman occasioned visits to his new family, and he recruited followers for his *zawiya* from the region of Palestro. He traveled armed, the subprefect noted.[65] Many marabouts by their nature sought out followers, often among kin, and only the most unwise traveled through colonial Algeria unarmed. In short, his lack of permit aside, Kouider's behavior stood out in no particular way from the common behavior of marabouts. It *was* the common behavior of marabouts, and as such gave rise to the subprefect's concern. By the spring of 1882, before his deportation to Corsica, Kouider ben Amar attempted to call attention to his plight, writing: 'I the undersigned Kouider ben Amar have the honor of informing M. le Préfet that since the fourth of May I have been in prison without knowing the reason. I ask your benevolence in freeing me or making me know the reason.'[66] His ignorance of the cause of his imprisonment seems sincere; in halting French, he explained, 'I am a schoolteacher at Beni Rateni Cabili [sic] where you can ask for information about me', apparently genuinely not realizing that it was precisely his capacity as a schoolteacher (of *tolba*s, Qur'anic students) that aroused suspicion.[67] In another, more linguistically confident letter, he traced his troubles to the Palestro administrator's demand for his travel permit.[68] His failure to secure such permission functioned less as administrative oversight than actual crime in the context of the French colony: he did, indeed, need such a permit to travel, particularly in order to gain adherents to his *zawiya*. As late as January 1882, however, a representative of the governor general himself remarked on Kouider's admission to this crime, and recommended, further information not forthcoming, merely to return him to his own community. The prefect 'asked [the governor general] . . . to give you instructions about this native who you have incarcerated at the civil prison in Algiers. I have the honor of informing you, Monsieur le Préfet, that on this occasion I have no particular instructions to address to you.'[69] The minimalist punishment suggested by the governor general's office contrasted sharply with the escalation that the deportation to Corsica, a scarce two-and-a-half months later. I have, apparently like Kouider himself, found no additional information in

---

[65] 'Au sujet d'un marabout arrêté dans les Beni Khalfoun', no. 1012, Secretary of the Sub-Prefecture of Palestro to Prefect of the Department of Algiers, Palestro, 12 November 1881, ANOM, ADA, 2U/23.

[66] Kouider ben Amar to Prefect of the Department of Algiers, 21 March 1882, ANOM, ADA, 2U/23.

[67] Kouider ben Amar to Prefect of the Department of Algiers, 21 March 1882, ANOM, ADA, 2U/23. Kouider's correspondence was in French. Aside from the occasional letter, Arabic texts, with the exception of rather formulaic 'talismans' or 'amulets' given by marabouts for healing or protection purposes, are vanishingly rare in the colonial archive on maraboutism.

[68] Kouider ben Amar to Prefect of the Department of Algiers, 27 March 1882; see also ADA, 2U/23, Kouider ben Amar to Prefect of the Department of Algiers, 12 March 1882, ADA, 2U/23.

[69] Affaires indigènes, no. 44, 'Au sujet de l'arrestation à Beni Khalfoun du Marabout Si Kouider ben Amar', Councillor of Government for the Governor General to Prefect of the Department of Algiers, 5 January 1882, ADA, 2U/23.

the otherwise very complete file to indicate its motivation. Even the January letter from the governor general's office betrayed some exasperation with the lesser officials: 'the preventive detention of this marabout cannot be prolonged in current conditions'.[70]

If something about 'current conditions' changed, the archive took little note of it. Only certain facts recurred in each retelling of Kouider's crime. He acknowledged his laxity in securing permission to travel—'vagabondage' in the words of colonial criminality. However, because of his status as marabout, administrators presumed to add to this the crime of 'propagande religieuse', long prohibited in colonial Algeria for fears that it would excite religious resistance, fears to which the increasing secularization of the Third Republic gave greater credence.[71] They confessed to no real knowledge of the nature of his teachings, and he himself had little compunction about using, unwisely as it turned out, his status as schoolteacher to attempt to exculpate himself and attest to his character. The mere fact of his maraboutic identity, as far as the admittedly incomplete and unsatisfactory archival record indicates, compounded his crime.

## CONCLUSION

The scholar-administrators who published on maraboutism drew extensively on such reports.[72] Louis Rinn, the archetype of such writers, suspected marabouts as a general category of 'religious monomania', inherently dangerous and worthy of severe repression.[73] 'This severity is only, in sum, prudence', especially in regards to those only feigning piety, he wrote, continuing: 'These pseudo-marabouts are always dangerous, and one would have avoided more than one insurrection, if one had always considered as very serious, from the beginning, the malevolent ramblings of the exalted as of then still without influence, and who later served as the flag or chief for numerous insurgents.'[74] Rinn nearly conflated religious monomaniacs and their seeming opposite, the dissemblers. Both, for the administrator, posed a potentially fatal threat to colonial control. True religious obsession and pretensions to it could serve equally to rally opposition to the empire.

As early as 1870, a major text aimed at introducing the colonial project in Algeria to a broader audience described marabouts as 'mystical cynics who can permit themselves the most enormous monstrosities', accusing them of 'charlatanism…to procure money'.[75] In 1897, Octave Depont and Xavier Coppolani,

---

[70] Affaires indigènes, no. 44, 'Au sujet de l'arrestation à Beni Khalfoun du Marabout Si Kouider ben Amar', Councillor of Government for the Governor General to Prefect of the Department of Algiers, 5 January 1882, ADA, 2U/23.

[71] 'Vagabondage et propagande religieuse:' ANOM, ADA, 2U/23, Sureté Général, no. 3968, Prefect of the Department of Algiers, 2 December 1881, Algiers, ANOM, ADA, 2U/23.

[72] Trumbull, *An Empire of Facts*, chs 1 and 2.     [73] Rinn, *Marabouts et khouan*, 128.

[74] Rinn, *Marabouts et khouan*, 130.

[75] Behaghel, *L'Algérie*, 290; another *œuvre de popularisation* offered a similar interpretation, see M. J. Baudel, *Un an à alger: Excursions et souvenirs* (Paris, 1887), 92.

devoted colonial bureaucrats and authors of a major text of Islamic mysticism designed to update that of Louis Rinn, drew on the observations of hundreds of administrators to claim that 'Muslim saints, however disinterested they seem in the joys of the world, have yet more religiosity than religion'.[76] Such generalizations responded to and compounded administrative fears that marabouts would prey upon local populations, stir up religiously motivated dissent, and pursue political agendas in lieu of pious quiescence.

The legacy of the Depont and Coppolani study, however, proved more decisive for colonial policy. Their charge to supplement Rinn's work required commissioning large-scale and intensive studies at the most local level, of religious notables across Algeria. Like Rinn's *Marabouts et khouan*, the Depont and Coppolani text intensified colonial surveillance on and interference in the activities of marabouts and Sufis. These milestones in the production of French knowledge about Islamic mysticism corresponded to stricter political surveillance of mystics and the collection of information depended on information gathered by local, largely rural, administrators. Subsequently, the colonial government's insistence on the utility of the texts for administrators meant that works by scholar-administrators in large part determined the kinds of inquiries other administrators would undertake.

Ultimately, Edmond Doutté, the most serious and devoted colonial scholar of maraboutism, most succinctly summarized the ambiguities, anxieties, and politics surrounding France's relationship with the marabouts of the Maghrib. They 'are the principal element of Maghrebi Islam', he wrote, asserting: 'Maraboutism will never become an instrument [for the French colonial] Government: a benevolent neutrality, interrupted from time to time by some severe repression, if hostilities manifest themselves; such is the policy to follow.'[77] Kouider ben Amar would surely have contested the benevolence of colonial surveillance of marabouts, and repression, no matter how severe, never succeeded in reconciling the entirety of marabouts in their tremendous diversity to empire in North Africa.

Hence, the profoundly ambiguous and often contradictory colonial understanding of the definition, role, sincerity, piety, and politics of marabouts in Algeria never crystallized into one particular policy or discursive form. The marabout remained charlatan, holy woman, madman, prostitute, trickster, all at once, and all in one. The French reckoning with popular Islam never quite came to a conclusion about maraboutism. Nor, perhaps, could it, given that the manifold forms of popular piety, after all, aimed at responding to personal needs, individual callings, and a deep and at times profoundly solitary relationship with the divine, and such responses mapped most imperfectly on to the interests of the colonial state. Not surprisingly, French administrators largely failed to formulate coherent policy on the transcendent. Despite its political uses by both Algerians and French, maraboutism remained best understood through the lens of the deeply subjective, transient experiences that individuals had of their God.

---

[76] Octave Depont and Xavier Coppolani, *Les confréries religieuses musulmanes* (Algiers, 1897), 147.
[77] Doutté, *Islam algérien*, 136–7.

# 14

# Islam and the European Empires in Japanese Imperial Thought

*Cemil Aydin*

## INTRODUCTION

This chapter examines Japanese debates about Islam and policies towards the imagined unity described as *Kaikyô Sekai* ('Muslim world') during the peak of Japanese imperialism. Focusing on the era of Japan's fifteen-year war—from the Manchurian Incident of 1931 to the end of the Second World War—the chapter argues that the boom in Japanese research into Muslim societies across the world was closely linked to the crisis of Japanese imperialism during the 1930s. Japan's pan-Asianism, as a discourse of both internationalism and imperialism, shaped the way Japanese scholars proclaimed a non-Eurocentric and hence 'better' understanding of Islam and of Muslim societies. Japan's imperial policymakers and scholars of Islam routinely referred to the policies of the European empires towards Muslim societies, claiming that the Japanese empire would impose superior methods of rule on Muslims since their view of Islam was independent of Western prejudices. This Islamophile vision allowed Japanese scholars to produce a different perspective on Muslim societies, mostly through the critical rereading of European Orientalist texts. Japanese scholars both reproduced and questioned the Orientalist notion of an East–West civilizational divide in their writings on an imagined 'Muslim world'. The history of Japan's Islamic studies before the Second World War also illustrates how internationalism, imperialism, and Orientalism interacted in discourses of Japanese–Islamic solidarity. In fact, Japan's imperial officials at various levels relied on Asianist notions of solidarity between the 'Muslim world' and Japan in their various propaganda efforts directed towards Muslim societies. Finally, this understanding of a monolithic anti-Western 'Muslim world' sympathetic to Japan helped shape imperial policy with regard to Muslim populations in China and in Southeast Asia.

During the most turbulent years in the history of the Japanese empire, from the Manchurian Incident of 1931 to the end of the Second World War, Japan hosted a surprisingly vibrant and productive community of scholars in Islamic studies. In fact, Japan's most prominent radical nationalist, imperial thinker, and pan-Asianist, Ôkawa Shûmei (1886–1957), was also an expert on Islam, and indeed published a general introduction to Islam, *Kaikyô Gairon* (*Introduction to Islam*) in 1942, at the peak of the Greater East Asia War. During the 1930s and 1940s, there was a boom in research in Islamic studies. Although the Japanese public knew little about Islam, Muslim countries became one of the most studied cultural geographies in these years.[1] Between 1931 and 1945, almost 1,700 books and articles on Islamic issues were published.[2] From 1938 to 1944, Japanese scholars published three regular journals on Islamic studies and maintained four research centers devoted to this subject.[3] These intellectual efforts accompanied a vibrant discussion on imperial policies towards Islam, which regularly referred to the imperial policies of the Italian and German empires in the Muslim world. Japanese imperial thinkers and policymakers perceived Islam and the Muslim world as the Achilles' heel of the European empires, while assuming that an Asian Japanese empire would not experience resistance from its Muslim subjects in China and Southeast Asia.

From the outset, the purposes and functions of Islamic studies in Japan could be directly linked to the needs and visions of the Japanese empire, which included large populations of Muslim subjects in Manchuria, China, and Southeast Asia during the era of the Greater East Asia Co-Prosperity Sphere. In fact, wartime intelligence reports of the Allies classified various programs of Islamic studies as part of a Japanese attempt at the 'infiltration' of the Muslims of European-ruled Asia.[4] Compared with negative European imperial discourses on Muslims, Japanese writings on Islam and Muslims generally reflected a positive outlook. This association between Islamophilic studies of Islam and the Japanese empire illustrates that empires can have very different and sometimes opposing political relationships with Muslim societies while sharing many of the basic globally circulating scholarly assumptions about Muslims. For example, writings by Ôkawa Shûmei and other scholars of Islam during the Greater East Asia War involved diverse subjects and arguments that cannot simply be categorized as useful knowledge for the sake of the Japanese empire. Japan's experts on Islam even identified themselves with Muslims as fellow Asians in a common struggle against the Western hegemony in

---

[1] A developed field of Islamic studies, for example, represented Muslims in a much more sophisticated way than the politicized stereotypes that characterized the representation of Jews during the interwar period, see David Goodman and Masanori Miyazawa, *Jews in the Japanese Mind* (New York, 2000).

[2] The statistical account is as follows: 1905–30: 907 items; 1931–45: 1,685 items; 1945–49: 67 items; 1950–59: 902 items. The peak of publications on Islam was reached during the 1939–41 period: 1939, 260 items; 1940, 196 items, 1941, 217 items, see *Bibliography of Islamic and Middle Eastern Studies in Japan, 1868–1988*, compiled and published by Tôyô Bunko (Tokyo, 1992).

[3] The journals were *Kaikyô Sekai*, *Kaikyôken*, and *Kaikyô Jijyô*. The research centers were Greater Japan Islam League Research Bureau, the Institute of Islamic Studies, the Foreign Ministry Research Section on the Muslim World, and the East Asian Economic Research Bureau. There will be more detailed discussion of these journals and institutions in the following pages.

[4] OSS reports included all the leading Islamic studies experts in its list of Japanese agents for propaganda and infiltration, see Office of Strategic Services Research and Analysis Branch (OSS), *Japanese Infiltration among the Muslims Throughout the World*, published by *Office of Strategic Services, Research and Analysis Branch*, R&A No. 890 (15 May 1943); see also OSS, *Japanese Infiltration among the Muslims in China*, R&A No. 890.1 (15 May 1944); and OSS, *Japanese Infiltration among Muslims in Russia and Her Borderlands*, R&A No. 890.2 (August 1944). Copies of these reports can be accessed at Japanese National Diet Library in Tokyo.

Asia. They also had an internationalist agenda, as they sought to make Japanese society more cosmopolitan and less Eurocentric by educating their own citizens about Islamic history, culture, and faith.

Japanese imperial research on Islam and Muslim societies raises important questions about the racial and civilizational identity of a particular empire in relation to various Muslim societies. The following pages enquire into the extent to which Japanese imperial discourse about Islam differed from or shared the characteristics of similar European discourses. Did Japan's non-white and non-Christian racial and civilizational identity influence the content and ideals of Japan's scholarship on Islam? What was the impact of Japan's pan-Asianism in the formation of its policies towards Muslims? While answering these two questions, the article will discuss how a number of Japanese policy experts tried to promote the idea of Japan as a 'patron of Islam' in order to undermine European colonial power across Muslim Asia.

The first two parts of this chapter deal with the relationship of early Islamophile pan-Asianist Japanese activists, showing how and why their vision of the Japanese empire became relevant during the 1930s. As the third section demonstrates, during the late 1930s when the Japanese empire entered into a period of crisis, various government circles appropriated earlier Asianist Islamophile views in their strategic and imperial policy calculations. In the final section, the chapter looks at more detached academic and scholarly writings on Islam, which was encouraged with additional government funding, to clarify its commonalities and differences in relation to military circles and traditional Asianist groups in Japan.

## PAN-ASIANIST ISLAMOPHILIA AND THE ROOTS OF JAPAN'S IMPERIAL POLICY TOWARDS ISLAM

The idea of developing a special policy towards the 'Muslim world' can be traced back to the period after the Russo-Japanese War of 1905, originating with a small group of Japanese Asianists, most of whom were connected with the ultra-nationalist Asianist organization Kokuryûkai. The policy towards Islam adopted by Japanese authorities during the late 1930s, when Japan was ruling Muslim populations in East and Southeast Asia, can therefore not be regarded solely as an immediate response to the specific colonial situation or the crisis of their empire, particularly given the absence of comparable policies towards Christians and Hindus. The activities of Kokuryûkai members who were involved in the early propagation and networking for Japanese–Muslim solidarity has already been the subject of an excellent discussion by Selçuk Esenbel.[5] It should be noted, however, that the ideas and activities

---

[5] Selçuk Esenbel, 'Japan's Global Claim to Asia and the World of Islam: Transnational Nationalism and World Power, 1900–1945', *American Historical Review*, 109/4 (2004), 1140–70; Esenbel, 'Japanese Interest in the Ottoman Empire', in Bert Edström (ed.), *The Japanese and Europe: Images and Perceptions*, (Richmond, 2000), 112–20; and El-Mostafa Rezrazi, 'Pan-Asianism and the Japanese

of this small group of advocates for a policy towards Islam within the Kokuryûkai were not taken very seriously by military and government authorities between 1905 and the early 1930s.

It was only after Japan's decision to withdraw from the League of Nations in 1932 that some officials in the military began to show an interest in the idea of a special policy towards Muslims in China and those living under European imperial rule.[6] The change in the relationship between Kokuryûkai activists and the Japanese government is reflected in the memories of Wakabayashi Han (*d.*1936), who had been interested in Islam ever since his 1912 visit to India, where he was accompanied by a Buddhist monk and Burmese nationalist Sayadaw U. Ottama.[7] Wakabayashi's encounter with Indian Muslims led him to undertake further research on Islam in Asia. For twenty years, he worked closely with a small circle of Islam experts within the Kokuryûkai led by Tanaka Ippei (1882–1934).[8] According to Wakabayashi, the activities of his group neither achieved any research results, nor did they receive any support from the government, leaving him pessimistic about the project.[9] Then, in 1932 Wakabayashi was sent by the Kokuryukai to observe the meeting of the League of Nations in Geneva. During his trip back to Japan, having witnessed the vital decision to withdraw from the League, Wakabayashi got a chance to talk with Isogai Rensuke, a lieutenant-colonel in the Japanese army, and he seized the opportunity to explain the benefits that attention to the 'Muslim world' could bring to Japan's policy in Asia.[10] Isogai Rensuke became interested and, when back in Japan, contacted Wakabayashi to introduce him to Army Minister Araki Sadao.[11] Wakabayashi's story of the developments that followed this meeting, as reflected in his memoirs, is a narrative of triumph: the Japanese army began to implement a policy towards Islam and to support the work of the Kokuryûkai group. It is clear from Wakabayashi's story that Japan's withdrawal from the League of Nations in 1932 was a turning-point in the Japanese government's attitude to the ideas of a policy towards Islam. As Japanese elites began discussing more seriously a potential conflict with the European empires in Asia, they increasingly regarded Muslims as allies whose active resistance against

Islam: Hatano Uhô: From Espionage to Pan-Islamist Activity', *Annals of the Japan Association for Middle East Studies*, 12 (1997), 89–112.

[6] Japan's withdrawal from the League of Nations was announced in late 1932, though it officially left the League on 27 March 1933.

[7] Sayadaw U. Ottama (1879–1939) was an influential figure in Burmese nationalism. Influenced by the Indian National Congress and the Japanese model, Ottama denounced British colonial rule. He was imprisoned by the British authorities for a very long time, ultimately dying in prison. For Ôkawa's praise of Ottama, see Ôkawa Shûmei, 'Ottama Hôshi o Omou', in Ôkawa Shûmei Zenshû Kankokai (ed.), *Ôkawa Shûmei Zenshû* (*Collected Works of Ôkawa Shûmei*), 7 vols (Tokyo, 1961), ii, 913–15.

[8] Tanaki Ippei was a scholar of China and Buddhism. He converted to Islam and made pilgrimages to Mecca in 1925 and 1933.

[9] For Wakabayashi's reflections on the history of the Kokuryûkai circle of Islam policy advocates, see Wakabayashi Han, *Kaikyô Sekai to Nihon* (*The Muslim World and Japan*) (Tokyo, 1937), 1–3.

[10] Isogai Rensuke (1886–1967) later became a general in the Japanese Imperial Army and served as governor of Hong Kong under the Japanese occupation between 1942 and 1944.

[11] Han, *Kaikyô Sekai to Nihon*, 3–7. Araki Sadao (1877–1966) was a leader in the Imperial Way faction of the army.

the European rule could be beneficial to Japanese interests. Wakabayashi's account also demonstrates that, had a vocal group of Kokuryûkai activists not existed to advocate the potential political benefits for Japan of the sympathy of the Muslim populations, it is probable that an organization such as the Greater Japan Islam League (*Dai Nippon Kaikyô Kyôkai*, from now on, GJIL) would not have come into existence by 1939.

Sakuma Teijirô and Ariga Bunpachirô were two other figures representing the continuity of ideas in the Asianist commitment to Japanese–Muslim cooperation. Both converted to Islam during the 1910s without abandoning their ultra-nationalistic patriotism. Sakuma had been assigned by Kokuryûkai to study Islam, and he lived in Turkey for three years.[12] He was primarily an expert on Chinese Muslims, among whom he was known as a convert with the name Ilyas. Sakuma established the first important Japanese-sponsored Islamic organization in Shanghai in 1923, aiming to inspire Chinese Muslims to rise 'from their age-old lethargy to unite them in a great pan-Islamic movement'.[13] As early as the mid-1920s, Sakuma outlined a program for bringing the Islamic religion to Japan through the agency of Chinese Muslims, arguing that if Japan could cooperate with the pan-Islamic movement, Russian penetration into the Muslim world could be checked and the entry of communism into Japan prevented.[14] The Japanese assumption that Muslims would be naturally anti-communist and anti-Russian was confirmed by the attitude of Muslim refugees from the Soviet Union who settled in Manchuria and later Japan.

Ariga Bunpachirô had a unique profile among Japanese Muslims.[15] He converted to Islam through his encounter and relations with Muslims in British India, and just a few months after the China Incident in December 1937, published a highly ambitious pamphlet titled *Nihon Isuramukyô no Setsumei* (*An Explanation for Japanese Islam*). The striking aspect of this missionary manifesto to the Japanese nation was its political stance emphasizing Japan's isolation in the event of a fight between civilizations. Regarding a final war between the white race and colored races as an almost inescapable culmination of the conditions of the 1930s, Ariga expected that Japan would naturally take on the leadership of the 'colored peoples'. He believed, however, that Japan on its own could not prevail in a global struggle for long without allies. As a missionary for Islam, he produced a doctrine of Japanese leadership of Islam against the 'world domination of the white race'.[16]

---

[12] Derk Bodde, 'Japan and the Muslims of China', *Far Eastern Survey*, 15/20 (1946), 311–13, 312.

[13] Sakuma Teijirô, *Shina Kaikyôto no Kakô, Genzai Oyobi Shôrai* (*Past, Present and Future of the Chinese Muslims*) (Tokyo, 1924). This book was highly praised by eminent scholars in the field, such as Naitô Chishû, for its analysis of the reality of Muslims in China. For Naitô Chishû's positive assessment of the book, see the introduction to Sakuma Teijiro, *Kaikyô Kaisetsu* (*Explanation of Islam*) (Tokyo, 1935).

[14] Sakuma Teijirô, *Kaikyô No Ugoki* (*Modern Trends of Islam*) (Tokyo, 1938).

[15] Ariga Bunpachirô was once praised by Kasama Akio as a 'progressive Muslim with a Japanese Spirit' whose religious commitment 'springs from the abiding spirit of patriotism of the Japanese, while he does away with the superficial and petty rules and regulations blindly followed by the Turks and the Arabs', see Kasama Akio, *Kaikyôto* (*Islam*) (Tokyo, 1941), 113.

[16] Ariga Bunpachirô, *Nihon Isuramukyô no Setsumei* (*Explanations on Japanese Islam*) (Tokyo, 1937), 2.

Ariga's connections with Muslims in British India strengthened his conviction that Japan should support the anti-British decolonization efforts of Muslims on the subcontinent. Ariga's writings and activities show that a kind of pro-Muslim anti-colonial discourse was consistently articulated by pan-Asianist circles at the height of the Japanese war in China.

Ariga Bunpachirô's patriotic advocacy of Islam as a universal religion to facilitate Japan's leadership of Asia raises questions about the nature of the Japanese approach to the Islamic faith within an Asianist framework. How was it that some Japanese Asianists could be very confident about converting to a new religion while preserving their nationalist loyalties and imperialist visions? An answer to this question can be found in a commentary written by Sakurai Masashi, a scholar of Buddhism and religious studies, on the subject of the future of Islam in Japan. Sakurai looked favorably on the efforts of an increasing number of Japanese Muslims to combine the Japanese national and imperial mission with the Islamic faith. He also categorically identified Islam, described as a religion of Asia which was 'born and developed in Asia', with the colored races in opposition to his identification of Christianity with the white race. For him and many others in Japan, Islam virtually represented a racial identity for many people in Asia, and they saw the imagined Islam–Christian West conflict as part of a broader conflict between the Christian white race and all the colored races in Asia. Accordingly, he believed that Japan could count on the support of Muslims within the East Asia Co-Prosperity Sphere against the Anglo-American powers.[17] Sakurai depicted the Muslims in China who fought against Japanese rule as 'puppets of the whites', believing that Japan could, in the end, rely on Muslim support on the basis of their racial solidarity. Meanwhile, Sakurai was so confident in the strength of Japanese identity that he did not expect Islam to offer any further cultural and religious appeal to the Japanese people beyond its immediate political utility in international relations.[18] Japanese advocates of pro-Muslim Asianist policies, such as Teijirô and Bunpachirô, were initially marginal voices in their country, with little impact on foreign policy decisions. But their ideas found acceptance among military and civilian elites in their country once Japan left the League of Nations in 1933 and Japanese political elites were seeking to create a new international order in East Asia under their leadership.

## FORMULATING AN IMPERIAL POLICY TOWARDS ISLAM

The major motive for wartime research on Islam was the need for accurate information about the peoples of Asia under Japanese rule and beyond. There was

---

[17] Sakurai Masashi, *Dai Toa Kaikyô Hattenshi* (*Development of Islam in Greater East Asia*) (Tokyo, 1943), 8.

[18] Masashi, *Dai Toa Kaikyô Hattenshi*, 269–70.

also a secondary interest in understanding Islam or Muslims as a weak spot of the European empires, which were competing and clashing with Japan in Asia. Although this imperial interest was not the sole motivation behind Islamic studies, there were institutions and scholars for whom the quest for knowledge of the 'Muslim world' had to have a useful function for their empire. The group that best represented this functional approach to research was the Greater Japan Islam League. Established in 1938, the organization soon had some 250 members, which included scholars as well as individuals from the military and the bureaucracy. The president of the organization was General Hayashi Senjûrô (1876–1943), whose presence was indicative of its connection with the military establishment.

The mission statement of the GJIL emphasized the new circumstances created by the war for a new order in East Asia and the imperial principle of *hakkô ichiu* ('eight corners of the world under one roof') as the main factors that made a more intense study of the 'Muslim world' necessary.[19] A message from Prime Minister Konoe Fumimaro (1891–1945), dated 19 September 1938, stands as evidence of the political support that GJIL was receiving from the government. The main purpose of GJIL was to develop, advocate, and implement a 'policy towards Islam' (*kaikyô seisaku*). More specifically, GJIL identified among its primary goals the promotion of research in Islamic studies, the introduction of Japanese culture to the Muslim world, the development of mutual trade ties, and the formulation of relevant international policies. The single greatest political purpose was to gain the loyalty of Muslims in China and to respond to the perceived pro-Chinese and anti-Japanese sentiments in 'the Muslim world'. They were also concerned about the Chinese nationalist sentiments of Chinese Muslims, which were seen as favoring the Allied powers during the war.

The leaders of GJIL were eager to distinguish themselves from the Institute of Islamic Studies (*Kaikyôken Kenkyûjo*). While the latter was devoted solely to scholarship, the former focused more on the promotion of cultural exchange and policy research.[20] The leaders of GJIL also explained that their organization neither represented a religious association of Muslims, nor did it have any similarity to Christian organizations.

The GJIL hosted a sizable and prolific research bureau, a result of its merger with the Islamic Culture Association (*Isuramu Bunka Kyôkai*), a previously existing research center led by Naitô Chishû, who was a prolific scholar interested in Muslim societies from the perspective of a putative clash of civilizations.[21] In their translation projects, the GJIL showed an interest mainly in the works of Muslims and in German scholarship on Islam. For example, they published a Japanese translation of Paul Schmitz's work *All-Islam! Weltmacht von Morgen* (*All-Islam! World*

---

[19] Dai Nippon Kaikyô Kyôkai, *Dai Nippon Kaikyô Kyôkai no Shimei ni Tsuite* (*On the Mission of Greater Japan Islam League*) (Tokyo, 1939).

[20] Dai Nippon Kaikyô Kyôkai, *Dai Nippon Kaikyô Kyôkai ni Tsuite no Mondô* (*Questions and Answers About the Great Japan Islam League*) (Tokyo, 1939).

[21] Naitô Chishû published the journal *Isuramu: Kaikyô Bunka* (*Islam: Muslim Culture*) from October 1937 to January 1939; on his geopolitical vision, see Naitô Chishû, *Nittô Kôryu Shi* (*A History of Turkish–Japanese Relations*) (Tokyo, 1931).

*Power of Tomorrow*), a work that was influential among German policy experts.[22] The experts of the GJIL believed that German and Muslim scholars would offer a more impartial view than British and French experts in Islamic studies.[23]

The GJIL was very prolific and regularly released policy papers. Its memorandum 'On the Necessity of Developing a Policy Towards the Muslim World' begins by describing the great potential for political and economic power latent in the Islamic world, even though the majority of Muslims at the time were living under European colonial rule.[24] It stressed Japan's economic interests in the 'Muslim world' and the role of natural resources, especially oil. In addition, large Muslim populations were regarded as a potential economic market for Japanese exports. To prove the importance of the 'Muslim world' as a trading partner, the literature of the GJIL contained detailed charts listing the populations and balances of trade for Muslim countries and the quantity of their imports from Japan. In the discussion of political concerns, the GJIL assumed that Muslims would naturally support Japan in the fight against the Anglo-American powers, Western empires in general, and communism. A GJIL pamphlet entitled 'Muslim Nations as an Ally (of Japan)' noted with regret that Muslims in China and elsewhere had, on the whole, adopted an anti-Japanese stance in the wake of Japan's war against China. The memorandum attributed the negative image of Japan to the influence of anti-Japanese propaganda, including the influence of Chinese Muslims in Mecca on pilgrims from across the Muslim world.[25] In its conclusion, the GJIL suggested a policy for the 'correction' of Muslim views of Japan that would entail fostering human ties between the two cultures and promoting scholarly study of the 'Muslim world'. The policy paper clearly appealed to the Japanese government and military authorities. With a self-deceptive naivety, the memorandum emphasized its assumption that Muslims would be willing to cooperate with Japan rather than with the Anglo-American powers or the Soviet Union if Japan's 'universal message' was properly delivered. The idea of a synthesis between 'Eastern and Western civilizations' (*Tōzai Bunmei no Yūgō*) was introduced as one of the ideals of Japan's world mission, since it was thought to have the potential to appeal to Muslims and lead them to a pro-Japanese position in international politics. However, this emphasis on Asianism, frequently noted in other publications on

---

[22] Paul Schmitz, *All-Islam! Weltmacht von Morgen* (Leipzig, 1937), under the title *Kaikyō no Zenbō: Ashita no Sekai Seiryoku* (Tokyo, 1938). Schmitz also worked as the Egypt correspondent of the NSDAP paper *Völkischer Beobachter*. On Schmitz and his role in Nazi Germany's policy towards Islam, see David Motadel, 'Germany's Policy Towards Islam, 1941–1945' (PhD, University of Cambridge, 2010), 35–8.

[23] Halide Edip Adivar's *Inside India* was translated into Japanese, see Halide Edip Adivar, *Rutsubo ni Tagiru Indo Kaikyōto* (Tokyo, 1938). When the GJIL published the translation of Syed Ameer Ali's *A Short History of the Saracens*, both the introductions by General Hayashi Senjurō and by the translators emphasized the need for understanding the Islamic world in the context of a new Greater East Asia heralded by the Pearl Harbor attack. See Syed Ameer Ali, *Kaikyō Shi*, trans. Tsukamoto Gorō and Takei Takeo, foreword by General Hayashi Senjurō (Tokyo, 1942).

[24] Dai Nippon Kaikyō Kyōkai, *Sekai Kaikyōto Seisaku no Hitsuyōsei ni Tsuite* (*On the Necessity of Developing a Policy Towards the Muslims of the World*) (Tokyo, 1939).

[25] Dai Nippon Kaikyō Kyōkai, *Sekai Kaikyōto Seisaku no Hitsuyōsei ni Tsuite*, 3.

Islam in the same period, was overshadowed by the view that the anti-Comintern pact between Japan, Germany, and Italy would shape a new international system.[26] The GJIL advocated the classification of Islam as one of the officially recognized religious faiths in the Japanese empire.[27] The group took great pride in its political impact when the Eighty-First Imperial Diet discussed the 'Muslim problem' and revised its legislation on religious organizations to include Islam within the category of recognized religions.[28] As part of the promotion campaign for this policy, the GJIL even sponsored several exhibitions on the 'Muslim world' at the Tokyo-Ueno and Osaka-Nihonbashi branches of the Matsuzakaya Department Store from November to December 1939.[29] The GJIL often saw the small Muslim community in Japan as an ally in formulating their Islam-friendly policy and as evidence of Japanese–Muslim solidarity, and regularly sought their cooperation. In fact, the Tokyo Muslim Community was also involved in the organization of the exhibitions, with additional support being received from various governmental ministries, the consulates of several Muslim nations, and the Manchurian embassy. The exhibitions attracted great public interest. Among the guests of honor for the opening ceremony were several Muslim leaders from Indonesia.

The GJIL advocated an aggressive anti-Soviet policy and urged the government to benefit from the allegedly anti-Communist sentiments of Asian Muslims. According to a policy paper published in 1939, the GJIL claimed that Muslims could be expected to join voluntarily in the international fight against the communist 'threat' in support of the anti-Comintern pact.[30] The authors divided the colonized Muslim world into two categories, separating those under British and Dutch imperial rule from those in Soviet territories. While hinting that Japan could not ignore the Muslim colonies of the British empire in the context of its policy towards Britain, its main focus was on the benefits of cooperation with the Muslims of Central Asia in a conflict against the Soviet Union.[31] At the time when the memorandum was published, there were two major schools of thought regarding Japanese military policy in Asia. One body of opinion advocated an active military front with the Soviet Union, while the other proposed a southward advance into the British, French, and American colonies of Asia. Eventually, the southern-advance policy was adopted and Japan did not attack the Soviet

---

[26] Saitô Tôkichi, 'Nobi Iku Nihon to Kaikyô Minzoku' ('Awakening Japan and the Muslim Peoples'), *Nihon Oyobi Nihonjin*, 345 (1937), 50–4; Suzuki Takeshi, *Nihon Ni Tai Suru Sekai Kaikyô no Sakebi* (*Crying Message from World Muslims to Japan*) (Tokyo, 1939); and Takisawa Toshiaki, 'Nihon Kaikyôken ni Hairu' ('Japan Enters the Muslim World'), *Shokô*, 118 (1938), 1–3.

[27] Dai Nippon Kaikyô Kyôkai, *Kaikyô Kônin Ga Waga Kokumin Ni Ataeru Eikyô Ni Tsuite no Mondô* (*Questions and Answers About the Impact of Official Recognition of Islam in Our Country*) (Tokyo, 1939).

[28] Dai Nippon Kaikyô Kyôkai Chosabu (ed.), *Dai 81 Kai Teikoku Gikai Ni Okeru Kaikyô Mondai No Shingi* (*Deliberations on Muslim Problem in Eighty-First Imperial Diet Meetings*) (Tokyo, 1943).

[29] Dai Nippon Kaikyô Kyôkai-Tokyo Isuramu Kyôdan, *Kaikyôken Tenrankai* (*Exhibition on the Muslim World*) (Tokyo, 1940).

[30] Dai Nippon Kaikyô Kyôkai, *Higashi Hankyû ni Okeru Bôkyô Tebbeki Kôsei to Kaikyôto* (*Muslims and the Fight Against Communism*) (Tokyo, 1939).

[31] Dai Nippon Kaikyô Kyôkai, *Kunô Suru So-Ren Kaikyô Minzoku* (*Sufferings of the Muslim Peoples of Soviet Union*) (Tokyo, 1939).

territories in the Far East and Central Asia. Yet, in 1939, the argument of GJIL about the utility of Muslim cooperation with Japan could be applied to both the Muslims ruled by the Soviet Union and the British empire. The policy suggestions were enthusiastic and over-optimistic:

> The majority of the Muslims live in Asia. They have the self-consciousness of being oppressed colored peoples, and they hold, very sincerely and fiercely, anti-Bolshevik and anti-Western ideas. Meanwhile, they keep very warm feelings towards our country as an Eastern nation and as the leader of Asia. Even concerning the present China Incident, the Muslims attitude is different from the Western and Soviet position as they hope to get the support of a strong Japan in order to revive their homelands.[32]

The GJIL compared Japan's policy towards Islam to those of other great powers, quickly dismissing the policies of Britain, France, and the Soviet Union as failures with reference to rising anti-colonial, anti-Christian, and anti-Communist trends prevalent in the Muslim world. Generally, the policy papers of the GJIL assumed that Shinto or Buddhist Japanese could be more friendly to the Islamic faith than Christians or Communists, because Muslims and Japanese shared the identity of being colored Asians. Thus, they stressed a common racial and continental identity over religious differences between the Japanese and Muslims. Japan's policy-makers were aware that Italy and Germany also had specific policies towards Islam, declaring their countries 'friends of Islam'. As early as 1898, the German emperor had used his visit to Damascus to declare himself a 'friend' of all Muslims, while Mussolini made the claim that he was 'a protector of Muslims' during his 1937 visit to Libya.[33] Nonetheless, in the eyes of GJIL officials, Italy's policy towards Islam was largely a failure, mainly as a consequence of the legacy of the Ottoman–Italian wars and the Italian military expansion into North Africa. Only Germany's policy towards Islam was considered by GJIL as a partial success. In contrast with the policy failures of the European empires in relation to Islam, Japan seemed to be in an ideal position to become the patron of Islam, given that Japan had no negative colonial history in the 'Muslim world'. This policy paper also argued that both Italy and Germany supported Japan's Muslim policy in Asia.[34] Nevertheless, the GJIL believed that Japan had yet to exploit the untapped potential of its presumed prestige in the Muslim world. As the only evidence for this argument, the memorandum referred to a call for collaboration with Japan issued over the course of an interview with a Prince Husayn of Yemen, the third son of Imam Yahya of the

---

[32] Dai Nippon Kaikyô Kyôkai, *Kunô Suru So-Ren Kaikyô Minzoku*, 13.
[33] Italy's policy towards Islam was also described and discussed as a potential model for Japan by Sakurai Masashi, *Dai Toa Kaikyô Hattenshi* (*Development of Islam in Greater East Asia*) (Tokyo, 1943), 8.
[34] Dai Nippon Kaikyô Kyôkai, *Sekai Kaikyôto Seisaku no Hitsuyôsei ni Tsuite* (*On the Necessity of Developing a Policy Towards World Muslims*) (Tokyo, 1939). There were Muslim nationalists exiled from Russia who were supported by both Japan and Germany, see Matsunaga Akira, 'Ayazu Ishaki to Kyokutô no Tatarujin Comuniti' ('Ayaz Ishaki and the Tatar Community in the Far East'), in Kindai Nihon to Toruko Sekai (ed.), *Ikei Masaru and Sakamoto Tsutomu* (*Modern Japan and the Turkish World*) (Tokyo, 1999), 219–63.

Zaydi ruling family, who visited Tokyo in 1938 to attend the opening ceremonies of the Tokyo Mosque.[35]

Besides publishing policy papers and organizing exhibitions on the 'Muslim world', the GJIL accomplished its most tangible work by issuing a monthly journal entitled *Kaikyô Sekai* (*Muslim World*). Launched in April 1939, the journal was primarily devoted to introducing Islamic culture, history, and civilization to a Japanese readership, and included assessments of international affairs. It argued that nationalist movements in the Muslim world should cooperate with the Axis powers and Japan if a war were to break out in Europe.[36] In contrast with the idealist pan-Asianists of Japan, the GJIL did not make any normative commitment to the decolonization of Asia. Instead, it concentrated on pragmatic political issues, most notably on forming an anti-communist alliance against the Soviet Union and on strengthening Japan's policy in China. Its publications assumed that Muslims are by nature very religious and that they would naturally be anti-communist and anti-Soviet due to the atheist doctrine of this regime.

In short, for the military and civilian expert members of GJIL, knowledge of Islam and the 'Muslim world' was primarily for the sake of advancing Japanese imperial interests. They wanted active Japanese imperial officers, from the level of top generals down to the position of civil bureaucrats, to be informed about the acceptability and legitimacy of Japanese imperial rule over Muslim populations, and to recognize the potential of Muslim support in a war against the Western empires in Asia. However, in their self-referential repetitions of several misleading assumptions of Muslim sympathy for Japan, the GJIL promoted an unsubstantiated optimism that the Japanese empire would find natural allies in the Muslim populations of Asia in the case of a military confrontation with the Western colonial powers.[37]

## JAPANESE SCHOLARS OF ISLAM ON ASIANISM, INTERNATIONALISM, AND IMPERIALISM

Japanese imperial policy towards Islam was not just shaped by military and civil officials. There was a powerful group of Japanese scholars of Islamic studies during this peak period of Japanese imperialism who, in various ways, contributed to the content of this policy. The leading pan-Asianist thinker of interwar Japan, Ôkawa Shûmei, was very influential among military officers. In fact, Ôkawa Shûmei was indicted at the Tokyo War Crimes Tribunal as an ideologue of Japanese

[35] In May 1938, Prince al-Husayn Yahya bin Hamid al-Din, the third son of Imam Yahya bin Hamid al-Din, visited Japan to participate in the opening ceremony of Yoyogi Mosque in Tokyo and met Japan's Showa Emperor to submit a letter from Imam Yahya. Prince Hussein stayed in Japan until January 1939, and he did preparatory negotiations for a trade agreement between Japan and Yemen.

[36] For an example, see Sôsa Tanetsugu, 'Ôshu Senran to Kaikyô Ken no Dôkô' ('European War and the Inclinations of the Muslim World'), *Kaikyô Sekai*, 1/7 (1939), 1–8.

[37] For a good example of self-referential Japanese imperial view of Muslim policy, see Kato Hisashi, *Kaikyô no Rekishi to Genjo* (*The Present Conditions and Future of Muslims*) (Tokyo, 1941).

expansionism, though the charges against him were dropped due to his deteriorating health on the first day of the trial. Even before the peak of Japanese imperial power in East Asia, Ôkawa had already established a reputation as an advocate of increased scholarly attention to Islam and Muslim nationalism in Asia, with extensive coverage of Turkish, Iranian, Saudi, Egyptian, and Afghan nationalism featured in his two previous books, *Fukkô Ajia no Shomondai* (*Problems of Resurgent Asia*) of 1922, and *Ajia no Kensetsusha* (*The Founders of Asia*) of 1941. As an activist intellectual writing since the 1910s, Ôkawa urged his readers not to be misled by the popular image of Islam as limited to the deserts of Arabia, reminding them of the presence of Muslims in China and Southeast Asia. In 1922, Ôkawa visited Indonesia for three months on a research assignment for the Manchurian Railway Company, his only travel experience to a Muslim society other than his encounters with Muslims in China.

Ôkawa Shûmei's wartime classic work introducing Islam to the Japanese audience, *Kaikyô Gairon,* offered a first-rate scholarly introduction to the Islamic religion and history. He began the book by explaining the political and intellectual significance of understanding the religion and history of Muslims, reminding readers that Japan's expansion into Southeast Asia and China had brought a sizable portion of the world's Muslim population under the control of the Japanese empire. He urged the Japanese public to become better informed about the different cultures of Asia, given Japan's claim to and preparation for leadership in the region. Contrary to what might be expected from an Asianist intellectual, Ôkawa's discussion first emphasized how Islamic culture was essentially 'Western', with the shared Hellenistic legacy of Muslim and Christian societies making the Islamic world historically much closer to the West than to East Asian civilization. This thesis of Ôkawa seems similar to the ideas of German Orientalists such as Carl Heinrich Becker, who argued for the common heritage of Islam and Occidental culture. Ôkawa Shûmei might have been familiar with Becker's ideas, as German Orientalist books on Islam were available at the research libraries that he helped accumulate. However, based on this new interpretation of Islamic civilization in the historical context, Ôkawa Shûmei particularly criticized European Orientalism for categorizing Islam as an 'Oriental' civilization and for neglecting mutual contributions and interactions between Muslim and European societies. He placed special emphasis on the medieval period, when the Christian West learned much from a superior Islamic civilization, in spite of their military conflict during the crusades. Ôkawa underlined how Muslim states were tolerant of Christian subjects, in addition to pointing out that Muslims and Christians always shared much in philosophy, culture, and theology. This observation led him to challenge the European view of Islam as an Oriental religion:

> Islam is frequently called an Oriental religion, and its culture is called an Oriental culture. However, Islam is part of a religious family that includes Zoroastrianism, Judaism, and Christianity...if we consider India and China as Eastern, Islam clearly has a Western character in contrast to the Eastern religions.[38]

---

[38] Ôkawa Shûmei, *Kaikyô Gairon* (*Introduction to Islam*) (Tokyo, 1942), 12.

In addition to writing impressive scholarly books on Islam, Ôkawa also tried to train a new generation of Japanese colonial officers to become familiar with Islam and to lead Muslims against European imperial rule. Ôkawa even received government funds to establish a special school offering instruction in Asian studies. This school, the most concrete product of Ôkawa's work, was established in May 1938 as a teaching institute affiliated with the East Asian Economic Research Bureau in Tokyo. It was funded by the Manchurian Railway Company, the army, and the foreign ministry. All expenses of the admitted students were paid by the school, which was widely known as the *Ôkawa Juku* (*Ôkawa School*), although its official name was *Shôwa Gogaku Kenkyûjo* (*Shôwa Language Research Institute*). In return for receiving tuition and a stipend for two years, the students were obliged to work for the Japanese government in overseas regions such as Southeast Asia for approximately ten years. Each year, the school recruited twenty students around the age of seventeen. In their first year, they had to learn either English or French as their primary foreign language, along with an additional language to be selected from among Urdu, Hindu, Thai, and Malay. After the second year of the school, Arabic, Persian, and Turkish were added to the elective language course offerings.[39] The school represented a practical implementation of Ôkawa Shûmei's long-held pan-Asianist vision of merging a colonial cultural policy with anti-colonial ideology. He aimed to educate a corps of Japanese bureaucrats who could understand the culture and language of Muslim peoples and take a position of leadership among them. According to his students, Ôkawa often noted the apparent unreadiness of the Japanese empire for a great pan-Asian cause, underlining the urgency he perceived in his teaching mission. He encouraged students to form personal friendships with Muslim and Asian peoples, and establish bonds of solidarity that would last even if Japan lost the war. Indeed, one can see traces of this ideal of solidarity in Japan's actual policy towards Islam and Muslims during the war.[40]

Japanese academic research on Islamic studies at the Institute of Islamic Studies (*Kaikyôken Kenkyûjo*) represented the complex relationship between ideals of Pan-Asianism, internationalism, and Japanese imperial policy. The Institute of Islamic Studies was Japan's primary academic center for research on Islam, hosting the largest number of scholars and the best library facilities of the four such centers in existence.[41] Although the institute was established in March 1938 by Ôkubo Kôji, Matsuda Hisao, and Kobayashi Hajime, its origins can be traced back to 1932, when almost all the Japanese scholars with an interest in Islamic studies established the Institute of Islamic Culture (*Isuramu Bunka Kenkyûjo*) and

---

[39] For Ôkawa's students at this imperial policy school, see Tazawa Takuya, *Musurimu Nippon* (*Muslim Japan*) (Tokyo, 1998), 145–6.

[40] On Japan's policies towards Muslim societies under their colonial rule, see Harry J. Benda, *The Crescent and the Rising Sun: Indonesian Islam under the Japanese Occupation, 1942–1945* (The Hague, 1958).

[41] The other three centers were: the Research Bureau of the Greater Japan Islam League, the East Asia Economic Research Institute in Tokyo, and the Research Section of the Foreign Ministry.

published a periodical called *Isuramu Bunka* (*Islamic Culture*).[42] The approach of Japanese scholars to Islamic studies was described in the introductory editorial of the journal as the pursuit of an understanding of Muslim societies independent of the negative influence of Western prejudices (*Ôbeijin no Henken*). In an English-language manifesto-like declaration summarizing these aims, which was appended to the first issue of *Isuramu Bunka,* it was declared that:

> In sincere estimation we, the Japanese nation as a branch of the Asiatic, hold Islam and the Musulman nations as a powerful religion in the East and the nations belonging to the East. But once very rare were the chances for us to get into direct contact with them. Unfortunately, as we happened to know the Christian Civilization previous to the Islamic, even though the former is very much antagonistic to the latter, when the latter were not so well situated politically in the world in modern ages, our understanding on Islam has been too much crooked mostly because of the anti-propaganda on the part of the Christian nations. As it is, the time is now with us at last when we can hold our cordial hands forth to Muslim people. Friendship is ensured, and our door is open to the Islamic nations including Turkey, Persia, Afghanistan and Egypt. Traffic is now vivid between them and us: we may fully grasp a true idea of them through direct and non-prejudiced media.[43]

The Institute of Islamic Studies started to publish the monthly journal *Kaikyôken* (*The World of Islam*), which distinguished itself as the most scholarly journal on Islam, compared with the two other major periodicals on Islamic issues, *Kaikyô Sekai*, published by the Greater Japan Islam League, and *Kaikyô Jijyô*, published by the Foreign Ministry research section. Even after *Kaikyôken* was terminated due to the wartime shortage of paper, the institute itself continued its activities until 24 May 1945, when approximately 10,000 books in its library holdings were burned during the intense bombing of Tokyo. In its seven years of activity, the Institute of Islamic Studies hosted an average of ten full-time researchers from different ideological orientations, published high-quality academic books, organized public conferences, produced documentary films, sponsored radio talks, and coordinated research projects in China and Indonesia, thus indisputably representing a vibrant intellectual center, despite the nationalist mood of wartime conditions.

The peculiar Asianist coloring of Japanese Islamic studies during the wartime era becomes clear in the work of the Institute director Ôkubo Kôji. Kôji's study of modern Islamic history had particularly emphasized the East–West encounter and gave a sympathetic account of Muslim revivalist movements and pan-Islamism. Unlike many European observers, Ôkubo presented the movements for Islamic revival not as forms of religious-nationalist xenophobia, but as a Muslim response to European imperialism, frequently invoking images of the Meiji Restoration and Japan's own encounter with the West. Muslim modernists

---

[42] For the charter of Isuramu Bunka Kenkyûjo, see Kawamura Kôrô, 'Isuramu Gaku: Senzen No Nagare' ('Islamic Studies: Postwar Trends'), in *Kaikyôken* (Fukkokuban) (*The Muslim World* (Reprint)) (Tokyo, 1986), 1–11, 2.

[43] Kaikyôken Kenkyûjo (Institute of Islamic Studies), *Manifesto, Isuramu Bunka,* 1/1 (1932). The text was printed on the back cover of the journal.

such as al-Afghani, Muhammed 'Abduh, and Rashid Rida were depicted as heroes who embodied a powerful anti-imperialist ideology and the successful Islamic appropriation of modernity. Ôkubo expressed strong optimism in relation to the synthesis of Islam with modernity, writing favorably of rising Muslim nationalism, modernist-revivalist movements in contemporary Islamic thought, and the diverse paths of modernization taken by Muslim nations such as Turkey, Iran, and Afghanistan. In another article, he argued that Japan's 'sacred' war against the British empire would open the way for the rebirth of the Muslim awakening and solve the problems faced by Muslim nationalism, while Muslims living within the Greater East Asia Co-Prosperity Sphere would become role models for the rest of the 'Islamic world':

> The purpose of the construction of the New Order in East Asia reflects the world policy of our nation. This means a change in world history by the liberation of East Asia from the Anglo-American powers and the establishment of a new order in East Asia with Japan as its center. From a different point of view, we should not forget that this implies a great advantage for the liberation of the Muslim world, and reflects Japan's leading position in the rationalization of world history.[44]

Looking at the writings of Ôkubo Kôji from a broader perspective, it would be inaccurate to characterize even his wartime scholarship as based merely on a desire to further Japan's imperial interests. In fact, he maintained an internationalist agenda to introduce an unfamiliar culture to the Japanese public and to propagate an Asianist vision of decolonization throughout his career. His support for Japan's Asia policy during the period of the Greater East Asia Co-Prosperity Sphere was derived more from his own Asianist convictions. Ôkubo did not have any affiliation with nationalist organizations, and did not share the strong ideological commitments of figures such as Ôkawa Shûmei. However, he did believe in the existence of two conflicting civilizations, East and West, and he saw Japan as having a 'liberating mission' in Asia, even to the extent that he condoned Japan's war in China as an effort to save the Chinese nation from European hegemony.[45]

## CONCLUSION

Japan's imperial policy towards Islam relied on the globally circulating notions of the 'Muslim world' and its stereotyped characteristics, most notably the notion of an anti-Christian and anti-European pan-Islamism. But, for the imperial policymakers in Tokyo, the idea of an inherently anti-colonial 'Muslim world' was also associated with pan-Asianism and pro-Japanese sympathies. With the support of pan-Asianist networks, Japanese imperialists created their own version of an imperial policy towards Islam, convinced that Japan as an Asian and non-Christian empire could attract the necessary Muslim support to defeat both Chinese

---

[44] Ôkubo Kôji, *Gaikan Kaikyôken* (*General View of the Muslim World*), 334–5.
[45] Ôkubo Kôji, 'Seisen' ('The Sacred War'), *Kaikyôken*, 1/4 (1938), 2.

nationalism and Western imperial hegemony. The assumptions that Muslims as a separate non-Western religiously defined group would never be loyal to Christian imperial rule, and that they would naturally be sympathetic to Japan shaped many policy assumptions.

Beyond imperial policy circles and organizations concerned with Islam, the Japanese empire also hosted a vibrant community of scholars of Islam, only some of whom were pan-Asianist. While Islamic area studies carried out by Japanese experts during the Fifteen Years War included the production of useful knowledge for the purposes of the Japanese empire, the effort clearly cannot be reduced to this single aim alone. Japanese scholars of Islam displayed a high level of identification with and sympathy for the Muslim societies which they studied. Furthermore, they depicted change and religious reform movements in the 'Muslim world' as a successful Islamic response to modernity, rather than as a deviation from the essence of Islam. Yet, while their approach assumed that Japanese and Muslims shared a common Asian civilization, they had a tendency to reaffirm the knowledge categories of Orientalist epistemology, even at a time when some Japanese scholars were vehemently advocating academic freedom from European Orientalism. Ironically, Japanese scholars could produce a deliberately anti-Orientalist agenda of scholarship on the 'Muslim world' when they were primarily relying on the writings of European Orientalists. Their scholarship shows that both Islamophilic Japanese writings and allegedly anti-Islamic European scholarship could rely on the same epistemological assumptions about the unity of all Muslims and their anti-Western emotions. However, even within a rigid framework that relied on an ontological distinction between Orient and Occident, Japanese scholars succeeded in producing a new perspective on Muslim societies that, in the long run, resembled the line of thinking that dominated the scholarship on Muslim societies in the postcolonial period.

# Index